Human Resource Management

This textbook introduces readers to an array of concepts and current practices of human resource management (HRM). It provides an understanding of the current problems in the area that require pragmatic research and realistic solutions.

Using a blend of diverse concepts, theories, tools and techniques, the book discusses contemporary practices of HRM and the challenges related to acquiring and training people, human resource development, compensation and reward, employee relations, technological changes, HR records, audit, research and more. Supported by the authors' rich experience of over five decades in academics as well as in the corporate sector and case studies, the book will enhance conceptual understanding of HRM, throw light on recent developments in this subject area and offer management strategies for problems and challenges related to human resources.

This book will be an essential textbook for students, professionals, corporate trainers and researchers of business studies, management studies, marketing, human resource management, resource management, work and organisational psychology, human resource development, risk management, economics and finance.

R. C. Sharma is the Founder Vice Chancellor of Amity University Gurugram, India, and Ex-Professor Emeritus of Amity Business School, India. His name is featured in the World Scientists and University Rankings (2021) at rank number 14 in the world and at rank number 2 in India and Asia. He possesses over five decades of experience in teaching, research and the corporate sector. He has published works extensively and has been editor-in-chief of *Amity Management Analyst* for a decade. Besides being honoured with many awards for his research contributions, he was also a gold medallist for securing a First Class First in PGDPM (Kurukshetra University).

Nipun Sharma is CEO of Jeeves Consumer Services and F1 Info Solutions (both Flipkart companies). He brings over 30 years of experience in senior roles at companies such as Flipkart, Airtel, Vodafone, Tata Tele, and Usha. His academic credentials include a BTech (Hons) in Electronics and Communication Engineering, a PGDMM (gold medallist), an MBA, and a PhD in Management. He also has executive education from IIM Ahmedabad, ISB Hyderabad and the University of Michigan. He is a certified Tata Business Excellence Management assessor and a certified SHL internal assessor. He has published many research papers and articles on HR and management-related topics and has been a guest speaker at several institutes and organisations.

Human Resource Management
Concepts, Theories and Contemporary Practices

R. C. Sharma and Nipun Sharma

LONDON AND NEW YORK

Designed cover image: © Irina_Strelnikova / Getty Images

First published 2025
by Routledge
4 Park Square, Milton Park, Abingdon, Oxon OX14 4RN

and by Routledge
605 Third Avenue, New York, NY 10158

Routledge is an imprint of the Taylor & Francis Group, an informa business

© 2025 R. C. Sharma and Nipun Sharma

The right of R. C. Sharma and Nipun Sharma to be identified as authors of this work has been asserted in accordance with sections 77 and 78 of the Copyright, Designs and Patents Act 1988.

All rights reserved. No part of this book may be reprinted or reproduced or utilised in any form or by any electronic, mechanical, or other means, now known or hereafter invented, including photocopying and recording, or in any information storage or retrieval system, without permission in writing from the publishers.

Trademark notice: Product or corporate names may be trademarks or registered trademarks, and are used only for identification and explanation without intent to infringe.

British Library Cataloguing-in-Publication Data
A catalogue record for this book is available from the British Library

ISBN: 978-1-032-62316-0 (hbk)
ISBN: 978-1-032-62837-0 (pbk)
ISBN: 978-1-032-62842-4 (ebk)

DOI: 10.4324/9781032628424

Typeset in Sabon
by Apex CoVantage, LLC

Contents

List of Figures — vii
List of Tables — ix
Preface — x
Acknowledgements — xii
List of Abbreviations — xiii

PART I
Introduction — 1

1 Human Resource Management: In Retrospect and Prospect — 3
2 Importance, Nature, Scope, Objectives, Principles and Functions of HRM and HR Policy — 35

PART II
Acquiring Human Resources — 63

3 Human Resource Planning — 65
4 Job Analysis and Design — 109
5 Recruitment, Selection, Placement and Induction/Socialisation — 133

PART III
Training and Developing Human Resources — 185

6 Training — 187
7 Executive Development and Training, Managing Careers, Promotions and Transfers — 226

PART IV
Compensation and Reward Management — 261

8 Performance Appraisal and Potential Appraisal — 263

Contents

9	Wage and Salary Administration and Employee Compensation	300
10	Divergent Systems and Institutions for Wage Determination in Practices in Indian Organisations (with Special Reference to Job Evaluation)	334
11	Fringe Benefits and Services, and Internal Audit of Compensation and Benefits (I)	367
12	Fringe Benefits and Services, and Internal Audit of Compensation and Benefits (II)	396

PART V
Integrating, Maintaining and Retaining Human Resources — 429

13	Employee Motivation	431
14	Job Satisfaction, Employee Morale and Communication	464
15	Supervision and Leadership	500
16	Managing Employee Discipline and Handling Grievances	530

PART VI
Employee Relations and Personnel Records, Audit and Research — 557

17	Human Relations and Industrial Relations	559
18	Collective Bargaining and Workers' Participation in Management	584
19	Trade Unions	622
20	International Human Resource Management	650

Bibliography	673
Glossary	679
Index	699

Figures

1.1	The Matching Model of HRM	23
1.2	David Guest Model of HRM	24
1.3	The ARDM Model for HRM	25
3.1	Relationship Between Corporate Plan and HR Plan	68
3.2	Determining the Relationship Between School Size and the Number of Non-teaching Staff	77
3.3	Factors in HR Forecasting	78
3.4	A Simple SHRP Model	85
4.1	Sources of Job Information	112
4.2	Process of Job Analysis	113
4.3	Uses of Job Analysis	117
6.1	Training: Education Continuum	188
6.2	Training and Development	203
6.3	Competency Pyramid Model	210
7.1	Methods of Executive Development	233
7.2	Stages in Career Development	244
8.1	Objectives of Performance Appraisal	266
8.2	Methods of Performance Appraisal	268
8.3	The Philips Model	294
9.1	Structure/Types of Rewards	324
9.2	Non-monetary Rewards	325
10.1	A Wage-Trend Line	340
10.2	Factor Scales of a Factor Comparison System	341
10.3	Job Pricing through Intersection of Demand and Supply Curves	342
10.4	A Price (Wage)-Trend Line	343
10.5	Job Classes (Grades)	343
10.6	Flat Rates Wage Structure for Each Class of Jobs	344
10.7	Varying Rates Wage Structures for Each Job Class	344
13.1	Need-caused Human Behaviour	433
13.2	Maslow's Order of Priority of Needs	443
13.3	Maslow's Hierarchy of Needs	444
13.4	Expectancy Model	449
13.5	Model as Given by Urwick	451
13.6	Financial and Non-financial Incentives	455
14.1	Elements of Communication Process	479
14.2	Main Types of Communication	483

14.3	Informal Communication Network	488
15.1	Position of First-line Supervisors in the Management Hierarchy Organisation	502
15.2	Supervisor as a Person in the Middle	503
15.3	Supervisor as the Marginal Man	503
15.4	Supervisor as Another Worker	503
15.5	Supervisor as a Human Relations Specialist	504
15.6	Supervisor as a Keystone in the Organisational Arch	504
15.7	Managerial Grid Leadership Style	523
15.8	Reddin 3-D Styles	524
16.1	Model Grievance Procedure	546
17.1	Effective Human Relations	560
17.2	Organisational Chart of Central Safety Committee	565
17.3	Industrial Relations as a Three-Dimensional Affair	571
18.1	Forms of Collective Bargaining	587
19.1	Objectives of Trade Unions	624
20.1	Sources of Staffing International Organisations	654
20.2	Approaches to Managing and Staffing Subsidiaries of MNCs	656

Tables

3.1	General Education Level of Labour Force (PS+SS) in the Age Group 15–59	86
10.1	Minimum Wages (Category-Wise) Revised with Effect from October 2022 in Different States/Union Territories	353
10.2	The Delhi Minimum Wages Notification (October 2022)	354
18.1	Details of Areas Covered by Agreements Reported by EFI Survey 1963	595
18.2	Subjects Covered by the Collective Agreements of the EFI Survey 1969	595

Preface

An economic analysis conducted for Korn Ferry by the Centre for Economics and Business Research, a global people and organisational advisory firm, reveals the tremendous financial value people bring to the global economy. The analysis finds that human capital represents for the global economy a potential value of $1.2 quadrillion, which is 2.33 times the value of physical capital, which is valued at $521 trillion and includes tangible assets, such as technology, real estate and inventory. Not only this, but human capital is also the greatest value creator available to organisations because for every $1 invested in human capital, $11.39 is added to the GDP. Besides, people, if considered assets, appreciate, whereas physical assets, which operate at a limited maximum output, typically depreciate over time. It is, therefore, unfortunate that when an innovation strikes gold, the connection between the value that is created and the team behind the technology is often lost. It is keeping the said facts into consideration that both the theoretical foundations and practices pursued in the corporate sector to manage human resources have been deliberated upon in the present textbook to enable the policy formulators and decision-makers to choose the best course of action in the realm of procurement, development, compensation, integration, and maintenance of human resources.

The book is organised into six parts. The first part, titled 'Introduction', comprises two chapters and deals with human resource management (HRM)—in retrospect and prospect—and the basics and fundamentals of HRM, such as its importance, nature, scope, objectives, principles and functions. The second part, 'Acquiring Human Resources', contains three chapters and addresses human resource (HR) planning, job analysis, job design, recruitment, selection, placement and induction/socialisation. The third part, 'Training and Developing Human Resources', consists of two chapters examining the issues of training, executive development, and managing careers, promotions and transfers. The fourth part, 'Compensation and Reward Management', having five chapters, deals with the issues of performance appraisal and potential appraisal, wage and salary administration and employee compensation, divergent systems and institutions for wage fixation and fringe benefits. The fifth part, 'Integrating, Maintaining and Retaining Human Resources', comprising four chapters, dwells in the areas of employee motivation, job satisfaction, morale and communication, supervision and leadership, employee discipline management, disciplinary action and grievance handling. The sixth and last part, 'Employee Relations and Personnel Records, Audit and Research', focuses on human relations and industrial relations, collective bargaining, workers' participation in management, trade unions, international HRM (IHRM), technological changes, industrial accidents, industrial hygiene, working environment and fatigue, and HR records, audit and research.

Preface xi

In the aforesaid endeavour, a large number of exhibits, tables, case studies, practical examples, recent developments, probable management strategies, individual and group exercises, authentic facts and figures, references, relevant questions, explanation of various terms used in the text, footnotes, annexures, subject and authors' indices and so on have been provided to make the reading of the present textbook more factual, realistic, illustrative, beneficial, interesting and meaningful. The book is intended to be extremely useful not only to the postgraduate students and faculties of HRM, public administration, social work, business economics and other allied fields but also to professionals and researchers to gain conceptual clarity and information on various topics and to understand the current problems in the arena of HRM, which require pragmatic research and realistic solutions. It is expected that this textbook will meet the requirements of all concerned in the field of HRM.

The authors look forward to receiving feedback, including suggestions and recommendations, from all the stakeholders, by emailing one of the authors at rcsharma25544@gmail.com, nipunshrm@yahoo.co.in or contacting the publishers, to add more value to the present volume.

Acknowledgements

The authors gratefully acknowledge the inspiration, guidance and support that they were fortunate to receive from a good number of intellectuals, learned authors and experts, legal luminaries, corporate and government authorities, universities, peers, students, secretarial staff, various journals, periodicals, newspapers, government and private publications, and so on. Thanks are due to the Office of the Labour Law Reporter, New Delhi, for permitting to use their two case studies; Professor (Dr) Padmakali Banerjee, vice chancellor, IILM University, for allowing to include her recently introduced and a very popular concept, 'Optimism Index: Oi 1.1—A Predictive Tool for Success'; and Dr P. J. Phillip, ex-professor, National Institute of Technology, Kurukshetra, for permitting to use a case study based on his PhD research work. The authors are thankful to Dr Rishipal, professor of pedagogy and dean, pedagogy and Capacity Building, SV Skill University, for providing thoughtful insights on several occasions. The authors feel indebted to all the authors of various texts, research papers and articles published in books, journals, periodicals and newspapers that have been referred to or quoted from in the present text.

Dr Ashok K. Chauhan, founder president of Ritnand Balved Education Foundation (RBEF), and Dr Aseem Chauhan, chancellor at AUG and additional president at RBEF—two distinguished intellectuals and superb educational planners and administrators—genuinely deserve a deep sense of gratitude from the authors. They have always been inspiring, encouraging and supportive.

Dr Sulabh Sharma, head of model line (commuters) and senior general manager of R&D, Centre for Innovation & Technology, Hero MotoCorp Ltd, who was instrumental in providing the authors very useful inputs from the corporate scenario, also deserves thanks for his contribution. Idhant Sharma, area sales manager at Pidilite Industries Limited, and Ms Misha Sharma, Psychology (Hons) student at Flame University, too, deserve thanks for their creative inputs.

The authors would like to put on record their special thanks to the entire team of Routledge India (Taylor & Francis Group, London)—renowned international publishers—for completing the whole job of publication of this book very efficiently and effectively within the stipulated period.

In the end, the authors are thankful to all the visible and invisible forces that have been helpful to them directly or indirectly, though the same could not be named here due to paucity of space.

Abbreviations

ABS	Amity Business School
ABSSC	Amity Business School Study Centre
ADR	alternative dispute resolution
ADRDE	Aerial Delivery Research and Development Establishment
AFWA	Asia Floor Wage Alliance
AIBAS	Amity Institute of Behavioural and Allied Sciences
AIBEA	All India Bank Employees Association
AIEO	All India Employers Organisation
AIMO	All India Manufacturers' Organisation
AIOE	All India Organisation of Employers
AIRMA	All India Rice Millers Association
AITUC	All India Trade Union Congress
AIUTUC	All Indian United Trade Unions Centre
APAC	Asia-Pacific
ASBS	Amity School of Business Studies
ASCI	Administrative Staff College of India
ASSOCHAM	Associated Chamber of Commerce and Industry of India
ATS	Apprenticeship Training Scheme
AUH	Amity University Haryana
B2C	business-to-consumer
BARS	behaviourally anchored rating scales
BDI	behavioural description interview
BHEL	Bharat Heavy Electricals Ltd
BIB	biographical information blank
BMS	Bharatiya Mazdoor Sangh
CAP	competency alignment process
CBT	Central Board of Trustees
CDO	chief digital officer
CIE	Council of Indian Employers
CII	Confederation of Indian Industry
CIO	chief information officer
CITU	Centre of Indian Trade Unions
CIU	Confederation of Indian Universities
CMO	chief marketing officer
CMQ	common metric questionnaire

COVER	Commonwealth of Vocational Education and Research
CPI	consumer price index
DA	dearness allowance
DGE&T	Directorate General of Employment and Training
DGFASLI	Directorate General Factory Advice Service & Labour Institutes
DOT	Dictionary of Occupational Titles
EEAR	emergent economic ameliorative relief
EFI	Employers' Federation of India
EPFO	Employees' Provident Fund Organisation
EPSS	electronic performance support systems
ESI Act	Employees' State Insurance Act, 1948
ESI Scheme	Employees' State Insurance Scheme
ESMA	Essential Services Maintenance Act
ESOPs	employee stock option plans
EVP	employee value proposition
FAIFDA	Federation of All India Foodgrain Dealers Association
FICCI	Federation of Indian Chambers of Commerce and Industry
FJA	functional job analysis
GCs	global corporations
GHRM	global HRM
GHRS	global HR system
H&M	Hennes & Mauritz
HCNs	host country nationals
HCR	human capital risk
HMS	Hind Mazdoor Sabha
HR	human resources
HRD	human resource development
HRIS	human resource information system
HRM	human resource management
HRP	human resource planning
HSDC	Health Survey and Development Committee
IAEWP	International Association of Educators for World Peace
ICEM	International Federation of Chemical, Energy, Mine, and General Workers' Unions
IDV	individualism vs collectivism
IFL	Indian Federation of Labour
IHRM	international human resource management
IIMs	Indian Institutes of Management
IIPM	Indian Institute of Personnel Management
IJMA	Indian Jute Mills Association
ILC	Indian Labour Conference
ILO	International Labour Organisation
INTUC	Indian National Trade Union Congress
IPA	Indian Post Association
IR	industrial relations
ISB	Indian School of Business
ITeS	information-technology-enabled services
ITPA	Indian Tea Planters Association

JCCM	Joint Consultative Council of Management
JDCs	Joint Department Councils
JIT	job instruction training
JMCs	Joint Management Councils
JWC	Joint Workers Council
KAIM	Kedarnath Aggarwal Institute of Management
KGWI	Kelly Global Workforce Insights
KR	knowledge of results
KSAOs	knowledge, skills, abilities and other human attributes
LMIS	Labour Market Information System
LOUD	live out our dream
LPF	Labour Progressive Federation
MBO	management by objectives
MC	municipal corporation
MHRD	Ministry of Human Resource Development
MoLE	Ministry of Labour and Employment
MPDQ	management position description questionnaire
MPFB	Minnesota Paper Form Board Test
MSI	Monster Salary Index
MSMEs	micro, small and medium enterprises
NAB	National Apex Body
NCCTU	National Council of Central Trade Unions
NFITU	National Front of Indian Trade Unions
NGT	nominal group technique
NITL	National Institute for Transport and Logistics
NSDC	National Skill Development Corporation
NSQF	National Skill Qualification Framework
OBM	organisational behaviour modification
ODRS	on-demand recruiting services
OJT	on-the-job training
OT	overtime
PAQ	position analysis questionnaire
PCNs	parent country nationals
PF	provident fund
PMKVY	Pradhan Mantri Kaushal Vikas Yojana
PSBs	public sector banks
PTO	paid time off
RBEF	Ritnand Balved Education Foundation
RDAT	Regional Directorate of Apprenticeship Training
RJP	realistic job preview
ROE	return on equity
ROI	return on investment
RPM	Reinventing Performance Management
SBI	State Bank of India
SCOPE	Standing Conference of Public Enterprises
SHRM	strategic human resource management
SHRP	strategic human resource planning/plan
SI	situational interview/interviewing

SLC	Standing Labour Committee
SMEs	small and medium enterprises
SOP	standard operating process
SSBEA	State Sector Bank Employees Association
STEM	science, technology, engineering and mathematics
TA	transactional analysis
TBEM	Tata Business Excellence Management
TCNs	third country nationals
TCS	Tata Consultancy Services
TIMT	Tilakraj Chadha Institute of Management and Technology
TNCs	transnational corporations
TQM	total quality management
TSMG	Tata Strategic Management Group
TUCC	Trade Unions Coordination Centre
TWI	training within industry
UAI	Uncertainty Avoidance Index
USES	United States Employment Service
UTUC	United Trade Union Congress
W&S	wage and salary (adjective only)
WPM	workers' participation in management
YMCA	Young Men's Christian Association

Part I
Introduction

1 Human Resource Management
In Retrospect and Prospect

Learning Objectives

After studying this chapter, you should be able to do the following:

1. Describe the concepts, meaning, definitions and basics of personnel management, human resource management (HRM), human capital management, human resource development (HRD) and strategic human resource management (SHRM).
2. Distinguish between Theory X and Theory Y.
3. Discuss the phase-wise evolution of the philosophy of personnel/HR management.
4. Identify the challenges of HR strategy and also explain the changing environment of HRM.
5. List and describe the HRM challenges with special reference to individual challenges.
6. Explain the role of an HR manager and how the role of an HR manager is changing over a period of time.
7. Explain the main models of HRM.
8. Discuss the development of personnel/HR management in India.

Introduction

The origin of human resource management (HRM) can be traced back to the roots of personnel management, the need of which was felt in order to seek willing and effective cooperation of people at work for accomplishing the objectives of an enterprise. Following the growth and development of personnel management, the concept of HRM and subsequently the concept of human resource development (HRD) came into prominence. Later, the concept of human capital management attracted attention, and of late, strategic human resource management (SHRM) has started ruling the roost, which is likely to be confronted with a lot of challenges in the future. The aforesaid various concepts, though similar in many ways, have been discussed in the present chapter.

DOI: 10.4324/9781032628424-2

Personnel Management

Personnel management is that important branch of the science of management, which is concerned with the behaviour and organisation of the people working at a particular enterprise. The dealings and behaviour of managers towards employees have always been affected by the views of the management about human nature. It is from the philosophy of personnel management that we get a clue about the technique the management would employ to make the personnel work. According to Michael J. Jucius,[1] in broad terms, a personnel philosophy may take either of two courses. First, labour may be viewed as a factor that tries to resist managerial leadership. Hence, the management must mould and control people to achieve the company's objectives. Second, labour may be viewed as a factor with inherently constructive potentials. Therefore, what the management is required to do is to provide an environment in which the personnel will exert themselves to their maximum. Based on this concept, we can divide the philosophy of personnel management into two groups: (a) conventional philosophy and (b) modern philosophy.

Until recently, the first of these two philosophies generally prevailed in business organisations. Following this philosophy, the management adopted a pattern of close control and strict or task-oriented supervision of personnel. This philosophy has been associated with Theory X, which takes a pessimistic view of human nature. However, of late, the confidence in the effectiveness of this philosophy has been shaken; people have started realising that it is not always possible to obtain good results through a tough stance towards employees.

Obviously, this thinking gave rise to the modern philosophy of personnel management, which propagates that the constructive forces in people can be better realised through a participative or democratic attitude impacting personnel programmes. This modern philosophy holds an optimistic view of human nature, and instead of close control and strict supervision, it lays emphasis on participative management. This modern philosophy is reflected by McGregor's Theory Y.

The core of Theory Y is to integrate the goals of individuals with those of the organisation and to create those conditions in which the members of an organisation can best achieve their goals by directing their efforts towards achieving the organisation's goals. In such a concept, while high standards are expected, emphasis is laid on least control and self-direction. For self-direction, it is necessary that there should be integration of the goals of individuals and of the organisation. This is possible only when at the time of the determination of an organisation's goals, workers are also consulted and taken into confidence. When the objectives of the organisation are determined after thoughtful consideration and in consultation with the employees, the employees also integrate their goals with those of the organisation, and in such a state, there is no need of outside control or supervision and the workers become self-directed and contribute with maximum capacity. This sort of system—the modern philosophy of management, as it is popularly called—has been given different titles by different modern authors. For example, Peter Drucker[2] preferred to call it 'management by objectives' (MBO), while Rensis Likert[3] called it 'participative or supportive management'. Douglas McGregor's[4] Theory Y and Chris Argyris's management by integration and self-control are some of the other examples.

Theory X and Theory Y: A Contrast

Some comments are now presented in order to point out the major differences between Theory X and Theory Y, or for that matter between the conventional (or traditional) and modern systems of management. Theory X recognises the economic man only, while this is not the case with Theory Y; Theory X lays emphasis on close supervision and strict control, but Theory Y supports democratic or participative leadership; Theory X supports centralisation of authority and power, but Theory Y emphasises decentralisation of authority; Theory X regards employees as one of the factors of production, but Theory Y considers employees as a live factor of production, regards them as responsible and faithful co-operators and lays emphasis on taking them into confidence in the decision-making process. Further, Theory X takes into consideration only economic or financial motivators, whereas Theory Y lays emphasis on all sorts of motivators, including financial, social and self-actualising. Theory Y asserts that unless an individual has job satisfaction and contentment in other aspects too, he/she will not offer his/her effective cooperation towards the accomplishment of organisational objectives. It is primarily for this reason that in the modern philosophy of management, a lot of emphasis is laid on motivators such as ego satisfaction, achievement, social acceptance, responsibility and self-actualisation.

Factors Responsible for Emergence of Modern Philosophy of Management

Some of the factors responsible for the emergence of the modern philosophy of management are the development of collective bargaining and trade unionism, rapid increase in the size and complexity of modern organisations, social and political changes, and increasing importance of professional management. Although the modern techniques of management are exercising great pressure for changes in the techniques and systems of conventional management, the fact remains that most personnel managers, especially in a country like India, in practice follow conventional techniques. It is a different matter that theoretically they accept and approve of the modern philosophy of management and thus recognise the significance of self-control, self-direction, self-discipline, co-partnership, participative leadership, employee development programmes, performance appraisal and MBO, but when it comes to practice, most of them become indifferent to these things.

Evolution of the Philosophy of Personnel/HR Management

Although it is difficult to trace the origin of the modern philosophy of personnel management, certain stages of its development can be determined. Broadly speaking, the stream of the philosophy of personnel management can be divided into five phases. A brief account of these phases is discussed further here.

First Phase: Earlier Philosophy of Personnel Management

The history of personnel management can be traced to England, where masons, carpenters, leatherworkers and other crafts people organised themselves into guilds. They used their unity to improve their work conditions.[5] During the first phase, an attempt was made by industrialists like Robert Owen to pay attention towards improving the working and living conditions of workers.

J. S. Mill and Charles Babbage,[6] who were contemporaries of Robert Owen, also contributed towards the development of personnel management. Although Babbage was a mathematical management scientist, he took equal interest in the human element also. He stood for the integration of management and workers' interests. He stressed that workers should get a fixed pay according to the nature of their work, plus a share in profits and bonuses for their suggestions for improving productivity.

6 Introduction

The contribution of Henry Varnum Poor lies in his recognition of human factor for the success of an enterprise. Subsequently, the human factor has started getting the desired importance by and by.

Second Phase: Movement for Increasing Efficiency and Productivity

Towards the end of the 19th century, there developed a scientific approach towards management. At that time, there were several difficulties in the way of industrial production and thus in the way of accomplishing the desired objectives of the organisation. It was with the intention of solving these problems with the help of science that the scientific approach came into popularity. During the second phase, an employee was considered as an 'economic man', there was an introduction of scientific methods in recruitment, selection and training was recommended, and the human element in industry was recognised. Frank Gilbreth, Lillian Gilbreth, F. W. Taylor and Henry L. Gantt were other main authors who contributed towards the growth of personnel management.

Henry L. Gantt stressed that in all problems of management, the human element is the most important. Edward A. Filene was another noted contributor in this direction. He was very much concerned with human elements in his business.

Third Phase: Beginning of Welfare and Industrial Psychology

Around 1900, there started a chapter of labour welfare in the labour movement. This movement was aimed at the physical, economic, social and educational betterment of the workers. Hence, employment departments started coming into existence for the recruitment and selection of workers. To begin with, these departments were entrusted with the job of recruitment and selection of workers and the maintenance of employee records. However, later, these departments were asked to look after the training, labour welfare administration, and lay-off and retrenchment of workers. The employment departments can be called the precursors of the modern personnel departments. Thus, during the third phase, the labour welfare movement was initiated, the human element in industry was recognised, and a personnel department was established in an organisation for the first time in 1914. Hugo Munsterberg, who is acknowledged as the father of industrial psychology, applied psychology in the service of industry.

Henry Ford, the well-known industrial autocrat, established a personnel department called the Sociological Department in 1914. He was concerned about the attitude and behaviour of workers and worried about labour turnover.

Fourth Phase: Growth of Human Relations Concept

Initiation of human relations approach in personnel management was the major contribution during the period. Human relations approach in personnel management was a reaction to the dehumanising aspect of scientific management started by Taylor and his associates and followers. Due to mechanical approach of the management towards workers, they lost their overall involvement in the organisation and pride in their job. But to say this is not to say that Taylor and others had been totally indifferent to the cause of workers. The point is that their primary concern was to increase efficiency and productivity of the workers through scientific methods. But at the same time, they also made efforts in the direction of giving physical and mental ease to the workers in the discharge of their duties. They also laid emphasis on the mutuality of interest between the management and the workers. What was mainly lacking in the scientific approach was the indifference towards the individuality of the worker. He was primarily considered as an 'economic man'. Not much heed was paid to his emotions, sentiments, group behaviour, personality and so on. Although a beginning in this direction had already been made by Hugo Munsterberg, Lillian Gilbreth, Walter Dill Scott, Henry Ford, B. Seebohm Rountree, Edward D. Jones, Harrington Emerson, Oliver Shelton and so on, it was Elton Mayo, F. J. Roethlisberger and their associates who, after conducting the famous Hawthorne experiments at Hawthorne plant of the Western Electric Company between 1927 and 1932, stated that an organisation is a social system and that in order to accomplish the desired objectives of the organisation, the management should adopt human relations approach towards its personnel. Elton Mayo is regarded as the father of human relations approach, the focus of which was 'to study human behaviour at work'. Douglas McGregor,[7] W. F. White, Lyndall Urwick,[8] Mary Parker Follett and so on were the other authors who contributed to the human relations approach.

The crux of the human relations approach was that a worker should not be considered only as a factor of production. He/she is a human first and worker afterwards. Hence, he/she has his/her own desires, wants, attitude, emotions, sentiments and so on. It is, therefore, the primary responsibility of an effective management to adopt a human relations approach towards its personnel.

Economic depression, growth of trade unions, the Second World War and the management literature published during this period also gave impetus to human relations approach. This led to the establishment of personnel department in various organisations. Today, everybody, including the psychologists, sociologists, economists, managers and so on, recognises the significance of the study of human relations and tries to understand the human behaviour. They, instead of regarding a worker as an 'economic man', extend a humanly treatment to the worker considering him a lively thing who is motivated by desires, ambitions, hobbies, likes and dislikes, and so on. The role of behavioural sciences in the field of personnel management is also getting momentum, especially since 1960.

Fifth Phase: Modern Period (1950–Present)

Remarkable advancement of human relations approach, MBO, HRM, HRD, human capital management, SHRM and so on are some of the major contributions during the fifth phase of personnel/HR management. The fifth phase started in 1950. This period is usually called as a period of refinement and extension of earlier achievements. There has been an equally remarkable advancement in the human relations approach as is evident from the rapid development in the field of personnel management, industrial relations and the allied areas. One of the latest developments is MBO. In it, specific objectives are jointly established by the supervisor and his/her subordinates. These objectives should be related to the need of the organisation, realistic and attainable, expressed as far as possible in quantitative terms and controllable. A periodic review of the achievements of these objectives is again done jointly, and necessary corrective steps are taken if the achievements are below the target. However, this system of MBO has its own limitations.

The renowned authors who have contributed in this period include R. B. Blake and J. S. Mouton,[9] Douglas McGregor,[10] Rensis Likert,[11] Chris Argyris,[12] Harold Koontz and Cyril O'Donnell,[13] L. R. Sayles,[14] F. E. Fiedler,[15] G. E. Kimball[16] and so on. It is difficult to prepare a complete list of the contributors. However, today, management is quite a developed science as well as an art.

In the recent decades, a new wind is blowing in management literature which is fast driving out the traditional term 'personnel management' and substituting a new term 'HRM'.[17] A lot of developments have taken place in the realm of HRM, including international HRM and SHRM. Human *capital* management is a recent development.

Definitions and Basics of Personnel Management, HRM, Human Capital Management, HRD and SHRM

Personnel Management

It is difficult for any definition to describe fully any concept or subject. Obviously, it is not an easy job to give a precise definition of personnel management also. Different authors have defined personnel management in their own ways. According to Michael J. Jucius, personnel management is that field of management which has to do with planning, organising, directing and controlling the functions of procuring, developing, maintaining and utilising a labour force in such a way that the objectives for which the company is established are attained economically and effectively and the objectives of all levels of personnel and society are served to the highest possible degree.[18] This definition obviously lays emphasis on the achievement of specified objectives through proper planning, organising, directing and controlling by the management. Thus, it clarifies that personnel management is a responsibility of management. The management should plan a personnel programme and should not only specify necessary operative personnel functions but also point out how such functions are to be performed. For carrying out the plan effectively, proper organisation is needed, that is, how and from where the resources are to be procured, what should be the system of purchases, communication and so on. Personnel management also owns the responsibility of directing the organisation, that is, supervising, motivating, training and guiding the personnel engaged in the establishment at different levels. For effective direction, qualities of leadership must be there. Ultimately, the management is required to control, that is, evaluation of the result, keeping in view the specified objectives and targets. Failure in achieving objectives and targets reflects inefficiency of the management. For achieving the specified objectives, the management is to see that the necessary workforce is procured, developed, maintained and utilised appropriately. This involves a lot of responsibility as it covers a vast field such as recruitment, selection, training, promotion, transfer, wages, dearness allowance and fringe benefits. While producing a service or commodity at reasonable profits to the establishment, the personnel management should make necessary contribution and discharge its obligations towards not only the region and the nation but also the whole community of the world.

The views of E. B. Flippo are also noteworthy in this regard. According to him, the personnel function is concerned with the procurement, compensation, integration and maintenance of the personnel of an organisation for the purpose of contributing towards the accomplishment of organisation's major goals or objectives.

In this regard, the views of Professor Thomas G. Spates are worth mentioning. According to him, personnel administration is a code of the ways of organising and treating individuals at work so that they will each get the greatest possible realisation of their intrinsic abilities, thus attaining maximum efficiency for themselves and their group, and thereby giving to the enterprise of which they are a part of, its determining, competitive advantage and its optimum results.[19]

According to this definition, good personnel management helps individual workers to realise and utilise their capacities to the full and organisation to achieve its desired goals.

M. W. Cumming has also emphasised the same viewpoint while he says that personnel management is concerned with obtaining the best possible staff for an organisation and having got them, looking after them so that they will want to stay and give their best to their jobs.

Edison has preferred to call personnel management as 'the science of human engineering'. According to Professor Dale Yoder, who is an eminent authority on personnel management, personnel management is that phase of management which deals with the effecting control and use of manpower as distinguished from other sources of power.

Some authors and institutions have laid more emphasis on human relationship in personnel management. As a matter of fact, personnel management includes both the welfare side, which is concerned with the physical amenities necessary for the comfort of the workers, and the personnel side, which extends to psychological study of human personality embracing all aspects of human relationship.

There are some other authors also who have defined personnel management. According to John Shubin, an eminent author on personnel management, personnel administration is the systematic recruitment of a competent workforce whose human resources are effectively used through the control of the occupational environment in a manner that develops employees' potential and enables them to contribute valuable services to the organisation of which they are an integral part. Thus, personnel administration is related with the control and improvement of human element in the organisation. The Bombay Textile Inquiry Committee also held similar views. According to it, personnel administration is a method to control the human factor in the industry intelligently and equitably.

From the foregoing account, it is obvious that it is not possible to coin a definition of personnel management[20] which may be acceptable to all. However, the fact remains that personnel management is primarily concerned with the methods of recruitment, selection, training, education, terms of employment, wages, working conditions, amenities, and industrial and human relations in the industry.

Thus, personnel management is a functional area of general management which manifests the following:

- It is the management of people at work.
- It is people-oriented.
- It is action-oriented.
- It is globally-oriented.
- It is future-oriented.
- It is interdisciplinary.
- It is both science and art.
- It is a staff function.
- It is development-oriented.
- It is concerned with the effective use of personnel of the organisation.
- It is concerned with the accomplishment of common goals.
- It tries to integrate individual and organisational goals.
- It aims at the best fit among individuals, their job, the organisation, and the environment.
- It is a continuous function.

Human Resource Management

'Personnel management' and 'HRM' are almost synonymous concepts because there are a lot of similarities between the two. While the 1930s are known as the personnel administration stage, the period of the 1940s and 1950s is known as the developing stage during which a whole range of personnel activities emerged. The period of the 1960s and 1970s is known as the mature stage of personnel management during which personnel management not only got increasingly professionalised but also got sophisticated. However, studies on human resource were initially guided by Taylor's scientific management principles and then graduated through the Hawthorne studies conducted by Professor Elton Mayo, to behavioural school based on the theories of Abraham Maslow, Frederick Herzberg, Douglas McGregor and so on.

HRM Phase I started in the early 1980s. During the 1980s, HR and business strategy were integrated to evolve SHRM approach. HR managers became more business- and management-oriented. HR directors in big companies started getting representation on corporate boards. During HRM Phase II (the 1990s and onwards), more emphasis is being laid on processes such as culture management, teamwork, learning organisations, empowerment, more flexible and delayered organisations, downsizing, strategic approach, evolving desired HR policies, and borrowing and emulating best practices. In India, since the 1990s, HRM is getting magnified on account of the initiation of the process of globalisation and liberalisation because of which the form and content of capitalist relations between the various factors of production are undergoing a sea change, leading to a new era of HRM.

Definition of HRM

HRM is the planning, organising, directing and controlling of the procurement, development, compensation, integration, maintenance and separation of human resources to the end that individual, organisational and social objectives are accomplished.

Thus, HRM is concerned with the people dimensions in the management and looks after both the qualitative and quantitative aspects of human resources of an organisation. It is basically concerned with acquiring the manpower for the organisation, developing its skills and competencies, motivating its commitment and retaining it. HRM is primarily concerned with how to make people at work more productive and contented (see Exhibit 1.1).

Exhibit 1.1   HRM Is the Effective Management of People at Work

Human resource management (HRM) is the effective management of people at work. HRM examines what can or should be done to make working people more productive and satisfied.

Source: Ivancevich, *Human Resource Management*, 1.

Human Capital Management

The significance of human resources has been realised to such a great extent that, of late, some people have started using the terms 'human capital' for 'human resource'. As a matter of fact, 'capital' is a type of asset that allows a business to make more money or otherwise further its goals. 'Human capital' which is the sum total of an employee's skills, knowledge and competencies, is what an organisation uses to further its goals. In every organisation, some of the employees have general level of human capital, such as the ability to collect and process information in various ways, the ability to critically think and solve problems, communication skills and motivating skills. On the other hand, some of the employees have specialised knowledge, such as software engineering and management skills. Of course, many a time human capital needs to be refined as treacle is refined into alcohol or spirit. Human capital management ensures how to attract, cultivate and develop, and retain human capital in an organisation. Human capital can be increased through education, training and providing opportunities to people to learn and groom themselves.

Irrespective of the industry, in today's global scenario, all enterprises are confronted with keen competition and, therefore, in order to secure an upper edge over their competitors, enterprises must leverage on their manpower as a competitive weapon. They strategise in a way as may make their manpower more productive through appropriate human capital development programmes so that it may yield higher returns to the enterprises and ensure their long-term sustainability.

The ever-changing business environment requires organisations to strive for superior competitive advantages via dynamic business plans which incorporate creativity and innovativeness, which is an essential requirement for their long-term sustainability. It is now an established fact that human resource inputs are instrumental, to a great extent, in increasing the competitiveness of an enterprise. Human capital enhancement will result in greater competitiveness and performance. In countries like India, which is a labour surplus country, the surplus labour can be transformed into human capital with effective inputs of education, skill development, moral values and so on. The transformation of raw human resources into highly productive human resources with the aforesaid inputs is the process of capital formation. Another worth-mentioning point here is that it takes human capital to create some other forms of capital.

Definition of Human Capital

Human capital refers to processes that relate to training, education and other professional initiatives in order to increase the level of knowledge, skills, abilities, values and social assets of an employee which will improve the employee's satisfaction and performance and eventually improve the firm's performance. Besides, human capital is also instrumental in promoting personnel and economic welfare. It has also been observed that enterprises that possess and cultivate their human capital outperform other enterprises lacking human capital.

According to Dessler, human capital refers to the knowledge, education, training, skills and expertise of a firm's workers. That is why the centre of gravity in employment is moving fast from manual and clerical workers to knowledge workers.

Human Capital Risk (HCR) Management

Although companies in India find HCR to be an urgent board-level concern, only very few have a formally defined risk control strategy (see Exhibit 1.2). HCR in India makes it to the top of risks for businesses (see Exhibit 1.3).

Per the study done by the Confederation of Indian Industry (CII) in which about 100 CEOs, CHROs and other senior executives in India from a diverse set of industries participated, 74% of the respondents pointed out that vacant key positions were likely to lead to missed targets and disrupted business continuity. Seventy-seven per cent of the respondents said that high attrition of critical workforce segments also affected businesses in many ways, posing obstacles to business growth and raising succession/transition risk.[21]

Exhibit 1.2 Companies Find HCR Management to Be an Urgent Board-level Concern

Rising HR challenges like workforce planning, retention, succession planning and skill gaps will drive organisations to prioritise human capital risk management (HCR). A study done by CII called the State of Human Capital Risk in India says, '62% companies find HCR to be an urgent board-level concern'.

Source: Hindustan Times, 3 May 2016

Exhibit 1.3 HCR at the Top Among Risks for Businesses

Human capital risk in India made it to the top of list in the survey conducted recently. As quoted in *Hindustan Times*, 84% of the companies considered human capital factors (high attrition and attraction) as the greatest business risk.

Source: Hindustan Times, 3 May 2016.

Human Resource Development

HRD, both as a concept and practice, is still ambiguous and ill-determined in our country. However, broadly speaking, HRD aims at developing competence (knowledge, skills, abilities, attitudes, values) of an employee which helps in meeting out the requirements of not only his/her current job but also of the job(s) that he/she is likely to undertake in not-so-distant future. HRD helps in discovering and exploiting inner potentials of an employee for his/her own as well as organisational development and brings about an integration of individual and organisational goals besides developing organisational culture of trust, openness, teamwork and collaboration.

In order to meet the challenges posed by the ever-increasing and rapid changes, there is a need of proactive HRD because proactive HRD practices can positively contribute to set the journey in the right direction. They set the tone with creation of right attitudes and help in building capabilities, commitment and culture of self-responsibility. Quest for proactive HRD, including intensive initiatives from top management as have been taken by Tatas (e.g. in Tata Steel), could bring forth ways and means to strengthen the involvement and effectiveness of teams through building core competencies and essential skills

Strategic Human Resource Management

While the term 'HR strategies' refers to the specific HRM courses of action an organisation follows to achieve its strategic objectives, SHRM means formulation and execution of HR policies and practices that create and develop human capital the organisation requires to accomplish its strategic objectives. First, keeping in view the external environment (opportunities and threats), the organisation formulates the strategic plan depending on which the organisation's HR department prepares its HR strategies and implements them so as to support the accomplishment of strategic objectives of the organisation. The basic process of aligning HR strategies and actions with the business strategy involves (a) assisting in the formulation of the business strategy and its proper understanding, (b) identifying the employee behaviour required to produce the outcomes that will help the organisation accomplish its strategic aims, (c) formulating HR strategic policies and actions to produce these employee behaviours and (d) developing measures to evaluate the HR department's performance.

Today, employees are central to achieving competitive advantage, which has led to the emergence of a new field known as SHRM. A competitive advantage is defined as having a superior market position relative to competitors.[22] SHRM means accepting the HR function as a strategic partner in the formulation and implementation of an organisation's strategies through HR activities, such as acquiring, training, developing and rewarding manpower.

Today, because of recognition of the crucial importance of people, HRM in an increasing number of organisations has become a major player in developing strategic plans.[23] HR people should take up the responsibility of influencing the hearts and minds of the employees of the organisation, though consistent with the culture of the organisation concerned, to such an extent that the employees care more about their business than competitors care about theirs.[24]

It can also be said that SHRM is the pattern of planned HR deployments and activities in such a fashion that an organisation achieves its goals and objectives in order to improve business performance and develop organisational cultures that foster innovation and flexibility.

Gary Dessler has also remarked that whereas SHRM recognises human resources' partnership role in the strategizing process, the term 'HR strategies' refers to the specific HR courses of action the company plans to pursue to achieve its aims. For example, a company may like to achieve its aim of better levels of customer service and high profitability through highly committed workforce, preferably in a non-union environment.

Challenges of HR Strategy

The main challenges an organisation comes across while developing an effective HR strategy include developing HR strategies suited to unique organisational features, maintaining a competitive advantage, reinforcing overall business strategy, coping with the environment, seeking top management commitment, avoiding excessive concentration

14 Introduction

on routine problems, implementing the strategic plan, combining intended and emergent strategies, accommodating change and so on.[25]

Selecting HR Strategies to Increase Performance of the Organisation

As stated earlier also, the effectiveness of HR strategies depends on the situation or context in which they are used as no HR strategy is good or bad. The effect of an HR strategy on the performance of an organisation depends on how well it fits with other factors.[26] Hence, an HR strategy should fit with the following:

1. Organisational strategies (vertical fit)
2. The environment
3. Organisational characteristics
4. Organisational capabilities
5. Strategies of other departments of the organisation (horizontal fit)

The Changing Environment of HRM

In today's highly competitive global environment, a lot of changes are happening concerning HRM, which are as follows:

1. **Technological changes:** Today's highly sophisticated technology is replacing human factor with mechanised and automatised processes. Even robots have started playing a vital role. Due to technological changes, there is a substantial rise in productivity, leading to reduction in cost of production and increase in profitability. But technological changes have also resulted in shifting employment from some occupations to others. Computers and the Internet have brought about revolutionary changes.
2. **Empowerment:** Today, empowerment of the frontline employees and the like is becoming more important, and authority is being delegated to them.
3. **Knowledge-based industries:** Due to rapid technological changes, explosion of knowledge and innovative approach, knowledge-based industries have started ruling the roost.
4. **Basis of power:** Today, formal authority is in the background. It is the team leader who has become more powerful.
5. **Workforce diversity:** Today, bias and differences based on gender, caste, religion, age, values and so on are disappearing. More women, minorities, disabled people and migrants are available for employment. Even state laws are supportive of workforce diversity.
6. **Globalisation:** Today, production and marketing are becoming globalised. Human capital is also shuttling from one country to another according to the demand for and supply of it.
7. **Trade unions:** Trade unions have become more aware of their strengths, privileges, rights and so on. However, in some industries, such as IT and other knowledge-based industries where greater weightage is being attached to individual or team performance, trade unions have become irrelevant or started losing ground.
8. **Nature of work:** Technological changes are also impacting the nature of jobs and work. IT, information-technology-enabled services (ITeS), various communication devices, quick transport facilities and so on have enabled many organisations to relocate their operations in low-wage regions. The nature of work has been greatly impacted by the aforesaid factors in industries like knowledge industry.

9. **Statutory obligations:** The intervention of the government is on an increase. Labour reforms are taking place. Many labour laws are in the churning process, making things more complex for management.
10. **Other changes:** The traditional, pyramid-shaped organisation is being substituted by flattened organisation. Virtual organisations are also coming into being.

Thus, we see that frequent and rapid changes are taking place in the environment of HRM, putting forth a lot of challenges before the HR managers. Some of the main challenges are as discussed further.

HRM Challenges

Only those organisations are likely to sustain themselves and prosper whose managers would be able to deal with the challenges discussed further.

Environmental Challenges

Organisations need to monitor the opportunities and threats being posed by the external environment, which, of course, are beyond the control of organisations. These challenges include the following:

1. **Fast and frequent changes:** Causing stress and requiring innovation, hard work, work–life balance, more sacrifices and so on.
2. **Technological developments and the Internet revolution:** The most revolutionary change ever happened, and which has dramatic impact on organisations and their employees is the Internet. It is leading to 'web economy'. The Internet requires investment, expertise, concentration, greater written communication skills, online learning, focus on human resources, redefining of jobs, flexible working hours, and so on. Use of software has also posed several challenges (see Exhibits 1.4 and 1.5). Today, companies suddenly have a lot of data they can look at. For instance, those who are performing better, those committing fraud, those who are at good at management and so on—they want to learn about these and what they can do with this information to run the company better.[27]
3. **Globalisation:** It has led to worldwide competition, cross-cultural problems, virtual workforce, global mergers, acquisitions, alliances and so on.

Exhibit 1.4   Popularity of Cloud-based Analytics in Human Resources

Over the last three to five years, roughly half of the big companies globally have replaced their core technologies with cloud-based software. Our research shows that the number of companies using tools in HR and analytics has doubled. So, a lot of the software is being sold to facilitate that. These are massive projects where companies have taken entire employee record out of old systems and moved them into clouds. During this time they have had the opportunity to clean up data and rationalise all the information about people.

Source: The Economic Times, 5 August 2016.

> **Exhibit 1.5 It Is Difficult to Run Human Resources Without Tech**
>
> According to Josh Bersn, most HR software available today look at goals, performance appraisals, career, working your way up and training programmes, etc. But HR people are seeking answers on how to adapt and reward people better and deal with the new digital kind of organisation.
>
> *Source: The Economic Times*, 5 August 2016.

4. **Workforce diversity:** Due to globalisation, high rate of literacy, economic pressures, and technological developments workforce diversity is steadily improving, giving rise to more dual working couples, females, minorities, disabled people, tribal people and so on in the workforce. All these issues need to be dealt with by HR people in the organisations.
5. **Skill shortage:** Due to fast technological changes, there is an acute shortage of required skills, which affects organisations a great deal.
6. **Work–life balance:** Due to employment of dual couples and ever-increasing share of female workers in the workforce, and greater stress, employees now require work–life balance. This issue also needs greater focus.
7. **Rise of service sector:** The growth of service sector and its contribution to GDP, almost all over the world, is phenomenal. Technological changes, need for professionalisation, changes in consumer tastes and performances, and so on are instrumental to a great extent for the rise of services sector.
8. **Government intervention:** Of late, the governmental intervention has also been on the rise. Labour reforms and labour legislation, economic policies and plethora of government rules and regulations are some of the other challenges.

Organisational Challenges

It is relatively easier to monitor organisational problems as compared to environmental problems. Organisational challenges primarily include the following:

1. **Labour costs:** These constitute a significant chunk of total cost of production. Because of ever-increasing competition, labour costs need reduction by every organisation.
2. **Quality of the production:** It needs continuous improvement because of greater awareness among consumers.
3. **Innovation:** Only those organisations are likely to survive whose workforce is innovative and comes forward with novel ideas.
4. **Self-managed work teams:** These are replacing the traditional supervisory system. Bossism is coming to an end. The future of self-managed work teams, which, of course, have their own issues, is bright.
5. **Organisation culture:** Every organisation has its own culture—its philosophy, norms, values, feelings, observed behaviour, rules of the game and so on—which a newcomer needs to learn and adapt himself/herself to become an accepted member.

6. **Outsourcing:** The extent and nature of outsourcing are also problematic issues these days. The organisation must take a thoughtful decision as to which part of operation is to be outsourced and for how long.
7. **Organisational restructuring:** Tall organisations are now on the way out, yielding place to flat-structured organisations. The number of hierarchies is getting reduced. Mergers, acquisitions, takeovers, joint venture, alliances and so on have become order of the day, which give rise to cultural and HR problems.
8. **Downsizing:** The recent economic recession of 2008 and global competition have been putting pressure on organisations to reduce cost of production, which, in turn, force organisations to go for downsizing. Consequently, problems such as retrenchment, rehabilitation, outplacement and the like must be tackled by the HRM.
9. **Decentralisation:** Today, the traditional top-down form of organisations is no more popular because of its inflexibility and involving more cost in its operation and is, therefore, being replaced by decentralisation. How to bring more flexibility is another challenge.
10. **Technological advancements:** The rapid technological advancements giving rise to the problem of training, retraining, retrenchment, rehabilitation, outplacement, heavy investment and so on are also posing a variety of challenges (see Exhibits 1.6 and 1.7).

Exhibit 1.6   Human Resources Need a Lot of Technology Tools Today

You can't run HR without technology. Today there is a huge army of disruptive tools that are being developed by little companies to create goals, regular feedback surveys and more.

Source: The Economic Times, 5 August 2016.

Exhibit 1.7   India Is Lagging Behind in Using Automated Processes for Strategic Decisions

There is a culture in India of adopting technology. But where India is behind is in using the automated processes for strategic decisions. More companies bought software and implemented it but didn't know what to do with it. The adoption of HR technology in India is nearly 15% higher compared to global companies.

Source: The Economic Times, 5 August 2016.

Per an estimate, about 80–90% of the companies have bought software in India to reduce staff. Human resources have the tendency, if they are not managed well, to balloon staff, and there are a lot of HR people running around in companies trying to help people do their jobs. A lot of technology being built is to reduce the number of HR people. There is going to be a huge shrinkage in HR staff, and it will become more consultant-based work. There will be a shift in service delivery towards strategic consulting.[28]

Today, organisations have data, big data and instant data, which they are using for making decisions on selecting the right kind of talent and even averting resignations.

Several large organisations around the world have started using data analytics, something that HR experts club with artificial intelligence (see Exhibit 1.8) to manage people and power talent decisions more effectively. Instead of having HR managers personally reviewing and evaluating resumes, companies are using technological screening tools to assess the true capabilities of candidates chosen from talent pools, ensuring that the person is a right fit for the job. It is also called identifying potential accurately, going as far as to determine through psychological profiling whether the candidate will be interested in the job in the first place. Companies are also using technology to automate manual processes such as scheduling interviews and sending out job offers.[29]

Exhibit 1.8   At Work, Artificial Intelligence Is Coming into Play

Incorporating technology in HR processes is 'the need of the hour' for organisations, helping them make quick decisions.

While most HR experts agree that the use of artificial intelligence for talent management is a 'reality', 'the need of the hour', 'a moment of truth', something which enables quick insights and faster decision-making, others are of the opinion that it cannot replace common sense and will never be able to understand culture and assess a candidate's fit with corporate culture. That's an aspect which requires human intervention.

Source: Hindustan Times, 4 October 2016.

Per the inputs from experts debating on the topic artificial intelligence for autonomous talent management at the recently concluded SHRM India Conference held in Delhi, data sciences are no longer a differentiator but a necessary tool for managing business planning and strategy. Artificial intelligence in HR processes plays a critical role in managing talent and people and can power talent decisions far more effectively, reducing risks and driving success in decision-making around talent management and organisational performance.[30]

Today, most organisations like Accenture are investing in HR technology (see Exhibit 1.9).

Accenture was using technology as retention modelling. It has used data to identify that if an individual has seen three supervisor changes in an 18-month period, there is a great chance that he/she is going to leave. Data also helped the company identify that the 57th day was important for women who came back and re-joined work after maternity leave. Data revealed that it is on the 57th day that they start contemplating resignation. Using that data, we decided to increase the maternity leave by another two months which helped us hugely in retaining talent.[31]

Today, many CHROs are looking for ways to provide employees the technology they have at home for digitisation of human resources (see Exhibit 1.10).

For today's employer, it has become desirable to provide employees the technology they have at home. That is the recipe to retain talent. While you can put a price on the cost it takes to integrate user experience into your solutions, the value gained from providing a simple intuitive interface is unquantifiable. This is why many CHROs are looking for ways to create quality experiences that will delight—not frustrate—employees.[32]

Exhibit 1.9   Accenture Using Technology (Retention Modelling)

Today there was no choice left for HR but to invest in technology Unmesh Pawar, global MD TA, Accenture, said, 'HR is all going to be about digital personalization if you want to create that great experience for your customer who is your employee. Most organizations today are trying to figure out how to go digital and leverage the power of data analytics'.

Source: Hindustan Times, 4 October 2016.

Exhibit 1.10   Digitisation of Human Resources

The concept of HR is much more complicated than before. Today, we have to recognise that most employees will not stay with one organisation for more than three to five years, and we have to get the best and most out of them during that period of time and retain them for as long as possible.

Source: The Economic Times, 3 February 2017.

Exhibit 1.11   HR to Go Digital

According to Anuranjita Kumar, CHRO, CITI South Asia, HR has witnessed exponential progress in the use of technology. Mobile applications and social networking platforms for recruiting, virtual interviews and employee social networks, as well as predictive analytics and crowd learning together form the new norm.

As digitisation and analytics become more fundamental to business advisory, resulting in innovative and agile people management practices to stay competitive, HR will have truly gone digital.

Source: Quoted in The Economic Times, 8 January 2016.

Human resources have witnessed a good amount of progress in the use of technology, but human resources are yet to go truly digital (see Exhibit 1.11).

In the near future, HR professionals will have to embrace technology and leverage data-driven decision-making to redefine talent management, employee engagement and people policies. HR big data capabilities will become more intrinsic to the function, and technology will enable employee and business interactions, driving an overall culture shift.[33]

Leading HR analyst Josh Bersin said that India has a culture of adopting technology, but it lags in using automated processes for strategic decisions. In an interview by Bersin, the founder of Deloitte said that HR people are seeking answers to how to adapt and reward people better and deal with the new digital kind of organisation.[34]

11. **Capability gaps:** Capability gaps are a big challenge today in industry and need immediate solution (see Exhibit 1.12).

Exhibit 1.12   Capability Gaps is a Big Challenge

Per the State of Human Capital Risk in India—a study done by CII—Suresh Neotia Centre of Excellence for Leadership in association with Wills Towers Watson, capability gaps with respect to emerging business technology was a matter of concern. Seventy-four per cent of respondents said skill gaps significantly hurt business performance.

Source: Hindustan Times, 3 May 2016.

Other organisational challenges may include the following: workplace design will be driven by the innovation and collaboration agenda in addition to addressing workforce needs of informality, flexibility and sociability; technology may be the medium, but the outcome will be towards creating a space that connects people across diverse backgrounds and skill sets to work as a cohesive unit; social media and mobile will become as enabling as email; and so on.

Partnerships and extended ecosystem alliances will change the way talent is sourced (talent-on-tap, contingent workforce forums, open recruiter networks), developed (rapid reskilling and reinforcement) and engaged (diverse career opportunities provided across the ecosystem).[35]

Individual Challenges

1. **Brain drain:** The loss of high-talent key individuals to competitors or elsewhere leaves a vacuum in the organisation which becomes very difficult to fill up. To overcome such problems, many companies have started giving stock options, the quantum of which increases with the length of service in the organisation.
2. **Job insecurity:** In case the jobs are not secured in the organisation, the rate of labour turn gets increased, causing serious problems for the HR department.
3. **Productivity:** How to attract and retain ability and competence is another challenge, more so in knowledge-based industries, because it affects productivity directly. Keen national and global competition requires high productivity, but in our country, workforce productivity is very low (see Exhibit 1.13).
4. **Matching people with their job and organisation:** Again, how to attract and retain employees who best fit their jobs, the organisation culture and objectives is another challenge for HR people.
5. **Other issues:** There are several other challenges like individuals' expectations from the organisation in terms of its social responsibility, ethics, treatment towards its employees and so on.

> **Exhibit 1.13 Low Workforce Productivity: A Big Challenge***
>
> A low workforce productivity is a big problem. Many studies have confirmed a direct correlation between corporate financial performance and workforce productivity. Failing to enhance employee productivity can result in unmet business targets, lower profits and higher HR costs as less productive workers are replaced. It can also foster an organisational culture lacking in performance-oriented work processes and systems, further dampening performance levels.
>
> *Source: Quoted in Hindustan Times, 3 May 2016.*

*See the State of Human Capital Risk in India, a study conducted by CII, S. N. Centre of Excellence for Leadership, in association with Wills Towers Watson.

Role of HR Manager/Changing Role of HR Manager

It is not easy to profile the job of an HR manager in definite terms. It differs from organisation to organisation and even within the same organisation from time to time, depending on situations. He/she needs to play several roles such as an advisory role, guidance role, service role and so on.

Some of the main roles played by an HR manager are as follows:

1. Conscience role: Reminding the management of its moral and ethical obligations towards its employees
2. Line and staff role: Line role within the HR department and staff role for the rest of the organisation
3. Media specialist's role
4. Counsellor's/advisory role
5. Spokesperson of the HR department/company role
6. Group facilitator's role
7. Programme designer's role
8. Programme administrator's role
9. Role of the evaluator of utility of a personnel programme or service
10. Mediator's role
11. Theoretician's role (developing and testing theories of learning, training and development)
12. Trainer and developer's role
13. Strategic role
14. Change agent's role
15. Task analyst's role
16. Marketer's role
17. Decision-making role
18. Role of assimilation and dissemination of information
19. Functional role (procurement, development, compensation, integration and maintenance)
20. Image-building role

21. Leadership role
22. Performance-boosting role
23. Employee advocacy role
24. Need-analysing role
25. Others

Of late, the role of an HR manager is changing. Unlike in the past, now he/she is expected to provide significant inputs to the top management while the strategy for the whole organisation is being formulated. It is not only in the formulation of the strategy of the organisation that he/she is supposed to play a vital role but also in the strategy implementation. An HR manager is also supposed to prepare an HR strategy which should not only be 'vertically fit' but also be 'horizontally fit'. He/she is now seen as a strategic partner in the organisation.

Today, an HR manager is supposed to play the role of an expert in identifying the needs of employees and frame not only the HR plan and training and development programmes appropriately but also formulate wage, benefit and services programmes which should be pragmatic and prove effective in delivering the desired results.

Today, an HR manager is supposed to be a quality professional, knowledgeable and highly enlightened, as today both the employees and the management have become highly conscious of their rights and privileges and the HR manager is supposed to maintain the balance between the two.

An HR manager these days is supposed to be an expert in HR planning (HRP) and is supposed to keep it aligned to the strategic plan of the organisation. Today, he/she is to play the role of an expert psychologist who is well versed in various methods of psychological tests and selecting the right person at right jobs.

Today, he/she is supposed to play the role of a mentor of high order and take full care of the employees.

Models of HRM

Today, a large variety of models of HRM are available. An insight into these models helps an HR manager to get inputs in formulating a tailor-made HRM model for his/her own organisation. Kandula has discussed a good number of HRM models[36] including Baldrige model of HRM, Harvard model of HRM, Michigan model of HRM, Ten C model of HRM, Ten Commandments model of HRM, triarchic model of HRM, Toyota model of HRM, business process model of HRM, competitive advantage model of HRM, e-business model of HRM, HRM model for dynamic organisations, model for business–HRM alignment, model linking HRM with strategy and structure, paralleling HRP with business planning, model for matching HRM with life cycle of organisation, model for linking HRM practices with organisational stages, model for world class HRM systems, model for effective HRM practices, model for capability-driven HRM practice, model for customer-focused HRM, model for HRM scoreboard, model for re-engineering HRM, ten-step HRM model for strategic alliances, seven-step HRM model for take-overs, people-capability maturity model (P-CMM), HRM as shareholder value, human potential model and so on.

The highlights of some of the HRM models are as follows:

1. **The Harvard model:** The Harvard model was postulated at Harvard University. Per this model of HRM, situational factors, such as workforce characteristics, business

strategy and conditions, managerial philosophy, labour market, unions, technology, laws and societal values impact interests of stakeholders, such as shareholders, management, employee groups, government, community and unions, and both situational factors and stakeholders' interest together affect HRM policies, such as reward systems, work systems, HR flow, employee influence and so on, which, in turn, affect HR outcomes, such as commitment, competence, congruence, cost-effectiveness and so on. HR outcomes, in turn, affect long-term consequences like individual well-being, organisational effectiveness, and societal well-being. Long-term consequences affect both situational factors and stakeholder interests.

2. **The Michigan/matching model of HRM:** The Michigan model was developed at the Michigan Business School. This model suggests that business strategy affects organisational structure, both business strategy and organisational structure affect HR strategy and all the three are impacted by economy, political and cultural forces as shown in Figure 1.1.

3. **The Guest model:** The Guest model was propounded by David Guest in 1987. This model is a fusion of aspects that resemble both a hard and a soft approach of HRM. Guest proposes four crucial components that underpin organisational effectiveness, which are as follows:

    a. **Strategic integration:** There must be congruence between the business strategy and the HR strategy for the organisation to achieve its goals. Strategic integration shows the harder side of the Guest model.
    b. **Flexibility:** Flexibility can show the soft side of HRM through the same example given earlier. Flexibility in this case is concerned not only with the need to achieve business objectives but also with the need to treat its employees fairly.
    c. **High commitment:** This is concerned with the need to have both behavioural commitment, which is the ability to go an extra mile, and attitudinal commitment, which is reflected through a strong identification with the organisation.
    d. **Quality:** Quality assumes that the provision of high-quality goods and services results from a quality way of managing people.

According to this model, organisational effectiveness is dependent on strategic integration, high commitment, quality and flexibility as shown in Figure 1.2, which is self-explanatory.

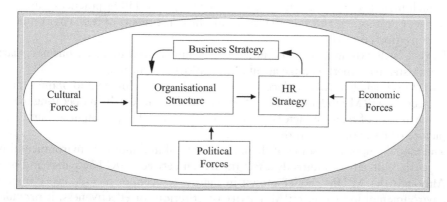

Figure 1.1 The Matching Model of HRM

24 *Introduction*

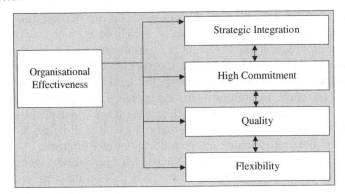

Figure 1.2 David Guest Model of HRM

4. **Model of John Storey (1989):** He believed that HRM is a holistic approach with a set of interrelated policies with an ideological and philosophical underpinning. The model by John Storey is based on four aspects.
    a. **Beliefs and assumptions:** The model is premised on the notion that HRM is based on a set of beliefs and assumptions, which make it a distinctive approach; for example, it is believed that it is the human resource among all the other factors of production which gives the difference.
    b. **Strategic qualities:** HRM is strategic in nature and, therefore, requires the attention of senior management and top executives.
    c. **Role of line managers:** Line managers have a very important role to play in people management.
    d. **Key levers:** There is a strong belief that culture management is important than managing procedures and systems. This is primarily important because culture management brings consensus on overall organisational values, beliefs and assumptions.
5. **Contextual model of HRM:** This model focuses on context. Per this model, the constituents of environmental context (which comprise international context, national context and national HRM context) and the constituents of organisational context (which include corporate strategy, HRM strategy and HRM practices) interact and impact one another, and so is the case with the constituents of both environment and organisation contexts.
6. **Dave Ulrich HR model:** This model views human resources as business partner, administrative expert, change agent and employee advocate.
7. **ARDM model:** The ARDM (*a*cquiring, *r*ewarding, *d*eveloping and *m*aintaining and protecting) HRM model with a strategic (overall) focus can help operating managers home in a set of relevant factors. It offers a map that aids a person in seeing the whole picture or parts of the picture.
   The model emphasises some of the major external and internal environmental influences that directly or indirectly affect the match between HRM activities and people. Although the ARDM model shown in Figure 1.3 cannot include every important environmental influence, HRM activity or criterion for effectiveness, it provides an orderly and manageable picture of what HRM activities intend to achieve.

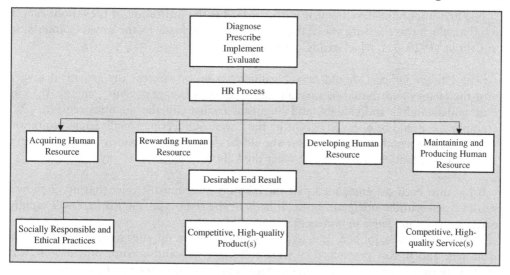

Figure 1.3 The ARDM Model for HRM

8. **The integration–devolvement model:** This model which is being followed by ten European countries is also worth mentioning. In the said model, while UK, Italy and Germany have low integration as well as low devolvement and, therefore, fall in the 'professional mechanic' square, Norway, France and Spain are categorised as 'guarded strategist' because of their high integration and low devolvement. As far as the Netherlands and Denmark are concerned, they fall in the 'wild west' square because of their low integration but high devolvement, while Sweden and Switzerland are in the category of 'pivotal' because of their high integration and high devolvement.

Development of Personnel/HR Management in India

The development of personnel management is an important event in the history of industrial growth. It was around the beginning of the 19th century that the term 'personnel management' came into existence and was popularised by Elton Mayo. Prior to this, most of the industrial management experts usually laid emphasis on scientific management and mechanisation and remained indifferent towards human factor. However, Elton Mayo not only recognised but also popularised the importance of human factor in the process of production and thus gave rise to human relations approach in industrial management. India also could not remain unaffected by this new development in the field of labour in the developed countries of the West. Today, Indian industries are aware of the importance and modern techniques of personnel/HR management, though much remains to be done.

Personnel management is not a new thing to Indian industries, though its progress has been very slow. It is due to the long reign of foreign rule on our country. It is primarily during the last four to five decades that a considerable progress has been made in this direction.

The first important development in this regard is the institution of the labour officer in India, which was the outcome of the recommendation made by the Royal Commission on Labour (1929–31), which reads as follows:

> [The Labour Officer] should be subordinate to no one except the general manager of the factory and should be carefully selected. Integrity, personality, energy, the gift of understanding individuals, and linguistic facility are the qualities required. No employee should be engaged except by the Labour Officer personally, in consultation with departmental heads, and none should be dismissed without his consent, except by manager himself, after hearing what the Labour Officer has to say.[37]

It has also been recommended that the labour officer must 'ensure that no employee is discharged without adequate cause: if he is of the right type, the workers will rapidly learn to place confidence in him as their friend'.

During those days, jobbers used to play the main role in the engagement and dismissal of labour, and in this process, they were following evil and corrupt practices. It was partly with the objective of shunting these jobbers out of the process of employment that this recommendation was made. The qualities recommended by the Royal Commission for a labour officer are almost the same which a modern personnel officer is required to possess. Besides, the independence recommended for a labour officer in his/her working is also noteworthy. He/she should be subordinate only to the general manager of the factory. This goes to establish the importance of a labour officer.

Although after this recommendation was made, the employers started realising that workers are also one of the important pillars on which the progress of industries is based, no practical step was taken until the initiative was taken by the state governments.

It was in 1934 that the Bombay Disputes Conciliation Act, providing for the appointment of a government labour officer to deal with labour grievances, was passed. The government persuaded the Bombay Mill Owner's Association also to appoint a labour officer of its own. Thereafter, the individual cotton textile mills also started appointing labour officers. It was estimated by the Bombay Textile Labour Enquiry Committee that by 1940, there were at least 26 labour officers in the Bombay textile mills.

The widespread strike of 1937 in the Bengal jute mills compelled the provincial labour minister to think that every jute mill employing more than 1,000 workers should appoint a labour officer. At almost the same time, the Government of Bengal appointed a labour commissioner. Then as a result of the negotiations between the representatives of the workers, the management and the government, one labour officer was appointed in 1938 and another five in 1939.

The Indian Jute Mills Association showed a keen interest in the labour welfare work. It established a Labour Department. It also prepared a sort of syllabus for the labour officers to be appointed by its member mills. Hence, the institutes and the universities also got inspiration to prepare such syllabi.

The Indian Engineering Association, the Indian Tea Association, the Chamber of Commerce and other employers' organisations also followed the example of the Bombay Mill Owners' Association in this regard.

At this stage, the labour officer, at times, had to perform the police functions also in the sense that the strained relations between the employers and the workers were often considered a law-and-order problem. However, as stated earlier, the labour officers besides looking after the employment function started taking keen interest in the welfare of the workers.

The recommendations made by the Labour Investigation Committee, 1946, added many new chapters to the history of labour welfare. Keeping in view the recommendation made by the committee, the government passed the Industrial Employment (Standing Orders) Act, 1946, and the Factories Act, 1948. Under the Factories Act, 1948, it was made obligatory on the part of every factory employing 500 or more employees to appoint a labour welfare officer.

After 1948, there was rapid progress in this field. The Calcutta University started a training programme for labour officers. In 1949, the Xavier Institute of Labour Relations was established, which imparts postgraduate diploma in labour relations, which is recognised by several state governments. Today, there are several institutes and bodies spread over the entire country imparting instructions in labour welfare, labour relations, labour administration, personnel management and allied fields.

As the industrial relations situation got alarming, the personnel administration also took over the responsibility of maintaining good industrial relations.

Although it is difficult to pinpoint any date or year when the term personnel management came to be recognised in India, perhaps it was in 1951 in our country when a chemical concern in Bombay appointed a personnel officer and assigned him modern personnel management functions that it became popular. Since then, organisations in the private sector have started establishing personnel/HR departments headed by personnel/HR managers or personnel/HR directors. Today, most private corporations, such as DCM, Hindustan Lever Ltd and Bata Shoe Company, have full-fledged personnel/HR departments. Similarly, in the big undertakings of the public sector, such as IFC, BHEL and HMT, we have modernised personnel/HR departments.

Thus, we find that the personnel officers, by whatever name they have been called from time to time, were in the earlier days primarily concerned with the recruitment and dismissal of the workers. In this way, the evil institution of jobbers was done away with. The labour officer, as they used to be called those days, however, also had to do the unpleasant job of dismissing the workers according to the wishes of the employers, which used to be, usually, unjust and unfair. It used to be done in an authoritarian manner. It was the time of 'hire and fire the workers' according to the interests of the employers. This was feasible because those days, the workers were, by and large, not united. Unions, if any, were not strong. Workers were not enlightened.

But with the passage of time, labour movement got momentum, trade unions started getting stronger and workers more enlightened. The result was that labour officers were, in addition to employment function, assigned the job of labour welfare also. The change in the function was due to the enlightenment among the management, strong recommendations made by renowned authors, managers and behavioural scientists, and the ever-growing resistance among the workers.

Due to the ever-growing strength of the trade unions, industrial relations also showed a trend of getting strained. Hence, the personnel managers were assigned the job of industrial relations and legal matters also. This shows that the activities of personnel/HR managers are becoming wider. In future, the scope of personnel/HR managers may get more widened. It is, therefore, necessary that we may bring sophistication and refinement in the personnel management. Labour movement is likely to get more strengthened and production more mechanised, more automatised and more computerised/robotised.

Obviously, the job of personnel/HR managers will also become more complex as it will have to take care of both internal and external environments. If it fails to do so, the government will have to interfere and labour will also agitate. In order to check this, we shall require more effective personnel/HR managers in future.

Whatever personnel/HR managers we have got in India, a considerable number of them cannot be called effective. Examples are not rare, where though the company has a personnel/HR department, the personnel/HR practices followed are traditional ones. There is not much innovation in any of the personnel/HR functions.

As our future requirement of personnel/HR managers is substantial, it is necessary that all concerned authorities should assess their yearly requirement and arrange for quality and effective professional education at the college, institute or university level followed by practical training at places where adequate facilities are available. The future of industrial development in our country depends, to a large extent, on important factors such as developing an efficient, effective and willing labour force, and good industrial relations. In the absence of these two factors, we cannot think of any substantial development in the industrial field. It is the job of personnel/HR departments to take care of these factors. They are required to procure right kind and number of people at right time. They are also required to arrange for necessary training and development programmes, motivate the employees and coordinate their activities. Thus, the demand for the profession of personnel/HR management in India appears to be very high in the future to come.

Chapter Review

1. The origin of HRM can be traced back to the roots of personnel management, the need of which was felt to seek willing and effective cooperation of people at work for accomplishing the objectives of an enterprise. Following the growth and development of personnel management, the concepts of HRM and HRD came into prominence. Later, the concept of human capital management attracted the attention, and, of late, SHRM has started ruling the roost, which is likely to confront with a lot of challenges in the future. The aforesaid various concepts, though similar in many things, have been discussed in the present chapter. Personnel management is that important part of the science of management which is concerned with the behaviour and organisation of the people working at a particular enterprise. It helps in seeking willing and effective cooperation from the people at work.
2. The philosophy of personnel management is divided into two groups: (a) conventional philosophy, which is associated with Theory X, and in which management practices close control and task-oriented supervision of people at work, and (b) modern philosophy of personnel management, which is associated with Theory Y and, therefore, believes in the constructive forces in people, realisation of goals through participative management and certain psychological assumptions about human nature based on the classification of needs—physiological, security and safety, affiliation, esteem and self-actualisation needs, as suggested by A. H. Maslow.
3. Evolution of the philosophy of personnel management can be divided into five phases. The first phase started from the beginning of the 19th century when

Robert Owen initiated improvement in the living and working conditions of people at work in his factories. J. S. Mill, Charles Babbage, H. V. Poor and so on were the other contributors towards the philosophy of personnel management in the first phase. In the second phase, F. W. Taylor, the father of scientific management, regarded workers as 'economic men' and recommended the use of scientific methods in recruitment, selection, training and development of workers, and the use of time study, motion study and fatigue study to improve the lot of workers. The other contributors in this phase include Henry L. Gantt, Frank Gilbreth, E. A. Filene and so on, who were all concerned with human element in industry. The third phase, started around 1900, gave rise to the concept and practices of labour welfare. Hugo Munsterberg, the father of industrial psychology, Lillian Gilbreth, Walter D. Scott, Henry Ford and so on were the other main contributors who suggested the importance of human element and how to improve its fate in the industry. The fourth phase saw the growth of human relations concept. The main contributor during this phase was Elton Mayo whose Hawthorne experiments (1927–32) encouraged the study of human behaviour at work and concluded that an organisation is a social system and that the work behaviour of an employee is impacted by the work group he/she belongs to. Douglas McGregor, W. F. White, L. Urwick, Marry Parker Follett and so on were the other contributors during this phase. The fifth phase (modern phase), which started around 1950 and onwards, has been witnessing remarkable advancements in HR approach and MBO approach. The renowned contributors during this phase include R. B. Blake and J. S. Mouton, Douglas McGregor, Likert, Chris Argyris, Harold Koontz, Cyril O'Donnell, L. R. Sayles, F. E. Fiedler, G. E. Kimball and so on.

4. In the recent decades, the term 'personnel management' is being replaced by 'HRM', and the concepts and practices of HRD, human capital management, and SHRM are getting popular.
5. While 'personnel management' is the art of acquiring, developing, and maintaining a competent workforce for accomplishing the functions and objectives of the organisation in an economic and efficient manner, HRM is the planning, organising, directing, and controlling the procurement, development, compensation, integration and maintenance of the people at work to achieve the betterment of all concerned. Of late, the management of 'human capital', which is the sum total of an employee's skills, knowledge and competencies and which is used by an organisation to further its goals, is also coming into prominence. Another prominent development during the recent decades is the concept and practice of 'HRD', which aims at developing competencies of an employee which help him in meeting out the requirements of not only his/her current job but also of the job(s) that he/she is likely to undertake in a not-so-distant future.
6. A very important development during the recent decades is the emergence of the concept and practice of SHRM, which focuses on the formulation and extension of HR policies and practices that create and develop human capital needed by an organisation to accomplish its strategic objectives. Today, SHRM means accepting the HR functions as a strategic partner in the formulation and implementation of an organisation's strategies through HR activities.

7. The main challenges of HR strategy include developing HR strategies suited to unique organisational features, maintaining a competitive advantage, reinforcing overall business strategy, seeking top management commitment, implementing a strategic plan, accommodating change and so on.
8. The environment of HRM is changing because of technological changes, workforce diversity, emergence of knowledge-based industries, change in the basis of power, empowerment of front-line employees, globalisation, trade unionism, statutory obligations and so on.
9. HRM challenges comprise environmental challenges, organisational challenges and individual challenges. An HR manager needs to play a multifaceted role which has been changing due to several factors.
10. A good number of models of HRM have come up. An organisation needs to prepare its own tailor-made HRM model to enable it to accomplish its strategic objectives.
11. The development of personnel/HR management is not a new thing to Indian industries, though its progress has been a little bit slow. The important landmarks in the history of development personnel/HR management in Indian industries include (a) the appointment of labour officers (as a result of recommendations of Royal Commission on Labour, 1929–31); (b) enactment of the Bombay Disputes Conciliation Act (1934), Industrial Employment (Standing Orders) Act (1946), Industrial Disputes Act (1947) and Factories Act (1948); establishment of Xavier Institute of Labour Relations in 1949, followed by the establishment of a number of institutes and universities imparting courses in personnel/HR management and industrial relations; appointment of personnel officer in a chemical concern in Bombay in 1951 for the first time, followed by such appointments in a number of organisations later on; constitution of Ministry of Human Resource Development in the country; enactment of a large number of labour laws; and labour reforms being undertaken by the NDA government as also by state governments.

Key Terms

affiliation needs
behavioural science
brain drain
competitive advantage
conscience role
conventional philosophy of personnel management
decentralisation
downsizing
economic man
esteem needs
globalisation
HR strategy
human capital
human element
human relations approach
human resource development (HRD)
human resource management (HRM)
industrial psychology
labour welfare
line and staff
modern philosophy of personnel management
participative management

physiological needs
productivity
scientific management
security needs
self-actualisation needs
service sector
statutory obligations
strategic HR policy
strategic human resources management (SHRM)
work–life balance

Questions

1. Discuss the difference between 'conventional' philosophy and 'modern' philosophy of personnel management.
2. Discuss how Theory Y is an improvement over Theory X and how psychological assumptions of Theory Y are based on the classification of needs made by A. H. Maslow.
3. Discuss the evolution of the philosophy of personnel management with special reference to its development since the 1950s.
4. Discuss the concept of HRM as we as compare it with the concept of personnel management.
5. Discuss the correlation between human resource and human capital. Also discuss the concept of HRD.
6. Discuss why SHRM should recognise HR's partnership role in the strategising process.
7. Discuss the challenges of HR strategy and how to select HR strategies to increase the performance of an organisation.
8. Discuss how the environment of HRM is changing.
9. Discuss the environmental, organisational and individual challenges of HRM likely to emerge in the near future.
10. Discuss the role of an HR manager and how it is changing.
11. Discuss the main landmarks in the development of personnel/HR management. Also discuss a few HR models.

Individual and Group Activities

1. As an individual or in a group of three, visit some large organisations and discuss with the HR officials whether their respective organisation is following the conventional or modern philosophy of personnel/HR management and the reaction of employees towards the same.
2. As an individual or in groups, discuss with the HR officials of some big manufacturing organisation about the HRD activities being undertaken by their organisation.
3. As an individual, visit some large-scale organisation in your close vicinity and discuss with the HR manager how his/her department formulates strategic HR policy and prepare a brief note based on your discussion with him/her.

4. As an individual or in a group of two members, discuss with the HR officials the changes they are experiencing in the environment of HRM, and prepare a brief report.
5. As an individual, visit a big organisation, discuss with the HR officials the environmental, organisational and individual challenges they are anticipating in the near future, and prepare a detailed report.
6. Affiliation needs: These are social needs such as the need to be accepted by others.
7. Competitive advantage: It is defined as having a superior market position relative to competitors.
8. Conventional philosophy of personnel management: It takes a pessimistic view of human nature and believes in the pattern of close control and strict or task-oriented supervision of personnel.
9. Economic man: Economic man is one who is governed by materialistic considerations.
10. Esteem needs: These needs refer to the want to be held in esteem both by a person and by others.
11. HR strategies: HR strategies refer to the specific HR courses of action the company plans to pursue to achieve its aims.
12. Human capital: Human capital is the sum total of an employee's skills, knowledge and competencies which an organisation uses to further its goals.
13. Human resource development (HRD): HRD aims at developing competencies which help in meeting out the requirements of not only a person's current job but also of the job(s) that he/she is likely to undertake in not-so-distant future.
14. Human resource management (HRM): HRM is the planning, organising, directing and controlling of the procurement, development, compensation, integration, maintenance, and separation of human resources to the end that individual, organisational and social objectives are accomplished.
15. Labour welfare: Any activity of management that leads to economic, physical, social or educational betterment of employees.
16. Modern philosophy of personnel management: It propagates that the constructive forces in people can be better realised through a participative or democratic attitude impacting management's personnel programmes.
17. Participative/democratic management: In it, employees are associated in the decision-making process.
18. Physiological needs: These are the basic needs necessary for sustaining human life.
19. Productivity: Ratio of output to input.
20. Security needs: These needs refer to the security of job, property, food, shelter, physical protection and so on.
21. Self-actualisation needs: These needs are related to the desire to become what one is capable of becoming.
22. Statutory obligations: Obligations which have to be discharged because of legal requirements.
23. Strategic human resource management (SHRM): SHRM means formulation and execution of HR policies and practices that create and develop human capital the organisation requires to accomplish its strategic objectives.

Application Case 1.1

Lapses in the Formulation of Strategy

Due to keen competition with other organisations functioning in the same field, the top management of XYZ company observed that their company's sustainability in the market is not very secured unless they increase the scale of production so as to take advantage of economics of large-scale production. Hence, the top management convened a meeting of all middle- and senior-level managers of production and purchase departments, and after deliberating all production issues, they prepared a strategy to double the quantity of the output of the company. Hence, they placed the purchase orders for additional raw material, tools, equipment, other required accessories and so on. The company did not realise that other competitive companies might also be thinking of increasing the scale of their product.

Very soon, the top management of the company realised that the required type of trained manpower was in short supply, and as such, it may not be possible for the company to procure the desired type of manpower in adequate number to increase the scale of production to the desired extent. Since the top management had not associated the HR manager in the process of formulation of its strategy, the latter could not be held accountable for the non-availability of the desired type of manpower in adequate number. Because the HR department was not associated as strategic partner in strategy formulation, it had formulated its HR strategy in the routine manner as it did in the previous year because it did not have any specific idea about the organisation's strategy as also about the strategy of the purchase department which was responsible for the purchase of raw material and other requirements.

It took almost eight months to procure the adequate desired type of manpower. In the meantime, the company had to incur substantial amount of financial loss on purchase and storage raw material and other items needed for doubling up its production.

Questions

1. Where did the fault lie in the mess up of strategic planning?
2. Do you find 'vertical fit' and 'horizontal fit' in the HR strategy? Yes or no, how?
3. What lesson should the top management learn from its lapse?

Notes

1 M. J. Jucius, *Personnel Management* (Homewood, IL: Richard D. Irwin, Inc., 1971).
2 P. F. Drucker, *The Practice of Management* (New York, NY: Harper & Row, 1954), 63, 101.
3 See Rensis Likert, *New Patterns of Management* (New York, NY: McGraw-Hill Book Company, 1961); Rensis Likert, *The Human Organisation* (New York, NY: McGraw-Hill Book Company, 1967).
4 See D. McGregor, *The Human Side of Enterprise* (New York, NY: McGraw-Hill Book Company, 1960).

34 Introduction

5 J. M. Ivancevich, *Human Resource Management*, 9th ed. (New Delhi: Tata McGraw-Hill Company Ltd, 2003).
6 See C. Babbage, *On the Economy of Machinery and Manufacturers* (London: Charles Knight, 1832).
7 See McGregor, *Human Side of Enterprise*.
8 See L. Urwick, *The Elements of Administration* (New York, NY: Harper & Row, 1944).
9 See R. B. Blake and J. S. Mouton, *The Managerial Grid* (Houston, TX: Gulf Publishing Company, 1964).
10 See McGregor, *Human Side of Enterprise*.
11 See Likert, *New Patterns of Management*.
12 See, for example, Chris Argyris, *Integrating the Individual and the Organisation* (New York: John Wiley & Sons, Inc., 1964).
13 See Harold Koontz and C. O'Donnell, *Management: A Systems and Contingency Analysis of Managerial Functions* (New York, NY: McGraw-Hill, 1976).
14 See G. Strauss and L. R. Sayles, *Personnel: The Human Problems of Management* (New Jersey: Prentice-Hall, 1960). Also see L. R. Sayles and M. K. Chandler, *Managing Large Systems* (New York, NY: Harper & Row, 1971).
15 See F. E. Fiedler, *A Theory of Leadership Effectiveness* (New York, NY: McGraw-Hill Book Company, 1967). Also see F. E. Fiedler and M. C. Martin, *Improving Leadership Effectiveness* (New York, NY: John Wiley & Sons, 1977).
16 See G. E. Kimball, *Methods of Operations Research* (New York, NY: John Wiley & Sons, 1951).
17 P. C. Tripathi, *Personnel Management in Industrial Relations* (New Delhi: Sultan Chand and Sons, 2008), 1.13.
18 See Jucius, *Personnel Management*, 5.
19 Thomas G. Spates, *An Objective Scrutiny of Personnel Administration*, Personnel Series No. 75 (New York, NY: American Management Association, 1944), 9.
20 Personnel management is sometimes also known as personnel administration, manpower management, HRM and so on.
21 See *Hindustan Times*, 3 May 2016, Organisations not managing people-related risks effectively, *Hindustan Times*, 3 May 2016. Retrieved from https://www.pressreader.com/india/hindustan-times-delhi/20160503/282664686589170 (Accessed on 26 October 2017).
22 See A. I. Kraut and A. K. Korman, eds., *Evolving Practices in Human Resource Management: Response to Changing World* (San Francisco, CA: Jossey Bass, 1999).
23 A. Mayo, *The Human Value of the Enterprise* (New York, NY: Nicolas Publishing Ltd, 2001).
24 See J. Fitz-Enz, 'Do People Really Add Value?', *Workforce Online*, 7 October 1999.
25 For details, see L. R. Gomez-Mejia, D. B. Balkin, and R. L. Cardy, *Managing Human Resources*, 3rd ed. (Delhi: Pearson Education, Inc., 2003), 22–24.
26 For details, see Ibid., 29–37.
27 See *The Economic Times*, 5 August 2016.
28 For details, see *Hindustan Times*, 5 August 2016.
29 *Hindustan Times*, 4 October 2016.
30 Ibid.
31 Ibid.
32 See *The Economic Times*, 3 February 2017.
33 *The Economic Times*, 8 January 2016.
34 *The Economic Times*, 5 August 2016.
35 CHRO, Genpact, quoted in *The Economic Times*, 8 January 2016.
36 For details of models, see Srinivas R. Kandula, *Human Resource in Management in Practice* (New Delhi: Prentice-Hall of India Pvt Ltd, 2013), 1–39.
37 See Report of the Royal Commission on Labour in India, 1931, H. M. Stationery Off., London.

2 Importance, Nature, Scope, Objectives, Principles and Functions of HRM and HR Policy

Learning Objectives

After studying this chapter, you should be able to do the following:

1. Explain the significance of human resource management (HRM).
2. Describe the nature of HRM.
3. Explain the scope of HRM.
4. List and describe the objectives of HRM.
5. Discuss the principles of HRM.
6. List and describe the functions of HRM.
7. Explain the complete anatomy of HR policy.

Introduction

The changes experienced by organisations around the world include growing global competition; rapidly expanding technologies; increased demand for individual, team and organisational competencies; faster cycle times; increasing legal and compliance scrutiny; and higher customer expectations.[1] In order to manage these changes, we need highly competent and dedicated workforce. It is here that the HRM comes into picture.

Importance of HRM

The rapid industrialisation during the last couple of centuries has given rise to a new civilisation, popularly known as 'industrial civilisation'. Whereas this civilisation has led to material prosperity of the world, it has not paid adequate attention to human values. As the modern industrial structure is gradually getting complex, human problems in industry are also assuming new forms. It is rather unfortunate that human factor which is a living and an active factors of production and which also activates the passive factors of production, i.e. land, capital and so on, and is the foundation pillar of industrial development has not received adequate attention. As a matter of fact, the development of human factor is more important than that of other factors of production because the use or misuse of other factors of production depends on the human factor. Thus, the importance of HRM, which aims at seeking willing and effective cooperation of human factor towards the accomplishment of the objectives of an organisation, hardly needs any elaboration.

DOI: 10.4324/9781032628424-3

While management gives due consideration towards the development of technical skills required for human factor to achieve higher production, it should not be forgotten that man possesses other attributes as well. When a worker enters the factory, it is not only the two hands and a few heat units of energy that he/she carries with him/her but also a live personality throbbing with aspirations and anxieties. He/she has various feelings, desires, perceptions, motives, values and drives. His/her personality, ambitions and aspirations, attitudes and perceptions affect his/her working because all personnel in the organisation are concerned about their status, roles, personal and family needs, security, and relations with their fellow workers. In case the management does not take care of all these factors, the efficiency of the workers will be adversely impacted, and it may be quite difficult to obtain their willing and effective cooperation. On the other hand, if all the dimensions of human factor are taken care of, the workforce will be more effective in the working situation. Here comes the HRM into picture.

Human resources must, therefore, be dealt with as both a technical factor and a human being. An individual is a complicated creature. He/she is a combination of perplexing forces. He/she manifests himself/herself through his/her individual actions as well as group interactions. His/her human aspects are subjective and changeable, qualitative and dynamic, and usually, with the passage of time, vary with several factors such as economic events, personal background and cultural environment in which he/she has been brought up. An effective HR manager takes care of all dimensions of the human factor and makes it a willing and effective contributor towards the accomplishment of the objectives of an organisation. The HR manager never forgets that while a worker is a technical machine in his/her physical, manipulative, muscular and effort-exerting operations, he/she is also emotional and creative. In other words, the HR manager takes care of psychological dimensions of the personnel employed in the organisation and tries to bring about an integration of individual and organisational objectives.

However, the job of a modern HR manager has become difficult because of ever-growing level of education of community members, rise of strong trade unions, rapid advancement in technology, increasing size and complexity of the organisations, consciousness among workers, tendency towards increasing obligations towards society, and interference of the government in labour management affairs. All these factors have been causing a change in the role of the HR manager during the recent past. Today, the role of HRM in organisations is centre stage. Thus, an HR manager needs to be very dynamic and needs to be well-equipped in the field of subjects such as psychology, management, sociology, economics and philosophy besides possessing other relevant qualities. Such an HR manager would prove effective in performing his/her changing role, which will be in the interest of the organisation and other stakeholders.

Some of the modern writers on management have considered both the management and HR administration as one and the same thing. According to them, these two cannot be separated from each other. They feel that the management is meant for HR development. In case adequate attention is paid to the betterment and development of personnel, many of the problems of the management would be solved automatically. HRM is always busy making efforts in this direction. By taking care of physical, mental, social and intellectual development of the employees, the HR manager makes persistent efforts to increase contentment, efficiency and effectiveness of the workforce so that it may contribute substantially towards the achievement of the organisational goals.

Another plus point of human factor is that while the constant use of other factors of production leads to depreciation in their value, human factor gets enriched because with the passage of time it acquires experience and efficiency which lead to higher productivity.

Hence, an all-round development of human factor is highly desirable, which is one of the main objectives of HRM.

The significance of recruiting, selecting, training, developing, rewarding, compensating, motivating, increasing employee's job satisfaction, self-actualising, quality of work life, managing changes, managing increased urgency and faster cycle time, and helping the organisation reach its goals is recognised today by managers in every unit and functional area of an organisation. Gary Dessler and Biju Varkkey have, therefore, rightly remarked that HR activities, such as hiring, training, appraising and developing employees are part of every manager's job.[2] It is because of this that it is said that HRM belongs to all organisations.

Thus, through efficient and effective procurement, development, compensation, integration and maintenance of human resource in an organisation, an HR manager creates and retains an effective workforce which, in turn, creates services and goods. Hence, an HR manager is expected to be a successful psychologist, philosopher and guide also. Only then he/she can be successful in his/her mission. An HR manager is the greatest friend of workers. It is because of this that the HR department has assumed the place of a necessity rather than of comfort in an organisation. That is why, around the world, managers recognise that human resources deserve attention because they are a significant factor in top-management strategic decisions that guide the organisation's future operations.[3]

HRM as a Closed-Loop System

HRM is a closed-loop system as shown in Exhibit 2.1, which is self-explanatory. HRM is made up of several mutually dependent parts or sub-systems, which on the basis of certain inputs received from the external environment produce certain outputs. The central process which returns the information from the outputs to inputs makes the system 'closed' (see Exhibit 2.1).

Exhibit 2.1 A Systems View of HRM

Inputs (Stimuli)	HRM Process	Outputs (Responses)
Company objectives, plans, strategies and policies	Procurement	Individual need fulfilment
	Development	
Organisation structure	Compensation	Satisfaction
Communication, reward and decision-making processes	Integration	Organisational output and productivity
Environmental obligations	Maintenance	
	Feedback	

Nature of HRM

An organisation is formed for the fulfilment of its objectives. For example, a manufacturing firm aims at producing goods at the lowest cost and thus earns profits. This process involves activities such as production, sales and finance. These functions are controlled by different line managers. However, the entire work is done by the employees in different departments. Therefore, the primary function of every line manager is to seek cooperation of the employees of his/her department. Only then he/she can do his/her job effectively. In this way, HRM acquires a higher place than production management, sales management, materials management, finance management and the like.

As far as the nature of HRM is concerned, there are many views. According to one view, HR administration is a line responsibility and a staff function. Departments contributing directly to primary objectives of the organisation are often designated as 'line departments', and the departments that do not contribute directly towards the primary objectives but rather do so indirectly by facilitating and assisting in the performance of line work, are designated 'staff departments'. However, much confusion has arisen both in literature and among managers as to what 'line' and 'staff' concepts mean. One widely held concept of 'line' and 'staff' is that 'line functions are those which have direct responsibility for accomplishing the objectives of the enterprise' and the staff 'refers to those elements of the organisation that help the line to work most effectively in accomplishing the primary objectives of the enterprise'.[4] According to this concept, production, sales and finance are classified as line functions, and purchasing, accounting, human resources, plant maintenance and quality control as staff functions. However, the confusion is regarding the determination whether a particular activity is directly related to the accomplishment of primary objectives of the enterprise. For example, purchasing is auxiliary to the main goals of the business as it is not directly essential as production is. But all the same, purchasing is very important for accomplishing enterprise objectives. Thus, it is difficult to categorise whether a particular activity should fall under the purview of line function or staff function.

Another view, which appears to be more convincing, is held by J. D. Mooney,[5] Harold Koontz and Cyril O'Donnell,[6] and so on. According to this view, line and staff are simply a matter of relationship. In line authority, there is a supervisor with a line of authority running to a subordinate. This hierarchical arrangement is referred to as the 'scalar principle' in an enterprise. Thus, the nature of line authority is related to the relationship in which a superior exercises direct supervision over a subordinate, that is, an authority relationship in direct line or steps. The nature of the staff relationship is advisory. According to Mooney, staff is auxiliary. He states, 'Any duty in organisation that cannot be identified as an actual link in the scalar process is an auxiliary function, adhering to the line like sidings along the main track'.[7] According to Dessler and Varkkey,[8] the HR manager carries out three distinct functions: (a) a line function, where the HR manager directs the activities of the people in his/her own department and thus exerts the line authority; (b) a coordinative function, where the HR manager coordinates personnel activities and exerts functional authority/control; and (c) staff (assist and advise) function, where the HR manager assists in hiring, training, evaluating, rewarding, counselling, promoting and firing employees. Here, he/she also plays the role of an innovator, role of employee advocacy and administers various benefit programmes and handles employee grievances.

Anyway, without probing further this difference of opinion, the fact remains that, by and large, every subsidiary unit adopts both types of organisation. Thus, the departments are organised either on the line basis or on the line and staff basis. However, it is also possible that one department within itself be a line organisation, while for another department it may be an auxiliary. Hence, HR department may be one such department. Within the HR department, it may have line organisation, while for other departments it may be auxiliary. Hence, HR department involves both line and staff activities. But, by and large, it has staff relationship because while, on the one hand, it procures efficient and effective personnel for other departments, imparts training to them, develops their productivity, improves their working conditions, maintains personnel records and determines their wage policies and method of wage payments, on the other hand, it provides adequate protection and security to the workers.

Besides, as Urvic has also pointed out, personnel (HR) management cannot be completely separated from other functions of the organisation. As personnel management is responsible for maintaining good industrial relations in the organisation, it is concerned with every department and with all managerial decisions in the organisation. Another important point is that all the functions of personnel management cannot be specialised, though in order to make the subunit a modern one, specialisation can be adopted to a limited extent.

Urvic has further suggested that the formation of personnel policies should be a centralised activity, that is, such decisions should be taken by the administration. It has also been suggested by him that the personnel management should be accountable to the board of directors or the chief executive. It has also Importance, Nature, Scope, Objectives, Principles and Functions of HRM and HR Policy been stated by him that all the units doing different activities of the personnel department, such as recruitment and selection, training and development, industrial relations, wage and salary administration, and labour welfare should be in the line control of the personnel manager. However, regarding three of the important aspects of the personnel function, namely, determination and maintenance of the relations between the employees and the organisation, negotiations with the trade unions, and promotion and development of higher executives, the personnel manager should act only as a staff expert, and it should be within the purview of the chief executive to discharge these functions.

Next important point about the nature of HRM is that its utility is universal. It is a universal activity and has a universal utility. Its general principles are applicable everywhere—in trade; industry; political, religious and social fields; and so on and for everyone. Functions of HRM are as important in the offices, government departments, political organisations and other trade organisations as in the industrial organisations, the reason being that every organisation whose aim is to accomplish its objectives through collective efforts utilises the services, efforts and efficiency of its employees, and such activities fall under the purview of HRM. In an industrial enterprise, every department depends for its success on the HRM because the success of the department is directly related to the willing and effective cooperation of the employees of that department. It is here that the HR manager comes into picture, and it is because of this that it is said that in order to be a successful and effective manager, one is required to have qualities of a good HR administrator. Glean Gardiner was very correct when he stated that by centralising the personnel function in a personnel department, too many people have assumed that you can centralise human relations. That was perhaps the error in the thinking of the production people and general managers who felt that it would be very helpful if we could just put all our personnel headaches into one and let somebody else worry about them for all of us.

Another important view regarding the nature of HRM is that HRM is a profession. In order to discuss whether HRM is a profession or not, it is necessary to understand the meaning and characteristics of the term 'profession'. Professionalisation involves certain variables (see Exhibit 2.2).

Thus, professionalisation is based on scientific knowledge and a temper for service. Professional people are well-equipped with the knowledge of their field, are adequately trained and have scientific outlook towards their profession. While we analyse HRM in the light of the aforementioned characteristic features of a profession, we can unhesitatingly assert that HRM is a profession as it possesses all the aforesaid characteristics/features of a profession. According to writers such as R. P. Kalhan and F. B. Miller, personnel management is a profession. An HR manager has got wide moral responsibilities, and in order to discharge these responsibilities properly, he/she is required to have high intelligence, good personality, adequate training, calibre and knowledge of principles of management and social psychology. The HR manager does not merely owe a duty to management or the enterprise but also owes his/her duty to the employees, the government and the community at large. The society can even alter its assignment of responsibilities. For example, the society can state that the enterprise should enhance the material standard of living but that this must be accompanied by affirmative action to assist culturally disadvantaged groups within the society. HRM has a lot of social responsibility.

Exhibit 2.2   Variables of Professionalisation

- The right mental attitude
- The acquisition of basic knowledge and training of the subject
- The blending of managerial knowledge and efficiency
- The presence of service motto in addition to earn money for one's livelihood
- The financial reward is not the only index of the success of the profession.

Scope of HRM

That the term 'HRM' is called by several names, such as 'personnel management', 'employee relations', 'manpower management', 'industrial relations', 'labour management' and 'human capital management' speaks for the fact that the scope of HRM is very wide. As HRM is concerned with the 'human beings at work', it is basically concerned with the recruitment, retainment and retirement of manpower and, therefore, takes care of the manpower from recruitment to retirement. That is why it is said that HRM takes care of the employees from 'womb to tomb'. Different authors have expressed their opinions regarding the scope of HRM in their own ways. For example, Dale Yoder[9] has classified the scope of personnel management (HRM) in terms of the following functions:

- Laying down general and specific management policy for organisational relationship and establishing and maintaining a suitable organisation for leadership and cooperation
- Collective bargaining
- Staffing the organisation
- Taking care of self-development of employees
- Developing and motivating employees by offering them some incentive
- Reviewing and auditing of workforce of the organisation
- Industrial relations
- Research aiming at explaining human behaviour and, consequently, improving workforce management

Putting forward the same contention in different words, Strauss and Sayles[10] have included, under the support of HRM, the subject matters such as recruitment, selection and placement, job analysis and evaluation, compensation and performance appraisal, personnel records, welfare, safety, training, education and development, labour relations and public relations.

However, according to the Indian Institute of Personnel Management (IIPM),[11] the scope of personnel management comprises the following three aspects:

1. Welfare aspects related to working conditions, housing, education, recreation and so on
2. Personnel aspects related to acquiring, placing, remunerating, promotion, productivity and so on
3. Industrial relations aspects related to trade union negotiations, joint consultations, collective bargaining, settlement of industrial disputes and so on

Thus, it can be stated that all functions related to the acquiring, developing, compensating, integrating and maintaining of workforce constitute the scope of HRM, whether the organisation is big or small, commercial or non-commercial, private or public. It is also concerned with the well-being of the society to whatever extent it is possible.

Objectives of HRM

HRM must aim at making employees effective contributors to the success of the enterprise. In case the enterprise is not successful, it can neither continue to exist nor can be useful for either employees or management. Thus, the primary objective of the HRM is to seek willing and effective cooperation of the workers towards the accomplishment of the organisational objectives. According to M. W. Cuming, personnel management aims at achieving both efficiency and justice, neither of which can be pursued successfully without the other. It seeks to bring together and develop into an effective organisation the men and women who make up an enterprise enabling each to make his/her own best contribution to its success both as an individual and as a member of a working group. It seeks to provide fair terms and conditions of employment and satisfying work for those employed.

HRM aims at creating, maintaining and utilising a competent and motivated workforce, securing integration of individual and organisational goals, satisfying employee needs, enriching human capital, involving workers in decision-making, maintaining good human and industrial relations, providing a conducive work environment, providing effective leadership, reducing employee grievances and, above all, seeking willing and effective cooperation of the workforce.

In order to seek willing and effective cooperation of the employees, the HRM aims at attracting and securing right kind and right number of people at the right time by offering adequate compensation and services. It also aims at maximum development of the personnel engaged in the enterprise and utilising them most effectively. The HRM aims at the fulfilment of both financial and non-financial needs of the personnel because it is only then that the willing and active cooperation of the employees can be obtained. The HRM aims at recruiting the most suitable and effective candidates, inducting them properly in the organisation, arranging for their training and development, paying them adequate remuneration and incentives, arranging for adequate social security and welfare measures, and ultimately conducting HR research so that more and more facts may be revealed.

The HR manager should also aim at ensuring moral, social and ethical standards of the employees. He/she should review the impact of his/her HR programmes on the personality of the employees. He/she should lay emphasis on those human values which carry social and economic significance in the long run. He/she should aim at generating a feeling among the employees that they are co-partners in the organisation. All these factors will lead to the upliftment of their mental and moral standards.

The HR manager also aims at generating mutual goodwill and cooperation between the employees and the management. This is possible only when the HR manager has the confidence, cooperation and support of both the parties—namely, labour and management. The employees should regard the HR manager as their well-wisher, whereas the management should consider them an important link between the labour and itself. The HR manager should make the management realise that labour is not a commodity but a living thing, bubbling with certain ambitions, aspirations and feelings and, therefore, in order to accomplish the objectives of the organisation, it is necessary that it should be attached due importance and its personality recognised. Similarly, the labour should also be made to realise that the interests of both the labour and the management are common, and therefore, the labour should contribute its maximum towards higher production at the greatest economy. Thus, the HR manager should aim at integration of objectives of both the labour and the management.

The HRM also aims at contributing adequately towards social needs and norms, because an enterprise is not only an economic institution but also an inseparable part of social complex. Therefore, an enterprise must like and behave according to the best interests of its regional and national location and act like a good neighbour in its immediate locality. If possible and wherever applicable, it should not lag discharging its international obligations.

The aforesaid objectives may seem somewhat idealistic, and most management, especially in countries like India, may not be paying adequate heed to these objectives. However, the fact remains that an organisation cannot be successful unless it has certain ideals before it. This statement can be further corroborated by the fact that most successful enterprises in the world have had the HR programmes closely in line with the objectives stated previously.

The objectives and goals of an HR department must be derived from the objectives of the entire organisation. Ralph C. Davis[12] has classified the objectives of a business organisation as discussed further.

Primary Objectives

The primary objectives of HRM include creating and distributing a product or service, satisfying personal objectives of the members of the organisation and meeting community and social obligations (see Exhibit 2.3).

Secondary Objectives

The secondary objectives of HRM include the following:

1. Economy of operation in meeting the primary objectives
2. Effectiveness of operation in meeting the primary objectives

In order to accomplish 'product or service objectives', it is necessary that personal objectives of the employees should be accomplished because it is the personnel who produce or create service. Thus, the HR department always aims at fulfilling the personnel objectives because if the personal objectives of all individuals or all groups are not realised, the basic objectives of the enterprise will also suffer because in that case there may be greater labour turnover, higher rate of absenteeism, low morale, indifferent attitude and so on. Thus, there lies a great responsibility on the shoulder of the HRM because it aims at fulfilling not only monetary but also non-monetary personal objectives.

Importance, Nature, Scope, Objectives, Principles and Functions of HRM and HR Policy

---

Exhibit 2.3   Primary Objectives of HRM

1. Create and distribute a product or service
2. Satisfy personal objectives of the members of the organisation such as:

    a. Profits for owners
    b. Salaries and other compensation for executives
    c. Wages and other compensation for employees
    d. Psychic income for all, including:

        i. Pride in work
        ii. Security
        iii. Recognition
        iv. Acceptance

3. Meet community and social obligations such as:

    a. Protection and enhancement of the human resources of society
    b. Protection and enhancement of the physical resources of society

---

The objectives of the HRM can also be studied in terms of the management process—planning, organising, staffing, motivating and controlling aspects. Thus, under the head 'Planning of HR Requirements', the objectives of the HRM can be to assess the future requirement of personnel and attract potential candidates to meet the manpower requirement of the organisation as and when necessary. Similarly, under the head 'Organisation of Human Resources', the objective of the HRM can be establishment of relationships among (a) various personnel engaged in the industry, (b) men and their job, (c) men and machinery, and so on, that is, to determine the structure of the organisation. The HRM also aims at screening the qualifications and capability of candidates to ascertain their suitability for the jobs concerned and ultimately placing them at right jobs, clearly specifying their duties and responsibilities. Then, under the head 'Staffing', the HRM's objectives may be to arrange for 'workers' training programmes, supervisors' training programmes and executive development programmes so that all these personnel could effectively contribute towards the accomplishment of the overall objectives of the organisation. Under this head, another objective of the HRM can be to 'improve the efficiency and effectiveness of the personnel through promotions, transfers, individual development programmes and so on'. Next comes the head 'Directing' or 'Motivating'. Under this head, the HRM's objective can be to work out fair and equitable wage rates through job evaluation and so on, to improve communication system, to encourage healthy trade-unionism, to provide recreational facilities and to improve human relations and industrial peace. Coming to the head 'Controlling', the objectives of the HRM can be to ensure that everything is going on per plan, and if not, then taking corrective steps.

Principles of HRM

Usually, some people confuse a principle with a policy. A principle is discovered by research, investigation and analysis and generally stated in the form of a cause-and-effect relationship. A principle thus becomes a fundamental truth. However, the principles and laws of social sciences may not always prove as exact as those of physical sciences, the reason being that social sciences primarily deal with 'human beings' who have individual differences. A policy, on the other hand, is a rule or a predetermined course of action. It is framed to guide and help an organisation to achieve its objectives. However, in order to be effective, policies should be based on known principles, though these may change according to the changed situations.

As far as the principles of HRM are concerned, they all are not the outcome of research, investigation or controlled experiments. Many of the principles of HRM have been the result of general observation and practices. As many of these practices have withstood the test of trial in realistic and practical situations, these have become as good as any fundamental truth. Moreover, the concept of HRM is based on an interdisciplinary approach. As such, the controlled experiments in behavioural sciences have also brought an element of truth and certainty in the principles of HRM, though some sort of adjustment would still be required to become suitable to actual practice. These principles or guidelines should be amended as conditions change and as more is revealed and learned about the behavioural patterns of human beings, whether individually or in groups.

Although it is not possible to prepare a complete list of the lines along which a set of principles could be built, still some of the important points may be enumerated as discussed further.

The first important thing is that the HRM should deal with an employee as a complete individual, that is, in their totality. Although the people are hired by an organisation primarily for their economic usefulness or technical capabilities, the management cannot extract the best out of its employees unless it also takes care of their personal feelings and attitudes, culture and ethics, social and political environment, and so on. Hence, while dealing and interacting with or taking decisions regarding employees, the HRM should attach due weightage to the aforementioned factors.

Second, it has been observed that at times, some of the employee programmes have failed to yield the desired results. Usually, it is mainly because managements have not bothered to take the feelings and reactions of the employees into consideration while framing such programmes. So, in order to make employee programmes effective, the HRM should assess the feelings, reactions, needs, and the like of the employees by conducting opinion surveys or through personal contact with the representatives of the employees and so on. Simply spending money on employee programmes designed by the management according to their own whims is not going to serve the purpose.

The third important point is adequate and fair remuneration to the employees. If wages are paid at fair levels, then the employees develop a sense of belongingness and contribute much towards the achievement of organisational goals. There is no doubt that 'fair level' is always a controversial issue, yet the personnel management should try to be as fair as possible; otherwise, the employees lose their confidence in the management. Besides, simply, to be fair is not enough. The HRM should also appear to be fair. Even if the HRM is fair but does not appear to be fair, then the desired results cannot be achieved.

Fourth, reasonably good working and living conditions should be created. Needless to mention that a contented labour force is a must to achieve the organisational goals. Working conditions may include working hours, rest pauses, noise, illumination, humidity, dust, gases, temperature, music, seating arrangement, safety measures and so on. All these things should be at appropriate levels.

Next comes the recognition of the personality of the employee. All individuals and groups want to be recognised, that is, they should be attached due importance. The HRM should create an environment in the organisation, whereby each employee may feel that he/she is making some contribution towards the achievement of the objectives of the organisation and that the management is conscious of that contribution. In order to have higher productivity, it is necessary that the personnel engaged in the organisation must have a feeling of accomplishment, feel pride in their job and have harmonious relationship with other personnel.

Fifth, there should be an effective communication system so that the employees may get all relevant information. It is in the overall interest of the organisation. It has been observed that it is difficult to keep important information from employees. It is bound to be leaked out sooner or later and thus may weaken the confidence of the personnel in their organisation. In case all relevant information is made available to the employed, they feel that their organisation has nothing to hide from them, and this feeling generates confidence among the employees towards their organisation. Thus, a free flow of communication in an effective manner goes to serve the ends of the organisation.

The next important point is that the HRM should give the impression to the employees that whatever reward they have received has been earned by them and not gifted by the management. Every employee of self-respect would like to earn his/her reward rather than receive it as a gift. Some research studies have revealed that gifts are no incentives for extra efforts as after some time, the employees start claiming them as a matter of right. A worker should not be put in a position of feeling grateful for the reward received by him/her. This is possible only when he/she earns his/her reward through his/her efforts. It strengthens the sense of self-respect among the workers which, in turn, boosts their morale.

Again, the HRM should not underestimate its employees either in intelligence or in strength. At times, they may be slow in action, but they can rise to the occasion any moment and create an unexpected situation. It will, therefore, be desirable to associate employees in the decision-making affecting their interests. Some people point out that employees are not wise enough to be allowed to participate in the decision-making process. This may not be true. Employees exert an influence upon every decision of the management, though mostly it may be in an indirect manner. Sometimes it may go against the interest of the organisation. So the ways and means may be found out for associating employees in the decision-making, especially in matters affecting their interest.

The real test of the principles lies in the fact whether an organisation's day-to-day activities and acts of executives are based on these principles. Only the actions will show the real significance of the principles.

Functions of HRM

The functions of the HRM can be studied under two heads: (a) managerial functions and (b) operative functions.

Managerial Functions

The HR manager is basically a manager and as such must perform the basic functions of management which are as follows:

1. **Planning:** Defined in its simplest terms, planning is the determination of anything in advance of the action. It involves scanning of the external and internal environment, setting up of goals and objectives, preparing an action plan to achieve these objectives/goals, laying down policies and procedures, formulating standards of evaluation and allocating resources. It requires anticipation, forecasting, predictions and so on. Thus, planning is a deliberate and conscious effort to utilise the resources to achieve the given ends. Planning is a link between the present and the future and is a continuous and never-ending process. The goals set up under planning may be (a) short-term and (b) long-term. Besides, these objectives may be (a) financial, (b) non-financial and (c) mixed. Above all, planning should be flexible so that necessary adjustments could be made as and when needed. Thus, planning provides the basis for effective and most economical action in the future. It leads to integrated action and reduces considerably the probability of unanticipated crisis. It also leads to the use of effective and efficient methods and helps in accomplishing the desired goals of the enterprise through better control and coordination.

   As far as an HR manager is concerned, he/she is required to determine in advance an HR programme that will contribute towards the achievement of goals specified for the organisation. Thus, it involves planning of manpower requirements and related issues. Obviously, it is necessary that the HR manager should be an expert in the field of HRP.

2. **Organising:** After plans have been developed and the course of action determined, organising is next in order. The process of organising is essential for accomplishing the objectives of the enterprise. Organising involves the establishment of an organisation structure through determination and grouping the activities, the assignment of activities to the specified individuals and departments, defining their role, establishing relationships, the delegation of authority to carry out the responsibilities and provision of coordination of men and work. As far as an HR manager is concerned, in order to execute the HR plans and programmes, he/she must also form an organisation. He/she is required to design the structure of the relationships among (a) various jobs, (b) various personnel, (c) jobs and men, (d) men and machinery, (e) a specialised unit and the rest of organisation and (f) other physical factors. In case the relationships among these are well defined, it will leave practically no scope for any sort of confusion and thus lead to smooth sailing of the organisation towards the specified goals. The HR manager is expected to procure the resources necessary to carry out the HR programme, design an appropriate system to carry out such a programme and establish lines of authority and communication between the various people working with or receiving benefits from the HR programmes. However, the development of sound organisation requires certain principles.

3. **Staffing:** Staffing is a process of manning the organisation and keeping it manned. Needless to mention that the future of any enterprise is governed by the quality of the hired personnel. In case the enterprise has failed to get right man for the right job, the accomplishment of the objectives of the enterprise will be quite difficult. As far as an HR manager is concerned, he/she is required to recruit, select, train, place, compensate, promote and retire the personnel of the organisation at the appropriate time in a manner most conducive for accomplishing the objectives of the enterprise. The HR department itself is all about staffing.
4. **Directing:** Having a plan and an organisation to execute it, the next step is getting the job done. As the process of management is concerned with getting work done through and with people, they require proper motivation. The management is required to lead, guide, motivate, supervise, communicate and inspire them towards improved performance.

    An HR manager is also expected to do all these things in getting people to go to work willingly and effectively. Although all managers must unavoidably direct their subordinates, the HR manager should possess exceptional expertise in this regard.
5. **Controlling:** Controlling is a very important function of management. In an undertaking, control consists in verifying whether everything occurs in conformity with the plan adopted, the instructions and the principles laid down. In this way, controlling is a measuring and corrective device. Through control, we evaluate the performance against the goals and the plan. Two important things in the process of control are (a) comparing actual performance as against standards and (b) taking corrective actions.

    As far as the HR manager is concerned, he/she needs evaluate the results of the personnel activities in comparison with the desired objectives. Through control, he/she measures the progress of the HR programme along the lines laid out in the programme and determines how effectively the desired HR objectives were attained. Thus, we can say that through direct observation, supervision report, records, audits and so on, the HR manager ensures that the enterprise is carrying out the HR programme on the desired lines and, if necessary, takes corrective steps.

Operative Functions

Management functions, as stated earlier, are common to all types of managers. Operative functions, on the other hand, are the specialised functions related to a particular field or functional area. Operative functions in the case of HRM arise out of the fact that a workforce must be procured, developed, compensated, integrated and maintained. These functions may also be called 'service functions' or 'staff functions', as the role of an HR manager is primarily advisory in nature. Operative functions of the HRM are discussed further.

Procurement of Personnel

This is the first operative function of an HR manager. It is concerned with the obtaining of proper kind and right number of personnel at the right time and at the most economical rates so that the organisational goals could be easily accomplished. It deals especially with subjects such as HRP, job analysis, recruitment and selection, induction, and placement. Hence, it involves the following: (a) An HR manager must anticipate manpower requirements in future. This can be possible by estimating future vacancies to be caused

48 Introduction

by future promotions, transfers, resignations, dismissals, retirements, deaths, technological change, organisation's policies and programmes, government policies and so on. (b) An HR manager must adopt scientific methods and techniques in the process of recruitment and selection—an effective HR manager is supposed to locate sources of supply of potential candidates and attract them to apply in as large a number as possible. For this, he/she is required to be well informed to adopt appropriate techniques of advertisement and preparation of job analysis (job description and job specification). In the process of selection, he/she is required to conduct an initial or a preliminary interview, prepare an application blank, check references, arrange for psychological tests, hold an employment interview, get the candidate approved by the super-visor or his/her immediate boss, get him/her physically examined and ultimately select the candidate(s). (c) An HR manager must induct, that is, introduce or orient, the new employee to the organisation. It may be done by telling the new employee something about the nature of the company and its products, specific employee services such as safety measures and welfare programmes and introducing him/her to the important personnel of the organisation. Then the new employee may be handed over to his/her supervisor for further induction, in technical aspects. And (d) an HR manager must placing the new employee at the right job.

Development of Personnel

Having obtained personnel, the next step is to develop them. Due to rapid changes in technology, the realignment of jobs and even growing complexities, training and development programmes are unavoidable; otherwise, the enterprise cannot compete with other organisations. Development programmes involve workers training programmes, supervisory training programmes, executive development programmes, promotions and transfers, good communication and suggestion system and the like. Obviously, the HR manager is required to assess the needs of training and development at different levels of workers, supervisors and managers; plan and prepare training and development programmes for different levels of personnel; provide training material, staff and other related things; conduct the training and development programmes followed by evaluation of results; and make suggestions. The HR manager is required to move very cautiously.

Compensation

The compensation function involves the payment of adequate and equitable remuneration to the employees for their contribution towards the accomplishment of the objectives of the enterprise. No doubt, non-financial incentives play their own role in boosting the morale of personnel, yet the importance of monetary compensation cannot be undermined: Wages are still a potent motivator. The compensation function includes things such as job evaluation, wage policies, wage system, incentive and premium plans, bonus policy and so on. As monetary income plays an important role to fulfil the physiological and some of the psychological needs, it highly proves a morale booster.

Integration

Having procured, developed and adequately compensated the personnel, there comes the problem of integration of individual, societal and organisational interests. In the absence of adequate and reasonable reconciliation among these interests, it is difficult to achieve the desired objectives of the organisation. Integration, thus, refers to prevention of conflicting interests to keep harmonious relations between both the elements in the enterprise: the capital and the labour. This function primarily emphasises on labour–management relations, free flow of communication, grievance handling, maintaining discipline in the industry and so on. Thus, a personnel manager is required to prepare rules and code of conduct, administer disciplinary measures, use effectively the existing machinery for prevention and settlement of disputes and grievances, arrange for employee counselling, encourage collective bargaining and so on.

Maintenance of Personnel

This last function of HRM is perhaps the most important function. It refers to sustaining and improving the conditions that have already been established. This, of course, means that all the functions referred to earlier should remain in continuance. Still, this function involves the maintenance of physical conditions and positive attitudes of employees towards the enterprise. Obviously, the HR manager is required to arrange for proper health/medical services—namely, providing medical treatment and periodical medical check-up for employees; taking preventive steps against infectious and epidemic diseases; educating the employees in health matters through talks, literature, documentary films and so on; and arranging for adequate safety and security measures by seeing that the concerned personnel are imparted safety instruction and that the safety rules and instructions are properly and effectively enforced. He/she is to ensure that statutory requirements regarding safety measures that these are met out both in letter and spirit, periodical safety inspections by competent people are regularly conducted, and all possible preventive steps are taken. Similarly, the HR manager is to arrange for the security measures both for the personnel and the organisation, especially against fire, theft and sabotage. In order to do this, he/she is required to arrange for security guards, alarms raising devices, firefighting equipment and adequate force of trained personnel for fire-extinguishing and framing of security rules and so on. The HR manager is also required to ensure reasonably good working conditions, undertake welfare measures by chalking out effective welfare plans having provision for indoor and outdoor games, cultural and social activities, recreational activities, picnics and so on. The maintenance function also requires research on HR policy and practices to ensure betterment in future. The ultimate objective of all the functions both managerial and operative is to attain the objectives of the enterprise. The existence of HRM in an organisation can be justified only when along with procurement, development, compensation, integration and maintenance of personnel, it also contributes substantially towards the accomplishment of the basic objectives of the enterprise on the one side and discharges its responsibility towards the community on the other side.

HR Policy

Needless to mention, the performance of HR functions is significantly conditioned by HR policies. It is also certain that all organisations have policies, though it is a different matter whether the policies are written or unwritten, complete or incomplete, sound or unsound, followed or not followed, and understood or not understood. It is so because in the absence of a policy, it is almost impossible to delegate authority since a subordinate manager cannot make decisions without some kind of guidelines.

Meaning and Nature of Policies

According to Edwin B. Flippo, a 'policy is a rule or pre-determined course of action established to guide an organisation towards its objectives'.[13] Thus, a policy guides the course of future actions of the management. Similarly, an HR policy also indicates the line of action or the attitude the management is likely to adopt in future towards its personnel and their problems. An industrial organisation should form and declare its HR policy well in advance so that it may have a basis to take decisions regarding future HR problems. According to Calhoon, personnel policies constitute guides to action. They furnish the general standards or bases on which discussions are reached. Their genesis lies in an organisation's values, philosophy, concepts and principles.[14]

Thus, an HR policy will also be helpful in making decisions routine on frequently occurring HR problems.

Michael J. Jucius has also expressed his opinion on the nature and purposes of personnel policies. According to him, 'policies are basic rules established to govern functions so that they are performed in line with desired objectives'.[15] While clarifying this definition, Jucius has pointed out that policies are guides to action and not the action. It is the functions and procedures that constitute the action. This point can be illustrated with the help of an example. Suppose a selection policy states: 'For the posts of Clerks, only graduates or the equivalent are eligible'. Here, hiring would be done through the selection process; the policy simply restricts those going through the hiring process. Another point of clarification suggested by Jucius is that policies simply guide action towards objectives, but they are not the objectives. Thus, in the aforementioned example, policy is helpful in achieving effectiveness in hiring as it restricts some candidates from the selection process who presumably are not suitable. The third point of clarification mentioned by the learned author is that while personnel policies are a tool of management, they cannot think for or replace management. As a matter of fact, management is supposed not only to design appropriate policies but also to see that they are properly applied.

Based on the foregoing discussion, we can say that policies serve two main purposes. First, policies restrain subordinates from performing undesirable functions or from mishandling specified functions. In order to illustrate the former, we can quote an example. Suppose a policy states that the office-bearers of the trade union shall not collect membership subscription from the member workers on company premises. Here, the policy restrains such an activity from being performed. Second, policies are positive in nature as they provide standard decision when an action must be taken. In this way, the subordinates are not required to enquire from the superiors how a given problem is to be tackled. For example, suppose a personnel policy states that all employees should be medically checked up after every six months to ascertain their physical suitability for the post occupied by them. Thus, this policy states specifically when the employees can expect to be medically examined, which, of course, in the absence of such a policy, is not definite. Thus, with the help of this policy, any personnel executive can give a prompt and definite answer if asked about the frequency of medical check-up.

Another important thing regarding the nature of policies is that they should not be construed as fundamental or unchanging truth. Policies should be based on the principle of flexibility so that whenever a change in policies is necessary to accomplish the organisational objectives, it may be given effect to.

Need and Justification of HR Policies

Having understood the meaning and nature of HR policies, it is natural to put a question of whether it is necessary to have HR policies. Raising of doubt about the utility of HR policies may not be totally irrelevant as there are some enterprises which are working successfully, though they have never framed policies. The answer to this question is that it is not always necessary to have policies in writing. The mere fact that a policy has not been written down in an enterprise does not mean that none exists. Informally or subconsciously, if not openly, policies exist in every enterprise. There are some authors who contend that once HR policies are framed, the management is handcuffed. The management cannot take any liberty. As such, they consider policies as obstacles in the freedom of their functioning and decision-making. They think that it is sheer wastage of money to reduce HR policies in writing. Their contention is that every HR manager knows how he/she has to behave with his/her employees. Then why to become bound by declaring the HR policy? These and such other statements declare HR policies as totally useless and unnecessary.

However, a close observation of facts will reveal that these statements are simply misleading and confusing and have no relevance in the modern context of management. Instead of limiting freedom in the decision-making process, the HR policies bring uniformity and rationality in the decision-making of managers. The significance of HR policies can be highlighted with the help of the following points:

- **Sound basis for decisions**: HR policies offer a sound basis for taking decisions regarding HR problems. Once a policy has been laid down, any executive can take a decision easily based on that policy.
- **Facilitate meaningful and effective HRM**: Once HR policies are framed and declared, everybody knows the course of action regarding different HR problems. Hence, there will be least confusion and HRM will be more effective.
- **Restrain discrimination and undesirable behaviour towards employees**: With the declaration of HR policies, the management cannot discriminate with the employees. It must maintain a standard behaviour towards all.
- **Restrain injustice**: After the declaration of HR policies, practically no scope is left for the management to exercise its discretion or sweet will. Hence, even biased management cannot take undesirable decisions.
- **Help in decentralisation of authority**: HR policies ultimately lead to decentralisation of power and authority. As a policy matter, the middle-level or lower-level HR staff may be delegated authority in certain spheres. This eases the job of senior or top-level management.
- **Distinguish policy from procedure**: Although some HR executives know how to tackle the employees, they often confuse a policy with a procedure. A policy is meant for general guidance, whereas a procedure is the implementation of the policy on a particular problem. A manager should know the distinction between policies, rules and procedures. Many of the companies' policy manuals are often a mishmash of policies, rules, and procedures. According to Harold Koontz and Cyril O'Donnell, some policies are rules and recognised as such; other so-called policies are really procedures designed to channel action, not thinking.[16] Therefore, for good planning, good human and industrial relations, and for workable delegation of authority, it is necessary that these three types of guidelines—policies, rules and procedures—must be carefully and correctly separated.
- **Save time**: As the HR policies serve as guidelines, there is no need of analysing and discussing all problems separately and individually. The problems can be grouped together and solved according to guidelines contained in the HR policies.
- **Bring continuity and uniformity**: Once the policies are formed, whether these are in the field of finance, or human resources, or sales, or distribution and so on, there will be no difficulty if the manager is replaced by a newcomer. Thus, the policies bring

continuity and uniformity which, in turn, encourage the morale and faithfulness of the workers.
- **Help in accomplishing the organisational goals**: As the formation and declaration of HR policies lead to the contentment among workers, they offer their willing and effective cooperation in accomplishing the desired objectives of the organisation.

Framing HR Policies

HR policies may be of two types: formal and informal. About informal HR policies, Michael J. Jucius[17] has rightly observed that many personnel policies undoubtedly have just grown. In such instances, everyone seems to know, without being told and without knowing where it originated, that a certain type of decision will be made in certain situations. Such policies are informal, and as such their framing or establishment cannot be analysed.

However, some useful comments can be made about formal policies.

Most of the HR policies should be framed by the higher level of management with the advice and assistance of staff of the HR department. Framing of HR policies is also affected by the consultation and advice of employees, day-to-day problems by the management, social and political changes, international happenings and so on. It is the responsibility of an efficient and effective HR manager to frame HR policies and make necessary changes and amendments from time to time, whenever necessary. In the framing of HR polices, weightage should be given to the views, advice and suggestions of such people who are likely to be impacted by those HR policies. Such people make a lot of relevant information available for the formation of HR policies. When the rough draft is made, it should be sent to the representatives of employees, departmental heads and experts for their perusal, comments and suggestions, if any. Maximum attention should be paid to the comments, criticism and observations made by the employees because these are the people who are most effected by HR policies. Then ultimately, the HR policies should be finally drafted and declared. There is every justification for framing the HR policies by the higher level of management in consultation with other agencies mentioned earlier.

It brings consistency and uniformity in the decisions and actions of the organisation. It can be illustrated with an example. Take the matter of awarding punishment for the acts of indiscipline. In an organisation, practically every executive must take disciplinary actions at one time or another. In case there is no HR policy laying down the nature and quantum of punishment for different types of acts of indiscipline, every executive will have to use his/her own discretion in awarding the punishment. Obviously, it will differ from executive to executive, and cases will not be wanting in which the nature and quantum of punishments may differ widely, though the offence may be the same. This may lead to discontentment among employees and, thus, may prove an obstacle in the way of the accomplishment of the desired objectives of the organisation. Hence, it will be a better proposition if policies on such matters are framed by higher-level management to cover all parts of the organisation so that there may be uniformity and consistency in the decisions and acts of the management.

While framing HR policies, we should also keep in view the objectives, cost and utility of the policies as also the reaction of trade unions. The successful implementation of a policy needs the sincere cooperation of trade unions. Hence, trade union leaders should also be taken into confidence while framing HR policies or for that matter any policy. The principles of justice, democracy and equality, and the recognition of the needs of employees, should also be taken care of in the preparation of HR policies. The policies framed having kept in view the aforementioned points, usually, prove effective.

Once the HR policies are framed, there comes the problem of their transmission and application. As a matter of fact, it is the middle management and the first-line supervisors who will be more concerned with the transmission and application of HR policies. Middle management should be responsible for communicating the policy formulation to operating levels. Here, communication involves a lot of functions such as interpretation of policies, clarification of areas of uncertainty and misunderstanding imparting training to lower-level staff in policy application. Regarding the form in which HR policies should be communicated, it may be mentioned that many policies are stated in oral or may be informal, but it is better if policies are in writing. Written policies are decidedly an improvement over oral or informal policies. There is no doubt that written policies need more time and labour to prepare, but they are worth it, because written policies impart precision, permanence and ease of transmission. They can be produced for auditing or evaluation whenever required without any loss of time. They can also be used as training manuals. Hence, it may be suggested that it is always desirable to prepare policies with a careful selection of words and having clarity and should be in printed form.

As far as the line supervisors are concerned, they should be responsible for applying HR policies. In some cases, the HR department should also be responsible for applying HR policies in their respective fields.

Types of HR Policies

HR policies may be classified into several categories as shown in Exhibit 2.4.

Contents of an HR Policy

An HR department primarily deals with recruitment and selection, training and development, job evaluation, wages and incentives, and labour welfare policy. Hence, an HR policy should have brief but complete statements on all the points referred to earlier. The major outlines of the HR policy of a medium-sized organisation may be as follows:

Exhibit 2.4   Types of HR Policies

HR policies may be any of the following:

- Originated policies: These are formulated by the top management to guide executive thinking.
- Appealed policies: These are usually based on the request of subordinates to deal with certain peculiar situations not yet covered by already-existing policies.
- Imposed policies: These are usually formed because of external pressure like dictates from the government.
- General policies: These reflect the basic philosophy of the top management providing base for the organisation's growth.
- Specific policies: These cover specific issues like recruiting, rewarding, and written and implied policies and reflect management thinking on paper. These are inferred from the behaviour of members, for example, not losing temper while at working and so on.

- **Recruitment and selection policy:** To procure suitably educated and efficient personnel by offering them tempting wages, good working conditions, safety and security, and better prospects.
- **Training and development policy:** To make available all possible facilities for the training and development of employees to enable them to do their job efficiently and to prepare themselves for future promotions; to take effective steps, including training and development programmes, to equip the employees in the latest techniques of production, management and so on; to get the performance appraisal done; and to provide adequate opportunities and facilities for the development of employees.
- **Job evaluation, wage and incentive policies:** To determine reasonably good wage rates and dearness allowance, and to work out incentive plans for workers after undertaking job evaluation and other necessary steps as well as keeping in view the prevalent wage rates for similar jobs in other industries.
- **Labour welfare policy:** To improve industrial relations by evolving a suitable machinery for the settlement of disputes; to encourage mutual negotiations; to prepare and execute labour welfare programmes; and to arrange all possible facilities for the health, education and other welfare programmes.

However, there is no rigidity with these elements. These elements can be contracted or expanded depending upon local conditions and other social and political factors. Even sub-policies can be prepared for each of these elements, if need be. These elements and statements are just the guidelines. Adjustments are always possible.

Characteristics of an Ideal HR Policy

An HR policy should clearly define the attitude, outlook and trend of future behaviour of the management towards employees. However, it should be very simple, precise and clear. There should not be any ambiguity about it. It should aim at improving industrial relations and contribute towards the accomplishment of the organisational goals. It should also specify the place of the workers in the organisation so that they may feel proud of it and feel involved in the affairs of the organisation. It should make adequate provision for the development of employees. It should also create consciousness and generate confidence and cooperation among employees. It should be capable of taking full advantage of the capabilities of the employees. HR policies should be in writing. They should also be flexible. They should be distinguished from rules and procedures.

Policies should be taught. They should be controlled. Above all, the policies should be practicable. Thus, an ideal HR policy should have the following qualities:

- **HR policy should contribute to organisational objectives**: An ideal HR policy should be such that its implementation may help in the accomplishment of the desired objectives of the organisation.
- **HR policy should make the employees conscious of their importance and place in the organisation**: This makes the employees feel proud that they also have a place in the organisation and that the organisation realises their importance.
- **HR policy should be in writing**: An ideal policy should be in writing. Putting policies in writing is the best way of putting them to work. Management should not feel that written policies lead to rigidity. Written policies eliminate vagueness and inconsistency. By more precise communication in writing, the difficulty of communicating intentions and desires is reduced considerably. A major management consulting firm has summarised the importance of a written policy as follows:

It builds on proved decisions of the past, conserving executive energy for new decisions. It creates an atmosphere in which individual actions may be taken with confidence. It speeds administration by reducing repetition to routine. It supports consistency of endeavour across a large group through the years. It stabilises the enterprise. It frees top management so that more creative consideration can be given to the problems of today and the new programmes of tomorrow.[18]

- **HR policy should create a sense of security**: An ideal HR policy should create a sense of security among the employees. They should feel that the management has a policy whereby it ensures the security for employees.
- **HR policy should encourage cooperation between the management and the employees**: An ideal HR policy should aim at fostering the spirit of cooperation between employees and the management. It should create an environment in which there is no place for suspicion or doubt against each other.
- **HR policy should be flexible**: Although policies should not change frequently, an ideal HR policy is one which has the element of flexibility; that is, if the objectives of major plans of the organisation change, then policies should also be reconsidered to meet the changed circumstances. However, if an HR policy is disregarded quite often, then it shows that the policy is not sound, and it must be reframed.
- **HR policy should aim at creating opportunities for the development of employees**: An ideal HR policy should aim at creating opportunities for the development of employees. Such a policy would win the heart of the employees, and they would work very sincerely.
- **HR policy should be consistent**: An ideal HR policy should be consistent; otherwise, it is unlikely to help in the accomplishment of the desired objectives of the organisation. Although everybody agrees with this contention, in practice, it is violated quite often. An HR policy should be clear on all matters and may be suitable even in unusual situations. An ideal HR policy should have the quality of clarity, leaving nothing to chance. It should be able to withstand unusual situations.
- **HR policy should be controlled**: As HR policies are likely to be misinterpreted or getting obsolete, it is necessary that they may be controlled. The job of controlling the HR policies can best be done by the top management. It should be controlled by a top executive who is well versed in writing, teaching, familiar with the history and operations of the organisation and has a lot of experience of administrative work. Harold Koontz and Cyril O'Donnell have also favoured the control of policies.[19]
- **HR policy should be taught**: Simply issuing a policy or statement is not enough. As stated earlier, a policy is likely to be misunderstood or misinterpreted, and we know the consequences of a misunderstood policy. Hence, a policy must be explained and taught. Wherever and whenever needed, it should be interpreted.

Thus, an ideal HR policy should have the aforesaid features to serve its desired purpose.

Should HR Policy Be Declared?

There has always been a controversy among the HR managers regarding the declaration of HR policies. On the one hand, there are some managers who do not favour the declaration of HR policies. They object to reducing them to a written form. But this does not appear to be a correct approach. Everything has both advantages and disadvantages, but in the present case, merits far exceed the demerits. In case while framing an HR policy, care has been taken of its objectives, language, tone, clarity and so on, the policy

56 Introduction

can prove very effective in achieving the desired goals of the enterprise. The declaration and publicity of the HR policy create confidence and goodwill among the employees. They feel that the management has nothing to hide from them and that its (management's) cards are open. They feel that the management has no intention of manipulation or bungling because the HR policy is open to everybody. When the employees feel that the management is impartial, they feel highly motivated towards their jobs and develop a feeling of cooperation. They start liking to work in groups. Declaration of the policy leads to decentralisation of power. It is also an indication that the management is interested in the welfare of the employees and is not biased against any individual or group of individuals. It raises the morale of the employees besides proving instrumental in seeking their willing and effective cooperation towards the achievement of the desired objectives of the organisation.

Implementation of HR Policy

The successful implementation of an HR policy depends much on the management. In case the intentions of the management are good, there is every possibility of the successful implementation of the policy. It is a matter of common knowledge that in industrial organisations, both executive and judiciary powers rest in the hands of the management. Hence, in the case of any difference of opinion on any clause of the policy, it will be better if the matter is entrusted to a third party who may be an impartial man or body. In this way, the trade union leaders will feel better, and a climate of harmony will be sustained. Simply to implement a policy impartially is not sufficient. It should also appear to be impartial. In case the management must depart from the declared policy in any matter due to its unusual or emergent nature, it will be in the fitness of things if the management explains the background of that case, reasons for taking an exceptional view and justifies its stand in a convincing manner. If the trade union leaders are also taken into confidence, then it will be still better. Besides, the policies should change with the passage of time depending on the change in the objectives, targets, values and principles of the organisation. Necessary changes should be made only after soliciting the views, advice and suggestions of the representatives of the employees and the well-known experts of the field concerned. Otherwise also, the policies should be reconsidered periodically, say, after every three years or so, and if need be, changes should be made to make it more meaningful and effective. The moment the management feels that the declared policy is not serving the desired purpose, it should be revised, amended or dropped as the situation demands.

Exhibit 2.5   HR Policies Must Match Employee Expectations

Formal programmes and policies aiming to cultivate inclusion must match up with the daily reality of employees, connecting the dots between what the organisation says it is doing and what employees feel they are experiencing.

Source: Hindustan Times, 20 December 2016.

HR Policy Control

For making the HR policies more effective, it is necessary that they are established in accordance with good standards. Besides, as stated earlier, they should be reviewed from time to time. There should be a set of standards to check the effectiveness of a particular HR policy. Michael J. Jucius[20] has suggested some guidelines to check whether a policy will be effective or not. According to him, the checks or guidelines may be whether the policy is based upon a careful analysis of the objectives and ideals of the company; whether it is definite, unambiguous, complete and accurately stated; whether it is reasonably stable and not subject to change because of temporary changes in existing conditions; whether it has sufficient flexibility to handle normal variations in changed conditions; whether it is related to policies of other sections of the company so that proper balance of complementary policies is established; and whether it is known and understood by all who must work with it or are affected by it. In case the answers are in affirmative, it means the policy would be good and vice versa.

HR policies must match employee expectations. Policies aiming to cultivate inclusion must match up with the daily reality of employees (see Exhibit 2.5).

Through its new research report, 'The Day-to-day Experiences of Workplace Inclusion and Exclusion', Catalyst, a USA-based non-profit organisation that promotes inclusive workplaces for women, discovered three critical lessons about employee experiences: (a) inclusion and exclusion happen at the same time for many employees, (b) inclusion is really difficult to grasp and define and (c) exclusion is powerful and easy to recall.[21] Through its cross-regional study, the report captures the voices of employees across 42 organisations in 5 countries—Canada, China, India, Mexico and the USA—to better understand their everyday interaction. The three critical lessons Catalyst discovered often create a dilemma for many leaders because they must both create inclusive cultures while rooting out exclusionary behaviours.[22]

HR policies should also be periodically reviewed. This will help determining which HR policy needs to be dropped or changed or whether there is a necessity of having an additional policy. For this, Michael J. Jucius[23] has suggested a variety of appraisal methods such as all policies should be subject to some, if not extended, evaluation annually; some policies should be reviewed at specific times such as when collective bargaining agreements must be renegotiated; policies of each department may be reviewed when budgetary requests are made; spot or overall appraisal of policies may be made by outside consultants (this could be done after trouble develops, but preferably, it should be a constructive preventive measure); policies should be subject to review when the desirability is indicated by employee suggestions, employee grievances or unsatisfactory reports on employee performance or behaviour; and policies should be subjected to review whenever a company plans a major expansion or contraction, a change to a new location or a change of methods.

Thus, we find that Michael J. Jucius has very aptly suggested certain tests to check if the policy will prove good or not. Similarly, a variety of appraisal methods suggested by him for effecting periodical review of policies and introducing changes wherever necessary have immense practical utility.

Chapter Review

1. For managing changes which are far and wide and complex, we need highly competent and dedicated workforce. It calls for an efficient and effective HRM.
2. HRM is important because it takes care of all the dimensions of human factor and makes it a willing and effective contributor towards the accomplishment of

the organisational goals. HRM activities are a part of every manager's job and are recognised by managers in every unit and functional areas of an organisation. Strategic HRM is instrumental in making an organisation efficient, effective, sustainable, competitive, and profitable.
3. Regarding the nature of HRM, it is recognised that HRM is a line responsibility and a staff function, though line and staff are simply a matter of relationship. The utility of HRM is universal as it belongs to every organisation at all places. HRM possesses almost all the features of a profession.
4. The scope of HRM is very wide, developing and dynamic. According to IIPM, the scope of HRM comprises welfare aspects, personnel aspects and industrial relations aspects.
5. The primary objective of HRM is to motivate employees in such a fashion that they offer their willing and effective cooperation towards the accomplishment of the organisational objectives. HRM aims at creating, maintaining, and utilising a competent and motivated workforce, securing integration of individual and organisation goals, satisfying employee needs, enriching human capital, involving workers in decision-making, reducing their grievances, creating and maintaining conducive working and living environment, providing effective leadership and so on. The HRM objectives can be divided into two groups—primary objectives and secondary objectives.
6. HRM can deliver the desired results if certain principles are followed. These include dealing with the employee in totality; assessing the needs, feelings and reactions of employees; ensuring fair and equitable remuneration to employees appropriately; ensuring conducive working and living environment; recognising the personality of employees; ensuring effective and free flow of communication; associating the employees in decision-making process, especially in matters which affect them; making them feel that the reward they have received is not a gift but it has been earned by them; and so on.
7. HRM performs two types of functions: (a) managerial functions, which are performed by all managers irrespective of their specialisation or area of function. These functions include planning, organising, staffing, directing and controlling and performed by HRM in the context of HR activities, and (b) operative functions.
8. Operative functions in the context of HRM include (a) procurement of manpower of right kind, in right number, as and when they are required and at right wages; (b) development of manpower through appropriate training and grooming; (c) compensation, that is, reward and incentives, ensuring that the employees get fair and equitable wages and salaries; (d) integration of individual, organisational and social goals; and (e) maintenance of good and comfortable working and living environments and so on.
9. Every organisation should have its HR policies as the same indicate the action or the attitude the management is likely to adopt in future towards its personnel and their problems, though there are some authors who contend that once HR policies are framed and declared, the management is handcuffed. However, this does not sound logical as HR policies offer a sound basis for taking decisions regarding HR problems. HR policies may be (a) formal, which are

deliberately and consciously formulated—usually by top management—and (b) informal, which have just grown—everyone seems to know these without knowing where the same originated from. HR policies may contain recruitment, selection, training and development, job evaluation, wage, incentives, and labour welfare policies.

10. An ideal HR policy should preferably be in writing, contribute towards the accomplishment of the organisational objectives, create sense of security, be flexible to be declared and so on. The HR policy should be implemented in both letter and spirit and be properly controlled.

Key Terms

compensation	managerial functions
controlling	operative functions
development	organising
directing	personnel aspects
executive development	planning
human capital	procurement
industrial relations aspects	profession
industrialisation	recognition
integration	staff functions
line functions	staffing
maintenance	welfare aspects

Discussion Questions

1. Discuss the fast changes the organisations are experiencing around the world and how these can be managed through efficient and effective HRM.
2. Discuss how the HRM can be effective in seeking willing and effective cooperation from the employees towards the accomplishment of organisational goals. Also discuss why it is said that HRM belongs to all organisation.
3. Discuss what is meant by 'line' and 'staff' people.
4. Discuss that HRM works as both line and staff.
5. Discuss how HRM is a profession.
6. Discuss that the scope of HRM is very wide and it continues developing and changing per requirement.
7. Discuss the main objectives of HRM. Also discuss the primary as well as secondary objectives of HRM.
8. Discuss why it is said that principles of HRM are not absolute.
9. Discuss the managerial and operative functions of HRM.
10. Discuss the characteristics of an ideal HR policy and the importance of HR policy to both employees and the management.

Individual and Group Activities

1. As an individual or in a small group of three members, visit some big manufacturing company and find out from some of its managers how HRM helps their organisation.
2. As an individual, pay a visit to the HR department of a big organisation and discuss with the HR officials what and how they perform line functions and who is responsible for these functions in their organisation. Prepare a brief report of your discussion with them.
3. In a group of two members, discuss with the HR officials of some big company the objectives of their HRM and how far they have been successful in accomplishing them.
4. As an individual or in a small group, visit the HR department of a big organisation and discuss if they follow all the main principles of HRM and what are the difficulties they come across in implementing these principles.
5. In a group of two members, visit and discuss with the HR officials of a big manufacturing company the operative functions being performed by them and find out the hurdles, if any, they come across while doing so.
6. In a small group, visit some big manufacturing company, talk to its HR officials and discuss the main features of the training and development policy of the company.

Application Case 2.1

Significance of Maintenance Function

Abhisk, the son of a traditional businessman, established his own enterprise for manufacturing locks for automobiles. Being highly ambitious, he wanted to have the best of human resources to secure a place for his organisation in the markets. He, therefore, gathered data regarding wages and salaries being paid by other organisations in the same industry as also in the neighbouring industrial areas. He was able to attract good number of competent people by offering them slightly better than competitive rates of wages and salaries. However, within a couple of years, he was shocked to note that most of such competent employees had left his enterprise and the remaining ones also appeared to be in a mood not to continue for long in his enterprise.

Perturbed over the high per cent rate of employee turnover, he called his HR manager and asked him that in future, he should not relieve any employee unless his/her exit interview was conducted. He asked his HR manager to frame such questions to be answered by the outgoing employees as may reveal the exact cause(s) of their leaving the organisation. Within the next two months, another five employees left his enterprise—all of whom had faced the exit interview conducted.

An analysis of the responses of the outgoing employees who had left during the aforesaid two months revealed that while none was dissatisfied with his/her wage or salary, all felt that except their wages or salaries which were reasonably good, no other facilities were available to tempt them to continue with the enterprise, so they left. In other words, the HR department was indifferent towards discharging the maintenance function, which is essential to retain employees.

Questions

1. As an HR manager, what aspects would you include under the maintenance function to retain employees in future?
2. Who is accountable for not paying adequate attention towards high rate of attrition during the last two years?

Notes

1 Ivancevich, *Human Resource Management*, Importance, Nature, Scope, Objectives, Principles and Functions of HRM and HR Policy.
2 See G. Dessler and B. Varkkey, *Human Resource Management*, 11th ed. (New Delhi: Pearson Education Inc., 2009), 3.
3 Ivancevich, *Human Resource Management*, Importance, Nature, Scope, Objectives, Principles and Functions of HRM and HR Policy.
4 L. A. Allen, 'Improving Line and Staff Relationship', *Studies in Personnel Policy*, no. 153 (1956): 12, 20, National Industrial Conference Board, Inc.; see also L. A. Appley, 'Staff and Line', *Management News* 29, no. 5 (May 1956): I; R. C. Sampson, *The Staff Role in Management* (New York, NY: Harper & Row, 1955), 42–44.
5 See J. D. Mooney, *Principles of Organisation* (New York: NY: Harper & Row, 1947), 14–15.
6 See Koontz and O'Donnell, *Management: A Systems and Contingency Analysis of Managerial Functions*, 332–35.
7 Mooney, *Principles of Organisation*, 35.
8 Dessler and Varkkey, *Human Resource Management*, 4–5.
9 For details, see D. Yoder, *Personnel Management and Industrial Relations*, 6th ed. (New Delhi: Prentice-Hall of India Pvt. Ltd, 1972), 10.
10 For details, see G. Strauss and L. R. Sayles, *Personnel: The Human Problems of Management* (New Delhi: Prentice-Hall of India Pvt. Ltd, 1977).
11 For details, see Sen Gupta, R. M. *National Institute of Personnel Management, Personnel Management in India* (Mumbai: Asia Publishing House, 1961), 29–30.
12 R. C. Davis, *Industrial Organisation and Management* (New York, NY: Harper & Row, 1957), 26.
13 Edwin B. Flippo, *Principles of Personnel Management* (Tokyo: McGraw-Hill Kogakusha Ltd, 1976), 8.
14 Richard P. Calhoon, *Personnel Management and Supervision* (New York: Appleton Century Crafts, 1967), 21.
15 Jucius, *Personnel Management*, 65–66.
16 See Koontz and O'Donnell, *Management: A System and Contingency Analysis of Managerial Functions*.
17 Jucius, *Personnel Management*, 67.
18 As stated by Booz Allen Hamilton, and quoted by Louis Cassels and Raymond L. Ramdall, 'Written Policies Help Nine Ways', *Nation's Business* 47, no. 12 (December 1959): 84–87.
19 See Koontz and O'Donnell, *Management: A Systems and Contingency Analysis of Managerial Functions*.
20 Jucius, *Personnel Management*, 68.
21 *Hindustan Times*, 20 December 2016.
22 Ibid.
23 Jucius, *Personnel Management*, 68–69.

Part II
Acquiring Human Resources

Part 2

Acquiring Human Resources

3 Human Resource Planning

Learning Objectives

After studying this chapter, you should be able to do the following:

1. Explain the linkage of human resource planning (HRP) to corporate plan, and also the forms an of HRP.
2. Explain the meaning and need for HRP.
3. Explain the linkage of HRP to corporate plan, and also the forms of HRP.
4. Explain the process of HRP.
5. Explain the techniques of forecasting demand for and supply of human resources.
6. Discuss factors in HRP.
7. Explain the concept of strategic HRP.
8. Discuss the various facets of labour turnover.
9. List and describe, in brief, the models of HR strategies emerging from the approaches to business strategies/HR planning.

Introduction

An organisation's performance and resulting productivity are directly proportional to the quantity and quality of its human resources. It is all right that although nothing can be done about the past performance, perhaps even about the present performance, tomorrow's performance can certainly be made as excellent as the organisation desires, provided due care is taken today to plan for the quality and quantity of tomorrow's manpower. It is perhaps because of this that the first operative function of HRM is the procurement of personnel or human capital for the organisation. In order to achieve the desired results, there must be a mechanism in the organisation whereby the right type of people in right number could be made available as and when the necessity arises. In a small organisation, this function can be taken care of by the manager who can do the recruitment, interviewing, placement and so on without any specialised assistance. However, in a big organisation, it may not be possible for the manager to do all this. Therefore, in such organisations, much of the procurement function is delegated to specialists like an employment section of an HR department. Anyway, in both the cases, recruitment is preceded by HRP, that is, determining the kind of personnel and their skills, knowledge

DOI: 10.4324/9781032628424-5

and education desired as well as specifying the number of personnel required for each job at different levels and at different times.

Meaning of HRP

Planning, in general, involves determining the future course of action under given circumstances. Similarly, HRP (also called employment/personnel/human capital/manpower planning) involves formulating plans for manpower, visualising the kind and number of personnel possessing specified skills and knowledge required at different times, determining the possible sources of supply of the required manpower, preparing training and development plans, working out programmes for effective use of the human resources and so on.

According to Geisler,[1] manpower planning (or HRP, as it is usually called today) is the process—including forecasting, developing and controlling—by which a firm ensures that it has the right number of people and the right kind of people at the right places at the right time doing things for which they are economically most useful.

Almost similar views have been expressed by Miner and Miner. According to them, manpower planning attempts to ensure that the right number and the right kind of people will be available at the right places at the right time in the future, capable of doing things needed so that the organisation can continue to achieve its goals.

According to Coleman, manpower planning is the 'process of determining manpower requirement and the means for meeting those requirements in order to carry out the integrated plan of the organisation'.[2]

C. Wikstrom[3] has interpreted manpower planning as a series of activities consisting of (a) forecasting future manpower requirements, in terms of either mathematical projections of trends to the economy and developments in the industry or judgemental estimates based upon specific future plans of the organisation; (b) preparing an inventory of the present manpower resources and analysing the extent to which these manpower resources are employed optimally; (c) anticipating or visualising manpower problems, by projecting present resources into the future and making comparison of the same with the forecast of requirements, to determine their adequacy both quantitatively and qualitatively; and (d) planning the necessary programmes of recruitment, selection, training, development, utilisation, transfer, promotion, motivation, compensation and so on to enable the organisation to meet its future manpower requirements.

As a matter of fact, HRP helps an organisation to have the right number and the right kind of personnel at the right places at the right time in such a fashion that both the organisation and the personnel receive the maximum advantage. In other words, an HR plan is a document based on which the management of the organisation can strive to have the right number of people possessing the right type of skills at right times, in right jobs and at right places with a view to enabling the organisation to achieve its both short- and long-term goals.

According to Gary Dessler,

[Employment planning] refers to planning to fill any or all the firm's future positions, from maintenance clerk to CEO. It is the process of formulating plans to fill future openings based on an analysis of the positions that are expected to be open and whether these will be filled by inside or outside candidates.[4]

However, it should not be forgotten that the most significant factors affecting planning involve the goals of the controlling interests in the organisation. As stated by Ivancevich, 'If planning and effective utilization of human resources are not a significant goal for the organisation, employment planning will be done in a slipshod manner'.[5] For example, if the goals of the organisation embrace rapid expansion, diversification or other factors with a significant impact on future employment needs, then HRP will be more important than if the goals of the top management include stable growth.

Thus, we observe that HRP plays a key role in the achievement of goals in an organisation. If handled attentively, HRP can boost the health of the organisation as also of its personnel.

Need for HRP

The pace at which changes are occurring in the 21st century has made the business environment of organisations more complex and dynamic as compared to what it used to be a decade or two earlier. Some people have even questioned whether it is possible for organisations to develop future business plans when so many unexpected changes are happening in the present age of discontinuous change! No matter what some people may say, planning remains critical, though more challenging and demanding better expertise than in the past. Since all the changes in the business environment have implications for HRM, HRP assumes added significance.

HRP is essential for every organisation because of the following:

1. It helps in detailing the number and kind of personnel required for carrying out the operations or rendering services or conducting business in an organisation.
2. It spells out the qualifications, skills, expertise, knowledge, experience, physical abilities, occupation groups and so on of personnel required in an organisation.
3. It gives adequate lead time for recruitment, selection, training and development of personnel because it anticipates the need for various types of skill requirement and levels of personnel, well in advance.
4. It can be effective in reducing the cost of production as through it, the labour can be effectively controlled and utilised.
5. There is a constant need for replacing people who retire, die, resign or get physically incapable of reporting for duty, or are promoted or dismissed.
6. It is essential for meeting the fresh demands of personnel caused due to business growth or expansion of the organisation.
7. There may be a need for appointing new hands from external sources or for imparting vigorous training in the case of drastic technological changes. Such problems can be tackled through HRP.
8. It also helps in detecting the surplus or shortage of skills and knowledge and suggesting solutions to such problems.
9. It is essential to make training and development programmes more effective.
10. Through HR inventory, the organisation can get information for the internal succession of key personnel in the case of sudden turnover of such personnel.
11. It helps an individual employee to improve his/her education, knowledge, skills and concepts and utilise his/her capabilities and potential in the best possible manner.

HRP: Whose Responsibility?

It is the responsibility of the HR department to prepare an HR plan in consultation with the heads of all major departments and the top management. However, as in the case of other types of plans, though the overall responsibility of the HRP rests on the shoulders of the top management, it is the HR department which owns the responsibility to prepare the HR plan in consultation with various departmental heads and top management. The HR department is responsible to prepare short-term, medium-term and long-term HR plans, keeping in view the HR needs of the organisation over a specified period. It is the responsibility of the HR department to get the objectives set by the top management, to collect and analyse data relating to HRP, to provide necessary research and development and to keep effective control over the execution of HRP.

Linkage of HR Plan to the Corporate Plan

In creating an HR plan, it is to be ensured that it is an integral part of the corporate plan. It must also mesh with plans in other functional areas. In other words, it should be both 'vertical fit' and 'horizontal fit'. After all, any organisation requires manpower for achieving its corporate objectives. For example, sugar industry employs the proper kind of personnel in proper numbers in order to reach the planned production of the desired level of quality during the stipulated period. Thus, the dependence of the HR plan on the corporate plan is evident. The relationship of the HR plan with the corporate plan can be as shown in Figure 3.1.

Forms of HRP

HRP can be of two types, as discussed further.

Short-term HRP

This mainly aims at two things, as discussed further.

Matching Employees to Their Present Jobs

The resources of an organisation cannot be effectively and purposefully utilised unless the employees of the organisation match to their jobs. Such an eventuality may arise in

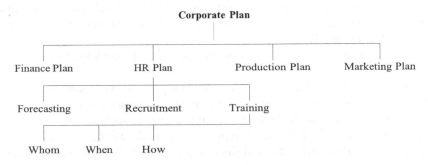

Figure 3.1 Relationship Between Corporate Plan and HR Plan

two cases: (a) when an employee is less qualified than the job requirement and (b) when the employee is more qualified than the job requirements. In both the cases, matching the employee with his/her present job is essential because the ultimate objective of HRP is the full utilisation of human resources. In the aforesaid two situations, the following measures can be undertaken:

1. **In case when the employee is less qualified than the job requirements**: Under such a situation, the following steps can be undertaken:
   a. Imparting training to develop the desired skills and expertise.
   b. Effecting changes in the job so that a part of the job, for which the employee is not suitable, may be transferred to some other employee or section.
   c. Providing assistant to the employee temporarily so that the assistant could help the employee in that part of the job in which the employee is lacking. Such steps are usually undertaken in the case of a high-ranking job in which the employee is an expert in a particular field.
   d. Changing the incumbent in case the desired skills and competence cannot be developed in the incumbent even after imparting training. The incumbent may be transferred to some other suitable job or in extreme case may be even demoted.
   e. Removing the incumbent in case the employee is incapable of serving the desired purpose even after imparting training and taking other steps. In such a situation, the employee can be terminated after taking necessary precautions.

2. **In case when the employee is more qualified than the job requirements**: There may be cases when some employees may be overqualified than their job requirements. In order to take full advantage of their skills and expertise, the following steps can be undertaken:
   a. **Job enlargement:** The job can be enlarged keeping in view the expertise and convenience of the employee.
   b. **Counselling and control:** The employee can be entrusted with job counselling and controlling others in his/her own field.
   c. **Temporary assignment:** The employee can be assigned some other job temporarily in case no other more suitable hand is available.
   d. **Promotion:** The overqualified employee can be considered for higher jobs involving more responsibilities.

Filling Unexpected Vacancies from among the Existing Employees

Sometimes certain jobs fall vacant unexpectedly due to sudden death, resignation, transfer, dismissal, disability or proceeding on long leave. In such cases, the vacancies need to be filled immediately, and usually, it is difficult to get readily the suitable people from outside. It may also happen that suitable hands may not be available even from within the organisation. Hence, the problem is of matching the man with the job. In order to overcome such problems, the following steps can be considered:

1. Entrusting additional responsibility to the existing employee(s) temporarily or if the vacant job can be divided into small parts, the so divided parts can be assigned to different employees.

70   Acquiring Human Resources

2. Promoting temporarily a relatively better existing employee to the vacant job with a clear understanding to the employee that it is purely a stopgap arrangement so that when the employee is reverted to his/her original job, he/she may not feel demoralised.
3. Abolishing the job itself. In case the job can be abolished without affecting the performance and efficiency of the organisation in any way, such a step can also be taken.
4. Imparting short-term training to the relatively more competent existing employee to bring him/her up to the mark.

Thus, in any organisation, certain jobs may fall vacant suddenly and the aforesaid steps can be undertaken to overcome the problem temporarily, and later, desired steps can be undertaken.

Long-term HRP

Although long-term HRP can be of any duration from three years and onwards, forecasting beyond ten years involves a little too much of crystal-gazing. It would be wise in most cases to settle for less. A five-year period appears to be more reasonable. However, this five-year HR plan should be a rolling plan. In other words, every year, a five-year HR plan should be made. Only in this way the plan can be kept realistic and functioning. The environment changes fast. Business must bring about internal adjustments to speedily and effectively adapt to these changes. Care must be taken that these adjustments reflect themselves in the HR plan; otherwise, adaptation will not take place, and there may be a possibility that the organisation may go out of tune with the environment and subsequently perish. Preparing an HR plan requires a great deal of tenacity, persistence and vigilance on the part of HR managers. There are mainly two objectives of long-term HRP. First, bringing about a situation in future where the personnel of the organisation match with their job requirements, and second, after forecasting the future manpower requirement, making the desired personnel available through both internal and external sources. In the long-term HRP, we may include three types of programmes as discussed further.

Forecasting HR Requirements

In order to achieve the desired objectives over a long range of period, the management has to visualise and estimate the future structure and size of the organisation over a period of time for which the management will have to take into consideration a large number of factors such as increase, expansion and growth of the organisation; the economic, political and social environment; government policy; business forecasts, design and structural changes; technological development; price structure; and so on. All these factors play a vital role in determining and shaping the future structure and size of the organisation over a specific time period. Having visualised the future structure of the organisation, estimates for future HR requirements will have to be made in terms of different functional categories, the number of personnel required and the levels at which they will be required. In order to give precision to the aforementioned estimates, we will have to take into consideration factors such as growth of the organisation, predictable turnover, for example, due to retirement, death, accidents, resignations, dismissals and so on.

Matching People with Requirements

Having prepared the list of future manpower requirement, it must be ascertained that how many of the existing personnel would be qualified or suitable to meet the required manpower needs in future. Having done this, it can be easily estimated how many people will have to be procured from external sources.

In order to fill vacancies in future, matching of existing personnel with future job requirements must be done so that the right man could be available at the right time. In this regard, we may come across three types of personnel and jobs:

1. Those future job requirements which almost match with the qualification and so on of existing personnel who, when need be, can take over the assignments.
2. Those future job requirements which can be injected into the existing personnel after imparting necessary training.
3. Those future job requirements which even after imparting training to the existing personnel cannot be met and, therefore, will have to be met out from external sources.

Based on this classification, it becomes clear that how many people would be available to meet the future job requirements from within the organisation without needing any training, how many will be matching the future job requirement after getting training and how many will have to be procured from external sources.

Planning Individual Development

From the aforementioned classification, it is obvious who and how many of the existing personnel can meet the future job requirements with or without training, and if training will be required, then what the ingredients of training and so on should be. For this purpose, a gap sheet, clearly indicating the areas where the employee is lacking and needs training, is prepared in respect of the employee likely to be assigned a new job in future after imparting training to him/her. At the time of training, the gap sheet proves very helpful because the areas where the employee is lacking can be taken care of.

Some organisations impart more than the required amount of training to certain employees for future vacancies, and those who prove up to the mark are finally selected for future assignments. There is also a possibility that an employee may be very efficient at his/her present job but may not prove to be so at a higher post because in some cases, there is a fundamental difference in the nature and demands of the existing and future jobs.

Thus, both the short-term HRP and the long-term HRP go on simultaneously in an organisation. The main difference between the two is that in the case of short-term HRP, due to non-availability of adequate time, it is difficult to make satisfactory arrangements permanently, whereas in the long-term HRP, enough time is available to the desired arrangements. However, as in the case of planning in other departments, in the HRP also, certain changes are to be incorporated because long-term planning is based on certain assumptions which may change due to certain disturbances in the internal and or external environments. Hence, HRP should not be rigid or static; it should be amenable to modification, review and adjustments in accordance with the needs of the organisation or the changing circumstances.

72 Acquiring Human Resources

In other words, it should be flexible. Although the long-term HRP may not be fully successful in matching people with the future job requirements, it brings dynamism due to which short-term HRP works very effectively.

Bases of HRP

The future requirements of human resources depend upon several factors. As a matter of fact, forecasts of manpower depend upon the following:

1. Economic forecasts
2. Sales forecasts
3. Expansion programmes
4. Employee market forecast

Processes of HRP

Basically, an HRP process entails working out HR demands and identification of the sources of supply to meet these demands, yet an HRP process is a very complex and multi-step process and embraces within its folds things such as determining objectives, going through business plan, forecasting future HR requirements, manpower auditing, carrying out job analysis and preparing an HR plan taking into consideration both internal and external sources. A brief description of all these are discussed further here.

Environmental Scanning

Environmental scanning is the first step in the process of HRP. In order to have an HR plan, the external environment which basically comprises economic factors, labour market, technological changes, demographic trends, socio-cultural-political factors and so on must be thoroughly studied and closely monitored. It is essential to scan changes in the external environment and align the business of the organisation and HR plans with the environmental demands.

Laying Down Objectives of HRP

Laying down the most common objectives of an HR plan are as follows:

1. **Making correct estimates of manpower requirements:** In every organisation, labour turnover, resignations, retirements, dismissals, promotions, transfers, technological changes, deaths and so on are common happenings which ultimately result in fresh demand for personnel which may not be met unless there is proper HRP.
2. **Making a sound recruitment and selection policy:** A sound and effective HRP helps in formulating a sound recruitment and selection policy, which may result in reducing the cost of recruitment and getting right type of people for all jobs.
3. **Making a sound training and development policy:** HRP spells out who, how and when personnel are to be trained or developed. A properly trained and or developed employee is a boon for the organisation.
4. **Managing the manpower according to the requirement of the organisation:** HRP helps in providing the right type of people in right number for the organisation.

Thus, it does not let the organisation suffer from the evils of overstaffing or understaffing of the organisation. Under the present labour-oriented policy of the government, it is very difficult to terminate the services of any employee even if he/she is in surplus. Therefore, it is essential to avoid appointing any person in surplus. It is possible only through effective HRP.

5. **Maintaining production level:** Production is always adversely affected if some employees remain absent, or go on leave, or do not turn up on duty for one or the other reason. It has been a common observation that there is usually a difference in the number of people appointed and the number of people present on duty. The bigger the gap between the two, the larger will be the loss to the organisation. However, this gap can be minimised through effective HRP by conducting workload analysis and workforce analysis.
6. **Maintaining good human and industrial relations:** HRP lays down clear-cut policies of recruitment, selection, promotion, dismissals and so on. Hence, if the HRP is effectively executed, there will be least grievances to the personnel in the organisation, and this may obviously be helpful in maintaining and developing good human and industrial relations.
7. **Getting information about the way in which the existing personnel are deployed:** HRP helps in getting this type of information also.
8. **Making proper and effective use of existing manpower:** HRP offers an inventory of the existing employees to an organisation by skill, qualifications, expertise, level, training, experience, salary and so on. It will, therefore, be possible to utilise the existing personnel more productively in relation to job requirements before going for additional manpower.
9. **Spelling out both short- and long-term objectives clearly:** Manpower planning spells out both short- and long-term objectives without any ambiguity to avoid any confusion.

Exhibit 3.1 Main Objectives of HRP

- Searching for and recruiting highly skilled and especially qualified employees
- Getting the best employee and assigning him/her the right work so that efficiency and production can be maximised
- Anticipating the changed requirements of personnel and being prepared for it organisationally
- A forward-looking activity plan that will help the management in identifying organisational needs in developing employees and in providing them growth opportunities

---

Thus, the main objectives of HRP are as shown in Exhibit 3.1.

Mello[6] identified the following major objectives of HRP:

- To prevent overstaffing and understaffing
- To ensure employee availability
- To ensure that the organisation is responsive to the environment.
- To provide direction to all HR activities
- To build line and staff partnership

Business Plan

Having determined the objectives of the organisation, the next important step in the process of HRP is to get involved in the business plan, that is, to arrive at the scale of business activity over a specific period to be able to estimate the structure and size of the organisation over a period of time. This is to be done keeping in view all the factors of internal and external environment.

Forecasting Future HR Requirements

Having estimated the structure and size of the organisation over a specific period, the next exercise to be done in the HRP process is forecasting the future manpower requirement. These days, a lot of forecasting techniques, many of which are highly mathematical, statistical and sophisticated, have been developed. But these sophisticated forecasting techniques are of greater value in the case of big organisations. In smaller organisational units, even simpler methods can serve the purpose and often may be more effective. In order to ensure that a forecast is effective and useful, the manpower estimates should be made as follows:

1. **The functional category:** That is, the estimates should be made category-wise depending on the tasks that have to be carried out and the special qualifications, training or experience required. It serves no purpose anticipating that the organisation will need 100 personnel during the next five years unless we know whether we need them, say, in the case of a sugar factory, mechanics, foremen, engineers, chemists and so on. In other words, forecast must be in terms of functions, departments or divisions.
2. **The number required:** That is, simply to know whether we shall be needing mechanics, or foremen, or engineers or all of them is not enough. We shall have to estimate the number of each category of personnel that will be required in future.
3. **The levels at which they are required:** Again, simply to estimate the functional categories and number of personnel required in such categories for the organisation in future is not enough. We shall have to estimate the various levels at which these will be required. For example, if it is estimated that the organisation will need 20 engineers in the next five years. This alone will not do, unless we also estimate how many of them should be of junior level, middle level and senior level. Only then a fruitful action can be followed.

The aforementioned estimates must be assessed under the following heads:

1. **Growth of the establishment:** It may be due to the following reasons:
    a. Increase in the demand for goods and services due to increasing population
    b. Rise in the standard of living of people causing more demand for goods and services for the existing products as also new products
    c. Rate of growth of the enterprise
    d. Competition in the market, giving rise to large-scale production for reducing the cost of production
    e. Change in production techniques/technology
2. **Turnover:** It may be of two types:
    a. Predictable: It may include retirement and so on.
    b. Unpredictable: It may include quits, deaths, transfers, promotions, dismissals, demotions, disabilities, accidents, resignations, lay-offs and other factors.

Unpredictable turnover should be assessed based on experience and the knowledge of environment.

Techniques of Forecasting Demand for Employees

Today, several techniques are available to organisations to forecast demand for manpower. A brief account of main forecasting techniques is discussed further.

Qualitative Methods of Forecasting HR Demand

These methods are judgemental and comprise the following:

1. **The expert estimate**: Based on his/her experience, guts, guesses, intuition and personal assessment of available economic and labour force indicators, an expert or a penal of experts can provide the organisation with estimates of HR requirements for future. Estimates from experts may be combined in several ways:

    a. **Delphi technique:** Since an individual's ability has limitations, the expert's estimate may not be accurate. Hence, to overcome the limitations, organisations may use the Delphi technique which was originally developed by the RAND Corporation.[7] Per this technique, estimates are sought from several individuals in an interactive manner; estimates are then revised by every individual based on the knowledge of other individuals' estimates, and in this way, a final estimate is worked out which is expected to be more accurate as compared to a single expert estimate.
    b. **Nominal group technique (NGT):** It is another method of forecasting HR requirement. In it, after individuals have generated estimates, there is a group brainstorming session in which all the individuals who have generated estimates interact and reach a group decision. Every individual enjoys equal opportunity to express opinions, thus eliminating domination by any individual in the group decision-making.
    c. **Averaging**: This method involves simple averaging of forecasts made by individual experts. The method has the advantage of taking into consideration diverse viewpoints. The main shortcoming of the method is that extreme views are marked when averaged.

2. **Sales force estimate**: This method is usually used when new products are introduced by the organisation. In it, sales personnel estimate the number of employees required based on their estimates of the demand of the product. The method has a plus point because the sales personnel who estimate the demand are familiar with the field. However, its major shortcomings are that the estimates are subjective and judgemental, and there is always a possibility of bias.
3. **Managerial judgement**: Initial forecasts made are likely to be impacted by factors like technological and administrative changes, causing enhanced productivity or decisions made to improve the quality of output or the decision made to penetrate int the new markets and so on. As such, managerial judgement will come into power play to modify the initial forecasts.
4. **Unit-demand forecasting**: This is a bottom-up approach because normally it is the unit manager at the departmental level or the leader of the project team or any other group of personnel who analyses person-by-person, job-by-job needs in the present as well as the future. It is then followed by improving the estimates by an HR executive responsible for forecasting the HR requirement, in consultation with unit managers.

76 Acquiring Human Resources

If there is any big difference between the forecasts made if both bottom-up and top-down approaches are made use of, the managers may reconcile by averaging the two total or by making use of the Delphi technique or NGT or simply averaging.

Quantitative Methods of Forecasting HR Demand

These methods involve the use of mathematical or statistical techniques and are as follows:

1. **Trend analysis and projection**: This is based on past relationship between a business factor related to employment and employment level itself. This relationship can be used in several ways as follows:
   a. **Simple long-run trend projection/analysis**: This is the second top-down technique to forecast manpower requirements. It is the study of an organisation's past employment levels over a period of years, say, the last five years or so, to forecast future manpower requirement. For example, in many organisations, sales levels are related to employment needs. A table or a graph showing the past relationship between sales and employment can be developed, which will be indicative of a trend in the past. Thus, this method extrapolates the past relationship between the volume of the business activity and employment levels into the future. As such, the main advantage of this method is that it recognises the linkage between employment and business activity. This trend will be valuable as an initial estimate. However, employment levels may not solely depend on the passage of time. These may be affected by several factors such as productivity and type of technology used. Thus, it ignores multiplicity of factors influencing employment levels. Hence, trend projections may have to be modified accordingly. Besides, this method assumes that the volume of business activity of the organisation for the forecast period will continue at the same rate as previous years which in the real world may not happen.
   b. **Regression analysis**: Regression is a statistical tool with the help of which we can estimate (or predict) the unknown values of one variable from known values of another variable. With the help of regression analysis, we can find out the average probable change in one variable given a certain amount of change in another.[8]

2. **Simulation models**: Simulation models use probabilities of future events to estimate future employment levels. The models make several assumptions about the future regarding both the internal and the external environment. However, it is a complicated method and involves a lot of cost.
3. **Workload analysis**: This method makes use of information about the actual content of work based on a job analysis of the work. In it, HR requirements are based on expected output of the organisation, and productivity changes can also be investigated. However, the method is a little bit difficult to apply. Besides, job analysis may also not be accurate.
4. **Markov analysis**: This method uses historical rates of promotions, transfers and turnovers to estimate future availabilities in the workforce. Based on past probabilities, one can estimate the number of employees who will be in various positions with the organisation in future. The model gives good results in a stable environment, but normally the environment does not remain stable. Besides, the assumption of the

model that the nature of jobs has not changed over time also appears to be unrealistic in the real world.

5. **Ratio analysis**: Ratio analysis is a forecasting technique for determining future manpower needs by using ratios between some causal factors (e.g. sales volume) and number of employees required. For example, suppose in an organisation a salesperson usually generates Rs. 400,000 in sales and that in each of the last two years, eight salespersons were required to generate Rs. 3,200,000 in sales. If it is expected that the sales volume of the organisation in that year (i.e. third year) will be increased by Rs. 1,600,000, additional four salesperson will be needed to generate the extra sales volume. The technique works when we assume that other things like productivity will remain the same. If other factors do not remain the same, then the estimate will have to be modified accordingly.

6. **Scatter plot**: A scatter plot is a graphical method which is used to identify the relationship between two variables. For example, a 1,000-student school expects to become a 2,600-student school over the next four years. The principal of the school, in order to forecast the requirement of non-teaching staff for 2,600-student school, contacts the four similar schools of various sizes and gets the following figures:

Size of the School (Number of Students)	Number of Non-teaching Staff
1,000	20
1,400	24
1,800	27
2,200	29
2,600	30

Having fitted the line (see Figure 3.2), one can project how many people will be needed, given the projected volume of the organisation.

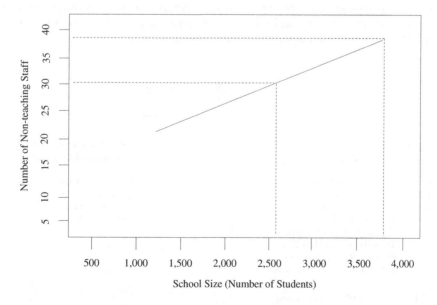

Figure 3.2 Determining the Relationship Between School Size and the Number of Non-teaching Staff

78 *Acquiring Human Resources*

7. **Stochastic method**: A significant statistical method as the stochastic method is, it refers to a process which develops in time, thereby suggesting that the future cannot be predicted with certainty. Only probabilities can be worked out because while projecting workforce requirements, two types of variables are present: (a) which are initiated by organisations and are usually certain and (b) which are initiated by individuals and are normally unpredictable (e.g. resignation by current employees). The stochastic method can handle both the certain and the unpredictable variables.
8. **Computerised systems**: Computerised systems are also used to forecast manpower requirements through which the information required to develop a computerised forecast of manpower requirements is compiled by an HR specialist.[9] Based on typical data like labour hours to produce one unit of product and three sales projections minimum, maximum and probable for the product line in question, a typical programme generates a figure on 'average staff levels required to meet product demands' as well as separate forecasts for direct labour (such as assembly workers), indirect staff (such as secretaries) and exempt staff (such as secretaries).[10] The estimate of projected productivity and sales levels so generated can be quickly translated into forecasts of manpower needs.

Factors in HR Forecasting

The future requirements of human resources depend upon several factors. The forecast of manpower depends upon the following factors:

As a matter of fact, the quantity of personnel is workforce analysis and quality of personnel is workload analysis; some details regarding the same are discussed further (see also Figure 3.3).

Workforce Analysis

The job and manpower requirements must be quantified as well as described. In many companies, steps are taken to find replacements only after vacancies occur or are likely to occur. This method of estimating a future manpower requirement is very simple and

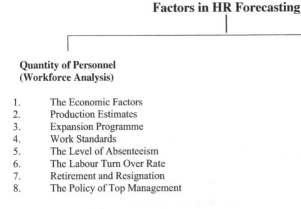

Figure 3.3 Factors in HR Forecasting

easy. However, its use aggravates interruptions to production and tends to result in hurry and hence poorly evaluated selection of replacements. The effectiveness of hiring can be increased by forecasting manpower requirements of different categories of personnel—operative, technical and executives—based on the following factors:

1. **Economic factors:** The economic forecasts relating to national economy, international economic scenario and future perspectives must be made thoroughly in order to determine future manpower requirements. If prospects of future economic situation are good, then the future sales and production prospects will also be good, resulting into more hands to obtain that level of activities. Inflation, deflation and increases in costs of inputs and raw materials are a few examples of such economic contingencies having their influence on the short-term and long-range plans of all business organisations.
2. **Production estimates:** Manpower requirements in some cases vary closely with fluctuations in production. Hence, forecasts of the latter are basic to estimates of the former. Production forecasts depend upon sales forecasts. Hence, sales forecasts are the basis upon which the estimates of manpower requirements are built. Thus, how much manpower is needed in a certain department of a company depends upon factory schedules, which, in turn, are worked out from sales forecasts and storage policies. Most companies do not produce strictly to the sales curve. Instead, a production schedule is prepared which levels out somewhat the peaks and valleys of sales estimates. The degree to which the production schedule is established in comparison with sales curve is largely dependent upon the storability of the products and their non-susceptibility to the style factor. After factory schedules are computed, department workloads can be established. These departmental schedules provide the basis for determining future manpower needs of each department.
3. **Expansion programmes:** If expansion programmes are on hand, then it will create more needs of different types of personnel. Therefore, such possibilities should also be taken into consideration while calculating future manpower requirements.
4. **Work standards:** A change in work standards due to a negotiation between trade unions and management may also create demand for labour. For example, if standard production of 50 units per worker per day at present is reduced to 40 per worker under a settlement, then it will require proportionately more workforce than at present in order to maintain the same level of production.
5. **Existing manpower inventory:** After making economic forecasts and production estimates, total manpower requirements may be determined keeping in view the work standards also. Now, it is necessary to ascertain how much manpower of various kinds is available to produce the output scheduled for the specific period in question. These two classes of information can be compared to compute the manpower to be added to or removed from the payroll. It can also be put as follows:
Total manpower requirements less existing or available manpower. Manpower to be added (or to be removed from the payroll, if economic forecast is gloomy).
6. **Labour turnover rate:** One of the oldest devices of estimating future manpower requirements in any company is through the computation of labour turnover ratio. In as much as vacancies are created by employees leaving the company, it is wise to estimate statistically how many are likely to leave. Thus, it may be possible to learn about the number of job vacancies, even though who specifically is/are to leave cannot be ascertained. Such estimates are best made in terms of past turnover. Such

turnover rates may be calculated either by separation method, replacement approach or flux method. But, however, knowing trends of turnover is an excellent means of approaching how many vacancies are likely to occur in the future (for details on labour turnover, see discussion under the head 'labour turnover' towards the end of this very chapter).

7. **Retirement and resignations:** In estimating future manpower requirement, the expected losses which are likely to occur through retirements, deaths, transfers, promotions, demotions, dismissals, disability, resignations, lay-offs and other separations should also be taken into consideration. Changes in the human quality resulting from the experience gained in the jobs during the period and the training undergone also need to be considered. After making the adjustments for wastages, anticipated and expected losses and separations, the real shortage or surplus may be found out.

8. **Changes in management:** Changes in management philosophy and leadership styles and the use of mechanical technology (such as the introduction of automatic controls or the mechanisation of materials handling functions) necessitate changes in the skills of workers as well as changes in the number of employees needed. Very often, changes in the quality or quantity of productive services also require a change in the organisation structure.

Workload Analysis

Workload analysis is a technical aspect of HRP. It involves the study of nature and composition of existing workforce, that is, auditing of human resources, study of work standards, demand analysis and so on. Auditing of existing manpower requires and initiates the preparation of a skill inventory. A skill inventory contains data about each employee's skills, abilities, work preferences and other items of information. It assists us in examining the nature and composition of existing workforce and estimating the future type of requirements of different categories of personnel. Some organisations prepare organisation charts for it, while others compile and maintain employee information card for this purpose. For determining the quality and type of personnel required, the study of work standards is essential. It is necessary to prepare a job analysis which records details of training, skills, qualifications, norms, abilities, experience, responsibilities and so on, which are needed for a job. Job analysis includes the preparation of job descriptions and job specifications. The study of work standards also removes the possibilities of underestimation of the quality and number of employees required leading to shortfalls in performance.

As an example of factors in forecasting personnel needs, Dessler[11] has pointed out that in a manufacturing firm, in addition to production or sale demand, the following factors will also have to be considered:

1. Projected turnover
2. Quality and nature of employees of the organisation
3. Decision to upgrade the quality of products or services or to enter into new market
4. Technological and administrative changes
5. The financial resources available to the department

Among factors in HRP, Saiyadain has included governmental factors, social factors, economic factors and technological changes.[12]

HR Audit and Forecasting the HR Supply

Having determined the HR needs of the organisation over a specific period, the next step in the process of HRP is to audit the existing HR in the organisation. (The primary objective of auditing the existing HR is to come to know the full details of what exists in the stock and what is needed to be added to that stock.) In other words, it gives an indication of the gap that needs to be filled in through external sources. It is therefore, very essential that human resource information system (HRIS), which is one of the important ingredients of the HRP process, should be very effective so that every bit of information about the manpower could be gathered. However, for cost consideration, we can do only with selective information. For this purpose, we can prepare 'skill inventory' or 'organisation charts'. A skill inventory may contain information about each employee such as personal factors (name, age, sex, place of birth) education and training (institutions/universities attended, examinations passed with years period, type and duration of training and so on), experience and skills (job areas, job titles, field of specialisation any other expertise, knowledge of foreign languages and so on) and any other information (existing total emoluments, scale of pay, action taken in the past, integrity, behaviour towards colleagues and confidential report or performance appraisal and so on).

From the information thus collected, we should prepare a 'manning table', clearly indicating (a) the number of the employees in each category in the organisation and (b) each employee's information card, or a 'personal inventory', classifying personnel into different groups and also relevant information about each individual worker, which can be computerised, and necessary results, especially fitness for promotion, obtained to be utilised at the appropriate time.

Thus, auditing of existing manpower should result in classifying employees into different categories and in each category further classifying them according to their status, levels of skills and so on.

Forecasting the Supply of Human Resources

Having forecast the HR requirements and conducting manpower audit, the next step in the process of planning is to forecast the supply of human resources. The forecast of the supply of human resources can be discussed under following two heads:

Forecasting the Supply of Inside Candidates

It is usually possible to meet, at least, a part of the demand predicted for HR requirements from internal sources. In this regards, qualifications or skill inventory can facilitate forecasting the supply of inside candidates.

Qualifications/skills inventories: Many organisations maintain such inventories separately for managerial and non-managerial personnel. The maintenance of such inventories tell us what kinds of abilities, skills, qualifications, experience and training the employees currently have. It helps in determining if a particular skill or ability will be available when it is needed by the organisation. Such inventories are also instrumental in helping the organisation identify the employees who need training and what type of training or who needs grooming and of what type(s) of skills need to be developed. Skill inventories also help an organisation identify what type of skills would be needed by the current employees to replace who stand retired or fired or have resigned or if any one or more than one has/have to be relocated, whether in their home country or abroad.

The contents of the skill inventories may differ from organisation to organisation and are usually tailored according to the requirements of the organisation concerned. Still, most such inventories contain details such as the name and designation of the employee, employee number, date of birth, date of joining, present location, job classification, educational qualifications, professional qualifications, expertise, foreign language(s) known, publications (including research-oriented ones), patents, performance appraisal reports, career goals and objectives, and geographical preferences, if any. The contents of the skill inventory can be categorised under relevant heads such as the summary of the skills the employee possesses at present, summary of the potential of the employee which can be tapped for future requirements and so on. However, today's skill inventories are highly sophisticated and include information on issues such as 'Do workers have necessary skills for developing and introducing new and innovative products?' or 'Who is available to become mentor for other employees?' and so on. The information to be included in the skill inventories can be collected through either getting the relevant 'questionnaire' filled in or 'interviewing' the personnel. The data so collected must be maintained in a planned manner and be updated monthly, twice a year or annually according to the relevance of the same.

According to the size, status and complexity of the organisation, the data can be maintained through any of the following systems:

1. **Manual systems**: Any of the several types of manual system can be used to store data about the employees' qualifications, training undergone at the present company level, language the employee can speak and write, career preferences and so on, which can be made use of while determining the availability of current employees for filling projected openings.
2. **Personnel replacement charts**: These charts display the performance record of the employees and their promotability for each potential replacement for vital positions. They reflect clearly which internal employee can be promoted for which position.
3. **Position replacement cards**: Some companies develop position replacement cards. In this system, a card is developed for each position displaying possible replacements, current performances, potential for performance and whether any training will be required by each probable employee.
4. **Computerised information systems**: In case the size of the organisation is big employing hundreds or thousands of personnel, it is not possible to do with manual systems. In such cases, the data regarding employees' work experience, codes, formal education, foreign languages, expertise, training undergone, product knowledge, industry experiences, career and development interests, performance appraisals, relocation limits (if any) and so on are stored on disk and are utilised whenever needed. There is no fixed limit of the data elements in HRIS which can be 100 or even more. It depends on the size and complexity of the organisation. However, adequate steps should be taken to ensure employees' right to privacy and identity thefts. Promotions, job-posting and succession planning are some of the internal sources of candidates.

Forecasting the Supply of External Candidates

It is usually not always possible to get candidates through internal sources to fill up adequately the gap between the demand for and supply of human resources. Hence, the organisations must look forward to outside candidates. In order to forecast the supply of outside candidates, the organisations must anticipate local market conditions, that is, what the status of local labour market and general economic conditions will be including the rate of unemployment as the later may affect the rate of supply of labour. A lot of secondary data about economic conditions are available through both government and private publications. Occupational market conditions will also have to be anticipated while making forecast regarding supply of outside candidates. At times, there is shortage of certain types of technical skills, while certain skills may be available in abundance. In this regard also, forecasts are available in various publications.

Job Analysis

Once manpower auditing is done and forecasting of supply of human resources has been made, the list of future vacancies over a certain period is prepared, and sources of manpower supply are identified. It is essential to prepare a job analysis. Job analysis provides information about the nature of the job (job description) and the characteristics and qualifications that-are desirable in the job holder (job specification).

The job description is a source of basic information for the HRP.

The information provided by the job description and job specification—the two ingredients of job analysis—is essential for selection, training, workload, incentives and salary administration. Job analysis has been dealt with in detail separately (see Chapter 4).

Development of Plans for Action

Having analysed the demand for and supply of human capital in the stipulated future period, it is time to choose a course of action to fill up the gap between demand for and supply of human resources. Here, there are two possibilities:

1. In case of shortage of employees: There are several options to meet the shortage of employees:

    a. Regularising the part-time workers
    b. Making the workers work overtime, of course, against payment and within the framework of current legislation
    c. Recalling the laid-off employees
    d. Using subcontractors
    e. Imparting the desired training
    f. Promoting the deserving current employees
    g. Using independent professionals in recruiting less skilled employees

2. In case employees are in surplus: It has often been observed that in times of economic recession or because of economical or technological constraints, it may be unavoidable not to do away with surplus manpower. Here also, several options are available to the employers, which are as follows:

    a. Early retirement/voluntary retirement scheme
    b. Lay-offs
    c. Retrenchments/termination
    d. Demotion
    e. Not filling positions falling vacant due to resignations, retirements and so on

84 Acquiring Human Resources

However, in our country, there are legal constraints in retrenching and laying off the employees. The employer must, therefore, observe necessary formalities before taking any such step. Trade unions resist retrenchment and lay-off tooth and nail. Hence, there should be proper HRP to enable the organisation to run smoothly.

Experience has revealed that it is always better, if it is feasible, to procure the desired manpower from within the organisation even if it involves some expenditure on the training and development of personnel. It creates a sense of belongingness towards the organisation among the workers, and promotional opportunities serve the purpose of potential incentives and make the personnel feel involved in the affairs of the organisation. Internal promotions are especially recommended for jobs of higher level involving great responsibilities. However, in the case of jobs of lower level, we can tap external sources as well. Therefore, a thorough knowledge of and close liaison with the labour market are necessary requirements on the part of the HR manager because the labour market, especially in developing countries like India, is usually unorganised and highly unstructured, mostly dealing in illiterate, immobile and ignorant workers, varied rate of wages for the same job, various methods of recruitment of labour and so on.

Strategic Human Resource Planning

HRM has become the only differentiating factor for firms for enhancing competitiveness and performance in today's knowledge-driven global economy. As human capital is considered as the most valuable asset, its nurturing, management and development have assumed greater significance for all kinds of firms. It is important that HR professionals appreciate the role of strategic planning in their organisation and understand the language and terminology of strategic planning. A strategy is the determination of the long-term goals and objectives of an organisation and the allocation of resources necessary for carrying out these goals. Business strategies usually focus on building a strong competitive position. Since an HR policy affects the organisation's profitability directly, human resources must 'fit' strategically with the mission of the organisation. An effective HR plan should, therefore, work in partnership with the strategic plan and strategy of the organisation (see Figure 3.4). For example, if the business strategy focuses on cost leadership, then the strategic HR plan (SHRP) should focus on internal promotions, training and hiring and training only for specific capabilities. Similarly, if the business strategy focuses on differentiation, then the SHRP should focus on external staffing and hiring and training for broad competencies. There should be a perfect alignment between the business strategy and SHRP so that when the SHRP is implemented, it is instrumental in accomplishing the objectives enshrined in the strategy of the organisation. HRP does not take place in isolation. It should be strategically guided by the goals and objectives of the organisation and be both 'vertical fit' and 'horizontal fit'.

Exhibit 3.2   SMEs' Contribution to Indian Economy

The SME sector has been recognised the world over as an engine of economic growth. In India, it is the second largest source of employment, after agriculture. Its contribution is significant as it accounts for more than 45% of the industrial output, 40% of exports and 42 million in employment and produces more than 8,000 quality products for the domestic and global markets.

Source: The Economic Times, 22 December 2015.

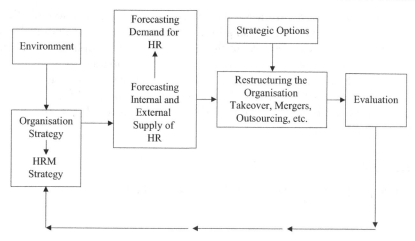

Figure 3.4 A Simple SHRP Model

Having learnt from the experience of some other developing countries such as China, Taiwan and Thailand that integrating HR management with strategic goals and objectives for improving business performance and developing organisational culture fostering innovations and flexibility is the key of success, Indian small and medium enterprises (SMEs) are developing a holistic HR perspective that focuses on talent management, training and skill development, retention, harnessing technology, greater employee engagement and a balance between employers' vision and employees' expectations. Expressing his views on emerging HR trends in SMEs for the contribution of SMEs (see Exhibit 3.2), the vice president and head HR, Power2SME, writes that it has been established that firms displaying greater congruence between HR practices and business strategies gain comparative advantage and enjoy superior performance. Growing significance of human capital and knowledge has made it pertinent for SMEs to integrate an HR perspective in their business strategies. Policies such as work timing, entry and exit procedures, safety and security regulations and compensation make the workforce more inclusive. Going further, he says that value creation, therefore, has become a formidable task for HR practitioners, especially in the SME space. They are expected to manage the employee as well as the employer perspectives and, in the long term, creativity holds the key to success while dealing with the limited resources and budgets.

In that context, outsourcing of the basic day-to-day functions such as human resources and payroll, strategic structured hiring and workforce planning have become new and necessary trends for SMEs. The HR piece in the SME growth story is vital to optimise and accelerate economic growth. The SME workforce will be the catalyst for change and, to keep them motivated, will be the key challenge of the HR function, in the years to come.

Of late, the Indian economy has become one of the fastest-growing economies, marching towards a $5 trillion economy by 2025. Coupled with globalisation, this is creating huge opportunities for SMEs for expansion and diversification across the country.[13]

Changing Environment and SHRP

In today's highly volatile environment, HRP should be strategy-oriented so that it may withstand the onslaught of the fast changes taking place these days in the environment.

86 *Acquiring Human Resources*

There is a highly competitive business environment both nationally and globally, manufacturing economy is gradually increasing by giving space to service economy, knowledge economy and knowledge workers are on the rise, technological sophistication is increasing rapidly, productivity is going up, labour market and demography are also witnessing changes, labour reforms are taking place and labour legislation is under the churning process. All these changes have HR implications and, therefore, call for suitable strategy in the HRP, which must be strategic and a little bit flexible as to take care of changes taking place in the environment.

Perspectives of HRP

There are two perspectives of HRP, which are discussed further here.

Macro Perspective

A macro perspective seeks to predict the types of skills needed by the industry in the future and compares these with what is or will be available nationally. In our country, the Twelfth Five Year Plan (2012–17) focuses on demand-aligned skill development and aims at significantly stepping up growth in employment in manufacturing. Hence, the manufacturing policy for the Twelfth Plan is to create 10 million additional jobs[14] in the manufacturing sector by focusing on labour intensive manufacturing and by suitable amendments to the labour regulatory framework. Not only this, the Twelfth Plan hopes to make the manufacturing sector a genuine engine of growth which could generate 100 million[15] work opportunities by 2022. Ambitious government initiatives such as Make in India and Smart Cities Mission are likely to create more than 0.5 million jobs in the financial year 2017 on the project side.[16]

Boston Consultancy Group's study in 2007[17] had clearly indicated that by 2020, while India will have surplus of 56 million working people, the rest of the world will encounter a shortage of 47 million working people. Hence, this opportunity can be availed by adequately training manpower in different required skills and creating abilities (see Exhibit 3.3), though the National Skill Development Corporation (NSDC) has been able to identify only 5% candidates who got placed after being trained under the Pradhan Mantri Kaushal Vikas Yojana (PMKVY), that is, only 82,183 out of 1.707 million students

Table 3.1 General Education Level of Labour Force (PS+SS) in the Age Group 15–59

	Agriculture and Allied	Manu-facture	Non-manufacture	Service	Total
Not literate	87.36	9.56	14.42	13.65	124.99
Literate without formal schooling	1.23	0.25	0.21	0.42	2
Below primary	57.62	12.69	12.47	18.32	101.10
Middle	36.20	10.27	8.67	18.98	74.12
Secondary	21.30	7.02	4.27	18.21	50.79
Higher secondary	10.36	3.21	1.45	12.43	27.45
Diploma/certificate course	0.58	1.16	0.53	3.12	5.39
Graduate	3.84	3.01	1.25	17.82	25.93
Graduate and above	0.74	0.73	0.24	7	8.70
Total	219.23	47.90	43.50	109.96	420.59

Source: Computed from NSS (66thRound), 2009–10.

trained for jobs got placement.[18] However, the government intends to provide skill training to 0.4 billion by 2022 and set a special Board for Assessment and Certification.[19]

An idea about the level of education by sectors can be had from Table 3.1.

As far as skill targets for the Twelfth Plan (2012–17) are concerned, it has been proposed that during the Twelfth Plan, 50 million non-farm employment[20] opportunities will be created and at least an equivalent number of people would be provided skill certification. The existing annual training capacity in the country is 4.5 million.[21] Therefore, it needs to be more than doubled if the target is to be achieved.

The National Policy on Skill Development, 2009, envisions empowering all individuals through improved skills, knowledge, and nationally and internationally recognised qualification to gain excess to decent employment and ensure India's competitiveness in the global market. The key features of the policy for addressing the challenges in the skill space, strategies for expanding and scaling up the skill development in the Twelfth Plan, and major functions of proposed National Skill Development Authority are shown in Exhibits 3.3–3.6.

Exhibit 3.3   Implementation Strategies for Expanding and Scaling Up the Skill Development in Twelfth Plan

Implementation Strategies:

- Expanding outreach to bridge all the divides
- Improving quality through better infrastructure, new machines and technology and better trainers
- Defining standards for outcome-driven training programmes and ensuring regular monitoring
- Introducing flexibility by adopting global standards and dynamic processes to suit the requirement of both national and international users
- Developing strong partnerships between all stakeholders; encouraging private partners providing incentive
- Creating enabling environment and monitoring the training programme to achieve outcomes

Source: Planning Commission, *Twelfth Five Year Plan*, 151.

Exhibit 3.4   Skill Policy for Promoting India's Competitiveness in the Global Market

Objectives

- Expanding the outreach by adopting established and innovative approaches to ensure equitable access to training to all irrespective of any gender, regional, social and sectoral divide
- Promoting greater and active involvement of all stakeholders, including social partners, and forging a strong, symbiotic, private–public partnership in skill development

- Developing a high-quality demand-driven skilled workforce/entrepreneur relevant to current and emerging employment market needs.
- Enabling the establishment of flexible delivery mechanisms that respond to the characteristics of a wide range of needs of stakeholders
- Enabling effective coordination between different ministries, the Centre and the States and public and private providers
- Creating institutional mechanism for research, development, quality assurance, examination and certification, affiliation and accreditation and coordination of skill development across the country

Source: Planning Commission, *Twelfth Five Year Plan*, 143.

Exhibit 3.5 Operational Strategies for Expanding and Scaling Up the Skill Development in Twelfth Plan

Operational Strategies:

- Replicability and scalability; strengthening existing centres
- Linking training with outcome
- Affordability across economic levels
- Stress on inclusivity and technology and innovation
- Flexibility in course content; qualification standards; quality trainers
- Focus on delivery

Source: Planning Commission, *Twelfth Five Year Plan*, 151.

Exhibit 3.6 Major Functions of Proposed National Skill Development Authority

1. To launch a National Skill Development Mission to, inter alia, skill five crore persons during the Twelfth Plan through appropriate strategies, including support to State Governments/State Skill Missions, and for active engagement with the private sector, NGOs and so on
2. To lay down strategies, financing and governance models to expedite skill development activities and coordinate standards of skill development working in close coordination with regulators concerned like NCVT, AICTE, Sector Skill Councils and so on
3. To assist Central Ministries in enhancing their skill development capacities
4. To act as a nodal agency for guiding State Skill Development Missions and providing funds to them to increase level of skill development activities
5. To act as a nodal agency for the launch and operations of National Skill Qualification Framework (NSQF) and keeping the NSQF constantly updated and ensuring its implementation of the same

6. To monitor, evaluate and analyse the outcomes of various schemes and programmes relating to skill development through a technology-enabled national monitoring system, and suggest/initiate mid-course corrections, additions and closure of parts or whole of any specific programme/scheme
7. To promote greater use of technology in the area of skill development
8. To oversee the advocacy campaign to ensure that aspirational aspect and enrolment in skill development programmes continue to rise
9. To advise as well as take required measures in various matters related to skill development, like training of trainers, apprenticeship training, assessment, accreditation, certification systems and national occupational standards and so on
10. To discharge any other functions and assume any other responsibility related to skill development as may be assigned to it by the Government of India.
11. To oversee and support the ongoing skill development efforts of central and state UTs ministries and departments and ensure that the estimated training target of 5 crore during the Twelfth Plan is achieved.

Source: Planning Commission, *Twelfth Five Year Plan*, 151.

As far as the coverage of the National Skill Policy is concerned, it aims at promoting the following forms of delivery of skills: institution-based skill development including private/vocational schools/technical schools/polytechnics/professional colleges; learning initiatives of sectoral skill development organised by different ministries/departments; formal and informal apprenticeships and other types of training by enterprises; training for self-employment/entrepreneurial development; adult learning, retraining of retired or retiring employees and lifelong learning; non-formal training including training by civil society organisations; and e-learning, web-based learning and distance learning.[22]

As far as the finances of the national skill development are concerned, all stakeholders, the government both at the centre and states, the enterprise—public and private—and the direct beneficiary (the individual), would share the burden of mobilising financial or in-kind resources for skill development.[23]

Micro Perspective

It is one which is the process of forecasting demand for and supply of human resources for a particular organisation which has been discussed in detail in the foregoing pages of this chapter.

Emerging Trends/Recent Happenings/Development and Projections

While formulating an HR plan, the following trends, happenings and other relevant information should also be kept in view.

Plan to Raise Manpower by up to 15%

Per the survey 'Hiring, Attrition and Compensation Trends', which is conducted every year by Genius Consultants, 43 out of the 779 companies across sectors plan to increase their

90 Acquiring Human Resources

manpower by up to 15% in the current fiscal (2016–17); 46.9% of companies across the country said that the southern region has the brightest hiring scenario followed by the northern, western and eastern zones.[24]

Manufacturing Pips IT to Be Top Employment Generator

Per a TimesJobs study of 700 employers, it was revealed that manufacturing is the top employment generator as the year unfolds.[25] The mid-year job outlook survey also saw demand for mid-level managers picking up. The other finding of the survey is that IT/telecom and manufacturing and engineering take the lead as key employment generators[26] (see Exhibit 3.7 for more findings of the job study).

Exhibit 3.7 Employers' Forecasts Regarding Generation and Other Related Issues, per TimesJobs Study of 700 Employers

1. IT/telecom and manufacturing and engineering take the lead as key employment generators.
2. Sales/business development the functional area will be most in demand.
3. Mid-level and senior managers will be most in demand.
4. Employers do not perceive a threat from start-ups.

Source: The Economic Times, 10 June 2016.

Some other forecasts in this regard include metros and tier II and III cities to witness maximum hiring, employers to remain cautious on staff levels, and employers to focus on upskilling existing workforce.[27]

India Inc. Faces Talent Crunch at Mid-level

A survey of 350 CXOs and business heads in Mumbai, Bengaluru and Delhi, conducted by Singapore-headquartered Emeritus Institute of Management, has revealed that India Inc. faces a dearth of talent at the middle management level across sectors and locations that could derail the entire country's growth prospects. Around 88% of CXOs said that hiring is the biggest challenge, followed by skill gaps, retention of high potential employees and talent development. Innovation and strategic thinking is the most important skill gap to be addressed nationally. Around 82% of the respondents across the three metros agreed on the need to provide lifelong learning to employees.[28]

Ninety-Five Per Cent of Indian Labour Force Lacks Vocational Skills

According to the City & Guilds Group Skills Confidence Report which is a global study among 8,000 employees in India, the UK, the USA and South Africa, about 95% of India's labour force lacks formal vocational skills. In India, the study was conducted by Censuswide during May 2016 with 2,055 respondents, including 272 CEOs or senior leaders, 532 middle managers and 1,251 general employees.[29] There exists a serious skill gap that needs to be filled as early as possible (see Exhibit 3.8). A panel of HR leaders shared their perspectives on the themes mentioned in Exhibit 3.8. Held in Chennai, the panel discussion was led by C. Ram Kumar, head HR, TCS; Prem K. Thomas, chief HR manager, Blue Dart Aviation; and Vijay Iyer, chief business officer, HCL TalentCare, among others.[30]

Exhibit 3.8 Bridging the Skill Gap Is Necessary

In the 37th edition of Shine HR Conclave, organised by Shine.com in partnership with The Hindu in the second week of March 2016, addressing issues related to the changing needs and expectation of employers, the conclave talked about the efforts needed to bridge the skill gap.

Source: Hindustan Times, 15 March 2016.

Exhibit 3.9 Top Ten Skills in Demand

Per 'The Future of Jobs' report released by the World Economic Forum on 18 January 2016, the top ten skills in 2020 as compared to 2015 will be as follows:

In 2015	*In 2020*
1. Complex problem solving	1. Complex problem solving
2. Coordinating with others	2. Critical thinking
3. People management	3. Creativity
4. Critical thinking	4. People management
5. Negotiation	5. Coordinating with others
6. Quality control	6. Emotional intelligence
7. Service orientation	7. Judgement and decision-making
8. Judgement and decision-making	8. Service orientation
9. Active listening	9. Negotiation
10. Creativity	10. Cognitive flexibility

Source: World Economic Forum, *The Future of Jobs* (Geneva: World Economic Forum, 2016).

Top Skills in Demand

There will be a shift in top skills in demand by 2020 (see Exhibit 3.9).

In its report entitled 'Future Skills', S. P. Jain School of Global Management pointed out the top skills of the future as displayed in Exhibits 3.10 and 3.11.

Exhibit 3.10 Top Skills of the Future

- Managing complexity
- Innovative mindset
- Dealing with ambiguity

Source: The Economic Times, 19 July 2016.

Exhibit 3.11 Top Five Skills Considered Most Important by Indian Employees, for Prospects in Five Years' Time (as Revealed in the Report by City & Guilds Group)

- Leadership skills (79%)
- Management skills (72%)
- Technical skills related to current job role (64%)
- Communication skills (62%)
- IT skills (59%)

Source: The Economic Times, 17 June 2016.

Indians See Tech Risks to Career Prospects

In its first Skills Confidence Report, based on a study of 8,000 employees in the UK, the USA, South Africa and India, the global skill development firm City & Guilds Group mentioned that India was the only market in the four-nation study where 91% employees felt that their skills would become obsolete in the next five years[31] as automation, artificial intelligence and so on could replace a number of current jobs. The skill gaps in Indian organisations were the most among the four nations covered under the study. Per the study, the top five skills that India employees consider are shown in Exhibit 3.11.

IT Sector to Lose 0.64 million Jobs to Automation by 2021

A USA-based research firm (HFS) is predicting that by 2021, the IT industry worldwide would see a net decrease of 9% in headcount, or about 1.4 million jobs, with countries such as the Philippines, the UK and the USA also taking hits.[32] India's IT services industry will lose 30% (or about 0.64 million) of low-skilled jobs to automation in the next five years.[33] Low skills are those that follow a set process and are repetitive and do not require much in the way of educational qualifications. Medium skills require some amount of human judgement in the process, dealing with more challenging problems.

Highly skilled jobs, which require creative problem-solving and analytical and critical thinking, will rise by 56%. Thus, there will be some impact of automation, but overall technology adoption will lead to more job creation across sectors.[34]

Plan to Increase Formal Workforce

The Twelfth Five Year Plan (2012–17) is to increase formal workforce. India has a total workforce of around 500 million.[35] Out of this, over 90% is in the unorganised sector, often deprived of social security benefits.[36]

Digital/Chief Digital Officers Will Be Much in Demand in Future

Today, a chief digital officer (CDO) is one of the top three important roles in many firms. In the last few years, it has become a critical role; CDOs report to the CEO and are often given the same status as the chief marketing officer (CMO) or the chief information officer (CIO). Per Gartner's CIO Survey—a few highlights of which have been published by *The Economic Times*—a CDO has become a much-in-demand role, with companies scrambling to get the right talent onboard. Demand for their skills coupled with a supply scarcity has led to salaries at the top end and shooting up to 35 million and beyond in some cases. The report further points out that during 2016, 20% of Indian organisations were opting for CDO roles, whereas the comparable percentage globally was just 9%. Reliance, Mahindra, Aditya Birla Group, RPG Group, Birla Sun Life Insurance, J10, InfoTech, L&T and Raymond are just a few of the organisations that have hired digital talent for their top deck recently.[37]

Indian Companies Still Most Bullish on Hiring

Per Manpower Employment Outlook Survey of 5,100 employers across the country, conducted by the ManpowerGroup, Indian employers have emerged as the most bullish in the world in terms of recruitment for the fourth consecutive quarter, as the survey has found that payrolls are expected to grow in all four regions and seven industry sectors—the services sector having reported the strongest hiring prospects, with a net employment growth outlook of 44%, followed by transportation and utilities sector with an outlook of 38%,[38] and so on. It is heartening to note that India's prospects remain comparatively positive even around the global economic slowdown. The survey found that there is a growing demand for young leaders predominantly in consumer goods, IT and financial technology, apart from new age sectors like e-commerce. With firms observing a growing gap between skills that candidates claim and actual skills required for many roles, there is a need for proper skill mapping and identification of the future requirements to build a talent pool for the emerging trends in the job market.[39]

All HR planners should, therefore, keep the aforementioned trends and developments while formulating HR plans.

Workforce Diversity/Gender Bias

Decades of research by organisational scientists, psychologists, sociologists, economists and demographers show that socially diverse groups (i.e. those with a diversity of race, ethnicity, gender and sexual orientation) are more innovative than homogeneous groups. People who are different from one another in race, gender and other dimensions bring unique information and experiences to a working environment. While all diversity dimensions are important, it is increasingly being recognised that women do bring substantive diversity to the organisation in terms of skill sets and experiences, in turn bringing in differential styles of leadership. Although women constitute a substantial part of the total population of our country, their participation in workforce is nowhere near the appropriate mark (see Exhibits 3.12 and 3.13).

It is relatively less in top jobs of the organisations across the country, though the Constitution of India guarantees equality of opportunity to all including women. While it is easier to improve gender diversity at lower levels, companies across industries are finding it difficult to increase the numbers at the top. As they move up the hierarchy, women managers drop out due to several reasons. However, of late, a growing tendency of increasing the share of women, especially at the mid- and top-cadre management, is being observed. A few of the cases at hand are shown in Exhibits 3.14–3.19.

It may also be pointed out that at Zensar, women make up 50% of the staff at the entry level. The company plans to increase it to 60% this fiscal year. In the middle-management level and above, women account for 29% of the workforce, which Zensar plans to increase to 50% by 2020. The company has 13% women at the vice-president level and 10% at the top-management level.[40]

Exhibit 3.12   India Ranks Low in the World in the Female Participation in Top Positions

According to a study carried out by EMA Partners in 2009, about 11% of 240 large companies have women CEOs. In comparison only 3% of the Fortune 500 companies have women CEOs. About half of these CEOs are in the financial services sector, but the manufacturing sector, which traditionally did not attract too many women, is now increasing by appointing lady CEOs.

Source: Hindustan Times, 1 August 2016.

Exhibit 3.13   India Ranks Among the Lowest in the World in the Female Labour Force Participation

India ranks among the lowest in the world in female labour force participation, behind even relatively low-income countries such as Bhutan and Bangladesh. According to the World Bank, India's female labour force participation is at 27%, compared to Bhutan's 67% and Bangladesh's 58%. Since the beginning of the of the reforms programme in 1991, India's female labour force participation has fallen from 35% to 27%.

Source: Hindustan Times, 1 August 2016.

Exhibit 3.14   Zensar Nails IT! Keen on 50% Women Staff

Zensar Technologies, which has more than 8,300 employees and is a digital solutions and technology services company, is looking to double the proportion of women in middle management and above to 50% in four years by attracting diverse talent right at recruitment, both from campuses and lateral hiring, incentives to search consultants for identifying high potential women candidates, flexible hours, work-from-home policy and time-off scheme when organisations grow women from within that you have true inclusion happening.

Source: The Economic Times, 17 June 2016.

Human Resource Planning 95

Exhibit 3.15 Tatas to Groom 300 Women Leaders for Top Posts Across Group Companies

In March 2014, the Tata Group—$109-billion India's largest conglomerate—launched 'Tata Lead' initiative for the conglomerate to double the number of women employees and also have at least 1,000 women leaders by 2020. While in 2014, there were 1.15 lakh women employees, in 2016 this number increased to 1.45 lakh. Overall gender diversity ratio is 24%, with 10% of at the top level. It is intended to increase the number of women employees to 2.30 lakh by 2020, which will account for 30% of the Group's workforce, including 1,000 women leaders. The project will have 300 high potential women executives mentored by 180 CXOs and CEOs from 45 Group companies.

Source: The Economic Times, 19 July 2016.

Exhibit 3.16 Mastercard Needs More Women as it is a Business Case for Them

A few years ago, Mastercard had less than 100 employees in India; today it has close to 1,500 and plans to grow 10% every year. Mastercard today has 60% men and 40% women employees globally. Mastercard feels it necessary to add more women to its workforce because the percentage of buying choices made by women across the globe is more than 85%.

Source: Hindustan Times, 21 June 2016.

Exhibit 3.17 Ericsson to Have 30% Women on Its Board

Ericsson's aim for 2020 on gender diversity is that 30% of workforce is female (up from 22% at present), represented in leaders and executives (top 250 leaders). Ericsson, which has 1,16,000 employees from 171 nationalities, has an inclusive approach and hires employees independent of gender, age, nationality, sexual orientations or disability.

Source: Hindustan Times, 21 June 2016.

Exhibit 3.18 Marriott to Hire More Women for Senior Roles

US hotel chain Marriott International currently employees over 1,200 women across India. Of these, 25% are managers and the company is working to improve percentage of women managers. The company introduced diversity and inclusion goals in India in 2015. The chain has hired women leaders in positions like director of operations, market directors of sales and marketing during the last four months.

Source: The Economic Times, 4 July 2016.

Exhibit 3.19   Women to Make Up 30% of Headcount in Five Years at Edelweiss

Edelweiss Financial Services (EFS) has embarked on a strategy to increase the number of women working in the diversified financial services conglomerates to 30% of the workforce, from the current 19%, in five years. It has identified 60 high-potential women with five-to-ten-year experience who are being mentored.

Source: The Economic Times, 4 July 2016.

Besides, Zensar's gender diversity strategy aims to deliver balanced leadership through balanced gender distribution across all levels. Further, in the last few years, the company claims to have moved mid-level women managers' retention from 88.5% to 94%, reduced voluntary attrition of women from 17% to 10%, increased the percentage of women returning from maternity leave from 85% to 100%, increased the percentage of women at entry level from 33% to 50%, and developed women leaders and increased the number of women function heads from 5 to 16.[41]

It should also be pointed out that Zensar is in the process of identifying 200–300 female executives in the company who can be potential leaders and part of the management committee. The company will invest in mentoring these women and get industry leaders to mentor them to help them play to their strength. The company is also working with its learning and development team to design an in-house learning and development programme (LDP) for women, because there are areas such as networking and business leadership where women need specific inputs. These initiatives are a part of the company's Vision 2020 programme.[42]

Women at the Top of Some of India's Biggest Companies

Today, we come across many women leaders who are leading some of the big companies—pharma, health care, banking and so on.

To mention a few examples of women leaders, first we can mention the name of Mrs Namita Thapar, CFO, Emcure Pharmaceuticals, whose key achievements include expanding global footprint and making five global acquisitions in the past three to four years. She has also launched a programme to raise the number of women in the company. Second, Ms Zahabia Khorakiwala, MD, Wockhardt Hospitals, is known for turning around the hospitals business of Wockhardt. Next is Tara Singh Vachani, CEO and MD, Antara Senior Living, who built the Antara Business from scratch and has convinced the family and the board of Max Group that homes for senior citizens is a viable business. Next, Samina Vaziralli, executive director, Cipla, is incubating and growing the consumer business at Cipla and steering the company into the next phase of growth. She feels that women have extreme levels of commitment. She introduced workers-centric reforms in the first week she joined Cipla. Then, Ameera Shah, MD, Metropolis Labs, wanted to convert a doctor's practice into an organisation, and she succeeded and made it pan-India business. She built the business from scratch.[43]

In order to achieve the desired objectives, the mentoring programme is in the process of being rolled out. Handholding by experienced mentors can be a vital support to help women grow as senior leaders. The programme reinforces the group's commitment to women and encourages them to stay and be an integral part of its future leadership pool. It acts like a retention tool, shielding women managers from dropping out. It has also been pointed out that the programme will not just be restricted to India but also be applicable in the 100 countries where the group operates.[44]

Mastercard is taking several initiatives. For example, it is rolling out globally flexi work, increased parental leave benefits, increasing maternity leave in India from 12 weeks to 16 weeks and paternity leave from 2 weeks to 8 weeks. Mastercard has 30% women at senior to top management and ensures that women's and men's pays are balanced.[45]

In order to move ahead in this regard, Ericsson is partnering with universities and further expanding its cooperation with organisations such as Grade Hopper (for women in computing) and Girls in ICT. Today, Ericsson has talented female leaders in the early stages of their careers and higher up in the organisation and is providing them growth opportunities and buying to make female employees work in an inclusive working environment in which everyone feels valued and welcome. It is focusing on a culture of constructive dialogue around diversity and inclusion and having policies supportive for women.[46]

The other initiative includes mentorship for grooming women to higher positions of leadership. Fortunately, today more and more hotel chains are making diversity an integral part of their hiring strategy and are giving out specific mandates for hiring women at senior levels across functions. Hyatt, Hyatt Regency Kathmandu and Hyatt International Corporation have also appointed women on every senior position recently.[47]

The company implements the mentorship programme by 30 senior women who are mostly in their 40s. The programme creates a platform for women to network and link across hierarchy and age groups. There is a plan to stop women from leaving around mid-career, by providing them with mentoring support and charting out a clear career growth path to retain high-potential female professionals. There is now a focus on hiring more women at the entry level—freshers and those with two to three years' experience—besides incentivising the group heads to hire women at the entry level.[48]

The Government of India is also thinking to give a boost to deployment of women officers in warships, leading men's teams and raising all women battalions (see Exhibit 3.20).

The defence minister also indicated that women officers might lead men's team. He also pointed that the idea of allowing girl cadets at the National Defence Academy as well as Sainik Schools is also being considered.[49]

Exhibit 3.20   Debate on All-women Units/Regiments and Women in Combat Role

The defence minister has recently reignited the debate on the role of women in combat duties. He has mooted the idea of raising all women battalions in the army and indicated that warships could shortly see women officers on board during missions.

Source: The Economic Times, 5 July 2016.

> **Exhibit 3.21 Women in STEM Perceive Gender Bias**
>
> Globally, women in STEM (science, technology, engineering and mathematics) jobs are highly ambitious and driven, but gender bias and hostile work cultures make them feel stalled and hasten their decisions to quit sooner than their male counterparts.
>
> *Source: Hindustan Times*, 12 July 2016.

MakeMyTrip, which is an online travel company, has launched a programme, Back To Future. The programme is specifically designed for women professionals who have been on a career break for at least two years and are ready to make a career back. In doing so, it joins companies such as Goldman Sachs, Genpact, Target and Intuit, which have launched similar programmes to help women transition back to work.

MakeMyTrip has been focusing on improving gender diversity numbers for many years now; currently, women make up approximately 30% of their workforce. The company is still looking to bring up these numbers and making concentrated efforts to do so by tilting the scale towards women during campus recruitments.[50]

Women Employees Perceive Gender Bias

In the fields of technology, science, engineering, mathematics and so on, women employees leave their job due to gender bias and hostile work culture (see Exhibit 3.20). In India, childbearing years and 'double burden syndrome' are also responsible for making women leave their jobs at mid-management levels. Consequently, very few women are visible at senior-management level or board of directors (see Exhibit 3.21).

> **Exhibit 3.22 Very Few Women at Top-management Level in the Corporate Sector**
>
> According to the latest Kelly Global Workforce Insights (KGWI) survey on women in STEM, it was found that only a few women are left to fill roles at the top. This glaring disparity is clearly visible in publicly traded companies as early as 2015, 12% of the companies had failed to fulfil the mandate of having at least a woman representative on their board.
>
> *Source: Hindustan Times*, 12 July 2016.

In India also, 81% of women in STEM perceive a gender bias in performance evaluation. The latest Kelly Global Workforce Insights (KGWI) survey on women in

STEM found that women in India tend to drop out of the workforce at key phases in their lives, most notably around childbearing years and later at mid-management level.[51]

It is also noteworthy that while women represent 46% of all undergraduate students in STEM, not many continue to pursue careers. Compared to 17% of men, 41% of women in technology companies leave after ten years of experience. This is a very worrying scenario.[52]

Since a good number of women leave their job at mid-management level, we come across a very limited number of women employees at top-management level or board of directors (see Exhibit 3.22).

It is discouraging to note that of the 50 companies in the NIFTY index, only five had two female directors. As many as 53% met this directive by appointing directors who were either wives or sisters of executives and not really independent members.[53]

A global study says that there would be a beneficial impact on the global economy if more investment is made in developing female leaders (see Exhibit 3.23).

Gender bias is also evident from the fact that right from the boardroom to the C-Suite, female leaders around the world are seriously scarce. Thus, the message is that gender imbalance is alive and well in the corporate landscape.[54]

It is unfortunate that Indian women earn 25% less than men (see Exhibit 3.24).

About 68.5% of women at Indian workplaces also feel that gender parity is still a concern and management needs to 'walk the talk'. According to Vishalli Dongrie, head of People and Change Practice, KPMG India, the issue of gender pay gap arises for complex reasons in India, and some reasons make it unique to the country, given its deep-rooted philosophies and industrial employment practices. There need to be policy changes to combat gender-based stereotypes in employment and promote equal pay between men and women at the workplace, especially at junior-to-middle-management levels.[55]

In a sectoral analysis, it was revealed that the largest gender pay gap in 2016 was found in the transport, logistics and communication sector (42.4%). The lowest (14.7%) was recorded in education and research, where women earned 3.4% more than men. The gender pay gap at supervisory level dropped from 2015 to 2016 by 8.1 percentage points (from 28.1% to 20%). Contrary to this, the gap at the non-supervisory level had grown by 5 percentage points between 2015 and 2016. The average gender pay gap in the manufacturing sector stood at 29.9%.[56]

Exhibit 3.23   More Female Leaders Could Mean More Profits

A global study, conducted by Ernest & Young (EY) and Peterson Institute of International Economics, reveals that an organisation with 30% female leaders could add up 6% of its net margin. The first of its kind study analysed 21,980 publicity-traded firms spanned a wide variety of industries and sectors from 91 countries. It would be a beneficial impact on the global economy if more companies invested in developing a robust pipeline of female leadership.

Source: The Economic Times, 15 March 2016.

> **Exhibit 3.24 Indian Women Earn 25% Less than Men**
>
> Women in India earn 25% less than men, proving that gender continues to be a significant parameter in determining salaries in the country according to the Monster Salary Index (MSI) on gender for 2016. While men earned a median gross hourly salary of 345.8, women earned 259.8 in 2016. The gap has narrowed by two percentage points from 27.2% in 2015 and is closer to the 24.1% in 2014.
>
> *Source: Hindustan Times*, 7 March 2017.

Labour Turnover

HRP has an important aspect of turnover. Workers sometimes leave the firm or industry at their own instance and occasionally they are ousted from the firm or industry. New workers are employed in their places and thus the composition of labour force changes from time to time. Hence, turnover is the rate of displacement of the personnel employed in an organisation due to resignation, retirement, retrenchment and so on. If the rate of labour turnover is high, then this is a sign of instability, and it adversely affects the efficiency of employees as well as the profitability of the firm. According to Flippo, 'Turnover refers to the movement into and out of an organisation by the workforce. This movement is an index of the stability of the workforce'.[57]

Experienced workers go out of the firm and new and inexperienced workers come in who are to be trained. The work suffers thereby, and the cost of labour increases. Therefore, the labour turnover proves to be very costly for the business, and every effort should be made to keep its level as low as possible.

However, a moderate labour turnover is always good for the firm. It equips the firm with new, young and energetic blood. New people bring new ideas, experience and new outlook with them.

Causes of High Rate of Labour Turnover

The factors responsible for the labour turnover may be put as follows:

1. Unavoidable factors

    a. Personal betterment
    b. Illness or accident
    c. Death or retirement
    d. Discharge due to insubordination
    e. Marriage (in case of female workers)

2. Avoidable factors

    a. Lack of congenial and healthy atmosphere in the factory
    b. Lack of proper facilities and amenities
    c. Low wages, ill treatment and so on
    d. Lack of opportunities for employee growth and promotion
    e. Redundancy due to lack of planning and foresight of higher management
    f. Others

Human Resource Planning

If the people leave the organisation due to personal reasons, then it is not a matter of anxiety. However, they should be provided opportunity for promotion within the organisation according to their seniority and merit It will not only motivate them, but the organisation will also be benefited by their experience, sincerity and loyalty. If workers leave the organisation due to lack of good working conditions and uncordial industrial relations, then it is a matter of great anxiety. The management should the causes and try to improve physical and mental environment of the organisation so that people may like to stay and contribute their maximum for the attainment of its objectives.

Measurement of Turnover

The measurement of turnover is an important problem for determining the numbers of people to be recruited at a particular point of time. Its knowledge assists the management in several ways. It may be measured by any of the following methods. The choice of a particular method will depend on whether emphasis is given on labour separations, replacements or both.

1. **Separation rate method**: This is the most commonly used method.

    According to this method, turnover rate is measured by dividing the usual number of separations during a period by the average number of workers on the payroll during the same period:

    $$\text{Turnover rate} = \frac{\text{Number Of separation in a period}}{\text{Average number of workers in the period}} \times 100$$

2. **Replacement method**: This method takes into consideration only the actual replacement of employees, irrespective of the number of people leaving. It is to be noted that in case new workers are employed on account of expansion of the business, they should not be included in replacements.

    $$\text{Turnover rate} = \frac{\text{Number of replacements in a period}}{\text{Average number of workers in the period}} \times 100$$

3. **Flux rate method**: This method takes into consideration both the number of replacements and the number of separations.

    $$\text{Turnover rate} = \frac{\text{Number Of separations} + \text{replacement}}{\text{Average number of workers in the period}} \times 100$$

It is to be noted that turnover can neither be completely avoided nor is it desirable. However, its rate can be kept at a considerably low level by taking such steps which improve employee morale and create a congenial atmosphere in the organisation.

Significance of Turnover Rate

The study and calculation of turnover rate is very significant in HRP. It helps the management in preparing manpower inventory sheet for future, in determining the type and number of workers required at a time and in future, and in proper recruitment, selection, training and so on. The management should always keep a strict eye on its rate and should prepare HRP policies accordingly. The management must also try to keep turnover rate

102 Acquiring Human Resources

as low as possible because an excessive movement is undesirable and expensive. When the employee leaves the firm, the following costs are incurred:

1. Hiring costs involving time and facilities for recruitment, interviewing and examining a replacement.
2. Training costs.
3. The pay of a learner is more than what is produced.
4. Accident rates of new employees are often higher.
5. Loss of production in the interval between separation of the old employee and replacement by the new one.
6. Production equipment is not fully utilised during the hiring interval and the training period.
7. Scrap and waste rates rise because of new employees.
8. Overtime pay may be raised to get the work completed with alienated number of employees. Keeping in view all the costs, the firm should try to control it as far as possible.

Models of HR Strategies Emerging from the Approaches to Business Strategies and HRP

In order to understand the alignment of HR strategies with business strategies, it is desirable to understand the following models that explain the relationship between human resources and strategy:[58]

1. **Model of best practices**: For implementing strategic plans, an organisation confronts the problem of selecting best practices. While an HR strategy is concerned with implementing strategic plans, it is also helpful in securing long-term benefits for the organisation through effective staffing, including HRP, maintenance and development of human resources. The model of best practices developed by Tyson and Doherty helps in analysing best practices that a business can adopt according to its strategies. Tyson and Doherty have also devised a best practice that a business can adopt according to its strategies. Tyson and Doherty have also devised a best practice virtuous circle which demonstrates the influence of an HR activity on the business strategy. According to their model, in order to achieve the desired outcomes, HRM has to work at the following three levels: (a) At the strategic level, the HR department is supposed to form policies and programmes in such a fashion as may be instrumental in realising the organisation's strategies and which can be integrated with the production service delivery systems. (b) At the operational level, in order to give a competitive advantage, competencies are created by developing sound recruitment and retention strategies and also by overcoming shortcomings in the performance through training. (c) At the business level, the HR department ensures that equal weightage has been given to all the stakeholders and that the policies are fair and impartial. Efforts are made to involve employees in the formulation of policies.

    At all levels, best practices should be developed to control cost and assist in designing workflow as also in designing jobs.
2. **Models integrating strategic change and HRM**: One of such models, which is flexible, was developed at the Harvard University and is known as the Map of HRM Territory. The model suggests that while developing HRM strategies, organisations

should keep in view the legitimate interests of the shareholders in the organisation and the same should be aligned with the HR strategy and business strategy. Based on the Harvard model, Guest developed a model that has four propositions: strategic integration, high commitment, high quality and flexibility.

Based on this model, Hendry and Pettigrew developed the model of strategic change and HRM which integrates all the models of HRM—staffing, recruitment, training and so on—keeping in view the various internal and external forces that have an impact on the organisational strategy.[59]

In another model called 'Ideal Type', Storey discussed how organisations are shifting from personnel practices to HRM practices. Storey classified these differences into four areas: beliefs and assumptions, strategic concepts, line management and key lives.[60]

HRM Strategy Regarding HRP

Since HRP is the first important step in the process of HRM, the HRM should be very vigilant and conscious in formulating its strategy regarding HRP. An HRP strategy should be in alignment with the organisational strategy to contribute significantly towards achieving the strategic goals of the organisation. HRM should follow the process of HRP and move step by step. It should scan the external environment, study the strategy of the competitive organisations, especially the number and kind of people being employed by them for producing a specific quantity of product or service, and prepare a benchmark. The HRP strategy should always keep this benchmark into consideration. The technique(s) to forecast the demand for and supply of manpower should be chosen keeping in view the size, nature, objectives and finances of the organisation. Only those techniques which can be implemented easily and which are economical and time-saving should be used. The organisation should also try to know the techniques being used by its competitors. An HRP strategy should be able to acquire right type of people for right jobs in right number at right time and at competitive rates of wages to secure an edge over its competitors.

Chapter Review

1. In order to achieve the desired results, it is necessary that the organisation should have the right type of people at right jobs in the right number and at reasonable rates of pay. This is what the HRP is all about. HRP involves making future manpower plans for the organisation, visualising the demand for and supply of human resources.
2. HRP helps in procuring, training and developing at the minimum cost. It is basically the HR department which should prepare the HR plan in consultation with various departmental heads and top management. It should also be ensured that there is a proper linkage between the HR plan and the corporate plan.
3. Forms of planning include both the short-term plan, in which action is taken to match employees to their present job and to fill unexpected vacancies from among existing employees, and the long-term plan, which includes forecasting

manpower requirements, matching people with requirements and planning individual development. The bases of manpower planning include the economic forecasts, sales forecasts, expansion programmes and the employee market forecasts.
4. The process of HRP is a multi-step one. It comprises environmental scanning, laying down objectives of HRP, involving business plan, forecasting future manpower requirements (functional category-wise, specifying the number of employees required in each category and at each level), manpower audit and forecasting the supply of manpower, conducting job analysis, and preparing development plans for action.
5. As far as techniques of forecasting demand for employees are concerned, these can be divided into two groups: (a) qualitative methods, which comprise the expert estimate (Delphi technique, NGT, averaging, sales force estimate, managerial judgement, unit-demand forecasting and so on), and (b) quantitative methods, which include trend analysis (simple long-run trend projection and regression analysis), simulation models, workload analysis, Markov analysis, ratio analysis, scatter plot, stochastic method, computerised systems and so on.
6. Forecasting the supply of human resources is done in two respects: (a) forecasting the supply of inside candidates for which an organisation must depend on data collected through manual system, personnel replacement charts, position replacement cards and computerised information systems, and (b) forecasting the supply of external candidates for which the organisation has to anticipate local labour market conditions, general economic conditions and so on.
7. An SHRP should have a perfect alignment with the strategic plan of the organisation and should be vertically and horizontally fit. It should be guided by the goals and objectives of the organisational plan.
8. Perspectives of HRP include both the macro perspective and the micro perspective.
9. Any HR plan should take care of labour turnover, which can be due to unavoidable and avoidable factors. Since unavoidable factors are usually beyond the control of the organisation, every effort should be made to monitor and regulate avoidable factors.
10. Depending on the emphasis laid by an organisation, turnover can be measured through either separation rate methods or replacement method or the flux rate method or a combination of any two or all the aforesaid three methods. Anyway, knowing turnover rate helps in reducing costs incurred on procurement, training, development, production and so on.

Key Terms

averaging
business plan
computerised information systems
Delphi technique
employment planning
gap sheet

horizontal fit
human capital planning
human resource planning
job analysis
job description
job enlargement

job specification
labour market
labour turnover
lay-off
manning table
manpower planning
Markov analysis
nominal group technique
personnel replacement charts
position replacement cards
ratio analysis
regression analysis
retrenchment
scatter plot
simple long-run trend projections
simulation models
skill inventory
stochastic method
strategic human resource management
strategy
trend analysis
unit-demand forecasting
vertical fit
workforce analysis
workload analysis

Discussion Questions

1. Discuss how HRP helps in the accomplishment of organisational goals.
2. Discuss that HRP is instrumental in procuring right people for right jobs in right number, as and when required, and at right cost.
3. Discuss that it is vital that HRP has proper linkage with corporate plan.
4. Discuss the steps undertaken to match employees to their present jobs in a short-term HRP.
5. Discuss the various types of programmes that can be included in a long-term HR plan.
6. Discuss the steps, in proper sequence, undertaken under the process of HRP.
7. Discuss the techniques, both quantitative and qualitative, used for forecasting the HR demand.
8. Discuss the techniques used for forecasting the HR supply.
9. Discuss why there should be perfect alignment between the HR plan and the corporate plan.
10. Discuss the causes of high rate of labour turnover as well as the significance of labour turnover in the context of HRP.

Individual and Group Activities

1. Working individually or in groups, visit a large organisation and find out from its HR department how it formulates the objectives of the HR plan of the organisation.
2. Working individually or in groups, discuss with the HR manager of a big organisation what techniques they make use of in forecasting the HR demand for their organisation.
3. Working individually or in groups, discuss with the officials concerned what techniques they use in forecasting the HR supply.

4. Working individually or in groups, discuss with the HR officials how they conduct the exercise of linking their HR plan with the corporate plan.
5. Working individually or in groups, visit some big organisation in your close vicinity and find out from the HR officials the labour turnover rate during the last five years in their organisation as well as find out if they make any effort to keep it low. If yes, then what?

Application Case 3.1

Varying Trends in the Demand for Labour from Season to Season

A mega sugar mill located in West UP has been in existence since the 1950s. At present, the mill employs around 500 permanent employees, 1,500 seasonal workers and a number of contractual workers during the crushing season. The overall performance of the mill has never been steady. One of the major problems of the mill relates to manpower due to a number of factors. For example, it has never been certain about the actual acreage on which sugarcane crop is sown, as it varies from year to year, from where the mill gets its raw material, that is, sugarcane. Even if some estimates of total output are made, then they are rarely correct as the output of sugarcane is dependent on several factors such as duration of winter season, frequency and intensity of frost, conditions of weather, rains or availability of water supply (which, in turn, depend on the availability of electricity), quality of sugarcane (which is often affected by various crop diseases) and so on. Availability of contractual workers and continuity of seasonal workers, in some cases, are also not certain.

As a result of the aforesaid uncertainties, the output of the mill has not been consistent and so is the case with its profits. Since labour cost constitutes a significant portion of the total cost of production, it must be monitored appropriately, but, in practice, it has never been possible due to aforementioned reasons.

The management of the mill has had several rounds of discussion on the topic but has not been able to overcome the problem and is in a great dilemma.

Questions

1. Summarise the main causes responsible for the fluctuating trend in the number of workers required by the mill from season to season.
2. Which technique(s) of forecasting demand for and supply of human resources should be used to mitigate the problem?
3. Do you think that the mills should have a separate section of HRP which should consist of experts in the field of HRP, even if it is a little bit costly proposition, to overcome the problem? Yes or no? Why? Justify with logical arguments.

Notes

1. See E. B. Geisler, *Manpower Planning: An Emerging Staff Function* (New York, NY: American Management Association, 1967).
2. B. P. Coleman, 'An Integrated System for Manpower Planning', *Business Horizon* 13, no. 5 (1980): 89–95.
3. W. S. Wikstrom, *Manpower Panning: Evolving Systems*, Conference Board Report No. 521 (New York, NY: The Conference Board Inc., 1971), 2.
4. G. Dessler, *Human Resource Management* (New Delhi: Prentice-Hall, 1998), 119–20.
5. Ivancevich, *Human Resource Management*, 135.
6. J. A. Mello, *Strategic Human Resource Management* (Singapore: Thomson Asia Pvt. Ltd, 2003), 135–36.
7. See N. Dalkey, *The Delphi Method: An Experimental Study of Group Opinion* (Santa Monica, CA: Rand Corporation, 1969).
8. S. P. Gupta and M. P. Gupta, *Business Statistics*, 15th ed. (New Delhi: Sultan Chand & Sons, 2008), 238.
9. See Glenn Bassett, 'Elements of Manpower Forecasting and Scheduling', *Human Resource Management* 12, no. 3 (Fall 1973): 35–43, reprinted in Richard Peterson and Lane Tracy, *Systematic Management of Human Resources* (Reading, MA: Addison-Welsey, 1979), 135–46.
10. Dessler, *Human Resource Management*, 122.
11. Dessler, *Human Resource Management*, 120.
12. Mirza S. Saiyadain, *Human Resource Management*, 4th ed. (New Delhi: Tata McGraw-Hill Publishing Company Ltd, 2009), 64–66.
13. See *The Economic Times*, 22 December 2015 and 24 January 2018.
14. Planning Commission, Government of India, *Twelfth Five Year Plan (2012–2017): Social Sectors*, vol. III (New Delhi: SAGE Publications, 2013), 137.
15. Ibid., 138.
16. *The Economic Times*, 29 January 2016.
17. Planning Commission, *Twelfth Five Year Plan*, 141.
18. *Hindustan Times*, 1 June 2016.
19. Ibid.
20. Planning Commission, *Twelfth Five Year Plan*, 141.
21. Ibid., 142.
22. Ibid., 143.
23. Ibid.
24. *The Economic Times*, 3 June 2016.
25. *The Economic Times*, 10 June 2016.
26. Ibid.
27. Ibid.
28. Ibid.
29. *The Economic Times*, 21 June 2016.
30. *Hindustan Times*, 15 March 2016.
31. For details, see *The Economic Times*, 17 June 2016.
32. *The Economic Times*, 5 July 2016.
33. Ibid.
34. Ibid.
35. *The Economic Times*, 21 June 2016.
36. Ibid.
37. *The Economic Times*, 17 June 2016.
38. *The Economic Times*, 14 June 2016.
39. Ibid.
40. For details, see *The Economic Times*, 17 June 2016.
41. Ibid.
42. Ibid.
43. For details, see *The Economic Times*, 19 July 2016.
44. For more details, see *The Economic Times*, 19 July 2016.
45. See *Hindustan Times*, 21 June 2016.

46 Ibid.
47 For more details, see *The Economic Times*, 4 July 2016.
48 Ibid.
49 *The Economic Times*, 5 July 2016.
50 *The Economic Times*, 7 April 2017.
51 For more details, see *Hindustan Times*, 12 July 2016.
52 Ibid.
53 Ibid.
54 For details, see *The Economic Times*, 15 March 2016.
55 For details, see *Hindustan Times*, 7 March 2017.
56 Ibid.
57 Flippo, *Principles of Personnel Management*, 127.
58 See R. Viswanathan, *Strategic Human Resource Management* (Mumbai: Himalaya Publishing House, 2010), 16–18.
59 For details, see Chris Hendry and Andrew Pettigrew, 'Human Resource Management: An Agenda for the 1990s', *International Journal of Human Resource Management* 1, no. 1 (1990): 17–43.
60 For details, see J. Storey, *Development in the Management of Human Resources: An Analytical Review* (Oxford: Blackwell Publishers, 1992).

4 Job Analysis and Design

Learning Objectives

After studying this chapter, you should be able to do the following:

1. Distinguish between the terms, 'task', 'position', 'job', 'occupation' and 'job families'. You should also be able to explain the term 'job analysis' and its uses.
2. List and explain the various sources of job information.
3. Explain quantitative techniques that help in obtaining information about job duties and knowledge, skills, abilities and other human attributes required to execute a job well.
4. Explain the steps involved in the process of job analysis.
5. Explain the relationship between job analysis and SHRM, job analysis and competencies, and job analysis and work–life balance.
6. Explain the term 'job description', its contents and characteristics of a good job description.
7. Describe the term 'job specification' and its contents.
8. Explain the meaning of job design and various approaches to job design.
9. Explain the meaning of 'job analysis in a jobless world'.
10. Identify and explain the future challenges in the context of job analysis.

Introduction

Procurement of personnel for the organisation is the first operative function of HRM. Therefore, before recruitment takes place, it is necessary to determine (a) the duties, responsibilities and requirements of a particular job (job description) and (b) the minimum acceptable human qualities necessary to perform that job properly and effectively (job specification). Job description and job specification are the two immediate products of job analysis, which will be dealt with in detail in this chapter.

Meaning and Definition of Job Analysis and Other Relevant Terms

The term 'job analysis' is a combination of two words 'job' and 'analysis', that is, to analyse the job. Therefore, before we may study the process of job analysis, it is essential to understand the meaning of the term 'job' and some other related terms.

DOI: 10.4324/9781032628424-6

First, tasks are coordinated and aggregated series of work elements used to produce an output such as a unit of production. A position consists of responsibilities and duties performed by an individual. A job, on the other hand, is a collection or aggregation of tasks, duties and responsibilities that, in toto, is regarded as reasonable assignment to an individual employee.[1] A job needs to be distinguished from a position. A position is a group of tasks assigned to one individual.[2] A job, however, may include many positions, for a position is a job performed by an employee and hence related to a particular employee.

According to Dale Yoder, an employee has his/her position, but many positions may involve the same assignment of duties and constitute a single job.[3] It is perhaps for this reason that a job has also been defined by Mamoria as 'when the total work to be done is divided and grouped into packages, we call it a job'.[4] As a matter of fact, a job is an assignment of work calling for a set of duties, responsibilities and conditions that are different from those for other work assignments.[5]

Another related term is 'occupation'. An occupation is a group of jobs that are similar to the kind of work and are found throughout an industry or an entire country.[6] Thus, an occupation is a category of work found in many firms. According to Michael J. Jucius, the term 'occupation' refers to a group of jobs with common characteristics.[7] For example, a group of closely related selling jobs may be considered as an occupation. In other words, an occupation is a generalised job.[8]

'Job families' is another term used to cover the idea of groupings of similar jobs.[9] According to Dale Yoder, job families or occupational families are groups of jobs or occupations having similar personnel requirements.[10]

Job analysis is the procedure by which the facts with respect to each job are systematically discovered and noted. It is sometimes called job study, suggesting the care with which tasks, processes responsibilities and personal requirements are investigated.[11] Job analysis provides information about the nature of the job and the characteristics or qualifications that are desirable in the job holder. It refers to the anatomy of a job. According to Edwin B. Flippo, 'Job analysis is the process of studying and collecting information relating to the operations and responsibilities of a specific job'.[12]

Some other definitions of job analysis are as follows:

Job analysis refers to the process of gathering information about the operations, duties and organisational aspects of jobs in order to write up specifications or, as they are called by some, job descriptions.[13]

Job analysis is the process of critically evaluating the operations, duties and relationships of the jobs.[14]

According to Mamoria:

Job analysis is a procedure and a tool for determining the specified tasks, operations and requirements of each job.[15]

According to R. Viswanathan:

Job analysis is the process of determining and recording all the pertinent information about a specific job, including the tasks involved, the knowledge and skill set required to perform the job, the responsibilities attached to the job and the abilities required to perform the job successfully.[16]

According to H. L. Wylie:

Job analysis is a complete study of a job, embodying every known and determinable factor, including the duties and responsibilities involved in its performance, the conditions under which the performance is carried on, the nature of the task, the qualities required in the worker, and such conditions of employment as pay, hours, opportunities and privileges.[17]

In other words, job analysis is usually a complete and detailed account of job description and job specification. Thus, job analysis is basically a process of data collection.

According to Dale Yoder, job analysis provides information in seven basic areas:

1. **Job identification**—that is, its title and code number, if any.
2. **Distinctive characteristics of the job**—that is, details regarding its location, physical setting, discomforts, union jurisdiction, supervision and hazards.
3. **What the typical worker does**—that is, specific operation and tasks that make up an assignment, their relative timing and importance, their simplicity and routine complexity, and the responsibility for others, for property and for funds.
4. **What materials and equipment will be used by the worker**—that is, whether plastics, yarns, metals, milling machines, lathes or cornhuskers and so on.
5. **How the job is performed**—that is, what are the operations involved in the performance of the job, for example, handling, lifting, feeding, cleaning, removing, drilling and so on. In other words, it refers to the nature of job.
6. **Required personal attributes**—that is, apprenticeship, training, experience, coordination, physical strength, physical demands, mental capabilities, aptitudes, social skills and so on.
7. **Job relationships**—that is, in its simplest form, such information indicating experience required, opportunities for advancement, and patterns of promotion, essential cooperation, directions or leadership from and for other jobs.

Sources of Job Information

Usually, one or more of the types of information are collected via job analysis as shown in Exhibit 4.1.

As mentioned earlier, job analysis is principally the activity of collection of various types of information pertaining to a job. Obviously, it is very important to have an idea about the various sources of information for job analysis. There are mainly five sources of job information (see Figure 4.1), which are as follows:

1. **Job holders' questionnaires:** Information may be gathered from the job holder personally or through a job questionnaire, which should be as short as possible, be simple, explain for what purpose the questionnaire is being used and be tested before using it.
2. **Other employees who know the job:** This may include supervisors and foreman who may be given special training and be asked to analyse the job under their supervision.
3. **Independent observer:** This is the person who observes the employee performing the job. Special job-reviewing committees or technically trained job analysts can be assigned the job and necessary information collected from them.

Exhibit 4.1 The Types of Information Collected via Job Analysis

- Work activities
- Human behaviours
- Machine, tools, equipment and work aids
- Performance standards
- Job context
- Human requirements

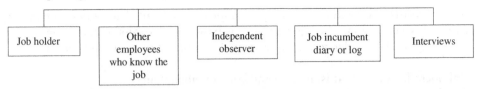

Figure 4.1 Sources of Job Information

Exhibit 4.2   Typical Interview Questions Usually Asked for Job Analysis

- What is the job being performed?
- What are the major duties of your position? What exactly do you do?
- What physical locations do you work in?
- What are the education, experience, skill and (where applicable) certification and licensing requirements?
- In what activities do you participate?
- What are the job's responsibilities and duties?
- What are the basic accountabilities or performance standards that typify your work?
- What are your responsibilities? What are the environmental and working conditions involved?
- What are the job's physical demands? Also, what are the job's emotional and mental demands?
- What are the health and safety conditions?
- Are you exposed to any hazards or usual working conditions?

---

4. **Job incumbent diary or log:** If the job incumbent keeps his/her diary or log updated recording his/her job duties, his/her frequency and when the duties are performed, these can also provide very useful information.
5. **Interviews:** Information may also be gathered through interviews of the people concerned. Some typical questions[18] asked in the interview are shown in Exhibit 4.2.

Quantitative Techniques for Obtaining Information

The aforesaid sources of data collection for job analysis form the basis for construction of specific techniques, the use of which can provide systematic and quantitative procedures that are helpful in spelling out which job duties are being performed and what knowledge, skills, abilities and other human attributes (KSAOs) are required to execute the job well. Although there are many quantitative techniques, the following three techniques are more popular.[19] These include the following:

1. **Functional job analysis (FJA):** In this, after getting the description of a job from the Dictionary of Occupational Titles (DOT), the job analyst can use the FJA to elaborate and describe exhaustively the content of a job in a common language.

2. **Position analysis questionnaire (PAQ)**: It was developed at Purdue University and contains 195 items placed in six major sections, which should be filled out by a trained job analyst and then with the help of computerised programmes PAQ ratings are scored, enabling the development of profiles for job analysed and the comparison of job.
3. **Management position description questionnaire (MPDQ)**: It is used for conducting job analysis for managerial jobs in a checklist of 208 items related to the concerns and responsibilities of managers and is designed to be the comprehensive description of managerial work.

Some other quantitative techniques/systems being used include the common metric questionnaire (CMQ) and occupational informational network.

Who Should Conduct the Job Analysis?

Who should conduct the job analysis may differ from organisation to organisation. For example, in case an organisation has only occasional requirement for job analysis, a job analyst from outside can be hired on purely temporary basis. However, in the case of other organisations, full-time job analysis experts will have to be employed. Of course, some organisations may use their own supervisors or job holders and so on to collect information related to job analysis. Anyway, whosoever collects the data, he/she should understand the jobs, people and organisation thoroughly and select the best methods and procedures to conduct the job analysis. He/she should also make use of (a) the organisation chart which presents the relationship among various departments and units of the organisation and spells out line and staff functions and (b) the process chart which spells out how a specific set of jobs is related to another.

Process of Job Analysis

Job analysis is a staff function. In order to carry out job analysis, we need a trained and highly efficient job analyst. The job analyst can be a member of the HR department, provided we have such an expert in the HR department. If need be, a practice expert can be arranged from outside the organisation also. Some big organisations employ full-time trained job analysts. The job analyst should be impartial, trained and well-equipped in the modern techniques of job analysis.

The process of job analysis is basically one of data collection. It involves a number of steps, as outlined in Figure 4.2, and can be divided into parts as discussed further.

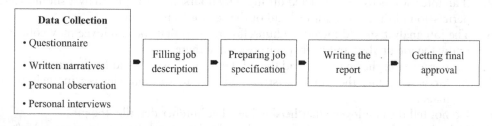

Figure 4.2 Process of job Analysis

Data Collection

As getting and stating facts as accurately as possible is only a part of the job analyst's assignment, the first step is to gather factual material about the job. In order to carry out this, following methods can be adopted:

1. **Questionnaires**: Collection of information through questionnaires is often found to be incomplete and unorganised because this technique presumes that the job holder has necessary ability to furnish the desired information properly, whereas in most cases, including even employees holding high posts, this sort of ability is missing. However, the information collected through job questionnaire(s) can be gainfully utilised at the time of interviewing the employee.
2. **Written narratives**: In this method, detailed written information is collected from the job holder and his/her supervisor. The job holder can also be requested to record daily full details of his/her major duties, including the time taken in doing each task. Unless supported by follow-up interviews, the technique does not serve the desired purpose.
3. **Personal observation**: This technique is relatively better than the former ones. In this technique, working conditions, equipment and materials used, skills required and so on are observed personally by the job analyst so that a clear picture may emerge. However, this technique may be helpful in the case of only routine and repetitive jobs and not in the case of complex jobs. It is always desirable if personal observation is followed by follow-up interviews.
4. **Conducting personal interviews**: Although this technique involves more expenditure and is also time-consuming, if any one or a combination of two or more of the aforesaid three techniques are used by the job analyst for gathering information for a job analysis, then it is always desirable that these techniques should be supplemented by personal interviews of the employees concerned. A combination of personal observation and interview is supposed to be a better proposition. Since interview is the prime method for collection of job information, the job analyst needs a certain amount of organisation sense, considerable aptitude insight, experience as an interviewer, courtesy, thoroughness, objectivity and efficiency because in a sense, the job analyst is an ambassador in this regard.

The job analyst should take care of the following suggestions:

1. As far as possible, interviews should be conducted when the employees are free and off the duty so that neither the employee nor the organisation suffers on this count.
2. If an interview is to be conducted during duty hours, then the job analyst should seek permission of the supervisor or head of the section/department.
3. The job analyst should introduce himself/herself so that the employee may come to know the job analyst and his/her purpose to be there.
4. Keen interest in the employee and the job being analysed should be shown.
5. As far as possible, the job analyst should talk to the interviewees in their own language.
6. Do not tell the employee what he/she does. Let him/her describe the job.
7. Help the employee to organise his/her thoughts but avoid putting words into his/her mouth.

Job Analysis and Design

8. Help the job holder to talk about what he/she is paid for rather than what he/she does.
9. Do not try to tell the job holder how to do the job.
10. The work should not be confused with worker.
11. The job analyst should verify the job information collected from one job holder by consultation with other job holders handling the same job.

Filling Job Descriptions

After collecting information through aforementioned techniques, the job analyst makes his/her file up-to-date and then fills the standard job description pro formas, which are separate for separate jobs.

As is clear from the title, these pro formas are descriptive in nature and contain vital information regarding the existing and future jobs.

While writing job descriptions, the following precautions should be taken:

1. Every sentence should start with a functional verb.
2. These should be written in present tense.
3. These should be brief and accurate.
4. These should be in a simple and lucid style.
5. These should have examples of work performed.
6. It should specify the extent of direction received and supervision given.
7. Avoid statement of opinions.
8. Describe in adequate detail each of the main duties and responsibilities.
9. Give a clear, concise and readily understandable picture of the whole job.

Contents of Job Description

A job description includes the following:

1. Job identification
2. Job summary
3. Duties to be performed
4. Extent of supervision to be given/received
5. Machines, tools and equipment to be used
6. Working conditions
7. Relation to other jobs
8. Organisation relationship
9. Hazards involved
10. Pay
11. Training and promotion
12. Required qualifications of the worker
13. Comments

Preparation of Job Specification

Like a job description, a job specification is also an immediate product of job analysis. It is also prepared based on information collected in the process of job analysis, but preparing a complete and correct job description is relatively simpler as compared with preparing a complete and correct job specification. A job specification is the 'statement of the minimum acceptable human qualities necessary to perform a job properly'. It contains two important things: (a) job identification and (b) required human qualities and qualifications.

Writing the Report

Having prepared the job description and job specification, the job analyst has to prepare a report. Hence, he/she puts his/her notes together and prepares a draft which should be shown to the departmental supervisor and/or head of the department/manager of the organisation and their suggestion can be solicited. The job analyst now revises his/her first draft, incorporating any new information or suggestion that can make his/her analysis more accurate or more informative. If there is a union in the organisation and if the management policy is to review the job analysis with the union representatives before issuing the details of the job analysis, then the complete draft may now be reviewed and/or discussed with top office-bearers of the local union. In such cases, the management's intention is not to get the union's approval of the draft, but it is just like informing the union in advance that the draft is ready for approval by the management. However, the management may consider the suggestion, if any, made by the union.

Getting Final Approval

Although getting final approval of the job analysis is usually not considered as part of the process, no such document becomes official until it has been approved by the line manager or staff expert who is considered the final authority in this matter. Hence, getting final approval of the job analysis from the competent authority is equally important.

Uses of Job Analysis

Job analysis is a very important and effective activity of HRM (see Exhibit 4.3).

The job information provided by job analysis is very vital in almost all-important programmes of HRM. In brief, the main uses of job analysis (see Figure 4.3) are as follows:

Exhibit 4.3   Job Analysis as a Necessary Part of HRM

Job analysis is a necessary part of HRM and in many respects is the foundation upon which all other HRM activities must be constructed. Understanding exactly what constitutes any particular job is critical to developing HRM activities that support the organisation's mission.

Source: Ivancevich, *Human Resource Management,* 151.

Uses of Job Analysis

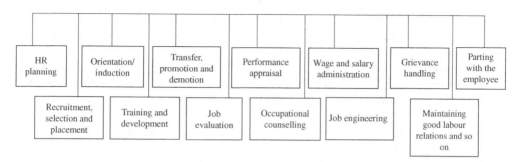

Figure 4.3 Uses of Job Analysis

1. **In HR planning**: We forecast the HR requirement over a period of time, keeping in view the duties, responsibilities and capacity of the personnel to do various jobs and so on. Job analysis provides us necessary information about duties, responsibilities and requirements of different jobs.
2. **In recruitment, selection and placement**: A job description tells us the duties, responsibilities and requirements of a particular job. Similarly, a job specification tells the minimum acceptable human qualities necessary to perform a job properly. These are the various pieces of information which constitute the basis of recruitment, selection and placement.
3. **In orienting and inducting new employees**: A job description helps to clarify what the employee needs to know about his/her job and thus prevents avoidable misunderstanding. Since job descriptions are in writing, they can prove a reliable and dependable guide which can be referred to if the new employee is confused on any issue of the job.
4. **In training**: In training also, description of duties, materials and equipment used are of considerable help in working out the contents of training programmes.
5. **In transfer, promotion and demotion**: A job description provides necessary information in deciding whether an employee should be moved up or down, and if yes, then how far or whether the nature of his/her present job fits him/her for transfer to a vacant position because his/her proven abilities equip him/her to meet requirements in other jobs grouped in the same job family.
6. **In job evaluation**: Job descriptions and specification of human requirements are weighed in terms of worth and are helpful in determining rupees value of various jobs.
7. **In performance appraisal**: A job description provides an excellent checklist, one that can be objectively discussed between the worker and his/her immediate supervisor. Without such a guide for realistic thinking, performance appraisal is likely to be affected by subjective judgement of the supervisors.
8. **In occupational counselling**: A job description may play an effective role by advising an employee who does not seem suited to the present position. He/she can also be counselled about other types of jobs that exist in the environment.
9. **In wage and salary administration**: For hourly rated employees as also office employees, job descriptions are widely made use of. The written descriptions and job analysis can be helpful in avoiding wage and salary inequality and making sure that pay is in line with going rates for comparable jobs in the industry or in the community. Job

descriptions constitute factual basis for conducting wage and salary surveys, grading jobs and developing a fair wages and salary structure.
10. **In job re-engineering**: Job analysis provides information which may be instrumental in changing job to permit their being filled by personnel with special characteristics, for example, physically handicapped.
11. **In preventing dissatisfactions**: Sometimes, contents of a job or a group of jobs may be changed to the extent that revision of job becomes unavoidable. In such cases, the revised job description should be reviewed by the supervisors with the incumbents. Doing so may prove helpful to an employee in understanding such matters as why his/her rate of pay has been altered. Such a timely explanation may prove effective in preventing employees' dissatisfaction.
12. **In maintaining good labour relations**: Job descriptions prove helpful in detecting if any employee has violated the standard fixed in the job description. If yes, then he/she can be informed, advised and reformed, and thus, misunderstanding can be avoided.
13. **In retirement**: If due to advanced age or some other physical disability or health reasons, the performance of a job holder is not up to the laid-down mark, then he/she can be asked to retire, and the worker may also appreciate the stand of the management.

Thus, we find that a job description and job specification, which are the immediate products of job analysis, have multiple uses in a well-planned HR programme.

Job Analysis and SHRM

Environmental changes are taking place at a fast pace. There will be greater flexibility in work environment. New responsibilities will be assigned to jobs from time to time. Functional areas will, therefore, not be as important as they used to be in the past to design a person's job.

Re-engineering of one kind or another will be needed from time to time to meet the requirements of the job and enable the organisation to be competitive. Hence, the strategic job analysts also must be to be capable of capturing both the present and the future.[20]

Competency-based Job Analysis

In a high-performance work environment in which employees are required to seamlessly move from job to job and exercise self-control, job descriptions based on lists of job-specific duties may create roadblocks in the flexible behaviour required by companies. Hence, today entrepreneurs are moving towards new approaches for describing jobs. One such approach is competency-based analysis in which job descriptions are based on competencies instead of job duties. It emphasises what the employee must be capable of doing rather than on a list of the duties he/she must perform.[21] Competencies are observable and measurable behaviours comprising part of a job.[22] As against traditional job analysis, which is job-focused, competency-based analysis is worker-focused and takes into consideration what he/she is competent to do.

Why Competency-based Analysis?

In the traditional job analysis, a worker is not inclined to be flexible and is always ready to say 'That is not my job' if he/she is required to do anything over and above his/her narrowly defined job in line with traditional job analysis, whereas today, a worker is required to be enthusiastic about leaving and moving among jobs. Then, in today's typical environment, it is desirable to describe the job in terms of the skills, knowledge and competencies as it is more strategic. Finally, measurable skills, knowledge and competencies support the organisation's performance management process.[23]

Scope of Job Analysis

The scope of job analysis refers to the information collected in the process of job analysis. The information so collected can be divided into two categories: (a) information pertaining to the identification of job, duties and responsibilities, working conditions, relationship with other jobs and so on (i.e. job description) and (b) information regarding minimum acceptable human qualities and qualifications and so on to enable the job holder to perform his/her duties properly (i.e. job specifications). Now, we shall study both job description and job specification in detail.

Job Description

As the title indicates, a job description is a document which is basically descriptive in nature and contains very vital information about the job. It is the first immediate product of the process of job analysis. It is, therefore, prepared by the job analyst. A job description generally describes the work performed, the responsibilities involved, the type and extent of skill or training required, working conditions, relationship with other jobs and so on. In other words, a job description is a word picture (in writing) of the duties, responsibilities and organisational relationships that constitute a given job or position. It defines continuing work assignments and a scope of responsibility that are sufficiently different from those of others to warrant a specific title. Some of the other important definitions of a job description are as follows:

According to Edwin B. Flippo, 'A job description is an organised, factual statement of the duties and responsibilities of a specific job'.[24]

According to M. W. Cumming, a job description is a broad statement of the purpose, scope, duties and responsibilities of a particular job.

In sum, a job description should tell what is to be done, how it is to be done and why it is to be done. It describes the contents of a job.

Contents of Job Description

The following things are mentioned in a job description:

1. **Job identification**: It may include the job title, alternative titles, department, division, plant, the unit where it exists, code number of the job and so on.
2. **Job summary**: It is a condensed statement of the primary functions of the job. It may also include a short definition, which may be useful as additional identification information if the job title is not sufficient for identification of the job.
3. **Duties performed**: It is a brief description of the functions performed by the employee, that is, what is being done, how it is done, why it is done and how much percentage of time is to be devoted to each major duty. Job responsibilities are also described, such as those for the custody of funds, for supervision of other workers, for training subordinates and so on. This section of job description is perhaps most important and is relatively difficult to write.

4. **Extent of supervision given and received**: How many employees and holding what jobs are to be supervised. The nature and extent of supervision, that is, whether it will be general or close supervision.
5. **Machines, tools and equipment used**: The trade names, types, models of machines, tools and equipment are also mentioned, for example, working on lathe machine or drilling machine and so on. What raw materials are to be used and the like are also mentioned.
6. **Working conditions**: The conditions in which the job holder is to work, such as noise; temperature; postures, such as standing, sitting, stooping, walking, climbing, lifting and so on; illumination; working hours, that is, during day time or night hours, over-time, hours of work, rest intervals, dirt and so on; oil; location of the place of work, such as the office, factory, inside, outside, underground, solitary, gang and so on.
7. **Relation to other jobs**: Whether it is at the horizontal level or otherwise and details about the flow of work and procedures.
8. **Organisational relationship**: The position or status of the job in the organisational structures; its position in job hierarchy and vertical relationship; the jobs which are immediately above or below this job; responsibility and accountability to the extent of authority delegated and so on.
9. **Hazards involved**: Accident risk and health hazards such as nerve strain, eye strain, physical strain, acid, exposure to weather and so on.
10. **Pay**: Method of payment—hourly, daily, weekly, monthly, piece rate—range of pay from minimum to maximum, bonus and so on required to do the job well.
11. **Training and promotion**: Whether training or apprenticeship required; if yes, then of what type and duration, basis, and line of promotion.
12. **Required qualifications of the worker**: Skills, experience, education, mental and physical standards, aptitude, attitude and so on.
13. **Comments**: The job analyst can make his/her comment or additional remark concerning the job.

Almost all good organisations use standard printed forms for filling the job description. A specimen of a general-purpose job description form is given in Exhibit 4.4.

Exhibit 4.4   A General-purpose Form for Job Description
(Name of the Organisation)

1. Department

    a. Section.......................... Title of Job........................
    b. Job Number.................... Job Code.........................

2. Work Performed

    (Description of specific duties, showing approximate percentage of time spent on each major task)
    a. Principal duties (functional specialties)
    b. Subsidiary duties (including those which are often sub-delegated)
    c. Combination tasks (in coordination with personnel in other units, sectors and departments)

3. **Organisation Relationship**
   a. Supervises (nature, type and extent of supervision given, job titles of the personnel to be supervised)
   b. Reports to (including the type and extent of supervision received)
   c. Coordinates with

4. **Conditions of Work**
   a. Time (day, night, shift, probability of overtime, peak loads)
   b. Location (factory, workshop, office, outside, inside, underground, solitary or in group and so on)
   c. Speed (quick, slow, moderate)
   d. Posture (sitting, stooping, standing, moving, climbing and so on)
   e. Accuracy (precise, medium, ordinary)
   f. Accident risk (nil, less, more)
   g. Health hazards (dirt, noise, heat fumes, temperature, humidity, illumination, acids, ventilation, physical strain, hours of work, rest pauses and so on)

5. **Minimum Job Requirements**
   a. Sex preferred
   b. Age (minimum, maximum)
   c. Physical requirements (physique, height, weight, strength, eyesight, stamina)
   d. Education (high school, graduate, postgraduate, technical qualifications, professional qualifications)
   e. Training and experience (type, duration, level)
   f. Language (written, spoken, both)
   g. Specialisation
   h. Special rating (leadership, initiative, drive, cooperation, appearance, culture, mental alertness, emotional stability, mechanical aptitude and so on)

Signature of Job Analyst

Comments   Date

Exhibit 4.5   Writing Job Description Through Internet

Today, writing job descriptions through Internet is getting more popular. The process is simple search by alphabetical title, keyword, category, or industry to find the desired job title. This will take you to a generic job description for that title. Then you can use the wizard to customise the generic description for this position.

Source: www.jobdescription.com

Using Internet for Writing Job Description

Normally, employers write their own job descriptions but, of late, more and more employers are switching over to the Internet (see Exhibit 4.5).

Characteristics of a Good Job Description

There are primarily two main objectives of preparing job descriptions: (a) to help at the time of recruitment and (b) to help at the time of job evaluation. A good job description should have the following characteristics:

1. **Proper title**: The job title should be apt and so framed as to make the qualities expected in the job holder quite clear. If the job title is appropriate, then it can be easily separated and compared with other job titles.
2. **Comprehensive job summary**: The job summary[25] should give a bird's-eye view of primary responsibilities, indicating and distinguishing principal and primary duties. The relationship with other jobs and for coordinating with other people should be clear and comprehensive.
3. **Completeness**: A detailed description of a job should be as concise as is compatible with completeness. Every detail should be very precise.
4. **Elasticity**: Job descriptions should be elastic so as to have scope for making them up-to-date from time to time. We know it well that most jobs tend to be dynamic, not static. Therefore, a job description can quickly go out of date. Hence, jobs have to be constantly revised and kept up-to-date. That is, there should be scope for elasticity in the job description.
5. **Other characteristics**: Job descriptions should clearly specify the qualities required by the job holder. The limitation of the job activities and the time taken in different operations of the job should be clearly stated.

A job description having these characteristic features will prove effective and present the description of the job in a very realistic manner.

Advantages of a Job Description

1. Helpful in recruitment and selection
2. Helpful in working out training and development programmes
3. Helpful in transfers, promotions and demotions
4. Reduces frustration among workers to a great extent
5. Reduces grievances of workers to a considerable extent
6. Helps in giving directions to newly recruited workers
7. Helps in determining wages and allowances
8. Helps in matching the workers with the job

Although written job descriptions have been developed by many companies as an attempt to define clearly and without ambiguity the duties and responsibilities of each job, a job description can be either an asset or a liability, depending on the way it is used. Job descriptions can be assets if they cover every position in the organisation, offering an operational view of the whole and showing that every job in the enterprise has been designed and analysed as an integral part of a total effect. Job descriptions can be more useful for the organisation in case these are supplemented by coaching on the job so that every employee has a position guide. However, if the job descriptions are incomplete, immaculate, ambiguous, out of date or giving rise to suspicion or confusion, then these can be a liability. Besides, simply singling out only lower-level job for job descriptions is also not a good practice.

Job Specification

According to Edwin B. Flippo, a job specification is 'a statement of the minimum acceptable human qualities necessary to perform a job properly'.[26] In contrast to the job description, it is a standard of personnel and designates the qualities required for acceptable performance. According to Dale Yoder, a job specification is a derivation from a job description. It places major emphasis on the personal characteristics required by the job. It is essentially a set of specifications for people, somewhat comparable to materials specifications. It is more difficult to prepare a complete and correct job specification than to prepare a complete and correct job description. There may always be differences of opinion regarding the minimum human requirements for doing a job properly, satisfactorily and effectively. For example, it is always controversial as to what degree of intelligence is required for doing a given job. So may be the case regarding educational qualifications, training and experience and so on. As a matter of fact, systematic and scientific personnel research can provide information that can lead to realistic human requirements for a particular work. A sound HR practice requires that all stipulated minimum human requirements for different jobs have a foundation of fact rather than intuition.

A general specimen of job specification may be as given in Exhibit 4.6.

Exhibit 4.6   Job Specification

Name of the Company..
Payroll Title...
Classification Title..
Department...
Occupational Code..
Foreman/Supervisor...
Telephone/Mobile No..
Job Summary...
....
....
....
Educational Status..
....
....

Experience required ....
....
....
Maturity ....
....
....
Knowledge and Skills Required ....
....
....
Special Abilities ....
....
....
Physical Requirements ....
....
....
Energy Level and Tempo ....
....
....
Personal Requirements ....
....
....
Creativeness ....
....
....
Self-reliance ....
....
....
Marital Status ....
Dominance ....
Sex ....
Citizenship ....
Age (minimum–maximum) ....
References Required   (1) Work ....
                      (2) Character ....
                      (3) Any Other ....
Wage Code ....
....
Hours .... Days ....
.... Shift ....
....
Tests   (a) Aptitude .... (b) Trade ....

Signature

Contents of Job Specification

Broadly speaking, besides mentioning job title, department, occupational code, name of the supervisor or boss, wage code, hours, days, shift and job summary, a job specification lays special emphasis on the following points:

1. **Physical requirements**: Various kinds and degrees of physical capacities are required on different jobs. Hence, all those physical qualifications which are called for a given job are to be listed. These may include strength, height, voice, colour discrimination, eyesight, physical impairments permitted and so on. Some special-purpose job specifications, developed as an aid in selection and placement of handicapped workers, must go into much greater details, for example, levels of strength, vision and hearing and so on. They also indicate the proportions of time spent in sitting, standing, stooping, moving, pushing, lifting, climbing, using right and left hands and feet, and so on.
2. **Mental requirements**: Various mental processes are called for different jobs. Hence, job-wise mental requirements are to be specified. These include the following:

    a. **Education:** Common school and desired college, number of years required, degree(s) required and professional technical training required—its nature, duration and type.
    b. **Language ability:** Reading, writing and speech.
    c. **Special ratings:** Leadership, initiative, drive, cooperativeness, accuracy and ability in developing men.
    d. **Test rating:** Mental alertness, aggressive–submissive, extrovert–introvert, interest, mechanical aptitudes, trade skills, IQ, memory, solving arithmetic problems, planning and decision-making.
    e. **Experience:** Kinds, levels and duration of experience.

    According to Michael J. Jucius,[27] some specific types and degrees of mental characteristics to be specified may include general intelligence; memory for names, places and abstract ideas; oral directions; written directions; spatial relations; ability to estimate quantities and qualities and to plan; arithmetical abilities; reading abilities; scientific abilities; judgement; ability to concentrate; and ability to handle variable factors.
3. **Emotional and social requirements**: These may include emotional stability, personal appearance, social adaptability, social contacts, social responsibility and so on. These days, it is being felt that perhaps the most important aspects of personal requirements are those pertaining to emotional and social characteristics.
4. **Behavioural requirements**: These may include concern for the problems of others, sensitivity to the feelings of others, greeting and meeting visitors, judgement, creativity, teaching ability, physical behaviour, dress, extent of freedom allowed to subordinates, maintaining good human relations and so on.

Job Analysis in a 'Jobless' World

In today's highly changing environment, the concept of a job stands changed significantly because today, jobs tend to be more varied and loosely defined than what they used to be in the past. Last few decades have made job enrichment, job enlargement and job or position rotation quite common, and therefore, the concept of job instead of being static has become dynamic. The companies are getting 'dejobbed'. Dejobbing refers to broadening the responsibilities of the company's jobs and encouraging employees not to limit themselves just to what is on their job description. Again, companies are organising tasks around teams and processes instead of specialised functions as used to happen hitherto. Self-managed teams, which are getting popular today, also expect an employee not to be tied down to his/her job description. Then because of re-engineering, usually, an employee's job tends to change besides making an employee collectively responsible for overall results instead of just for their own tasks. Today, a job has become like a hat which has lost its shape because of it being used by different people. Individual jobs are becoming broader and much less specialised. Hence, organisations do not want employees to be limited by a specific set of responsibilities mentioned in a job description, and job descriptions are becoming broad-based rather than static.

Why Managers Are Dejobbing Their Organisations?

Technological changes, global competition, deregulation, political turmoil, demographic changes, shift to service economy and such other challenges being confronted by the companies these days require them to be flexible, responsive and competitive. This, in turn, has weakened the meaning of job as a well-defined and clearly delineated set of responsibilities because requiring employees to limit themselves to narrow jobs runs counter to the need to have them willingly switch from task to task as job and teams-assignments change. Today, there are several organisational factors that contribute to encouraging workers not to limit themselves to narrowly defined job[28] (see Exhibit 4.7).

Exhibit 4.7 Sample of Organisational Factors Encouraging Workers Not to Limit Themselves to Narrowly Defined Jobs

- Flatter organisations
- Self-managing work teams
- Re-engineering
- Others

The Challenge

In the current scenario, self-directed teams are getting popularity, and efforts are also on how to ensure that employees make use of skills. In this regard, a competency alignment process (CAP) can prove of great help in determining current skill levels of employees in order to identify skill gaps which can be bridged through training, outsourcing and so on. The big challenge is to acquire such job analysts and HR professionals as may be able to meet the onslaught of re-engineering processes.

Job Design

Meaning and Approaches

As a matter of fact, job design is the process of organising work into tasks required to perform a specific job. It is difficult to suggest one best way to design a job. While some approaches to job design stress on providing satisfaction, the others lay emphasis on performance. Hence, the job design will be dependent on the more critical needs of the firm. Of the four main approaches to the job design, the first two, the perceptual-motor approach and the biological approach, stress on the integration of human–machine systems and suggest that equipment design should be as suits the operations. The third approach, the scientific management and machinistic approach, focuses on productivity and is best illustrated by F. W. Taylor's scientific management for whom productivity was the main concern. He, therefore, suggested a job structure, per which the job should be broken down into simple repetitive tasks to improve the efficiency of the workers. The fourth approach, that is, the motivational approach, to job design focuses on satisfying employee needs and is best illustrated by Herzberg's two-factor theory of work motivation. His contention was that employees feel motivated by jobs that increase their feelings of self-worth. Hence, job design should result in increasing the worth of the job. Job enrichment may play an important role in this direction. Work simplification, job enlargement, job rotation, job commitment and learning-based design can be the other approaches to job design.[29]

Work–Family Balance and Job Design

The changing demographics of workforce—bringing more woman workers, dual-career couples, single parents, telecommuting and so on to its fold—call for flexible work arrangements such as flexitime, job sharing, telecommuting and so on. In the hope that employees are enabled to balance their work–home demand if they are given more control over their work lives, today more and more organisations are offering flexible work arrangements to all their employees, training and rewarding those managers who encourage their subordinates to accept the flexible work arrangements without any fear of adversely affecting their standing in their firms. More ways will have to be devised to maintain work–family balance according to changed circumstances from line to time and job analysts will have to keep it in mind. In India, this has already been happening in some organisations, especially in IT and ITEs organisations, and feedback received is encouraging.

HRM Strategy Regarding Job Analysis and Job Design

Since job analysis provides information which is useful in almost all the areas of HRM, HRM's strategy regarding job analysis and job design should be perfectly aligned to the business strategy and be helpful in the accomplishment of organisational goals. After HRP has identified a job which has to be filled up by the organisation, the management selects such sources of data collection which are reliable, dependable and economic, besides less time-consuming. It is always advisable, especially in the case of big organisations, to have a full-time, well-trained job analyst who knows how to conduct job analysis and from where he/she can get expertise, if need be. It is again desirable to have printed job description pro formas and job specification pro formas, which should be prepared by experts. Such pro formas can be separate for separate categories of jobs. It will make the job easy for the job analyst, and comprehensive information can be obtained through these pro formas.

Regarding job design, the HRM may follow any of the four approaches or more than one approach while preparing the job design. However, the job should be so designed as

Chapter Review

1. After an HR plan has been formulated, the next step in the process of acquiring human resources is to conduct job analysis which is the systematic process of collecting information about a specific job—its duties, responsibilities, relationship with other jobs and so on. It collects information in seven basic areas: job identification, distinctive characteristics of the job, what the typical worker does, what materials and equipment will be used by the worker, how the job is performed, required personal attributes and job relationships.
2. The aforementioned required job information is collected through job holders, other employees who know the job, independent observers, job incumbent dairy or log and interviews. There are various techniques such as FJA, PAQ, MPDQ, CMQ, occupational informational network and so on that help in obtaining information about job duties and KSAOs required to execute the job well.
3. Job analysis can be conducted either by a job analyst from outside on purely temporary basis or a full-time (permanent) job analysis expert or by the company's own supervisor/job holders, depending on the circumstances and requirement of the organisation.
4. The process of job analysis is a multi-stepped one which usually comprises collecting data, filling of job description pro formas, preparing job specification, writing the report and getting final approval from the appropriate authority.
5. Job analysis provides useful information for HRP, recruitment, selection, training and development, promotions and transfers, job evaluation, performance appraisal, occupational counselling, wage and salary administration, maintenance of good labour relations and so on.
6. Since jobs are changing very fast, new responsibilities are being assigned to jobs from time to time and jobs are re-engineered frequently, it is necessary that the strategic job analyst capture both the present and the future and be able to contribute to make the organisation competitive.
7. As far as job analysis and competencies are concerned, since jobs are being re-engineered and teamwork is emphasised, it is necessary to have competencies which are broad-based and include attributes needed by employees to do well across multiple roles. The job analyst will have to pinpoint the requirements in ways that extend beyond the specific job itself.
8. As far as scope of a job analysis is concerned, it comprises (a) job description and (b) job specification. A job description is a written statement that identifies, describes and defines a job in terms of its duties, responsibilities, working conditions and specifications. The main contents of a job description include job identification, job summary, duties and responsibilities, job specifications and so on.

9. Regarding job specification which spells out what human traits and experiences are required to do a particular job well, it lays special emphasis on identifying physical, mental, emotional and behavioural requirement to be successful on a specific job.
10. Job design is the process of organising work into tasks required to perform a specific job. The main approaches to the job design include the perceptual-motor approach, biological approach, scientific management machinistic approach and motivational approach.
11. Due to changing demographics of workforce, especially women, dual-career couples, single parents and so on joining the workforce in substantial numbers, organisations will have to provide flexible work to enable the workforce to maintain balance between work and family demands, and the job analyst will have to keep it in mind while conducting job analysis.
12. Today, there is job analysis in a jobless world because owing to fast changes, it is difficult to have a permanent job description of any specific job. Job enlargement, job enrichment, job rotation, re-engineering and so on are getting so common that the concept of job has become dynamic instead of being static. Hence, a job analysis needs to be broad-based.
13. Today, self-directed teams, re-engineering and how to make proper use of skills and abilities of workforce are some of the challenging issues. The job analyst will have to make concrete contributions in that direction.

Key Terms

common metric questionnaire
competencies
demographics
Dictionary of Occupational Titles (DOT)
flexitime
functional job analysis (FJA)
job analysis
job description
job design
job families
job incumbent diary or log
job re-engineering
job specification
job study
management position description questionnaire
occupation
occupational counselling
organisation chart
performance appraisal
position
position analysis questionnaire
process chart
strategic human resource management
work–family balance
written narratives

Discussion Questions

1. Discuss the importance of job analysis in almost all the areas of HRM.
2. Discuss the pros and cons of various sources of job information.

3. Discuss who should conduct job analysis in a big manufacturing organisation employing around 5,000 people and having approximately different types of jobs.
4. Discuss the process of job analysis.
5. Discuss what precautions should be taken by a job analyst while conducting job analysis.
6. Discuss what should be the main contents of a job description.
7. Discuss the main contents of a job specification.
8. Discuss what job design is all about.
9. Discuss how job design can be instrumental in balancing work and life demands.
10. Discuss the big challenge today in the context of job analysis.

Individual and Group Activities

1. As an individual, visit a medium-scale manufacturing organisation and contact its HR officials. Find out from them if they conduct job analysis, and if yes, then how frequently and who conducts the job analysis in their organisation.
2. As an individual or in a group, contact the production manager of a large manufacturing organisation and find out from him/her if job analyses conducted in the past in their organisation have served the desired purpose and how?
3. As an individual or in a group, visit some service organisation and discuss the contents of the job description pro forma(s) being used by it for different positions.
4. As an individual or in a group, prepare a job description for the position of sales managers to be used by an automotive organisation.
5. As an individual or in a group, visit some big manufacturing organisation and find out from the officials concerned how they prepare job designs in their organisation.

Application Case 4.1

Recruiting Without Having Job Specification

Joe, an MBA (HR) with two years of experience as assistant HR manager in a manufacturing organisation, had joined an automotive company as the HR manager about a couple of years back. The number of industrial conflicts had been rising ever since he joined this company as his company was situated in the belt where many other automotive companies were also located and where industrial disputes, strikes and lockouts were common phenomena. Many a time, he had to attend proceedings in the office of conciliation officer, labour court and so on, telling upon heavily on his time and personal health on account of excessive physical and mental exertion. When he found that it was not possible for him to cope with the legal work in addition to his routine duties in the HR department, he approached his

CEO, who was MTech (mechanical engineering), and pleaded for an additional hand to take care of legal issues.

After a lot of discussion, the CEO agreed to sanction a post of assistant manager (legal) and asked Joe to go ahead with the recruitment for the aforesaid post. With the intention of getting immediate relief, Joe advertised the post next day, laying down that the applicant should be a first-class law graduate and be readily available to join the company, if selected. Within a period of three weeks, Robin, a fresh law graduate, was appointed as he had scored the highest percentage of marks in his law degree among all the candidates who had applied for the job and subsequently interviewed.

Robin reported for his duty within a week of his selection for the post. However, Joe found that instead of proving a helping hand, Robin proved to be a liability to him because he was a raw hand and had no practical exposure in handling the legal issues. He used to approach Joe very frequently to seek background of the case, legal formalities to be observed and implications related to every case. Joe felt so much overburdened that he resigned from his post.

Questions

1. Identify what went wrong in the appointment of Robin.
2. What policy should be followed by the company in future in order to avoid the pitfalls experienced in the case of Robin?
3. Prepare a brief job specification for the position of assistant manager (legal) for the organisation Joe was working at.

Notes

1. Yoder, *Personnel Management and Industrial Relations*, 280.
2. Flippo, *Principles of Personnel Management*, 110.
3. Yoder, *Personnel Management and Industrial Relations*, 280.
4. C. B. Mamoria, *Personnel Management* (Mumbai: Himalaya Publishing House, 1980), 134.
5. Jucius, *Personnel Management*, 90.
6. Flippo, *Principles of Personnel Management*, 110.
7. Jucius, *Personnel Management*, 91.
8. Yoder, *Personnel Management and Industrial Relations*, 280.
9. Jucius, *Personnel Management*, 91.
10. Yoder, *Personnel Management and Industrial Relations*, 280.
11. Ibid.
12. Flippo, *Principles of Personnel Management*, 110.
13. Jucius, *Personnel Management*, 91.
14. W. D. Scott, R. C. Clothier, and W. R. Spriegal, *Human Resource Management* (New Delhi: Tata McGraw-Hill Publishing Company Ltd, 1977), 140.
15. Mamoria, *Personnel Management*, 135.
16. Viswanathan, *Strategic Human Resource Management*, 37.
17. See H. L. Wylie, *Office Organisation and Management* (New Delhi: Prentice-Hall of India Private Ltd, 1961), 254.
18. Dessler and Varkkey, *Human Resource Management*, 134.

132 *Acquiring Human Resources*

19 For details, see Ivancevich, *Human Resource Management*, 166–71.
20 B. Schneider and A. M. Konz, *Human Resource Management* (Boston: Irwin McGraw-Hill, 1989), 51–63.
21 Dessler and Varkkey, *Human Resource Management*, 151–60.
22 Ibid.
23 For details, see Dessler and Varkkey, *Human Resource Management*, 159–61.
24 Flippo, *Principles of Personnel Management*, 110.
25 See also J. V. Grant and G. Smith, *Personnel Administration and Industrial Relations* (London: Longmans Group Ltd, 1977), 10–20; British Institute of Management, *Job Evaluation: A Practical Guide for Managers* (London: British Institute of Management, 1970), 77.
26 Flippo, *Principles of Personnel Management*, 111.
27 Jucius, *Personnel Management*.
28 See Dessler and Varkkey, *Human Resource Management*, 158.
29 For details, see Gomez-Mejia, Balkin, and Cardy, *Managing Human Resources*, 63–64.

5 Recruitment, Selection, Placement and Induction/Socialisation

Learning Objectives

After studying this chapter, you should be able to do the following:

1. Define the term 'recruitment' and explain the factors affecting the recruitment process.
2. List and discuss the main internal and outside sources of HR supply as also their advantages and disadvantages.
3. Point out the various methods of recruitment an discuss the recruitment practices in Indian industries.
4. Define the term 'selection' and explain the factors influencing selection. Explain the process of selection with special reference to psychological testing and interviewing.
5. Explain the objectives and processes of induction and socialisation.
6. Explain the competency-based selection as well as the competency-based interview.
7. Point out the recent development/emerging trends in the field of recruitment and selection.

Introduction

After completing the process of job analysis which defines the duties and human requirements of the company's jobs,[1] the next step is to procure the desired human capital for the organisation which involves the processes of recruitment and selection of employees for the organisation, followed by their placement, induction/socialisation and transfers, if required. Procurement of right kind of human capital having appropriate levels of education, knowledge, skills and professional competence is one of the most important operative functions of the HR department.

Recruitment

Recruitment of human capital is not just placing the advertisements or calling consultants or employment agencies. It is a much more complex exercise. We must ensure that the human capital to be recruited matches the strategic plans of the organisation. Which

134 *Acquiring Human Resources*

method of recruitment would suite more to attract the desired human capital is another issue. Should the organisation go for pre-screening to reduce the number of applicants to be interviewed? Can the organisation afford to pay slightly more than the ongoing rates of wages and salaries in the market as it helps in attracting the quality human capital? What is the image of the organisation in the market? All such issues affect the exercise of attracting the desired human capital.

Meaning

Recruitment is the process by which several prospective candidates are attracted by various methods to apply for the positions available. According to Edwin B. Flippo, recruitment is the process of searching for prospective employees and stimulating them to apply for jobs in the organisation.[2]

As the objective of recruitment is to attract several potential candidates for the jobs available, it is considered a positive concept. Selection, on the other hand, is often considered negative because it tends to eliminate applicants, leaving only the best to be appointed.

The successful working of an organisation depends to a great extent on the policy and methods of recruitment of human capital. In case only the right kinds of candidates, in right number, on right wages and on right conditions are appointed, the future of the organisation is likely to be bright. It is basically for this reason that every organisation has an employment department called by different names in different organisations.

Employment Section/Department

The employment department, normally existing in big organisations, is usually headed by an employment manager. The employment department is mainly responsible for procuring the best available personnel on reasonable terms and conditions, whenever and whatever number required. Hence, the important functions of an employment department or employment office[3] are as follows:

1. Forecasting manpower requirements
2. Determining employment standards
3. Advertising vacancies
4. Making initial contact with prospective employees
5. Initial interviewing
6. Testing
7. Arranging physical examinations
8. Final interviewing
9. Keeping record of the service of personnel
10. Induction
11. Placement of worker
12. Following up the employee

Centralised vs Decentralised Recruitment

In the case of large organisations, there may be centralised or decentralised recruitment of human resources depending on certain factors. In the centralised recruitment, the organisation conducts recruiting company-wide from its central recruitment office, whereas in the decentralised recruitment, recruiting is done by the organisation's various offices. The centralised recruitment is preferred because in addition to reducing duplication and producing synergies, it enables the organisation to apply organisation's strategic priorities organisation-wide. However, decentralised recruitment is preferred where familiarity with the local language or such other things play a vital role because of the geographical and educational diversity. For example, in the case of people required for sales, retail, non-voice BPO operations and so on, decentralised recruitment can be more fruitful.

Should Recruitment Function Be Independent?

Whether recruitment function should be independent depends on several factors. However, in normal course, it has been observed that in case the scale and size of recruiting activities are vast, the organisation may have an independent recruitment department, having technical experts in the relevant field. It may be instrumental in procuring human resources of the desired quality in the desired numbers. However, in our country, recruitment is normally conducted by the HR department of the company.

Factors Affecting the HR Recruiting Process

There are several external factors, such as composition of labour force, labour market conditions, government rules and regulations, economic conditions, state of competition, location of the organisation, strength of union(s) and so on, and internal factors, such as organisation goals, organisation strategy, organisation's policies and practices, organisation's image, work groups, leadership, nature of the task, organisation culture, especially work culture, and so on, that may affect the human capital recruiting process. However, both the external and internal factors should be properly diagnosed, prescribed, implemented and evaluated so that desirable end results may be obtained.[4]

Policy of Recruitment

Every organisation should have a well-thought-out and well-laid recruitment policy. The best recruitment policy should have the following features:

1. All employment activities must centre in one place. In case all requisitions go through one centre and all employment records are kept up-to-date, there is maximum possibility for efficiency and for the type of follow-up that may progressively improve employment methods by checking on the success of previous hiring. A busy line manager normally does not have enough time and skill to perform the recruitment and selection process himself/herself, so he/she can benefit by the assistance of a central staff agency.
2. The creation of a new post and sanction for appointment on the same should be authorised by the competent authority.
3. The number of selected people should not exceed the number of effective vacant positions.
4. Job analysis should take place well before recruitment.
5. The qualifications and the like of the candidates should match the job requirements.

6. Recruitment and selection should be fair.
7. A comparative study of different sources of recruitment should be made from time to time, and only the best source should be tapped.
8. As far as possible, all candidates should be taken from one source.
9. No false information or assurance should be given at the time of selection.
10. Recruitment and selection should be done only by trained, experienced and efficient staff.
11. The recruitment policy should clearly lay down the long-term career plans for the employees.
12. It should keep in view the public policy.
13. It should clearly indicate the firm's attitude towards employment of and reservation for minorities, women, the physically handicapped and so on.
14. It should clearly state the basis and extent of promotion from within the organisation.
15. It should attach due importance to audit and research on matters like recruitment ratio as the number of actual people hired per hundred applicants in the firm as well as in other firms.

Sources of HR Supply

Sources of HR supply can be divided into two groups: (a) internal sources and (b) external sources.

Internal Sources

It is not always possible to rely on external sources to fill all HR requirements. No doubt, certain jobs are similar from one organisation to another, but most jobs require specialised knowledge that can be obtained only within a particular organisation. Even those jobs which do not appear to be unique require familiarity with the procedures, policies, people and special features of the organisation in which they are performed. Therefore, internal sources play an important role in providing manpower to a great extent in a good number of organisations, large and small.

Job posting and bidding approach plays an important role in internal recruitment of human capital. Earlier, job posting was just like the use of bulletin boards and company publications for advertising vacant positions, but today, job posting has become an innovative recruiting technique and is considered an integrated component of an effective career management system. In job posting, postings are computerised and are, therefore, easily accessible to employees. Computer software allows the employees to match an available job with their skills and experience and then highlights where the there are gaps, so the employees know what is necessary if they wish to be competitive for a given job.[5]

However, observation suggests that the policy of recruitment from internal sources is generally accepted in clerical, supervisory and, to some extent, even managerial ranks in many organisations. In some organisations, such a policy is stated in collective bargaining agreements.

Broadly speaking, internal sources refer to the present workforce of an organisation. Whenever any job position falls vacant, someone already working in the organisation is upgraded, promoted, transferred or even demoted. There are some authors[6] who are of the view that not only the people who are already on the payroll should be included in the internal sources but also those who may not be on the payroll of a particular organisation but are in employment of a subsidiary or affiliated organisation, as also those who were once on the payroll of a particular organisation but plan to return or whom the organisation could like to rehire, such as those who quit voluntarily or those who are on production lay-offs and so on. Succession planning which is the ongoing process of systematically identifying, assessing and developing organisational leadership to enhance performance is also used to fill key positions whenever they fall vacant and intended to be filled in by internal employees.

Advantages

1. It avoids the problem of people coming in by one door of the organisation while highly similar talent leaves by another.
2. In increases the general level of morale of employees by assuring them that whenever there is any vacancy, they would be given preference over outsiders.
3. It motivates the present employees to prepare themselves for higher posts. Hence, their efficiency goes up.
4. It promotes loyalty and a sense of belongingness among the workers because they feel that their seniority, merit, sincerity and so on will be duly rewarded at the appropriate time.
5. The present employees are already-tried people and, therefore, more reliable.
6. It reduces rate of labour turnover.
7. The employer is in a better position to evaluate those presently employed than outside candidates. However, this would be possible only if the organisation maintains a proper record of service experience, progress, conduct and so on.

Disadvantages

Some of the demerits of this system are as follows:

1. In case the company does not maintain proper record of the progress, achievements, experience, service, punishments and so on, internal sources may degenerate into an undeserved monopoly of those on the payroll.
2. During the period of rapid expansion requiring large and different types of people, internal sources may not be adequate.
3. The advantages of infusion of new blood from outside the organisation are not available.
4. It has all the disadvantages of inbreeding; for example, the learner rarely develops ideas which differ widely from those of the instructor; hence, there is little scope of surprising innovations which are of special importance in the field of designing, advertising, marketing and so on.
5. As seniority plays an important role in promotions, duly capable hands may not be available.
6. Personal likes and dislikes of the management play an important role in the selection of candidates from internal sources.

Thus, it is obvious that internal sources of manpower supply can be more effective if proper record of service of the existing employees is kept in the desired manner and they are given enough notice of preparing themselves for new assignments. However, if we need personnel possessing those specifications which the present employees do not have, then we shall have to look forward to external sources.

External Sources

Few firms can fill all their manpower requirements from within. Over a period of years, a firm should go to external sources, may be for lower-entry jobs, for expansion or for positions whose specification cannot be met by the present employees. Staffing policy must, therefore, assume that some recruitment will look to sources outside the organisation. Hence, every organisation must be acquainted in some degree with the kinds of external sources available. One of the main advantages of recruitment from external sources is that we can have right type of candidates having necessary education, experience, training, expertise and aptitude in required number, as well as at economical rates of wages. However, sometimes certain companies indulge in the unethical practices of raiding other firms in their community or industry. For example, DCM Management used to have its grievance that it imparts training and expertise to the newly recruited management and other trainees, but after these newly recruited are duly trained, they are lured away by some other companies. The major external sources of manpower supply are as follows.

Advertising

Advertising is one of the most common recruitment practices. How much advertising is done will normally depend on the immediacy of the need of labour. Although many kinds of advertising can be done, for example, hand bills, billboards, newspapers, subway and bus cards, telephone, classified advertisements, radio, television and so on, it is basically newspapers which play an important role in this respect. In case there is shortage of time, daily newspapers will be more suitable for advertisement because daily newspapers reach the maximum number of readers in the shortest period. However, if enough time is available, then it will be better to publish advertisements, especially for professional/managerial positions, in trade and professional publications as they remain in circulation for a longer period thus are in a better position to attract large number of potential applicants. Besides, trade publications are usually gone through by the people of related fields.

There are many advantages of inserting advertisements in newspapers or trade publications and so on. First, it leads to self-screening by the applicants because through advertisement, the employer can publish relevant information about job specification, the company, the future prospects and so on. So, only really deserving candidates will move their application. Second, advertisements may contribute towards image and prestige building of the company because some details of the policies, status and so on of the company are also highlighted in the advertisement. Third, advertisements inserted in trade journals or professional magazines reach only the desired group of people and thus only right type of applicants are attracted. However, there are also certain shortcomings of recruitment through advertisement. First, it is a costly affair, especially when advertisement is to be inserted in different newspapers or inserted repeatedly in the same newspaper or published in well-reputed and standard trade publications. Second, sometimes due to wide publicity through newspapers and so on, several applications are received, the processing of which is very time- and money-consuming. Third, a longer lead time is required for their publication. Other shortcomings of this source are its uncertainty and the range of candidates that are attracted. Again, if the advertisements are not well written and appropriately timed, they may not play the desired role. Not only this, but even if several potential candidates have been attracted through effective advertisements, the desired purpose may not be served if it is not followed by good selection techniques. In developing a recruitment advertisement, a good place to begin with is the corporate image.[7] The advertisement should be seen as an extension of the organisation and represent the values that the organisation is looking forward to in the applicants. The advertisement should also create a sense of pride in the applicants and their profession or jobs. Recorded want ads are another innovative way of attracting human capital, in which job seekers are enabled to pick up a telephone and hear a two-to-three-minute recorded recruiting message that may include a job description, job specification and details about how to contact the organisation.

Employment Agencies

Additional screening of applicants can be affected if we use employment agencies. These are usually of two types.

Public Employment Agencies

The public employment agencies have achieved a significant role in the field of recruitment. In our country, these are better known as employment exchanges or labour exchanges. In the USA, these are known as the United States Employment Service (USES). In our country, employment exchanges refer to the special offices set up for bringing together as quickly as possible those workers who are looking forward to having some employment and the employers who are looking for workers. The job seekers get themselves registered with these employment exchanges, giving full particulars of their qualification, training, experience, nature of job required and so on. On the other hand, the employers send their manpower requirements to these employment exchanges. Then employment exchanges forward the names of suitable unemployed candidates registered with them to the employers concerned for their further and fine screening. Thus, the employment exchanges bring about an adjustment between the supply of and the demand for labour and try to provide right man for the right job. They help in avoiding involuntary unemployment as well as in giving each registered candidate the job for which he/she is best suited.

The main functions of employment exchanges as summarised by Saxena[8] are as follows:

1. Employment exchanges work as an intermediary between employees and employers, leaving both settle the terms of employment.
2. They bring about an adjustment between the supply of and demand for labour.
3. Employment exchanges eliminate bribery and corruption in recruitment by offering a free service to all.
4. They also collect statistical information regarding unemployment and manpower to build up a composite picture of a labour market in the country.
5. They help in increasing the mobility of labour by directing the surplus labour in one area to other deficit areas. Thus, uneven distribution of labour due to paucity of adequate amount of communication is reduced.
6. At times, they help in the implementation and operations of schemes, such as rehabilitation of displaced people, decasualisation of labour and unemployment insurance.

7. Although employment exchanges cannot create jobs, they decidedly reduce frictional unemployment by reducing the time lag between occurring vacancies and their filling up.
8. Employment exchanges also provide training facilities and give vocational guidance.
9. They also provide employment counselling to people or parents and guardians about their wards.

Some of the public employment agencies in some of the countries provide a selective placement service for handicapped workers to match their capacities to demands of various jobs. Minority groups and the underprivileged are also helped in finding jobs and to be trained for employment. These agencies play a significant role at the time of acute labour shortage, especially during wartime. Some agencies provide special service for college, technical and professional applicants. They also help military veterans in seeking to match their skills with civilian jobs. These public agencies are more effective in the fields of unskilled, semi-skilled and skilled operative jobs.

Private Employment Agencies

Private agencies are brokers/head-hunters/executive recruiters/consultants who bring employers and job seekers together, for which they charge fees either from the employers or the job seekers or sometimes even from both. Charging for this service is legitimate. However, normally, these agencies charge much more than the reasonable amount. It is because of this that in many countries, state agencies and other public controls have come into existence to check the malpractices in which private employment agencies usually indulge. For example, in our country, private employment agencies dealing in foreign employment are misusing their position. Wherever there is a competition between the public and the private employment agencies, it has led to a considerable improvement in the employment services. Legislation, including provisions for public inspection and licensing of private agencies, may also encourage improved practice.

It is basically in the technical and professional areas that the private agencies appear to be doing most of the work. They have specialised in different fields such as sales, accounts, computers, engineering and executive jobs. However, some private agencies deal only in lower levels of worker skills. They are of special use if the employer needs unskilled workers in large number, or for a short duration, or for a season, or on purely temporary basis or at places which are far from labour markets.

Special private employment agencies assist firms in their search for executive people. These agencies are usually known as management consultants. They raid the firms in which they find the required candidates. Such agencies are getting very popular in the USA.

Recommendations of Present Employees

Certain organisations encourage present employees to suggest candidates for employment and to assist them in filing applications. It is expected that when employees recommend friends, relatives or other close acquaintances for jobs, they do it with some degree of care. They know it well that to recommend someone who is not good will reflect upon their own judgement. They also know that a friend or relative and so on will not appreciate a lead that does not result in a good job. Besides, when present employees recommend anybody, a preliminary screening takes place automatically because the present employee knows both the firm and the acquaintance and, therefore, would try to please both. This source also helps in maintaining goodwill among present employees. However, the risk involved in this practice is that recruitment based on recommendations made by the present employees may encourage family cliques, nepotism, inner circle of close friends and discrimination. Consequently, it may be difficult to get right candidate for the right job. Anyway, in the case of acute shortage of labour, the present employees may be given some financial reward for recommending the desired candidates.

Employee referrals are a great way to get new hires. Employees are the best ambassadors. Referrals work for an organisation because employees are the best brand ambassadors. It is an indication that employees are happy with their workplace. It helps speed up the hiring process as HR people do not have to spend money and time in talent hunting. According to HR experts, hiring or filling up vacancies through referrals works in the company's favour because it helps in hiring candidates speedily and at a low cost.

More than anything else, it gives companies a chance to strengthen bonds with existing employees, especially if it gives them an incentive for referring their friends.

Interestingly, employee referral, employee branding and quality of hire were among the top recruitment priorities for the year in LinkedIn India's Recruiting Trends 2016.

In fact, 55% of talent leaders stated that employee referral programmes were the top source of quality hires, and 42% considered social professional networks as equally important. Both sources were said to be long-lasting and were thus preferred. Many companies give incentives to those employees who refer their sources (see Exhibits 5.1 and 5.2).

Schools and Colleges

Many firms make special efforts to establish and maintain constructive relationships with schools and colleges. These firms send their representatives to interview the candidates at the schools and colleges. In our country, this practice is very common in case of technical colleges where the experts of different firms come and interview the candidates. This technique enables the company to present an attractive picture of the employment opportunities as well as to advance screening of candidates. The better candidates may be further interviewed at the company's premises later. In companies like Airtel, campus hiring is a crucial channel for fresher recruitment. The company generally does not hire fresh graduates if they do not clear its campus process. About 10% of its overall hiring is done through campus placements. However, this technique is expensive, perhaps the most expensive recruitment practice. Besides, it is also possible that some representatives may misrepresent job and opportunities.

According to a TimesJobs study that had complete responses from over 600 employers, there has been a 25% increase in the number of organisations with dedicated campus recruitment strategies. The study has revealed that 34% of the respondents go for communication skills, 30% look at domain knowledge, 22% look at analytical skills, 15% go for creativity and 12% look at leadership skills.[9] Some of the other findings are shown in Exhibit 5.3.

However, the biggest challenges include joining ratio/dropout ratio, employment quotient, training costs and budgetary allocations.

Exhibit 5.1 Employee Referrals Are the Most Popular Source of Hiring Talent

According to Shine.com survey, employee referrals are the most popular source of hiring. In fact, while 47% participants said they were given *incentives* for suggesting hires, 25% said their HR did not believe in this system, and 28% said they did refer their sources but were not given any incentive.

Source: Hindustan Times, 17 May 2016.

Exhibit 5.2 Ericsson to Continue Incentives for its Referral Programme

Swedish telecom equipment maker Ericsson will continue to provide incentives to its staff for referring potential recruits, after this mechanism helped hire 45% of the people added to its workforce in India in 2015. According to the company, 2016 also is looking promising for the programme. Since 2013, when the programme was launched, the number of employees hired through referrals has gone up 20%.

Source: The Economic Times, 4 July 2016.

In our country, this practice is very common in case of technical colleges where the experts of different firms come and interview the candidates. This technique enables the company to present an attractive picture of the employment opportunities and to do advance screening of candidates. The better candidates may be further interviewed at the company's premises later. In companies like Airtel, campus hiring is a crucial channel for fresher recruitment. The company generally does not hire fresh graduates if they do not clear its campus process. About 10% of its overall hiring is done through campus placements. However, this technique is expensive, perhaps the most expensive recruitment practice. Besides, it is also possible that some representatives may misrepresent job and opportunities.

According to a TimesJobs study that had complete responses from over 600 employers, there has been a 25% increase in the number of organisations with dedicated campus recruitment strategies. The study has revealed that 34% of the respondents go for communication skills, 30% look at domain knowledge, 22% look at analytical skills, 15% go for creativity, and 12% look at leadership skills.[10] Some of the other findings are shown in Exhibit 5.3.

Exhibit 5.3 Campus Hiring Gains Pace but Dropouts Big Challenge for Cos

Some of the findings of a Times.com study reveal that of all the respondents:

- 40% would go far only renowned B-school for campus interviews.
- 60% would go for lesser known/upcoming institutions.

- 40% found campus interviews cost-effective.
- 35% found campus interviews helpful in brand building.
- 05% found it time-saving.
- 65% have a formal campus recruitment programme in place.

Source: The Economic Times, 21 June 2016.

However, the biggest challenges include joining ratio/dropout ratio, employment quotient, training costs and budgetary allocations.

Labour Organisations

Labour unions have been playing an important role in providing labour to the firms, especially in the industrially advanced countries of the West. There, in some industries, labour unions have carried the responsibility of supplying employers with needed skilled employees. In closed-shop relationships, all recruits must be union members, and employers often call on unions to supply whatever additional employees may be needed. There is no doubt that it is to management's advantage to be able to tap a ready supply of skilled, experienced workers just by lifting the phone and calling the union. This saves management expense of recruiting and screening.

Casual Applicants

A part of the manpower requirement can be met from the unsolicited applications received through the mail or at the gate. No doubt this source is uncertain, and applicants may cover a wide range of abilities.

Hence, it needs a careful screening. Anyway, it is an inexpensive source because the applicants come to the door or apply at their own. Sometimes, very capable hands may also be available. Hence, those who apply at their own, their letters must be replied promptly and courteously, and, similarly, those who come at the gate of the company must be well treated.

Leasing On-Demand Recruiting Services (ODRS)

In order to meet short-term urgent requirements of specialised human capital, leasing personnel by the hour or day can also be a source of procurement of personnel. In addition to obtaining desired personnel, the firm also escapes from the liabilities of making payment for insurance, pensions and such other obligations towards its employees. ODRS, which is a service that provides short-term specialised recruiting to support specific projects without the expense of retaining traditional search firms,[11] handles recruiting, analysing and pre-screening and leaves the client with a short list of qualified candidates to put through the employer's own internal screening process.[12]

Minority Groups

Some companies, especially in the industrially advanced countries of the West, seek candidates from minority groups. In such cases, usually the companies rely upon their own employees of minority groups to suggest ways and means of finding candidates.

Obviously, in order to tap these sources, special attention should be given to the sentiments, feelings and viewpoints of minority members in attracting, interviewing and communicating with them.

Special Events Recruiting

At times of shortage of desired human capital or when the organisations are not well known, some organisations organise special events, such as conducting symposia on college campuses, staging open houses, sponsoring cultural events and so on, and advertise these events in appropriate media. Some organisations together organise job fairs where each of these organisations has a booth or stall to publicise the jobs available.

E-recruiting/Recruiting via the Internet/Networking Sites

E-recruiting is increasingly becoming very popular as a recruiting method for attracting appropriate human capital. It has, therefore, been rightly said that 'perhaps no method has ever had as revolutionary an effect on organisational recruitment practices as the Internet'.[13] In the USA, more than 95% of all companies now utilise the Internet for some or all their recruitment-related activities. There are thousands of websites devoted in some manner to job posting activities. The Internet as a method of recruitment is preferred because it is a relatively inexpensive way to attract human capital besides enabling immediate access to thousands of prospective applicants. The Internet method of recruitment is very beneficial to job seekers as it allows for searches over a broader array of geographic and company postings than was ever before possible.[14] There are available several online services, including more specialised online sites focusing on jobs in particular areas like higher education.

Many companies are having their own HR web page on the Internet as it serves as an effective addition to their overall recruitment strategy. Such organisational home pages may include not only the employment opportunities and application procedures but also the general background information about the organisation, its products and services, and so on. The Web has revolutionised job hunting and recruitment in the current century. Today, employers can electronically screen candidates' soft attributes, direct potential hires to a special website for online skills assessment, conduct background checks over the Internet, interview candidates via videoconferencing and manage the entire process with Web-based software. There is no doubt that such innovations are welcomed at a time when there is acute shortage of manpower in certain areas, but there are also legal risks associated with the unbridled use of e-recruiting. It is recommendable that while developing and executing an e-recruiting programme, an enterprise should ensure that job opening is conveyed to a substantial chunk of the targeted population. Besides, the enterprise should also identify a way in which applicants who apply for on-the-job postings can be properly tracked.

Networking sites are just one among the many avenues to recruit the right talent. In the war for talent, employers are turning to social networking sites and other digital mediums to find and hire new talent. With the advent of these new avenues, hiring managers and recruiters find that they need to be more proactive in their approach by engaging with talent across a wide range of social and networking platforms.

Social media is now playing a key role in the evaluation of individuals. There should be more and more social networking sites and the reasons for this is that people get used to understanding the rules of the game for a given site. (Also, there are many other tools to analyse the social media behaviour of a candidate, whether it is the written part or otherwise.) But the information available on professional site is certainly not enough to find the right fit for a job.

If we need to recruit freshers or people with two to four years of experience or if we are doing mass hiring and if we believe that our training programme is strong enough to get the desired result from a candidate, then social media can play a huge role in hiring fast and in large numbers. But if we are looking for people in higher position involving decision-making and be strategic, then the reliance on face-to-face interaction becomes very important. Similarly, if we need to find out the attitude of the person along with his/her ability and achievements, then we will have to take help of other tools. Besides, the networking sites have inherent disadvantages like the issue of privacy. Many people may not be willing to put everything online. Thus, how effective these sites are for recruiting depends on many factors. Whether hiring through networking sites will replace conventional means of hiring candidates is a big question mark.

Summer Internships

Some organisations hire students studying in their final year as interns during the summer or part time during the school year. The organisations get specific projects done by these interns besides exposing them to talented potential employees, who may also become their 'recruiters' at their institutions. The organisations can also decide if they would like to have these interns or some of them as their full-time employees afterwards. Thus, internships enable organisations to attract the best talent as well as to improve the diversity of their recruitment efforts. Summer internships are useful to students also in as much as they get a job with pay (though for a short duration) besides getting an opportunity for a real work experience and a possible future job.

Walk-ins

Direct applications made at the office of the organisations or directly coming for interview at the office of the organisation is also a big source of recruitment. Walk-ins should be treated courteously and carefully. Walk-ins are effective to a great extent in attracting mainly good local applicants.

Offshoring/Outsourcing White-collar and Other Jobs

Of late, outsourcing and hiring workers abroad have also been showing an increasing trend. Although sending jobs abroad is contentious, but managers will have to deal with outsourcing. Cultural misunderstanding, language, special training, military tensions, political instability, security, privacy and so on are some of the concerns that the HR managers will have to keep in mind while formulating plans to outsource jobs abroad.

Virtual Workforce

Some of the firms tap skilled foreign labour but not moving those workers to their own country. The Internet is making this possible with little additional expense.[15]

Poaching

Although poaching is ethically not justified, a good number of companies are used to it, especially for middle and higher-level managerial jobs, either directly or through their consultants (see Exhibits 5.4 and 5.5).

Exhibit 5.4 Amazon Raids Rivals for Talent

In an aggressive hiring spree arrived at consolidating its gains as well as expanding the scope of its business in India's fast growing online retail industry, the American online retailer Amazon India has hired half-a-dozen top managers who will lead payment business, drive special initiatives for sellers, head sales for fashion, food and grocery, head for accessories or act as director of product management and so on.

Source: The Economic Times, 26 February 2016.

Exhibit 5.5 Ethically Wrong Practices of Recruitment

Zspacev, a cloud security firm, drove a van with a 'we are hiring' banner continually around the building of its 'target' competitor, Blue Coat, in order to entice the competitor's employees into leaving.

Source: John Sullivan, 'The War for Talent is Returning; Don't Get Caught Unprepared', *Human Capital* 18, no. 2 (July 2014). Available at https://www.ere.net/the-war-for-talent-is-returning-dont-get-caught-unprepared/ (Accessed on 31 January 2018).

It may be noted that from November 2015 until February 2016, Amazon, which competes with market leader Flipkart and SoftBank-backed Snapdeal, had roped in a diverse cast of top executives from companies such as McKinsey and MakeMyTrip.[16]

Attracting Prospective Employees Through Employee Value Proposition (EVP)

Candidates can be attracted through EVP as well.

Meaning and Importance of EVP

EVP takes its name from a marketing idea known as unique value proposition; the value the company provides to customers that differentiates it from its competitors. An EVP is the unique value that the company brings to employees. It must be unique, relevant and compelling if it is to act as a key driver of talent attraction, engagement and retention.

Minchington defines an EVP as a set of associations and offerings provided by an organisation in return for the skills, capabilities and experiences an employee brings to the organisation. EVP is, thus, the value that employees gain in return for working at their organisations.

It is vital for organisations to build unique brands of themselves in the eyes of their prospective employees. This essentially implies developing a statement of 'why the total work experience at their organisations is superior to that at other organisations'. The value proposition, therefore, should outline the unique employee policies, programmes, rewards and benefit programmes that prove an organisation's commitment to people and management development. In other words, it should define an employee's 'Why should I join this organisation?' Today, it is a well-known fact that there is more to an employee satisfaction than just his/her salary and benefits. EVP has been proven crucial to attracting, hiring and retaining the best talent in the industry.

EVP should, therefore, be well communicated in all hiring efforts of the organisation. As such, it may be duly reflected on the company's website, job advertisements and letters extending employment opportunities.

Building EVP

While thinking about creating an employer band, we first think about how it looks. Hence, we focus on a logo or the type of font to use as this is what our prospective employees see first. However, simply having an attractive face may not suffice. It should be lively as well as having its own personality. It is here that EVP comes into picture because the EVP is how life can be put into your employer band. According to Mike Bensi, a meaningful value proposition can be developed by taking the following steps:

1. **Dig**: First, you should identify what your company offers to employees today. It is not only the wages or salaries that employees get. They get much more. Hence, you should investigate the details of the total rewards package.
2. **Listen**: You should listen to employees what they say about why they joined, why they are continuing with your organisation and why they like to work in your organisation. Also listen what the employees have to say about what drives employee engagement as well as about what issues exist that, if improved upon, would lead to greater employee engagement. It is equally important to listen to employees as to what they say about why employees leave the organisation. Employee turnover data and exit interviews can indicate the issues that need improvement. Also listen to about what your competitors are doing so that you may do better and prompt job seekers to join your organisation.
3. **Analyse**: By analysing the data you have obtained so far, find out what employees expect and value and whether the benefits being extended by your organisation meet their requirement. This will also help you to know if you are offering the right benefits. Investment on any benefit that is not attracting the desired talent may be discontinued and instead be made on another appropriate benefit.
4. **Decide**: Discuss with all other relevant stakeholders and go deeper into the finding to get further insight into the key themes emerging out of listening (step 2). The feedback so obtained may be instrumental in solidifying your EVP and take you to the 'build' stage.
5. **Build**: Based on research and insight, coin the words and phrases reflecting your company and its culture and values. It may be just one statement that defines your employment brand. The EVP will be marketable if it is inspirational, aligned, differentiated and simple.

6. **Codify**: The last step starts with implementation part. It needs the value proposition to be codified across the whole employee experience—from your recruitment until the exit stage and finally to your employment brand. Efforts should be made to ensure that your brand promise can be delivered on by creating a strong EVP.

Methods of Recruitment

Having discussed the internal and external sources of human capital supply, we now come to the methods of recruitment which can be divided into three categories.

Direct Method

- Job posting/recruiting at the gate of factory
- Sending recruiters to:
  - Educational and professional institutions
  - Conventions and seminars
- Sending mobile officers or recruiters to the desired centres

Indirect Method

- Advertising in:
  - Newspapers
  - Trade publications
  - Radio
  - Television
  - Subway
  - Bus card
  - Telephone

Third-party Methods

- Public employment agencies
- Private employment agencies
- Inviting biodata and/or recommendations from schools, colleges and professional institutions
- Friends and relatives of present employees
- Casual applicants
- Leasing/ODRS
- Labour unions
- Minority groups
- Special events recruiting
- E-recruiting/Internet/networking sites
- Summer internships
- Walk-ins
- Offshoring/outsourcing white-collar and other jobs
- Miscellaneous

Recruitment Practices in Indian Industries

Recruitment practices in Indian industries differ from industry to industry. In addition to recruitment from internal sources, some of the prevalent practices of recruitment from external sources are as follows:

1. The usual practice is putting up a notice at the factory gate that so much labour is required, then the recruiting officer comes to the gate and selects the necessary labour.
2. Attracting labour through the present employees.
3. Recruitment through intermediaries or jobbers, such as Sardar, Mistry, Mukadam, Tindal, Chowdhary, Kangany, Naikins, Mukadamins and so on.
4. Recruitment through labour officers.
5. Recruitment through contractors.
6. Badli or temporary workers
7. Recruitment through public and private employment agencies/consultants.
8. Recruitment through labour unions.
9. Recruitment through advertisement.
10. Recruitment through polytechnics, engineering colleges, IITs, NITs, institutes of management, universities and so on.

Limitations of External Sources

1. **Boundaries of labour market:** A labour market refers to a geographical area in which the supply of and demand for labour interact and thus determines the wages of labour. The labour market boundaries decide the availability of manpower to a great extent. For example, in India, married women looking forward to some employment may be reluctant to take jobs at distant places and so on.
2. **Bad reputation of the company:** In case a company is known for its fair dealings, such as high rates of wages and salaries and bonus, tempting fringe benefits, quick promotions and so on, it may not have any major problem in getting adequate manpower from external sources. However, if a company has just the opposite image, then it may not get the desired candidates.
3. **Paucity of desired skill(s) and expertise:** The desired skill and expertise either may not be available at all or may be available to a limited extent.
4. **Location of the company:** In case a firm or company is situated in an area or region where there is acute shortage of unemployed manpower, it may not be easy to get required number of people.
5. **Practice of 'raiding' or 'hunting':** In case the company does not believe in the practice of hiring, raiding or hunting employees from other companies in its community, it may not get adequate number of desired employees.

Recruitment Evaluation/Measuring Recruiting Effectiveness

Despite a substantial expenditure involved in recruiting human capital, only a few organisations evaluate the effectiveness of their efforts of recruiting human capital. In this regard, the first thing that we should measure is: 'How many applicants did our recruiting procedure generate through each of our recruitment sources?' All the same, it does not mean only in terms of number. The applicants so generated should not only be available but also hireable and competent enough. Another simpler plan to evaluate sources of human capital supply can be to use such measures as job success, turnover, grievances and disciplinary actions. For example, if a correlation is discovered between successful personnel and particular labour sources, then efforts should be made to develop such sources. Again, by classifying turnover data according to the original sources of manpower supply, it is possible to contrast the relative merits of sources of supply. The same results may be obtained if we tabulate grievance and disciplinary actions according to classes of hiring source. Not only this, even within the same source, we can pinpoint a particular unit or units which can provide better human capital. For example, in the case of schools, colleges and professional institutes, the company may find that a particular school or college or professional institute provides better human capital for its purpose than other schools, colleges or professional institutes.

Periodical evaluation of sources of recruitment in terms of cost per applicant, the applicant hiring ratio, tenure, performance appraisals, grievances, disciplinary action and so on should, therefore, be carried out, and the sources of manpower supply best suited for the organisation should be identified and developed accordingly. The organisations can also look forward to applying best practice management techniques. Besides, employers can also improve their recruiting efforts by using guidelines revealed by research.

Recruiting a More Diverse Workforce

Recruiting a diverse workforce in today's globally competitive environment has become almost unavoidable. Organisations must also recruit women candidates, disabled candidates, older workers, minority candidates, single parents, candidates from reserved categories and so on. Recruiters have, therefore, to understand and formulate appropriate plans and implement the same per the requirement of the organisation and legislation.

Alternatives to Recruitment

Some organisations for meeting their requirement of human capital make use of the following alternatives to recruitment[17] as the same prove relatively less costly:

1. Overtime
2. Employee leasing
3. Contingent/temporary employment

Realistic Job Previews

It has been observed that recruiters, instead of giving a truthful and realistic presentation about their organisations, give a very rosy picture and glowing description of their organisations. It should be a rather realistic job preview (RJP) and, therefore, should provide the prospective employee with pertinent information about the job, free from any exaggeration, a full picture with its positive and negative features, so that the new hires do not feel disappointed afterwards and think of quitting their jobs.

Attributes of an Effective Recruiter

A recruiter is viewed by the applicants and viewed as an extension of the organisation. He/she represents his/her organisation and is, therefore, seen by the applicants as a primary example of the kind of person the organisation is looking forward to recruit. An effective recruiter should, therefore, convey an image that reflects favourably on the organisation. He/she should possess good interpersonal skills, know a lot about his/her organisation, be self-motivated and good salesperson, take interest in applicants and have experience in the specialisation he/she is looking forward to recruit for.

Recent Developments/Emerging Trends

Time Taken by HR Department to Fill Up Vacant Positions

Per the findings of the Shine.com survey, HR tends to act quickly to fill up vacant senior management positions and takes its own sweet time to replace entry and middle-level staff. At times, there is even continuous cribbing that there is terribly shortage of staff, and no concrete results are available from the HR department, which affects the performance of the organisation. For findings of a survey in this regard, see Exhibit 5.6. In today's digital age, filling up vacancies should not take more than a week as talent is barely a click away. HR either has the option to send out to employees with the list of vacancies they hope to fill internally or simply post the job openings on their websites. Besides, there are certain recruiting trends as shown in Exhibit 5.7.

Exhibit 5.6 Initiative Taken by HR Department to Fill Vacant Positions

Does HR play a protective role only at certain level?

- HR is quick to fill up top positions   33%
- It takes time to fill mid-level roles   43%
- Filling entry-level jobs takes a few months 24%

Does HR regularly monitor terms that are short of hands?

- No, this does not happen   41%
- Yes, we get constant feedback   35%
- Can't say   24%

Source: Hindustan Times, 17 May 2016.

Exhibit 5.7 Top Five Recruiting Trends

- Social networks are the fastest growing services.
- Employer branding is getting more important.
- Data use is crucial to making good hires.
- Internal recruitment is on the rise.
- Mobile hiring is calling for more investment.

Source: S. C. Saha, 'Tapping the Hiring Trendo-Meter', *Human Capital* 17, no. 9 (February 2014).

152 *Acquiring Human Resources*

Exhibit 5.8 Companies Going Digital for Quick Recruitment Processes

- Social media makes access to talent easier and provides a rich repository of information on potential candidates.
- Firms are using non-traditional sourcing routes like posting jobs through tweets, sending details of job openings to their customers and organising technology competitions.
- By using social media platforms, companies can reach millions of candidates.
- The personal touch enables deeper engagement with the talent pool.
- Digital transforms recruitment processes and lightens the administrative burden of HR.

Source: Hindustan Times, 12 July 2016.

Companies Going Digital for Quick Recruitment Process

An organisation's ability to identify, attract and recruit the right talent when and where needed is the foundation for success. Getting the right quality talent, on time, has traditionally been an uphill task. Organisations typically turn to job sites, referrals and head-hunters to source candidates. However, these three and other traditional methods of recruitment leave much to be desired. To gain a competitive edge in the light of changing dynamics, including the new characteristics feature of the millennial generation (millennials are tech-savvy digital natives and are always online), many organisations are now moving to gamification-based talent-spotting solutions. A gamification approach utilises elements of game play to build real-life work-context interactive games within which a candidate's skills are assessed. When applied to organisational settings, this application of gamification is also called 'serious games' (see Exhibit 5.8).

Selection

Meaning and Definition

Selection is the process by which all candidates are divided into two groups: those selected and those rejected.[18] Through a series of steps such as the scrutiny of applications, obtaining references, administration of tests and holding of interviews, a process of elimination is continued until the right kind of people are selected to fill the positions available. In other words, all the activities designed to find out whether a person is suitable for a job collectively constitute the selection process. It usually starts with the scrutiny of application forms and ends when a final opinion is expressed regarding the suitability of a candidate. The purpose of selection is to assess the suitability of the candidates for certain positions in the firm. The emphasis throughout should be on suitability and not only on ability. In other words, the purpose of selection is to assess role–person compatibility. Selection begins by close reference to job specifications, preferably those that outline not only immediate job requirements but also other qualities regarded as desirable for long-term employment in the organisation.[19] The common personal qualities that can be regarded as the bases for selection may comprise education, training, experience, skill, intelligence, initiative, drive, ingenuity, aptitude, attitude towards work, maturity, emotional stability, personality, physical appearance, age, sex, marital status, physical characteristics and so on.

Preliminary Requirements

Before we can initiate the selection process, we must first ensure that there is an authority to hire. Second, we must ensure that, as far as possible, we have a standard of personnel with which we can compare the applicants. Third, we must have adequate number of applicants. For ensuring these things, we need to carry out an analysis of the workload as well as of the workforce, prepare job specifications and chalk out a well-planned recruitment programme.

Pseudoscientific Methods of Selection

Since evaluation of abilities of an applicant is a very complicated and difficult task, the selection procedures of big companies are very long and complicated. Although more and more scientific and precise techniques are being adopted, the use of some of the following practices of quick appraisal, which saw their growth particularly in the 19th century and are popularly known as pseudoscientific methods, have not been eliminated completely. The pseudoscientific techniques may include the following:

1. **Astrology:** Establishing relationship between date of birth and vocational aptitude.[20]
2. **Phrenology:** Evaluating qualities of a person by an analysis of the skull and its shape, protrusions, bumps and so on.[21]
3. **Graphology:** Determining characteristics of the applicant by means of his/her handwriting.[22]
4. **Physiognomy:** Evaluating a person based on his/her facial features.[23]
5. **Caste and creed:** Assumption that some jobs are discharged better by people belonging to certain castes and creeds.
6. **Pigmentation:** Based on the blonde–brunette theory—that is, blondes are positive and brunettes are negative.[24]
7. **Height and weight:** Determining suitability based on height, weight and so on of the applicant.

Need for Scientific Methods of Selection

Since pseudoscientific methods of selection suffer from certain drawbacks, there is a need of scientific methods of selection because of the following reasons:

1. Scientific methods of selection aim at reducing the margin of error to the minimum in selecting the most suitable candidates for the organisation.
2. Scientific methods of selection reduce the cost of selection and development.
3. The cost of training and development is also reduced if the scientific methods are used in the selection process.
4. Scientific methods of selection boost the image of the organisation in the external environment because scientific methods of selection make it known to the people that the organisation's approach is more merit-oriented and it believes in equal opportunity to all.

Steps Required to Improve the Accuracy of Selection

Edgar H. Schein[25] has suggested the following steps to improve the accuracy of selection:

1. Develop criteria: The actual performance on the job must be in some way measurable and the organisational roles or positions to be filled in must be described in detail to the person(s) responsible for selection.
2. Determine the predictor variable: The variables which are supposed to be good predictors of performance should be determined and the applicant should be adjudged in respect of those variables.
3. Obtain sufficient candidates to ensure adequate variation on the predictor variables.
4. Hire an unselected group of candidates.
5. Rate candidates on actual job performance.
6. Correlate scores or observations on the predictor variable with criterion performance in the unselected group of candidates.
7. Select from further candidates only those who reach a certain score on the predictor variables.

If we follow these steps, then we can ensure accuracy of selection to a great extent, though the improvement in selection which results from the aforesaid steps depends on a number of factors in the situation. Some of such important factors[26] are as follows:

1. The actual variation in job performance (the criterion) between best and worst workers
2. The reliability of the criterion
3. Success in locating predictor variables
4. Enough candidates to be able to select and to ensure variability in the predictor
5. A correlation high enough to improve the selection process

Factors Influencing Selection

There may be several factors related to the external environment that may determine the kind of selection system to be utilised by an organisation, such as the size, composition and availability of local labour market. In case there is an oversupply of qualified human capital in the labour market, the selection strategies will be different as compared to when the supply of the human capital is tight. Besides, the economic, political and social compulsions also play their own roles.

Similarly, in the context of internal environment, the typical features of an organisation such as its size, technology used, policy about hiring from within, complexity, work culture and so on may also play their roles in determining the type of selection system to be used to hire employees. For example, in case an organisation believes in and adheres to its liberal policy of hiring from within, it will have to follow different techniques and different criteria as compared to the other organisation which believes tapping external sources of supply of human capital.

Reliability and Validity of Selection Criteria

After choosing a set of selection criteria, a technique for assessing each of these must be selected. By whatever method the information about the applicants has been collected, the organisation must ensure that it is reliable as well as valid. Test–retest reliability and alternative-form reliability should be determined. Similarly, regarding validity, which addresses the questions of what a test measures and how well it has measured, the HR specialist should be aware of content validity, construct validity and criterion-related validity.[27]

Selection Procedure

Since it is very difficult to measure the personality and real worth of a candidate, different methods of selection are being used by different organisations to elicit as much significant information about the applicant as possible. The information so obtained is compared with the job specification, and the applicant found most suitable for the organisation is selected. Although it is difficult to evolve a standard procedure of selection, the following steps in the selection procedure are quite popular.

Initial Contact

Initial contact with the candidates is usually made through their applications for employment. Every big organisation keeps several printed blank application forms. These forms may differ according to the nature and status of different jobs.

Screening

Having received applications, the first step in almost all programmes of selection involves screening. Screening implies a rough, crude shifting of applicants to avoid further concern about those who are obviously unsuitable. In the initial screening, what is generally done is to weed out those who do not possess the minimum requirements laid down for the vacant positions, the most important of which are generally indicated through the 'job descriptions' and the 'job specifications' given in the advertisements or subsequently supplied. In screening, most organisations use some sort of initial or preliminary interview and one or more types of application blanks.

Initial or Preliminary Interview

Some sort of interview is usually included in the preliminary stages of selection. Such an introductory interview is normally quite short and aims at the elimination of the obviously unqualified. Such an initial interview may take place across the counter in the firm's employment office and may be conducted by the receptionists, secretaries and so on. In such initial interviews, information regarding the company's interest in hiring and the applicant's reason for enquiring is exchanged. The applicant may be asked why he/she has applied for this job in this organisation. What are his/her expectations regarding salary? A rough idea about his/her educational and technical qualifications, previous experience and so on can be had in a nutshell. Applicants who pass this crude screening, that is, who appear to have some chance of qualifying for existing vacant positions, are asked to fill up application blank.

Application Blank

The application blank is, no doubt, one of the most common tools used in the selection process. It is a universally accepted device for gathering relevant information from the applicant which may be of vital importance to the management in making a proper selection. The information gathered in this manner provides a clue to the need of and a basis for other selective processes. The application blank is rarely used as the only criterion for selection. Its main utility is to provide information for interviewing, testing and checking of references and so on. It also tests the applicant's ability to write, organise his/her thoughts and present facts. Although application blanks differ from organisation to organisation depending on the nature of jobs, there is remarkably high degree of similarity among the blanks of various companies. Most probably, this uniformity is caused by the fact that these blanks deal with basic information that all organisations consider vital. According to Michael J. Jucius,[28] the following classes of information are usually sought through the application blank:

- Identity information such as name, address, telephone number and social security number
- Personal information such as marital status and dependents
- Physical characteristics such as height, weight, health and defects
- Education
- Experience, usually through the last three or four employers only
- References, personal and business
- Miscellaneous remarks and comments

According to another author,[29] a properly designed application blank has the following advantages:

- It constitutes a simple test of the candidate's ability to spell, write legibly and answer factual questions rapidly and accurately.
- Along with the information collected later during testing, it gives the employment manager a line on the candidate before the main employment interview begins.
- For many applicants, it is easier to think out answers alone than to answer those very questions when interviewed.
- It gives satisfaction to the applicant that his/her request for employment and his/her CV are on the record of the firm.

The aforesaid advantages are possible only if the application blank is brief so that even if the applicant is not used to doing much writing, he/she is not put to disadvantage. Besides, the application blank should comprise only those items which are correlated with job success. The information submitted in an application blank should help predict the candidate's chances for making a success of his/her job. As far as possible, the application blank should not include any embarrassing question or use of such words or questions which may cause any ambiguity or misinterpretation. In order to ensure accuracy of information, usually, the application blank carries a threat of dismissal at any time after employment if the information furnished by the candidate proves incorrect at any stage.

A specimen of a short application blank for unskilled workers is given in Exhibit 5.9.

A specimen of a long or usual application blank which may serve the purpose for a variety of jobs is given in Exhibit 5.10.

Per the Constitution of India, discrimination in employment based on caste, religion, nationality, colour, sex, previous arrests and so on is prohibited. Hence, all those questions which are likely to reveal such information are deleted from the application blanks.

Crucial indicators may be helpful in saving much time if large numbers of applications are to be examined. Such items may be prominently mentioned in the application blank, and the information furnished by the applicant in these columns may play a decisive role to a great extent regarding his/her suitability for the post. For example, for stability and long service in the organisation, the distance between the living place and the working place, age and sex may be considered crucial indicators. Some organisations also use 'biographical information blank' (BIB), which is a supplement to the traditional application blank and comprises many more items than a typical application blank. BIB asks for such information as is related to a much wider array of attitudes and experiences. BIB items are based on the assumption that these prior behaviours and experiences will be strongly related to an applicant's future behaviour.[30]

Exhibit 5.9   Specimen of a Short Application Blank for Unskilled Workers

(Name of the Firm)

Name (in Capital Letters) Mr/Miss/Mrs:......................................

Address:..

Marital Status (Single/Married/Married with Children):.........................

Age:...

Job Position Applied for:..

Past Experience:

Name of the Employer	Designation	Nature of the Job	From–To	Salary	Reason for Leaving

Physical Disabilities, if Any:...
....

Selected/Rejected...................Department............................

Due to Start..

Signature of the Interviewer

Exhibit 5.10   Specimen of (Long) Application Blank

(Name of the Organisation)

Post Applied for:....................Advertisement No.....................

Date:..............

 1. Name (in Capital Letters) Mr/Miss/Mrs:...............................
 2. Father's Name:..

3. Present Postal Address:..
4. E-mail ID:..
5. Permanent Home Address:...
6. Date of Birth:..
7. Place of Birth:...
8. Nationality:...
9. Whether Belongs to SC/ST/BC:....................................
10. (a) Marital Status:..................(b) No. of Dependents:.......................
11. Languages:

Speak	Speak and Read	Speak, Read and Write

12. Educational/Technical Qualifications from Matriculation Onwards:

Exam Passed	University/Board	No. of Attempts	Roll No.	Year of Passing	Division (with Percentage of Marks)	Subjects Offered

13. Apprenticeship/Practical Training:

Nature of Training	Company in which Undergone Training/ Apprenticeship	Period From	Period To	Remarks

14. Past Experience:

Name of the Employer	Designation of the Post Held	Period From	Period To	Nature of Job	Salary and Allowance	Reasons for Leaving

15. Field of Specialisation:
16. Minimum Salary Acceptable:
17. Time Required for Joining (if Selected):
18. Have You Ever Applied/Been Interviewed in This Company Before? If Yes, Get Details:..
19. Is Any of Your Relatives/Friends/Acquaintances Employed at This Company? If Yes, Give His/Her Name and Designation:..
20. Have You Ever Been Prosecuted, Kept under Detention or Bound down, Fined, Convicted by a Court of Law of Any Offence or Debarred/Disqualified by Any University, Public Service Commission from Appearing at Its Examinations/ Selection? If Yes, Give Details:..

21. Is There Any Case Pending Against You in Any Court of Law at the Time of Filling Up This Application Form? If Yes, Give Full Particulars of the Case:..
22. No. of Symposia/Conferences Attended:............................
23. List of Research Publications:...................................
24. References (Other than Relatives):

   a.
   b.

25. List Below the Certificates and Testimonials (Attach Self-attested Copies):

   a.
   b.
   c.
   d.
   e.

I certify that the foregoing information is correct and complete to the best of my knowledge and belief. I am not aware of any circumstances which may impair my fitness for employment.

Place....................
Date.....................   (Signature of the Candidate)

(To Be Filled in by the HR Department)

Interviewed   (a) On
               (b) By
                    1.
                    2.
                    3.
                    4.
Comments...
Appointed/Rejected:
If Appointed

1. Date of Appointment:
2. Salary Fixed:
3. Post/Department to which Appointed:
4. Temporary/Permanent:
5. Period of Probation:

                                   Signature of the Appointing Authority

Weighted Application Blank

In order to make an application blank more effective, some organisations study such items as age, marital status, number of dependents, education, earnings and years on previous jobs of the employees and correlate them with success on the job. Based on the experience, a scoring system may be worked out for all such items and a cutting score may be established for the total. Such a weighted form may be extremely useful in expediting selection. As a matter of fact, certain qualities of both successful and unsuccessful existing personnel are studied carefully. If it is found that the group of successful employees possesses certain qualities which are not possessed by the group of unsuccessful employees, then these qualities become distinguishing qualities, and thus weights can be determined for such qualities. For example, if it is found that bachelors are more devoted to their job, then bachelorhood can be given due weightage.

However, due care should be exercised in the use of weighted application blanks. First, we must pinpoint the objectives, that is, whether we are interested in job proficiency or stability of workforce and so on, and only after that we must attach weightage to the related factors. Second, each organisation must prepare its own weighted form. Third, the weighted application blanks must be revised and updated because with the passage of time, there is a possibility of consistent decrease in the predictive accuracy of the weighted application blank. Besides, a few important factors which have been assigned weightage in the application blank should not be the only criterion for selection. Other information elicited through tests, interviews and so on should be attached due importance in the process of selection.

References

References are letters of recommendations usually written by teachers, guides, supervisors and previous employers. It is believed that a great deal can be learnt about the applicant if the references are checked in the right manner.

Sometimes, even that information can be elicited from the references which perhaps even interviews or different types of tests cannot furnish. It is perhaps for this reason that a majority of application blanks in current use include a request for the names of references.

Types of References

References may be of the following three types:

1. **School references**: In case the students are to be hired directly from the college or the university, references of their teachers may provide some useful information about the intelligence, honesty, regularity, sincerity, general discipline and so on of the student concerned.
2. **Character references**: Such references are listed as potential source of information with respect to the general character, integrity and reputation of the applicant. However, character references are of very little significance in applying for jobs these days.
3. **Work references**: It is usually the work references which are attached greater significance these days. In such references, the impressions and recommendations of the last employer of the applicant are obtained.

Letters of recommendation have been classified into two categories:[31] first, special letters, which are directed to a specific employer with respect to the specific applicant; second, general 'to whom it may concern' letters, which are taken by the applicant and shown to his/her would-be employer as a testimony to his/her efficiency, conduct and experience.

Edwin B. Flippo[32] has pointed out the following ways of obtaining the required information on a reference check:

- Letters of reference sent to the hiring company at the request of the applicant
- Letter of reference sent to the hiring company at the request of the hiring company
- Seeking information on telephone from the reference giver
- Seeking information from the reference given through personal visit or contact

Limitations of References

These days, there is a lot of controversy regarding the value of checking applicant references. Many employment mangers hold that most of the employers are reluctant to reveal exact information about their former employees and, therefore, practically no usable information is available from references. Anyway, some of the drawbacks in obtaining usable information from references are as follows:

- References are selected by the applicant. Hence, he/she would suggest only those from whom he/she expects favourable response.
- School references are not of much use as the information provided by the teacher is not of much significance in hiring.
- In order to get rid of unsatisfactory employees, the last employer may give good recommendation to the hiring company.
- Employers are reluctant to divulge exact information about the applicant, lest the remarks become known to the applicant.
- References do not want to be an obstacle in the way of progress of the applicant.
- References may not take due care of the request of the hiring company.
- The former employer might have formed a misconception of the qualities of the individual and even dismissed him/her for unsound reasons. Even the employer's recollections might be faulty. Hence, exact information may not be forthcoming.

The aforesaid limitations can be overcome to a great extent if the hiring company gets closer to the reference giver. Therefore, in order to get more accurate and valuable information about the applicant, the hiring company should check all work references by telephone or personal conversation or by sending an officer of the HR department to the former employer. However, if it may not be possible to use the aforementioned techniques, the hiring company should ask specific questions, through mail, which can be answered in a brief form by the former employer of the applicant. Such questions can be as follows: Was Mr/Miss/Mrs (applicant) employed by your company? What was the duration of his/her stay with your company? What was the post held by him/her? What was the nature of his/her job? Did he/she resign at his/her own? Did he/she advance in his/her position with you? Did he/she follow instructions satisfactorily? What may be the reasons for his/her leaving job with you? Would you rehire him/her, if available? Did he/she have any financial difficulties? Did he/she have any domestic trouble? How did he/

162 Acquiring Human Resources

she behave with his/her immediate boss, associates, customers and so on? What about his/her integrity, morals and character? Could you say he/she was a perfect worker? Do you think he/she would fit in our type of organisation? What is his/her accident record?

Thus, references cannot be transformed into an accurate selection device. They can simply be helpful in the selection process.

Psychological Tests

Psychological tests play a significant role in establishing the suitability of the applicant for the post. Since psychological tests involve a lot of expenditure, it is usually the large organisations which can bear with this device.

Psychological tests and employment interviews are two of the more important devices used in hiring procedure. In the present chapter, we have tried to indicate their place and importance in the HR programme as well as suggest some basic principles and approaches to be utilised in their administration. We take up psychological tests first.

Psychological testing represents an additional tool in the kit of the employment office.[33] Of late, an increasing number of enterprises have started using psychological tests evolved to measure physical dexterity, mental alertness, achievement, typical attitude and so on. However, these tests are by no means a tool for measuring the suitability of job applicants. Tests seek to eliminate the possibility that the prejudice of the interviewer or supervisor, instead of potential ability, will govern selection decisions.[34] They may help in revealing qualifications and talent that would not be detected by interviews or by listings of education and job experience.

A test of a particular ability does not measure that specific ability alone but also a class or group of abilities. For example, in a test of numerical ability, the candidate need not only grasp the relation between various data presented and to deduce something new to reach an answer but also be able to read and comprehend the question. All tests, therefore, are first psychological and then tests of specific abilities.[35]

An employment test is an instrument designed to measure selected psychological factors.[36] Such factors may include the ability to reason, capacity for learning, temperament and personality, specific aptitudes, manual dexterity, hand–eye coordination and so on.

Some people define an employment test as a systematic procedure for sampling human behaviour. Psychological tests help us in measuring what we feel to be a representative sample of human behaviour and utilising that measurement to predict future behaviour. In other words, the objective of this measurement process is to enable one to predict what a person is likely to do in the future. As a matter of fact, psychological tests are essentially an objective and standardised measure of a sampled behaviour.

By such measurement, we can determine how well a person has done something or may do something in the future. However, these measurements can be of two types: (a) intangible or qualitative and (b) quantitative. In the former, we simply indicate the quality or our impression about a person or an object. For example, after talking to a person, we can say that he/she appears to be dependable. In the latter, we express our findings in quantitative terms. For example, after testing a person, we can say that his/her IQ is 105.

Areas of Usage of Psychological Tests

Psychological tests are used in a variety of fields:

1. In the selection of personnel for the organisation: Psychological tests help in selecting suitable candidates. Through testing, training costs can be reduced by eliminating poor learners.

Recruitment, Selection, Placement and Induction/Socialisation   163

2. In vocational guidance: With the help of tests, it can be found out for what field of endeavour one is best suited. For example, tests of arithmetic, reasoning, reading, comprehension and reaction speed can tell us whether one is suitable for the job of an accountant or not.
3. In the placement of personnel: Tests help us in deciding who should be placed where.
4. In imparting training to personnel: Tests tell us who should be trained, where training should begin, what should be the contents of training and whether training has been adequate. Tests also help in reducing the cost of training.
5. In research into human behaviour and personality: Tests tell us about an individual's sociability; dominance; cooperativeness; tolerance; emotional stability; attitude towards life, individuals and society; control and intensity of feelings; and general level of activity.
6. In counselling employees.

Basic Principles of Testing

Following are the important basic principles of testing:

1. Tests should be selected based on job analysis. We should select or design tests to measure those requirements which have been suggested under a job specification.
2. Tests must have the characteristics of validity. The selected tests should be valid or the objective of measuring the desired requirement of the job, in a particular situation. In other words, validity refers to the extent to which a test measures what it is designed to measure. Since a particular test may be valid for one objective and invalid for another and further that a test may not have equal validity in different situations, most firms develop their own tests to ensure validity of the test. Validity may be of three kinds: predictive validity, concurrent validity and synthetic validity.
3. Reliability is another principle of testing for employment. According to Edwin B. Flippo, reliability refers to the degree of consistency of results obtained.[37] A reliable test is one which yields the same result even if a person is tested for the second or third time, provided the test and situation remain the same. In the case of change of time limit, instructions, subject's state of mind and health, room temperature, pencils and erasers or any other testing condition, the consistency of results may not be obtained even in the case of most reliable test.
4. In order to make test results comparable, the administration of tests must be controlled and standardised. There must be uniformity of procedure in administering and scoring the test as well as of testing conditions.
5. Objectivity of tests is another important principle. It refers to quality of opportunity for those taking the test. A test should not discriminate against caste, creed, sex and other factors. Besides, objectivity also refers to the job relatedness of the test; that is, tests should also possess face validity.
6. Tests should not be the only criterion for selection. They should instead supplement other instruments of selection.

Types of Tests

Tests used in selection can be classified into five categories: achievement, aptitude, interest, personality and intelligence tests.

1. **Achievement tests:** Achievement tests measure the job knowledge of the applicants in the areas such as marketing, HR and economics. When an applicant claims to know

something, an achievement test is given to measure how well he/she knows it. It is for this reason that achievement tests are also known as proficiency tests or performance tests. Achievement tests are a refinement of the work sample technique and are used to measure what the applicant can do and what tasks he/she can perform right now. Adaptability tests, abstract reasoning tests, Stanford–Binet Scales, Miller Analogies Test and the Purdue test for machinists and machine operators are some of the examples of such tests. Trade tests are the most common type of achievement tests given; for example, in a typing test, matter to be typed is provided to the candidate, and the time taken by the candidate in typing that matter and also the errors made by him/her are noted down, and thus, his/her proficiency in typing is measured. Similar tests are available in shorthand, calculating machines, operating calculators, simple mechanical equipment, and dictating and transcribing apparatuses.

2. **Aptitude tests:** Aptitude tests are also known as potential ability tests and specific cognitive tests and are used to measure the latent ability of a candidate to learn a given job if he/she is given the required training. Aptitude tests have special significance where the new recruit has little or very less experience along the lines of the job opening. Specific aptitude tests need to be designed for jobs that require mechanical, clerical, musical, academic, linguistic and motor capacities and abilities. The Bennett Test of Mechanical Comprehension and the Stenquist Mechanical Aptitude Test are some of the examples of popular mechanical aptitude tests. Aptitude tests for clerical jobs lay emphasis mainly on arithmetic, handwriting, spellings, vocabulary, checking and so on. Aptitude tests help in detecting peculiarities or defects in the applicant's sensory or intellectual capacity.

3. **Interest tests:** Interest in a job or task contributes to success on the job. A person interested in his/her job is likely to do better than one who is indifferent or uninterested. Interest tests have been designed to discover a person's field of interest and to identify the kind of work that will satisfy him/her. They are, in a sense, inventories of the likes and dislikes of the people of some occupations.

   Although the interest tests have been mostly standardised, some organisations have developed tests to suit their own requirements, especially when there is a continuing demand for se new personnel for a single job. Such developed tests are also known as tailor-made tests.

   Most widely used interest scales are Kuder Preference Record, Strong Vocational Interest Blank, mechanical reasoning tests and so on.

4. **Personality tests:** These tests aim at measuring the basic make-up or characteristics of an individual. They assess his/her introversion motivation, emotional reactions, emotional maturity, stability, mood, value system, ability to adjust, interpersonal relations, self-image, self-confidence, ambition, tact, optimism, decisiveness, sociability, objectivity, patience, fear, distrust, suspicion, judgement, dominance, impulsiveness, integrity, stability and so on. Industrial psychologists usually emphasise the 'big five'[38] personality dimensions as they apply to personnel testing.

   Theses dimensions are as follows:

   - Extraversion (sociability, activeness, energy, zeal and so on)
   - Emotional stability (poor conditions, adjustment, insecurity, hostility, anxiety and so on)
   - Agreeableness (trust, caring, gentleness and so on)
   - Conscientiousness (achievement and dependability)
   - Openness to experience (imagination, unconventionality and autonomy)

Recruitment, Selection, Placement and Induction/Socialisation 165

These are normally conducted for selecting supervisors and higher executives. These are pen-and-paper tests.

5. **Intelligence tests:** These tests aim at measuring the general level of intelligence of the applicant. This is done by measuring the IQ of the applicant. In addition to this, they also measure a range of abilities such as numerical ability, vocabulary, memory and verbal fluency. However, intelligence is usually measured with individually administered tests, such as the Wechsler Adult Intelligence Scale, Wonderlic Personnel Test, Stanford–Binet Test, California Test of Mental Maturity (Adult Level), Kaufman Adolescent and Adult Intelligence Test, Minnesota Paper Form Board Test (MPFB), Comprehensive Test of Verbal Intelligence, Wide Range Intelligence Test and Slosson Intelligence Test.[39] Some organisations also conduct the polygraphy and honesty tests.[40]

6. **Motor and physical abilities tests:** Such tests usually measure the speed and accuracy of simple judgement as well as the speed of fingers, hands and arms movement. Some of the popular tests in this regard include the Stromberg Dexterity Test, the Crawford Small Parts Dexterity Test, the Minnesota Rate of Manipulation Test and so on.

Tests are also divided into the following three categories:

1. **Objective tests:** These tests measure neurotic tendencies, self-sufficiency, dominance, sub-mission and self-control.
2. **Projective tests:** The candidate is asked to project his/her own interpretation into certain standard stimulus situations. The way he/she responds to these stimuli depends on his/her own values, motives and personality (e.g. Rorschach blot test and thematic apperception test).
3. **Situation tests:** These tests measure the applicant's reaction when he/she is placed in a peculiar situation. Normally, in a leaderless group, problem is presented, and solution is to be found out. A situation test requires the examinees to respond to situations representative of jobs. Video-based simulation is a situational test in which an examinee responds to video simulations of a realistic job situation.

Employment Interviewing

Interviewing is perhaps the oldest method of selection. The primary objective of the employment interview is to obtain significant information about the candidate. If given a choice of single device for selection, perhaps every hiring company will choose interviewing.

Interviews are so important that hundreds of research studies have been generated on the topic of interviews. Interviews may be structured and unstructured.

In a structural interview, almost similar questions are asked and these questions are predetermined and prepared in advance. Hence, there is a standardised list of questions with the interviewer.

As against structured interviews, there are unstructured interviews which have no predetermined script or protocol. Through an unstructured interview, a highly expert interviewer can elicit useful insights about the applicant. Of late, two types of unstructured interviews have come into prominence: (a) the behavioural description interview (BDI) in which the interviewee is prompted to relate actual incidents from his/her past relevant work experience and the like because past is the best predictor of the future and (b) the situational interview (SI) in which questions asked are such as may encourage applicants to respond to hypothetical situations they might come across on the job for which they are being interviewed. With the help of SI, an attempt is made by the interviewer to find out whether the applicant possesses job knowledge and motivation. Although both structured and unstructured interviews are good at their own place, research has revealed that structured interviews are generally more reliable and valid than unstructured interviews.

Interviews can be very useful as well as harmful. It has been rightly said that 'interviews are the most used, misused and abused tool in the process of selection'.

Approval by the Supervisor

The principles of line and staff relationships require that after a candidate has been okayed by the HR department, he/she should be handed over to the supervisor concerned for acceptance or rejection, even though this third interview may involve some amount of overlapping of the preceding interview. It will not be fair to hold the supervisor accountable for the performance of an employee who has been selected without his/her approval. Hence, the approval by the supervisor appears to be quite desirable. Besides, in this third interview, the supervisor finds an opportunity to detect whether the applicant has all those essential qualities which the other personnel on similar jobs in the department have got. If he/she feels that the applicant does not possess those minimum requirements and that it will be difficult for the applicant to develop those characteristics in a reasonable time period, he/she can well recommend the rejection of the candidate. Many organisations seek the approval of the supervisor early in the process of selection to eliminate needless testing, reference checking and so on in case the candidate is not acceptable to the supervisor.

Physical Examination

Most organisations require that an applicant goes through a physical examination before he/she can be finally accepted for employment. There cannot be two opinions about the utility of an applicant going through a physical examination. It is in the interest of both the hiring company and the applicant himself/herself. It will be a costly process for the hiring company to assign a job to a person who though may be mentally qualified for it but physically unfit for the same. It is equally costly for the recruit to be assigned a job for which he/she is not physically qualified when he/she might be readily assigned to other work for which he/she is qualified in every way. Besides, physical examination of the applicant may be helpful to prevent communicable diseases from entering the organisation. In addition to this, physical examination also safeguards the interest of the hiring company against payment of claims under compensation law. That is why, some of the companies get the heart and lungs of the applicant examined through a fluoroscope or get the lungs X-rayed. However, such practices are not general and differ from industry to industry and from organisation to organisation.

Ordinarily, the physical tests involve the following:

1. Physical measurements, such as weight, height and chest expansion
2. Quick examination of eyes, ears, mouth, throat and so on
3. Testing for bronchial problems leading to nervousness, tuberculosis and hernia
4. Examination of respiratory system

5. General check-up of lungs and chest
6. General check-up of skin and muscles
7. Check-up of blood pressure
8. Laboratory tests of urine, stool, blood and so on

The physical examination may vary somewhat from post to post, from company to company and from post to post within the same company. Personnel required to do heavy labouring work will be tested more for physical strength, freedom from hernia, heart action and general health. On the other hand, for typists, special emphasis will be laid on eyesight, fingers, lungs and so on. In order to reduce the cost on this step of selection (physical examination), it is usually conducted near the end of the procedure of selection because at this point, the number of applicants left is much less than the number of applicants who fill out application blanks. Many employers conduct drug screening (substance abuse screening), especially when there is a reason to believe that the applicant has been using drugs.

Use of Digital Tools

These helps companies rate employees and identify top performers. Predictive analysis will go a long way in helping managers hire people whose personalities fit the role and the value of organisation. It also aids in forecasting which employee will produce better results than others and achieve success (see Exhibit 5.11).

However, while predictive analytics can be helpful in improving hiring and retention rates, this needs to be viewed in conjunction with evaluation methodologies. There are factors that could affect its results, including the employees' performance and their retention.

Competency-based Selection

Competency-based selection is a process based on the ability of candidates to produce anecdotes about their professional experience which can be used as evidence that the candidates have a given competency. Candidates demonstrate competencies on their application form, and then in the interview, which in this case is known as competency-based interview. The process leaves little scope for any discretion to be exercised by the recruiter as the required competencies are clearly laid down and tested at the time of interview.

Exhibit 5.11   Digital Tools Help Companies Rate Employees and Identify Top Performers

The explosion of analytics in the digital world has changed the future of business. It also guides the managers to hire workers personalities fit the core values and perceptions of the company.

It also works as it finds the right fit for each role and helps companies recognise the type of people who could succeed in its environment and the kind of sources that will produce better.

Source: Hindustan Times, 21 March 2017.

168 *Acquiring Human Resources*

Assessment Centres

An assessment centre is a process where candidates are assessed to determine their stability for specific types of employment, and it came into existence in early 20th century (see Exhibit 5.12).

The candidates' personality and aptitudes (see Exhibit 5.13) are determined by a variety of techniques, including group exercises (see Exhibit 5.14), presentations, examinations, psychometric testing and interviews (see Exhibit 5.15). These assessment centres exercises assess how close the candidate's behaviour is to the requirement for the role match. The process lasts usually from half a day to two full days, depending on the level of position applied for.

A Competency-based Interview

Many organisations have started using behavioural competencies as well as organisational and job fit, rather than the more traditional '100% match' with skills, technical knowledge and experience. A competency-based interview can be effective if it is supported by a well-planned process, starting by analysing the available position to ensure that the competencies required for the aligned task are identified and the associated behaviours are accurately quantified. It should also be ensured that the information gathered from candidates is meaningful and complete. Again, interview guides must provide guidance and support to everyone involved in the competency-based interview.

There must be available bona fide, validated, fair and unbiased standards against which to assess applicant competencies to perform in the targeted role/job. The transparency of the selection process may be improved, clearly communicating the behaviours employees must display for success in the role/job. The process of a competency-based interview can be made more effective by contributing to the design of a well-articulated, efficient and effective recruitment and selection process. Work managers who are likely to conduct competency-based interviews must have required knowledge and skills and must be exposed to behavioural interviewing and SI. They should have been trained for the purpose.

Besides, there should be no pressure on the interviewers to fill up the job urgently, and they should be allowed to take their own decisions. Questions like 'tell us about yourself' should be avoided because the question is too broad and at times may allow the candidate to take control of the interview. The interview guide must clearly indicate the competencies needed for the job—which competencies are 'must have' and which are 'nice to have'—and as well as contain a clear scoring system.

Besides, the interviewers should not allow a single competency to overshadow the lack of others—or the opposite. The interviewers should not make snap decision about candidates based on information from the CV, the candidate's dress sense or their handshake or the like. Although interviewers should focus on the core skills needed for the job, all the same, they should pay adequate attention to the motivational aspects of the position and the interviewee.

In short, there should be analysis of jobs, drafting needed competencies and specifications for different roles, preparing competency-based interviewing guides which may include appropriate questions and rating scales, and proper training to interviewers who should possess necessary skills and knowledge along with adequate exposure to behavioural interviewing and SI.

Exhibit 5.12 Beginning and Growth of Assessment Centres

In modern times, the German army introduced assessment techniques for selecting its officers in the 1930s.

- Assessment centres were created in World War II to select officers and are still commonly used in military recruitment today.
- AT&T created a building for recruitment of staff in the 1950s. This was called the Assessment Centre and was influential on subsequent personnel methods in other businesses. Some of the renowned employers which feature an assessment centre in their graduate recruitment process include Accenture, Ernest and Young, KPMG and PwC.

Source: Wikipedia: The Free Encyclopedia.

Exhibit 5.13 Typical Individual Assessments Used at Assessment Centres

- Personality tests
- Aptitude tests
- Presentations
- Written exercise
- Case study
- E-tray exercise
- In-tray exercise
- Professional conduct questions

Exhibit 5.14 Typical Group Assessment Used at Assessment Centres

- Case study
- Role exercise
- Role play

Exhibit 5.15 Typical Interviews Used at Assessment Centres

- Competency interview
- Partner interview
- Technical interview
- Panel interview

Cost–benefit Analysis of the Selection Decision

Cost–benefit analysis is one of the cardinal principles of management. An organisation should assess the utility including the statistical utility and organisational utility of the selection decision and find out whether the return coming for the selection system is more than its costs including both direct and indirect costs. If yes, then it should continue; otherwise, drop it or improve it.

Recent Developments/Emerging Trends/Feedback

Optimism Index Oi 1.1: A Predictive Tool for Success

The word *optimism* is derived from the Latin word *optimus*, which means 'best'. Optimism has been defined by Martin Seligman (1995) as being proactive in reacting to the problems with positive attitude and confidence and effectively working towards the same. Thus, optimism is the innate belief system of an individual, and it suggests that an optimist would always look for the best and is positive that good things will certainly happen. Optimism is also a major dimension of emotional intelligence, which, if developed and inculcated, may lead to enhanced quality of life of an individual.

To measure optimism, an assessment tool with sturdy psychometric properties—Optimism Index Oi 1.1—has been developed by Padmakali Banerjee. This index rates the optimism level of an organisation, group or individual.

This test is not only a measure of present performance but also a predictive measure of success. It is being popularly used as a screening tool for selection and as a developmental tool for training in organisations. The various dimensions of optimism as measured by this test include positive emotions, engagement, relationship networks, meaningfulness and accomplishment. This test can be taken online at www.optimism-index.com

Based on the analysis of the optimism index scores, individuals are classified into ten categories: collaborator, entrepreneur, energetic, synergist, networker, analyst, innovator, go-getter, expert and leader. This classification highlights the attributes and strengths of individuals and creates distinction. This helps them in making career choices and engaging in suitable professional roles. Knowledge of results (KR) on this test benefits not only the individual but also the organisation in decision-making related to talent management.

Participate in a Contest, Get Hired

Some companies, of late, have started a hiring game, whereby they are now running contests for college graduates, fast-tracking job interviews for winners and hiring some as trainees (see Exhibits 5.16 and 5.17).

Exhibit 5.16 Participate in a Contest, Get Selected

Deloitte Maverick is one such contest in which candidates are asked to solve actual organisational issues. Senior professionals at Deloitte monitor the solutions provided and the well performing candidates are given pre-placed interview opportunities. Godrej, too, over the last four years, has been organising Godrej LOUD (Live Out Ur Dream) for first-year students across B-schools. As part of the initiative, students need to write about their unfulfilled dreams and eight to ten 'best dreamers' are given 1.5 lakh to fulfil that dream.

Source: Hindustan Times, 2 August 2016.

Exhibit 5.17 National-level Contest: Winners Receive Pre-placement Interview Offer

Microsoft organises Build the Shield, an annual national-level security contest for graduates or undergraduates pursuing major in computer science, information technology or electronics and communication engineering. The winners receive pre-placement interview offer from the organisation.

Source: Hindustan Times, 2 August 2016.

There is a provision that students participating in the LOUD programme can join Godrej Industries Ltd and associate companies as summer interns, and the talented ones are recruited as management trainees after they graduate. They are later hired as permanent employees based on their performance. Godrej management trainee programme is called Gallop, and it is a major source of leadership hiring at entry level. Every year, on average, 30% of summer interns are recruited through LOUD, and 80% of management trainees are recruited through the summer internship programmes.[41]

Blind Audition to Help Remove Gender Bias in Recruitment

According to a recent survey,[42] of late, some companies are embracing the concept of 'blind audition' to do away with the powerful gender bias, such as in management consultancy.

Capgemini is set to adopt blind sieving to prevent bias in the first phase of recruitment, by masking information on gender, ethnicity, age and other such non-job-specific elements related to candidates to help recruiters make unbiased choices. Another example is of software exporter Infosys where the company gives candidates an option not to disclose information unrelated to selection process. Another example relates to consultancy Ernst & Young which withholds information on gender when hiring in bulk.

The hiring practice of not revealing information regarding gender is prevalent in Nordic countries. In India also, per the law of the land, companies cannot force the applicant to share gender-sensitive information initially that can influence the decision of the company. If the companies insist on gender-related information, then it is a malpractice. According to the founder chairman of Forum for Women in Leadership, such biases will only disappear once employers are penalised for such offences.

Blind audition hiring allows any form of conscious or unconscious bias to be removed from the hiring process, thereby allowing companies to hire purely based on skills. Of course, it helps improve gender diversity and ethnic diversity. However, it is impersonal and difficult to implement on scale.

It misses cultural fitment. Besides, it lacks competency to manage and use the technique. Despite all this, its usage will increase, and it will take two–three years for this concept to make a mark in India and usage will be limited.

Are Start-ups Hiring Right and Do They Need to Simplify Their Interview Process?

Start-up companies in India need to put in place innovative as well as tried-and-tested hiring policies if they want to attract and retain talent.[43] In many start-ups, we come across bizarre hiring processes which have been put in place in some of India's start-ups.

Well-thought-out recruitment processes are not being followed in many start-ups. In most cases, such faulty processes are leading to mass lay-offs. According to the director general of National HRD Network, an HR management forum, the main fault on the part of the founders of these start-ups is to think that an individual would be an expert in everything. In the absence of adequate manpower, they tend to assign specialised functions even to non-specialised people. Multi-skilling is certainly good, but it cannot be applied unitarily.

The start-up founders are very diligent when it comes to hiring the first few employees who come from the friend and family pool. As soon as the time to hire employee number 11 comes, the cracks start showing. As work is not structured or defined, they tend to start hiring people based on gut feel. Since there are no written roles or key tasks for prospective employees, they make a 'judgement call' without having hard data to support the call. The interview questions are flimsy, and first-time founders, most of the time, do not even know if they are making a mistake. During hiring, it is best for gut feel to remain in the gut. Companies do not want to appoint specialist sourcing consulting firms because they do not want to pay handsome fees and deal with questions which they do not want to answer.

The start-ups are, therefore, required to take a lot of precautions and preparations for interviewing the candidates (for what needs to be done by start-ups, see Exhibit 5.18).

Start-ups need to improve their recruitment processes as applicants are also consumers in the same marketplace. In case they do not treat or respect the candidate, they have lost a customer forever. Negative feedback from interviews when shared by interviewees with friends and relatives reflects negatively on the company. In case the companies are in the business-to-consumer (B2C) space and selling in India, they need to map the interview experience. The start-up founders or HR should not hide behind the volume of applicants and the usual cliché of 'we are doing our best'.

Exhibit 5.18 What Needs to Be Done: A Few Pointers for Start-ups

- Failing to do their research about company and role
- Not looking interested with the interviewer
- Not dressing appropriately
- Lying about achievements
- Being too quiet/not asking questions
- Confused/vague responses
- Making up answers
- Complaining about their current employer

Source: The Economic Times, 5 January 2016.

It is not only that many employers fail to conduct interviews properly but also that candidates appearing for interview come without doing any research on companies. A TimesJobs survey of 500 recruiters on Interview Blunders has revealed that over 50% of candidates fumble during job interviews. Per the survey, the entry-level candidates (44%), middle-level candidates (36%) and senior-level candidates (20%) fumble during job interviews.[44] The most common interview mistakes committed by interviewees are shown in Exhibit 5.19.

Exhibit 5.19 Most Common Interview Mistakes Committed by Interviewees

- Failing to do their research about company and role — 71%
- Not looking interested with the interviewer — 50%
- Not dressing appropriately — 43%
- Lying about achievements — 36%
- Being too quiet/not asking questions — 28%
- Confused/vague responses — 16%
- Making up answers — 15%
- Complaining about their current employer — 12%

Source: The Economic Times, 5 January 2016.

Exhibit 5.20 Increasing Trend in Adoption of Psychometric Instruments

In its study 'Psychometrics in Indian Organisations' (2013), Tata Strategic Management Group (TSMG), the largest Indian-owned management consulting firm finds that the Indian companies are progressively employing psychometric instruments for addressing behavioural changes to support decisions for talent processes like recruitment and selection, leadership development, succession planning, high performance identification, team allocation, etc. The survey conducted by TSMG, suggested that adoption rate of psychometrics was likely to increase to 87% by 2016 in the Indian organisations.

Source: Tata Strategic Management Group, 'Psychometrics in Indian Organisations—A Report presented by Tata Strategic Management Group', *Human Capital* 18, no. 2 (July 2014).

It is, therefore, necessary for the candidates also to prepare for their job interviews. They should research the company, read job description, think possible tough questions, be well versed with their resume and prepare their own queries.[45]

Adoption Rate of Psychometric Instruments

The adoption rate of psychometric instruments is showing an increasing trend (see Exhibit 5.20).

HRM Strategy Regarding Recruitment and Selection

As labour cost constitutes a significant part of total cost of production, an HRM strategy regarding recruitment and selection should be formulated taking all precautions. For example, regarding which sources of HR supply should be used. Such sources should be such as may not only be feasible, economical and dependable but also competitively better. Similar is the case regarding method(s) of recruitment. While taking a decision, HRM strategy should always keep in view the past experiences of outside organisations. The selection strategy should also aim at choosing the best possible candidates at competitive rates of wages and salaries. The strategy should have provisions for periodical evaluation of sources and methods used and suggest remedial steps. Efforts should be made to make use of the latest and sophisticated methods of selection, if economically feasible. All exercises in this regard should be carried out, keeping the stand being taken by competitive organisations. It must also be ensured that the HRM strategy regarding recruitment and selection should be in alignment with the overall strategy of the organisation and be instrumental in accomplishing the objectives of the organisational strategy.

Placement

Placement is the determination of the job to which an accepted candidate is to be assigned. It is matching of what the supervisor has reasons to think he/she can do with the job demands (job requirements), it is matching of what he/she imposes (in strain, working conditions) and what he/she offers in the form of payroll, companionship with others, promotional possibilities and so on.[46]

Normally, applicants are hired for a specific position in a department of the company. In case the number of people hired for the same position is large, there may arise a problem of placement, that is, who should be placed under which supervisor and so on. Proper placement is important for both the supervisor and the newly appointed employee. In view of added significance being attached to human relations and reducing high rate of turnover of the newly appointed personnel in the first few months of their appointment, good relations between the supervisor and their newly appointed subordinates are very essential.

It helps the new subordinates to adjust with the other employees and accept them as co-workers. To aid this process, some companies have very exhaustive induction and orientation programmes.

Induction/Orientation

Induction or orientation as it is often called is the process of receiving and welcoming an employee when he/she first joins a company and giving him/her basic information he/she needs to settle down quickly and happily and start work.[47] Induction is concerned with the problem of introducing or orienting a new employee to organisation. No doubt, during the process of selection, the interviewer imparts much information regarding the history, traditions, policies and products of the organisation that develops confidence and interest on the part of the worker. But the process of introducing the worker to his/her work and of integrating him/her with his/her position in order to create a well-balanced worker, naturally continues after the actual selection of the worker has been completed.[48] Employee orientation provides new employees with the basic background information they need to work in the company. It has been rightly observed that the adjustment begins with the hiring interview and continues so long as the employee faces new situations, even though he/she may be an 'old timer'. The organisation must see that the new employee is imparted all that information and that point of view which will make him/her a confident, interested and capable hand. According to E. W. Bakke,[49] induction constitutes a significant part of fusion process,

> which is a simultaneous operation of the socializing process by which the organisation seeks to make an agent of the individual for the precise achievement of organisational objectives and of the personalising process by which the individual seeks to make an agency of the organisation for the achievement of his/her personal objective.

Through induction, we aim at integrating the organisation and the personal goals.

Objectives of Induction

1. To define the terms and conditions of work
2. To acquaint the employee with the requirements of the job
3. To inculcate in the employee a confidence in his/her own ability to do the job and also a confidence in the organisation
4. To bring about integration and agreement between organisational goals and personal goals
5. To inform the new employee about training facilities[50]
6. To provide the information and opportunity required by all new employees to satisfactorily adjust themselves to their work and help them to develop an enthusiasm for the organisation and its ideals, policies and responsibilities
7. To put the new employee at his/her ease

However, the details involved in carrying out these objectives may differ from company to company, as well as with different classes of people within the same company. For example, the emphasis in a company which is highly centralised may vary substantially from the one which has decentralised responsibility. Similarly, the personnel belonging to different categories and cadres need different handling. The details of an induction procedure usually depend on (a) the number of personnel to be oriented and (b) the level of business activity.

Of late, there is a strong movement in the direction of handling induction process with great care because turnover among new employees is higher than among workers with greater seniority. Besides, if the organisation fails to induct an employee to his/her work situation and to the company's policies properly, then the employee, even if he/she may be having creative faculties, high ambitions and aspirations, may turn into a questioning worker with thwarted ambitions and aspirations. Therefore, a worker needs to be oriented not only in his/her specific tasks, rules and regulations of the plant but also in the policies, traditions and objective of the firm.

An induction programme mainly lays emphasis on the following points:

1. **To provide information about the job requirements:** It is the duty of the employment interviewer and the supervisor to tell the new employee the nature of his/her job. The new employee should be given the relevant occupation description to go through it and know his/her job requirements. It will be in the fitness of things if the new

employee is taken round the place where he/she is to work to enable him/her to see for himself/herself the nature of the job, the machines and the plant he/she is to work on and so on. The supervisor or the head of the unit/section/department should give the new employee a complete and faithful conception of his/her work.

2. **To explain the conditions of employment:** It is basically the duty of the HR manager to impart complete knowledge of terms and condition under which he/she is to serve. He/she must be told about his/her wages, allowances, overtime, hours of work, sickness benefits, rules of conduct, penalties, fines and so on. The supervisor too should orient the new employee regarding the terms and conditions of employment.

3. **To infuse confidence in the new employee:** The new employee is obviously more interested in his/her future than in his/her present. A fair and clear picture about the opportunities for promotion and increase in salary and so on may create confidence in the employee. The new employee is keen to know the personnel policies, working condition and so on. If the employee is given a just, precise and fair statement about all these and if the employee finds them suitable, then he/she develops confidence and interest in his/her job.

4. **To provide instruction on an induction procedure:** Having studied the aforesaid three items to be laid emphasis upon during an induction programme, we can now discuss the items that should generally be covered under an induction procedure. As far as the HR department is concerned, it should take care of items such as history of the firm, policies of the firm, products of the firm, organisation of the firm, merit rating, union relationship, industrial relations policies, safety and health group insurance, lease and holidays, medical vacation, pension and gratuity schemes, income tax deductions and pay cheques, suggestion system, incentive schemes, employee activities and bonus rules. As far as the supervisor is concerned, he/she should orient the new employee regarding departmental objectives, plant facilities (parking, lockers, transportations, cafeteria, restrooms and so on), probation period, working hours, union, job routine, company, plant, departmental regulations and so on.

Induction: Whose Responsibility/Process of Induction

Process of induction in a small organisation, especially having little centralisation of functions, is usually handled by the supervisor concerned. However, in large organisations having central agencies to handle various functions such as HR and inspection, the first phase of the induction process is carried out by the HR department and the second phase is conducted by the job supervisor.

1. **Role of the HR department in the induction programme:** It is usually the HR department which conducts the first phase of the induction programme. Although during the employment interview and at other stages of the selection procedure, a number of details are made known to the new employee, the new employee should be formally oriented in all concerned things. The nature of the company and its products are to be explained. If possible, a motion picture depicting the history and operations of the company may be shown to the new employee. This will create in the employee a sense of pride and interest towards the organisation. The representative of the HR department may give an indoctrination talk to the group of new employees. Here, they can make use of different people. For example, the medical officer may be invited to orient the new employees in medical system prevailing in the organisation.

Recruitment, Selection, Placement and Induction/Socialisation

The safety officer may talk about safety measures. The HR manager may cover other items and policies of the organisation. In some organisations, the employment interviewer or some other suitable person of the HR department makes it a practice for first few days to stop near the table or machine of the new employee for a moment's chat to enable him/her to seek clarification to his/her doubts, confusion or misgivings. This is also a very good procedure.

2. **Role of the supervisor in the induction programme**: In the second phase, the induction is conducted by the job supervisor. However, if the supervisor is too busy to spare time for this purpose, then some older and experienced employee of the department can be assigned this job. Induction at this stage is quite specific and requires skill on the part of the job supervisor. He/she needs to see that there is successful fusion of the employee with his/her fellow workers, the company, the supervisor and so on. The candidate should be taken to his/her workplace; introduced to his/her fellow workers; told of the location and other details of the locker rooms, cafeteria, restrooms and so on; and informed about the duration and frequency of rest pauses, uniform, usual practice regarding lunch and so on. As a matter of fact, he/she should be told about all those things that will be helpful to him/her to adjust himself/herself to the new job and environment. In all this, the supervisor has a primary responsibility for getting his/her new employee start off properly.

Methods of Giving Information to the New Employee Under the Induction Procedure

It may differ from company to company. Yet some of the common methods used in this process are as follows:

1. Motion pictures and sound slides
2. Lectures
3. Written material either in the form of booklets or included in one book
4. Trips through the plant
5. Trips to the department or division or section
6. Illustrated catalogues, especially designed for the purpose
7. Models of finished products
8. Display/notice boards
9. Showcases exhibiting the assembled and disassembled products of the company
10. Charts showing the number of employees, rate of absenteeism and turnover
11. Charts displaying total output during the last few months/years
12. Counsellors meeting and escorting the new employee to his/her workplace
13. Surprise and frequent visits by the supervisor to the workplace of the new employee

Follow-up Interview

The complete induction programme includes a follow-up some weeks after the initial hiring and orientation. This follow-up interview may be conducted by any responsible line or staff executive. The objective of such an interview as a part of induction programme is to ascertain the mental status of the worker. Whether he/she is reasonably well satisfied with his/her job or has certain fears, or misgivings, or confusion. If he/she has got any such thing, then there is no better technique for removing fears and doubts than talking things over with someone in authority. However, such follow-up interviews should also include the first-line supervisor to find out how well satisfied he/she is with the inducted employee.

Socialisation

Orientation is an important aspect of socialisation stage of the staffing process[51] and at times is used synonymously by many authors. However, the main difference between the two is that while orientation/induction is a short-term programme and usually continues for a day or two or so, socialisation is a long-term process as this enables the new employees to acclimatise themselves to the new organisation, know what is expected of them by their company and understand the culture of their company. Although socialisation is generally taken as informal, it needs a systematic approach to make the new employees affected and enable them to contribute their best towards the accomplishment of the organisation objectives. It should, therefore, start to make them know the mission of their organisation, to whom they need to report in the hierarchy and how the whole system of the organisation works.

Although there is no formal phase categorisation of socialisation, according to L. R. Gomez-Mejia, D. B. Balkin and R. Cardy, it can be divided into three phases:[52]

1. **Anticipatory phase,** during which an RJP should be presented so that the new employees may understand the realities of the organisation's expectation from them, actual demands of the job and the realities of the work environment. This will help in removing misconception or confusion the new hires may have regarding their prospective about the organisation.
2. **Encounter phase** starts when the new employees have started their work and are coming across the reality of the job. In this stage, the new hires should be presented on relevant information about their practical work, reporting relationships, rules and regulations, policies and procedures followed in their organisation, and so on to create a feeling among them that the company values them.
3. **Settling-in phase,** during which the worker starts feeling himself/herself as a part of the organisation if he/she is satisfied with his/her job and the role assigned to him/her. In case he/she does not feel settled and is uncomfortable with his/her job or the role that he/she has been playing, the new hire will not develop a sense of belongingness. In this phase, mentoring can play an effective role.

Thus, socialisation is a long-term process and may continue for about a year or so. However, it is worth it.

Chapter Review

After completing job analysis, the next step in the process of procurement is recruitment which involves searching for and stimulating the potential candidates to apply in as large a number as possible for the vacant positions in an organisation. This exercise is usually undertaken by the employment section of the organisation.

1. There can be centralised or decentralised recruitment depending on the requirement of an organisation. Similarly, the answer to the question 'whether the

recruitment function be independent' depends on the size of the recruiting activities in the organisation. Besides, both the external factors, such as labour market and government rules and regulations, and the internal factors, such as organisational goals and policies, affect the recruitment process.
2. Every organisation should have a well-thought-out, properly crafted recruitment policy, preferably formulated in consultation with the workers' union.
3. There are both the internal sources of HR supply, such as job posting, present workforce, old workers, retrenched workers, succession planning, and transfers and promotion, and the external sources, such as advertising, employment agencies, recommendations by present employees, schools and colleges, labour organisations, casual applicants, leasing ODRS, minority groups, e-recruiting/recruiting via the Internet, summer internships, walk-ins and offshoring/outsourcing white-collar and other jobs. Both the internal and external sources of HR supply have their advantages and disadvantages. The methods of recruitment include direct method, indirect method and third-party method.
4. It is desirable that there is periodical recruitment evaluation and remedial steps taken. Recruiting a more diverse workforce is almost unavoidable these days because of keen global competition and socio-politico-legal compulsions. The alternatives to recruitment comprise overtime, employee leasing and temporary employment. Besides, an effective recruiter should possess certain attributes such as good interpersonal skills, self-motivation, awareness about his/her organisation and interest in applicants.
5. After recruitment starts the process of selection. In the selection process, all the activities are designed together to find out whether a person is suitable for a particular job. Before starting the selection process, we ensure preliminary requirements, such as authority to hire, adequate number of employees and so on. The pseudoscientific methods of selection have now almost lost their relevance and stand replaced by scientific methods, which are relatively more useful in finding out the right person at the right job and reducing the cost of training and development. Necessary steps should also be taken to ensure accuracy of selection.
6. Selection is affected by both the external factors, such as labour market and socio-economic scenario of the country, and the internal factors, such as the policies of the organisation and work culture of the organisation. Besides, the selection criteria should be both valid and reliable.
7. The selection process consists of several steps such as initial contact, screening (preliminary interview, application blank and so on), references (such as school references, character references and work references), psychological tests (such as achievement tests, aptitude tests, interest tests, personality tests and intelligence tests), interviewing (which can be structured or structured), approval by the supervisor and physical examination. There should be periodical cost–benefit analysis of the selection decisions.
8. Having selected the candidates, they should be properly placed, that is, what job should be assigned to each of them, who should be placed under which supervisor and who should be placed at which plant of the organisation if the plants are located at different places.

9. Induction or orientation (which is a short-term process) of the new hires is a must as it leads to their integration into the organisation and adds to their confidence, morale and a feeling of ease. There may be two phases of induction programme—first to be conducted by the HR department and the second to be conducted by the supervisor concerned. There are several methods of giving information to new hires under the induction programme. Socialisation, which includes induction also, is a long-term programme and may take around a year. Socialisation aims at enabling the new hire to acclimatise himself/herself to the new organisation, its work culture and so on. Socialisation may consist of three phases: anticipatory stage, encounter stage and selling-in stage. Overall, socialisation is worth it.

Key Terms

Behavioural	E-recruiting	Orientation	Socialisation
Casual applicants	Head-hunters	Placement	Structured interviews
	Induction	Rehire	
Centralised recruitment	Interview	Realistic job preview (RJP)	Succession planning
	Job posting		
Decentralised recruitment	On-demand recruiting services (ODRS)	Recorded want ads	Unstructured interviews
		Recruitment	
Description	Open job bidding	Situation tests	Walk-ins

Discussion Questions

1. Discuss the functions of employment department in the context of recruitment, as well as the positive and negative points of centralised and decentralised recruitment. Also discuss the features of a good recruitment policy.
2. Discuss the various internal sources of HR supply and their advantages and disadvantages.
3. Discuss the various external sources of HR supply, with special reference to e-recruiting, and their merits and demerits in the context of large organisations.
4. Discuss the various recruitment practices prevalent in Indian industries. Also discuss how to evaluate recruiting effectiveness.
5. Discuss the preliminary requirements that should be present in an organisation before initiating the selection process. Also discuss the steps required to improve accuracy of selection and the importance of validity and reliability of selection criteria.
6. Discuss the importance of testing and interviewing in the selection process.
7. Discuss the benefits of proper placement accruing to the new hires as well as the organisation.
8. Discuss the difference between induction and socialisation and how these two are beneficial to both the employees and the organisation.

9. Discuss the stages involved in the process of induction.
10. Discuss the various phases of socialisation.

Individual and Group Activities

1. Working individually or in groups, contact the HR department official of a big organisation and discuss the details of the recruitment policy of their organisation. Then contact the trade union office-bearers and find out their reaction towards the recruitment policy and thereafter prepare a brief report.
2. Working individually, contact the trade union leader(s) of a big organisation and find out from him/her if the workers are satisfied with the selection process of their organisation. Yes or no? Find out the reasons and seek their suggestions for improvement.
3. Working individually, visit a big organisation and find out how it places its new hires.
4. Working in a group, interact with some of the new hires of a big organisation and find out if they are satisfied with the induction programme conducted by the management. Also seek their suggestions to improve the existing system of induction in the organisation.
5. Constitute a group of three members and visit a big organisation. Contact a few employees who have been in this organisation for a year or two and find out from them what were the informal ways in which they could help them in acclimatising themselves to their new organisation and its culture.

Application Case 5.1

Lack of Genuineness in Reference Letter

Sundran, a BTech (mechanical engineering) and MBA (marketing), joined a big manufacturing company, producing two-wheelers, in 2008 as an assistant purchase officer. The company had a turnover of 120 billion. It employed around 5,000 employees, of which about 600 were in the supervisory and the managerial cadre. The company had been in existence for the last about one and a half decade. Sundran proved his worth and was appreciated for procuring the desired ancillaries for the company at reasonable rates. Within a short span of two years, he was promoted as purchase officer, and in 2012 he was further promoted as deputy purchase manager. However, his super boss, Nandkarni, director of purchase, started suspecting the integrity of Sundran as he noticed a very high standard of living of Sundran, which was much beyond the salary he was receiving from the company. Nandkarni tried his best to get some proof leading to the establishment of corruption against Sundran. Although he could not get any proof, he was more than convinced that Sundran was not above board.

After a few months, Sundran received a call for interview for the post of senior purchase manager from a company which was also in the manufacturing of two-wheelers and was a competitor of the company Sundran was working at.

Kumar, the deputy director of HR, was responsible for recruitment of senior officers in the company Sundran received the interview call from. He formed a very favourable impression about Sundran as his CV was quite impressive, especially the reference letter Sundran had from Nandkarni. Nandkarni had appreciated the achievements of Sundran and also recommended his candidature to whomsoever it may concerned. Nandkarni had issued that letter of recommendation not because that he wanted to favour Sundran but because he (Nandkarni) wanted to get rid of Sundran as the integrity of the latter was suspected by the former. Nandkarni did not mention anything about his suspicion of integrity of Sundran in his letter of reference.

Kumar, along with other members of the selection committee, interviewed Sundran for about 45 minutes. Attaching a great weightage to the letter of recommendation Sundran had attached with his CV, Kumar selected him. Kumar's office did not make any other effort to verify the credentials, especially the integrity of Sundran.

Sundran joined the new organisation as senior purchase manager and delivered good results. However, after about a year, Kumar came to know that for certain considerations, Sundran was showing favour to a supplier who used to supply ancillaries in bulk to the new company Sundran had been working with. Kumar alerted his office and asked it to get the matter investigated confidentially and within a couple of months it was established that Sundran was indulging in unfair practices. Consequently, Sundran was asked to find job elsewhere.

Questions

1. What went wrong in the selection process followed by the new company where Sundran was interviewed for the post of senior purchase manager? Also, who should be held responsible for the lapse in this connection?
2. What remedial steps should be taken by the company so that this lapse is not repeated in the selection process in future?
3. How would you comment on the genuineness of Nandkarni with reference to letter of recommendation issued by him in favour of Sundran? Does it have any unethical element involved in it?

Notes

1. Dessler and Varkkey, *Human Resource Management*, 170.
2. See Flippo, *Principles of Personnel Management*, 131.
3. For details of physical environment of employment office and personnel in employment office, see W. D. Scott, R. C. Clothier, and W. R. Spriegel, *Personnel Management*, 6th ed. (New Delhi: Tata McGraw Hill Publishing Co. Ltd, January 1984), 70–72.
4. See Ivancevich, *Human Resource Management*, 192–96.
5. Milan Moravec, 'Effective Job Posting Fills Dual Needs', *HR Magazine* 50, no. 2 (September 1990): 76–80.

6 For example, see Jucius, *Personnel Management*, 109–10.
7 Ivancevich, *Human Resource Management*, 200.
8 R. C. Saxena, *Labour Problems and Social Welfare* (Meerut: Jai Prakash Nath & Co., 1986), 53.
9 *The Economic Times*, 21 June 2016.
10 Ibid.
11 See Dessler and Varkkey, *Human Resource Management*, 193.
12 Ibid.
13 M. Piturro, 'The Power of E-Recruiting', *Management Review* 89, no. 1 (January 2000): 33–37.
14 Ivancevich, *Human Resource Management*, 202.
15 Gomez-Mejia, Balkin, and Cardy, *Managing Human Resources*, 7.
16 See *The Economic Times*, 26 February 2016.
17 For details, see Ivancevich, *Human Resource Management*, 208–9.
18 Yoder, *Personnel Management and Industrial Relations*, 327.
19 K. K. Jacob, 'Scientific Approach to Personnel Selection', *The Personnel and Guidance Journal* 55, no. 9 (May 1977): 35–37.
20 For details, see Flippo, *Principles of Personnel Management*, 137–38.
21 For details, see A. Monappa and M. S. Saiyadain, *Personnel Management* (New Delhi: Tata McGraw-Hill Publishing Co. Ltd, 2007), 110.
22 Ibid., 107.
23 Ibid., 106–7.
24 For details, see Flippo, *Principles of Personnel Management*, 138.
25 Edgar H. Schein, *Organisation Psychology* (New Delhi: Prentice-Hall of India Pvt. Ltd, 2001), 23–24.
26 For details, see Ibid., 23–24.
27 For details, see Ivancevich, *Human Resource Management*, 218–22.
28 Jucius, *Personnel Management*, 128.
29 P. Pigors and C. A. Myers, *Personnel Administration*, 5th ed. (New York, NY: McGraw-Hill Book Co., 1969).
30 See Ivancevich, *Human Resource Management*, 223.
31 Yoder, *Personnel Management and Industrial Relations*, 347.
32 Flippo, *Principles of Personnel Management*.
33 Yoder, *Personnel Management and Industrial Relations*, 336.
34 Strauss and Sayles, *Personnel*, 420.
35 Monappa and Saiyadain, *Personnel Management*, 114.
36 Flippo, *Principles of Personnel Management*, 153.
37 Ibid., 154.
38 See J. Salgado, 'The Five Factor Model of Personality and Performance in the European Community', *Journal of Applied Psychology* 82, no.1 (1977): 30–43.
39 For details, see Dessler and Varkkey, *Human Resource Management*, 225; Ivancevich, *Human Resource Management*, 229.
40 For details, see Ibid., 239–41.
41 *Hindustan Times*, 2 August 2016.
42 See *The Economic Times*, 12 April 2016.
43 *Hindustan Times*, 5 January 2016.
44 See *The Economic Times*, 5 January 2016.
45 For details, see *The Economic Times*, 17 June 2016.
46 Pigors and Myres, *Personnel Administration*, 256.
47 See M. Armstrong, *Handbook of Personnel Management* (London: Kogan Page Ltd, 1976), 180.
48 See Scott, Clothier, and Spriegel, *Personnel Management*, 272.
49 E. W. Bakke, *The Fusion Process* (New Haven, CT: Yale University Labour and Management Centre, 1955), 5.
50 Armstrong, *Handbook of Personnel Management*, 161.
51 Gomez-Mejia, Balkin, and Cardy, *Managing Human Resources*, 285.
52 Ibid.

Part III
Training and Developing Human Resources

Part 2

6 Training

Learning Objectives

After studying this chapter, you should be able to do the following:

1. Distinguish between training, education, learning and motivation.
2. Explain the importance of training and how it is beneficial to both employees and employers.
3. Explain the principles of training, challenges in training and types of training.
4. Explain on-the-job and off-the-job methods of training.
5. Prepare a training programme for reducing cost of production by operative staff of a big organisation.
6. Explain the essentials of a good training programme and also how to evaluate the effectiveness of a training programme.
7. Explain the concept of learning organisation.
8. Describe the concept of competency mapping, methods of competency-based training needs identification and competency models.
9. Point out the recent developments/latest trends/emerging trends in the field of training.

Introduction

After the selection, placement and induction of the employee, the next function of HR department is to provide him/her with training and development facilities needed for him/her not only to match the present job but also for possible future jobs requiring extra skills and abilities. The complexities of modern industrialisation and technological changes have all the more enhanced the need of systematic training programmes in all types of organisations. As a matter of fact, today, no organisation has a choice of whether to train or not; the only choice is that of method.

Meaning and Definition

The term 'training' refers to any process by which the aptitudes, skills and abilities of an employee to perform specific jobs are increased.[1] It is a short-term process utilising a systematic and organised procedure by which non-managerial personnel learn technical knowledge and skills for a definite purpose. It is basically related to instructions in

DOI: 10.4324/9781032628424-9

technical and mechanical operations meant for operatives or non-managers. According to Campbell, training courses are typically designed for a short-term stated set purpose, such as the operation of some piece(s) of machinery.[2] Teaching a worker how to operate the drill press is training.[3] Thus, training is the act of increasing the knowledge and skills of an employee for doing a particular job.[4] A formal training programme is an effort by the employer to provide opportunities for the employee to acquire job-related skills, attitudes and knowledge.[5] The objective of training is to achieve a change in the behaviour of those trained. Any behaviour that has been learnt is a skill. Therefore, improvement of skills is what training will accomplish.[6] In the industrial situation, this means that the trainee shall acquire new techniques, skill and problem-solving abilities and develop work attitude. However, it is expected that in the near future, in industrially advanced countries such as the USA and Europe, most of the jobs will require extensive use of knowledge and employees will be required to share and use this knowledge in an innovative manner to improve a product or render services to the customers[7] as the case may be. This broader perspective is known as high-leverage training which is linked to strategic business goals and objectives, uses and instructional design process to ensure that training is effective and compares or benchmarks the company's training progress against training programmes in other countries.

Training and Education

While training is concerned with increasing knowledge and skills in doing a specific job, the major burden of education, which falls upon the employer, is generally concerned with increasing general knowledge and understanding of our total environment, the responsibility of which is usually that of the formal schooling system of the state or the local administration. Teaching a worker how to operate a particular machine is training, whereas giving a course in economics is education. Edwin B. Flippo[8] has rightly observed that the difference between training and education is not precise. It resembles a continuum ranging from general to specific, that is, from general background for proper understanding to specific skill for proper execution as is clear from Figure 6.1.

There is also continuous learning which requires employees to understand the entire work system, including the relationships among their jobs, the work units and the company.[9] Thus, we find that the distinction between education and training is not that simple, the two overlap each other and many a time both occur at the same time.

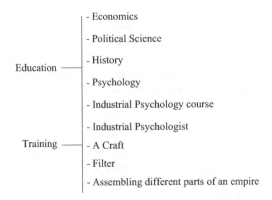

Figure 6.1 Training: Education Continuum

Learning Theory and Training

Training is a form of education. Hence, some of the findings regarding learning theory apply to training. These principles have relevance in the design of both formal and informal training programmes (for details, see 'Principles of Training' in this very chapter).

Training, Learning and Motivation

Training cannot be effective if the trainee lacks motivation to take advantage of it. In order to motivate and make him/her learn, in the very beginning of the training programme, the trainer should provide him/her an overview of the training material, present familiar examples to illustrate key points, offer opportunities for practice, let the trainee make mistakes, make the learning meaningful, make skill transfer easy, follow motivation principles for trainers, analyse training needs, conduct task analysis for assessing his/her training needs, go for performance analysis for assessing his/her training needs and so on.[10]

Need and Importance of Training

Training is a hallmark of a good management.[11] The effective operation of an organisation requires that the individuals involved learn to perform the functions of their current jobs at a reasonable level of proficiency which is possible only when there exist systematic training programmes in the organisation. Even under the last conditions, there is a need for some type of training and development activities for personnel in the organisation because all types of jobs in the organisation usually require some or the other type of training if their effective functioning is to be ensured. Training is needed not only for newly recruited employees who are to learn how to perform their jobs but also for the already existing employees because of rapid technological changes requiring new skills and expertise. Thus, training is important for new or present employees.[12]

Research studies show training to be important in enhancing competitive advantage. Training is also seen as a useful means of coping with changes fostered by technological innovation, market competition, organisational structuring and demographic shifts.

Training is a continuous process because, on the one hand, it imparts knowledge and skills to the newly recruited employees and, on the other hand, it serves as a refresher course in updating existing employees in the organisation. It is wrong to think that the absence of a scientific and systematic training programme results in the elimination of training costs. It will rather enhance the training costs because in that case, the employees will try to train themselves by trial-and-error method or by observing others which will naturally not only consume longer time but also may not enable the employees to learn the best operating methods. That is why, more and more companies are extending their training budget (see Exhibit 6.1).

Exhibit 6.1 Investment on Training: Showing an Increasing Trend

Companies like Accenture, Deloitte, IBM, Boeing, UPS, Qualcom, and many others invest heavily in corporate training to help build key skills such as supervisory and technical skills internally.

> Companies like Maersk (big shipping line) and even BMW pride themselves on their internal development, apprenticeship, and certification programmes.
>
> *Source*: Quoted in *Human Capital* 18, no. 5 (October 2014): 43. Available at http://www.humancapitalonline.com/PDF-Issues/October_14_Issue_Lowrespdf.pdf (Accessed on 15 November 2017).

It is worth mentioning that Deloitte launched a $500 million new education centre focused exclusively on providing world-class education and training to its global consulting workforce.[13]

The need and importance of training to any organisation is clear because these lead to the following:

1. **Higher level of productivity:** It is reflected through an improvement in the quantum of output or quality or both which, in turn, depends on the updated knowledge and skills of the employees in their current jobs which is possible only through systematic programmes of training.
2. **Reduced learning time:** As stated earlier also, in the absence of systematic training programmes, employees have to learn by trial-and-error method or by observing others which usually takes longer time, and even then one may not learn the best methods and techniques. Thus, systematic training programme not only reduces learning time but also teaches the best way of doing a thing.
3. **Heightened morale:** According to Edwin B. Flippo, possession of needed skills helps to meet such basic human needs as security and ego satisfaction.[14] Morale can be heightened through an elaborate personnel and human relations programme only if there is a solid core of meaningful work done with knowledge, skills and pride.
4. **Reduced supervision:** Although training does not eliminate the need for supervision, it reduces the need for constant and detailed supervision because the trained employee is one who can perform with limited supervision. Training makes an employee self-reliant in his/her work, requiring very little of supervision.
5. **Reduced absenteeism and turnover:** Trained employees can experience the direct satisfaction associated with a sense of achievement and knowledge. While working, they feel that they are developing their inherent capabilities of work. Hence, they find little scope for dissatisfaction, frustration or remaining absent or leaving their jobs and so on.
6. **Reduced accidents:** Research studies have established that most of the industrial accidents take place because of deficiencies in employees rather than of flaws in equipment or working conditions. Training improves both job skills and safety attitudes which ultimately result in reduced number of accidents.
7. **Reduced wastage and less damages to plant and machinery:** As training teaches the best way of doing a job and handling of machines, it results in less wastage and least damages to equipment and so on. Trained personnel always make better and economical use of materials and equipment.
8. **Increased organisational stability and flexibility:** An organisation is considered stable only when it has the ability to sustain its effectiveness, despite the loss of its key personnel which is possible only through the creation of reservoir of trained replacements. Similarly, the flexibility of the organisation requires its ability to accommodate short-run variations in the volume of work. This can also be achieved by developing

multiple skills among its personnel through training. Such trained personnel can be easily transferred wherever the volume of work is more.
9. **Standardisation:** Well-trained workers are less likely to make operational mistakes. Hence, with the help of training, the work methods can be standardised and made available to all concerned, which will result in better performance and production the standardised goods.
10. **Helpful in performance appraisal:** Training plays a very useful role in the performance process. Training effort must make sense in terms of what the organisation wants each employee to contribute to accomplish the organisational goals. Establishing a linkage between learning and organisational performance is a critical issue for training professionals. That is why, 'the issue of workplace learning and performance'[15] has assumed added significance.
11. **Meeting special manpower requirement:** Many a time, the organisation may need new skills. In such eventualities, it will be a better proposition to train promising personnel from within the organisation in the new skills rather than to go for fresh recruitment from outside the organisation.
12. **Beneficial to employees:** As employees acquire new knowledge and job skills through training, they increase their market value and earning power. The possession of useful skills enhances their value to their employer and thereby increases their job security. Training may also qualify them for promotion to higher and more responsible jobs. Obviously, this will increase their pay and status.
13. **Obsolescence prevention:** Training and development programmes foster the initiative and creativity among employees and help in preventing manpower obsolescence which may be due to age, temperament or lack of motivation or the inability of a person to adapt himself/herself to technological changes.
14. **Helpful in gaining acceptance from peers:** Learning a job quickly and being able to pull their own weight is one of the best ways of gaining acceptance from one's own colleagues.
15. **Reduced labour turnover:** It has also been observed that employees properly trained by an organisation are less likely to leave their organisation (see Exhibits 6.2 and 6.3).

Exhibit 6.2   Training and Turnover

A Hackett Benchmarking and Research Report shows that companies that spend $218 per employee on training have more than 16% voluntary turnover, while companies that spend over $273 per employee have turnover of 7%.

Source: Quoted in Human Capital 18, no. 5 (October 2014): 42. Available at http://www.humancapitalonline.com/PDF-Issues/October_14_Issue_Lowrespdf.pdf (Accessed on 15 November 2017).

Exhibit 6.3   Training and Turnover of the Employees

A Louis Harris and Associates poll reports that among employees with poor training opportunities, 41% planned to leave within a year, whereas of those who considered their company's training opportunities to be excellent, only 12% planned to leave.

Source: Quoted in Human Capital 18, no. 5 (October 2014): 42. Available at http://www.humancapitalonline.com/PDF-Issues/October_14_Issue_Lowrespdf.pdf (Accessed on 15 November 2017).

Exhibit 6.4 Training and Productivity

Motorola calculated that every dollar spent on training yields an approximate 30% of gain in productivity within a three-year period. Motorola also used training to reduce costs by over $3 billion and increase profit by 47%.

Source: Quoted in Human Capital 18, no. 5 (October 2014): 43. Available at http://www.humancapitalonline.com/PDF-Issues/October_14_Issue_Lowrespdf.pdf (Accessed on 15 November 2017).

---

16. **Beneficial to management:** With the help of trained personnel, a manager is in a better position to plan, organise, direct and control his/her affairs more effectively because trained personnel understand, cooperate and involve themselves in the direction of achievement of organisational objectives. With a trained workforce, executive effort will tend to shift from the disagreeable need of correcting mistakes to the more pleasant task of planning work and of encouraging expert employees. Besides, trained personnel are less likely to leave the organisation (see Exhibit 6.3). Training also helps in reducing the cost of production and increasing productivity and profits (see Exhibit 6.4).

The simplest argument in favour of a formal training programme is that a company pays for training whether it has a programme or not. People do not come complete into an organisation. They must learn to adjust to a new environment, increase and sharpen the skills they have, become understanding participants in organisational endeavours and meet the challenges of changing conditions. It has been noticed that during economic slowdown, many companies stop their training programmes (see Exhibit 6.5).

For all this, training is a must. It has been widely accepted as a problem-solving device. Thus, training is a top priority in an organisation dedicated to creating a learning environment. A successful organisation and managers view employee training as an investment in their people, not an expense.[16]

Exhibit 6.5 Status of Training in a Tough Business Scenario

It is unfortunate to note that in a tough business scenario, one major cost that gets axed is training budget. No arguments hold water when confronted with the harsh realities of cost pressures.

Source: H. Raju, 'Learning in Tough Times', *Human Capital* 17, no. 11 (April 2014): 30.

Principles of Training

Based on research, certain principles have been evolved which play a very important role while imparting skills or knowledge to the trainees. These principles of training can be briefly summarised as follows:

1. **Motivation:** Various research studies have demonstrated that the more highly motivated a trainee, the more quickly a new skill is learnt. The trainee must, therefore, want to learn. That is, his/her motivation to learn a new skill or to improve his/her job performance must be pretty high. Motivation can be increased by the prospects of some reward at the conclusion of training, for example, a job or a better job, promotion, recognition, more money and status. Besides, it is much easier to motivate a new employee than an older employee.
2. **Feedback:** The consequences of a trainee's learning should be checked by the trainer and the trainee be told whether he/she is learning correctly or incorrectly and why. This is known as 'feedback'.
3. **Reinforcement:** After the trainee has learnt the desired skills, the effect should be reinforced by means of incentives or disincentives. Positive reinforcements may include rise in pay, promotion, appreciation and so on. Such rewards must be given on the successful completion of training. Rather, in the beginning, the trainee must be rewarded after each time success is attained. However, in the case of undesired behaviour, punishment may be suggested but experience has shown that such penalties earn ill will and resentment in the long run. Therefore, only positive reinforcement which may be dispensed on a variable ratio schedule may be a better proposition.
4. **Active participation:** In order to learn a skill or acquire knowledge or develop particular type of attitude, it is necessary that the trainee himself/herself participates actively. This is also known as 'learning by doing'. Needless to mention that practice makes a man perfect.
5. **Whole versus part:** Whether to teach the whole job at once or to teach the job in parts is still a controversial issue. However, the general consensus of opinion is that if the job is longer and more complex, it should be taught in parts.
6. **Individual differences:** Although it is easier to train an individual, because of economic considerations, group training has to be provided. In such cases, due attention should be paid to individual differences because individuals vary substantially in their intelligence, aptitude and physical strength.
7. **Specificity:** It is always desirable to impart more specific rather than general training.
8. **More use of supervisors:** Experience has shown that it is better to make greater use of supervisors or fellow workers in imparting substantial amount of training.

Sawyer and Eastmond[17] have suggested the following ways so that learning principles can be applied to job training:

- The trainee must be motivated to learn.
- The trainee must be able to learn.
- The learning must be reinforced.
- The training must provide material for practice.
- The material presented must be meaningful.
- The material must be communicated effectively.
- The material taught must transfer to do the job.

Methods of Training

The efficiency of a training programme depends upon selection of the most suitable training methods. Only those training methods should be used which accomplish certain training needs and objectives. Through the methods of job analysis, psychological tests, attitude and morale surveys, activity analysis and group therapy, training needs can be assessed. The following are the main methods generally used to provide training:

1. On-the-job methods

    a. On specific job

        i. Experience
        ii. Coaching
        iii. Understudy

    b. Position rotation
    c. Special projects
    d. Selective reading
    e. Apprenticeship
    f. Vestibule school
    g. Multiple management

2. Off-the-job methods

    a. Special courses and lectures
    b. Conferences
    c. Case studies
    d. Brainstorming
    e. Laboratory methods

        i. Simulation

            - Role-playing
            - Gaming

        ii. Sensitivity training

    f. Electronic performance support systems (EPSS)
    g. Tele-training
    h. Videoconferencing
    i. MP3/instant messaging
    j. Slides and videotapes
    k. Programmed learning
    l. Audiovisual-based training
    m. HRIS learning portals
    n. E-learning
    o. Mentoring
    p. Informal learning
    q. Distance and Internet-based training

On-the-Job Training (OJT) Methods

Numerous training methods can be used while a man is engaged in the process of productive work. OJT methods are suitable for all levels of personnel. In order to ensure the success of OJT, the steps[18] to be followed may be as shown in Exhibit 6.6.

Various methods of OJT are as follows:

1. **On specific job**: The most common and formal OJT programme is training for a specific job. The current practice in job training has been strongly influenced by the wartime training within industry (TWI), which was first designed to improve the job performance through job instruction. TWI also included training for supervisors to improve job performance.

Exhibit 6.6   Steps to Be Followed in OJT

- Prepare the learner
- Present the operation
- Do a tryout
- Follow up

Source: Based on OJT steps discussed in G. A. Dessler, and B. Varkkey, *Human Resource Management* (New Delhi: Pearson Education, Inc., 2009), 304.

These are the following methods of training on specific job:

a. **Experience:** It is the oldest method of OJT. Learning by experience cannot and should not be eliminated as a method of development, though as a sole approach, it is wasteful, time-consuming and inefficient. In some cases, this method has proved to be very efficient, though it should be followed by other training methods to make it more meaningful.

b. **Coaching:** On-the-job coaching by the superior is an important and potentially effective approach if the superior is properly trained and oriented. The technique involves direct personal instructions and guidance, usually with extensive demonstration and continuous critical evaluation and correction. The advantage is increased motivation for the trainee and the minimisation of the problem of learning transfer from theory to practice. The danger in this method lies in the possible neglect to coaching by superior.

c. **Understudy:** The understudy method is considered a somewhat different approach from those described previously in that a certain person is specifically designated as the heir apparent. The understudy method makes the trainee an assistant to the current job holder. The trainee learns by experience, observation and imitation. If decisions are discussed with the understudy, he/she can become informed on the policies and theories involved. The advantage of this method is that training is conducted in a practical and realistic situation. However, disadvantages are many. For example, the method tends to perpetuate mistakes and deficiencies of existing managerial practices. Moreover, the understudies are frequently neglected by those they assist.

One of the approaches to OJT is the 'job instruction training' (JIT) system, which was developed during the Second World War. Per this system, the trainers first train the supervisors, who, in turn, train the employees.

2. **Position/job rotation:** The major objective of job rotation training is the broadening of the background of trainee in the organisation. If trainee is rotated periodically from one job to another, he/she acquires a general background (see Exhibit 6.7).

The main advantages of this method are as follows: it provides a general background to the trainee, training takes place in an actual situation, competition can be stimulated among the rotating trainees and it stimulates a more cooperative attitude by exposing a man to other fellows' problems and viewpoints. There are also certain disadvantages of this method. The productive work can suffer because of the obvious disruption caused by such changes.

Exhibit 6.7 Philosophy of Job Rotation, and Case Study*

Whitney Daines Ltd is committed to provide opportunities for employee training and development. This goes hand in hand with the job rotation philosophy, and the case study showcases multiple examples to illustrate this. Investing in its employees certainly goes a long way in driving the right message in the organisation and also motivates employees that they have a career with the organisation.

Source: V. Singh, 'Case Study', *Human Capital* 18, no. 3 (August 2014): 58.
* See *Human Capital* 17, no. 11 (April 2014).

Rotation becomes less useful as specialisation proceeds, for few people have the breadth of technological knowledge and skills to move from one functional area to another.

3. **Special projects:** This is a very flexible training device. Such special project assignments grow ordinarily out of an analysis of individuals' work. The trainee may be asked to perform special assignment; thereby, he/she learns the work procedure. Sometimes, a task force is created consisting of a number of trainees representing different functions in the organisation. Trainees not only acquire knowledge about the assigned activities but also learn how to work with others.

4. **Selective reading:** Individuals in the organisation can gather and advance their knowledge and background through selective reading. The reading may include professional journals and books. Various business organisations maintain libraries for their own executives. Many executives become members of professional associations and they exchange their ideas with others. This is a good method for assimilating knowledge. However, some executives claim that it is very difficult to find time for much reading other than absolutely required in the performance of their jobs.

5. **Apprenticeship:** Appropriate training can be traced back to medieval times when those intended on learning trade skill bound themselves to a master craftsman to learn by doing the work under his/her guidance. In earlier periods, apprenticeship

was not restricted to artisans but was also used in training for the professions including medicine, law, dentistry and teaching. Apprenticeship is a process by which people become skilled workers, usually through a combination of formal learning and long-term OJT. Today's industrial organisations require large number of skilled craftsmen who can be trained by this system. Such training is either provided by the organisations, or it is imparted by governmental agencies. In order to regulate and control the training of apprentices, the Government of India passed the Apprentices Act, 1961,[19] the twin major objectives of which are promotion of new skills and improvement or refinement of old skills through both practical and theoretical training in a good number of trades and occupations. A number of substantial changes[20] are being effected by the government in the Apprentices Act, 1961. Most states now have their own apprenticeship laws with supervised plans for such training. Arrangements usually provide a mixed programme of classroom and job experience.

6. **Vestibule schools:** Large organisations frequently provide what are described as vestibule schools, a preliminary-to-actual shop experience. As far as possible, shop conditions are duplicated, but instructions, not output, are major objectives, with special instructors provided. Vestibule schools are widely used in training for clerical and office jobs as well as for factory production jobs. Such training is usually shorter and less complex than that adaptable to the apprenticeship system. Vestibule training is relatively expensive, but these costs are justified if the volume of training is large or if uniform, high-standard results are important.

7. **Multiple management:** Multiple management emphasises the use of committees to increase the flow of ideas from less experience managers and to train them for positions of greater responsibility. The programme was developed by the McCormick & Company of Baltimore, USA. The company claims that the plan has increased employee efficiency, reduced labour turnover and absenteeism, and enabled the company to pay higher wages than those prevailing in the area and industry. In this method, a junior board is authorised to discuss any problem that the senior board may discuss, and its members are encouraged to put their minds to work on the business as a whole rather than to concentrate to their specialised areas.

Off-the-Job Training Methods

In these methods, trainees have to leave their workplace and devote their entire time to the development objective. In these methods, development of trainees is primary, and any usable work produced during training is secondary. The following training techniques are used off the job:

1. **Special courses and lectures:** Lecturing is the most traditional form of formal training method. Special courses and lectures can be identified and arranged by business organisations in numerous ways as a part of their development programmes. First, there are courses which the organisations themselves establish to be taught by members of the organisations. Some organisations have regular instructors assigned to their training and development departments, such as Tata and Hindustan Lever in the private sector and Life Insurance Corporation, State Bank of India and other nationalised commercial banks, Reserve Bank, Hindustan Steel, Fertilizer Corporation and many others in the public sector. The second approach to special courses and lectures is for organisations to work with universities or institutes in establishing

a course or series of courses to be taught by instructors of these institutes. The third approach is for the organisations to send personnel to programmes established by the universities, institutes and other bodies. Such courses are organised for a short period ranging from two or three days to a few weeks. The first such programme was the Slogan Fellowship programme, established in 1931 at the Massachusetts Institute of Technology, USA. In India, such courses are organised frequently by the Institutes of Management, Administrative Staff College of India (ASCI), National Productivity Council, National Institute for Transport and Logistics (NITL), All India Management Association and some other organisations and universities.

2. **Conferences:** This is also an old method but still a favourite training method. In order to escape the limitations of straight lecturing, many organisations have adopted guided discussion-type of conferences in their training programmes. In this method, the participants pool their ideas and experience in attempting to arrive at improved methods of dealing with the problems which are common subject of discussion. Conferences may include buzz sessions that divide conferences into small groups of four or five intensive discussions. These small groups then report back to the whole coherence with their conclusions or questions. The conference method allows the trainees to look at the broader angle. These conferences, however, have certain limitations. Unless the discussion is directed to the felt needs of the participants, they may well feel that the whole session is useless.

3. **Case studies:** This technique, which has been developed and popularised by the Harvard Business School, USA, is one of the most common forms of training (see Exhibit 6.6). A case is a written account by a trained reporter or analyst seeking to describe a real decision-making situation in the organisation. Some cases are merely illustrative; others are detailed and comprehensive, demanding extensive and intensive analytical ability. Cases are widely used in a variety of programmes. This method increases the trainees' power of observation, helping him/her to ask better questions and to look for a broader range of problems. Trainers are supposed to study the case, identify the problems, analyse the problems, offer solutions, choose the best solution and implement it. The instructor acts like a catalyst and facilitator and gets all the participants involved in finding out solution to the problem. The incident method is one variation of the case method in which only bare outlines of a problem are put forth initially and the participants are given a role in which to view the incident. In case any additional relevant information is sought by the participants, it is provided to them. Initially, each participant solves the case followed by formation of groups based on similarity of solutions. Each group so formed is expected to formulate a strong statement of position. Then groups debate their solutions followed by comparison of their solutions with the results. Finally, participants are supposed to try to apply this knowledge to their job situations and be benefited accordingly. A well-chosen case may promote objective discussion, but the lack of emotional involvement may make it difficult to effect any basic change in the behaviour and attitude of trainees.

4. **Brainstorming:** This is the method of stimulating trainees to creative thinking. This approach, developed by Alex Osborn, seeks to reduce inhibiting forces by providing for a maximum of group participation and a minimum of criticism. A problem is posed and ideas are invited. Quantity rather than quality is the primary objective. Ideas are encouraged and criticism of any idea is discouraged. Chain reactions from idea to idea often develop. Later, these ideas are critically examined. There is no trainer in brainstorming, and it has been found that the introduction of own

experts into it will reduce the originality and practicability of the group contribution. Brainstorming frankly favours divergence, and its fact may be sufficient to explain why brainstorming is so little used as yet in developing countries where no solutions ought to carry the highest premium. It is virtually untried, even though its immediate use is limited to new ideas only, not change in behaviour.

5. **Laboratory training:** Laboratory training adds to conventional training by providing situations in which the trainees themselves experience through their own interaction some of the conditions they are talking about. In this way, they more or less experiment on themselves. Laboratory training is more concerned about changing individual behaviour and attitude. It is generally more successful in changing job performance than conventional training methods. There are two methods of laboratory training: simulation and sensitivity training.

    a. **Simulation:** An increasingly popular technique of management development is simulation of performance. In this method, instead of taking participants into the field, the field is simulated in the training session itself. Simulation is the presentation of real situations of organisations in the training session. It covers situations of varying complexities and roles for the participants. It creates a whole field of organisation, relates participants through key roles in it and has them deal with specific situations. There are two common simulation methods of training: role-playing and business game.

        i. **Role-playing:** Role-playing is a laboratory method which can be used rather easily as a supplement of conventional training methods. Its purpose is to increase the trainee's skill in dealing with other people. One of its greatest use is in connection with human relations training, but it is also used in sales training. It is spontaneous acting of a realistic situation involving two or more people under classroom situations. Dialogue spontaneously grows out of the situation, as it is developed by the trainees assigned to it. Other trainees in the group serve as observers or critics. Since people take roles every day, they are somewhat experienced in the art, and with a certain amount of imagination, they can project themselves into roles other than their own. Since a manager is regularly acting roles in his/her relationship with others, it is essential for him/her to have role awareness and to do role thinking so that they can size up each relationship and develop the most effective interaction position. Role-playing has many advantages. By this method, a trainee can broaden his/her experience by trying different approaches, while in actual situation, he/she often has only one chance.

        ii. **Gaming:** Gaming has been devised to simulate the problems of running a company or even a particular department. It has been used for a variety of training objectives, from investment strategy and collective bargaining techniques to the morale of clerical personnel. It has been used at all levels, from the executives to the production supervisors. Gaming is a laboratory method in which role-playing exists, but its difference is that it focuses attention on administrative problems, while role-playing tends to emphasise mostly feeling and tone between people in interaction. Gaming involves several teams, each of which is given a firm to operate for a number of periods. Usually, the period is short, one year or so. In each period, each team makes decisions on various matters such as fixation of price, level of production and inventory level. Since each team is competing with others, each firm's decision will affect the results of all others. All the firms' decisions are fed into a computer, which is programmed to behave somewhat like a real market. The computer provides the results, and the winner is the team which has accumulated largest profit. In the light of such results, strength and weaknesses of decisions are analysed.

    b. **Sensitivity training:** Sensitivity training is the most controversial laboratory training method. Many of its advocates have an almost religious zeal in their enhancement with the training group experience. Some of its critics match this favour in their attacks on the technique. As a result of criticism and experience, a somewhat revised approach, often described as 'team development' training, has appeared. It was first used by National Training Laboratories at Bethel, USA. The training groups called themselves 'T Group'. Since then, its use has been extended to other organisations, universities and institutes.

6. **EPSS:** EPSS are sets of computerised tools and displays which automate training, phone support and documentation. They are used to help employees in not learning and memorising a substantial chunk of details, which are difficult to memorise, but are otherwise necessary.
7. **Tele-training:** In tele-training, groups of employees located at remote locations are taught by a trainer in a central location via television hook-ups. It is a very economical method.
8. **Videoconferencing:** Involving the use of audio and visual equipment, videoconferencing enables trainers sitting at one location to communicate live with trainees in other cities. PC-based video cameras play a vital role in this method. This method saves time and is economical also.
9. **MP3/instant messaging:** These days, some organisations encourage their employees to use instant messaging as a quick learning device. The organisation usually purchases iPods for trainees and the training department and then has an Internet audiobook provider create an audio learning site within the organisation's firewall. The employees use it to download training materials to their iPods.
10. **Slides and videotapes:** Slides and videotapes can be used either off the job or in special media rooms. Although this method is both thought-provoking as well as interesting, it does not have the provision for trainees to put questions or have interaction but, of late, these shortcomings are also being overcome by and by. Some organisations use slides, tapes, films and so on as a supplement to the programme.
11. **Programmed learning:** Programmed learning reduces training time. It lets the trainee learn at his/her own pace, though it provides immediate feedback on the accuracy of his/her answers to the questions presented to him/her after presenting facts and problems, which determines what will be the next question to the trainee. Some organisations follow intelligent tutoring systems which indicate which questions and approaches prove effective or ineffective and then adjust the instrumental sequences accordingly.
12. **Audiovisual-based training:** Although a little bit more expensive, it appears to be interesting to the trainees/learners. The techniques such as films, PowerPoint presentations, videoconferencing, DVDs and videotapes are commonly used these days as they usually prove quite effective. The use of audiovisual-based training techniques is

recommended when there is a need to expose trainees to events which are not easily demonstrable in live lectures or when it is a costly proposition to move trainers from place to place and that too frequently.
13. **HRIS learning portals:** Through its business portals, the learners can get the tools needed to analyse data inside and outside their organisation and see the customised content they need. These days, many employers conduct the training through learning portals. Learning portal suppliers create special courses for an organisation's employees and customers. These days, organisations are making efforts towards integrating e-learning system with the organisation's overall enterprise-wide information systems. This may enable the organisation to synchronise employees' training with their performance appraisal, succession plans, skill inventory and so on.[21]
14. **Using e-learning:** In this method, it has to be ensured that the trainee can use the extra control that Web-based learning should provide. It has also to be ensured that the trainee knows the control he/she has, and how he/she can use it, such as how to change the learning sequence. However, today, the trend is towards blended learning solutions and not a choice of conventional versus online training. Of course, e-based learning can be improved in a number of ways.
15. **Mentoring:** In mentoring, a senior manager assumes the responsibility for grooming a junior person. A mentor is a guide, counsellor, teacher, developer of skills and intellect, supporter and facilitator, who helps the mentee in realising his/her vision, attaining psychological maturity and getting him/her integrated with the company. Mentoring can be effective if the mentor is a patient listener, understands well, stimulates the learning, builds self-confidence in the mentee, counsels well, acts as a role model, encourages and shares his/her experiences in the right perspective. On the other hand, it is also necessary that the mentee is also a good listener, follows the advice given by the mentor, is a committed learner, is not an egoist, is open-minded and proactive and is willing to change. However, employees who serve as mentors frequently are not trained in effective mentoring skills or designing mentoring programme. They are most often busy with their responsibilities and expected to squeeze mentoring onto an already full plate. Once they take on mentoring duties, they are usually left to their own devices and have few avenues to discuss problems and challenges in their mentoring programmes or relationships. Employees, therefore, need training to be mentors and must be rewarded for a job well done.[22]
16. **Informal learning:** The employers do not arrange informal learning except that they can place certain tools in a common area which can be made use of for work-related discussion. In almost all organisations, some type of informal training does happen. Most SMEs prefer informal training because it involves less cost besides being at the heart of the SME culture and productivity outcomes. It can also be easily integrated into daily operations with presumption of being less costly.
17. **Distance and Internet-based training:**[23] This method involves the use of various forms of distance learning methods such as tele-training, modern Internet-based courses and videoconferencing. In case a large number of trainees located at different places are to be taught, this method proves very economical.

Challenges in Training

Training is not a simple process. It is full of challenges.

Gomez-Mejia, Balkin and Cardy[24] have pointed out the following challenges in training:

1. Is training the solution?
2. Are the goals clear and realistic?
3. Is training a good investment?
4. Will the training work?

Managers must answer these questions while they initiate the training process.

Types of Training

The most commonly used types[25] of training in industry are as follows:

1. Skills training
2. Retraining
3. Cross-functional training
4. Team training
5. Literacy training
6. Creativity training
7. Company in-house programmes
8. Company/local school programmes
9. Company/local or state government programmes
10. Crisis training
11. Customer service training
12. Diversity training

Avoiding Training Pitfalls

In order to make a training programme effective, the following things should be avoided:[26]

- Attempting to teach too quickly
- Viewing all trainees as the same
- Not providing time to practise
- Not frightening the employees
- Not providing the pat on the back

Relationship Between 'Training and Development' and 'Performance' of an Organisation

It has been established that training and development impact the HR outcomes—skills, abilities, knowledge, work behaviour, attitude, motivation, confidence, morale, and so on of the employees—which, in turn, affect the performance of the organisation in terms of its financial performance—return on investment (ROI), sales, productivity, return on equity (ROE) and so on—as well as non-financial performances, such as absenteeism, role of labour turnover and grievance as depicted in Figure 6.2.

Relationship Between Training Programmes and Employees Level

The basic need and objectives of a training programme for a particular level differ from that of other level. For example, rank-and-file employees need specific job training,

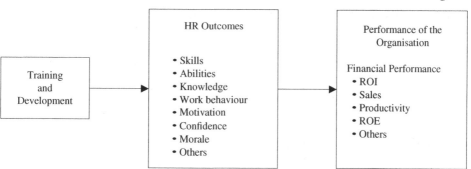

Figure 6.2 Training and Development

while the management group needs broad-based training. Thus, a particular training programme would be more suitable to a particular group of people. Moreover, within a particular group, an individual may need a particular training, while others may need some other programme. The determining factors would then be the level of an individual in the organisation and his/her own personality characteristics. However, in assessing the suitability of training programmes, the former factor is more emphasised. From this point of view, the entire personnel of an organisation may broadly be classified into three levels: rank-and-file employee, supervisory level and management level.

1. **Rank-and-file employees**: Most extensive of all training programmes are those designed to meet the needs of rank-and-file employees. Such employees may require training either at the time of entry or at subsequent time to keep pace with the technological development. Thus, the training is mostly of technological nature. Pre-employment training may involve preparation, not for a single job, but for many types of related jobs that may be given to workers subsequently. Retraining or refresher courses may be given as a means of avoiding personnel obsolescence.
2. **Supervisory level**: Candidates for frontline supervisory positions and incumbent supervisors need the same kind of training opportunities. People at this level need to know how to develop and carry out approved programmes within a budget to obtain and use service and staff help, and to meet the requirements of their superior managers. At this point where a trainee is assigned to a supervisory position, the practice of management begins. Over a range of time, the new incumbent practices with full responsibility for results what he/she has learnt about supervision and refines his/her peculiar techniques of interpersonal relationships. His/her further career depends upon his/her developed skills, and outstanding ones will become candidates for promotion to middle management positions.
3. **Management level**: Management differs from supervisory groups as far as the training need is concerned because people at the management level do not have any direct contact with the workforce. Their outlook is broad-based. The management group may further be divided into two levels: middle management and top management. The ones to enter the middle management group are generally supervisors who have had several years of on-the-job practice. They are the ones who need the knowledge of management theory the most. On the practical side, there is much about management that they know informally. Now, when they are about to manage managers and not technicians, no longer they can rely so much on their technical proficiency to get things done. To manage managers, they particularly need a comprehensive

understanding of the functions of managers because these are the means they must utilise to accomplish their job.

On the other hand, those to be trained for top management level are normally functional managers who are candidates for general management positions. Functional managers who have stepped up the promotion ladder within their division require training in the management of functions which are strange to them. The top managers are required to have a substantial background in the fundamentals and techniques of management. Moreover, the knowledge and technical aspects of managing are rapidly changing. Consequently, one of the objectives of top management training should be the review of management theory and principles and the updating of knowledge and technical developments in managing.

As far as training of CEOs is concerned, a survey revealed that CEOs crave training. Although 78% of CEOs said that they receive informal coaching and leadership advice from members of the board of directors, CEOs overwhelmingly indicated a desire for coaching from outside sources too (the Stanford survey).[27]

Recommended Training Programmes at Different Levels

On the basis of the previous discussion, some specific training programmes may be recommended for people at various levels:[28]

1. For rank-and-file employees

    a. Job training
    b. Apprenticeship
    c. Pre-employment training
    d. Retraining

2. For supervisory levels

    - Supervisory skill training
    - Coaching
    - Special course and classes
    - Conferences
    - Job rotation
    - Brainstorming
    - Case studies
    - Special projects and task forces
    - Simulation: role-playing
    - Sensitivity training

3. For management level

    - Coaching
    - Special courses and classes
    - Conferences
    - Job rotation
    - Brainstorming
    - Committee assignments

- Selective reading
- Understudy
- Case studies
- Multiple management
- Simulation: role-playing and gaming
- Sensitivity training

4. For all levels

- Job experience
- Induction and orientation

Process of Training in a Large Organisation

A well-organised training programme must comprise the following steps:

1. **Determining the training needs and setting objectives for these needs:** This is the starting point in managing a training programme in an organisation. The first step in the process of assessing training needs is to analyse organisation's needs; the knowledge, skill and ability required to perform the job well; and the job holder's needs. This requires examining both the short-term and long-term objectives of the organisation. Where does the organisation want to go? Is it capable of going there? The financial, marketing, social, growth and HR objectives can be accomplished only when the structure of the organisation, the talent that the organisation contains, the efficiency of the organisation and the organisational climate are adequate and up to the mark. It is, therefore, necessary to review organisational charts, efficiency, performance appraisal, quality of production objectives, ratios, absenteeism and so on of the organisation. The next step is to analyse the knowledge, skills and abilities required to perform the job well. Hence, questions such as 'What are the tasks to be performed?' and 'What are skills and knowledge needed to do these tasks well?' should be answered. Finally comes the job holder's needs. For this, we should ask them about their needs on the job. We should also ask them to perform the task which may help in getting information and data. Since training is to be imparted to job holders, it is important to focus on their needs.

   Analysis of production problems, anticipating future problems, using a checklist and so on also help in determining the training needs of employees. Donald Kirkpatrick[29] has suggested four ways for identifying employees' training needs: (a) observe employees, (b) listen to them, (c) ask supervisors about employees' needs and (d) examine the problems employees have.

   To state simply, it can be said that gaps between expected and actual results suggest a need for training. Donald Michalak and Edwin Yager[30] have pointed out nine steps in using a performance analysis to work out training needs of employees: determine behavioural discrepancy, do cost value analysis, ask whether it is a 'cannot do' or 'will not do' situation, set standards, remove obstacles, practice, train, change the job, and transfer or terminate.

2. **Contents of training:** Contents or scope of training are governed by the major types of employees who are to be trained. In this respect, four distinctive groups of employees may be noted: rank-and-file, supervisory staff, middle management and

top management. Rank-and-file employees have no administrative or supervisory duties. Supervisory staff is composed of specialised technical and professional people attached to the operating line to provide counsel and aid. Managerial people usually do decision-making and its implementation. Hence, on the basis of these distinctions, the various types of training should be outlined. 'Organisation analysis', 'operation analysis' and 'men analysis' techniques also help in determining the contents and scope of training.

3. **Selection of training method:** After preparing the estimates of the need of training, it should be ascertained with the advice of personnel manager and high officials that which system will suit the training (for details of methods, see discussion under the head 'Methods of Training' in the subsequent pages of this chapter).

4. **Preparation of training:** Here, we have to arrange for the following two things:

   a. **Choosing a trainer:** The trainer must be ready before the training starts. He/she should ascertain as to what is to be taught and by which method it is to be taught. Since the success of a training programme depends to a very great extent on the trainer, all precaution should be taken in choosing the trainer[31] so that he/she may prove effective in accomplishing the objectives of the training programme. The trainer should possess good communication skills, be able to organise effectively and be innovative and motivating.

   A training programme can be conducted by inside trainers or an HR specialist or an outside hired training expert/consultant or both. A good trainer should be able to motivate every individual trainee, know well the training techniques and know how to effect training delivery. He/she should also be duly exposed in all aspects of learning. Most organisations use their own managers and experts in training their employees.

   b. **Choosing the trainees:** The trainee is the person to whom training is to be imparted. He/she must be mentally prepared to learn. Training must always recognise individual differences in abilities, interests, learning speed and other significant personal characteristics. The training programme is framed according to the training needs of a particular category of employees. Hence, only those employees should be chosen as trainees who are going to be benefited by that particular programme. It can be a programme for new employees to be trained in certain skills or for retraining the old employees due to change in the use of technology. Some companies, when some employees are to be laid off or retrenched, arrange special training for outplacement of such employees. In case the trainees are likely to be promoted or have to get higher salary after their training is over, the management can use the same procedure for selection of trainees as is used when new employees are hired for similar posts.

5. **Conducting the training:** Having done all of these, the next step is conducting the training. While imparting training, the following points should be observed:

   a. The instructor must prepare a timetable of the training, and only one sub-job should be taught in one instance.
   b. All jobs should be orderly kept and this order should be made to understand, and time for each sub-job should be distributed.
   c. Every trainee should be personally cared.
   d. Work should be explained clearly and comprehensively. Important points should be stressed. For this, all orders should have clarity.

e. Work should be clearly and slowly told, that is, at a time, only one action or sub-action be explained.
   f. The trainee should be provided time for practice and repetition, if necessary.
   g. The trainee should be employed on work. He/she should be asked questions while working, and his/her difficulties, confusion and ambiguities, if any, should be removed.
   h. After sometime, he/she should be left alone for working and do his/her job.
6. **Examination of the trainee's job**: The trainee's job should be examined while working. Whenever he/she makes mistakes, he/she should be corrected. After that, he/she should be asked to repeat the whole work again. Let him/her repeat the work until he/she develops competence.
7. **Follow-up**: After the completion of the training, he/she should be allowed to work. But, later on, his/her work should be checked. In case of any difficulty, he/she should be provided necessary guidance and help. Regularity and vigilance are the key of a successful training programme.

Dessler and Varkkey[32] have suggested the following five steps in a training and development process:

1. Need analysis
2. Instructional design
3. Valuation step
4. Implementing the programme
5. Evaluation of the programme

Gomez-Mejia, Balkin and Cardy[33] have suggested three phases in the training process as follows:

1. Need assessment
2. Development and conduct of training
3. Evaluation

Raymond A. Noe has suggested a training design process comprising seven steps: conducting a need assessment, ensuring that employees have the motivation and basic skills necessary to master training content, creating a learning environment, ensuring that trainees apply the training content to the jobs, developing an evaluation plan, choosing the training method according to learning objectives, and evaluating the programme and taking remedial steps.[34]

Concept of Learning Organisation

A learning organisation is one which has an ideal learning environment perfectly in tune with organisational goals and which is a place where people continually expand capacity to create the results they truly desire, where new and expensive patterns of thinking are nurtured, where collective aspiration is set free and where people are continually learning to see the whole (reality) together. No organisation can flourish in case it does not have these traits as due to excessive global competition, the products of an organisation need constant improvement in quality and decrease in cost.

A learning organisation depends upon the mastery of five dimensions as follows:

1. System thinking: It involves treating an organisation as a complex system comprising sub-systems (smaller systems which too may be complex). Hence, it is desirable to have system maps that show how systems connect.
2. Personal mastery: It refers to a process where an individual endeavours to increase his/her vision, to focus his/her energy and to be in a constant state of learning.
3. Mental models: It refers to deeply ingrained assumptions, generalisations, or even pictures and images that influence how we understand the world and we take actions. These must be recognised and also challenged so that there emerge new ideas and changes.
4. Building shared vision: A leader's vision does not automatically become shared with his/her subordinates. It has to be consciously shared with him/her passing on a picture of the future to them in a storytelling fashion. It may also be passed on through dialogue, commitment, enthusiasm and so on and not by dictating.
5. Team learning: It refers to the state where team members think together to achieve common goals. It builds on shared vision, adding the element of collaboration.

It is the leader who plays a vital role in the creation of a learning organisation by playing the role of a designer and creates a common vision with shared values and purpose. He/she may also be instrumental in determining the policies, strategies and structures that translate guiding ideas into business decisions. He/she may also be instrumental in creating effective learning processes which will allow for continuous improvement of the policies, strategies and structures. He/she can also play the role of a teacher and act as steward and contribute significantly towards the effectiveness of a learning organisation.

Competency Mapping

Competency mapping is a process to identify key competencies for an organisation and/or a job and incorporating those competencies throughout various processes such as recruitment, job evaluation and training of the organisation. It may be worth mentioning here that a competency is defined as a behaviour rather than a skill or ability.

Steps Involved in Competency Mapping

The main steps involved in competency mapping are as shown in Exhibit 6.8.

Exhibit 6.8   Methods Involved in Competency Mapping

- Conducting job analysis
- Developing a competency-based job description (it will be based on the results of job analysis)
- Mapping the competencies based on competency-based job description
- Identifying in what competencies individuals need additional development or training needs which will help achieving the goals of the position and company

---

Methods of Competency Mapping

Following are the main methods of competency mapping:

1. Assessment centre[35]
2. Critical incident technique: This technique is useful for obtaining in-depth data about a particular role or set of tasks. For obtaining detailed feedback, we can use any of the two approaches: (a) unstructured approach and (b) moderate structured approach
3. Interview techniques
4. Questionnaires
5. Psychometric tests which may be aptitude tests and achievement tests

Methods of Competency-based Training Needs Identification

Because of highly competitive environment, it is becoming difficult for organisations to determine whether their employees have the capabilities required for success. Hence, a good number of companies are making use of competency models to help them identify knowledge, skills and personal characteristics needed for successful performance in a job. This, in turn, helps in identifying the training needs of the employees of the organisation.

First, identify the job or position to be analysed and identify if there are any changes in the business strategy of the organisation and whether such changes in the business strategy need new competencies or old competencies need to be altered. The next step to follow is to identify effective and ineffective performers using the approach(es) such as analysing one or more 'star' performers, surveying people who are familiar with the job and investigating benchmark data of good performers in other companies.[36] The final step involves validating the model, that is, whether the competencies included in the model are really effective in getting the desired results.

Competency Models

Before discussing competency models, it is desirable to understand the term 'competency'. According to Morrelli et al., 'A competency is a measurable human capability that is required for effective performance. A competency may be comprised of knowledge, a single skill or ability, a personal characteristic, or a cluster of two or more of these attributes'. This means that competencies facilitate and lead to superior results.

As far as a competency model is concerned, it lists the competencies required for delivering. It is essentially a model (see Figure 6.3) built on the foundation of inherent talents, incorporating the types of skills and knowledge, that can be acquired through learning efforts and experience.[37]

There are several competency models. Some of the main ones are as follows:

1. **Customised generic method:** Per this method, organisations use a probable list of competencies that are diagnosed internally to aid in their selection of a generic model and then validate it with the input of outstanding and average performers.
2. **Job competence assessment method:** This is generated using interviews and observations of outstanding and average performers to determine the competencies that differentiates between them in critical incidents.[38]

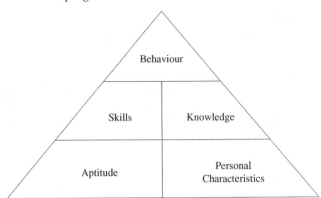

Figure 6.3 Competency Pyramid Model

Source: Suggested by S. Sanghi, The Handbook of Competency Mapping (New Delhi: SAGE Publications, 2011), 23.

3. **Flexible job competency model method:** This seeks to diagnose the competencies that will be required to perform effectively under different conditions in the future.[39]
4. **Accelerated competency system method:** This lays emphasis on the competencies that specifically support the production of output such as an organisation's products, services or information.
5. **Modified job competence assessment method:** This also identifies such behavioural differences as in the job competence assessment method, but to reduce costs, interviewees provide a written account of critical incidents.
6. **Systems method:** This method requires reflecting on not only what exemplary performers do now, or what they do overall, but also behaviours that may be important in the future.

Which model or approach or method should be chosen depends on the circumstances of the organisation concerned, but it should be ensured that it should be practically implementable and that the behaviours described in the model correlate with effectiveness on the job. In other words, it should be able to deliver the expected results.

Essential Features of a Good Training Programme

Whatever method of training is adopted and whatever type of training is organised for the employees, it should be characterised by the following features:

- The training programme must be so designed as to suit the nature of the organisation, the requirements of trainees and financial capability of the organisation.
- Since business strategy affects the type and amount of training, training should be aligned to business strategy.
- It must be flexible.
- It must be supported by the top management.
- Training must always recognise individual differences such as differences in their abilities, interest, age (see Exhibit 6.9), learning speed and other significant personal characteristics.

- Staff should be involved in the formulation and execution of the training programme.
- Training should reflect the information provided by job analysis, which indicates both the need for training and the nature of the training to be provided.
- Incentives are always important in training. Motivation of trainees cannot be taken for granted.
- A company should organise its training department, adopting to any one or more than one models of organising the training department: faculty model, customer model, matrix model, corporate university model and business embedded model.[40]
- Teachers and instructors for training must be carefully selected and must themselves be given special training, if necessary.
- Participation of executives and supervisors, as well as trainees, in training activities is an important means of enhancing motivation and interest in training.

Exhibit 6.9 The Great Learning Divide

There are four generations we come across in majority of organisations. These include the Silent Generation (born between 1933 and 1945, they are very less in number), baby boomers (born between 1946 to 1964), Generation X (born between 1965 to 1980) and Generation Y, or the millennials (born between 1981 to 2000). Each of these generations has its own cultural norms, which should be clearly understood and accepted by the HR professionals, and that understanding must be leveraged for successful training and knowledge.

Source: S. Ray, 'The Great Learning Divide', *Human Capital* 18, no. 4 (September 2014): 31.

Determining ROI on Training

Determining the costs and benefits will lead us to work out the ROI on training as follows:

1. **Determining costs**: Costs incurred at different stages of the training process can be compared across alternative training programmes. Accounting can also be used to calculate costs, which may be direct costs, indirect costs, development costs, overhead costs and compensation for trainees.
2. **Determining benefits**: First, the organisation should review the original reasons that caused the training programme and work out how far the programme was effective in giving the desired results. Trainees and their managers provide estimates of training benefits.

Finally, calculate the ROI on training. Phillips[41] has suggested the following steps to calculate ROI:

- Identify outcomes (e.g. quality and accidents).
- Place a value on the outcome.
- Determine the change in performance after eliminating other potential influences on training results.

- Obtain an annual amount of benefits (operational results) from training by comparing results after training to results before training.
- Determine the training costs (including all types of costs).
- Calculate the total savings by subtracting the training costs from benefits (operational results).
- Calculate the ROI by dividing benefits (operational costs) by costs. The ROI gives an estimate of the dollar return expected from dollar invested in training.

There is also a utility analysis which is a cost–benefit analysis method which can also be used.[42]

Evaluating Training Effectiveness in an Organisation

Evaluation of effectiveness of training and management development programmes is a highly delicate step. There has arisen a question among all types of enterprises about the productivity of training and development programmes. Especially, management wants to know whether it is being repaid for the expenses of various training programmes. It wants to know the degree to which their programmes accomplish the objectives for which they are established.

Many companies cite greater motivation, higher quality, changed attitudes and more open and honest communication as evidence that training is working but admit that proof of its effects on company profits is harder to find.[43]

Various authors and researchers have tried to find out the ways for evaluating training programmes. They have suggested many indicators for it. The effectiveness of a particular training programme is visualised in the context of the changed behaviour of participants after training. However, the behaviour of participants may also be affected by the organisational constraints, and the organisation may be too weak to use well-trained participants properly. Similarly, in a well-organised training programme, a particular participant may not be able to learn much because of his/her own inherent weaknesses. Thus, the effectiveness of training is determined by all three partners in it: the institution imparting formal training, the participants and the work organisation.

For evaluation of the training programme, the basic question is 'To what extent did the programme achieve what was set out to be achieved?' Any training programme is started with certain objectives. Hence, after the programme is over, its success can be measured in this context. Evaluation at the very end of the programme is about the new knowledge, understanding and skills that the participants have gained during training. The same kind of data at various stages of the post-training phase show how stable these gains are and to what extent they have survived transfer to the work situation.

McMurry has suggested eight tests that he feels must be met by any successful management training programme: it must (a) train candidates for specific positions, (b) define necessary qualities and skills, (c) include only trainees with adequate potential, (d) carefully determine which qualities can be developed through training, (e) use tested and proved techniques and procedures, (f) assure qualified trainers, (g) assure adequate trainee motivation and (h) demonstrate results of the programme. The effectiveness of any training programme depends on its objectives.

If the training objectives have not been appropriately formulated, then even a good training programme has no chance to be effective. Faulty job analysis sometimes leads to such result. Even if participants are shifted very frequently from one work to another, no training can be relevant to their future work. Thus, training failure happens whenever training objectives are not rooted or are improperly rooted in definite plans for changes on the job or when the change process as a whole fails due to inadequate organisational commitment and support. A deliberate policy is required which can guide the establishment and revision of training objectives. When the policy is realistic and clear, regular and frequent evaluation followed by marginal adjustments can keep training objectives in tune with shifting needs. This assumes a close relationship between the training institution and the work organisation. However, evaluation of training objectives is the responsibility of the work organisation in the first place. The training institution can contribute procedural experience and consistent and sustained interest. Collaboration between the organisation and the institution ensures rapid use of evaluation results in the selection and preparation of participants in programme designs and in preparing the organisation for change.

With the training objectives formulated clearly in terms of changes to be effected at work, the work organisation is in the best position to evaluate the effects of training on individual participants. The question remains: What is such evaluation for? The participant's evaluation can be done in the context of training objective, if precisely defined. This objective may be in terms of a changed behavioural approach. This behavioural approach may be immediate and direct, or it may be secondary, less direct and more obviously subject to hazards of contamination. The impact of training may be evaluated in parts by direct measurement of the time required for the trainee to reach the accepted standard level of productivity. It may also be expected to influence but less directly the behaviour of trainees, work attitudes, morale and turnover. All these secondary outputs may be subject to the influence of many other factors.

Some of these results of participation may not become evident for some time, while others may have a short life. The evaluators will have to decide whether their primary interest is in short-term or long-term behaviour change.

Models for Evaluation of Training Effectiveness

Gone are the days when measuring of learning effectiveness was based on multiple choice questions because this approach was based on short-term retention of knowledge. Today is the time of a long-term ability to apply knowledge. With the rapidly growing need to get employees educated and giving top performance, organisations are now looking at other ways to measure learning effectiveness. The following are the three main ways to measure training effectiveness:

1. **Skill assessment:** One of the three main ways of measuring training effectiveness, skill assessment, involves creating a visual assessment of an employee's skill set and performance both pre- and post-training and finding out the difference. Date analytics can help a lot in this direction.
2. **Social ownership:** The concept of social ownership puts learners in the position to teach others by showing how they apply concepts in their real world. It also gives training managers the ability to measure how concepts are being implemented with the organisation. Videography can also help in this direction by having the images of poor–peer workshops.
3. **Visual confirmation:** Today, with the help of technology (e.g. videos), learners have the ability to share visual confirmation that they have completed a task in real life.

The training manager, having access to the videos of the employees using knowledge from a workshop in real life, can measure the effectiveness of training undergone by the employees.

Difficulties in Evaluation

The evaluation of training programmes presents numerous difficulties. First, there are many intangible matters which may not be easily appraised. These may be matters of attitude, opinions and feelings. Second, difficulty of assessment may be accepted as justifying complacency with respect to evaluation. Third, the process of checking up on training programmes may overlap and be conflicting. It is very difficult to quantify the contribution of formal and informal training techniques. However, the views and experience of evaluators play a very prominent part in the process.

Strategic Context of Training

It should be ensured that the organisation's training programme has relevance in terms of organisation's strategic goals. It means that instead of following the traditional objectives of training, the organisation should help in identifying strategic goals and objectives and the skills and knowledge required to accomplish them. All concerned should assess whether the employees possess the required skills and knowledge. If yes, then okay. If not, then training needs should be worked out.[44]

Training Practices in India

India is moving rapidly on the road of industrialisation. For the industrial development on modern lines, the material and physical resources of the country are almost satisfactory. From the point of view of human resources, India, with a huge population of nearly 1.25 billion, is not short of manpower. Rather, a very small fraction of the total population constitutes the workforce engaged in the organised sector of the industries. Thus, with regard to the progress of industrialisation, the problem of human resources is not at all a problem of numbers, but rather it is a question of the quality, type of training and improving the skill of manpower required for industries. Hence, the need and importance of training facilities in India are unquestionable.

Various training facilities in India can be divided into three categories: training of lower-level workers, training of supervisory and middle-level personnel and, finally, training and development facilities of managerial personnel.

In India, workers' training is comparatively a new idea. It came to light mainly after the Second World War. But real progress in this direction has been made only after independence of the country.

In 1961, the Government of India enacted the Apprentices Act, and more than 500 industrial training institutes were established. For apprenticeship training, 300 centres were established. Some places have special training centres. Chennai has Advanced Training Institute, Kolkata has the Central Staff Training and Research Institute and Bengaluru had the Foremen Training Institute. The Directorate General of Employment and Training (DGE&T), Government of India, established many training centres under the Craftsmen Training Scheme. With this scheme, the National Apprenticeship Training Scheme was extended to other industrial houses also. During 1976, under Apprenticeship

Scheme, Child Training Scheme was initiated and now this has been extended to many new works.

The Apprenticeship Training Scheme (ATS) is implemented by Ministries of Labour and Employment (MoLE) and Human Resource Development (MHRD) under the Apprentices Act, 1961. About 254 groups of industries are covered under the act and 27,000 establishments engage apprentices. DGE&T is responsible for the implementation of the act in respect of trade apprentices in the central government undertakings and departments. It is done through six Regional Directorates of Apprenticeship Training located at Kolkata, Mumbai, Chennai, Hyderabad, Kanpur and Faridabad. It covers 15-to-18-year-olds who had completed at least eight years of schooling. The Department of Secondary Education in the MHRD is responsible for the implementation of the act in respect of Graduate, Technician and Technician (Vocational) Apprentices. This is done through four Boards of Apprenticeship Training located at Kanpur, Kolkata, Mumbai and Chennai and is targeted at 19-to-22-year-olds who are certificate or diploma or degree holders in engineering and management. The scheme has a focus on manufacturing or non-manufacturing industries and within that also, only the organised sector leaving the unorganised sector completely dependent on the informal system of apprenticeship.

Per the Twelfth Five Year Plan, the apprenticeship system is in need of major reforms in terms of enhancement in both physical and human infrastructure. There is a need to develop a centralised institutional mechanism at the Regional Directorate of Apprenticeship Training (RDAT) and a matching Web portal at the district/state/national levels with transparency in the process of filing applications for apprentice training. The Web-based portal would enable the employers to publish their trade-wise requirements of apprentices and facilitate apprentices to apply online. These processes may be facilitated by the Labour Market Information System (LMIS). The MoLE is proposing the Amendment in the Apprentices Act, 1961. The norms relating to engagement of skilled workers as apprentices under the Apprentices Act, 1961, need to be made flexible. The stipend paid may be enhanced and linked to minimum wages for the trade at the state level. Industry should be free to pay higher stipend to apprentices if it feels so. Given the need to train larger numbers as apprentices for eventual employment, the micro, small and medium enterprises (MSME) may explore the avenues for engaging apprentices. Further modular courses can be brought under the purview of the Apprentices Act.[45]

As regards private and public sectors, the private sector has, by and large, not implemented formal training programme properly among its workers. But many concerns have an induction programme for their new employees aimed at informing and educating them about the company, its products, policies, management and so on. These programmes are generally conducted by their personnel department, at times with the help of the supervisory staff. However, the public sector undertakings use their internal training facilities for training their non-supervisory employees. In some cases, employees are also encouraged to avail of the external training facilities. Sometimes they sponsor their candidature and meet the costs also. Some public sector organisations such as banks, insurance companies and railways have started their well-organised training programmes.

Now, many well-established private sector concerns are also conducting in-company training programmes based on their workers' needs and job requirements. So, we can say that India is marching ahead steadily in this direction.

As far as supervisory training is concerned, an organisation obtains its supervisors either by promotion from the ranks or by direct recruitment, the latter being the more widely followed practice in India, though promotion from the ranks is more common in

Western countries. Illiteracy and poor educational background greatly limit the possibility of promotion to supervisory jobs from the ranks in India. The problem of supervisory training has, therefore, to be tackled at the root and, in order to bridge the gap between the potentiality of a worker for supervisory work and the post itself, the level of general educational needs to be realised. Many organisations have undertaken, with a great deal of success, training of both junior and senior workers in mathematics, elements of science and so on, according to their requirements, through regular routine classes during working hours. Some supervisory training in also imparted through TWI, which was formally introduced in India with the help of International Labour Organisation (ILO) experts. A number of organisations, both in the public and private sectors, have had people trained by TWI centre staff so that they can undertake supervisory training in their respective organisations.

TWI programmes have had mixed results. Many managements, who have realised the importance of training for supervisors, have not been led into complacency by the simplicity of TWI. They have obtained highly successful results as a result of intensive supervisory training programmes. The Central Training Institute for Instructors has also an additional course meant for supervisors which covers non-technical subjects such as leadership, foundations for good relations, handling of problems, induction of new entrants, effective communication and so on. Some institutes, particularly Small Industries Service Institute, National Institute of Training in Industrial Engineering (NITIE) and so on, organise short-term training programmes for supervisors.

Coming to training and development of managerial personnel, it has attracted the greatest attention of both practising managers and academicians in this field. This is because of the fact that management has greatly lagged behind the imperative demand of the country. It has now been accepted that major gap in the developing countries is managerial rather than technological. While advanced technology can be imported, managerial competence has to be home-grown to suit the ethos, temper and needs of our society. In our country, the needs are to train the following:

1. Government administrators, who are concerned with law and order, as they have to contribute in the development programme as latter are being emphasised now
2. Professional managers, who take managerial positions in an expanding economy and fill the vacancies caused by people who are occupying important decision-making positions in both public and private sectors and are due to retire shortly

As far as the training facilities for administrative and managerial personnel in our country are concerned, the training and development of civil servants is being largely attempted through a basic course in the National Academy of Administration in Mussoorie and in the staff colleges run by various states. Refresher courses to meet specific objectives are also being organised. The needs of the industry are being met through (a) pre-recruitment training in management and (b) training and development of practising managers, particularly at senior and middle management levels.

1. **Pre-recruitment education and training in management:** The need and importance of management education and training have come to be accepted in our country in a shorter period as compared to the other areas of education. In 1957, when Andhra Pradesh organised the two-year programme in master's degree in business management, it was the first department of management education. Since then, the number

of such institutions offering two-year courses has increased enormously. It is not only the number of management institutions that has grown a great deal but also new and more effective methods of teaching have been evolved and awareness towards qualitatively better teaching has increased. The institutions imparting management education and training can be divided into two groups, besides private institutes including management training centre of large organisations both in public and private sectors. These are as follows:

   a. The first group comprises the institutes at the national level. These are Indian Institutes of Management (IIMs) at Ahmedabad, Kolkata, Bengaluru, Lucknow and many other places, and also some other national-level institutions for management education and development.
   b. The second group consists of universities having department of management running either two-year full-time MBA degree courses and/or three-year part-time courses for the same degree. The teaching of management courses is also receiving increased attention at undergraduate and postgraduate levels in commerce faculties.

2. **Training and development of practising managers:** There are two types of facilities for training and development of practising managers. First, business organisations employing managerial personnel impart such training either through their own management training institutes or through organising lectures, instructors being their own line and staff managers or faculty being taken from outside in some cases. These organisations recruit fresh management graduates and students from other disciplines also as management trainees. They are put through training process while working in the organisation. Hindustan Steel, Life Insurance Corporation, commercial banks, Fertilizers Corporation and many organisations in the public sector and Hindustan Lever, Tata and others in the private sector have their own management training institutes. Second, there are many management institutes, associations and other bodies which organise short-term management development programmes. Prominent among these are ASCI, Hyderabad; IIMs; All India Management Association and its local chapters; National Productivity Council and Local Productivity Councils; Indian Institutes of Bank Management; National Institutes of Personnel Management; NITIE; and so on. These bodies organise management development programmes of the varying duration ranging from two days to twelve weeks.

Evaluation of Training Facilities

The preceding discussion shows that training and development facilities have developed considerably, both for managers and operatives. In the case of former, however, the facilities have increased manifold during the last three to four decades. This is in term of management graduates being educated and the short-term management development programmes. We are constantly and steadily moving towards professional management. Old guards are changing their styles; they are changing to adopt new environment. Perhaps after independence, managers have developed themselves a great deal. As Minoo Masani has observed, 'There are very few success stories that can be told since the achievement of Indian independence. If one among these exceptions is the record of the farmer, another is the story of the manager'.[46] However, this success story has its own limitations when it is judged in the absolute terms of managerial needs of the country, their qualities and the qualities of institutions imparting managerial training.

Here, management training and development will be analysed in terms of quantity and quality.

Quantity: The combined efforts of all institutions having facilities for management training are not enough to meet the requirements of the country. Today, we have a large number of joint stock companies, many of which could be considered as large ones. In addition, we have a good number of small-scale industries and several lakhs of cottage and village industries spread all over the country. The present facilities are not enough even to meet the requirement of joint stock companies, though there is a considerable scope for improving the efficiency of smaller sectors. If we add the number of commerce graduates and postgraduates also, then the number reaches to a satisfactory level. However, then the problem of quality comes into picture.

Quality: It is ironical that our industries are facing shortage of managerial people while many MBAs remain unemployed for a fairly long time after completing their management courses. This shows a serious gap between the quality required by the industries and the quality produced by the institutes. This quality again can be measured in terms of facilities available with the management institutes and the type of management graduates being produced.

Educational facilities: Except IIMs and a few management institutes and universities, no other institutes have the right type of facilities to educate managerial graduates. There are several types of lacunae. There is a lack of adequate faculty, financial resources, equipment and other teaching materials, research work, liaison with business world and operational autonomy because of the university administrative structure. It is astonishing that many management departments are having just four to six faculty members running full-time MBA courses. On the other hand, IIMs are having adequate faculty in each area besides huge financial resources. Naturally, the quality of two types of management graduates has much difference. Another problem in this area is the availability of teaching materials based on Indian environment. Management courses being offered in India are generally based on the syllabi of American universities. The textbooks, books of reading and the journals used for imparting this education are usually the works of American authors. The validity and relevance of management concepts developed in foreign environment have not always been tested and adopted to suit Indian environment. Although the institutions such as the IIM, Ahmedabad; ASCI, Hyderabad; and some other institutes have done considerable work in the area of developing Indian case materials, much more remains to be done in this regard quantitatively. Management graduates are prepared for the jobs mostly in large joint stock companies. Not much attention is being paid to small and cottage industries. Moreover, the graduates have a tendency to go to multinationals and a few public and private sector organisations, where they feel that they would be able to work in a dynamic situation. This might be because of the promotional avenues and availability of elite class to which they themselves perceive to belong. Their expectations are quite high both in terms of financial compensation and social status. The management programmes tend to impart education meant to develop higher-level executives who can take important decisions without any practical experience, rather than people who would begin with effective management assistants and grow gradually in management hierarchy. Another factor which T. Thomas, Chairman, Hindustan Lever Limited, has pointed out is also worth consideration. He has observed that young managers seem to be professional and more task-oriented. They seem to have little orientation towards people, although they have a well-developed sense of social justice. Somewhere along the line, loyalty and feeling for people have to be developed in them.[47]

Emerging Trends and Latest Developments

Increasing Investment on Training

Of late, having realised the positive impact of training on productivity and success of an organisation, employers have started increasing their investment on training (see Exhibits 6.10 and 6.11).

Linking Training and Development Initiatives to Business Strategy

Of late, strategic training and development initiatives (such as aligning training and development with the company's strategic decisions; ensuring that the work environment is conducive to learning as well as transfer of learning; capturing strong knowledge; diversifying the learning portfolio; using technology in training, including informal training and so on; enhancing the speed of employees learning; extending development opportunities and communicating them to employees; improving customer service; and offering more learning opportunities to non-managerial employees) are being taken so that these may be instrumental in achieving business strategy objectives. These initiatives are normally learning-related actions and may differ from company to company. Many companies are undertaking training and development activities linked to strategic training and development initiatives.

Outsourcing Training

When a company assigns the responsibility and control of designing, developing, delivering and administering all or most of or any of a company's training activities, it is known as outsourcing of training.

Exhibit 6.10   Trend of Increasing Investment on Training

According to the 12th edition of the Conference Board of Canada's Learning and Development Outlook, between 2010 and 2012, Canada's organisations increased funding for training, learning and development. Spending was up $17 per employee.

Source: Quoted in *Human Capital* 18, no. 5 (October 2014): 43. Available at http://www.humancapitalonline.com/PDF-Issues/October_14_Issue_Lowrespdf.pdf (Accessed on 15 November 2017).

Exhibit 6.11   Increasing Training Budgets

A 2014 report from Bersin by Deloitte, The Corporate Learning Fact Book 2014: Benchmarks, Trends, and Analysis of the US Training Market says that businesses increased training budgets by an average of 15% in 2013, reflecting the highest growth in this area in the last seven years.

Source: Quoted in *Human Capital* 18, no. 5 (October 2014): 42. Available at http://www.humancapitalonline.com/PDF-Issues/October_14_Issue_Lowrespdf.pdf (Accessed on 15 November 2017).

220 Training and Developing Human Resources

The outsourcing training is showing an increasing trend. However, how much part of training is outsourced differs from company to company, though most companies who outsource training do not outsource complete training function. It is only the small parts of the training function which is usually being outsourced.

Use of Subject-Matter Experts (SMEs) in Assessment

In order to assess training needs, today, good organisations use academicians, technical experts, trainers, customers and suppliers, their own employees and managers who have in-depth knowledge about task for which the training is to be provided, the skills required to perform that task efficiently and effectively, about the conditions under which that task is to be performed as also about the tools and equipment to be used in the execution of that task. In order to find out whether employees have the capabilities needed for successful training, today, many companies are using competency models which identify the competencies necessary for each job, including the knowledge, skills, behaviour and personality characteristics underlying each competency.

HRM Strategy with Regard to Training

With today's constantly and rapidly changing technology, almost every worker needs some sort of training at the entry level and also retraining later on depending on the new technology adopted by the organisation from time to time. A trained worker is a relatively contended person and he/she is economical too to the organisation. Hence, HR should formulate an appropriate strategy with regard to imparting training to its employees. Keeping in view the environmental factors and also what is being done by the competitive organisations, the training strategy should be so formulated that it can answer such questions as the following: Who needs training and when? In what he/she needs to be trained and how to be trained? Who will train? How much financial burden will it cause on the organisation? What has been the past experience of the organisation in this regard? What has been the reaction of the workers so trained? And what has been the outcome of cost–benefit analysis in this direction? Answers to all the aforesaid questions should form the basis of the HR training strategy. The HR training strategy should be 'vertically fit' to the organisation strategy and 'horizontally fit' to other departments' strategies, and it should be helpful in accomplishing organisational objectives. Obviously, the training strategy will differ from organisation to organisation and from time to time within the same organisation depending on the situations.

Chapter Review

1. The complexities of modern industrialisation and technological changes have led to the realisation of the greater necessity of training, which is a short-term programme arranged to impart certain skills(s) and to enhance abilities to do a specific job well.
2. Training is beneficial to both employees and the organisation as it adds value to the worth of employees and yields economic gains to the organisation; the provided training is arranged following the well-laid-out principles of training.
3. Training methods comprise both the on-the-job methods (on specific job, position rotation, special projects, selective reading, apprenticeship, vestibule schools,

multiple management and so on) and off-the-job methods (special courses and lectures, conferences, case studies, brainstorming, laboratory methods, EPSS, tele-training, videoconferencing, MP3/instant messaging, slides and videotapes, programmed learning, audiovisual-based training, HR's learning portals, e-learning, mentoring, informal learning, distance, Internet-based training and so on).
4. There are several challenges in training like establishing clear and realistic goals for a training programme. There are several types of training imparted in industry depending on the requirement of the organisation. In case due precautions are taken, training pitfalls can be avoided.
5. The contents of a training programme depend on the level the trainee belongs to. Hence, the type and method of training should be decided keeping in view the level (in hierarchy) of the trainee into consideration.
6. Training is a multi-step process, mainly comprising determination of needs and objectives, deciding the conditions of training programme, selection of training method(s), preparation of training, examination of the trainee's job and follow-up.
7. There are certain essentials to make a training programme effective such as recognition of individual differences, motivated trainee, appropriate contents and method of training and feedback. A training programme should, therefore, be evaluated—especially its objectives—periodically and remedial steps taken.
8. A training programme should have relevance to the strategic goals of the organisation.
9. The training practices in Indian industries differ from industry to industry, organisation to organisation and even in the same organisation, depending on the objectives of a particular training programme.
10. There is a marked shortage of training facilities in Indian industries. However, training facilities are relatively more for administrative and management personnel.

Key Terms

apprenticeship
brainstorming
case studies
coaching
company in-house
  programme
crisis training
cross-functional training
distance and Internet-based
  training
diversity training
education e-learning
electronic performance support systems (EPSS)
gaming
grievance

grievance
HRIS learning portals
incident method
HRIS learning portals
incident Method
individual differences
  learning
mentoring
morale
motivation
multiple management
  obsolescence
position rotation
productivity
programmed learning
  reinforcement

retraining role-playing
sensitivity training
  simulation
skill training
team training
tele-training
training
training within
  industry (TWI)
understudy
vestibule school
  videoconferencing

Discussion Questions

1. Discuss the typical features of a training programme. Also discuss the difference between training, education and motivation.
2. Discuss how training is useful to both the employees and the employer.
3. Discuss which OJT methods are appropriate for operative staff of a large manufacturing organisation.
4. Discuss which off-the-job training method(s) of training are more useful for imparting training to supervisory staff.
5. Discuss the special features of each type of training usually imparted in Indian industries.
6. Discuss the various stages involved in the process of training in the context of a large service organisation like a bank.
7. Discuss what is it that makes a training programme effective and also how to evaluate the effectiveness of a training programme.
8. Discuss the strategic context of training.
9. Discuss the most commonly used training practices in Indian industries.
10. Discuss the adequacy of training facilities available in our country for administrative and management personnel.

Individual and Group Activities

1. Working individually, visit a large manufacturing organisation, and after finding out the OJT methods it has been using to train its operative staff, prepare a brief note.
2. Working individually or in groups, contact the training department of a big organisation of the telecom sector and find out from its officials which off-the-job methods of training they use and why.
3. Working individually or in groups, find out from the officials of the training department of a big organisation whether they follow the principles of training and with what outcome.
4. Working individually, interact with a trade union leader of a big manufacturing organisation and find out whether the employees are satisfied with the training methods being used by their organisation. Yes or no? Why?
5. Working individually or in groups, contact the officials of the training department of a big organisation and find out the process of training they follow in their organisation.

Application Case 6.1

Inadequate Personal Touch Between the Trainee and the Trainer During the Period of Training

Swamy has been serving as manager (training) in a mega steel company for the last ten years. The company has a turnover of around 300 billion and employs over

3,000 employees. The company has about 20% share in the market and is known for its quality product as it has been updating its technology from time to time.

In 2014, the company had selected a batch of ten mechanical engineers, all of whom had to undergo training for one year. Mr Yash, a BTech (mechanical engineering) from IIT Kanpur, was one of these trainees, whereas rest of them were the products of different B-grade engineering colleges of the country. All the trainees, per the company's practice, undergo first six months of training in different functional areas which is considered to be the core training of engineers joining in the mechanical trade. By then, the trainees are allotted the various sections/departments against the available or projected vacancies. Their further training in the next three months is planned according to the requirement of the jobs where they are placed. The last three months of the training are spent on the job.

After the first six months of his training, Mr Yash was allotted the maintenance section in the production department where he spent the remaining six months of his training. Mr Yash felt that all the trainees were treated equally without taking note of their performance during the first six months of the training. There was not much of the personal or informal contact between the trainees and the trainers as the training moved ahead in a mechanised fashion. Mr Yash was a very inquisitive, innovative and ambitious person. Although vacancies were there in the production section, mechanical section and R&D section, the trainees were not asked for their options and were allotted positions in these sections of the production department at random. By the time training was over, Mr Yash was depressed as he could not find any avenues to make use of his potential and innovativeness in the maintenance section. Hence, he started looking for another opportunity elsewhere, and within two months after the completion of his training, he tendered his resignation, which was accepted, and he was relieved without being asked to appear for any exit interview. Thus, the company lost a brilliant trained engineer without taking any advantage of the investment made by it on his training.

Questions

1. What was the flaw in the training process which led to the resignation by Mr Yash?
2. What steps would you suggest to overcome such a situation in future?
3. What was the shortcoming, if any, on the part of Mr Yash?

Notes

1 Jucius, *Personnel Management*, 225.
2 J. P. Campbell, 'Personnel Training and Development', *Annual Review of Psychology* 22, no. 1 (1971): 1–38.
3 Jucius, *Personnel Management*, 225.
4 Flippo, *Principles of Personnel Management*, 209.
5 Ivancevich, *Human Resource Management*, 399.
6 Ibid.
7 See A. P. Cornivale, 'America and the New Economy', *Training and Development* 54, no. 11 (November 1990): 31–52; R. Brinkerhoff and A. Apking, *High Impact Learning* (Cambridge, MA: Perseus Publishing, November 2001).

8. Flippo, *Principles of Personnel Management*, 211.
9. See V. Sessa and M. Condan, *Continuous Learning in Organisations* (Mahwah, NJ: Erlbaum, 2006).
10. For details, see Dessler and Varkkey, *Human Resource Management*, 300–3.
11. Ibid., 298.
12. Ivancevich, *Human Resource Management*, 399.
13. See 'Why Learning Still Matters! Facts, Statistics, Practices, Perspectives and More', *Human Capital* 18, no. 5 (October 2014): 43, Available at http://www.humancapitalonline.com/PDF-Issues/October_14_Issue_Lowrespdf.pdf (Accessed on 15 November 2017).
14. Flippo, *Principles of Personnel Management*, 210.
15. See B. Sugrue, T. O'Driscoll, and. D. Blair, 'What in the World is WLP?', *Training and Development* 8, no. 2 (January 2005): 51–54.
16. Gomez-Mejia, Balkin, and Cardy, *Managing Human Resources*, 259.
17. S. B. Sawyer and D. V. Eastmond, 'Learning Theories and the Design of E-Learning Environments', *Quarterly Review of Distance Review* 6, no. 1 (Spring 2005): 77–80.
18. Dessler and Varkkey, *Human Resource Management*, 304.
19. For details of the Act, see R. C. Sharma, 'Protective and Employment Legislation and Industrial Relations II', in *Industrial Relations and Labour Legislation* (Delhi: PHI Learning Private Ltd, 2016).
20. For details of the changes being effected, see R. C. Sharma, 'Labour Legislation and Labour Reforms', in *Industrial Relations and Labour Legislation* (Delhi: PHI Learning Private Ltd, 2016).
21. For details, see J. Thompson, 'The Next Generation of Corporate Learning', *Training and Development* 57, no. 6 (June 2003): 47.
22. S. Srivastava and D. Amandeep, 'Antecedents & Consequences of Mentor–Mentee Fit in Mentoring Relationships: An Exploratory Concept Study', *Indian Journal of Training and Development* 45, no. 1 (January–March 2015): 6.
23. For details, see M. Blotzer, 'Distance Learning', *Occupational Hazards* 62, no. 3 (March 2000): 53–54.
24. For details, see Gomez-Mejia, Balkin, and Cardy, *Managing Human Resources*, 261–63.
25. Ibid.
26. See V. S. Rao, *Human Resource Management*, Inf and 2nd ed. (New Delhi: Excel Books, 2006), 192.
27. Quoted in S. C. Saha, 'The Leadership Riot', *Human Capital* 17, no. 11 (April 2014): 35.
28. For operative staff, Edwin B. Flippo has suggested four training programmes: (a) OJT (b) vestibule school, (b)   apprenticeship and (c) special courses. For details, see Flippo, *Principles of Personnel Management*, 214–19.
29. See Donald Kirkpatrick, *Evaluating Training Programmes* (New York, NY: Berretl-KoePler, 1998).
30. For details, see D. Michalak and E. Yager, *Making the Training Process Work* (New York, NY: Harper & Row, 1979).
31. See P. G. Whitmore, *How to Make Smart Decisions about Training* (Atlanta, GA: CEP Press, 2002).
32. For details, see Dessler and Varkkey, *Human Resource Management*, 299.
33. For details, see Gomez-Mejia, Balkin, and Cardy, *Managing Human Resources*, 263.
34. A. Noe Raymond, *Employee Training and Development* (New Delhi: Tata McGraw-Hill, 2011).
35. For details, see discussion elsewhere in this very chapter.
36. See D. Dubois and W. Rothwell, 'Competency-Based or a Traditional Approach to Training', *Training and Development* 58, no. 4 (April 2004): 46–57; J. Kochanski, 'Competency-based Management', *Training and Development* 51, no. 10 (October 1997): 41–44.
37. S. Sanghi, *The Handbook of Competency Mapping* (New Delhi: SAGE Publications, 2011).
38. Ibid.
39. Ibid.
40. For details, see D. Laird, *Approaches to Training and Development*, 2nd ed. (Boston: Addison-Wesley, 1985); M. London, *Managing the Training Enterprise* (San Francisco, CA: Jossey-Boss, 1944).

41 J. J. Phillips, *Handbook of Training Evaluation and Measurement Methods*, 2nd ed. (Houston, TX: Gulf Publishing, 1991); J. J. Phillips, 'ROI: The Search for the Best Practices', *Training and Development* 50, no. 2 (February 1996): 42–47.
42 See J. E. Mathein and R. L. Leonard, 'Applying. Utility Analysis to a. Training Program in Supervisory Skills: A Time Based Approach', *Academy of Management Journal* 30, no. 2 (1987): 316–35.
43 P. K. Mohanty and S. Sahoo, 'Training and Its Effectiveness: A Study in State Bank of India', *Indian Journal of Training and Development* 45, no. 1 (January–March 2015): 20.
44 For details, see C. Ellis and S. Gale, 'A Seat at the Table', *Training* 38, no. 3 (March 2001).
45 See Planning Commission, *Twelfth Five Year Plan*, 154–55.
46 M. Masani, 'Indian Management Has Come of Age', *The Illustrated Weekly of India* 47 (November 1971): 15.
47 T. Thomas, 'Company Proceedings', *Hindustan Times*, 22 April 1978.

7 Executive Development and Training, Managing Careers, Promotions and Transfers

Learning Objectives

After studying this chapter, you should be able to do the following:

1. Define executive development and explain how it is different from training of non-managerial personnel.
2. Explain why management development is important for both employees and employers.
3. Explain what the contents of management development programme should be.
4. Describe the process and principles of management development.
5. Explain the executive development needs and the methods used to meet these needs.
6. Describe the procedure of executive development.
7. Explain the present position of management training in India.
8. Explain the elements involved in promotions and bases of promotion with their advantages and disadvantages.
9. Distinguish between various types of transfers and also explain characteristics of a sound transfer policy.

Introduction

Perhaps one of the most encouraging trends in HRM is the increasing role being given to executive development (see Exhibit 7.1). Prior to 1940, the acquisition of needed skills, knowledge and attitudes in higher levels of management used to be left to individual effort and the laws of chance.

But, of late, more and more organisations are giving increased attention to executive development at all levels, from supervisory through middle management to the top.[1] The process of training should be distinguished from that of development, though it is not always easy to tell where 'training' leaves off and 'management development' begins[2] because training is often used in conjunction with development. However, the two terms, 'training' and 'development', are not synonymous. While 'training' typically focuses on providing employees with specific skills or helping them with specific skills or helping them correct deficiencies in their performance,[3] 'development' aims at longer-term development, focusing on developing the capabilities of current or future managers.

DOI: 10.4324/9781032628424-10

The executive job is typically open-ended, fragmented, interpersonal, verbal and active.[4] No job description, if it should exist, can possibly capture the nature of the job in its entirety. Development activities are not only limited to the new employees but are also necessary for existing executives too. The present junior executives have to fill senior positions in future; the present middle-level as well as top-level managers need further development of skills and abilities to cope with the technical and social changes. Orientation in new development and skills does necessitate the training of existing staff and executives in new branches. That is why a lot of emphasis has been given to it in the last two to three decades. Management development programmes are very popular nowadays not only in foreign countries but in India too.

Definition of Executive/Management Development

The terms 'management development' and 'executive development' are used interchangeably. According to Dessler and Varkkey,[5] management development is any attempt to improve managerial performance by imparting knowledge, changing attitude or increasing skills.

According to Jucius, 'Executive development is the programme by which executive's capacities to achieve desired objectives are increased'.[6]

Gomez-Mejia, Balkin and Cardy have defined development as 'an effort to provide employees[7] with the abilities the organisation will need in the future'.

Thus, the process of executive development is important as it enables managers to develop their management skills. It improves their morale and motivation and equips them to shoulder more responsibilities easily at the time of their promotion.

Exhibit 7.1 Nurturing Talent

We grow only when our people grow with us and the key to any growth is by learning. In line with this spirit, Development Credit Bank has designed a programme named ASPIRE which has a two-fold objective of acknowledging the average performers in the talent pipeline as well as developing their skills to take up greater responsibilities.

Source: K. Kaushik, 'Nurturing Talent', *Human Capital* 17, no. 8 (January 2014): 53–54.

Training vs Development

While contrasting 'training' and 'development', Gomez-Mejia, Balkin and Cardy[8] point out that training focuses solely on current jobs, whereas in development, focus is on both the current and future jobs; time frame of training is immediate but that of development is long-term; the scope of training is individual employees, whereas it is the work group or organisation in the case of development; and finally, while the goal of training is to fix current skill deficit, in the case of development, the goal is to prepare for future work demands.

Need for and Importance of Management Training and Development in India

Management is a life-giving and dynamic element of business. No business can run without efficient managers. Although experience is also a way of achieving efficiency and success, it is a slow and expensive process. In this context, management training and development become very important. Henry Fayol, the staunch supporter of management education, developed the idea of management training and started the first school of management in Paris. Management is recognised as a social science today, and it has its organised body of knowledge, principles and techniques. This knowledge can be communicated to the young people who want to opt business management as a career. It is not only important for new people but equally important for lower-, middle- and supervisory-level managers to equip them with the new developments in the managerial skills.

Management training and development are especially significant in the context of industrial and organisational management. Among the live factors of production, management is the most important. It acts as a leader, and it takes out work from the other factors.

Management establishes effective coordination among different factors of production. Today, specialisation, automation and scientific management are given much emphasis. This has enhanced the importance of management because all these things can be made more effective through efficient management, and efficient management is possible through proper training and development. A large number of CEOs desire coaching from outside sources too (see Exhibit 7.2).

Exhibit 7.2   CEOs Desire Coaching from Outside Sources Also

A survey revealed that CEOs crave training. Although 78% of CEOs said they receive informal coaching and leadership advice from members of the board of directors. CEOs overwhelmingly indicated a desire for coaching from outside sources, too (the Stanford survey).

Source: S. C. Saha, 'Facts, Statistics, Practices and Perspectives and More . . .', *Human Capital* 17, no. 11 (April 2014): 35.

India is new to industrial field. Industrial development on modern lines has commenced in India after independence. India is a fast-developing country. For the development of new industries, more trained and developed managers are needed.

As the management specialisation is developing, new branches such as HRM, financial management, marketing management, materials management, production management and inventory management are coming into prominence, and new techniques and specialties are coming into existence.

In India, there is a shortage of efficient managers, especially in the public sector. This is the main reason for the loss in the public sector where general administrators work as managers and, therefore, are not efficient managers. Government has realised this fact, and now it is paying attention on the recommendations of the Administrative

Reforms Commission. Now trained managers are being appointed in the public sector undertakings.

Thus, it can be said that the following are the main factors that emphasise the need for executive development programmes:

1. **Technological and social changes**: The rapid rate of technological and social changes in our society has made it imperative to have managers who are trained to cope with these developments. Among the manifestations of these changes are automation, the fruits of accelerated research, electronic computers, intense market competition from foreign nations, new markets in emerging underdeveloped countries, enlarged voice and elevated role of labour in industry, government interference, greater interest by the public and government in the actions of business houses and exercising control over them, and so on.
2. **Professionally managed enterprises**: There has been a pronounced shift from owner-managers to employee-managers. Management has been recognised as a distinct kind of occupation consisting of teachable skills and a unified body of knowledge. Management is required to have updated knowledge and managerial skills to cope with the complexity of modern organisations.
3. **Research orientation**: Within the past few decades, there has been an ever-increasing amount of research-generated knowledge of the principles and techniques of administration. This applies to both general management and its various functional fields such as HR and industrial relations, production, finance, marketing and accounting. This newly acquired information has been favourably received by the industrial community, which has often sought to apply certain portions soon after it has been made available. Hence, to communicate and make use of this knowledge by the executives, it is necessary to groom them.
4. **Recognition of social and public responsibilities**: Today, managers are supposed to be aware about their social and public responsibilities requiring close ties with the community and the government. This has demanded new awareness, sensitivity and skills on the part of managers.
5. **Frequent labour management strives**: In order to overcome or at least to minimise labour management strives, it is necessary to have trained and developed management personnel.
6. **Increased size and complexity of organisations**: The increased size and complexity of most organisations—commercial, industrial, governmental or non-profit public services—require trained and developed managerial personnel.

Objectives of Management Training and Development

The following are the main objectives of management training and development:

1. Imparting the knowledge of basic principles of management
2. Training the future executives to act according to new scientific and timely methods
3. Getting the knowledge of general, industrial and managerial values
4. Developing the skills and competencies to analyse and take a decision related to any business problem
5. Implementing managerial principles through oral and written methods
6. Developing leadership qualities (see Exhibit 7.3)

Contents of a Management Development Programme

The contents of a management development programme depend to a large extent upon the needs of an enterprise. Such programmes are basically personnel development programmes which provide a framework for the consideration of problems in developing an executive or management development programme. The items generally covered are individual development techniques, organisation analysis and planning, managerial appraisal and inventory, and such other items which may increase the skill of existing managers so that they may shoulder more responsibilities easily after promotion and so on. Thus, a management development programme must have the following:

Exhibit 7.3 Leadership Development

When 500 executives were asked to rank their top three human-capital priorities, leadership development was included as both a current and a future priority. Almost two-thirds of the respondents identified leadership development as their number-one concern. Only 7% of senior managers polled by a UK business school think that their companies develop global leaders effectively, and around 30% of US companies admit that they have failed to exploit their international business opportunities fully because they lack enough leaders with the right capabilities (McKinsey & Company).

Source: S. C. Saha, 'Facts, Statistics, Practices and Perspectives and More', *Human Capital* 17, no. 11 (April 2014): 35.

---

1. A carefully considered plan and organisation for carrying out such a programme.
2. A periodic appraisal of each executive regarding his/her performance, skill and capabilities and need for further development.
3. After evaluation, the plans for individual development should be chalked out and then the programme should be organised.
4. Programme evaluation, in terms of its cost and time, is also essential.

As a matter of fact, the contents of development programmes should be based on the tasks the executives are most likely to encounter. That is why we find that most executive development programmes take up various subjects connected with handling people, that is, human relations. According to Michael J. Jucius,[9] under such programmes, the subjects such as the following ones are discussed:

1. Present-day labour management philosophy and policies
2. Working with others through organisational channels
3. Communicating up and down organisational channels
4. Employment policies and practices
5. Training and education policies and practices
6. Discipline, grievances, and rules and regulations
7. Employee services and recreation
8. Transfers, promotions, merit and seniority policies
9. The union contract—its meaning and implications
10. Community agencies and institutions

Executive Development and Training

As an executive has to work as a leader, the contents of an executive development programme should be related to the characteristics a leader should possess. Michael J. Jucius[10] has pointed the following characteristics to which attention should be paid in executive development programmes:

1. Ability to think
2. Ability to organise
3. Ability to handle people
4. Ability to plan
5. Ability to lead
6. Ability to obtain and interpret facts
7. Loyalty
8. Decisiveness
9. Teaching ability
10. Ability to solve problems
11. Courage
12. Self-motivation
13. Desire for achievement and prestige
14. Social balance and understanding
15. Sense of responsibility
16. Emotional balance and poise
17. Ability to influence people, individually and in groups
18. Attitude towards subordinates and associates
19. Attitude towards community and associations
20. Ability to solve problems
21. Attitude towards economic and political systems

While establishing its own development programme, an organisation should give consideration to outside practices and also take its own needs into consideration. This can be done by taking the following steps.[11]

1. Determine as precisely as possible the major objectives or tasks the company faces.
2. Make the inventory of the present executive capacities.
3. Compute the shortages of executive capacities.
4. Establish the content of training required by an individual executive to bring him/her up to desired standards.

Principles of Executive Development

Based on research and experience, a number of principles have been evolved which should serve as guides in creating and maintaining an effective executive development programme. Such principles are as follows:

1. **All development is self-development**: It means that people are developed not so much by others as by themselves. This principle highlights the importance of an individual candidate's inner motivation and basic abilities. The primary responsibility must rest upon the person to be developed.
2. **Development is closely akin to education**: Development is more closely akin to education than it is to specific training in skills because the development programme aims at overall growth of an individual to enable him/her to achieve the desired objectives.

232   Training and Developing Human Resources

3. **Gearing to individual differences**: Too much emphasis should not be laid on uniformity of development efforts. Instead, development efforts should be geared to individual differences. An individual must be helped, and the development programme should be so planned as can create an environment in which self-development is stimulated and facilitated.
2. **Long-range process**: An executive cannot be developed just by taking a course, holding a job, reading a book or attending a seminar or conference. Such development is rather a long-range process with individual development programmes running into many years.
3. **Adequate facilities**: For encouraging self-development, it is necessary to create an effective organisational climate, making all developmental facilities available.
4. **Adequate rewards**: The people who display interest and activity in development should be rewarded appropriately.
5. **Effective immediate supervisor**: The immediate supervisor exercises a key influence. The supervisor should emphasise on high-quality performance, supportive coaching and proper counselling.

Executive Development Needs

Edwin B. Flippo[12] has pointed out various types of development needs typically required by an executive position. According to him, such development needs can be categorised under the following heads:

1. Decision-making skills
2. Interpersonal skills
3. Job knowledge
4. Organisational knowledge
5. General knowledge
6. Specific individual needs
7. Other needs

In each of these categories, a number of alternative methods are available to achieve the desired objective.

Executive Development Methods

In order to fulfil the aforesaid development needs, many alternative methods may be adopted which have been depicted in Figure 7.1.

Decision-making Skills

The primary job of an executive is decision-making. Decision-making skills can be developed through the following methods:

1. **In-basket**: Each group of trainees is given a file of correspondence containing background information on the company, its products, organisation, key personnel and other data. Each individual studies the file, and if any other information is required, it is supplied to him/her. Having gone through the file, he/she makes his/

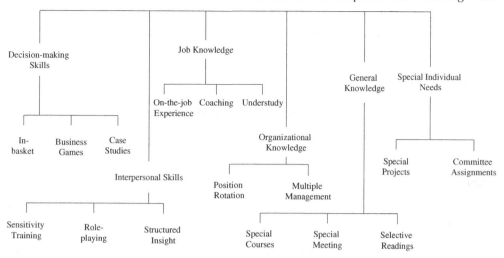

Figure 7.1 Methods of Executive Development

her observations on the situation. Then, the observations of each individual member are compared and conclusions are drawn and thereafter put down in the form of a report. In this method, decisions are objective and rapid, but all the same, it is a costly method.
2. **Business or management games**: A variety of business and management games have been devised and are being used with varying degrees of success in development programmes. A management game is a classroom exercise in which teams of students compete against each other to achieve common objectives. The game is designed to be a close representation of real-life conditions. The trainees are asked to make decisions about production, cost, research and development inventories, sales, and so on for a simulated organisation. Since they are often divided into teams as competing companions, experience is also obtained in teamwork.
3. **Case studies**: Case method is a means of simulating experience in the classroom. Under this method, the trainees may be given a problem to discuss which is more or less related to the principles already taught. This method gives the trainee an opportunity to apply his/her knowledge to the solution of realistic problems. Cases may be used in two ways: First, they can be used subsequent to the exposition of formal theory under which the trainees apply their knowledge of theory to specific situations. Second, the trainees may be assigned the cases for written analysis and oral class discussion without any prior explanation of pertinent concepts and theory. The case study places heavy demands upon the trainees and requires that they should have a good deal of maturity and background in the subject matter concerned.

Case studies are extensively used in teaching, law, personnel management, human relations, marketing management, business policy and so on in various educational institutions. Students learn that there is no single answer to a particular problem. The answers of each trainee may differ. Case discussions will help them to appreciate each other's thinking; that is why, case studies are frequently used for supervisory and executive training in businesses

> **Exhibit 7.4 Leadership Training and Behavioural Changes**
>
> A survey has revealed that leadership training is 3 times more effective as teaching knowledge than it is in changing behaviour.
>
> *Source:* S. C. Saha, 'Facts, Statistics, Practices and Perspectives and More', *Human Capital* 17, no. 11 (April 2014): 34.

Interpersonal Skills

Leadership training is not as effective in changing behaviour as in teaching knowledge (see Exhibit 7.4).

Behaviourists lay more emphasis on developing interpersonal competence among effective executives so that they may be able to get things done through 'others'. Interpersonal skills can be developed through the following methods:

1. **Sensitivity training or T-group training:** This means the development of awareness and sensitivity to behavioural patterns of oneself and others. It is an experience in interpersonal relationships which results in a change in feelings and attitudes towards oneself and others. T-groups are helpful in unlearning and learning certain things. They help the participants understand how groups actually work and give them a chance to discover how they are interpreted by others. It also aims at increasing tolerance power of the individual and his/her ability to understand others. The sensitivity training programmes are generally conducted under controlled laboratory conditions; this is quite a costly method in terms of time, money and psychological inputs.

2. **Role-playing:** The role-playing technique is used for human relations and leadership training, its purpose being to give trainees an opportunity to learn human relation skills through practice and to develop insight into one's own behaviour and its effects upon others. Thus, its objective is very narrow, that is, to increase the trainee's skill in dealing with others. It can be used in human relations training and sales training because both these involve dealing with other people.

   Under this method, a conflict situation is artificially created, and two or more trainees are assigned different parts to play. No dialogue is given beforehand. The role-players are provided with either a written or an oral description of a situation and the role they are to play. They being allowed sufficient time to plan their actions must then act out their parts spontaneously before the class. For instance, a role-playing situation may be a supervisor discussing a grievance with an employee or a salesperson making a presentation to a purchasing agent.

   Role-playing has a number of advantages. It provides an opportunity for developing human relations, understanding and skills and putting into practice the knowledge they acquired from textbooks, lectures, discussions and so on—it is learning by doing. The interview may be taped to provide the trainees a chance to listen/watch their performance and note their strengths and weaknesses. Thus, KR is immediate because the trainees as well as the listeners analyse the behaviour of the role-players.

3. **Structured insight:** Any systematic device that furthers understanding of one's actual behaviour in comparison with preferred behaviour can be called 'structured insight'. This method provides self-insight into leadership practice of top-level executives. Per this method, first of all, a manager is required to write about his/her espoused theory of leadership, that is, how he/she deals with other people. Then an actual meeting conducted by the manager is tape-recorded. Thereafter, all the managers involved in the development programme meet together, and each of the manager is asked to diagnose and describe the actual theory in use as revealed by his/her own tape. In the discussion that follows it, a comparison of the espoused theory with the theory actually in use as revealed by the tapes is made. The objective of this exercise is to reveal the difference between the stated belief and actual behaviour, if there is any. In case there is a difference, it is to be reduced by changing either the espoused theory or the theory in use.

Job Knowledge

In addition to decision-making and interpersonal skills, an executive needs to acquire knowledge regarding the actual job he/she is supposed to do. This can be done through the following methods:

1. **On-the-job experience:** Learning by experience is the oldest and an important method of development irrespective of the level an executive belongs to. Interactions with fellow professionals on the job are a major source of motivation as well as information, though experience alone is not sufficient. It needs to be supplemented by other desired things.
2. **Coaching:** This is also an old technique discovered anew. The distinctive feature of this technique is face-to-face counselling. The coach helps by explaining the relevance of information and also in generating alternatives for problems. Coaching also involves teaching by example. The success of coaching depends on the ability of the counsellor and also on the receptivity of the candidate.
3. **Understudy:** In understudy, a certain person is specifically designated as the heir apparent. The executive is expected to train this heir apparent to fill his/her (executive's) place when he/she (executive) may be away for some time or permanently because of business trip, illness, vacation, resignation or any other reason. This brings flexibility and stability in the organisation.

Organisational Knowledge

It is equally important that a trainee must have knowledge about the total organisation—that is, he/she must have exposure to information and events taking place in the entire organisation. This can be had through the following methods:

1. **Position rotation:** The major objective of job rotation training is the broadening of the background of a trainee in the organisation. If an executive is rotated periodically from one job to another job, he/she acquires a general background. The main advantages of this technique are as follows: it provides a general background in all functional areas of the business; training takes place in an actual situation; competition

can be stimulated among the rotating trainees; and so on. However, due to rapid specialisation, this technique has become less effective and less useful.
2. **Multiple management:** It is also known as committee assignment. Under this method, an ad hoc committee or a junior board of directors is constituted and is assigned a subject to discuss and make recommendations. The committee or the junior board has assigned objectives and responsibilities related to the work of the organisation. It will make a study of the problem and present its suggestions to the departmental manager. The committee or the junior board assignment can provide the necessary general background to the members because every member of the committee gets a chance to learn from others. The committee assignment is an important device of educating the executives to acquire general background and to change their behaviour towards the selected problem.

General Knowledge

General knowledge can be acquired considerably through formal educational institutions of various types. But in this regard, the main role is played by the following methods:

1. **Special courses:** It is a popular off-the-job method. The executives may be required to attend special courses which are formally organised by the enterprise with the help of experts from educational institutions. The executives may also be sponsored to attend the courses to be conducted by management institutes and the like. This method is gaining popularity these days. It may be noted that only the big enterprises can send their executives to the management development courses run by management institutes because the fee of these courses is very high.
2. **Special meetings:** This involves one- or two-day meetings or conferences or seminars on special subjects, organised by various associations, institutes, universities and other organisations. In such meetings and conferences, speeches or lectures are delivered by experts followed by questions and discussions. For example, in India, All India Management Association, Indian Society of Labour Economics and so on organise annual conferences where special topics are discussed. Similarly, a large number of universities, IIMs and so on organise many seminars and conferences. In a conference, a group meeting is conducted according to an organised plan in which the members seek to develop knowledge and understanding by obtaining a considerable amount of oral participation. It is an effective training for people in the positions of both conference member and conference leader. As a member, a person can learn from others by comparing his/her opinions with those of others. He/she learns to respect the viewpoints of others and to realise that there is more than one workable approach to any problem. As a conference leader, a person can develop his/her skill to motivate people through his/her direction or discussion. He/she learns the effect of closely controlling and dominating the discussion as compared to adopting a more permissive type of direction. Conferences provide an opportunity for the interchange of information and interaction among personnel of various organisations.

> The conference method overcomes certain disadvantages of the lecture method because here the participants play very active roles. They are not passive. Learning is facilitated through building upon the ideas contributed by the conference members. In fact, people learn from each other. Interest of the participants tends

to be high. The conference is ideally suited to learning problems and issues and examining them from different angles. It is the best method for reducing dogmatism employed in supervisory and executive development programmes.

3. **Selective reading**: Although shortage of time is an often-repeated explanation for not doing selective reading, proper organisation of daily routine task may make some time available for doing selective reading. Many organisations have their own libraries containing very useful books on different functional areas of management. Besides, they subscribe many useful magazines, journals and other periodicals. Top-class executives can be stimulated by an attractive book-reading programme. Some companies in the industrially advanced countries of the West provide their executives four to six weeks' time to read assigned books and thereafter arrange their face-to-face discussion with the authors of these books. Such discussions help in developing greater conceptional ability and broadening the executives' thinking, analytical faculty, and general knowledge and awareness.

Specific Individual Needs

Because of individual differences among the executives, development programmes should be tailored so as to meet the specific need(s) of the individual executive because it is difficult to have a standard development programme to meet specific needs typical to an individual executive. This problem is solved with the help of the following two methods:

1. **Special projects**: This is a very flexible method. Under this method, an executive may be assigned a project that is closely related to the objectives of his/her department and the specific need of the individual executive. For instance, a trainee may be assigned to develop a system of cost control in the execution of an order. The trainee will study the problem and make recommendations upon it. This project would also help in educating the trainee the importance of cost and to understand the organisational relationships with the accounting and other departments. Thus, the trainee acquires the knowledge of allied subjects also.
2. **Committee assignments**: It is also known as multiple management. Under this method, an ad hoc committee is constituted and is assigned a subject to discuss and make recommendations. The committee has assigned objectives and responsibilities related to the work of the organisation. It will make a study of the problem and present its suggestions to the departmental manager. A committee assignment can provide the necessary general background to the trainees because every member of the committee gets a chance to learn from others. It is an important device of educating the executives to acquire general background and to change their behaviour towards the selected problem.

Another way to classify development techniques, as suggested by Ivancevich,[13] is on the basis of the target area they are intended to affect. According to him, there are three major target areas:

1. **Individual**: Techniques involving 'good setting behavioural modification' improve an individual's ability to accomplish goals and use an individual's learning through reinforcement to affect behaviour respectively.
2. **Group**: Team-building techniques focus on the group.

3. **Organisation**: Total quality management (TQM), which is an organisation-wide technique, involves everyone in the organisation in developing and fine-tuning processes that are customer-oriented, flexible and responsive to improving the quality of every activity and functions of the organisation.[14]

Among development programmes, Dessler and Varkkey include succession planning, managerial OJT (job rotation, coaching/understudy approach, action learning), off-the-job management training and development techniques (case study method, management games, outside seminars, university-related programmes, role-playing, behaviour modelling, corporate universities).

These different methods are not mutually exclusive in nature. In fact, the typical programme of an executive development includes a number of methods both of on-the-job methods and off-the-job methods. But unlike training programmes for operatives, the primary emphasis in executive development should be on self-development. Development which occurs on or near the job has the advantages of providing motivation and of being practicable. As regards the question of choosing one method against the other, higher the position in the organisation, the more important become off-the-job methods. The managers are highly educated people, and they can learn soon newer techniques. Method is not important in this respect; the important thing is to realise the need and importance of such development programmes and to provide these facilities. However, in a good number of cases, leadership development programmes are not in keeping with the organisations' strategy (see Exhibit 7.5).

Exhibit 7.5   Lack of Alignment in the Leadership Development Programme and Organisation's Strategy

Forty-one per cent of leadership development programmes are not aligned with their organisation's strategy.

Source: S. C. Saha, 'Facts, Statistics, Practices and Perspectives and More', *Human Capital* 17, no. 11 (April 2014): 34.

Procedure of Executive Development Programme

The main stages involved in an executive development programme are as follows:

1. **Organisation planning**: Organisational development (OD) decides an organisation's present and future needs for different level managers. It also covers the assessment of potentialities of personal development.
2. **Programme targeting**: This is to focus the company's efforts on the most pertinent areas relating to management development.
3. **Ascertaining key positions requirements**: This is to stress the basic requirements of particular managerial positions.
4. **Managerial appraisals**: This is to evaluate periodically the abilities and performance of the individuals concerned, with a view to determining the managers' indicating potential for further development and their training needs. A test named Oi 1.1,

recently developed by Padmakali Banerjee, not only helps in measuring present performance but is also a predictive measure of success.[15] Moreover, based on the analysis of the optimism scores obtained through this test, individuals can be classified into ten categories: collaborator, entrepreneur, energetic, synergist, networker, analyst, innovator, go-getter, expert and leader. This test can be of immense help in determining the type and contents of the executive training and development programme for a particular executive so that both his/her competencies and potential can be utilised for his/her further development.

5. **Replacement of skills inventories**: This indicates people qualified for managerial replacements available from within.
6. **Planning individual development programmes**: It is to provide specific development programmes for promising managers. The top management should realise the fact that managers are also individuals and they differ in respect of their ambitions, desires, knowledge and personality traits. Hence, different types of programmes should be organised for different managers. The programme must be a skilful blend of theory and practice, requiring the use of both educated and practising managers on the faculty.
7. **Appraising the programmes**: This is to ascertain sources of improvement for incorporation in the future programmes. Each programme should be evaluated by the top management in terms of its unity, cost, time and so on.

The essential components of a comprehensive executive development programme may be explained as follows:

1. **Organisation planning**: This step is concerned with ascertaining development needs that calls for organisational planning and forecast of its needs for present and future growth. This is generally based upon a comprehensive programme of job analysis. The management should ascertain well in advance the future course of organisational development, the kind of executives needed and the kind of education, experience, training, special knowledge, skills, personal traits and so on required for each work. Most companies train their own executives except when they experience a critical shortage of specialised high-level talent. In the latter case, executives are hired from outside.
2. **Appraising present management talent**: It is made with a view to determining qualitatively the type of personnel that are available within an organisation itself. The performance of a management individual is compared with the standard expected of him/her. His/her personal traits are also analysed so that a value judgement may be made of his/her potential for advancement.
3. **Managing manpower inventory**: It is prepared for the purpose of getting complete information about each management individual's biodata and educational qualifications, the result of tests and performance appraisals. This information is generally maintained on cards, one for each individual. It may also be maintained on replacement tables or charts. From these, it can be known that several capable executives are available for training for higher positions.
4. **Planning individual's development programmes**: It is undertaken to meet the needs of different individuals, keeping in view the differences in their attitudes and behaviour and in their physical, emotional and intellectual qualities. The weak and strong points of an individual are known from his/her performance appraisal reports, and

on the basis of these, tailor-made programmes are framed and launched. Such programmes give due attention to the interests and goals of the subordinates as well as the training and development opportunities which exist within an organisation.
5. **Establishing training and development programmes**: This job is done by the HR department. A comprehensive and well-conceived programme is generally prepared, containing concentrated brief courses (often called crash programmes). Such courses may be in the field of human relations, time and motion study, creative thinking, memory training, decision-making, leadership courses, and courses in professional and academic institutions, depending on organisational needs and the time and the cost involved.
6. **Evaluating development programmes**: The evaluation of training has been defined by Hamblin as 'any attempt to obtain information (feedback) on the effects of a training programme and to assess the value of training in the light of that information'. According to him, the objectives of evaluating training are assessing the reactions of trainees, job behaviour, improvement in performance, contribution to organisational objectives and so on. The means of evaluating development programmes may include observation, ratings, surveys, interviews and so on.

Dessler has suggested a three-step process for management development: (a) assessing the company's strategic needs, (b) appraising managers' current performance and (c) developing the current and future managers.[16]

Management Training and Development in India

Human capital is of equal importance for industrial development as are the physical and financial resources. The Government of India has recognised this fact and is doing its best to develop the managerial talent in the country. Before independence, nothing was done for management training. In India, most of the industries were managed by managing agents coming from foreign land, and Indians were not given such opportunities. Hence, there was practically no management development in India before independence. It was only after independence that the Indian government paid attention on this subject. A committee was appointed in 1949 for educating in vocational management. It submitted its report in 1953. On its recommendations, All India Technical Education Society was established under the presidentship of Jehangir Gandhi. It had representatives of industry, trade, university, technical institutions, vocational institutes and the government. Its main work was to spread the management education in the country. On the advice of the Estimates Committee of Lok Sabha, a group was sent to America under the leadership of Y. A. Fazalbhai in the year 1959. This nine-member management education team undertook a two-month study tour there.

The members included representatives of seven leading Indian institutions where management training was being imparted, including the IIT Kharagpur, the University of Bombay (now University of Mumbai), the Indian Institute of Social Welfare and Business Management Calcutta (now Kolkata). The team visited[17] universities and 13 industrial organisations to study the techniques relating to management education in the USA. The team also met over 202 leading personalities engaged in training and education in management techniques in the USA. Full-time degree courses in management, including a master's degree, and an intensive management programme in close collaboration between industry and business and the universities were some of the important recommendations of the study team.

The industrial management courses have been started only by IIT Kharagpur. Up to 1960, there was a provision of courses in industrial psychology and industrial relations of one year's duration leading to the MTech degree. Courses in industrial management were also proposed to be started at the remaining three institutes of technology at Bombay, Madras and Kanpur. There is a provision of 20 seats at the Victoria Jubilee Technical Institute, Matunga, Bombay, for the postgraduate diploma in industrial management. The duration of the course is three years. The Indian Institute of Science, Bengaluru, has a provision for ME degree in industrial engineering and industrial administration.

Some short courses in management and in various subjects allied to management are being organised by a number of other institutions, organisations and universities. The universities of Agra, Aligarh, Ujjain, Rajasthan, Gorakhpur, Lucknow and so on provide certain courses in management of a limited nature.

Really speaking, such courses are meant only for familiarising the students of the faculty of commerce with the management studies. The University of Allahabad received a donation a few years back and the University of Bombay received a donation from the family of late Shri Jamuna Lai Bajaj for starting the courses in industrial management. Hence, management institutes have been established by these universities.

But the most important development in India in the field of training in industrial management has just crossed the planning stage. The first All India Institute of Management started functioning at Calcutta from September 1962. The Ford Foundation provided a grant of $434,000 for the institute for a period of two years. This included provision for service of four experts from the Massachusetts Institute of Technology and short-term consultants and also for training abroad of Indian faculty members.

The second IIM was established at Ahmedabad. Both the institutes are autonomous bodies. Boards of governors for them have been constituted. Thereafter, IIMs have been started at Bengaluru, followed by at Lucknow and many other places.

Present Position

In India, at present, there are three kinds of management training facilities, which are as follows:

1. **Full-time management courses**: Such type of management training is being imparted by many universities and institutions. The most popular name of such a course is MBA; its duration is of two years. Besides universities, there are certain all-India-level institutes and a good number of many other management institutes which provide management education.
2. **Refresher and short-term courses**: Such courses are organised for junior-level executives. These are organised by different institutions, such as All India Institutes of Management, Ahmedabad, Calcutta, Bangalore and Lucknow; National Productivity Council; and various professional organisations, which are as follows:

   Institute of Cost and Work Accountants
   Institute of Chartered Accountants
   Institute of Personnel Management
   Institute of Production Engineers
   Textile Research Associations
   All India Management Association

3. **TWI**: In the industry, practical training is imparted by various concerns in both public and private sectors such as DCM, Tata Enterprises, Bata Shoe Co. and Life Insurance Corporation. This system is based on mixed practical experience and training. Among the companies which have developed management training programmes, Hindustan Lever, Tata, DCM, Atlas Cycles and many others deserve special mention. Tata has started Tata Staff College at Pune and Hindustan Lever has started Unilever Training Centre at Bombay.

But if looked from the needs standpoints, these provisions are not sufficient. Although correct estimate for needs is not available in India, still it is hoped that the country will need a large number of trained managers during the coming 20 years. Hence, it requires more efforts as these institutes cannot cope up the demand. Although some universities have done an admirable work in this direction, it is also not enough. More sincere efforts, especially quality-wise, are required in this direction from all concerned. However, talent shortages are hindering leadership efforts of many organisations (see Exhibit 7.6).

Exhibit 7.6   Talent Shortage and Leadership Development Efforts

A global Talent Research survey found that more than 80% of 930 companies surveyed stated that talent shortages were hindering leadership development efforts.

Sources: S. C. Saha, 'Facts, Statistics, Practices and Perspectives and More', *Human Capital* 17, no. 11 (April 2014): 34.

Key Factors for the Success of Executive Development

Although there are several factors that support the success of executive development, there are a few which may be categorised as key factors, which may include (a) intense involvement of top management, (b) a clearly stated executive development philosophy and policy which is well understood by all concerned, (c) direct linkage between 'executive development policies and strategies' and 'business strategies, objectives and challenges' of the organisation, (d) successful executive development processes and (e) executive development as a responsibility of line management.

Executive Development in Global Organisation

It has been observed that there is a high rate of failures when executives are relocated overseas. Hence, it is necessary that employers develop managers for overseas arrangements. Besides other things, first of all, only those candidates should be selected for foreign assignments that are well qualified and possess required experience. They should also be able to adapt themselves to the new culture and environment. They should also be briefed on all relocation policies, be given a realistic preview of what the overseas assignment will entail and, above all, be provided with a suitable mentor who may be able to monitor their overseas careers.

Evaluation of Training and Development Programme

The evaluation step is the last phase of the training and development programme. This step may involve many things such as (a) cost–benefit analysis, (b) participants' (trainees') reaction, (c) behavioural modification, (d) learning by the participants and (e) results—that is, the effect of the programme on organisational dimensions, such as productivity, volume of sales, turnover and so on.

However, this phase is often bypassed by organisations. Also, there are several cases where vigorous evaluation may not illustrate qualitative improvements.

Career Development

Meaning

Through the last chapter and the foregoing pages of the present chapter, you have understood the significance and mechanism of training and development. Now it will be desirable to know about career development which refers to those personal improvements which one undertakes to achieve a personal career plan. Before we discuss about career development, it will be quite in the fitness of things for you to first understand about the following terms which will be used while discussing about career development.

According to Keith Davis, a **career** is all the jobs that are held during one's working life.

Career path: A career path is the sequential pattern of jobs that form a career.

Career planning: Career planning is the process by which one selects career goals and the path to these goals.

Career goals: Career goals are the future positions one strives as a part of career.

Career management: According to French and Bell, career management is the process of designing and implementing goals, plans and strategies to enable the organisation to satisfy employee needs while allowing individuals to achieve their career goals.

Career Today

Perceptions are changing fast. The way people used to views careers decades ago stands changed. The cut-throat competition, economic slowdown, globalisation and so on have led to the phenomena of downsizing, mergers, takeovers, mergers and consolidations, dual-career couples and outsourcing, all of which are responsible for the change of perception of people about careers. Today, in countries like India, most people unlike in the past are not confined to one or a few organisations for their upward movement. They may rather move anywhere to reinvent themselves. They may not only change their organisation but also, if need be, even the trade industry or even their profession. Today, people assure their employers that they will give their best to the organisation but, in return, expect a fast-track career.

Stages in Career Development

Super and Hall have pointed out the following five stages in career development (see Figure 7.2).

1. **Exploration**: The exploratory stage is the period of transition from college to work, that is, the period immediately prior to employment. It is usually the period of one's early 20s and ends by mid-20s. It is a stage of self-exploration and making preliminary choices.
2. **Establishment**: This career stage begins when one starts seeking for work. It includes getting one's first job. Hence, during this stage, one is likely to commit mistakes;

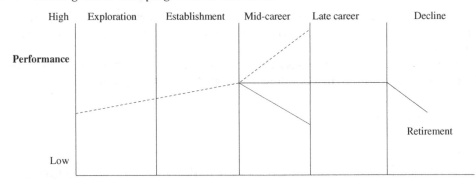

Figure 7.2 Stages in Career Development

one has also the opportunities to learn from such mistakes and may also assume greater responsibilities. He/she accepts job challenges and develops competence in a speculating area. He/she develops creativity and rotates into a new area after three to five years.

3. **Mid-career stage**: During this stage, the performance may increase or decrease or may remain constant. While some employees may reach their goals at the early stage and may achieve greater heights, some may be able just to maintain their performance. While the former may be called 'climbers', the later ones are not very ambitious though competent otherwise. During this stage, an employee tries to update himself/herself technically and develops skills in coaching others. He/she may rotate into a new job requiring new skills.
4. **Late career stage**: This stage is usually a pleasant one because during this stage, the employee neither tries to learn new things nor tries to improve his/her performance over that of previous years. He/she takes advantage of and depends on his/her reputation and enjoys playing the role of an elderly statesperson. He/she may shift from a power role to one of consultation. He/she starts identifying and developing successors and may also start activities outside the organisation.
5. **Decline stage**: Since it is the final stage of one's career, it ends in the retirement of the employee after putting up decades of service full of continuous achievements and success stories. As such, it is viewed as a hard stage.

Career Planning

Of late, it has been observed that organisations are finding it difficult to hold on to their employees as the latter are more concerned for their jobs than for the organisation. There has always been a trend, though in a varying degree, among employees of migrating to green pastures in terms of availing good opportunities. It is partly due to lack of opportunities in terms of occupational advancement, which are clear and easy to measure, in their present organisation. Besides, the employees may also feel stressed due to high demands from their present jobs and, therefore, may like a change of organisation also. Hence, there is a need for career planning, in the process of which the individual and the organisation should play their respective roles.

Career planning is the process that individuals use to assess their opportunities and their strengths and weaknesses and to develop goals and action plans that will move their careers in desired directions. Although career planning is an individual's responsibility, the organisation also can help the individual in this direction.

Let us now discuss the (a) organisational component and (b) individual component in career planning:

1. **Organisational component in career planning**
   An organisation can contribute by doing the following:
   a. Making available to the employee information about potential career opportunities and organisational perceptions of their current readiness or long-term potential to avail themselves of these opportunities.
   b. Having identified career paths, the organisation can provide employees with the tools, equipment and other required materials to enable them to enhance their skills.
   c. Creating a conducive environment for continuous learning.
   d. Rewarding suitably to encourage and motivate them towards their growth.
   e. Providing opportunities and facilities for self-assessment.
   f. Providing mentoring facilities.
   g. Integrating career performance with other HR performances.

2. **Individual component in career planning**
   As stated earlier, career planning is primarily an individual's headache. Therefore, an individual should do the following:
   a. Choose a field of employment.
   b. Collect all relevant information about opportunities finally available at present and also in future.
   c. Assess himself/herself.
   d. Develop himself/herself.
   e. Avail the opportunities.

In case the individual finds lack of opportunities in his/her present organisation and feels that his/her career is blocked or that the organisation is poorly managed or the future of the organisation itself is bleak or the compensation system is not good or that the present job is not likely to fulfil his/her aspirations, he/she can plan his/her exit from the organisation. In that case, he/she should organise his/her exit per his/her convenience. He/she should establish networking relationship while still on the job. He/she should not leave his/her present job until he/she finds another one and, finally, he/she should leave the organisation on good terms.

Process of Career Planning and Development

The various steps included in career planning and development are as follows:

1. Analysing the skills, aptitudes, knowledge, competence and so on of the employee
2. Identifying and analysing the career opportunities available in the organisation as well as outside the organisation

3. Analysing career demands such as skill, knowledge and competence
4. Relating specific jobs to different careers
5. Working out both short-term and long-term goals
6. Working out career strategies in the area of change or adjustment
7. Preparing action plan and acquiring resources
8. Executing the action plan

Steps and Policies in Establishing a Career Development System

A brief description of the steps and tasks involved in establishing a career development system and for which companies formulate policies is as follows:

1. **Needs:** To start with, an attempt is made to define the existing system and establish roles and responsibilities of all the employees including managerial personnel as also of the organisation. Then needs are worked out and target groups are identified. It is also found out that whether the company's policies to support career development programme are assessed. The philosophy of the career development programme is established. Thereafter, criteria of success are established.
2. **Vision:** The company then establishes the vision and objectives of the career development programme and designs interventions for itself as well as for employees and managers. The company then organises and makes the career information available, which is needed to support the programme.
3. **Action plan:** An action plan is formulated so as to achieve the vision. Resources and competencies available are assessed. An advisory group is also constituted and involved in various activities such as designing the programme, implementation, evaluation and monitoring. The company which believes in career development programme is supposed to have a policy of supporting the programme.
4. **Results:** The next step is to integrate the career development programme with the ongoing employee training and development programmes of the organisation. The programme is evaluated and redesigned, if necessary. Future trends and directions for the programme are examined.

Career Development Actions

It is very important that all employees must accept their responsibilities for career development because it is only then that various career development actions prove effective. The main career development actions include the following:

1. Adequate job performance if career progress is desired.
2. Exposure of skills, knowledge, achievements, performance and so on to the decision-makers regarding career development programme.
3. Resignation from the present job if new career opportunities are found elsewhere.
4. Change of jobs in the same of organisation if better opportunities are foreseen in that job. This happens when the employee views organisation loyalty more important than career loyalty.
5. Career guidance is necessary to find better job elsewhere.

Challenges in Career Development

Today, management comes across three major challenges while putting a career development programme in place. These are (a) who will be ultimately responsible for career development activities, (b) how much emphasis on career development is appropriate and (c) how the development needs of a diverse workforce will be met.

Meeting the Challenges of Effective Career Development

Career development which is an ongoing organised and formalised effort that focuses on developing enriched and more capable people at work is a continuing cycle of three phases: (a) In the assessment phase, employees' skills, interests, values and the like are identified either by the employees themselves or by the organisation or by both. (b) The direction phase involves determining the type of career that the employees of the organisation want and the steps they must take to make their career goals a reality. Employees may get individual career counselling or information for a number of sources. And (c) the development phase involves creating and enhancing skills to prepare for future jobs and foster this growth and self-improvement through coaching, monitoring, tuition assistance, job rotation, and so on.

Policies for Effective Career Development

Companies supporting career development programmes usually adopt the following policies so as to make the career development programme effective:

1. Assigning challenging jobs in the very beginning of the career
2. Collection and dissemination of career option information
3. Job positioning
4. Assessment centres
5. Career counselling
6. Career development workshops
7. Periodic job rotation
8. Education and training
9. Mentoring
10. Sabbatical leave
11. Management simulation
12. Sabbatical leave
13. Management simulation

Thinking Strategically About Career Development

Employees need to think strategically for their career growth. The following are the suggestions from some experts on how to set expectations and exploit opportunities to progress towards leadership roles:[18]

1. Have a clear vision
2. Take complete ownership
3. Write a plan

4. Plan for a role
5. Make investments

Practices Adopted by Some Organisations in Career Development

There is no uniform pattern in the practices adopted by organisations in our country in order to promote career development programmes, though the overall objective remains the same. All the same, we come across some similarities also in certain cases.

In the private sector organisations, career development activities are usually conducted for executives on a case-to-case basis and rarely on a group basis. An idea about the practices adopted by organisations in career development programmes in our country can be had from the following examples.

In some private organisations such as L&T, Godrej Soaps Ltd and Batliboi Ltd, career development programmes for executives are much more targeted and performance oriented than in the government organisations. In these three organisations, the career development patterns are almost the same, the reason being that big organisations are continuously looking forward to innovative schemes and borrowing HRD practices from each other. These organisations are conducting training and development programmes mostly in the areas of management behaviour, computer learning, programmes concerning HRD interventions, core development programmes, appreciation programmes and so on.

The procedure usually followed is that the request received by the HRD department from the executive is referred to the head of the department. After receiving the comment from the head of the department concerned, the HRD department decides whether the executive is to be trained and, if yes, in which area. The outcome of the training programme is reviewed from time to time, and changes are made in the contents of the programme according to the requirement of the executive. In other words, it can be said that a career development programme focuses on immediate needs of the executive so as to be helpful in the future growth of the executive. In Batliboi Ltd, there is a little difference. It selects one or two executives from the team and sends them for training and on the completion of their training, they are required to conduct training programme for others.

Due to limited resources earmarked for HRD in most private sector organisations, career development efforts are made very cautiously. Since the general feeling is that the development of the individual takes place primarily through his/her own efforts, the individual should continuously upgrade his/her skills and knowledge and also bring about the desired improvement in his/her behaviour and attitude. The immediate boss should council, coach and advise the executive, delegating some decision-making powers and involving in the process of decision-making and teamwork and team building. The organisation at its own part should support the executive through various techniques such as job rotation, job enrichment and enlargement, training and development and special assignments.

As against private sector organisations, in government and public sectors, promotion usually takes place according to seniority. For example, there are guidelines laid down in the National Training Policy and, therefore, in all the central government services, the same are followed.

In Indian Railways, there are training managers in different zones in different departments who look after training activities which differ from category to category. For example, Group A officers are normally subjected to three types of training programmes: (a) mandatory training, (b) functional training and (c) strategic management courses.

When all is said and done, there is no doubt that career development system is beneficial to both the parties: (a) the employees and (b) the organisation itself. Employees are benefited because they are able to have more realistic goals and expectations; better feedback about their performance; better communication, behavioural and functional skills; and better career decisions. The organisations are also benefited because of the improved skills and understanding of the employees, better communication within the organisation, greater retention of valued employees, greater clarification of organisational goals, increased effectiveness of personnel systems of the organisation and expanded public image of the organisation as a people developer.

Promotion/Advancement

Opportunities for advancement in service are one of the best incentives an organisation can provide to its employees. Practically, in all organisations, there are only a few employees who are always satisfied with their existing jobs. The desire to advance and increase one's status is a basic urge in all human beings. Satisfaction of that desire keeps most people striving for higher status and better pay, which in turn improves their standard of living, morale and job satisfaction. Thus, advancement is one of the best forms of incentives, which generates a sense of loyalty towards the organisation and keeps the employees busy in investing their sincere efforts in the hope of getting further advancement.

Meaning

Advancement within an organisation is ordinarily labelled as 'promotions'.[19] In general usage, promotion means the change to a higher job accompanied by increased pay privileges. In the words of Pigors and Myres, 'Promotion is the advancement of an employee to a better job—better in terms of greater responsibilities, more prestige or "status", greater skill, and specially, increase rate of pay or salary'.[20]

According to Flippo, 'Promotion involves a change from one job to another that is better in terms of status and responsibilities'.[21]

Thus, from the aforesaid definitions, it is clear that promotion involves the following three basic elements:

1. Better job and status
2. Greater responsibilities
3. Increase in pay and perks

However, all promotions do not possess all the aforesaid characteristics, for example, there may be no increase in pay in a promotion. Sometimes it may happen that the promotion may be a 'dry promotion'. A dry promotion refers to an increase in responsibility and status without an increase in pay. A company may have a formal as well as an informal promotion system, an open or a closed promotional system and so on. Promotion is distinguishable from transfer also in the sense that the latter refers to changes in jobs that involves little or no change in status, responsibility and pay.

Promotion Policy

Promotion from within is a very good policy. It is useful for both employees and organisation. Every organisation, therefore, needs a formal and systematic programme of promotion. The promotion programme can be said to be a promotional policy. A sound promotion policy should be invariably based on merit, but seniority should also be taken into consideration. In addition to the relative emphasis on merit and seniority, there are certain other elements which must be duly incorporated in a sound promotion policy. These other elements are as follows:

1. A statement of management's intention regarding filling up of vacancies of superior type either from within the organisation (i.e. by promotion) or by hiring from outside the organisation, or from both. This statement, if to be of some worth, must be faithfully followed.
2. An open job bidding system should be used to encourage internal mobility. This will encourage to permit capable employees to go for better jobs available elsewhere. If a good employee is held back, he/she is likely to remain a frustrated and dissatisfied employee.
3. A promotion policy should charter lines of progression ladders of promotion within the organisation.
4. A promotion policy should make a provision for use of job analysis to develop a chart showing the basic requirements of a job in terms of competency, experience, formal education and so on. Employees need to know what is expected on higher-rated jobs to prepare themselves for advancement.
5. To ensure check on the unfairness of promotions, the supervisor should propose promotions, which should then be subject to approval by the immediate boss in the line organisation.
6. A sound promotion policy should explicitly incorporate the provision of training for an employee falling within the promotion zone.
7. A sound promotion policy should make a provision for an employee or a union to challenge a particular promotion as made within the union agreement.
8. A sound promotion policy should not aim at forcing promotions of reluctant employees.

Benefits of a Promotion Policy

The formation of a formal and sound promotion policy in any organisation offers the following advantages:

1. It develops employees' loyalty by assuring their promotion within the organisation.
2. It increases job satisfaction and improves their morale.
3. It attracts good and efficient employees from outside also, if there is a provision for such an arrangement.
4. The policy of promotion from within is economical for organisation also.
5. It increases the effectiveness of the organisation too.
6. A sound and well-organised promotion policy, if followed in a non-partial manner, removes the chances of subjectivity in promotional decisions.
7. The efficiency of the employee and production of the organisation also go up.

Executive Development and Training 251

Bases of Promotion

There are two important bases of promotion: merit and seniority.

There has been a great controversy with regard to the question that whether the promotions should be based on merit, that is, qualifications and competence of the employee, or on his/her seniority.

Promotion on the Basis of Sincerity

Seniority is based on the total length of service of an employee and is counted from the date of his/her appointment in the organisation. The workers and their unions prefer 'seniority' as the basis for promotion, while the management prefers 'merit or competence'. Before reaching on a final conclusion, we must evaluate the respective merits and demerits of these bases.

Advantages of Seniority as a Basis of Promotion

Seniority is the oldest and most widely used basis of promotion. It has the following advantages:

1. In business and industrial undertakings, the system has been adopted with a view to patronise the employees.
2. Utilisation of seniority in making various employment decisions brings an objective means of distinguishing among personnel.
3. Seniority as the basis of promotion creates a sense of security in employees, for they can predict in advance when and how certain changes will be effected.
4. Seniority as a means of employment decisions creates more peace in the organisation for these decisions are always made strictly on the basis of seniority acceptable to all. This will keep employees satisfied and help in avoiding the charges of bias, favouritism and nepotism.
5. Seniority as a basis of promotion is also acceptable to management because it reduces the rate of labour turnover. Employees will remain within an organisation even when they are aware of better opportunities elsewhere, the reason being the loss of seniority resulting from quitting.

Disadvantages of Seniority as a Basis of Promotion

Although the aforementioned positive points usually establish a case, especially in unionised firms, to give more weightage to seniority in making promotions because workers attach great importance to length of service, this is not the whole truth because there are several reasons against the use of seniority, particularly when it becomes the sole base of decision-making. It has the following main disadvantages:

1. Seniority often ignores merit or ability because the employee with the longest service need not necessarily be the most competent.
2. It overvalues experience. If workers automatically qualify for better jobs by accumulating seniority, then it will bring no incentive to new employees to improve their performance.

3. It may enhance the rate of labour turnover. It may drive the ambitious and able man, with little service, out of the firm.
4. A rigid seniority system places a considerable burden on the hiring process. It makes extremely difficult to attract and recruit capable new personnel unless they are placed in the exempt category.
5. Since seniority places no premium on the merit of the employee; therefore, it fails to differentiate between efficient and inefficient employees.

Promotion on the Basis of Merit

If a promotion is given to an employee on the basis of his/her qualification, competence, ability or performance, ignoring his/her less seniority in the organisation, the promotion is called on the basis of merit. Merit-based promotion is, as a matter of fact, an incentive for excellent performance regardless of age or seniority. Management always favours promotions on the basis of merit and ability.

Advantages of Merit System

The following are the benefits from the promotion by merit system:

1. It recognises and rewards extra knowledge, competence and initiative of the employees. Even juniors can expect promotions.
2. It generates greater motivation in the competent employees as they do not have to depend on mere seniority for their advancement.
3. Competent employees are likely to be retained instead of being lost to the organisation.
4. It generally results in increased productivity as promotions will be based on an evaluation of the employee's performance.
5. It is a scientific and logical system for promotions. Managements prefer this system as it increases the efficiency and profitability of the enterprise.

We have discussed the relative advantages and disadvantages of seniority vs merit as the basis of promotion and we reach the conclusion that seniority or merit alone as a basis of promotion policy is inadequate. A sound promotion policy should be based on both seniority and merit. Although it is a general tendency in private sector enterprises to weigh merit more, seniority is given more weightage in government services and public undertakings. Hence, the best way is the mid-way, that is, a blend of these two should be used.

Transfer

Meaning

Transfers and promotions are the two important ways of personnel adjustments. When employees are transferred without any promotion or demotion, it is simply a transfer. In transfer, there is no material change in the status, responsibilities or pay of the employee. Although promotion and transfer may involve a change in the place of the employee, their objectives are different. The main aim of promotion is to fill a job from within the organisation, while the aim of a transfer is to make adjustment in the workplace and the employee. But both can do much for the morale of employees.

Transfer is a process of placing employees in positions where they are likely to be more effective or where they are likely to get more job satisfaction. Thus, transfer is a process of employee's adjustment with the work, time and place. In transfers, there is no material change in responsibility, designation or pay. For example, if a marketing manager finds the sales of north zone falling continuously, he/she may transfer some salespersons from other zones to the north zone in order to improve the situation as those salespersons are considered to be more experienced and trained in sales promotion. Sometimes transfer may be made as a disciplinary action also. In some organisations, it is a usual practice to transfer employees from one zone to another zone due to administrative reasons as in government services.

Types of Transfer

Transfers may be of different types depending on the purposes. Their main types are as follows:

1. **Production transfers**: These transfers are made from one department to another where labour requirements are reduced or increased or vacancies have been created due to partition. Such production transfers are also made to prevent lay-offs. It is not desirable to have in the same organisation lay-offs on one job and employees being in need in another department for a similar type of work. In this way, production transfers, at about the same occupational level, help to stabilise employment in an organisation and hence need some form of centralised control through the personnel department. Sometimes production transfers may involve downgrading. They should be prevented if possible.
2. **Replacement transfers**: These are similar to production transfers. These are used to replace a new employee with an employee who has been in the concern for a long time for a variety of reasons.
3. **Shift transfers**: Here, an employee is shifted from one shift to another on the same work. Workers dislike a second shift assignment as it affects their participation in community life. To minimise this, shift transfers are introduced.
4. **Remedial transfers**: These transfers are made to remedy the situation. If the initial placement has been faulty, or the worker cannot get along with his/her supervisor, then a transfer to a more appropriate job or a more agreeable supervisor might result in better performance.
5. **Versatility transfers**: It means to increase the versatility of the employee by shifting him/her from one job to another. In this way, the employee is given a varied and broader job experience. This helps the employee through job enrichment and enlargement. It can also help him/her get prepared for future promotion.

Objectives of Transfers

The following are some of the objectives of a transfer in a company:

1. To meet the exigencies of the company's business.
2. To meet the request of an employee.
3. To correct incompatibilities of employee relations.
4. To suit the age and health of an employee.

5. To provide creative opportunities to deserving employees.
6. To train the employee for later advancement and promotion. This involves actually job rotation.
7. To deal with fluctuations in work requirements or exigencies at work, such as situations when there is slackness in the work in one department and an overload of work in another; an employee from the first department may be temporarily transferred to the other department as found necessary.
8. To correct erroneous placement.
9. To place the employee in another department where he/she would be more suitable.

Transfer Policy

Every organisation must frame a systematic and sound transfer policy. It must be clear and unambiguous. It must be in writing and should give the following facts:

1. It must clarify the types and circumstances under which transfers will be made.
2. It should indicate who will be responsible for initiating and approving the transfers. For example, will this be the responsibility of the first-level supervisor alone, or should transfers be subjected to review by his/her immediate superior or the personnel managers?
3. It should prescribe whether the transfer can be made only within a subunit or also between departments, divisions and plants.
4. It should prescribe whether when an employee is transferred, his/her previous seniority will be restored or be affected.
5. It should indicate the basis for transfers. For example, where two people desire transfer to the same shift, would seniority be the main determining factor, or would skill and competence be the deciding criteria?
6. It should also point out the rate of pay the person involved should get when transferred.
7. It should provide for timely communication of the transfer decision.
8. Transfers should never be used as a tool for victimising the employee, though, sometimes, they may be remedial.
9. Sometimes, group transfers may be necessitated. In such circumstances, the workers' unions must be taken into confidence.
10. The type of expenses which will be reimbursed to the transferee when he/she is transferred.

Chapter Review

1. All managers need development, which is an ongoing process. Management/executive development is any attempt to improve managerial performance by imparting knowledge, increasing skills and changing attitude.
2. Technological and social changes, significance of professionally trained managers, research orientation, recognition of social responsibilities, labour problems, increased size and complexities of modern organisations, and so on emphasise the need and importance of management training and development in Indian organisations.

3. An executive development programme should be thoughtfully developed so that it may develop the desired skills and knowledge of the executives. It should also follow the principles of executive development.
4. Executives have various types of development needs such as (a) decision-making skills, which can be developed by in-basket, business games, case studies and so on; (b) interpersonal skills, which can be developed by sensitivity training, role-playing, structured insight and so on; (c) job knowledge, which can be increased through on-the-job experience, coaching, understudy and so on; (d) organisational knowledge, which can be increased by job rotation, multiple management and so on; (e) general knowledge, which can be increased through special courses, special meetings and selective readings; and (f) special individual needs, which can be met through special projects and committee assignments.
5. The procedure of executive development comprises organisational planning, programme targeting, ascertaining key position requirements, managerial appraisals, replacement of skill inventories, planning individual development programmes and appraising the programmes.
6. Before independence of the country, nothing was done for management training and development in India. But after independence, a lot of steps, such as establishment of management institutes, universities, IITs and IIMs imparting courses in management studies, have been taken to promote management training and development. The present position is that there are (a) full-time management courses (such as MBA and PGDBM) being taught at IIMs, IITs, universities and many other institutes, (b) refreshers and short-term courses being undertaken by professional bodies/association and (c) TWI.
7. Career development refers to those personal improvements one undertakes to achieve a personal career plan. There are five stages in career development: exploration, establishment, mid-stage, later career stage and decline stage. In order to meet their career growth, managers undertake career planning.
8. Career planning is the process that individuals use to assess their opportunities, strengths and weaknesses and to develop goals and action plans that will move their careers in desired directions. Career planning has two components: organisational component and individual component. The process of career planning includes analysing the skills, aptitude, knowledge, competence and so on; identifying and analysing the career demands; relating specific jobs to different careers; working out goals and career strategies; preparing an action plan and acquiring resources; and executing the action plan.
9. Steps and tasks involved in establishing a career development system include working out the needs, carrying out the visions and objectives of the career development programme, formulating an action plan, evaluating the results and taking remedial steps.
10. While putting a career development programme in place, there are three major challenges: who will ultimately be responsible for career development activities, how much emphasis on career development is appropriate and how the development needs of a diverse workforce will be met.

11. Promotion/advancement involves a change to a higher job, accompanied by higher status and increased salary and perks. Every organisation should have a well-thought-out, properly crafted, transparent and jointly formulated in consultation with workers' union(s) promotion policy. A promotion policy is beneficial to both the employees and the organisation. Promotions can be based on seniority or merit or a combination of both. All the three have their own advantages and disadvantages. Promotions are also helpful in filling certain vacant positions.
12. Transfers which involve a change but with no modification either in the status or salary and perks may also be helpful in filling some vacant positions. Transfers may be production transfers, replacement transfers, shift transfers, remedial transfers, versatility transfers and the like. A transfer policy in an organisation should preferably be formulated in consultation with the union and should be transparent and well communicated.

Key Terms

assessment centres
behavioural modification
business games
career
career counselling
career development
career development workshops
career goals
career management
career path
career planning
career strategy
case studies
coaching
committee assignments
decline stage
development
dry promotion
establishment
exploration
functional training
in-basket
individual component in career planning
late career stage
management manpower inventory
management simulation
mandatory training

mentoring
mid-career stage
multiple management
on-the-job experience
organisational component in career planning
organisational planning
position rotation
production transfer
programme targeting
remedial transfer
replacement transfers
role-play
sabbatical leave
selective readings
self-development
self-motivation
sensitivity training
shift transfer
skill inventories
strategic management courses
structured insight
total quality management (TQM)
training
training within industry
understudy
versatility transfer

Discussion Questions

1. Discuss the difference between 'training' and 'development'.
2. Discuss how executive development is useful for both the executives and the organisation.
3. Discuss what should be the contents of an ideal executive development programme and which principles are followed in the formulation and execution of such a programme.
4. Discuss what development needs are required by an executive position and how such needs can be developed. Discuss in the context of methods/techniques used for executive development.
5. Discuss the procedure of executive development programme.
6. Discuss the status of executive training and development in India.
7. Discuss the key factors responsible for the success of executive development.
8. Discuss the importance of career development and stages involved in career development.
9. Discuss what career planning is, with special reference to organisational component involved in it.
10. Discuss the challenges in career development and how these can be met.
11. Discuss the bases of promotion and their advantages and disadvantages to the employees.
12. Discuss the objectives of transfers and features of a good transfer policy.

Individual and Group Activities

1. In a group of two members, visit some big manufacturing organisation and find out from HR officials what methods/techniques they adopt to meet development needs required by executive positions.
2. As an individual, discuss with the HR officials of any well-established service organisation whether they follow principles of executive development.
3. In a group of three members, visit a big organisation and discuss with the officials concerned how they evaluate the executive training and development programme.
4. Visit a big organisation as an individual and find out the steps being taken there for career development. Prepare a brief report about the same.
5. As an individual, discuss with the HR officials of any well-established organisation the challenges they are visualising in the realm of career development.
6. Working in two groups of three members each, arrange a visit to a large manufacturing organisation by one group and of a service organisation by the other group. Both the groups should discuss the promotion policies of the respective organisations with some senior workers who have put in at least ten years' service in their organisation. Both the groups should prepare their reports of the highlights of the promotion policy of the organisation they visited and then compare and contrast their reports.

7. Working individually or in groups, contact a few employees of a big organisation and discuss the transfer policy of their organisation. Get feedback from them and prepare a brief report.

Application Case 7.1

Evaluation of Executive Development Programmes

Smith is the MD of a company dealing in sales and distribution of a few consumer goods. The company had a good reputation and had a 10% market share in the country until three years back, since when the company's revenue has been reflecting a decreasing trend. Despite all-out efforts of Smith to improve the health of the company, he has not been able to turn the tables of the lot of the company. About a year back, at the insistence of Smith, the company invested a substantial amount on the development programmes meant for its managers/executives so as to improve their job skills and decision-making skills.

The company was expecting good outcome because of improvement in the quality and contents of management development programmes. However, the results at the end of the year were not different from that of the previous year.

Distressed because of the prevalent situation, Smith contacted a leading consultant firm, well known for conducting quality executive development programmes. The consulting firm desired to have an audit of the development programmes and activities conducted during the last year. It deputed its team of two experts and requested Smith to spare one of his experienced senior executives to assist the expert team deputed by the consulting firm. Now it became a three-member team.

The expert team conducted a thorough evaluation of the executive development programmes and activities undertaken during the last year and, after an exercise of 15 days, came to the conclusion that none of the executive development programmes and activities focused on developing interpersonal skills, which are of utmost importance in the case of a sales and distribution company engaged in the business of consumer goods.

Questions

1. What was wrong with the company that it could not detect the absence of focus on developing interpersonal skills in its development programmes conducted during the last year?
2. Do you think that the evaluation of executive development programmes should be a regular exercise? Yes or no? Why? Give reasons.
3. Should the company replace its existing HR official responsible for looking after executive development programmes? Yes or no? Why? Give arguments.

Application Case 7.2

2012 LLR 1038
PUNJAB & HARYANA HIGH COURT
Hon'ble Mr Rajesh Bindal, J.
C.W.P. No. 15253/2012 (O&M), D/-9-8-2012
Vijay Kumar Wadhwa
vs
Life Insurance Corporation & Others

Important Points

*Transfer of an employee from one place to another cannot be stalled by the Court on the grounds of personal difficulties including illness as it is an incident of service.
*Mere distance is no ground to stall the transfer.

JUDGEMENT
RAJESH BINDAL J.

1. Challenge in the present petition is to the transfer of the petitioner from Branch Office, Ferozepur to Satellite Office, Patti.
2. The petitioner is working as an assistant administrative officer with Life Insurance Corporation of India. Earlier the petitioner had filed C.W.P. No. 11427 of 2012—Vijay Kumar Wadhwa v. Life Insurance Corporation of India in this court impugning the aforesaid order of transfer raising a plea that on account of illness, he may not be transferred to a far-off place. The writ petition was disposed of by this court on 1 June 2012 with a direction to the respondent therein for consideration of the representation of the petitioner. The representation of the petitioner was considered and the same was rejected vide order dated 16 July 2012 mentioning therein that transfers are general in nature as 36 other officers along with the petitioner have been transferred. There was allegation of sexual harassment to one Ms Paramjit Kaur on 25 November 2011, for which the petitioner had even appeared before the Women Committee formed at Divisional Office level at Amritsar on 27 February 2012. It is further noted in the aforesaid order that no medical report from 2009 onwards was submitted by the petitioner regarding his ill-health. Though the petitioner was relieved from Branch Office, Ferozepur, on 16 January 2012, but till date he has not joined at new place of posting despite repeated communications to him.
3. Learned counsel for the petitioner submitted that the petitioner being ill should have been transferred to a place close to Branch Office, Ferozepur, so that his family could be along with him.
4. After hearing learned counsel for the petitioner, I do not find any merit in the submission made. Transfer is a condition of service. The petitioner has been transferred from Branch Office, Ferozepur, to Satellite Office, Patti. Mere distance does not matter. It has been mentioned in the order passed after the earlier

writ petition was filed by the petitioner that from 2009 onwards, the petitioner has not placed before the authorities any record to show his ill-health.
5. Considering the aforesaid facts, I do not find any merit in the present petition. Accordingly, the same is dismissed.

Questions

1. Do you approve of the judgement dismissing the writ petition? Yes or no? Why?
2. Do you think that medical illness of the petitioner should have been given some weightage while considering his transfer from Ferozepur to Patti? Yes or no? Why? Give arguments.

Notes

1. Jucius, *Personnel Management*, 243.
2. Dessler and Varkkey, *Human Resource Management*, 313.
3. W. Fitzgerald, 'Training versus Development', *Training and Development* 46, no. 5 (1992): 81–84.
4. Flippo, *Principles of Personnel Management*, 225.
5. Dessler and Varkkey, *Human Resource Management*, 313.
6. Jucius, *Personnel Management*, 244.
7. Gomez-Mejia, Balkin, and Cardy, *Managing Human Resources*, 260.
8. Ibid.
9. Jucius, *Personnel Management*, 255–56.
10. Ibid., 256.
11. See Jucius, *Personnel Management*, 256–57.
12. For details, see Flippo, *Principles of Personnel Management*, 227–40.
13. See Ivancevich, *Human Resource Management*, 419–28.
14. See E. E. Lawler, S. A. Mohrman, and G. Benson, *Organising for High Performance* (New York, NY: John Wiley, 2001).
15. Dessler and Varkkey, *Human Resource Management*, 313.
16. For details, see Gomez-Mejia, Balkin, and Cardy, *Managing Human Resources*, 303–13.
17. For details, see *The Economic Times*, 7 April 2017.
18. Flippo, *Principles of Personnel Management*, 246.
19. Pigors and Myers, *Personnel Administration*, 308.
20. Flippo, *Principles of Personnel Management*, 248.
21. Ibid.

Part IV
Compensation and Reward Management

8 Performance Appraisal and Potential Appraisal

Learning Objectives

After studying this chapter, you should be able to do the following:

1. Define the term 'performance appraisal' and point out the objectives and importance of performance appraisal.
2. Define the term 'merit rating' and distinguish it from 'performance appraisal'.
3. List and describe the main methods of performance appraisal.
4. Explain the characteristics of a sound appraisal plan as well as the constraints of appraisal system.
5. Describe the concept of MBO.
6. Differentiate between 'performance appraisal' and 'performance management'.
7. Describe the process of performance appraisal and problems involved in appraising performance.
8. Explain the concept of appraisal interview.
9. Describe the concept of potential appraisal and also explain the methods of potential appraisal.
10. Describe the importance of potential appraisal.

Performance Appraisal

Introduction

After selection, training and development of employees and they being on job for some time, it is essential to appraise their performance which will give a fairly good idea about the effectiveness of the processes of selection, training and development undertaken by the organisation. The outcome of performance appraisal also indicates whether the organisation is going in the right direction or not.

It is perhaps for this reason that Edwin B. Flippo has rightly remarked,

> No firm has a choice whether or not it should appraise its personnel and their performance. Just as training must and does take place after hiring, it is inevitable that the performance of the hired personnel will be evaluated by someone at some time. The choice is one of method.[1]

The performance appraisal is very important in planning for an employee's development and in assessing his/her relative worth and merits. It is, as a matter of fact, an assessment of the employee which helps the management in finding out whether the selection of a particular employee was justified or not or whether he/she has been given just promotion or not and so on. Although the candidate's appraisal at the time of selection is a must and it serves many useful purposes, still performance appraisal on a continuing basis during the working life of such an employee is also desirable and useful. Although the appraisal of various employees is continuously done at an unconscious level—for example, employees evaluate their supervisors, fellow colleagues and subordinates also—here we are concerned with the periodic and systematic evaluation of an employees' performance which is done by the management in case of its employees at all levels.

Meaning and Definition of Performance Appraisal

Appraisal is the evaluation of worth and quality of merit. Appraisal should measure both performance in accomplishing goals and plans and performance as a manager. It is the evaluation of present performance and future capabilities.

Alford and Beatty have defined it as the evaluation or appraisal of the relative worth to the company of a person's services on his/her job.

As a matter of fact, performance appraisal is a systematic, a periodic and, as far as humanly possible, an impartial rating of an employee's excellence in matters pertaining to his/her present job and to potentialities for a better job.

Performance appraisal is a continuous activity. The management should plan it in a systematic and orderly manner. It must be conducted by some trained and experienced experts. If organised and operated carefully, it eliminates the chances of personal prejudices and subjectivity in the appraisal. Systematic appraisals are instrumental in boosting the morale of the employees as well as enabling them to know where they stand.

Difference Between 'Performance Appraisal' and 'Merit Rating'

Some people confuse performance appraisal with that of merit rating. Many use these two terms interchangeably. But these two are basically different. While in merit rating, an employee's internal merits and qualities such as his/her nature and bodily and mental abilities are studied, in performance appraisal, evaluation is made of quantitative factors based on production quantity and quality, quantity of accepted and unaccepted job, strata of work and so on. Thus, in merit rating, the stress is on 'what he/she is', while in performance appraisal, the emphasis is on 'what he/she does and what potentiality he/she possesses'.

The term 'merit rating' is designated by a variety of terms. Sometimes it is called 'efficiency rating', 'proficiency rating', 'service appraisal' and so on. But none of these has achieved so much popularity as 'performance appraisal'. The term 'rating' denotes the idea of some type of classification according to grade, rank or class. Thus, 'merit rating' is a system for discovering, analysing and classifying the differences among employees vis-à-vis job standards. Merit rating system, being a scientific tool to assess individual abilities of workers, forces their observations as conceived by the supervisor in a systematic manner with a view to bringing out differences among workers. Such an assessment is very useful in many HR decisions.

According to Ivancevich,[2] the potential purposes of evaluation of performance include development of the employees, motivating the employees, helping in HRP and employment planning, facilitating communication between superior and subordinates, legal compliance by way of legally defensible reason for promotions, transfer, dismissal and so on and HRM research.

Performance Appraisal vs Performance Management

While 'performance management' is a process that consolidates goal settings, performance appraisal and development into a single common system to ensure that the employee's performance is supporting the aims of the organisation, 'performance appraisal' is just a part of performance management, which is a process of evaluating an employee's current (and/or) past performance vis-à-vis his/her performance standards.

Why Appraise Performance?

Dessler and Varkkey[3] have suggested four reasons in favour of appraising subordinates' performance:

1. Most employers still base their pay and promotional decisions on the employees' appraisal.
2. Performance appraisal plays an integral role in the employer's performance management.
3. Performance appraisal lets the boss and the subordinate develop a plan for correcting any deficiency.
4. Appraisal serves a useful career planning purpose.

Importance of Performance Appraisal

The appraisal of performance is expected to provide answers to many of the questions in the management of people in the organisation. The people who make up a working organisation are evaluated for many reasons. Individually, managements may give different priorities to the purposes of performance appraisal, and their priorities may vary from time to time. A performance appraisal may serve the following objectives in the organisation:

1. A systematic performance appraisal provides information of great assistance in making and enforcing decisions about such subjects as promotions, pay increases, lay-offs and transfers. A research study has disclosed that performance appraisal is used for promotion in 73% cases, salary adjustment in 69% cases, deciding upon discharges in 46% cases and determining lay-off in 27% cases. Performance appraisal provides information in advance of time when it may be needed, thereby avoiding spot judgements when a decision must be made. Moreover, the systematic approach provides the information in a form that permits the making of comparisons.
2. A systematic performance appraisal serves to guide employee development. Today, more people like to know how they are doing. Appraisal programme provides this information which can be communicated to employees. Weaknesses of the employees revealed through the appraisal process can be removed through organising training

and development programmes. Thus, this provides opportunities of assessing an employee's training needs in the organisation.
3. Performance appraisal puts a psychological pressure on people to improve performance on the job. If the people are conscious that they are being appraised in respect of certain factors and their future largely depends on such appraisal, then they tend to present positive and acceptable behaviour. Thus, the appraisal automatically works as a control device.
4. Appraisal also serves to maintain fair relationships in group.

Thus, it is necessary for tactical and strategic planning, motivation, communication and equity.

Objectives of Performance Appraisal

Broadly speaking, there are twin objectives of performance appraisal: judgemental, that is, to judge or evaluate what the worker has done and what are his/her potentialities, and developmental, that is, to keep his/her performance and potentialities in view and formulate the plans for the development of the worker (see Figure 8.1).

However, broadly speaking, the objectives of performance appraisal are as follows:

1. To measure and improve the job performance of an employee and to identify his/her potentialities for other work.
2. To identify the need and areas for further training and development of the employees.
3. To reduce the grievances among the employees.
4. To make the compensation plans more scientific and rational.
5. To help in the proper placement of the workers after the completion of their training and probation.

Process of Performance Appraisal

Dessler and Varkkey[4] include three steps in the performance appraisal: (a) defining the job, (b) appraising performance and (c) providing feedback.

Establishing Evaluation Criteria

The dimensions of performance upon which an employee is evaluated are called the criterion of evaluation.[5] According to Ivancevich, an effective criterion of evaluation should

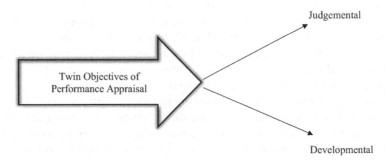

Figure 8.1 Objectives of Performance Appraisal

Performance Appraisal and Potential Appraisal

possess the characteristics such as reliability, relevance, sensitivity and practicality.[6] Only then and then alone the appraisal can be meaningful.

Who Should Appraise?

There are several options for appraising the performance of an employee such as immediate supervisor, peer appraisals, rating committees, self-rating, subordinates and 360-degree feedback.

Appraisal can be done by any of these or a combination of two or more.

Appraisal Interview

In an appraisal interview, the supervisor and subordinates review the appraisal and chalk out plans to overcome deficiencies and reinforce strengths. The following types of appraisal interview are more popular:

First is the unsatisfactory–uncorrectable: If the performance of the employee is unsatisfactory and the situation is uncorrectable, then there is no point in formulating a plan for him/her. Either his/her services can be terminated or he/she can be tolerated for the time being.

Second is the unsatisfactory–correctable: In such a case, a plan can be formulated for correcting the unsatisfactory performance.

The third is the satisfactory–not promotable: In such a case, steps should be taken that the employee maintains his/her performance. For this, steps such as enlargement of job, appreciation and a few incentives can be undertaken.

The fourth is satisfactory–promotable: In such a case, a specific action plan for the professional development of the employee concerned should be formulated, keeping in view, of course, the career plans of the employee.

While conducting an appraisal interview, an all-out effort should be made to let the employee speak the most. He/she should be encouraged to reveal more about himself/herself. Open-ended questions by the interviewer can be of great use in this direction. Queries and conversation should be direct and specific and not beating about the bush, for example, productivity records. The interviewer should also ensure that he/she does not get personal. For example, instead of comparing the employee's performance to that of other employees, it should be compared to the standards laid for the purpose. All the same, it should be ensured that at the end, the interviewee (appraisee) understands where he/she has gone wrong and how things will be better and within which time framework.

Appraisal Methods/Evaluation Techniques

When it comes to appraising the performance, there are two basic issues: (a) what to measure—usually, it is the quantity, quality and timeliness of work, but it is also desirable to measure performance with respect to developing one's competence or accomplishing the targets—and (b) how to measure—there are several ways to evaluate employees' performance/methodologies, but for the sake of convenience, these may be divided into three categories, as shown in Figure 8.2.

Casual, Unsystematic and Often Haphazard Appraisal

It is an old and very common approach, but of late, it is being replaced by the systematic and MBO approaches. Casual appraisal is more common among small organisations.

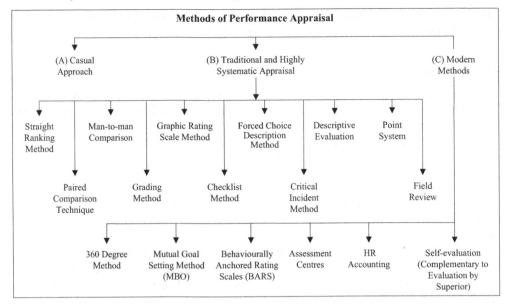

Figure 8.2 Methods of Performance Appraisal

Casual appraisal does not evaluate all performances in the same manner using the same approach. As a result, ratings obtained of separate personnel are not comparable. This approach lays more emphasis on the evaluation of the employee's worth as a person. In this approach, there is always a scope for human bias and prejudice. Besides, in this system appraisal is not made regularly after a fixed period.

Traditional and Highly Systematic Appraisal

Various studies have revealed that an increasing number of firms are opting for some formal type of appraisal. When formal programmes of appraisal are utilised, most organisations use one of the many traditional and systematic methods of appraisal. In a systematic appraisal, performance of all the employees of a particular category is evaluated in the same manner using the same approach so that the ratings obtained of separate personnel are comparable. The systematic appraisals are made at regular periodical intervals according to a predetermined plan. In a systematic appraisal, evaluation is made of what the person does rather than what he/she is.

Systematic performance appraisal is of great value in as much as it provides very useful and well-in-time information needed for making decisions at the time of promotions, transfers, pay increases and so on. Besides, it also provides the information in a form that permits the making of comparisons because all personnel have been appraised in the same manner using the same approach.

There are various traditional performance appraisal systems used by different organisations. The important ones are as follows.

Straight Ranking Method[7]

This is the simplest and oldest method of performance appraisal. Here, an employee is not treated separately from his/her job. One person is compared with all others for the purpose of placing them in a simple rank order of worth. In this way, all the employees are placed in order of their relative worth. Thus, this method separates the efficient from inefficient. However, this method suffers from several inherent defects. First, it does not appear to be desirable to compare one person with another because different people have different traits and qualities. Second, this method simply tells us who is better than the other, but it does not indicate how much better he/she is than the other. Third, this method may be used only in the case of small organisations. If a company employs several employees, then it may not be possible to rank all of them in order of their worth. Fourth, this system is based on snap judgement and does not have any systematic procedure to determine the relative worth of an employee. Hence, in order to overcome the defects of this system, the paired comparison method has been developed.

Paired Comparison Technique

Per this method, each employee is compared with every other employee of the organisation, one at a time. Suppose there are six employees in a particular firm. First, A's performance is compared with B's and a decision is taken as to whose performance is better. Then A is compared with C, D, E and F in order. Then, the next employee B will be compared with all other employees individually, and in the same way C, D, E and F will also be compared one by one with all other employees. Thus, in all, 15 decisions would be taken, involving only 2 employees in each decision. The number of decisions is determined by the following formula:[8]

$$\text{Number of comparisons} = \frac{N(N-1)}{2}$$

where N equals the number of personnel to be compared. The result of these comparisons can be tabulated, and in this way a rank can be created from the number of times each employee is found better.

This method of performance appraisal is also not practicable in the case of big organisations where several employees are engaged because in such cases, the number of judgements to be made becomes too large.

Man-to-man Comparison

In this method, for appraisal, more variables are ascertained, such as leadership, qualifications and faithfulness. After this, for each variable, a master scale is prepared in which for execution of each job, strata are maintained according to qualities. For that work, the most efficient person and the least efficient person are selected. These people are the two ends of the scale. After that, at a medium point, an average person is selected. Later, the two points are marked below and over the average. In this way, five points are ascertained. Comparing these points, a person's qualities are known. Thus, in this method, instead of comparing 'whole people' to 'whole people', personnel are compared to 'key people', one factor at a time. In performance appraisal, though this method is used to know the qualified person by the comparison of variables, the preparation of master scale is a difficult problem.

Grading Method

In this method, all people are grouped serially from best to least efficient for their every quality and are grouped as extraordinary, best, good, average, bad and worst (see Exhibit 8.1). These groups are also explained. These groups could be increased or lessened. An example of Grading Method Report is shown in Exhibit 8.1.

Graphic Rating Scales Method

It is the simplest and most popular method for appraising performance. Per this technique, the rater is presented with a set of traits such as job knowledge, quantity, quality and initiative and is asked to rate employees on each of these traits. The number of traits rated may vary from a few to many. The rating can be in a series of boxes (as shown in Exhibit 8.2), or it can also be on a continuous scale of 0–9 or the like, and in the case of using a continuous scale, the rater places a check above descriptive words ranging from none to maximum. These ratings are then assigned points such as outstanding may be assigned a score of 5 and unsatisfactory a score of 0. Total scores are then computed.

Exhibit 8.1   Grading Method Report

Name of the Appraise: ....
Designation: ....
Section/Department: ....
Date: ....
Name of the Evaluator: ....

Merit	Extraordinary	Best	Good	Average	Below Average	Worst
1. Type of Job						
2. Decision-making Power						
3. Hard Work						
4. Intelligence						
5. Expertise						
6. Experience						
7. Leadership						
8. Physique						
9. Communication						

Performance Appraisal and Potential Appraisal 271

Exhibit 8.2   Typical Graphic Rating Scale

Name of the Appraise:.................... Designation:..........................
Department:.......................................
Date:............

	Extraordinary	Above Average	Average	Below Average
Skills Professional related skill to the job	☐	☐	☐	☐
Output Of pre-prescribed specifications	☐	☐	☐	☐
Leadership Ability to influence subordinates work behaviour	☐	☐	☐	☐

Later, in order to make the scale more effective, two modifications are designed: (a) mixed standard scale in which the rater, instead of just rating a trait like 'job knowledge', has to tick one of the three statements given to describe that trait and (b) adding operational and benchmark statements to describe different levels of performance.[9]

Checklist Method

This is also known as questionnaire method. In this method, a checklist is prepared in which several questions related to performance of a particular job are included such as 'Is equipment maintained by him/her (ratee) in good condition?' 'Is he/she respectful to his/her superiors?' 'Does he/she listen sincerely to his/her subordinates?' The rater needs to simply mark a 'tick' against the column of 'yes' or 'no'. In other words, the rater simply reports the behaviour, and the evaluation of the 'reported behaviour' may be done by the HR department.

This system has the possibility of partiality as the rater does the work by himself/herself. Second, each department or work needs separate checklists as nature, character and responsibilities of different jobs have vast differences. Hence, it involves more work.

Forced Choice Description Method

This method reduces the chances of rater bias because the rater needs to make a choice between the two descriptive statements seemingly of equal worth. Out of each pair, the rater has to select one statement which according to him/her is the most characteristic of the employee who is being rated. For example, the rater will have to make a choice out of the following two questions:

1. Can he/she be relied upon to any extent?
2. Does he/she maintain good relations with his/her subordinates?

Only one statement in each pair is correct in identifying the better performance, and this scoring key is kept secret and is not known to the rater. After the rater completes his/her assessment, he/she sends it to the HR department where it is compiled, and the result is ready.

This is a simple method and is an improvement over the grading procedure. There is no partiality, but this method is not able to cast directions on the future development of the worker. At times the evaluator needs to take such decisions which he/she does not prefer.

Selection of Critical Incident Method

This method assumes that there are certain key acts of behaviour which are responsible for success on a job. The supervisor-rater keeps on recording such acts/events that take place in the performance of the ratee's job. These acts/events are the critical incidents. For example, the sales officer may keep on noting whether the salesperson has been courteous to the customers or whether he/she attends to telephone calls effectively and so on. All these acts may be considered as critical incidents. Thereafter, all the collected critical incidents may be ranked in order of importance or frequency or both. In this way, numerical weights can be obtained, thereby providing the basis for a rating score for the evaluation of performance of the ratee. Thus, we find that in this method, the supervisor-rater needs to be very vigilant, and each pertinent critical incident needs to be identified.

Descriptive Evaluation

In this method, the evaluator prepares a written report in relation to the execution of the job by the employee, containing details about the personality, merits, quantity and quality of work, and so on. The clarity and extensiveness of the report (description) play an important role in the effectiveness of evaluation.

Point System

In this method, for every unit of every work, some points are specified. A manual or a scale is used in which all units' description, points for evaluation and evaluation procedure are given. Generally, some units are determined as cleverness, responsibility, effort (mental or bodily) and job conditions. Each person's each merit is given the points from the maximum determined points. Afterwards, all the points are totalled, and that is the evaluation of that person.

Field Review Method

Under this method, the evaluator asks the supervisor questions about the workers working under him/her and gets his/her opinion and records it. These are signed by the supervisor and kept for future reference as a context.

Modern Methods of Performance Appraisal

Some of the modern methods of performance appraisal are as follows:

The 360-Degree Techniques

The process of 360-degree feedback was originally developed by NASA to evaluate their space programmes. Now most Fortune 500 companies use 360-degree feedback with considerable success. Consultant Peter Ward introduced this technique into Tesco (UK). Some other major companies using this process in the UK include WHSmith, Forward Trust and so on, while in the USA, companies such as General Motors, Mobil and Motorola fall in this category. In India, we can mention the names of some companies such as Reliance Industries Ltd, Godrej Soaps, Infosys and Wipro.

All this goes to illustrate that with its origins in the 1960s and 1970s, this approach has a growing number of exponents and fans.

'Multi-rater feedback', 'all-round feedback', 'peer appraisal', 'upward appraisal', '180-degree appraisal', '360-degree appraisal', '400-degree appraisal', '540-degree appraisal' and so on are the names by which 360-degree feedback has been labelled, the reason being that all these terms represent different ways of describing the same thing. The variation in the numbers indicates the variation in the rater groups used. For example, while 180-degree feedback describes top-down and bottom-up feedback, the 360-degree feedback includes feedback not only from the boss and the subordinates but also from peers and so on. The 540-degree feedback comprises feedback from almost all stakeholders even if they are from outside the organisation. Thus, it is a process of systematic collection and feedback of performance data on an individual or a group, derived from several stakeholders, in their performance. While the traditional performance appraisal involves bosses only assessing their staff, the 360-degree feedback is based on the concept that people other than bosses also, who really work with us, for example, subordinates, peers, customers and suppliers, may also provide for more vital, accurate and useful insights into our strengths, weaknesses and scope for development.

It involves collecting responses through structured questionnaires about a manager from his/her bosses, peers and subordinates. The techniques span over several parameters: performance as well as behaviour, how effectively a manager handles his/her boss and juniors, how effectively he/she communicates, how deftly he/she delegates and how abrasively he/she administers. Values, ethics, fairness, balance and courtesy—nothing is excluded from the ambit of appraisal and neither crucially is the question of how inspired a manager's leadership is.

The questions are formulated to elicit one of the five responses to the subject's rating on a parameter: significant strength, strength, meets requirements, developments required and cannot rate. Normally, questions relating to behaviour are more effective than performance-related queries. The latter requires judgement which can be not only difficult but also biased. By contrast, the former elicits reportage, which is simpler and more reliable.

Each manager is assessed by a minimum of 15 colleagues: at least 2 of them being his/her bosses, 4 of them peers and 6 of them subordinates. While immediate supervisors are best placed to evaluate performance parameters, peer judgement provides comparative and even competitive perspectives. And including juniors is crucial: many an apple-of-the-boss's-eye metamorphoses into a brutal bully with subordinates, often

274 Compensation and Reward Management

hoarding responsibility rather than delegating it. The best 360-degree system polls customers too.

Crunched and graphed by a computer, the responses are presented collectively to the subject of the appraisal, with specific comments being presented later. A bar chart for each parameter indicates what percentage of respondents in each category—boss, peer or subordinate—rated the subject. Then interpretations of what the findings are telling their subject follow. And finally, counselling sessions tackle ways to solve the specific problems and weaknesses identified by the 360-degree assessment.

In 360-degree feedback, the role of evaluation is shared, shifting the responsibilities from one individual to many, reducing the severity of any one person's shortcomings as an evaluator, including errors of leniency, personal bias, subjectivity and so on.

360-degree feedback reflects many directions from which information is provided on a set of predefined competencies. Feedback comes from many sources, and it provides a more balanced evaluation that is usually more acceptable as fair and objective. Peers and subordinates are regarded as credible feedback sources because they have greater opportunity to observe the manager's behaviour than supervisors do. This hot new form of assessment, known as 360-degree feedback, involves having a manager rated by everyone above, alongside and below him/her.

Every organisation wants to know everything about a person. That is why 360-degree method should be on top of CEOs' wish list and that is why the companies referred to earlier and some other are using this technique to find out home truths about their managers. Although deployed mostly as a fact-finding and self-correction technique, 360-degree feedback is also beginning to be used to design promotion and reward. It involves collecting responses through structured questionnaires about a manager from his/her bosses, peers and subordinates.

How does 360-degree feedback score over other forms of appraisals? Normal performance appraisal systems judge the outcome of a manager's efforts but ignore the road taken. They focus on achievements rather than the intrinsic qualities that a manager must have in order to lead. But these qualities are what the appraisal reveals. Remember, it will not tell your managers whether they have met their hard targets, but it will praise or warn them about their styles. It is like having a close look at yourself in the mirror. How will your managers benefit?

They will learn which of their techniques hurt more than help and learn that their subordinates thought they were insecure and, therefore, did not delegate. For example, Godrej Group's CEO Adi Godrej was amazed to realise that his managers wanted him to curb his authoritarianism.

Communicated to your managers, their ratings will push the onus for changing directly onto each of them. Says Adi Godrej, managing director of Godrej Soaps, the first manager in the company to take a 360-degree appraisal: 'It is a powerful tool for self-development, especially at the senior level, which is where one tends to get insulated'.

Naturally, your organisation will gain from the improvements that heightened self-awareness generated among your employees, among the other benefits that will flow.

Now the question arises that whom should you subject to a 360-degree assessment? Although applicable across functions and anywhere in the hierarchy, the tool is most effective when used from the top-down for the fact that the CEO and the top managers have been administered the test convinces everyone else to go through it too.

Of course, do not be surprised if the results are uneven, for individual reactions can vary, and not every manager in your company will accept and benefit from the findings.

According to R. R. Likhite, group senior vice president (HRD) of Mafatlal Industries, 'Such assessment may be applicable to some managers, but not all'.

Then the next question is that should your manager's pay cheques reflect their appraisals? Used to complement performance assessments, the feedback can be a useful compass for pointing out directions to compensation. But do not deploy it as the sole arbiter of reward. After all, performance in terms of meeting targets must be fundamental to evaluation. Manab Bose, director (Human Resource and Corporate Affairs, India Region) of GE remarks, 'You can't deduct five per cent of someone's increment because he trampled over two people to achieve his goals'.

All right, but how can you ignore, when determining increments, the leadership ratings the 360-degree test gives your managers? To resolve the contradiction, American Express uses a target-based performance appraisal to award a performance bonus at the year end. And the leadership rating of the 360-degree assessment is linked to promotions and increments.

Thus, managers need to make the numbers for a one-off reward and earn high grades on the 360-degree test for permanent gains. Approves GE's Bose: 'The high performer who shoots past targets but is low on leadership skill will be forced to change. Don't replace your current system with 360-degree assessment, therefore, but do add it to your appraisal arsenal'.

Merits

The 360-degree method is preferred because of the following reasons:

- It unfolds strengths and weaknesses in the managing style of the assessed.
- It forces inflexible managers to initiate self-change.
- It helps in creating team spirit.
- It reveals truths about organisational culture and ambience.
- It promotes democratic climate in the organisation and, thus, makes it more open and transparent.
- It focuses on customers and suppliers also.
- It suits flatter structures.
- It is useful because direct line managers may not know all the aspects of an individual's work.
- The predictive ability to 360-degree feedback approach highlights long-term success.

Demerits

- Colleagues' responses may be biased.
- It ignores performance in the terms of reaching goals.
- The assessees usually deny the truth of negative feedback and, at times, feel threatened.
- Linking findings to rewards may be unfair.
- It is time-consuming.
- It can be used to humiliate the assessees.
- It is a costly proposition.

In order to make the whole exercise meaningful, individual employees and functional groups should be encouraged to take charge of getting feedback from their constituents on a regular basis. This ensures an organisation-wide performance management system that is ongoing and decentralised.

Besides, traditional appraisal systems are organisational requirements. They establish role clarity, enable one to plan performance, establish abilities and facilitate performance monitoring, assessment and rewards. 360-degree feedback, on the other hand, is an awareness-building, impact-assessing, reflective and developmental tool. Interest and enthusiasm are very critical for success.

360-degree feedback offers promise for the development of managers. The essential prerequisite is how the individuals react to the feedback and a desire to profit by it. One has to look at oneself critically with a desire to accept shortcomings and try to overcome them. It is like having a close look at yourself in the mirror.

MBO Method

The second approach, MBO, has emerged as a reaction to the traditional management practices. In the famous phrase of McGregor, traditional measurement asks the supervisor to 'play God' and sit in judgement upon his/her fellows.[10] As against this, in the MBO programme, there is a special provision for mutual goal setting and appraisal of progress by both the appraiser and the appraise(s). The philosophy of MBO is based on the behavioural value of fundamental trust in the goodness, capability and responsibility of human beings.[11]

Behaviourally Anchored Rating Scales (BARS)

This method combines elements of the traditional rating scales and critical incidents methods. Using BARS, job behaviours from critical incidents—effective and ineffective behaviours—are described more objectively. In this method, services and expertise of those individuals are used who are familiar with a particular job to identify its major components so that they may rank and validate specific behaviours for each of the components.

Process for Constructing BARS: The following are the main steps involved in constructing BARS:

1. Collecting critical incidents
2. Identifying performance dimensions
3. Reclassifying incidents
4. Assigning scale values to the incidents
5. Producing the final instrument

Assessment Centres

It was the German Army that applied this method for the first time in 1930. It is a system where assessment of several employees is done by various experts using various techniques discussed in this chapter as well as other techniques such as transactional analysis (TA), role-playing, case studies, in-basket and simulation exercises.

In this approach, employees from different departments are brought together to spend two–three days and assigned the task which they would be expected to handle if promoted. The observers then rank the performances of every participant in order of merit.

HR Accounting

In it, we work out the cost and contribution of an employee. Cost of the employee is worked out based on money spent on him/her in terms of manpower planning, recruitment, selection, induction, placement, training and development, wages, benefits and so on. The employee's contribution is the money value of his/her services. If the percentage of surplus of contribution to cost of the employee is more, then it is considered positive.

Optimism Index Oi 1.1

As the test 'Optimism Index Oi 1.1', recently developed by Padmakali Banerjee, is a measure of present performance also, it can be used as a tool in the process of performance appraisal (for details, see Chapter 5).

Self-evaluation as a Complement to Evaluation by Superiors

Performance appraisal by the superiors has been the basis for promotion, training and development since long. But subordinates are critical of the assessment done by their supervisors when they feel that the superiors:

1. Judge them in terms of their own self-image and appraise low-level role performance by comparing it with their own high-level role performance.
2. Adopt different criteria of assessment in different cases.
3. Do not give them opportunity to explain the causes of their failures or unsatisfactory performance.
4. Keep their assessment confidential so that it may not be challenged.
5. Evaluate them based on certain incidents or happenings which may not be a regular feature of their behaviour or work situation.
6. Rely too much on past records and remarks by their predecessors.

Self-assessment by employees may be complementary to evaluation by the superiors. McGregor's theory is based on three important postulates: self-direction, self-control and self-appraisal. The average human being, according to him, learns under proper conditions not only to accept but also to seek responsibility. The capacity to exercise a relatively high degree of imagination, ingenuity and creativity in the solutions of organisational problems is widely, not narrowly, distributed in the population. People should be given a degree of freedom to direct their own activities to achieve the goals which are set in consultation with them. This would satisfy their egoistic and self-fulfilment needs and will make them less dependent on their superiors and assume more responsibility. Thus, the philosophy of self-assessment is based on the theory of human behaviour. Self-assessment is successful when it ensures that the subordinates rate themselves in an objective manner without fear of being victimised.

The pro forma for self-assessment should be designed in such a manner that the employee may have an opportunity to reveal about his/her performance on the job both in qualitative and quantitative terms, his/her interest and aptitude, his/her relations with the superiors, colleagues and subordinates, and so on. If the assessment is done in a free atmosphere, then he/she will not hesitate in pointing out his/her weak points as well as his/her expectations from the bosses to guide him/her in improving his/her performance and potentialities.

Self-assessment may result in subordinates.

1. Accepting the organisation goals and working activity for the same
2. Cooperating with superiors in implementing plans and policies
3. Maintaining discipline, giving due respect to superiors and working in harmony with colleagues
4. Improving productive efficiency and reducing waste
5. Improving employee morale

Some Practices of Performance Appraisal in Indian Industries and Feedback About Performance Reviews

As far as performance appraisal practices in Indian industries are concerned, there is no uniformity, and different methods are being followed by different organisations. Some organisations have been shifting from one method of appraisal to another. For example, recently three top IT firms—Wipro, TCS and Infosys—have abandoned 'bell curve' appraisal and adopted a new one. The central idea behind this shift is that not only do these companies want individuals and their teams to win but their victories should also contribute to the success of the organisation. To use a cricketing analogy, a century makes sense only if it helps the team win. For example, at Wipro, the new structure is different from the previous one, as the emphasis on performances of individual client accounts has been placed on employees working closely as a team (see Exhibit 8.3). The new structure will further underscore the importance of collaborative behaviour and bring teams together to work towards a common goal. Simply put, the company is not looking for individual heroes. It wants a team of champions. The new structure will be applicable to CEO Abidali Neemuchwala, his/her direct reports and a level below them across verticals and horizontals.[12]

Exhibit 8.3 Abandoning 'Bell Curve' Appraisal System

Under the previous incentive structure, Wipro rewarded employees and executives based on the performance of a particular client account and not that of particular business vertical or horizontal. Under that structure, managers were also rewarded on four parameters—revenue growth, profit growth, employee satisfaction and customer satisfaction.

Source: The Economic Times, 20 June 2016.

Exhibit 8.4 TCS Plans to Straighten Out the Bell Curve with New Appraisal System

There will be separate appraisal systems for IT and BPO employees and the company is even looking at how senior executives should be appraised. This is all being tested out now. Nothing firm has been decided. TCS is looking to adopt a system of continuous feedback, a goal that may be hard to achieve given the number of employees.

Source: *The Economic Times*, 25 November 2016.

As the Indian IT sector moves away from the relative ranking of its three million employees, most companies are bringing in new models. TCS is rebuilding its appraisal system from the ground up. It plans to strengthen out the bell curve with new appraisal system (see Exhibit 8.4). To begin with, some employees will be assessed after a project is completed instead of half-yearly (see Exhibit 8.4).

Indian IT services companies and large firms across the world will keenly watch how TCS manages its appraisals, given the scales of the exercise. KPMG, Microsoft, Accenture and Deloitte have abandoned the bell curve, a performance rating system that requires managers to rank employees against each other. It was reported earlier also that TCS was building a technology platform to manage the process of regular feedback. A TCS executive said that the company will modify an existing platform for IT appraisals, while for BPO employees, it would be more of social media system. Like the internal Knome platform that TCS uses, the system for BPO employees would be more based on social media. The change in the performance review process has started for some TCS employees. Earlier in November 2016, a subset of employees received an email detailing the modifications. 'This is with reference to certain changes being introduced in the Performance Management System. Stage-wise timeline for appraisal process were discontinued last year to encourage continuous feedback', the email said. TCS is now moving to having one appraisal cycle for entire year applicable for all employees.[13]

Exhibit 8.5 Introduction of New Structure Called iCount as Part of Infosys Performance Appraisal System

As part of iCount, employees will be offered feedback and subjected to reviews throughout the year rather than just an annual appraisal. An Infosys spokeswoman said the company had leveraged 'design thinking' to enable the changes as part of Chief Executive Vishal Sikka's broader 'new and renew' strategy.

Source: *The Economic Times*, 8 February 2016.

Instead of half-yearly appraisals, targeted employees would move to a project-end appraisal cycle—that the project could last anywhere from two months to a year. These appraisal cycle changes are in a beta mode and will get rolled out to other employees over time. TCS is not the only IT company building new platforms—HCL Technologies has one called iSuccess, and Wipro's is called Performance Next. Infosys launched its iCount platform this year and is building a mobile application to record real-time feedback.[14]

Infosys has put in place a new incentive structure called iCount as a part of its performance appraisal system for employees that seeks to disproportionately reward individual performers based on specific targets, an overall that comes months after India's second largest software exporters gave up the so-called bell curve assessment tool (see Exhibit 8.5).

Infosys had in September 2015 bid adieu to the bell curve method that fits categories of performers into a certain bracket depending on whether they have met their targets. Infosys has changed the way performance management is done, with higher focus on individual performance rather than relative performance. It has moved away from forced ranking curve and given its managers more flexibility and empowerment while still retaining focus on maintaining a high-performance culture.[15]

IBM recently adopted the 'checkpoint' model, in which employees are put through four reviews in a year instead of one annual appraisal.[16] Another global tech firm, Accenture has also ditched annual appraisals and the bell curve system.[17] HCL Technologies is also in the process of overhauling existing appraisal systems.[18] Microsoft, GEC and HCL Technologies have also moved away from forced rating in some form or the other.

As progressive organisations move towards creating the future workplace, there is a decisive case for companies to give up the punitive system of forced ratings. One's accomplishments should stand for what one really does, and not against what someone else does.

The removal of rating, however, does not mean that differentiation in recognition and reward will not happen. Organisations know that they need to differentiate and ensure higher rewards for performers in a globally competitive environment; it is all about impact. Teams that make an impact deserve to be rewarded. Otherwise, organisations will be left with low-performing, complacent teams.

Some Recent Innovations in Appraisals: Setting the Standards

Some of the recent innovations in performance appraisal[19] are as follows:

Axis Bank

Axis has introduced the Enhancement Program. This is a 'second chance' where employees can volunteer to take on stretch targets to get a retrospective upgrade in their rating. With this, the bank has managed to do away with employees' negative perceptions around lower performance ratings while keeping the meritocracy intact.

Deloitte India

Deloitte has launched Reinventing Performance Management (RPM)—a system that has no once-a-year review or 360-degree feedback tools. Instead, it is hallmarked by speed, agility, engagement and one-size-fits-one approach. It also offers the staff real-time performance feedback from the team leader. RPM also gives professionals, 80% of whom are millennials, instant feedback.

Godrej Industries

Godrej focuses on not only the achievement of specific goals (the 'what') but also how they are achieved with reference to Godrej Capability Factors, a set of key capabilities unique to the organisation (the 'how'). Technology is used to analyse performance of each team member and enable managers to cascade their expectations to team.

Sun Pharma

PRIDE was designed as the new global performance management process for Sun Pharma, enabling an employee to perform, reflect, invest, develop and excel. This process is tech-enabled and includes long-term professional development objectives, backed by a formal mid-year process.

Accenture

Accenture has shifted from an annual performance management process to perform achievement. The company has eliminated performance reviews, rating and ranking. The focus is on setting priorities, growing strengths and creating rewarding career opportunities for the people to help them be more successful. This means the leaders spend more time coaching and talking with employees. Performance appraisal in Indian industries leaves much to be desired. For example, in the bell curve system, large number of employees get antagonised that their managers, super managers and the organisation have all failed to acknowledge their hard work (see Exhibit 8.6).

Per TimesJobs survey performance reviews of over 1,000 employees, reported in *The Economic Times* of 1 December 2015, nearly 60% of India Inc. employees are unhappy with their performance reviews. Poor informal feedback and hypocrisy are reasons for dissatisfaction about performance reviews (see Exhibit 8.7).

Most of the respondents held their immediate reporting manager responsible for performance review dissatisfaction (see Exhibit 8.8).

The survey also revealed bad performance review on productivity at work (see Exhibit 8.9).

As far as satisfaction on performance reviews is concerned, the survey under discussion revealed that while 42% of the respondents were happy, 58% were not happy with the way they were reviewed (for more details, see Exhibit 8.10).

Exhibit 8.6   For Whom the Bell Tolls

'You are rated "3: Meets Expectations" this year'. With this one sentence, the world of a performer comes crashing down. She does not hear the rest of the feedback where the manager is telling her how diligent she is or how the organisation values her work ethics. Emotions are on the boil.

At that moment, she is antagonised that her manager; super manager and the organisation have all failed to acknowledge her hard work with: 'You have done well, but then ratings are a function of the bell curve. Others have done better than you'. That, in a nutshell, is the performance appraisal experience 65% of the employees go through at 75% of the companies in corporate India—65% because forced rating would usually put about 35% employees above the rating of 3 or whatever similar system an organisation has put in place.

Source: The Economic Times, 2 May 2016.

Exhibit 8.7 Reasons for Dissatisfaction About Performance Reviews

- 8% of respondents said there was a mismatch in self-appraisal and manager's review.
- 45% of respondents said there was poor informal feedback.
- 22% of respondents said there was rating bias.
- 25% of respondents said there was hypocrisy.

Source: The Economic Times, 1 December 2015.

Exhibit 8.8 People Primarily Responsible for Performance Review Dissatisfaction

- 12% of respondents held HR responsible for performance review dissatisfaction.
- 86% of respondents held immediate/reporting manager responsible for performance review dissatisfaction.
- 2% of respondents held CEO responsible for performance review dissatisfaction.

Source: The Economic Times, 1 December 2015.

For more details, see *The Economic Times*, 1 December 2015. For more details, see *The Economic Times*, 2 May 2016.

Exhibit 8.9 Effects of Bad Performance Review on Productivity at Work

- 40% of respondents said it kills the motivation to work.
- 33% of respondents said it has a distracting effect.
- 20% of respondents said it hampers productivity but is temporary.
- 7% of respondents said it did not hamper productivity.

Source: The Economic Times, 1 December 2015.

Exhibit 8.10 Satisfaction on Performance Reviews

- 42% of the respondents said they were happy with the way they reviewed.
- 58% of the respondents said they were not happy with the way they reviewed.
- 90% of staff in IT/telecom and internet/dotcom cos said they were not happy.
- 85% of employees in manufacturing said they were not happy.
- 90% of employees in automobile and retail said they were happy.

Performance Appraisal and Potential Appraisal 283

- 74% of employees in metros said they were not satisfied.
- 58% of employees from tier I and II locations said they were not satisfied.

Source: The Economic Times, 1 December 2015.

Exhibit 8.11 Qualities of an Ideal Performance Review Process

- 34% of the respondents cited fairness and transparency.
- 32% of the respondents said a lack of bias.
- 20% of the respondents said feedback shared regularly to update on performance hiccups.
- 20% of the respondents said a bottom-up approach to appraisals.

Source: The Economic Times, 1 December 2015.

For more details, see *The Economic Times*, 2 May 2016.

As far as qualities of an ideal performance review process are concerned, the survey revealed that 34% of the respondents cited fairness and transparency as the most important quality of an ideal performance review (for more details, see Exhibit 8.11).

PricewaterhouseCoopers dropped the bell curve evaluation for its 12,000 employees in India[20] earlier this year. At Persistent, performance is assessed objectively with the help of clear goals and measurable key result areas (KRAs).

A forced relative ranking like bell curve is yesterday's approach. It's antiquated and small thinking. If the goals are measurable and aligned with the organisation's goals, then it is good for us if talent meets the goals because that means the organisation meets its goals.[21]

Surprise Appraisals

Today, many organisations such as BookMyShow, KPMG, RPG Enterprises, IBM and HCL Infosystems have initiated a system of instant appraisals (see Exhibit 8.12).

Exhibit 8.12 Surprise Appraisals: It Could Happen to You Anytime

Working hard just ahead of the appraisal season may not be enough. Be prepared for surprise appraisals throughout the year. Many companies such as KPMG, RPG Enterprises and Book My Show, and technology giants such as HCL, Infosystems and IBM, have begun a system of instant appraisals.

Source: Hindustan Times, 15 August 2016.

The new assessment styles have also turned informal. While some companies have turned to quick, app-based appraisals, some of them do it over a cup of coffee. For example, KPMG India now allows managers to catch up with employees and have a chat on the performance as and when required.

The benefit is immediate feedback and guidance rather than delayed post mortem. It may be recalled that in appraisals, activities that one can recall from the last few months often tends to take precedent. The appraiser may not be able to attribute certain accomplishments to the defined metrics, thus throwing different results.[22]

There are also some other examples of instant appraisals. For instance, HCL Infosystems has introduced a weekly evaluation programme that uses a mobile-enabled platform to assess employees. The idea is to fill the binary responses to a set of short and crisp questions in the app; there is no appraisal form. The focus is on self-assessment for employees and course correction, wherever required, on a weekly basis. Everything is now instant, then why to wait for a year to fix loopholes.

Another such example is Book My Show which has a system of weekly appraisals, every Friday.

Managers get a reminder SMS that their team needs to be rated.

IBM also uses a mobile app to assess employees. The app ACE is used for instant feedback on employees. However, head-hunters confess that annual performance sessions still have relevance. According to KPMG, changes are taking place.

Of course, success is heavily dependent on the maturity of the organisation. A wrong sense could lead to the entire people strategy going astray.[23]

Introducing an Effective Performance Appraisal Programme

Performance appraisal programme has been evolved as a valuable tool of HRM because it offers several advantages to the employees as well as to the management. But caution is essential in the use and introduction of this technique. The following care or prerequisites should be observed before introducing an effective performance appraisal programme:

1. **Analysis of jobs and responsibilities**: The first step of performance appraisal is the assessment of a person's jobs and responsibilities. For reaching the extracts of rights and responsibilities, one should go through the details of jobs first.
2. **Ascertainment of the standard of job execution**: While ascertaining the standard, employees and supervisors should be consulted. Besides, one should study the evaluation programmes of other industrial concerns also. While ascertaining the standards, one should take into consideration special facts and features of those programmes.
3. **To look on job execution**: The evaluator must be fully trained for this purpose. Then alone, he/she can rightly evaluate the person.
4. **Guess of ability**: After preparing different statements of job descriptions and so on, necessary information should be obtained about the people so that their measure of ability by any one method may be done and their future progress may be estimated.
5. **Labour management discussions**: After this, there may be discussions with employees and supervisors, and clarification on the evaluation strata may be given. Based on filled report on the occasions, supervisors guide and train the personnel.
6. **Formulation of scheme of the development of employees**: The supervisor prepares the evaluation report of work of a subordinate employee. He/she submits this report

to the report committee and the committee reviews and accepts it. The supervisor or higher official based on that evaluation talks to the employee in private. Afterwards, higher official and supervisor both jointly plan the scheme for job amendments of the employee, if need be.
7. **Review of the progress**: At times, progress is subject to review and evaluation. An employee should be reviewed necessarily for the job execution and objectives he/she is assessed for.
8. **Technologies in the service of performance appraisal**: Today, technology plays the most crucial role in providing the platform to have fast and quick informal communication needed for performance appraisal, and the organisations are no longer required to write a long performance appraisal at the end of the year (see Exhibit 8.13).

Today, more and more companies are moving to real-time performance appraisal and that is why in their system, everything is shareable and real-time. And technology plays the most crucial role in providing the platform to have fast and quick and informal communication.

Shedding the Tag of Poor Performance

Nobody wants to be seen as a poor performer. There is always a reason that you are being perceived that way, and it is your job to find out the reason. There are five ways to shed the tag of poor performer (see Exhibit 8.14).

Regarding the first step, 'find the root cause', Swapnil Kamat, founder of Work Better Training, says that the first step towards shedding the tag is to dig deep to find out where the poor performance stems from. Is it the lack of skill to do the job or lack of motivation to perform? Once you know and accept why you are underperforming, it becomes relatively easy to take corrective action.

As far as 'seek feedback' is concerned, according to Vikramjit Singh, president of Lemon Tree Hotels, it involves seeking constant 360-degree feedback to understand your shortcomings and work on them. Analysing feedback in a positive manner will help you grow professionally and personally. Take criticism constructively and learn from past mistakes.

Exhibit 8.13   Role of Technology in Performance Appraisal

The most common cliché is 'performance appraisal is dead'. What it means is the annual performance appraisal is dead and most organisations today are adopting regular, real-time, anecdotal and casual feedback. Just as young people do not write emails anymore—they use WhatsApp—similarly we don't have to write a long performance appraisal at the end of the year.

Source: The Economic Times, 3 February 2017.

> **Exhibit 8.14   Shed Tag of Poor Performer**
>
> 1. Find the root cause.
> 2. Seek feedback.
> 3. Take initiative and deliver.
> 4. Work with high performers.
> 5. Take small steps
>
> *Source:* *The Economic Times*, 16 December 2016.

Regarding 'take initiative and deliver', Kamat says that if it is lack of ability or skill, you must take the initiative to train yourself on the specific skill you lack. Have an honest conversation with your manager and let him/her know that you need training to improve your skills, if that is what you are lacking. When an employee is proactive, managers are more than happy to help. Once you have been trained, apply your learning to the task at hand. Delivering consistently helps you come out of the shadow of being a poor performer.

As far as 'work with high performers' is concerned, Vikramjit Singh says that while working in teams or on group projects, seek to work with high-performing team members, or those whose work has been responded to positively in the past. This will help you learn from their experiences, as well as showcase your work in a positive light.

Coming finally to 'take small steps', Kamat says that the label of a poor performer comes when you have not been delivering over a specific time period. It is not easy to get rid of it. However, the quickest way of doing so is to perform well at smaller tasks that are more short term in nature. Some such small wins will help you be known as a good performer. When you become consistent, it leads to a change in how people see you.[24]

Characteristics of a Sound Appraisal Plan

The successful appraisal of any appraisal programme will be governed by the following factors:

1. It must secure full agreement of line management on the need and purposes of an appraisal plan.
2. Complicated plans should be avoided.
3. It must enlist the cooperation of supervisors not only in drawing up the appraisal form but also regarding weights to be assigned to each factor.
4. An appraisal plan must be fully explained in advance to those who will be affected in any way by its implementation.
5. The supervisors must be trained for it.
6. It must seek full line and staff cooperation and mutual checking of employee performance appraisal.
7. It must make provisions for checking and review of performance appraisals, if need is felt by the union representatives.

Performance Appraisal and Potential Appraisal

Advantages or Utility of Performance Appraisal

A performance appraisal programme is an important instrument of HRM. Its main advantages are as follows:

1. **Development of personnel**: Based on performance evaluation, the employer or the organisation or the two together can plan for the career development or development programme for the individual concerned.
2. **Mutual comparison**: Performance appraisal provides a scientific basis for the evaluation of all people. Based on this information, their relative abilities can be compared.
3. **High morale**: Generally, every worker is eager to know the management's opinion about his/her work and ability. A properly planned appraisal programme gives chance to a person to know about himself/herself and motivates him/her for development. This increases his/her mental strength and provides self-satisfaction.
4. **Advantage to supervisors**: By appropriate appraisal, the supervisor comes to know the efficiency of the personnel working under him/her, and he/she also comes to know their strengths and weaknesses. He/she suggests remedies to the management, on the one hand, and tries to overcome the weaknesses of the workers, on the other hand.
5. **Helpful in proper placement**: Appraisal is helpful in the placement of the personnel. This means that the personnel should be placed on the right jobs. Besides, the abilities of the workers kept on probation can be found out, and they may be placed at proper positions after probation or discharged or the probation period can be extended so that necessary improvements be made.
6. **Utility for management**: The main advantage of the performance management goes to management. They know the abilities of the people and on that basis, the management sets right the programme for their promotion, transfer, forced leave or discharge. It serves in determining a sound and suitable wage structure. Appraisals can be used to evaluate the training programmes also.
7. **Other advantages**: Appraisals prevent grievances and develop a sense of confidence among employees if they are convinced of impartial evaluations. Hence, it improves labour management relations.

Constraints of Appraisal System

Performance appraisals, although very widely used, have well-recognised shortcomings and limitations. Even when the process emphasises appraisal rather than counselling, it is far from universally satisfactory. There are certain barriers which work against the effectiveness of an appraisal system. The identification of these barriers is necessary to minimise their impact on the appraisal programmes. These barriers are (a) faulty assumptions, (b) psychological blocks and (c) technical pitfalls.

1. **Faulty assumptions**: Because of the faulty assumptions of the parties concerned—superior and his/her subordinates in appraisal system—it does not work properly or effectively. These assumptions work against an appraisal system in the following manner:
   - The assumption that managers naturally wish to make fair and accurate appraisals of subordinates is untenable. It is found that both supervisors and subordinates show tendencies to avoid formal appraisal processes.

- Another faulty assumption is that managers take a particular appraisal system as perfect and feel that once they have launched a programme, that would continue forever. They expect too much from it and rely too much on it. It should be recognised that no system can provide perfectly defensible appraisals devoid of subjectivity.
- Managers sometimes assume that the opinion is better than appraisal, and they find little use of systematic appraisal and review procedures. However, this 'management by instinct' assumption is not valid and leads to bias, subjectivity and distorted decisions based on partial or inaccurate evidence.
- Managers' assumptions that employees want to know frankly where they stand and what their superiors think about them are not valid. In fact, subordinates resist to be appraised, and their reaction against appraisal has often been intense.

2. **Psychological blocks**: The value of any tool, including performance appraisal, lies largely on skills of the user. Therefore, the utility of performance appraisal depends upon the psychological characteristics of managers, no matter whatever method is used. There are several psychological blocks which work against the effectiveness of an appraisal system. These are managers' feeling of insecurity, appraisal as an extra burden, their being excessively modest to treat their subordinates' failure as their deficiency, disliking of resentment by subordinates, disliking of communicating poor performance to subordinates and so on. Because of these psychological barriers, managers do not tend to become impartial or objective in evaluating their subordinates, thereby defeating the basic purpose of appraisal.

3. **Technical pitfalls**: The design of performance appraisal forms has received detailed attention from psychologists, but the problem of adequate criteria still exists there. At best, appraisal methods are subjective and do not measure performance in any but in the most general sense. The main technical difficulties in an appraisal fall into two categories: the criterion problem and distortions that reduce the validity of results.

    a. **Criterion problem:** A criterion is the standard of performance the manager desires of his/her subordinates and against which he/she compares their actual performance. This is the weakest point in appraisal procedure. Criteria are hard to be defined in measurable, or even objective, terms. Ambiguity, vagueness and generality or criteria are difficult hurdles for any process to overcome. Traits also present ambiguity. A particular trait is hard to be defined, and variations of interpretation easily occur among different managers using them.

    b. **Distortions:** Distortions occur in the form of biases and errors in making the evaluation. Such distortions may be introduced by the evaluator consciously or unconsciously. An appraisal system has the following possible distortions:

        i. **Halo effect:** This distortion exists where the rater is influenced by the ratee's one or two outstandingly good (or bad) performance, and he/she evaluates the entire performance accordingly. Another type of halo effect occurs where the rater's judgement is influenced by the work team or informal group with which a subordinate has associated himself/herself. If the group is not well liked by the rater, his/her attitude may affect the rating of the individuals, apart from the actual performance.

        ii. **Central tendency:** This error occurs when the rater marks all or almost all his/her personnel as average. He/she fails to discriminate between superior

Performance Appraisal and Potential Appraisal

and inferior people. This may arise from the rater's lack of knowledge of individuals he/she is rating, or from haste, indifference or carelessness.

iii. **Constant errors:** There are easy raters and tough raters in all phases of life. Some raters habitually rate everyone high; others tend to rate low. Some rate on potential, rather than on recently observed performance. In such a situation, the results of two raters are hardly comparable.

iv. **Rater's liking and disliking:** Managers, being human, have strong liking for people, particularly close associates. The rating is influenced by personal factors and emotions, and raters may weigh personality traits more heavily than they realise. Raters tend to give high rating to people whom they like and low rating to whom they dislike.

Overcoming the Obstacles

A systematic performance appraisal is a measurement process and, as such, must be reliable which means that it must be accurate and consistent. Two main obstacles come in the way of a reliable appraisal system—technical characteristics of the system itself and the abilities of the appraiser to exercise objective judgement and to apply the tools provided. Taking appropriate actions in this direction may reduce the impact of these obstacles if not altogether eliminate them. The following measures may be taken:

1. The reliability of a rating system can be obtained by comparing the rating of two individuals for the same person. It can also be obtained by comparing the supervisor's rating given now to another rating in future.
2. The appraisal system can be designed to help in minimising undesirable effects. The system should focus on objective analysis of performance in terms of specific events, accomplishments or failures. The raters may be required to give their ratings through as much continuous and close personal observation as possible.
3. The rating must be made by the immediate superiors. However, a staff department can assume the responsibility of monitoring the system. Although the staff department cannot change any ratings, it can point out inconsistencies to the rater such as harshness, leniency and general tendency.
4. The rating should be reviewed with the ratee. It helps him/her to know where he/she stands, what he/she is expected to do, what are his/her strengths and weakness, and what further actions he/she should take. This not only puts subordinates in a position to improve performance but also minimises his/her resistance to appraisal if a proper atmosphere has been created.
5. The most important factor in an effective appraisal system is the supportive management philosophy. Without an appropriate basic philosophy to generate the continuous support of all the managers, an appraisal system cannot succeed. According to Myers, a goal-oriented climate in the organisation proves to be more favourable for effective performance appraisal.

How to Give Negative Feedback to Employees?

Feedback at work is important for an individual's development. However, some people are oversensitive to negative feedback which makes it crucial for managers and leaders to understand how to convey it. There are some ways to convey it which are shown in Exhibit 8.15.

> **Exhibit 8.15 Ways to Convey Negative Feedback**
>
> Following are some of the ways to convey negative feedback:
>
> 1. Be objective.
> 2. Combine negative and positive.
> 3. Importance of feedback.
> 4. Choose words carefully.
>
> *Source: The Economic Times*, 9 December 2016.

As far as 'be objective' is concerned, it is necessary to ensure that the person receiving the feedback knows that the feedback is not a personal vendetta. According to Sudhir Dhar, director HR, Motilal Oswal Financial Services, such kind of fundamental attribution error has the employee linking the negative feedback to the person giving it. So if you ask someone reporting to you the reason for being late, he/she might interpret that you are a control freak. Sadly, nearly all the time, the attribution strains the relationship between the two parties.

Coming to 'combine negative and positive', according to Swapnil Kamat, founder of Work Better Training, the ideal way of giving feedback to someone who is extremely emotional is to go for sandwich method. Here, you sandwich the negative feedback between two layers of positive feedback. This helps in softening the impact of the negative feedback. By starting and ending in positive words, you ensure that the negative feedback has the right impact.

Regarding 'importance of feedback', according to Kamat, one should begin by highlighting the importance of feedback—both positive and negative—in a professional's life. You could then follow that up with an example of how constructive feedback has helped you or someone you know or the said employee knows positively and made that person a better professional. While doing this, always make sure that your tone is calm and composed and like that of a mentor, rather than a rude, condescending or angry one. Coming to 'choose words carefully', Kamat is of the opinion that rather than telling someone outright that they are bad at something, it is better when you word it in a less harsh manner as well as provide suggestions and solutions to help them get better at what they are currently bad at. According to Sudhir Dhar, sometimes, the most innocuous of sentences is perceived in a way which makes it seem threatening and derogatory. The key is to make the employee feel safe. Only when he/she feels safe would he/she be in a state of mind to understand and appreciate what you are saying.[25]

Getting Over the Fear of Negative Feedback

According to the product development manager, Work Better Training, when it comes to preparing oneself for the mid-year or annual or quarterly feedback, receptivity generally varies. For example, some get cold feet, sweaty palms and creases on their forehead, thanks to stress and fear, while others look forward to it. If you fall in the former, then it is apparent that your fear stems from the fear of being criticised and corrected. But then it is important to understand that regardless of whether it is positive or negative feedback, it helps you grow. You will learn from your mistakes and be guided to perform better. Worrying has not done anyone any good. Instead of worrying, you need to learn to get over your fears and only you can help yourself (for details, see Exhibit 8.16).

As far as 'think of it (negative feedback) as an opportunity' is concerned, you should stop thinking of review sessions as personal attack on your potential. It will only hurt you if you are unwilling to hear it or are reluctant to grow. Instead, look at it as an opportunity to get you act together. If you have made a mistake, learn from it, instead of brooding over it and assuming the world is plotting a plan against you from succeeding. Coming to 'trust the person giving you feedback', you should know that whether it is the first time or the tenth time you are being reviewed, you need to trust the reviewer and the feedback being given to you. Should you have any concerns, raise them. Reframe their statements to make sure you have got exactly what they mean. Regarding 'eliminate negative thoughts', why should you waste time dwelling on thoughts of being shamed during the meeting? Why imagine? Why presume? Why fear? You know the amount of hard work you have put in and that if you have done it right, then you will be praised for it, and if not, then you probably do deserve an appropriate response. Again, coming to 'acknowledge and admit where you went wrong', it may be pointed out that when discussing work-related scenario where you have erred, own up to where you went wrong and seek advice on what you can do to avoid a similar situation in the future. As far as 'make following up a habit' is concerned, once you have received a feedback, work on ways to improve your action points and ask your manager's opinion on how you're faring.[26]

Thus, negative feedback is an opportunity to get your act together.

Exhibit 8.16 Getting Over the Fear of Negative Feedback

- Think of it as an opportunity.
- Trust the person giving you feedback.
- Eliminate negative thoughts.
- Acknowledge and admit where you went wrong.
- Make following up a habit.

Source: Hindustan Times, 27 December 2016.

As a matter of fact, an average performer needs to know what exactly went wrong and the strengths which he/she could capitalise on. We are so focused on dishing out programmes for star performers that we need to have suitable interventions in place to take care of average performers who are in a true sense the backbone of the system. They should receive regular feedback all through the year to help them take corrective steps in time. This increases their motivation levels to push themselves.

It is also important to let the individual do a self-evaluation and introspect. Tools like 360-degree feedback help the individual understand how he/she is perceived from different perspectives—his/her managers, peers, subordinates and even customers.[27]

Many a time people may not be even aware that their performance is not at par and when the year-end performance review happens, this comes to them as a surprise. That is why it is very important to give timely feedback to employees on their performance.

At Persistent, there is a continuous performance feedback process where the focus is on frequent interactions between line managers and their troops to discuss goals and performance. This helps employees in getting feedback in real time. Employees are offered the opportunities to learn new skills so that they remain fresh and challenged.[28]

Organisations that trust each employee decidedly stand to gain. It has been often seen that average talent improves its performance considerably after appraisals. Transparency, meritocracy and clarity of role are the three most important factors that can boost the employee's performance. Identifying the gaps in employee performance, addressing these by providing the right learning platforms and undertaking coaching and mentoring sessions to sustain their performance are also critical.

It is important that organisations keep communicating with their people. There should be transparency regarding employee role, their career growth, organisational performance and how they perform.[29]

Should Appraisals Be Done Away With?

Although lots of things have been said about the ineffectiveness of appraisal and many research studies also corroborate this contention, the fact remains that it is not practical to do away with appraisals. You cannot drive everybody with same the rod (see Exhibit 8.17).

It is no surprise that companies such as IBM and Microsoft have decided to label the practice as ineffective in some countries. A report by researchers from the London School of Economics and Political Science, the University of Toulouse and the Warwick Business School says that most evaluators were unaware of the real policies they used to write evaluations. Other studies have found that negative reviews do not necessarily encourage performance improvement as much as they generate ill will and make workers less likely to strive to be better and more likely to leave the organisation.[30]

Exhibit 8.17 Performance Reviews Aren't Liked Much

It's no secret that the annual employee evaluation drill is dreaded and disliked, depending more on the evaluator than the employee being assessed.

And it's not just employees who wish there are no reviews. Most assessment administrator, who give feedback throughout the year, also rue the time that formal appraisals take. And there's not much evidence that formal performance reviews actually improve performance.

Source: Hindustan Times, 15 March 2016.

Exhibit 8.18 Performance Appraisal Do Not Impact Employee Productivity: Survey

In a survey of nearly 1,050 working professionals by TimesJobs on performance appraisals, 70% respondents said their bosses are not serious enough regarding the process and 65% feel it is not a true reflection of their work.

Source: The Economic Times, 11 April 2017.

Surprisingly, a substantial majority of appraises feels that bosses are not serious enough regarding the process and that performance appraisal does not reflect their work truly (see Exhibit 8.18).

Not only this, but also it was revealed that 90% of the respondents feel that performance appraisal does not have any impact on employee productivity. Only 5% said that it lowers productivity. Regarding the impact of performance appraisal as employee engagement and retention, 80% said that employee engagement and retention are affected by performance appraisal.[31]

Besides, employees want and need feedback regarding how they are doing, and appraisal provides an opportunity to give them that feedback. What is really needed is a fair and just appraisal system which can be effective and can yield results in today's quality-oriented and team-oriented scenario. In this regard, the TQM approach can play an important role.

Potential Appraisal

Meaning of, Need for, and Importance of Performance Appraisal

Of late, in addition to performance appraisal, more and more companies are moving towards conducting potential appraisal. Some of the renowned organisations that have started stressing on potential appraisal include Glaxo, Philips India, Cadbury India, Mafatlal Industries, Pfizer, Procter and Gamble, Sandoz, National Organic Chemical Industries and so on. Measurement of potential is a highly challenging job because people are like icebergs. What we see above the surface (i.e. performance) is only a small part. A large part of the attributes (i.e. potential) needed to perform excellently in a future job is not immediately visible. It is hidden below the surface. One needs to exert a lot to uncover the iceberg, but that is a must if the organisation is to survive because people need to be prepared to take up higher responsibility.

According to Dr Moorthy K. Uppaluri, MD and CEO of Randstad India, performance and potential are typically the two most critical factors that are considered to define employees. However, what differentiates an average employee from a talented one is the extent to which the latter is high on potential as well as on the performance compared to the former.[32]

Usually, the various parameters that are considered by organisations while looking to identify talent with potential are commitment, drive, ability to influence people, competency levels, willingness to learn and be a strong team player, and aspiration to take on higher responsibilities. These are usually unique characteristics that are considered as game changers for the organisation.[33]

According to Sameer Bendra, chief people officer of Persistent, as a policy at Persistent Systems, talent is defined not just based on past performance but along with the potential that the talent can contribute towards the organisation's overall growth.[34]

It is perhaps because of the increasing importance of potential appraisal that several companies have redesigned or are in the process of redesigning their systems, that is, to shift from simple performance-oriented appraisal to a potential-cum-performance-based appraisal system.

Methods of Potential Appraisal

Some of the popular methods/models of potential appraisal being used by big organisations are as follows:

Philips Hi–Lo Matrix

In it, a 2 × 2 matrix is used to evaluate performance and potential in a single process as depicted in Figure 8.3.

It is evident from Figure 8.3 that the low potential–low performance employees are considered question marks. If they fail to bring about the desired improvements in their performance, the organisation moves towards a planned separation of such employees. In the next quadrant of high potential–low performance come the problem children. Such employees require close monitoring and need a new scenario for work as a strategy as well as to tap their full potential. The third quadrant of high potential–high performance pertains to 'star performers' who need to be engaged with complex assignments and groomed for top positions in the organisation. The fourth quadrant of low potential–high performance relates to employees called 'solid citizens'. Such employees have high skills but low potential to go beyond their current jobs.

Philips NV Holland Model

This system includes a five-point scale, ranging from excellent to insufficient, and provides for evaluation of employees on the following four qualities:

1. Conceptual effectiveness
2. Operational effectiveness
3. Interpersonal effectiveness
4. Achievement motivation

The employee is also assessed by the management development team. Efforts are also made to identify star track career development, indicating the highest level they can reach, and then forecasts are made for five to ten years or even beyond that.

Psychometric Tests

Through such tests, which have been developed mostly abroad, we try to capture the abilities of the employee on several fronts such as aptitude, logic, deduction and inference. These tests, for example, are conducted at Glaxo where potential appraisals are a prerequisite to succession planning. At Glaxo, there is also a provision in the performance appraisal form for assessment of an individual's potential vis-à-vis attributes

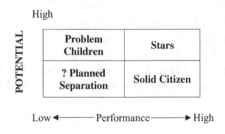

Figure 8.3 The Philips Model

such as initiative, attitude, commitment, accountability, ethics, leadership, judgement and drive by the superior of the employees. In addition to these, some other exercises are also carried out to identify the true potential of the employee.

Review Appraisal

Through such appraisal, which is carried out by the immediate supervisors and departmental heads, insights are obtained into the potential of the employee. This method, for example, is being used at Cadbury since 1993. The review process evaluates potential for growth as well as determines the action plans for career development. Then, efforts are made to rate the employee on six generic competencies: job knowledge, thinking clarity, goal setting and planning, relationships, leadership and innovation. These competencies are rated at a five-point scale.

There are also some other methods of potential appraisal, which are generally modified by the user companies to suit their requirements.

Best Practices of Potential Appraisal

The following are the best practices of potential appraisal being used by some organisations:

1. Ensure to distinguish reward for potential from reward for past performance.
2. Incorporate the appraisal and reward of potential in the assessment system.
3. Communicate potential appraisal to all the employees regularly.
4. Explain to all employees the attributes used for evaluating potential.

Thus, we find that potential appraisal, if used scientifically, can serve a very useful purpose in developing employees for their future assignments. The organisation also gets benefited from the efforts of so developed employees.

Chapter Review

1. Performance appraisal is a systematic, a periodic and, as far as humanly possible, an impartial rating of an employee's excellence in matters pertaining to his/her present job and potentialities for a better job. While in merit rating, an employee's internal merits and qualities such as his/her nature and bodily and mental merits are studied, in performance appraisal, evaluation is made of quantitative factors based on production quantity, quality and strata of work.
2. Performance appraisal is essential because (a) most employees still base their pay and promotional decisions on the employer's appraisal, (b) performance appraisal plays an integral role in the employer's performance management, (c) performance appraisal lets the boss and the subordinate develop a plan for correcting any deficiency, and (d) appraisal serves a useful career planning purpose.
3. Performance appraisal is important because it provides systematic and timely information about an employee's performance and his/her potential, which can

be used in different processes of HRM. Broadly speaking, there are twin objectives of performance approval—judgemental and developmental.
4. Defining the job, appraising performance and providing feedback are the three main steps in the process of performance appraisal. An organisation should, therefore, establish evaluation criteria which should be reliable, relevant, sensitive and practical.
5. Unsatisfactory–uncorrectable, unsatisfactory–correctable, satisfactory–not promotable and satisfactory–promotable are the four main types of appraisal interview.
6. The appraisal methods/evaluation techniques can be grouped under three heads: (a) casual, unsystematic and often haphazard appraisal, (b) traditional and highly systematic appraisal (straight ranking method, paired comparison technique, man-to-man comparison, grading method, graphic rating scale, checklist method, forced choice method, selection of critical incidents method, descriptive evaluation, point systems, field review method) and (c) modern methods. Self-evaluation should be taken as a complement to evaluation by superiors.
7. An effective appraisal programme is one that includes analysis of jobs and responsibilities, ascertainment of the standard of job evaluation, looking on job execution, labour management discussions, formulation of scheme of the development of employees, review of the progress and so on.
8. The main barriers in the way of an appraisal system are faulty assumptions, psychological blocks and technical pitfalls, which should be overcome by taking appropriate measures. However, with all its constraints, performance appraisal cannot be done away with.
9. Potential appraisal is very important because people are like icebergs. What we see above the surface (i.e. performance) is only a small part. A large part of the attributes (i.e. potential) needed to perform excellently in a future job is not immediately visible. It is hidden below the surface—it needs to be uncovered and traced.
10. There are four main methods of potential appraisal—Philips hi–lo matrix, Philips NV Holland model, psychometric tests and review appraisal.

Key Terms

360-degree appraisal
appraisal interview
career planning
central tendency
checklist method
descriptive evaluation
field review method
forced-choice-description method
grading method
graphic rating scale

halo effect
man-to-man comparison
merit rating
paired comparison technique
peer appraisal
performance appraisal
performance management
Philips hi–lo matrix
Philips NV Holland model
point system

potential
potential appraisal
psychological blocks
psychometric tests

review appraisal
selection of critical incidents
self-appraisal/evaluation/assessment
straight ranking method

Discussion Questions

1. Discuss the concept of 'performance appraisal' and how does it differ from 'merit rating' and 'performance management'.
2. Discuss why there should be performance appraisal and how does it help the employee and the employer.
3. Discuss the steps involved in the process of performance appraisal as well as the evaluation criteria, especially the performance interview.
4. Discuss the positive and negative points of traditional and highly systematic appraisal methods.
5. Discuss the philosophy of MBO.
6. Discuss the main features (characteristics) of a sound performance appraisal plan.
7. Discuss what should be done to introduce an effective performance appraisal programme.
8. Discuss the main constraints that come in the way of performance appraisal and how to overcome the same.
9. Discuss the concept of potential appraisal.
10. Discuss the methods available for potential appraisal.

Individual and Group Activities

1. As an individual, visit a big service organisation, contact HR officials there and find out which method(s) of performance appraisal their organisation follows.
2. As an individual or in a group of three members, visit some large manufacturing organisation and discuss with the HR officials of that organisation who conducts performance appraisal in their organisation. Is there a uniform pattern or is there any variation?
3. In a group of three members, contact the union officials in a big organisation and discuss with them if the employees are, by and large, satisfied with the appraisals conducted in their organisation. In case they have any suggestions to make in this direction, take a note of the same.
4. As an individual, visit some commercial organisation and find out from the HR department if there is a system of self-appraisal in their organisation. If yes, then what purpose is being served by it?
5. In a group of two members, visit some organisation of a large size. Discuss with the HR officials if they conduct potential appraisal of their employees. If yes, then which method do they follow?

Application Case 8.1

Non-recognition of Potential

Krishnamurthy is a fellow of IIM, Ahmedabad and Bachelor of Technology (Mechanical Engineering) from IIT Kharagpur. He has ten years of rich experience to his credit.

He joined a renowned company as its CEO and performed well in the first two years. He was successful not only in reducing overhead expenses but also in increasing the company's share in the market.

However, in the third year as CEO, he could not perform well and the company suffered loss for the first time in the history of the company. Although there were many reasons for the adverse results—for example, the number of the competitors of the company had increased substantially during the last two years, resulting in increase in the supply of the product the company and its competitors were producing and thus causing fall in its price; there was erratic supply of power throughout the year, affecting both the quality and output of the product of the company; due to heavy demand for raw material, its prices also went upwards; and the like—the main reason was that Krishnamurthy could not concentrate on his job as much as he was capable of and perhaps could have faced the storm. It was due to sudden and serious illness of his mother, to whom he was greatly attached. Nobody in the company was aware of it.

In the annual general body meeting of the shareholders of the company, the issue of financial loss incurred by the company was the first item on the agenda of the meeting. The issue was deliberated upon with all sorts of arguments. While a few members present in the meeting defended Krishnamurthy, the consensus of opinion was that Krishnamurthy was mainly responsible for the poor performance of the company during the year under review. Krishnamurthy, a man of self-respect, never brought the fact of the illness of his mother to the notice of the general body. Consequently, the next day he resigned from his position, and the same was readily accepted, and Krishnamurthy was relieved of his duties.

Questions

1. Was it appropriate on the part of shareholders to blame Krishnamurthy exclusively for the poor performance of the company ignoring his qualifications, rich potential, long experience, good performance in the company in the previous two years and adverse external factors? Yes or no? Why? Give arguments.
2. Was it desirable on the part of Krishnamurthy not to bring the fact of sudden and serious illness of his mother to the notice of top authorities and abruptly resign?
3. Were you a shareholder holding a large quantity of shares of the company, what would have been your reaction in the general body meeting?

Notes

1. Flippo, *Principles of Personnel Management*, 263.
2. For details, see Ivancevich, *Human Resource Management*, 253.
3. For details, see Dessler and Varkkey, *Human Resource Management*, 342.
4. Ibid., 343.
5. Ivancevich, *Human Resource Management*, 256.
6. For details, see Ibid.
7. For details of technical features of ranking method, see Edwin E. Ghiselli and C. W. Brown, *Personnel and Industrial Psychology* (New York, NY: McGraw-Hill, 1948).
8. Flippo, *Principles of Personnel Management*, 265.
9. For details, see Ivancevich, *Human Resource Management*, 264–65.
10. Douglas McGregor, 'An Uneasy Look at Performance Appraisal', *Harvard Business Review* 136, no. 16 (May–June 1957): 88–94.
11. Flippo, *Principles of Personnel Management*, 263.
12. See *The Economic Times*, 20 June 2016.
13. See *The Economic Times*, 25 November 2016.
14. Ibid.
15. Ibid.
16. *The Economic Times*, 8 February 2016.
17. Ibid.
18. Ibid.
19. *The Economic Times*, 7 April 2017.
20. *The Economic Times*, 27 December 2016.
21. *Hindustan Times*, 24 May 2016.
22. For more details, see *Hindustan Times*, 15 August 2016.
23. Ibid.
24. For more details, see *The Economic Times*, 16 December 2016.
25. For details, see *The Economic Times*, 9 December 2016.
26. See *The Economic Times*, 27 December 2016.
27. *Hindustan Times*, 24 May 2016.
28. Ibid.
29. Ibid.
30. For more details, see *Hindustan Times*, 15 March 2016.
31. For more details, see *The Economic Times*, 11 April 2017.
32. *Hindustan Times*, 24 May 2016.
33. Ibid.
34. Ibid.

9 Wage and Salary Administration and Employee Compensation

Learning Objectives

After studying this chapter, you should be able to do the following:

1. Understand the role of wage and salary (W&S) administration and also of employee compensation in enabling the employees to contribute their best to the organisation.
2. List and describe the objectives of W&S administration.
3. Explain the purpose and functions of W&S administration.
4. Define the term 'employee compensation' and its objectives and factors affecting employee compensation.
5. List and describe the components of employee compensation/industrial pay structure.
6. Explain the term 'wages' and how it differs from the term 'salary'.
7. List and describe various theories of wages.
8. Explain the national wage policy and the factors that have influenced it.
9. List and describe the various methods of wage payment and their advantages and disadvantages.
10. List and explain incentive or bonus (premium) schemes.
11. Describe the advantages and disadvantages of individual and collective incentive plans.
12. Explain the term 'wage differential' and their types.
13. List and describe the monetary and non-monetary rewards.
14. Explain the essentials of a satisfactory wage system.

Introduction

This is well said that while pay by itself is not necessarily the strongest motivator, any unjustifiable inequity or an unacceptable low level of reward causes great dissatisfaction to employees. Hence, it becomes obligatory on the part of HRM to ensure equitable compensation to employees for their contribution in the process of production. It is, therefore, very important that the process of wage and salary (hereafter W&S) administration should be in place in an organisation; otherwise, it will be difficult for it to accomplish its objectives. Only recently, British Airways staff decided to strike over pay dispute (see Exhibit 9.1).

DOI: 10.4324/9781032628424-13

Unite had scrapped calls for a walkout over the Christmas and Boxing Day holiday after British Airways proposed a new pay deal in talks at the UK's Advisory, Conciliation and Arbitration Service. Staff voted to reject the offer, and the company subsequently declined to extend the strike mandate, the union said, adding that members must legally act within 28 days of voting.[1]

W&S Administration

The most important thing that the W&S administration is to start with is to determine salary levels which are determined through the process of job evaluation (discussed in the next chapter). Having arrived at salary levels, the other obligations of the W&S administration are to (a) design and maintain salary structure, (b) operate salary progression systems, (c) administer and control salary reviews and (d) design and operate other allowances. A brief description of these obligations is as follows:

Exhibit 9.1   British Airways Staff to Strike Over Pay Dispute

British Airways flight attendants will walk out next week after the carrier declined to extend their right to strike in return for renewed pay talks following the rejection of the latest offer, according to the Unite union.

The so-called 'mixed fleet' cabin crew, who work on both short- and long-haul flights from London's Heathrow airport, will take action for 48 hours from Tuesday, 10 January 2017, the labour group said in a statement on its website.

A walkout would be the first since 22 days of action in 2010, after which crew accepted a deal including drastic pay cuts for new staff.

Source: The Economic Times, 5 January 2017.

Salary Structure

Salary structure of an organisation comprises its salary grades (or ranges) and its salary levels for a single job or group of jobs. It is the job evaluation that plays an important role in designing a salary structure into which all the jobs of an organisation can be appropriately graded based on their relative worth. While designing a salary structure, it is essential to provide for internal equity as well as maintaining competitive rates of pay. A salary structure can be either of the following or even a combination of both.

Graded Salary Structure

It has a sequence of salary grades, each having a defined minimum or maximum. There are two options: (a) to cover all the jobs of the organisation by the same structure of salary ranges or (b) to design different structures for different levels or categories of jobs. Each grade includes jobs of roughly the same value, and actual salary earned will depend on the performance or length of service of an individual. Regarding advancement through the structure, an individual has two options, that is, either by improving performance or by promotion. In normal course, employees move steadily from the start of the grade to the maximum limit of the grade, unless they move to a better grade. This progression may be classified into certain zones: (a) In the learning zone, an individual takes his/her own time, depending on his/her competence, ability and experience, to acquaint himself/herself with skills, knowledge, attitude and so on needed to become fully conversant and competent for the job. (b) In the qualified zone, having passed through the learning zone, an individual makes efforts to increase his/her capacity to improve his/her performance and efficiency. In this zone, in which the starting salary should match the market rates for the job, the mid-point of the grade should be such as is likely to be achievable by all competent employees. Thus, the mid-point in the grade should be higher than the market rate so that employees do not leave the organisation and would continue with it. (c) In the premium zone, in every organisation, there are some employees for whom appropriate promotion opportunities do not exist, despite their commendable and exceptional performance. Such outstanding employees are encouraged in this zone by rewarding them appropriately.

Salary Progression Curves

These curves are usually meant for professional, scientific or other highly qualified personnel, linking increases in their salary over a considerable long time to their increased maturity, expertise and experience. It is also possible to have more than one rate of progression to reward employees based on their potential and actual performance.

Salary Progression Systems

These refer to increases in salary in relation to merit or performance. In it, salary ranges are divided into defined zones through which an employee passes while he/she progresses. There are incremental systems which differ in their rigidity and flexibility. While the former indicates the rates at which employees can progress per merit or experiences, in the latter (flexible), management exercises its full discretion over the award as well as the size of increments with practically no guidelines. In between the rigid systems and flexible systems, there are middle-ranged, semi-flexi systems. It is highly desirable and in the interest of employees as also of organisation to ensure that employees are correctly placed in their range according to their performance and potential.

Administration and Control of Salary Reviews

While salary policies are executed, it is also necessary that salary costs against budgets are properly controlled because control is a vital element of salary administration. In salary budgets, it needs to be estimated that how many people will be working at different levels of activities during the budgeted period and how much financial resources will be made available. Another important thing in salary administration is salary reviews which can be either individual salary review or one annual review for all the staff, to decide on the merit increments. Then finally comes the fixing of salaries on appointment or promotion. While control on starting salaries is an important issue, salary fixation on promotion also demands adequate attention. The increase in salary on promotion should be adequate, and it should leave enough scope to reward good performance in the new job.

Designing and Operating Other Allowances

There are various forms of additional cash payments employers give to their employees over and above the basic salary in order to seek their commitment and active participation in the success of the enterprise, besides motivating them. This may be to compensate them for additional burden assigned to them or the like in the interest of the organisation. The reward may be in the form of bonus, medical facilities, holidays, sick pay, pensions and so on.

Purpose and Objectives of W&S Administration

In order to establish and maintain a fair and equitable wage structure and its proper implementation in an organisation, its W&S administration should aim at the following:

1. **Organisational Objectives**

    - To attract and retain competent manpower
    - To determine salary levels
    - To make provisions for incentives
    - To boost morale of the employees
    - To get the productivity increased
    - To ensure equity in pay for similar jobs
    - To be cost-effective
    - To be flexible to accommodate any organisational change, if need be
    - To have wage differentials
    - To ensure meeting legal obligations
    - To maintain a satisfactory public-related image

2. **Individual Objectives**

    - To treat every individual fairly and equitably
    - To pay every individual according to his/her worth and convince him/her of the same
    - To match or exceed the reward with the market rates (external equity)
    - To maintain internal equity

3. **Collective objectives**

    - To keep the workers' unions satisfied to the extent possible
    - To ensure that consumers' interests are duly protected
    - To abide by legal obligation and government policies

Functions of W&S Administration

A sound W&S administration is supposed to recommend to top management the wage policies for the administration of wage programme:

- Recommend changes in the wage policies as and when required.
- Design and maintain salary structure.
- Design and operate other allowances.
- Operate salary progression systems department-wise and remove anomalies, if there is any.
- Review the W&S scheme.

- Ensure that activities of W&S administration are in line with the company's policies.
- Ensure proper system of job description, job evaluation, job pricing and wage structure.
- Maintain internal and external relativities and individual worth in salary levels.
- Recommend to top management for its approval specific pay raises for executives above a specified limit.

Employee Compensation

Employee compensation is important to the employees because monetary compensation that they get as a reward for their contribution in the process of production is the only means of economic survival besides determining their social status. It is also significant for the employer as employee compensation usually constitutes the greatest single component of cost of production.[2] Employee compensation is important not only to the employees and the employers but also to the society because employee compensation plays a substantial role in determining the price of products which the members of the society need to pay, thus affecting the cost of their living. Hence, determination of employee compensation assumes added significance in HRM and, therefore, needs to be well planned and administered as it affects all the stakeholders in an organisation.

Meaning and Definition

First, the distinction between 'wage' and 'salary' needs clarification. The term 'wages' is used to denote payments to hourly rated production workers or wages are the remuneration paid for the labour of unskilled, semi-skilled or skilled operative workforce. In this type of labour, the element of corporal labour is much more in comparison to mental efforts and capabilities. ILO defined the term wage as 'the remuneration paid by the employer for the services of the hourly, daily, weekly and fortnightly employees'.[3] As far as the term 'salary' is concerned, it is used to denote payments to clerical, supervisory and managerial employees on a monthly or annual basis. Such employees usually contribute their mental labour to the organisation. Again, salaries are usually paid on monthly basis, while wages may be paid on daily or hourly basis. However, for our purpose, the distinction between the two carries no meaning because, broadly speaking, the same issues are involved in the administration of both W&S policies and all types of employees are treated as human resources. Of course, employee compensation is a complex issue as the process of compensation is a complex network of sub-processes directed towards remunerating employees for their contribution in the process of production of goods and services as also to motivate and retain them in the organisation. In this chapter, an attempt has been made to unravel the complexities of employee compensation.

Coming to the definition of employee compensation, it may be pointed out that it means different things to different people depending on an individual's perspective. From an employee's perspective, compensation may be considered as a return or reward for his/her efforts made for the organisation during a certain period. It also indicates the value the employer attaches to his/her skills, abilities, expertise, experience, education, training and so on. On the other hand, for an employer, since employee compensation is a major constituent of total cost of production, it needs to be judiciously determined so that it enables the organisation to be competitive and sustain itself meaningfully with good prospects. Thus, wages or salaries mean the amount paid to an employee for his/her services to the organisation.

Terminology and Concepts

In addition to wages and salaries, there are some other relevant terms used in this chapter, which are as follows:

Nominal/money wage: Nominal/money wage refers to the monetary form of wage payment.
Real wage: Real wage represents the actual exchange value of money wage, that is, the purchasing power of money wage.
Take-home salary: It refers to the amount of salary left to the employee after making authorised deductions, such as income tax, provident fund and life insurance premium.
Statutory minimum wage: It is the amount of remuneration fixed according to the provisions of the Minimum Wages Act, 1948.
Minimum wages: In the context of our country, minimum wages mean that minimum amount which the labour thinks necessary not only for the bare sustenance of life but also for the preservation of the efficiency of the worker. In other words, minimum wages are the amount or remuneration 'which may be sufficient to enable a worker to live in reasonable comforts, having regard to all obligations to which an average worker would ordinarily be subjected to'.[4]
Living wage: It represents the highest level of wages including all amenities which a citizen living in the modern civilised society is entitled to and expects when the economy of the country is sufficiently advanced, and the employer is able to meet the expanding aspirations of his/her workers. (The present level of our national income does not permit the payment of a living wage or standards prevalent in advanced countries of the world.)
Fair wage: According to the Fair Wages Committee, a fair wage is above the minimum wage but somewhat below the living wage, depending on the organisation's capacity to pay.
Basic compensation: It is the basic compensation that an employee receives for the work performed by him/her. It tends to reflect the value of the work and ignores differences in individual contribution. It is also known as basic pay.
Supplementary compensation: These are benefits for the time the employee did not work such as vacation and holiday pay and sick pay.
Variable compensation: It ties pay to productivity or profitability, usually as one-time lump sum. It keeps fluctuating depending on productivity or performance of an employee.

Objectives of Appropriate Employee Compensation

The twin main objectives of employee compensation are to attract and to retain qualified employees. However, to add a few more objectives, we can include to motivate employees, to maintain good industrial relations, to maintain efficiency of the organisation, to boost the image of the organisation and so on.

Factors Affecting Employee Compensation/Wage Rates/Wage Structure

There are several factors affecting employee compensation, the main being the following:

1. Demand for and supply of labour
2. Status of trade unions

3. Cost of living
4. Labour productivity
5. Collective bargaining
6. Company's wage policy
7. Prevailing wage rates
8. Job requirements
9. Ability of the company to pay
10. Wage legislation and government's wage policy
11. Wage boards
12. Region-cum-industry settlements
13. Internal pricing through job evaluation
14. Tribunal/court awards
15. Competition

The intermixture of these variables in a specific organisational context results in the wage structure/wage rates/employee compensation in a particular organisation.

Components of Employee Compensation/Wage Components/Components of Industrial Pay Structure

The major components or constituents of employee compensation may include the following:

Basic Wage

Basic wage is a stable wage paid over a specific time period which could be on a monthly, weekly or daily basis. This wage is the normal rate for a given level of output.[5] Thus, given a certain job, with all its attendant requirements of education, skills, training and expertise, it is the price to be paid to get it done. It is usually progressive over time—that is, it progresses more evenly over time if there is a running grade; otherwise, it remains fixed with no changes. It is the basic wage that provides a stable base to the wage structure.[6] The fixation of basic wage is affected by statutory minimum wage, recommendations of Indian Labour Conference, patterns set by the awards of industrial tribunals, directives of the Pay Commissions, collective bargaining, wage settlements, periodic job evaluation and so on. The basic wage may differ from job to job, depending on minimum educational and professional qualifications, training, skills, expertise, experience, skills and so on required by a particular job. It may also differ based on mental and physical requirements, responsibilities assigned, stress involved and so on.

Dearness Allowance

Starting from the First World War, the system of payment of dearness allowance (hereafter DA) aims at neutralising the impact of price rise on the wages and salaries of employees. DA protects the wage earners' real income by neutralising the increased cost of living due to increase in prices. However, some of the issues involved in this regard include whether the payment of DA should be automatic as soon as there is rise in the cost of living, and if it be so, what part of price should be compensated, that is, whether in full or partially, and whether the 'capacity to pay' of the industry is to be kept into consideration while deciding the payment of DA or increasing it. There are various methods of DA payment. For example, DA may be linked to consumer price index (CPI) in a specific region. Per this system, payment of DA is regulated based on actual price movement in a particular region/sector or industry. The system may have two methods: (a) a specified rate of DA is fixed for every point rise in the CPI irrespective of the income group an employee belongs to and (b) the DA is based on income groups and cost of living brackets or slabs. Per this system, the absolute amount of DA goes up with each higher income group. In it, DA does not change with every point in the cost-of-living index. Another example is that of flat rate system which provides a lump sum payment to the employees over a specific time period to set aside the impact of inflation.

Bonus

Since some authors consider bonus as a deferred wage, it may be considered as a constituent of wage structure. In our country, payment of bonus is regulated per the provisions of the Payment of Bonus Act, 1965.

Allowances

Another component of the wage structure are various allowances which vary from organisation to organisation, industry to industry and region to region. Some of these allowances have become statutory. Some of the popular allowances comprise house rent allowance, city compensatory allowance, leave travel concession, educational allowance, transport allowance, night duty allowance, hill allowance, shift allowance, book allowance, medical allowance, heat allowance, family allowance, uniform allowance, hazard allowance and so on.

Equity and Employee Compensation

Equity is concerned with felt justice according to natural law or right.[7] Equity generally exists when an employee perceives that the rate of outcome to input is in equilibrium, both internally with respect to self and in relation to others.[8] There should be maintained both the internal equity and the external equity; otherwise, the employee concerned feels psychological imbalance and, therefore, cannot contribute his/her best to the organisation and may not like to continue with the organisation for long.

Employee Compensation Planning

The steps involved in employee compensation planning are as follows:

1. Understand the company's wage philosophy, guidelines, policy and so on.
2. Define the boundaries and limits of employees in the organisation.
3. Know the expectations and want lists of the employees.
4. Estimate the cost of various alternative programmes and compare the same with the estimates of their effectiveness.
5. Perform a cost–benefit analysis of financial and non-financial rewards.
6. Recognise a part of compensation cost as investment in employees which pays for long.

7. Based on all of these, working out a final pay package including financial and non-financial rewards.

However, compensation planning is not a simple exercise. It needs to keep into consideration several things such as wage theories, job evaluation, job pricing, incentive plans, supplementary benefits and national wage policy.

Wages

Formulation and administration of wage policies and resultant determination of appropriate wage rates are an important exercise of HRM. Hence, this responsibility needs to be discharged effectively.

Meaning and Definition of Wages

According to Beham, wages mean the amount paid to the labour for his/her services to the employers. Employees consider wages as a means of satisfying their needs in terms of an expected standard.

Hence, they desire to receive at least as much remuneration as other individuals equipped with similar skills get for doing similar work. They have their own perception about wages. As a result, wages are a highly perplexing problem involving not only economic issues but also several emotional components.

Besides, wages may be of different types, such as 'money wage', 'real wage', minimum wage, living wage and fair wage, which have already been defined in the beginning of this chapter.

Theories of Wages

The main theories of wages can be divided into two categories as follows:

Economic Theory

Economic theories can be further subdivided as follows:

1. **Subsistence theory**: According to Ricardo (1772–1823), wages tend to settle at the level just sufficient to maintain the worker and his/her family at the minimum subsistence. The theory is no longer popular.
2. **Wage fund theory**: According to this theory, a fixed amount of wage fund is available for distribution at any one time and the level of wages depends on the number of labour-seeking employment. This theory also has lost its relevance because there is no justification to assume that the available fund would be constant.
3. **Marginal productivity theory**: This theory mentions that any industry would go on employing additional labour until the marginal productivity becomes equal to marginal cost. There is logic in this theory.
4. **Bargaining theory**: John Davidson feels that there are always upper and lower limits on wages. Therefore, wages will be somewhere between these two limits depending on the bargaining strength of the two parties, that is, the employer and the employees.
5. **Surplus value theory**: Due to typical characteristic of the capitalist form of production, there is the 'rate of exploitation', that is, the rate of surplus value, which is the ratio of surplus labour to necessary labour. In the capital wage systems, the supply

of labour is always tended to be kept in surplus, that is, in excess of the demand for it—thus, the workers do not get full compensation for the time and labour they spend on their duty.
6. **Purchasing power theory**: Per this theory, if the rates of wages are high, it will increase the purchasing power of workers, which will increase the aggregate demand for goods and services, which, in turn, will increase the level of output, and thus, the demand of labour will also go up and so will be the case with the wage rates which will further go up. Reverse will happen if the wage rates are low.
7. **Modern theories of wages**: Modern theories assume that, on the one hand, wages are governed by the laws of demand and supply, and, on the other hand, various external factors and constraints such as the institutions of trade unions and collective bargaining also affect the determination of wages.

Behavioural Theories

Factors other than money, such as internal and external equities, valence and contingency, also affect the determination of wages. In this regard, some of the main theories are as follows:

1. **Equity theory**: Per this theory, both internal and external equities should be maintained while determining wage rates; otherwise, it will be difficult to attract and retain good employees.
2. **Vroom's expectancy theory**: This theory states that the motivation of employees depends on an individual's expectations about his/her ability to perform tasks and receive the desired awards, its formula being:

   Motivational force = Valence × Expectancy

3. **Herzberg's two-factor theory**: Fredrick Herzberg, who propounded this theory, stated that awards have two aspects: (a) hygiene factors, whose absence creates dissatisfaction, and (b) motivation factors, which endue the employees to put in their best efforts. Hence, while determining wages, the role of the aforesaid factors should also be kept into view.

Although none of the economic and behavioural theories is perfect, all of them provide one or the other guidelines which may help in determining wage rates as appropriately as possible.

National Wage Policy in India

It is surprising that there does not exist any wage policy as such in India. It is through Five Year Plans and some other documents that one can form an idea about it. Over a specific time period, the following factors have influenced the thinking of the Government of India regarding wage policy:

- Payment of Wages Act (1936)
- Industrial Truce Resolution (1947)
- Industrial Policy Resolution (1948)
- Minimum Wages Act (1948)

- Constitution of India (1951)
- Directive Principles of State Policy (Article 43)
- Indian Labour Conference (1957)
- Payment of Bonus Act (1965)
- First National Commission on Labour (1969)
- Chakrabarty Committees (1974)
- Equal Remuneration Act (1976)
- Bhoothalingam Study Group (1978)

The highlights of the contribution of some of these are as follows:

Industrial Truce Resolution (1947): Capital and labour to share the product of their common efforts after having paid fair wages to the workers and a fair return on capital to employers and creating a reasonable reserve for the maintenance and expansion of the organisation concerned.

Industrial Policy Resolution (1948): Fair wage agreement in the organised sector and need-based statutory minimum wage in sweated industries.

Minimum Wages Act (1948): Fixation of minimum wages and its revision after prescribed period from time to time.

Directive Principles of State Policy (Article 43): Securing living wage for workforce.

15th Session of Indian Labour Conference: Wages to be determined based on the basic needs of workers.

First National Commission on Labour (1969): Recognised the need for a national wage policy.

Chakraborty Committees (1974): Need for setting up a National Wage Commission and a National Wage Board to evaluate all jobs, workout a grade structure based on skill differentials and fix wages for each grade.

Bhoothalingam Study Group (1978): Provided appropriate guidelines and principles to help in making corrections and adjustments within the framework of collective bargaining, raising steadily the areas of unduly depressed wages, as well as reducing disparities to the extent possible. It also made recommendations regarding the payment of bonus and DA.

Despite different perspectives of the trade unions, employers and the government with regard to wages as also the differences in the observations of different committees, agencies and commissions regarding wages, we cannot and should not escape the responsibility of formulating the national or public wage policy, which should be instrumental in linking reward to effort, sharing gains due to addition in the productivity, developing an inbuilt system to control wages, income and prices, promoting skill formulation and so on.

Wage Policy at the Organisational Level

Although an organisation can take some guidelines from the public policy, while formulating its wage policy and subsequent strategy, an organisation must take care of several factors, such as ongoing rates of wages in the market, its ability to pay, internal and external relativities, controlling of labour costs, motivation of workers and rate of productivity. In this regard, the major factors that may affect the wage policy of an organisation and need to be paid due attention at the time of formulation of organisational wage policy are as follows:

1. Internal equity
2. External equity
3. Productivity
4. Cost of living
5. Motivation level of workers
6. Pay vis-à-vis performance
7. National wage policy
8. Statutory obligations
9. Labour market conditions
10. Present rate of attrition of employees

Obviously, the wage policy may differ from one organisation to another depending on the status and context of the organisation concerned.

Wage Problems in India

India, being a poor country with, by and large, low rate of productivity and abundant supply of labour, has not been able to provide appropriate wages to its workforce even in the organised sector, not to speak of unorganised sector, which employs more than 90% of the country's total workforce. Hence, wage rates have always remained a burning issue as also a major irritant in the arena of industrial relations.

Wages are the only sources of income of Indian workers. Joint family system is rapidly giving way to nuclear family way of life. Workers are largely illiterate, ignorant and economically and socially backward. Employers are exploitative, especially in the unorganised sector. Social security system is either at most of the places non-existent or extremely weak whenever it does exist. There is a lack of standardisation of wages. Manpower is being replaced through the process of automation. Under the aforesaid circumstances, wage problem has always been attracting and continues to attract the attention of the concerned agencies. Statutory steps initiated by the government in the form of various wage-related acts passed so far, wage board constituted for different industries, Pay Commissions established, and the recommendations made by several committees, commissions, Indian Labour Conference and so on have not been able to solve the wage problems in our industries. It is, therefore, essential that all concerned should try collectively to overcome the wage problems to the extent possible.

Methods of Wage Payment

Of the two basic methods of wage payment, the first is based on of time spent on the job, popularly known as time rate method or time wages. The second method is based on output/result, popularly known as piece rate system or payment by results. The third method is of incentive plan or bonus (premium) scheme. The details of the aforesaid methods/systems are as follows.

Time Rate Method/Time Wages

This is perhaps the oldest method of wage payment. Per this method, an employee is paid based on time worked, that is, hourly, daily, weekly or monthly, irrespective of the quantity of work done. Of course, within that time, a certain standard of performance is expected. Payment by time rates is quite suitable where the pace of output is machine-determined or where the work done by an employee is difficult to measure, such as clerical, supervisory or managerial work. Under this system, wages are calculated based on attendance, that is, wages are computed by multiplying the time units spent by the predetermined time rate.

Merits

The merits of time rate system are as follows:

1. It is the simplest system—that is, the wages are easy to understand and calculate.
2. It helps in maintaining quality of the product as there is no time limit for the completion of a job.
3. In case production cannot be standardised and, therefore, the productivity of a worker cannot be measured precisely, time rate system is the best system of wage payment.
4. This system provides a sense of security of income to a worker because in the case of interruption of production, the worker will get his/her salary based on the time spent on the job.
5. This system is preferred by trade unions also; hence, there is no problem of industrial unrest.
6. This system does not create any ill will or jealousy among the workers because all workers doing the same type of work get the same salary.
7. This system involves less administrative control as the system is easy to operate.
8. There are least damages and depreciation of plant, machinery and tools and so on under this system as the same are handled properly because of there is no hurry in completing the job.
9. It promotes creativity among workers.

Demerits

However, there are several shortcomings in the time rate system, which are as follows:

1. Cost of production may be higher as there is no time limit to complete a job.
2. This system does not provide any incentive to an efficient worker. Hence, it decreases the morale of efficient workers.
3. There is relatively less output because the speed of workers gets slowed as there is no penalty for less output.
4. It requires close supervision to maintain output. Hence, supervisory costs may go up.
5. In this system, labour cost keeps fluctuating, and it is difficult to measure it.
6. Cost of production is likely to go up in this system. Hence, employers do not prefer it.

Thus, this system is suitable in circumstances where a worker's output is not measurable easily or precisely, quality of output is more important, nature of job changes quite frequently and interruptions take place frequently.

Piece Rate Methods/Payment by Results

It is also quite an old method of wage payment. Under this system, wages are paid based on the quantum of output of a worker. The worker is paid a fixed rate per unit of output as follows:

Wages = Number of units produce × Rate per unit

The rate is determined with the help of time or motion studies or based on analysis of previous performance and establishment of average performance of a particular standard of workmanship.

Merits

The main merits of piece rate system are as follows:

1. The calculation of wages is easy.
2. This system works as an incentive for workers to produce more.
3. It requires less supervision because in order to earn more, workers work at their own.
4. It becomes easier to estimate cost of production because piece rate is fixed.
5. Since the breakage of tools or machinery will reduce the output of workers, they handle the same cautiously; hence, there is the least amount of damage.
6. The idle time is minimised as the workers know that they will not earn anything during their idle time.
7. More scope of innovation because workers try to invent new methods of producing more.
8. More cooperation among team/group members so as to avoid interruptions in work.
9. Cost of product comes down due to bigger output by workers to earn more.
10. This system is more equitable than the time rate system as under this system, reward is related to effort.

Demerits

Some of the main disadvantages of this system are as follows:

1. This system may impact quality adversely as in the urge of more output and resulting more earnings, the workers may not bother for quality.
2. In the urge for more output, the workers may not bother for wastage of material and damage to machinery.
3. It may impact the health of the workers adversely because they may overwork to earn more.
4. If a worker falls ill, then he/she loses his/her wages for that period.
5. The rate fixed may be low, causing loss to the earnings of workers.
6. The earnings of workers suffer due to interruptions on account of power failure or machines breakdown.
7. The system is frustrating to less efficient workers and may spread feelings of jealously among workers against their follow workers.
8. There may be a problem of overproduction if the demand for products goes downwards.

For example, the Punjab National Bank wants performance to do the wage-hike talking. It has proposed performance-based remuneration (for details, see Exhibit 9.2).

> **Exhibit 9.2   PNB Wants Performance to Do the Wage-hike Talking**
>
> Times are changing and we have to change with the times. Now the time has come to recognise performance and it is also to retain talent.
>
> *Source: Hindustan Times*, 9 November 2016.

For decades, remuneration at government-owned banks has been linked to industry-wide negotiations irrespective of the performance of each employee. In contrast, remuneration at private banks is linked to performance and could vary significantly between two employees of the same rank. Performance-based remuneration was never considered.

The method of wage payment based on results can be any of the following:

1. **Straight piece rate**: In it, the worker gets depending on his/her actual output. His/her per-unit output is multiplied with the pre-fixed per-unit rate.
2. **Increasing piece rate**: Per this method, as the production increases, the per-unit rate also increases. For example, for the first 10 units, the piece rate may be 2 per unit; for 11–15 units, the rate may be 2.15; and for over 15 units, the wage rate per piece may go up to 2.25. The efficient workers prefer this system of wage payment.
3. **Decreasing piece rate**: Under this method, the rate of wages per unit goes down as the production increases. For example, for 10 units, the rate may be 2 per unit; for 11–15 units, the rate may be 1.90 per unit; and so on. Employers usually prefer this method of wage payment.
4. **Straight piece rate system with minimum wages**: In this system, a worker is paid minimum wages even if he/she produces less than the standardised output in a specific time; otherwise, he/she is paid based on straight piece rate.
5. **Balance and debt system of wages**: Under this method, a worker is paid minimum wages even if he/she produces less than the standardised output in a specific time, in the expectation that he/she will make up the deficiency of work in future by doing more work.

Incentive Plans or Bonus (Premium) Scheme

Any system of wage payment which induces a worker to produce more is known as incentive system. However, the worker is assured of a guaranteed minimum wage. The system correlates earnings to output, thus providing a special financial incentive for increasing effort while guaranteeing the minimum wages. Thus, this system has all the merits minus demerits of the earlier described two systems of wage payment: the time rate system and the piece rate system/payment by results.

The system offers several incentive plans which can be classified into two categories: individual incentive plans and group/collective bonus plans. A brief description of some of the main plans is as follows.

Individual Incentive Plans

The main ones are as follows:

Straight Piece Work Plan

This plan is just like 'straight piece rate' system, discussed earlier, but with the only difference that in straight piece work plan, hourly earnings are guaranteed. Hence, this plan resembles the 'straight piece rate system with minimum wages', which has also been described earlier.

Differential Piece Rate Plans

In such plans, differential piece rates are set for different amounts of outputs. There are the following important plans under this category:

1. **Taylor differential piece rate plan:** Initiated by F. W. Taylor, under this plan, there are only two-piece rates—high rate and low (or ordinary) rate—for each job or task. In other words, if a worker performs the work within or less than the standard time, then he/she is paid a higher piece rate, and if he/she does not complete work within the standard time, he/she is given a lower piece rate for low production, that is, he/she would be able to earn just an ordinary day's pay. This plan can be illustrated as follows:

    The following values are given:

    Task (standard output) = 20 units
    Actual output = 16 units

Rates:

   High rate = Rs. 3 per unit
   Low rate = Rs. 2.50 per unit

Calculations of earnings (E):
   In case actual output equals or exceeds standard output:

   E = 20 units × Rs. 3 = Rs. 60

In case actual output falls short of standard output (e.g. if actual output is 15):

   E = 15 units × Rs. 2.50 = Rs. 37.50

However, the system is possible where it is easy to relate effort to production; work is standardised, repetitive and measurable; production methods and machines are standardised; there is no interruptions in workflow; fixed expenses are more than variable expenses; and production control and supervision are well regulated.

2. **Merrick multiple piece rate plan:**[9] Instead of dividing the workers into two categories, as is the case in F. W. Taylor's differential piece rate plan, D. W. Merrick in his plan introduced three-piece rates and made the lowest piece rate equal to the ordinary piece rate, which becomes the base piece rate. The piece rates of wages suggested by him under his plan are (a) for less than 83% of output = basic piece rate,

(b) from 83% to 100% of output = 110% of basic piece rate, and (3) for over 100% of output = 120% of basic piece rate.

Thus, this plan is a modified form of Taylor plan and is more suitable for workers.

3. **Gantt task and bonus plan:**[10] In his plan initiated in 1901, which is a modified form of Taylor's plan, Henry L. Gantt introduced a better feature by mentioning that if a worker's output in a task time is equal to or more than the stipulated task, then he/she is paid a bonus at a certain percentage of guaranteed basic wage. The guaranteed basic wage is always a time rate wage. However, it is necessary that the basic wage rate and the task or the task standards should be determined with caution and care and further that tasks set should be reasonable and practical; otherwise, the plan may not be able to accomplish its objectives.

Gantt recommended that according to the nature of the work, the bonus may vary from 10% to 100% of the guaranteed wage per nature of work as follows:

1. Work not involving much physical labour combined with close and constant attention; for example, the work of machine attendants = 10–15%
2. Work in general machine shop or tool room = 35%
3. Work involving constant use of the eyes = 30–40%
4. Heavy work, including skilled work = 60–70%
5. Work requiring high skill, much physical labour or strain, ability to work under unpleasant conditions and involving acceptance of responsibility = 100%

Thus, it is obvious that more requirements of attention and the like for a job mean progressive increase in earnings. For this reason, Gantt system is also known as progressive rate system.

Apart from providing financial incentives in his plan, Gantt has put much emphasis on improving the efficiency of workers, on their training as also on making all possible arrangements so that workers may do their task without excessive exertion. Of course, it is not that easy for an employer to make all the arrangements as perfect as suggested in the plan.

Premium or Bonus Plans or Bonus Sharing Plans

A premium or bonus plan or a bonus sharing plan which is a unification of time rate and piece rate systems aims at providing suitable monetary incentives to both employers and employees of the time saved by the worker in completing his/her task. The main bonus sharing plans are as follows:

- **Halsey plan**: Under this plan, bonus is shared by the worker and the employer in some definite fixed proportions varying between 25% and 75%, though usually it is 50%. Per this plan, if the actual hours taken by a worker to complete his/her task are less than its stipulated standard hours, then the total wage for the time saved, calculated based on the guaranteed base ratio of worker, is shared by the worker and the employer. The worker gets his/her share of the time saved as follows:

Time wage = Time taken × Time rate + ½ (Time saved × Time rate)

Thus, the share of the wages of the 'time saved' given to the worker is his/her premium bonus. Obviously, in addition to this share, he/she will get usual guaranteed wage for the time spent by him/her on his/her work. An additional feature of this plan is that premium bonus is also given to foremen or supervisors who affect increase in the productivity of the workers working under their supervision.

Broadly speaking, 10–40% of employer's share of bonus is distributed among such foremen or supervisors.

- **Hasley–Weir plan**: Introduced by G&J Weir Ltd of Glasgow in 1990, this plan is another form of the Halsey premium bonus plan with the difference that, per this plan, a worker gets 30% of the time saved, that is, standard hours minus actual hours, whereas in the Halsey plan, the worker gets between 25% and 75%, which is usually 50%. Like the Halsey plan, a minimum wage is guaranteed under this plan also.
- **Rowan plan**: Keeping in view the guidelines of the Halsey plan, James Rowan of David Rowan and Company Ltd, Glasgow, introduced this plan in 1898. It is a variable bonus sharing plan, and the proportion of the bonus a worker earns varies if the time saved by the worker varies. Thus, the Rowan plan is a variable bonus sharing plan, its formula being as follows:

$$\text{Total Wages} = \underset{(i.e.\ Minimum\ guaranteed\ wages)}{\text{Time Taken} \times \text{Time Rate}} + \underset{(i.e. Bonus\ /\ Premium\ /\ Incentive)}{\left[\dfrac{Time\ Saved}{Standard\ Time}\right] \times \text{Time Rate} \times \text{Taken}}$$

For example, suppose the following information is given:

Task time (standard time) = 10 hours
Actual time taken = 5 hours
Hourly rate = Rs 2/-

In the case of above example, the total wages (i.e. minimum guaranteed wage bonus will be calculated as follows:

1. Calculation of minimum guaranteed wage:

    $5\ (T.T) \times 2\ \text{Time Rate} = 10$

2. Calculation of bonus or premium:

    $$\dfrac{5(TS)}{10(ST)} \times 2(\text{Rate}) \times 5(T.T)$$

    $$= \dfrac{1}{2} \times 10 = 5$$

    Total wages (i.e. Minimum guaranteed wage + Bonus/premium)

    $10 + 5 = 15$

The main advantage of this plan is that in addition to providing good incentive for relatively slow workers and learners, it protects the employer against loose rate setting as also enabling the employer to get a share in the benefit of increased output. However, the plan is more complex and expensive than the Halsey plan.

The other premium or bonus plans or bonus sharing plans are as follows:

- Bedeaux point premium plan[11]
- Emerson efficiency bonus plan[12]
- Barth variable sharing plan[13]
- Accelerating premium plan[14]
- Baum differential plan[15]
- Diemer system[16]

Group/Collective Bonus Plans

Such plans which are useful when individual workers' output cannot be easily measured aim at ensuring higher productivity, more production and creating a sense of cooperation. Today, several group/collective bonus plans are being practised. Some of the main ones are as follows:

Priestman's Production Bonus Plan

Adopted by Messrs Priestman Bros Ltd, Hull, in 1917, this plan provides that the bonus will be payable to that department which gives results higher than the standard output set jointly by a committee representing the management and the workers' union, well in advance every week or every month, per the following formula:

$$\text{Percentage of bonus} = \frac{\text{Increased production}}{\text{Stamdard production}} \times 100$$

Just to illustrate it, we can take a case where the standard production is 4,000 units and the actual output is 6,000 units, and the workers will be given a bonus equivalent to 50% of their wages as follows:

$$\text{Percentage of bonus} = \frac{2,000}{4,000} \times 100 = 50 \ percent$$

The plan suits especially to organisations where the cost of material is high.

Cost Premium Plan

Under this plan, if the actual cost of production comes less than its standard cost of production, then a part of the saving is distributed among the workers as their bonus.

Budgeted Expense Bonus

As per this plan, bonus is based on the savings in actual total expenditure compared with the total budgeted expenditure. The percentage of bonus is predetermined share of saving in budgeted expenditure.

Profit-sharing Plan

This plan provides for sharing of the profits of the enterprise with the workers in a predetermined ratio. The plan aims at motivating the workers to cooperate in increasing the profits of the enterprise.

Towne Gain Sharing Plan

Introduced by H. R. Towne in the USA in 1896, the plan provides for calculation of bonus on the reduction in costs (usually the labour cost) as compared with predetermined standard. An individual is entitled to half of the savings pro rata with wages earned. The supervisory staff also gets a part of this bonus.

Waste Reduction Plan

The plan has a provision to provide incentives to workers to reduce wastage. The plan takes the form of a percentage.

Advantages of Group/Collective Bonus Plan(s)

Group bonus plans provide incentives, besides guaranteeing time wages, to work cooperatively with the organisation to enhance output, reduce wastage and cost of production and so on. Besides, their administrative cost is also less as compared to individual bonus plans. Moreover, they need relatively less inspection and supervision.

Disadvantages of Group/Collective Bonus Plan

Since these plans provide bonus on collective basis, the efficient workers do not prefer it because they do not get due reward for their contribution. At times, the amount of bonus is too less to serve the purpose of the plan. Besides, how much amount should be given to which worker is also a problem.

Advantages of Incentive Plans

The main advantages of incentive plans can be studied under the following heads:

1. **Benefits to workers:** Due to incentive plans, the total earnings of workers are likely to go up, leading to improvement in their standard of living. Besides, their working capacity also gets a boost and morale also goes to a higher level.
2. **Benefits to employers:** It is not only the workers who are benefited by incentive plans, but the employers also get benefited by such plans. Since these plans motivate the workers to produce more, reduce cost of production, avoid wastage of material and so on, the cost of production goes down, and output goes up and so is the case with profits of the organisation. Besides, standards are fixed for everything which have to be achieved by workers in case they want to reap the benefits of these plans. The plans also lead to good industrial relations and so on.

Principles of Incentive System of Wage Payment

Incentive system is likely to sustain itself and prove effective if the following principles are adhered to:

1. An incentive plan must be thoroughly worked out, leaving no loopholes.
2. It should be properly conveyed and clarified to all concerned.
3. Bonus should be at least 15–20% higher than the hourly rates.
4. Standards should be based on logic and pragmatism.
5. Job evaluation must be rigorously carried out.
6. Periodic review must be there, and changes may be made as and when required.
7. Workers' unions should always be taken into confidence while standards are worked out or changes are introduced.

Prerequisites/Essentials for the Successful Working of Incentive Wage Plans

W. H. Spencer has suggested certain basic considerations while planning incentive wage plans. Some of such points are as follows:

1. The plan should have support from the top management.
2. It should be easily understandable by the workers.
3. It should have the constant attention of competent supervisory personnel.
4. An increase in the unit labour cost should be a matter of concern.
5. No premium for productivity below what should exist.
6. No increase in pay without a corresponding increase in productivity.

Comparison Between Individual and Group Bonus Plans

Group bonus schemes are better than individual premium plans where it is difficult to measure an individual's output. Group schemes are easier to implement than the individual premium schemes. Besides, group schemes develop greater cooperation and team spirit as compared to individual schemes. It is easier to understand a group bonus scheme. It is relatively easier to set targets for a group than for individuals.

Linking Pay to Performance

Of late, linking pay to performance is also getting popular. For an example, see Exhibit 9.3.

Exhibit 9.3 Campus Compensation: Companies Prefer to Link Pay to Performance (Variable Pay, Joining Bonus, Register Increase Across all Tiers of Business Schools)

Due to uncertain economic climate, organisations are forced to alter their approach towards campus compensation by reducing the fixed component and becoming aggressive in pay-for-performance and joining bonus. This is what has been revealed by the latest Aon Hewitt Campus Study.

The objectives are to foster a performance-oriented environment by linking pay with performance and to reduce the year-on-year burden of pay increases linked to the fixed pay component.

Source: The Economic Times, 31 March 2017.

Profit-sharing

It is said that the first profit-sharing plan was developed by Albert Gallatin, secretary of the treasury at a glasswork in New Geneva, Pennsylvania, in 1794. In a profit-sharing plan, a fixed percentage of total profit of an organisation is distributed among employees either in the form of cash bonus in which full payment is made to the employees after profits have been worked out immediately or quarterly or annually, or through deferred bonus system in which the bonus is credited to the employees' accounts, payable at the time of retirement, severance, death, disability and so on. It is also possible to have a combination of both.

Ownership Plans/Stock Options

Stock bonus plans were used originally in the 1920s. Stock options are offered to employees in the form of company stock with the objective of attracting, motivating and retaining them. Such plans are introduced for the same reasons as are offered profit-sharing schemes. The logic behind stock options is that after employees become partners in the company, they work harder, sincerely, efficiently and effectively, and the company's interests become their interests. Giving stock options is a common practice in telecom sector in our country. All leading telecoms, such as Bharti Airtel, have employee stock option plans (ESOPs).[17] Reliance Jio may also roll out ESOPs to reward and retain employees (see Exhibit 9.4). Initially, senior management may only get ESOPs.

Exhibit 9.4   Reliance Jio Plans to Reward Employees with Stock Options

Mukesh Ambani owned Reliance Jio Infocom is planning to roll out stock options for its employees, which could be a reward for the pace at which subscribers are being added as well as a talent retention and attraction strategy of the company.

The stock options programme is currently in the planning stage and could be rolled out later this year. Reliance Jio, with its 30,000-plus permanent employees, will possibly introduce stock options initially for senior executives. All leading telcos, such as Bharti Airtel, Idea Cellular and Vodafone India, have employee stock option (ESOP) plans.

ESOP is usually given once a year and can range between 10% and 200% of an employee's salary. These are over and above the compensation and act as a talent retention tool.

Source: The Economic Times, Mumbai, 10 January 2017.

Since its official launch in September 2016, Jio with its free voice and data offer has attracted about half a million subscribers a day and is believed to have already added over 65 million customers. The biggest challenge for Reliance Jio was to ensure that subscribers who had signed up did not migrate to rival telcos, once the free offer was withdrawn/modified. Since now the offer extended earlier stands withdrawn, its full impact will be known over a specific time period depending on the strategy of different telcos. And this is where ESOPs will come in handy, especially in retaining key people tasked with customers' retention. Jio has seen exits at senior levels in last one year, and ESOPs may help in retaining senior-level officers in future. In India, and indeed globally, telecom majors offer ESOPs to senior ranks. This move will help Jio retain employees for a longer period.

Stock appreciation rights are a bonus given to employees, which equals the rise in a company's stock value. Employees do not have to pay the exercise price and hence can receive proceeds from stock price increases, without coughing up anything.

Stock plans are employee benefit plans designed to pay their benefits in the form of company stock. In case the value of the stock increases, the stock owners (employees) could, by selling their stock, receive a good return.

Supplementary Compensation

Supplementary compensation (or benefits) is extended to employees over and above their wages, the objective being not only promoting their economic betterments but also providing psychic satisfaction to employees which is instrumental in boosting their morale (for a detailed study of supplementary compensation [or benefits], see Chapter 11, 'Fringe Benefits and Services').

Essentials of a Satisfactory Wage System

The survival and progress of an organisation depends on the efficiency and effectiveness of its employees, which, in turn, depends to a great extent on the total earnings the employees get from the organisation. An ideal wage system is instrumental in reducing the cost of production, improving the quality of the products/services of the organisation, increasing the productivity and profitability of the organisation and, above all, providing contentment to the employees. It is, therefore, vital that an organisation has a well-planned wage system, and it is also well administered. A wage system can be successful if the following conditions are met:

1. It is well planned.
2. It is simple and easily comprehensible by the employees.
3. It ensures guaranteed minimum wage to every employee.
4. It is motivating to employees, leading to cost and wastage reduction and quality improvement, and it is productivity-oriented and cost-effective so that it suits the employers also.
5. It is flexible so that it can accommodate any change.
6. It maintains internal and external relativities.
7. It is pragmatic.
8. It provides enough incentives to employees to put in their best.
9. It provides contentment to employees.
10. It has wage differentials.
11. It is easy to put into practice.

Wage Differentials/Wage Variation

Why is it that a certain job requiring a certain skill is paid more or less than another job requiring a different skill either in the same or some other industry? This is due to several factors which need to be known and well understood by all the stakeholders in an organisation. The factors contributing to variations in wage rates may include variance in the skills required to perform the job well, the type of training and experience required, the type and quality of expertise, the scarcity of the type of labour required, the working conditions under which the job is to be performed, the hazards involved, the place or region where the workplace is located, the physical or mental efforts involved in discharging work responsibilities, the amount of stress, statutory requirements, the demand for and supply of a particular type of skill, cost of living, ability to pay of the organisation or industry, local labour market conditions and so on.

Types of Wage Variations

Wage variations may be of the following types:

1. **Regional wage variations**: Wage rates may differ from region to region or from state to state. For example, the wage rates in textile mills in Uttar Pradesh are less as compared to their counterparts in Gujarat or Maharashtra. It may be due to several factors as discussed earlier.
2. **Industry-based wage variations**: Wage rates may also differ from industry to industry. For example, IT and ITEs industries pay higher rates to their employees as compared to employees employed in sugar industry. This may be because of several reasons explained earlier in this chapter.
3. **Time-based wage variations**: Wage variation may also be due to typical features of a particular economic period. For example, wage rates may be low during economic depression period as compared to inflationary period.

Reward System

You know it well that rewards are usually paid to those employees who make significant contribution towards promoting the interests of the organisation.

Aspects of Rewards

The following are the main aspects of rewards:

- Amount of rewards
- Value of rewards
- Timing of rewards
- Likelihood of rewards
- Fairness of rewards

Characteristics of Good Reward System

- It should comprise both monetary and non-monetary rewards. Such a system takes better care of the needs of employees.

324 *Compensation and Reward Management*

- The frequency, timing and precision of rewards should be ideal.
- The plan should be well communicated to the employees concerned.

Determinants of Rewards

Rewards are usually merit-based, though the term 'merit' is viewed differently by different authors. However, rewards are normally determined by the following factors:

1. Mental and physical efforts involved
2. Output
3. Skills possessed
4. Seniority
5. Discretionary time (a completely programmed and procedurised job needs little decision-making, hence less rewarding)
6. Job difficulty

Structures/Types of Rewards

There are two popular types of rewards which are as follows (Figure 9.1):

1. **Intrinsic rewards**
    - Greater responsibility
    - Greater authority
    - Diversity of activities
    - Participation in decision-making
    - Job autonomy
    - Opportunities for self-development
    - Job satisfaction

2. **Extrinsic rewards**: Such rewards can be further classified into following two categories:

    a. **Monetary rewards**—Monetary rewards can be sub-classified into two types:

      i. Performance-based rewards: Such rewards may consist of the following:
          - Performance bonus
          - Piecework

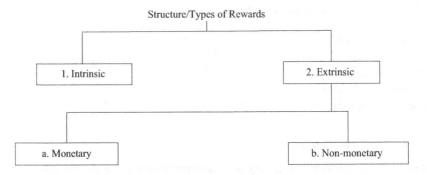

Figure 9.1 Structure/Types of Rewards

Wage and Salary Administration and Employee Compensation

- Merit pay plans
- Incentive plans
- Commission

ii. **Membership-based rewards**: These rewards comprise the following:

- Basic salary
- DA
- House rent allowance
- Pay for the time not worked, such as holidays and leaves
- Welfare and social security programmes

b. **Non-monetary rewards**: The main forms of non-monetary are reflected in Figure 9.2. However, G. B. Mohanty has identified the non-financial incentives related to effective work:

- Improved attitude
- Supervisory relationship
- Advancement and security
- Supervision
- Job satisfaction and enrichment
- Praise and blame
- Knowledge of result and experience of progress
- Experience of achievement
- Level of aspiration and nature of the goal
- Cooperation and competition

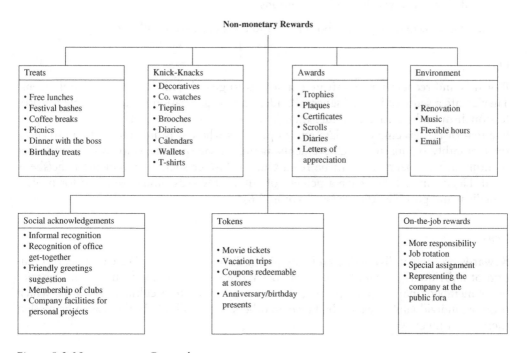

Figure 9.2 Non-monetary Rewards

Rewards in Indian Industries

Rewards in Indian industries differ widely. For example, incentives and rewards schemes in Godfrey Phillips India Ltd, Andheri, Mumbai, include the following:

- Production incentive
- Kaizen Telan ('continuous improvement' based on suggestions received from employees)
- Promotion of employees
- Attendance bonus
- Wage policy

In the Aerial Delivery Research and Development Establishment (ADRDE), Agra, rewards and incentives schemes include the following:

- Production-linked incentive
- Prime Minister's Shram Award
- Suggestion schemes
- Performance appraisal
- Transparency in management
- Wage policy

Thus, we see that performance appreciation, team rewards, suggestion schemes, production incentives, transparency in management, participation in management, tempting wage policies and so on are some of the common rewards.

Pros and Cons of Rewards and Recognitions

Rewards and recognitions have both pros and cons (also see Exhibit 9.5):

Pros

Rewards and recognitions motivate employees to give their best to their organisations. They create a sense of belongingness. Besides, if an organisation rewards people for professionalism and positive attitude, then it has a statutory effect. There are many jobs like that of HR executives or data entry operators where it is difficult for them to show their monthly or quarterly achievements against a salesperson, who can show his/her monthly achievements and can be rewarded for his/her such achievements if he/she is good. Hence, in order to have a percept of equity, rewards should be given for professionalism and positive attitude (see Exhibit 9.6).

Cons

Rewards promote individuality and may play a demotivating role. For example, recognition of individuals in team-based roles does more harm than good. In such a scenario, other members may stop supporting the winner.[18] In Eastern cultures, rewards, which promote individualism, leave a bad taste in others (see Exhibit 9.7), the reason being that there is not much work.

Exhibit 9.5 Rewards and Recognitions

Pros
- Motivate employees
- Employee satisfaction guaranteed
- Enhance organisations' productivity

Cons
- Promote individualism
- Foolproof process a challenge
- Demotivate other employees

Source: Hindustan Times, 12 January 2016.

Exhibit 9.6 Reward People for Professionalism, Positive Attitude

'If someone has performed under extreme pressure depending on the nature of the job he or she does, if someone has shown great patience during a public dealing. If someone has managed to defuse a crisis situation with a smile on his (or her) face, these are some personal attributes which should get a standing ovation in the company'.

'So, if good behavior and professionalism are rewarded suitably, others might not be demotivated', says Aman Attree, head HR, Hindustan Power projects.

Source: Quoted in *Hindustan Times,* 12 January 2016.

Exhibit 9.7 Do Awards Really Motivate?

Also, though some HR experts relate rewarding system with individual efforts, they say it is important to look at the difference in evolution of Eastern and Western cultures to understand the reward and recognition programmes.

In Western cultures, individuals are expected to survive on their own. It's common for children to be independent very early on, and this aspect of the socio-cultural background is evident at the workplace too. In Eastern cultures, rewards, which promote individualism, singling out one person as a hero, may not be the best choice, as it leaves a bad taste in others' mouths. Rewards which promote team collaborations and are given to groups have a higher significance in Indian culture. We have copied the West for its HR systems without considering our psychological background.

Source: Hindustan Times, 12 January 2016.

Profiles in which success can be attributed to one individual are rare since most senior-level positions require collaboration and support from other team members. Thus, if rewards and recognitions lead to individuality, they demotivate other employees. It is indeed difficult to have a foolproof process.

Hence, some precautions should be taken to make rewards and recognitions effective (see Exhibit 9.8).

HR heads believe that irrespective of job roles, reward systems can be implemented everywhere. According to Chandan Chattaraj, president of HR (Indian and global) at Uflex Limited, if someone does not deserve the recognition but he is recognised, then other team members will prove costly for the organisation. To make sure such things do not happen, there must be some rules for identifying suitable recipients, which start with identifying the values, goals and behaviour leading to success.

For Chattaraj, it is important that the parameters are well defined. 'For instance, in my company, we have different parameters for production, marketing and support functions. This is precisely to avoid overshadowing of the significant contribution made by support function employees' decisions'.[19] It is better not to run programmes for which you do not have adequate and proper measures to avoid preferential or subjective selection.

Some corporate leaders also believe that an employee should be awarded the moment there is a need to do so. Sometimes monthly and yearly awards do not achieve the desired purpose, they feel. 'Business activities and reward programmes need to be synced for success and for improving employee morale', says Gulshan Chib, HR head at Duet India Hotels.[20]

Exhibit 9.8   Handling Out Rewards: Do It Right

Don't start a reward programme because everyone's doing it. Take time to decide the core values you want to promote and thereafter reward those core values.

Make sure that the process is seen as fair and transparent.

Involve employees while working out ways in which selections are made for rewards and recognition.

Using rewards and recognition to drive desirable behaviour and efforts makes them more impactful.

Source: Hindustan Times, 12 January 2016.

Chapter Review

1. Although pay is not necessarily the strongest motivator, any unjustifiable inequity or an unacceptable low level of reward causes great dissatisfaction to employees. Hence, it is essential for an organisation to work out appropriate salary structure, have salary progression systems, administer and control salary reviews and design and operate other allowances justifiably. It is here that W&S administration comes into picture because all such things are taken care of by W&S administration.
2. There are organisational, individual and collective objectives of W&S administration. The main functions of W&S administration are to recommend wage policies and changes therein whenever required, to design and maintain salary

structure, to operate salary progression systems, to design and operate other allowances, to review W&S schemes and so on.
3. Employee compensation is important not only to employees but also to employers and the society. Employee compensation is the reward to an employee for his/her services to his/her organisation. Various wage concepts such as nominal and real wages, take-home salary, statutory minimum wage, living wage, fair wage, minimum wage, basic compensation and supplementary compensation should be known to all concerned. The objectives of employee compensation include to attract, motivate and retain competent employees; to increase productivity and profitability of the organisation; to maintain industrial peace; and so on. There are several factors affecting employee compensation, such as demand for and supply of labour, productivity, trade unions, collective bargaining, company's and government's wage policies and wage legislation. The main components of employee compensation or industrial pay structure comprise basic pay, DA, bonus and other allowances.
4. Both internal and external equities in the employee compensation should be maintained. Employee compensation planning should be there in an organisation, though it is not a simple exercise. It has to keep into consideration several things, such as wage theories, job evaluation and job pricing, incentive plans, supplementary benefits and national wage policy.
5. Wages are the reward paid to a worker for his/her service to the organisation. The main theories of wages can be classified into two categories: (a) economic theories (subsistence theory, wage fund theory, marginal productivity theory, bargaining theory, surplus value theory, purchasing power theory, modern theories of wages and so on) and (b) behavioural theories (equity theory, Vroom's expectancy theory, Herzberg's two-factor theory and so on). The national wage policy of our country has been influenced by several factors, such as the Directive Principles of State Policy, the Constitution of India, reports of various committees and commissions and legislative steps. As far as wage policy at the organisational level is concerned, it should be formulated keeping in view factors, such as internal and external relativities, productivity, cost of living and statutory obligations. The main wage problems in India relate to vast size of unorganised sector, ignorance of workers, weak trade unionism, emergence of nuclear family system, exploitative nature of employers, lack of adequate support from government and so on.
6. Time rate system, piece rate system and incentive system are the three main methods/systems of wage payment in our country. All the aforesaid three systems have their own positive and negative aspects.
7. Incentive plans or bonus (premium) schemes may be (a) individual incentive plans, which may be straight piece work plan, differential piece rate plans (such as Taylor differential piece rate plan, Merrick multiple piece rate plan and Gantt task and bonus plan) and premium or bonus plans or bonus sharing plans (such as Halsey plan, Halsey–Weir plan and Rowan Plan) or (b) group/collective bonus plans (such as Priestman's production plan, cost premium plan, budgeted expense bonus plan, profit-sharing plan, Towne gain sharing plan and waste reduction plan).

8. Incentive plans are beneficial to both the employees and employers as these plans, on the one hand, lead to increase in the earnings of the workers and, on the other hand, lead to more profitability of the organisation. In order to make an incentive plan a real success, the principles laid down for the purpose should be adhered to. The prerequisites for the successful working of incentive plans include support from the top management, simplicity, flexibility, maintenance of balance between increase in wages and increase in productivity and so on. Group bonus plans are preferable where it is difficult to measure an individual's output.
9. Profit-sharing develops among workers a sense of belongingness and involvement, motivates the workers and leads to industrial peace. Similarly, stock options to employees help in attracting, motivating and retaining employees. Supplementary compensation aims at benefiting the employees economically, motivating them and boosting their morale. In order to be a successful wage system, it should be simple, flexible, well planned, pragmatic, equitable and so on.
10. There are various factors such as skill requirement and competence required that cause wage differentials or variations. Wage differentials or variations may be of different types, such as regional wage variations, industry-based variations and time-based wage variations.

Key Terms

balance and debt system of wages
bargaining theory
basic wage
bonus
bonus (premium) schemes
bonus sharing plans
budgeted expense bonus plan
collective bargaining
cost premium plan
dearness allowance
decreasing piece rate
employee compensation
equity
equity theory
external equity
fair wage
Gantt task and bonus plan
graded salary structure
group/collective bonus plans
Halsey plan
Halsey–Weir plan
Herzberg's two-factor theory
incentive plans
increasing piece rate
Industrial Policy Resolution
Industrial Truce Resolution
industry-based variation
internal equity
learning zone
living wage
marginal productivity theory
Merrick multiple piece rate plan
minimum wage
modern theories of wages
money wage
nominal wage
piece rate method of payment of wages
premium plans
premium zone
Priestman's production bonus plan
productivity
profit-sharing plan/ownership plan
purchasing power theory
qualified zone
real wage
regional wage variations
salary levels
salary progression curves
salary progression systems
salary review
salary structure
statutory minimum wage
stock options plan
straight piece rate

straight piece rate system with minimum wages	time-based wage variation	wage and salary administration
straight piece work plan	time rate method of payment of wage	wage boards
subsistence theory	Towne gain sharing plan	wage differentials
supplementary compensation	tribunals	wage fund theory
surplus value theory	valence	wage variation
take-home salary	variable compensation	waste reduction plan
Taylor differential piece rate plan	Vroom's expectancy theory	

Discussion Questions

1. Discuss how W&S administration is helpful to both the workers and the employers.
2. Discuss the objectives and functions of W&S administration.
3. Discuss how employee compensation is important to employees, employers and the society.
4. Discuss the main components of employee compensation and also the factors that affect employee compensation.
5. Discuss the main theories of wages as also their limitations.
6. Discuss the highlights of national wage policy of India and the factors that have influenced it. Also discuss the factors that should be kept in view while formulating wage policy at the organisational level.
7. Discuss the various methods of wage payment and also their merits and demerits.
8. Discuss the main individual incentive plans.
9. Discuss the popular group bonus plans. Also discuss why there should be group bonus plans.
10. Discuss the concepts of profit sharing, stock options and wage differentials.

Individual and Group Activities

As an individual, visit a large manufacturing company employing more than 2,000 employees. Talk to the officials of the HR department of the company and find out the functions being performed by their W&S administration.

1. Constitute two groups of two members each and visit a large company. One group should discuss with the HR officials and find out from them the components of employee compensation. The other group should talk to trade union officials and find out the reaction of the members of trade unions about these components.
2. Either individually or in a group of two members, pay a visit to a big company and find out from the HR officials the factors that influence the wage policy of their organisation.

3. In a group of two members, talk to the trade union officials of a big company and find out the method(s) of wage payment operating in their company and have their reaction towards the same.
4. Form two groups of two members each and visit some big organisation. One group should talk to the HR officials and find out the incentive plans, if any, functional in their company. The other group should talk to the trade union officials and find out their reaction towards these schemes and also seek their suggestions.

Application Case 9.1

Perception of Equity

Michael, a diploma holder in mechanical engineering, has been working in a bicycle-manufacturing company for the last five years. Two of his classmates have also been working in the same industry elsewhere. All the three are in regular touch with one another, and they appear to be a satisfied lot as far as their salary is concerned. All the three are placed in the same grade and drawing almost an equal salary and perks. One day, both the friends of Michael came to his company on a courtesy call, and after taking a round of the company, all the three went to have a cup of tea in the company's canteen, where every item was available at a concessional rate. All the three were in a very happy mood and enjoyed their tea and snacks. In the meantime, they noticed that two people were talking with each other while taking tea in the same canteen and sitting next to their table. These three friends overheard the two sitting next to their table, who were speaking very proudly about their company, located in the same industrial area, producing gears needed in the automotive industry. The three got curious to know more about them and their company. Hence, after taking their tea, they got up and moved towards the two, who also regarded them favourably.

The three greeted them and, after shaking hands, started talking about their factory. During the course of their chatting, the three friends came to know that coincidently, the other two were also working as mechanics and that each of them was getting almost 30% more salary than what each of three friends was getting, along with a fairly good number of perks.

The three friends got upset when they came to know about higher salary the two mechanics were getting in the gear manufacturing company located in the same area. They started thinking about looking for job elsewhere.

Questions

1. Do you think that the main reason of the three friends thinking of leaving their present jobs was the disturbance in their perception of external equity? Yes or no? Why? Explain in brief.
2. What was the main shortcoming in the job evaluation and fixation of wages in bicycle-manufacturing company?
3. Were you the vice president of HR in the bicycle-manufacturing company, what steps would you take to overcome such problems in future?

Notes

1 *The Economic Times*, 5 January 2017.
2 R. C. Sharma, *Industrial Relations and Labour Legislation* (Delhi: PHI Learning, 2016), 307.
3 International Labour Organization, *Report of International Labour Office Conference*, 31 Session (Geneva: International Labour Office, 1948), 7.
4 T. N. Bhagatiwal, *Economics of Labour and Industrial Relations* (Agra: Sahitya Bhawan, 1984), 503–4.
5 A. Monappa, *Industrial Relations* (New Delhi: Tata McGraw-Hill Publishing Company Limited, 2007), 72.
6 See Sharma, *Industrial Relations and Labour Legislation*, 308.
7 Flippo, *Principles of Personnel Management*, 297.
8 Ibid.
9 For a detailed study, see H. L. Gantt, *Work, Wages and Profit* (New York, NY: Engineering Manufacturing Co., 1910).
10 For a detailed study, see D. V. Merrick, *Time Studies as a Basis for Rate Setting* (New York, NY: Engineering Manufacturing Co., 1919).
11 For details, see Sharma, *Industrial Relations and Labour Legislation*, 342–43.
12 Ibid., 344.
13 Ibid., 344–45.
14 Ibid., 345.
15 Ibid.
16 Ibid., 345–46.
17 *The Economic Times*, 10 January 2017.
18 Nitant Soni, quoted in *Hindustan Times*, 12 January 2016.
19 Quoted in *Hindustan Times*, 12 January 2016.
20 Ibid.

10 Divergent Systems and Institutions for Wage Determination in Practices in Indian Organisations (with Special Reference to Job Evaluation)

Learning Objectives

After studying this chapter, the reader should be able to do the following:

1. Explain the significance of appropriate fixation of wages.
2. List the divergent systems and institutions of wage fixations presently followed in Indian organisations.
3. Explain the role of job evaluation in designing pay structures.
4. Describe the process and methods of job evaluation.
5. List and describe the techniques/methods of job pricing.
6. Explain methods of pricing managerial jobs.
7. Describe bipartite wage fixation and the role of collective bargaining.
8. Explain the tripartite wage fixation.
9. Discuss statutory wage fixation and also wage fixation through third party.
10. Discuss the Code on Wages 2019.
11. Explain what should be the management's strategy with regard to wage fixation.
12. Point out the recent developments/emerging trends in the field of wages.

Introduction

Having gone through the wage and salary administration and employee compensation in Chapter 9, we can now move on to one of the major issues in the realm of compensating people at work in Indian organisations—namely, fixation of wages and practices being followed by them in this regard. Unfortunately, in our country there is a great disparity in the income of the people. According to the report titled, 'The Rise of India's Middle Class', authored by Rajesh Shukla, MD and CEO of PRICE (People Research on India's Consumer Economy), the number people who are deemed 'rich' (whose annual [2020–2021] household income is more than INR 30 lakh) has increased substantially consisting of 3% of the total households in the country in 2020–2021. The share of 'middle class' (whose annual [2020–2021] household income is more than INR 5 lakh–INR 30 lakh) doubled from 14% in 2004–2005 to 30% in 2020–2021. The number of households of 'aspirers' (whose annual [2020–2021] household income is more than INR 1.25 lakh–INR 5 lakh) and the 'destitute' (whose annual [2020–2021] household income is less than INR 1.25 lakh) constituted 52% and 15%, respectively, of the total households

DOI: 10.4324/9781032628424-14

in the country in 2020–2021. If we consider the number of households who are considered 'super-rich' (whose annual [2020–2021] household income is over INR 2 crore [a part of 'rich' class]), it increases from 9,800 in 1994–1995 to 1.8 million households in 2020–2021.[1] The report further states that by 2047, if the political and economic reforms have their desired effect, the India income pyramid will have a smallish layer at the bottom comprising the 'destitute' and 'aspirer' groups, a huge bulge of the 'middle class' and a big creamy 'rich' layer on top. These revelations suggest that the per household annual income is likely to go up in times to come, but all the same, the figures also show that there is a relatively vast disparity in the annual household incomes of different groups. (However, there is also a positive sign that per capita income of the population of India has increased in real terms by 33.4% in eight years since the enactment of National Food Security Act [NFSA], 2013, taking out large swathe of population out of the vulnerable section of the society.)[2] It is, therefore, necessary that the vast disparity should be minimised. In case wages are not appropriately fixed, workers are likely to suffer not only in economic terms but they get emotionally and psychologically disturbed a great deal—thus affecting their work behaviour (see Exhibit 10.1). Obviously, in such a scenario they cannot contribute their best to the organisation, which in turn is likely to cause loss to all the stakeholders in the organisation. Hence, wage fixation needs a thoughtful consideration and working out of an appropriate mechanism.

Exhibit 10.1 7 in 10 Employees Feel They Are Not Paid Fairly

Blame manager, HR team for pay disparity, shows a TimesJobs survey of more than 1,600 employees

7 in 10 employees feel they are not paid fairly. 30% said they felt they were paid fairly. 70% said they were not paid fairly.	**Who is to be blamed for the pay disparity?** 40% blamed their managers. 30% blamed HR. 15% blamed top management. 15% blamed themselves, since they need to reskill.	**Employer's expectations** 30% said they were clear about their employer's expectations from them and their profile. 70% said they were not clear.
6 in 10 do not see a long-term career in their current organisation. 35% said they saw themselves having a long-term career in their current organisation. 65% said they did not.	**Organisational support for growth and learning** 45% said they got support from the company to grow and learn. 55% said they did not.	

Source: The Economic Times, 6 March 2018.

Divergent Systems and Institutions for Wage Fixation in Practice in India

In our country, several systems and institutions for wage fixation are operational, the main ones are as follows:

1. Unilateral wage fixation
   a. In the organised sector (with special reference to job analysis and job evaluation)
   b. In the unorganised sector
2. Bipartite wage fixation
3. Tripartite wage fixation
4. Statutory wage fixation
5. Third-party wage fixation
6. Practices in vogue for supplementing base wages

A detailed discussion of the aforementioned systems is as follows.

Unilateral Wage Fixation

Unilateral wage fixation is common in both the organised and unorganised sectors.

In the Organised Sector

In most organisations in the organised sector, wage fixation is done unilaterally by the employer using the techniques of job evaluation and job pricing. These techniques are used to design pay structures as follows.

Job Evaluation

An employee is paid according to the worth of work that he does for the organisation. However, evaluating the worth of a work or job evaluation is not a simple task. It involves several problems. The technique of job evaluation is used to design appropriate pay structures which obviously influence employee behaviour and help the organisation to sustain its competitive advantage. Job evaluation involves what to value in the jobs, how to assess that value and what to translate it into a job-related structure.

Job evaluation establishes the relative value of jobs based on their contents, independent of link to the market. It is a tool or technique for evaluation and ranking of jobs to help an organisation to evolve a rational and scientific wage structure. Thus, job evaluation is a process of comparing jobs to determine the relative worth of each job with a view to determine what should be the fair wage rate for such a job. According to the ILO, job evaluation is an attempt to determine and compare the demands made by the normal performance of particular jobs on normal workers without taking into account the individual abilities or performance of the workers concerned.[3] According to the Bureau of Labour Statistics, United States, job evaluation is the evaluation or rating of jobs to determine their position in a job hierarchy.[4] However, it should be well understood that job evaluation is the technique for rating the job and not the man, that is, it does not take into account the individual's efforts and abilities. The immediate objective of the job evaluation process is to obtain internal and external consistency.[5]

1. **Single versus multiple plans:** Many employers design different evaluation plans for different types of work because they believe that work content is too diverse to be

usefully evaluated by one plan. For instance, production jobs may vary in terms of manipulative skills, knowledge of statistical quality control and working conditions, but these tasks and skills may not be relevant to finance and marketing jobs. Hence, a single universal plan may not suit employees or be useful to managers if the work covered is highly diverse.[6] The number of job evaluation plans used hinges on how detailed an evaluation is required to make pay decisions and how much it will cost. There is no ready answer to the question of 'one plan versus many'.[7] A good number of organisations use separate plans for major domains of work, whereas some, like Hewlett-Packard, use single plan.

2. **Process of job evaluation**: The process of job evaluation comprises certain steps, which are given as follows:

    a. **Job analysis**: Job analysis is the process of obtaining job facts through.

        i. **Job description**: It mainly describes the duties, responsibilities and nature of the job.
        ii. **Job specification**: It is a statement of human qualities required to perform the job well.

    b. **Selecting benchmark jobs**: The job evaluators should select benchmark jobs which should be representative of the level and type of jobs to be evaluated.
    c. **Job rating**: It is the use of some method to assign, with the help of job analysis, a relative score to each job.
    d. **Money allocation**: It involves assigning a rate of wages or salary (in terms of money) to each job keeping its rating into consideration.
    e. **Job classifications**: It grades different jobs into certain categories of the pay scale.

3. **Methods of job evaluation**: There are several methods of job evaluation, but for the sake of convenience, these can be grouped under the following two categories:

    a. **Non-analytical or non-quantitative methods**: These methods evaluate jobs as whole. There are two non-analytical methods, which are given as follows:

        i. **Job ranking method**: This is the oldest and the simplest of all methods of job evaluation. Per this method, each job is evaluated as a whole and is measured in comparison with other jobs in terms of their relative worth to the organisation. No specific factors are selected for consideration and job-to-job comparison is made. Thereafter, the total ranking is divided into a certain number of groups, say 6 to 10 or the like. All the jobs falling in one group will receive the same pay. The methodology adopted in this method to establish pay rate may be any of the following: first, the top and bottom jobs are selected as benchmarks for the remainder of the ranking process. The remaining jobs are rated according to their ranks between these two points. Per the second practice, a certain number of key jobs from different departments and of different functions are first rated and then all other jobs are broadly compared with these key jobs to establish a broad rating. Then, there is another technique also which is known as paired-comparison technique in which each job is compared with every other job, one at a time, and thus ranked in order of their merit, and wage rates are fixed accordingly.

        Job ranking method is simple, fast, inexpensive, and easy to understand and explain to employees, but all the same, it is suitable only for smaller organisations where the raters are fully conversant with the jobs which may not be possible in the case of bigger organisations where there are several jobs, some of which are of very complex nature. Another shortcoming of this method is that in this method subjective judgement comes into vogue.

ii. **Job classification or grading:** In this method also, jobs are measured as a whole, and a series of classes covers the range of jobs. Class descriptions are labels. A job description is compared to the class descriptions to decide which class is the best fit for that job. Each class is described in such a way that the 'label' captures sufficient work detail yet is general enough to cause little difficulty in slotting a job description into its appropriate class. The classes may be described further by including titles of benchmark jobs that fall into each class.[8] An example in this direction is as follows:

Job/Grade	Class Description
Unskilled	• No education or training required
	• Works under supervision
	• Little or no responsibility
	• Routine and repetitive task
Semi-skilled	• Some training is required
	• Some experience is desirable
	• Needs a little bit of initiative
	• Needs supervision
Skilled	• Very less or no supervision
	• Trains and guides subordinates
	• Takes initiative
	• Supervision of juniors

The result is a job structure made up of a series of classes with several jobs in each. The jobs within each class are equal or similar work and are paid equally. Hence, jobs in different classes should be dissimilar and may have different pay rate.

Though it is an improvement over ranking method and is an inexpensive and easy to understand, writing class descriptions, which is an art, is not an easy job. Besides, it does not suit an organisation which has several jobs of complex nature, or the jobs cover a wide range of responsibilities. However, this method can group a wide range of work together in one system, though descriptions may leave too much room for manipulation.

b. **Analytical or quantitative methods:** Under these methods, jobs are assessed, and numerical values are assigned under several compensable factors such as professional qualifications required, expertise needed, experience required and working conditions under which job is to be performed. Then by comparing total numerical values, assessors can assign pay rates to different jobs. The main analytical methods are as follows:

i. **Point method or manual system:** Developed by Merit Lott in 1923, point method is the most widely used job evaluation approach in the United States and Europe and is now quite popular in Indian organisations also. Point methods or point plans have three common features: compensable factors, factor degrees numerically scaled and weights reflecting the relative importance of each factor. The following are the main steps involved in this method.

• **Determining the compensable factors/job factors common to all jobs:** Initially, certain compensable factors which are usually common to all

Divergent Systems and Institutions for Wage Determination 339

the jobs are selected. The number of factors so selected may vary from organisation to organisation but the most common compensable factors (job factors) are (1) skills, (2) responsibility, (3) effort and (4) working conditions. Having determined the job factors, each of the same is divided into several smaller factors given as follows:

Skill	Responsibility	Effort	Working Conditions
Education	Machinery	Physical	Work environment
Professional training	Product	Intellectual	Hazards involved
Experience	Safety and security		
Creativity	Supervision of juniors		

ii. **Construction of a scale of values for each job factor:** The next exercise is to construct a scale of values for each factor so as to measure the factors in each job. For doing this, initially we have to decide the total number of points that will be utilised in the entire system. Thereafter, we will have to determine the percentage (of total number of points) to be allocated to each job factor. It can be explained with the help of following example:

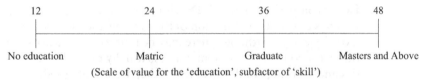

(Scale of value for the 'education', subfactor of 'skill')

Having determined the total value of each job factor, scales need to be derived. These scales comprise points and explanations of degrees of each of the factor. To illustrate, let us take the case of 'education' (which is a sub-factor of 'skill') and suppose that it has been assigned 48 points out of 160 points allocated to skill. Now, four degrees of 'education' may be established with an arithmetic progression of 12 points as follows:

Factor	No. of Points	Percentage
Skill	160	40
Responsibility	120	30
Effort	80	20
Working condition	40	10
Total	400	100

iii. **Assigning money value to points:** Points scored for sub-factors are added to find out the total value of a job and then its value is translated into terms of money as shown in Figure 10.1.

Per Figure 10.1, we have a line that approximates the going rates for all the jobs in the structure and now wage rates of all other jobs can be interpolated by reading up from the point values to the wage-trend line.

The point method is a very objective method and is therefore acceptable to workers. This method can handle several jobs and has long-lasting stability as the compensable factor remains relevant. Of course, the development and installing of this method involves heavy cost. Besides, it is a very complex and time-consuming process to define job factors and so is the case with determining factors' degrees.

340 *Compensation and Reward Management*

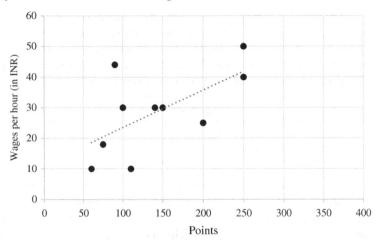

Figure 10.1 A Wage-Trend Line

iv. **Factor comparison method**: Developed by E. J. Bonge in 1962, this method, which is a sort of combination of the ranking and point systems, is less common these days. Although there may be four to seven factors that are used by the factor comparison system, but it is usually the skills, efforts, responsibilities and working conditions factors that are usually used.

Process: Following are the main steps involved in this method:

- Initially, it is the selection of job factors and their appropriate definitions that needs to be done very cautiously. As stated earlier, the factors selected may differ from organisation to organisation.
- Second, it is the selection of key jobs which should be fair, stable and relative to other jobs. The pay levels represented by the selected key jobs should be representative of a particular class of jobs.
- The next step involves determining correct rates of key jobs as is done in the point system explained earlier.
- In the fourth step, the key jobs are ranked by one factor at a time. It can be explained by giving the following example in which the rater ranks five key jobs (T, U, X, Y and Z):

Skill	Responsibility	Efforts	Working Conditions
T	U	Z	Y
U	T	Y	Z
X	X	U	X
Y	Y	X	U
Z	Z	T	T

v. In the next step, the correct rate of each key job is allocated among the job factors. For example, suppose the correct rate for job T is INR 24.00, it is divided among skill, responsibility, effort and working conditions (depending on the importance of each of these in job T) as shown in Figure 10.2

Thus, we have created a series of four sales—each scale consisting of 'key job titles' and 'money'.

Correct Job Rates	Skill	Responsibility	Effort	Working Conditions
T INR 24.00	T INR 13.60	U INR 8.00	Z INR 4.80	Y INR 4.00
U INR 22.40	U INR 8.80	T INR 7.20	Y INR 3.60	Z INR 3.60
X INR 17.60	X INR 7.20	X INR 4.80	U INR 3.20	X INR 3.20
Y INR 13.60	Y INR 4.00	Y INR 2.00	X INR 2.40	U INR 2.40
Z INR 11.20	Z INR 1.60	Z INR 1.20	T INR 1.60	T INR 1.60

vi. In the next step, other jobs are now evaluated by comparing them with the list of key jobs in each scale. For instance, if new job 'k' is most similar to U in skill (INR 8.80), Z in responsibility (INR 1.20), Y in effort (INR 3.60) and X in working conditions (INR 3.20), then its correct rate is INR 16.80.

vii. The final step involves designing, adjusting and operating the wage structure. If it is slightly different from any of these key jobs, then varying amounts can be allocated and the new job can be placed in the factor scale as a new level of that factor.[9]

Thus, this method is an improvement over simple ranking method as in this method (factor comparison method) comparisons are made on job-to-job basis, by factors, rather than as whole jobs. However, this method is a little bit complex, and therefore needs a group of specialists to monitor the system. Usually, the whole job can be carried out by a committee constituted for the purpose.

- **Choosing the best method:** A careful analysis of all the methods of job evaluation clearly reveals that none of the aforesaid methods is flawless, though the point method is the commonly used one. Hence, keeping in view the circumstances prevailing in an organisation, different methods may be used for different types of jobs.

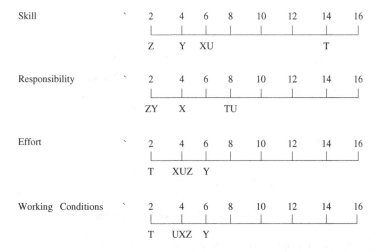

Figure 10.2 Factor Scales of a Factor Comparison System

Job Pricing

Job pricing is attaching a price tag to each job and creating a wage structure that equitably relates jobs to their calculated values.

1. **Methods or techniques of job pricing**: Following are the main methods of job pricing:

    a. **Supply and demand method**: Per this method, the price determination is the function of forces of demand for and supply of a certain type of job in the labour market, and therefore, other things remaining the same, the price of a job will be fixed, at a point where the demand curve and the supply curve intersect each other as shown in Figure 10.3

    b. **Converting the point values of job into monetary value**: This method requires wage surveys inside and/or outside the organisation to find out the going rates for various jobs based on point values assigned to jobs and then to key the entire structure to these rates in the organisation. For example, let us take the job of a mechanic, which has been assigned 100 points, the range of average rates for a mechanic's job is INR 10 per hour, which means that each point is currently priced at 10 paise per hour.

    To be more practical, point values are generally compared with the current prices of 10 to 20 key jobs. This requires, first, selecting a sample of organisations in the labour market, getting appropriate wage information from these sample organisations in respect of key jobs selected for the purpose, and then analysing and averaging the data so collected. The rupee value of key jobs is then plotted on the chart as shown in Figure 10.4.

    It is clear from Figure 10.4 that the price (wage)-trend line, which is closest to all points plotted, approximates the then going rates for all jobs in the structure. With the help of this, wage rates for all other jobs can be interpolated by reading up from the point values to the price (wage)-line.[10] However, many objections are raised against this system. For example, it is difficult to explain the whole mechanism to rank-and-file employees.

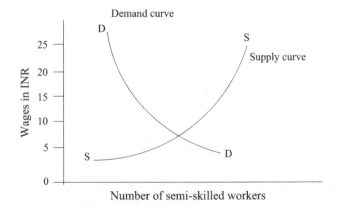

Figure 10.3 Job Pricing through Intersection of Demand and Supply Curves

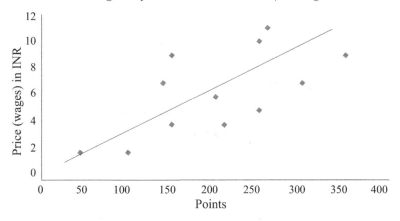

Figure 10.4 A Price (Wage)-Trend Line

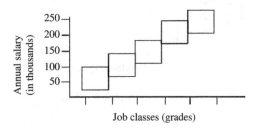

Figure 10.5 Job Classes (Grades)

c. **Establishing labour grades**: In any large organisation, individual wage rates for each job calculated from point values could create an undesirable multiplicity of fractional rupee–paise rates. Hence, labour grades are established, each grade representing a range of point values, with one wage rate or range for the entire grade.[11] In other words, instead of treating jobs separately, they are grouped to form a 'job class' and all jobs in a particular class are treated in the same way.

In a point system, job classes are created by dividing the point range into the desired number of classes. To illustrate it, we can say that from 50 to 100 points may constitute one class, 101 to 150 may constitute another class and the like shown as follows (see Figure 10.5)

An organisation has the option either to pay 'flat rates' for each job class (see Figure 10.6) or varying rates within a rate range of each class in which case the per wage structure will be as shown in Figure 10.7.

2. **Red circle rates**: When price tags are attached to job values, some current rates generally show up as distinctly out of line. Some jobs are being paid too much; others may be inadequately compensated. Many out-of-line rates may be due to personal factors, such as long services, blood relationship, friendship, personality and so on. Similarly, some may be due to environmental or technological changes. Such 'over' rates are red-circled and are temporarily regarded as personal rates which are to be protected

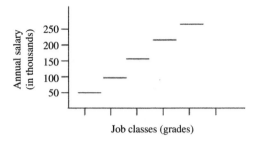

Figure 10.6 Flat Rates Wage Structure for Each Class of Jobs

Figure 10.7 Varying Rates Wage Structures for Each Job Class

as long as present employees remain in these jobs and are eliminated as soon as the employees concerned leave their jobs.

Executive/Manager Compensation (Pricing of Managerial Jobs in the Organised Sector)

Like engineers and scientists, managers are usually regarded as requiring distinctive reward programmes for high-level commitment. Thus, for both staff and line managers, the job evaluation programme is not considered a foolproof solution to problems of equity and holding high-level commitment. It is so because managers should be paid for their capability, that is, for what they can do rather than for job demands or measured output. Managers reflect a wide range of individual differences in performance and expectations. They may be different in that, as a group, they have more powerful desires for achievement, power and advancement.[12] Hence, great emphasis is placed on incentivisation through financial rewards. Managers rely principally on the daggling carrot of greater financial rewards to stimulate superior performance. Present or deferred monetary rewards are assumed to be the principal answer to the question of what makes the manager perform.[13] Hence, most employers, in the case of executive remuneration, supplement the base rate or range established by their job evaluation programme with a wide variety of bonuses, profit-sharing, fringe benefits, employee stock options and so on.

However, Indian executives are relatively paid less as compared to other countries in the Asia Pacific (APAC) region, as has been revealed by the research conducted by leading global advisory working and solutions company Willis Towers Watson.[14] For example, salaries even of the executives at Hindustan Unilever, the country's largest consumer goods maker, fell by a quarter in the fiscal year 2015–2016 (Exhibit 10.2).

It has been reported that about 129 Hindustan Unilever Limited managers took home more than a crore of rupees in annual salary in the year April 2015 to March 2016, against 169 managers a year ago. More than half of them are less than 40 years of age, equalling all of IT major Infosys' 53 eight-digit salary earners. According to Abneesh Roy, associate director, Edelweiss Securities, 'While the year hasn't been great for HUL, in terms of profitability, the final payout could have been impacted due to variable pay linked to sales, profit or market share. Also, payout depends on the company's outlook for next year'.[15] According to Anuj Roy, partner, digital practice at search firm Transearch,

> On an average, HUL salaries are higher by nearly 30% than second tier consumer companies. With part of bonus or employees' shares being vested for 3–4 years in general, many may have exercised the option last year which reflected in a higher number of people earning more than a crore.[16]

Exhibit 10.2 HUL's Crore-Plus Salary Club Shrinks by a Fourth

The number of executives at Hindustan Unilever who drew eight-digit salaries fell by a quarter last fiscal as the country's largest consumer goods maker fought slowing sales growth and declining profit in challenging macro-economic environment.

Source: The Economic Times, 17 June 2016.

According to some critics, the earnings of CEOs has been showing an increasing trend during FY 2018 to FY 2022 (see Exhibits 10.3 and 10.4)

Exhibit 10.3 Number of CEOs Earning $1mn⁺ (2018–2022)

Financial Year	Number of CEOs Earning $1mn+
2018	124
2019	146
2020	150
2021	125
2022	171

Source: The Times of India, 5 December 2022.

Exhibit 10.4 Rise in Total CEOs Compensation (in INR Cr) between 2018 and 2022

Financial Year	Total CEOs Compensation (in INR Cr)
2018	2,158
2019	2,457
2020	2,514
2021	2,549
2022	3,957

Source: *The Times of India*, 5 December 2022.

The top ten CEOs earning during FY2022 have also gone up considerably if compared to FY 2021 (see Exhibit 10.5).[17] There are nearly five crorepati executives per company in the BSE200 group with an average compensation of INR 5.5 crore.[18] The earnings of the ten top CEOs have also gone up considerably during FY 2022 as compared to FY 2021 (see Exhibit 10.5)

Exhibit 10.5 Top Ten CEOs Earnings (2021 and 2022)

S. No.	Name of CEO	Name of Organisation	Earnings During FY 2021 (in INR Cr)	Earnings During FY 2022 (in INR Cr)
1	Sajjan Jindal	JSW	85	146
2	Shantanu Khosla	Crompton	NA	118
3	Murli Divi	Divi's Lab	81	110
4	Sandeep Kumar Barasia	Delhivery	NA	93
5	Kalanithi Maran	SUN TV	83	88
6	Kavery Kalanithi	SUN TV	88	88
7	Pawan Munjal	Hero MotoCorp.	87	84
8	Thierry Delaporte	WIPRO	64	80
9	Salil Parekh	Infosys	50	71
10	S.N. Subramanyan	L&T	29	61

Source: *The Times of India*, 5 December 2022.

The amount of compensation given to senior executives who receive more than INR1 crore as salary grew 47% every year between FY15 and FY17, while the profit of the BSE 200 companies rose by 8%. HDFC Bank, India's largest bank by market capitalisation, had the largest number of senior executives (105) earning more than INR 1 crore, followed by TCS (91) and Bharti Airtel (82). In FY17, every 1 in 4 crorepati executive was from the manufacturing sector compared with 1 in 10 about two years ago. There was also a rise in the number of crorepati executives at midcap companies, such as Kajaria Ceramics and Bata India. The number of such executives at Kajaria Ceramics increased to nine in FY17 as compared with two in FY15.[19]

1. **Ratio of CEO's salary to average worker's salary**: The compensation of India Inc.'s top 100 senior executives other than promoters holding executive positions has a sharp increase. The average compensation of the sample increased by 12.1% to INR 9.8 crore in FY17.[20] Further, the median salary of the top senior executives is on average 243 times higher than the average salary of employees, according to the data of Capitaline and annual reports.[21]

Exhibit 10.6 RBI to Frame Rules for Bank CEOs' Pay

RBI is working on a set of rules that would link remuneration of banks CEOs to parameters like balance-sheet size of a bank, loan delinquency, profits and governance record.

The proposed framework is expected to provide a broad template to the board of directors of banks, while approving increase in salary, performance bonus and stock options to the senior most executive. The regulatory guidance that exists today is a general directive on the remuneration of senior officials in broad functions like 'business', 'control' and 'risk'. What is being considered is one that specifically relates to CEO compensation.

Source: The Economic Times, 14 January 2019.

---

2. **RBI to frame rules for bank CEOs' pay**: In order to put some check and link remuneration of bank CEOs to certain parameters, the RBI is working to frame a set of rules (see Exhibit 10.6).

    Even today, RBI clears the remuneration of a bank CEO and has powers to claw back a slice of it in case of non-performance or governance lapses. However, a framework would ensure that the board does not have to shoot in the dark while approving the package for the CEO and referring it to RBI for its clearance. Though such framework would be significant for private banks, it would also hold relevance for PSU banks, which are considering incentives and ESOPs for employees.[22]

    Central Bank officials have shared the idea with senior bankers during conversation. It is understood that the proposal was broadly agreed upon towards the end of Urjit Patel's exit. We tend to believe that RBI would pursue this under the new governor. Probably, it is also believed that given the turmoil in the banking sector, even a draft guideline on CEO pays giving out the broad contours would send the right signal.[23]

348 Compensation and Reward Management

3. **Shares of ESOP in total payout of top executives**: ESOPs are an effective tool in limiting attrition and improving engagement of executives since they align the growth of top employees' wealth with that of the company.[24],[25] The shares of ESOPs in the total remuneration of India Inc.'s top executives is on the rise.

   The companies make disclosure about ESOPs in the following two ways:

   a. When ESOPs are exercised, they are shown as part of the total compensation of the executive.
   b. When ESOPs are granted, the number of shares allotted as ESOPs that can be exercised in future is disclosed. For example, including the value of ESOPs in total compensation, C. P. Gurnani, CEO at Tech Mahindra, topped the pay charts in FY17. He received ESOPs worth INR 147 crore in FY17, taking his total payout to INR 150.7 crore. This was more than the salaries of the boards of IT peers TCS, Wipro

   > Among those who cashed in, Aditya Puri, MD at HDFC Bank, exercised ESOPs worth INR 57 crore in FY17, which had been granted and vested over the previous several years.[26] The pay ratio of the CEO and an average worker's salary in India was the second highest in the world after the United States, according to Bloomberg. The median remuneration of Indian employees was INR 565,748 in FY17, an increase of 8.5% from the year before. The average of global CEO salary is around $3.6 million (INR 23.6 crore), whereas it is $1.5 million (INR 9.76 crore) for Indian CEOs.[27]
   >
   > The group chairman of India's largest infrastructure company Larsen & Toubro was the highest paid key management professional, if employee stock option plans (ESOPs) are excluded, in FY17. He took home INR 78.91 crore in remuneration, an annual gain of 19.3%. Nearly half of his total compensation was due to retirement benefits. His remuneration was 1,102 times the median remuneration of the employees at the engineering giant. The CEO of Dr Lal PathLabs was next on the list with a payout of INR 33.20 crore in FY17, an increase of 12% year-on-year. In his case, perks account for nearly 90% of the total compensation.[28]

4. **Factors affecting pricing of managerial jobs**: Managerial compensation is influenced mainly by the following factors:

   a. Individual's performance (see Exhibit 10.7): Wipro, India's third-largest software exporter, has overhauled its incentive structure for top executives at the company and completely done away with the previous account-based incentive structure, as part of a broader strategy to regain growth momentum and revive growth. Per the new structure, Wipro is placing an equal amount of importance on both individual performances as well as the overall company's performance, as it urges top executives and employees to collaborate more closely and work as a cohesive unit.[29]

   For example, India's third largest software exporter, Wipro, has overhauled its incentive structure for top executives at the company and completely done away with the previous account-based incentive structure, as part of a broader strategy to regain growth momentum and revive growth.

   As part of the new structure, Wipro is placing an equal amount of importance on both individual performances as well as the overall company's performance,

Divergent Systems and Institutions for Wage Determination 349

as it urges top executives and employees to collaborate more closely and work as a cohesive unit (see Exhibit 10.7).

The new structure comes at a time when the broader $160 billion IT industry is taking a fresh look at traditional metrics and benchmarks previously taken into consideration to reward employees—which has for the better part of the last two decades seen revenue growth directly linked to manpower addition.[30]

Exhibit 10.7 Wipro Reworks Incentive Structure for Top Executives

Wipro president and chief human resources officer Saurabh Govil in an interview in early June said, 'Our incentive structure has undergone a fundamental shift. We have done away with the previous account-based structure. The new plan which came into effect on April 1, has two parts: 50% of the incentive will depend on the performance of the individual and his team while the balance 50% is linked to the performance of the organization'.

Source: The Economic Times, 20 June 2016.

---

    b. Organisation's performance
    c. Size of the organisation, that is, the number of people employed
    d. Nature of industry the managers are employed in
    e. Status of the industry in the economic/industrial structure of the country
    f. Status of the organisation concerned in the industry
    g. Manager's span of control, that is, the number of subordinates being supervised/controlled
    h. Responsibilities assigned
    i. Going rates of pay for subordinates

5. **Methods of pricing managerial jobs**: Different authors and practitioners have suggested various methods for pricing management jobs. For example, Yoder[31] has suggested the following:

    a. **Comparison data**: Executive and manager salaries are less frequently sampled and reported than those of production and office employees. Some of the largest, most inclusive top salary surveys do not give wide circulation to their findings. However, it should not be forgotten that a policy of full disclosure of salaries may have a net gain, despite the problems it can create. Such a policy might generate powerful pressures for improvements in compensation programmes.[32] Availability of adequate data can help in adopting the same technique(s) for pricing managerial jobs also as is done in the case of other employees for pricing their jobs.

    b. **Incentives for managers**: It is because of inclusion of formal incentive provisions, such as bonuses, profit-sharing, stock options, other special deferred payment fringes and a variety of non-financial payoffs in the salary of managers that complicates salary data in respect of managers. Hence, most organisations include one or more than one of the aforesaid formal incentives in the pay package of their managerial personnel.

c. **Distinctive fringes:** Several organisations include tax-exempt services, such as company car and driver, club memberships and other fringes in the pay packages of their managers. Some companies grant options to purchase stock and thus develop capital gains which are either non-taxable or taxable at a lower rate, though it is criticised that this encourages giving senior managers an unfair advantage over their juniors.
   d. **Pay package:** In order to maintain wage differentials in executive pay and also to maintain the essentials in the incentive of top managers, the idea of pay package has come into vogue, which comprises a base pay in determining which careful attention is paid to the going rate, some other programmes add a bonus, related to improvement in sales or profits or accomplishment of other stated objectives, to the basic pay. Still some other programmes provide opportunities for deferred benefits and capital gains, in addition to basic pay.

Today, the most common pattern is one that combines some or all of these in a special package. Thus, managerial pay packages include both financial and non-financial reward.

Wage Fixation in Unorganised Sector

In the unorganised sector, it is usually the employers who unilaterally fix the wages of workers. The number of workers engaged in the unorganised sector constitutes around 90% of the total workforce. In a good number of cases, even statutorily prescribed minimum wages are not paid to the workers; the main reason for this sorry state of affairs is the absence of trade unions in the unorganised sector. Even if there are unions anywhere in this sector, these are as good as non-existent. It is, therefore, the unorganised sector which needs immediate attention of the authorities concerned to take care of fixation of wages.

Bipartite Wage Fixation

Of late, collective bargaining which is a bipartite process has come into popularity regarding settlement of terms and conditions of employment of workers. It is primarily due to trade unions getting stronger and because of the realisation among the employers that they alone cannot work in and that without the cooperation of workers' unions they will not be able to accomplish the objectives of the organisations. The government is also interested in encouraging the institution of collective bargaining which is perhaps one of the best methods to ensure industrial peace.

In the process of fixing wages through collective bargaining, the trade unions present to the management their demand for a particular pay scale for a particular category of employees or different pay scales for different categories of employees in the organisation.

In case the management is not willing to accept the proposal of the trade union in toto, it puts forward a counter proposal keeping in view the interests of all concerned, to be followed by discussion, arguments, heated exchange of words, haggling, cajoling and whatnot.

Both the parties present facts and figures from different sources to support their contention. The discussion(s) may lead to different situation(s). For example, both the parties may totally reject each other's viewpoint and there may be deadlock. In such a scenario, efforts are made to resolve the issue through the conciliation machinery or adjudication machinery or even through arbitration.³³ Another scenario may be that the management may not be ready to accept the increase in wages in full as asked for by the union. In such a situation, the two parties can meet again to resolve the issue. In another case, the management may like to do exercise at its own once again regarding calculating the cost and other implications likely to be caused if the demand for increased wages is accepted. If this be the case, the negotiations may take place later. In another case, the management may accept the demand put forth by the workers' union but simultaneously put forth its counter demand to the union.

In the process of negotiations, there may be 'haggling bargaining' or 'Boulwarism bargaining' or 'continuous bargaining'.³⁴ There may also be 'attitudinal structuring', 'intra-organisational bargaining', 'distributive bargaining', 'integrative bargaining' or the like. Any of these approaches or a group of more than one approach may be adopted. Ultimately, both the parties, following the 'give and take' approach, may reach an agreement applicable for a specific period. For example, in a landmark agreement signed with Pune plant workers on 28 March 2017, Tata Motors, India's largest automobile company by revenues, has initiated a move to bring 15,000–20,000 blue-collar factory workers to a wage structure that is performance-linked.

The company concluded a long-term wage settlement agreement with its Pune workers' union that covers 6,400 workers, after 19 months of negotiations. Tata Motors then worked towards getting workers from Sanand, Lucknow and Jamshedpur factories to sign a similar agreement.³⁵ It is learnt that about 10% of the Pune plant workers salary is variable pay and is linked to the performance. The wage settlement for Pune plant workers had been signed for a period of three years—1 September 2015 to 31 August 2018. The agreement was implemented with immediate effect.

The total wage package is bifurcated as a fixed rise of INR 8,600 (in the ratio of 72%, 15% and 13% for a period of three years) and INR 8,700 non-actual, that is, a total of INR 17,300.35 According to the MD of Tata Motors, 'Here is a clear scheme, as far as performance-based rewards are concerned, just like how it translates for the management or white collar executives, in the same way the company is introducing performance linked pay for blue collar workers'.³⁶

In addition to the increment amount, the company has also agreed to pay a gratuity amount to the families of deceased workmen and a wristwatch be given to the spouse of an employee on the completion of 25 years of service. Additionally, various other facilities were agreed upon, including block closure days being increased by six days.³⁷

Tripartite Wage Fixation

It was the Royal Commission on Labour, 1931, and the First Five Year Plan (1951–1956) that had recommended the setting up of wage boards with a tripartite composition in each state and at the centre to resolve all aspects of wages. Now, let us have a brief description about wage boards.

Wage Boards

A wage board is a tripartite body having the representatives of both employees and employers appointed by the government in consultation with their organisations (unions/associations). The government also appoints an independent economist and an independent consumers' representative who should be a member of Parliament. The total number of members of a wage board has been varying between seven and nine in the past.[38] Wage boards are constituted with the objectives of working out standardised wage structure for the industry concerned and to protect the interest of consumers/community as also to promote industrial harmony. Thus, a wage board is expected to follow the principles of fair wage as laid down in the Report of the Committee on Fair Wage and to ensure laying down a wage policy enabling optimum allocation of resources and providing economic progress. These wage boards are set industry-wise and are in great demand by different industries. However, there is a great controversy regarding giving the statutory status to wage boards. It is because in some cases the recommendations of wage boards were not given effect to appropriately.

The issue has been alive since long. Although the Standing Labour Committee did not approve the idea of making wage boards as statutory bodies, it rather suggested that the parties concerned should implement unanimous decisions of wage boards. In case they do not, only then the government should give a statutory force to such recommendations. However, confronted with the problem of non-implementation of recommendations of some wage boards, the government thought of introducing a bill in 1961 to give a statutory force to the recommendations of the wage boards but postponed the matter. The matter was again taken up by the Standing Labour Committee in 1967 and constituted a committee to review the wage board system.

Regarding the working of a wage board, the procedure involves issuing an exhaustive questionnaire to get necessary information from the parties concerned, to be followed by assessing the views of the parties and finally making recommendations with regard to wage structure which remains in operation for a period of five years.

A good number of wage boards have already been set up for several industries since 1956. It was in May 1956 that the first wage board was constituted for working journalists, followed by for the cotton textile (March 1957), sugar (December 1957), cement (April 1959), jute industry (August 1960), tea plantations (December 1960), coffee and rubber plantations (July 1961) and so on. Second wage boards were also constituted for certain industries such as cotton textile (August 1964), cement (September 1964) and sugar (November 1965). Even more than two wage boards have also been constituted in certain cases, for example, the third wage board for working journalists was set up in February 1976 and the trend continues.

Wage boards have done a good job, though certain criticism is also there. But the fact remains that no other agency can do more justice than a tripartite body like a wage board because it is the platform where all concerned can put forth their viewpoints, argue and have an opportunity to justify their logic.

Statutory Wage Fixation

Since the wages constitute the only economic means of survival for industrial workers, it is essential that full justice should be done in the fixation of their wages. However, this has not been happening in a large number of cases. That is why the Government of India has been interfering from time to time and has undertaken the following measures in this regard:

Legislative Steps/Executive Order

To monitor wages of the workers, at least, to some extent, the Government of India has undertaken the following steps.

Enactment of the Minimum Wages Act, 1948,[39] and establishing the National Floor Level Minimum Wage, or Minimum Wages Act, 1948, empowers the appropriate government to fix minimum rates of wages payable to the persons employed for hire or reward to do any work, skilled or unskilled, manual or clerical and so on, in an employment specified in Part I or Part II of the Schedule appended to the act and also in an employment added to either Parts of the Schedule subsequently. Under Section 27 of the act, the appropriate government is empowered to extend the application of the act to any other employment in respect of which it thinks that the minimum rates of wages should be fixed under the act. This option is being made use of by several state governments, for example, the Government of Orissa did so in 2002. However, minimum wages were fixed for the first time in 23 employments (by union government [4], Kerala [6], Tamil Nadu [5], Karnataka [5], Maharashtra [2] and Chandigarh [1]). It is the inspecting officers of the Chief Labour Commissioner (Central) usually designated as Central Industrial Relations Machinery (CIRM), who ensure the compliance of the act in the central sphere. As far as the states are concerned, the enforcement of the act is ensured through the State Enforcement Machinery of the respective states. Besides, it is obligatory on the part of the appropriate government to review the minimum rates of wages from time to time under Section 3 (I)(b) of the act and revise the same, if required.

Adequate steps are also taken to protect minimum wages against inflation. For example, 26 of the states/union territories have made variable DA as a component of minimum wages. The central government too has made provisions of variable DA linked to consumer price index. Hence, minimum wages in respect of the concerned scheduled employments have been revised from time to time. For example, minimum wages in respect of different categories like unskilled, semi-skilled and skilled in different states/union territories in our country have been revised from October 2022, a few details of the same are as follows (see Table 10.1).

Table 10.1 Minimum Wages (Category-Wise) Revised with Effect from October 2022 in Different States/Union Territories

State	Zone	Unskilled Per Day	Unskilled Per Month	Semi-Skilled Per Day	Semi-Skilled Per Month	Skilled Per day	Skilled Per Month
Gujrat	I	363.30	9445.80	371.30	9653.80	380.30	9887.80
	II	355.30	9237.80	363.30	9445.80	371.30	9653.80
Bihar	—	366.00	9516	380.00	9880.00	463.00	12038.00
Madhya Pradesh	—	250.00	6500	271.42	7057.00	324.42	8435.00
Punjab	—	381.06	9907.68	411.06	10687.68	445.56	11584.68
Rajasthan (w,e,f. July 2021)	—	259.00	6734.00	271.00	7046.00	283.00	7358.00
Uttar Pradesh	—	374.73	9743.00	412.19	10717.00	461.73	12005.00
West Bengal (w,e,f. July 2021)	A	355.00	9239.00	391.00	10163.00	473	12297.00
	B	322.00	8380.00	354.00	9216.00	429	11154.00
Delhi		—	16792.00	—	18499.00	—	20357.00
Karnataka (w.e.f. April 2022)							
Maharashtra (w.e.f. July 2021)	I	440.42	11451.00	472.54	12286.00	502.38	13062.00
	II	417.50	10855.00	449.62	11690.00	479.46	12465.00
	III	394.54	10258.00	426.69	11094.00	456.54	11870.00

Source: https://www.simpliance.in/minimum-wages

354 *Compensation and Reward Management*

Table 10.2 The Delhi Minimum Wages Notification (October 2022)

Class of Employment	Class of Workers	Basic Per Month (in INR)	Variable DA Per Month (in INR)	Total Per Month (in INR)
Unskilled	NA	14,842	2,652	17,494
Semi-Skilled	NA	16,341	2,938	19,279
Skilled	NA	17,991	3,224	21,215
Clerical and supervisory staff	Non-matriculates	16,341	2,938	19,279
Clerical and supervisory staff	Matriculates but not graduates	17,991	3,224	21,215
Clerical and supervisory Staff	Graduates and above	19,572	3,510	23,082

Source: https://www.simpliance.in

Per the Minimum Wages Act, 1948, both central and state governments have dominion over the fixing of wages. As far as the state governments are concerned, they fix their scheduled employments and further release the minimum wages rates along with the Variable Dearness Allowance (VDA). Hence, the minimum wages rates in scheduled employments differ across states, sectors, skills, occupations and regions due to a lot of differentiating factors. It is therefore, obvious that there exist no single uniform minimum wages rates across the country and the revision cycle differs from state to state. The basic minimum (basic) wages per month effective in Delhi w.e.f. Oct 2022 per the Delhi Government Notification (Oct 2022) are per Table 10.2:

In addition these, Delhi government has been giving dearness allowance (DA) also, which is being constantly revised every six months. As such, the total minimum wages (basic + DA) per month as admissible in Delhi w.e.f. Oct 2022 in case of certain cases is as follows:

The Delhi government, in October 2022, has increased the Dearness Allowance for daily wage workers, resulting into taking up monthly wages for unskilled labourers from INR 16,506 to INR 16,729 per month. Similarly, for semi-skilled labourers wages have been increased from INR 18,187 to INR 18,499 per month (Table 10.3). The Dearness Allowance is being constantly revised by Delhi government every six months.

DA Calculation for Central Government Employees

For central government employees, the DA amount is calculated as a factor of current rate on employee's basic pay per 7th Pay Commission rules. According to the current percentage rate of 12%, this calculation would be as follows:

(Basic pay × 12)/100

DA percentage = 12-month Consumer Price Index (CPI) average – 115.76. The result will be divided by 115.76 and then multiplied by 100.

As far as the national 'floor level' minimum wage (NFLMW), introduced by the central government and which is the minimum wage below, which no state government can fix the minimum wage, is concerned, it is INR 178 per day or INR 5,340 per month. Wage rates vary depending on geographical areas and other criteria. While Indian national floor level minimum wage remained unchanged at INR 178 per day in 2022 from INR 178 per day in 2021,[40] the same is projected to trend around INR 185 per day in 2023 and INR 190 in 2024. A comparative study of monthly wages with regard to some of the other counties[41] is as follows:

Country	Minimum Monthly Wages (in INR)
India	5,340
China	29,837
Brazil	18,253
Egypt	4,176
Israel	1,24,038
Myanmar	3,744
Vietnam	15,444
Russia	14,515

Recent Developments

While the gig platforms show to adopt minimum wage policy,[42] the organisations like Coal India (CIL), Singareni Collieries (SCCL), have recently taken concrete steps to increase the wages to their non-executive staff.[43] Researchers in recent report have revealed that most of the gig platforms have been reluctant to publicly commit to, and operationalise, a minimum wage policy.[44] On the other hand, Coal India (CIL) and Singareni Collieries have recently agreed to pay a 19% wage hike to nearly 2.8 lakh non-executive employees of these two state run coal miners. The representatives of the two companies and four trade unions—BMS, HMS, AITUC and CITU—signed an MoU recently on 3 January 2023, envisaging the wage hike, described as 'mutual guaranteed benefit'. A formal pact for the 11th version of national coal wage agreement, effective from 1 July 1 2021 for a period of 5 years, is to be finalised after remaining issues are discussed.[45] The Karnataka government has also hiked the wages of the convicts in jails ranging from 165% to 200%, which will remain valid for three years or until a fresh order, so as to bring it at par with minimum wages fixed by the government. Jail inmates work mainly as carpenters, grow vegetables and fruits, or engage in handicrafts, making soaps, etc.[46]

For a long time the minimum wages have been under the purview of the Minimum Wages Act, 1948, but now this will be subject to the provisions of the Code on Wages Act, 2019, which was notified in August 2019. The new Wage Code, which replaces four labour legislations, viz. Minimum Wages Act, 1948; Payment of Bonus Act, 1965; and Equal Remuneration Act, 1976, prohibits employers from paying workers less than the stipulated minimum wage. Besides, there is a provision that minimum wages must be revised and reviewed at an interval of not more than five years by both central and state governments.

One of the main factors responsible for low wages in Indian industries is the low labour productivity (see Exhibit 10.8).

> **Exhibit 10.8 Labour Productivity**
>
> Labour productivity—defined as the ratio of output (GDP) per employed worker—varies widely in the economies of the APAC. Moreover, it can differ significantly from GDP per person due to the differences in the size of labour force relative to that of the total population.
>
> Labour productivity and output per person in select economies, 2014, are as follows:
>
> | Country | Labour Productivity (2011 PPP Dollars) | GDP (2011 PPP per Capita) |
> | --- | --- | --- |
> | Singapore | 131,595 | 78,429 |
> | China | 22,318 | 12,552 |
> | India | 13,091 | 5,439 |
>
> *Source: The Economic Times* (5 May 2016).

The remuneration given under Mahatma Gandhi National Rural Employment Guarantee Scheme (MGNREGS) in Haryana was increased from INR 251 to INR 259 per person per day on 1 April 2016, which is the highest in the country.

Records of job cards, muster roll, employment register, cash book and complaint booklet were initiated under MGNREGS. Of these, over 83,000 had been completed.[47]

Probability of Revision of Wages Under National Rural Job Schemes

The government considered revision of wages under the flagship of Mahatma Gandhi National Rural Employment Guarantee Act following a persistent demand for aligning wages under the scheme to minimum wages of individual states closer to the General Election of 2019.

Last time the two wages were aligned in 2009 after which there has been a divergence because several states have arbitrarily increased their minimum wages. Daily wages under MGNREGS for unskilled workers range between INR 168 in Bihar and Jharkhand and INR 281 in Haryana.[48]

However, minimum wage in Bihar, effective from April 2018, is INR 237, INR 210 in Jharkhand and INR 326 in Haryana. A high-level committee is likely to deliberate on the quantum of hike and its financial implications for the centre. The issue of lower wages came up at the regional conferences NITI Aayog had undertaken for the high-level group set up to lay out a road map for convergence of MGNREGS and agriculture.[49]

In the last few years, the government has set up two committees on MGNREGS wages in 2013 and in 2016. The committee recommended MGNREGS wages to be minimum wage fixed by the respective states or the current wage per the consumer price index for agriculture labourers (CPI-AL), whichever is higher. However, the Nagesh Singh committee said there was no need for aligning the two wages. The financial implication on the centre on aligning the two wages was estimated at INR 4,500 crore by the Singh committee, while shifting the index of calculation from CPI-AL to CPI-Rural would put an additional burden of INR 2,500 crore on the union.

The government allocated INR 55,000 crore under National Rural Employment Guarantee Scheme (NREGS) for 2018–2019. The scheme, launched by the UPA government in 2006, has seen 2,637 crore person days generated and total expense at INR 476,718 crore since inception. The scheme, executed by rural development ministry under the National Rural Employment Guarantee Act, provides minimum 100 days of employment out of 365 days in a year to every rural household willing to do unskilled manual work.[50]

The Delhi government was very sincere with regard to implementation of minimum wages.

Hence, it declared a whip in this regard on 5 December 2018 (see Exhibit 10.9).

Exhibit 10.9 Whip on Minimum Wage Violators

The Delhi government will launch a ten-day awareness and enforcement drive to implement minimum wages in the city, Labour Minister Gopal Rai said on Tuesday. As part of the campaign that begins on 10 December, ten enforcement teams of the labour department will inspect firms and factories to check if owners are paying government minimum wages, the minister said. According to the revised pay scale, workers in the unskilled category will get INR14,000 per month, semi-skilled INR 15,400 per month and skilled workers INR 16,962 per month.

If anyone is found violating rules, the government will initiate action in accordance with the Minimum Wages (Amendment) Act, 2017, the minister said. The government has issued a helpline number 011-155214 on which complaints can be lodged. The minister said employers found not paying minimum wages may be fined INR 50,000 or a jail term extending to six months or more according to the law.

Source: Hindustan Times, 5 December 2018.

Present Scenario of Rural/Agricultural Wages

The latest available data suggests that the nominal rural wage growth (for men) has fallen to its lowest level since November 2014. The value would be negative if one were to adjust for inflation. This means wages have fallen in real terms. A slightly long-term perspective shows a different picture. Rural wages rose sharply under the UPA government until 2011. This was followed by an equally sharp fall. While the down slide was arrested under the NDA, the quarterly wage growth has been stagnant.[51] Slow rural growth makes sense when seen in the context of poor agricultural growth. Also, wages have not risen appropriately despite most of the Centre's rural spending schemes meeting their targets. This shows that headwinds to rural wages, most of which are generated in the unorganised sector, due to policies such as demonetisation and GST, have overpowered the tailwinds that government spending must have generated.

Statistics show that caste is an important determinant in deciding whether a person employs agricultural labourers in rural area or get employed as one. Most of the upper caste and dominant Other Backward Class population belong to the former category, whereas an overwhelming majority of the Scheduled Caste and rural poor belongs to the latter. If a low growth in rural wages were accompanied by a high growth in agriculture, the former would have gained in a big way. Because this has not happened, neither of the groups is likely to have benefited. This could trigger rural discontent across the class and caste divide.[52]

Now that the oil cycle has been reversed, financial status is likely to change. If the government takes a haircut in its petroleum taxes to reduce prices, its ability to spend more in rural areas will decrease. This can put more downward pressure on rural wages. If it does not, growing fuel prices are bound to lead to an inflationary upsurge, to which rural labourers are among the most vulnerable.[53]

Coming to thinking about companies in any country is complicated but entrepreneurs essentially create two kinds of companies: a baby or a dwarf. Both are small but the baby will grow, whereas the dwarf will stay small. India is a nation of enterprise dwarfs; we have 63 million enterprises, of which 12 million do not have an address, 12 million work from home, only 6.4 million paid indirect taxes till GST, only 1.2 million pay social security and only 18,500 companies have a paid-up capital of more than INR 10 crore. Formality and size matter greatly for productivity; when you can rank manufacturing enterprises by size, there is a 22 times difference in productivity between somebody at the 90th and 10th percentile. With a 22 times difference in productivity, you will never pay the wage premium, but if you do not pay the wage premium, you will never be productive.[54]

Our low national productivity—it took 71 years for the GDP of 1.2 billion Indians to cross the GDP of 66 million Britishers—is a child of the Avadi Resolution of 1955 that unleashed the License Raj and ensured that firms did not have clients but hostages. Implementation of GST in 2017 is an important disruption; we added 4.7 million new enterprises in the last one year.

Not every enterprise will become a large employer, but this huge addition of enterprises substantially increases the odds of formal employment and India producing more babies.

Thinking about wages needs acknowledging three fault lines: gross versus net, nominal versus real and government versus market. The gross versus net transmission losses of 40% is highlighted by job seekers responding to salary numbers with the question 'Haath waali salary ya chitthi waali salary?', that is, the salary in the letter or in my hand. Nobody argues that gross should equal net but the current levels of confiscation for poor value for money schemes breed informality. The nominal versus real divergence is summarised through an incident whereby a kid in Gwalior said, 'Give me INR 4,000 per month in Gwalior, 6,000 in Gurgaon, 9,000 in Delhi and 18,000 in Mumbai; my bags are packed and tell me where you want me to go'.[55]

Bridging the Wage Gap between Genders

Is regulation the key to gender pay parity? The question was put to a panel of expertise at the ET Women's Forum. In a session on 'Gender and Pay: Towards Greater Parity', Shanmugh Natarajan, MD, Adobe India; Rostow Ravanan, CEO and MD, Mindtree; Sonal Agarwal, Managing Partner, Accor India; and Archana Vadala, Head of Staffing, Facebook India, thrashed out the issue and suggested possible solutions when it comes to closing the gender pay gap, and regulation alone is not enough. 'The drive to effect change should come from leadership'. Adobe announced in January that it had achieved pay parity in India, closing the wage gap between male and female employees.[56]

A few things can be better from the regulation perspective; for instance, a law in some states in the United States bars employers from asking job applicants their prior salaries. The objective is to narrow the gender wage gap. Closing the pay gap requires concerted efforts. For their part, companies can also decide to assign pay by roles. Plus, a woman can ask about median pay, while talking to a potential employer and even from her current one, Ravanan suggested, adding this would steer the conversation in the required direction. There is no denying that foresting gender diversity is a business imperative. 'In corporate board rooms, having a very diverse view may make it difficult to reach a decision'.

Recent 'Labour Reforms' and Wages

In his tweet on the passing of Labour Reforms Bill on 23.09.2022, PM Narendra Modi said, 'The new Labour Codes universalize minimum wages and timely payment of wages'.[57] For this purpose, the central government has amalgamated four labour laws in the Wage Code, 2019, which will ensure that all the workers of organised and unorganised sectors across the country will have the right to minimum wages.

Benefits Available in Labour Code (Wage Code)—2019

Per the Labour Code (Wage Code)—2019, the following benefits will be available to the workers of both organised and the unorganised sectors throughout the country:

1. The guarantee of minimum wages is available to 50 crore workers of organised and unorganised sectors.
2. Review of minimum wages in every five years.
3. Guarantee of timely payment of wages to all workers.
4. Equal remuneration to male and female workers.
5. For the first time, around 40 crore workers of unorganised sector in the country got this right. To remove regional disparity in minimum wages the provision of floor wage has been introduced. The determination of minimum wages has been made easy. It will be based on criteria such as skill level and geographical area.
6. From 28 August 2017, the Payment of Wages Act has increased the wage ceiling from INR 18,000 to INR 24,000.[58]

Pay Commissions

It is for fixing/revising the salaries of central government employees that Pay Commissions are constituted. So far, seven Pay Commissions have been constituted and their recommendations with necessary modifications, wherever the government thought it essential, have already been implemented. For example, the recommendations of the Seventh Pay Commission (see Exhibit 10.10) have come into force with effect from 1 January 2016. The state governments and some other agencies also usually adopt these recommendations—again with modifications if they so prefer. The minimum wage fixed by the Third Pay Commission was a need-based minimum wage based on dietary recommendations of the Indian Council of Medical Research Expert Group in 1968. This group had calculated dietary requirements for a family of three units as 7,600 calories.

However, it has also been pointed out that at times the recommendations of Pay Commissions tell heavily on the profits of concerned undertakings. For example, per the *Economic Times* reporters, the recommendations of the Seventh Pay Commission were viewed by Public Sector undertakings as a costly proposition (see Exhibit 10.11).[59]

Exhibit 10.10 Recommendations of the Seventh Pay Commission

The Commission report submitted in November 2015 recommended an overall 23.55% increase in salaries, allowances and pensions of which salaries could rise by 16% and allowances and pensions by 63% and 24%, respectively. The Commission also recommended a health insurance scheme for staff and pensions and doubled the gratuity ceiling to INR 20 lakh but retained the annual increment at 3%.

Source: Hindustan Times, 6 July 2016.

Exhibit 10.11 Pay Panel Suggestions May Dent PSUs' Profit

The Seventh Pay Commission recommendations may dent profit growth of PSUs who have limited ability to pass on their increased employee cost to customers. These include BHEL, BEL, BEML, SAIL, MOIL, NALCO, GAIL, HPCL, BPCL and IOC. Regulated return entities such as NTPC and Power Grid Corporation of India Limited (PGCIL) will have no effect as wage increase is a pass-through.

Source: Hindustan Times, 6 July 2016.

As a matter of fact, employee cost constituted on an average 60% of the total gross profit (revenue minus raw material) in FY 2016 for the sample. This ratio hovers in the range of 11% (for BPCL) and 154% (BEML), according to data compiled by the ET Intelligence Group from Capitaline.

The impact was more pronounced for companies such as BHEL, SAIL and BEML, where employee cost as a proportion of gross profit was more than 80%, and they were likely to feel the pinch more. For example, BHEL had a high percentage of slow-moving orders in the backlog that kept FY 2017 execution and margin under pressure; this meant an increase in employee cost would affect the company's margin even more. Analysts believed that BHEL had been using aggressive pricing to win orders and put its capacity to use. This together with the wage increase impacted profitability.

It may also be mentioned that the condition of public sector banks (PSBs) was not very encouraging either: the salary increase came at a time when their profits had been under pressure for the past few quarters due to higher proportion of non-performing assets and related provisions.

In the FY 2010, when the Sixth Pay Commission related wages were implemented, the cost–income ratio based on the aggregate financials of 12 leading PSBs had risen by nearly 460 basis points to 53.6%. This was the biggest increase in the ratio of the PSBs in the last eight fiscals. In contrast, for a sample of five prominent private sector banks, excluding Kotak Mahindra Bank, the measure had improved by 480 basis points in FY 2010 to 61%.[60]

Third-Party Wage Fixation

The third-party wage fixation method involves the role of the third party which usually is either 'adjudication' or 'arbitration'.

1. **Adjudication**: In case a problem related to wages is not resolved mutually between the employer and the workers' union or the collective bargaining fails to yield the desired results, the wage dispute may be referred to adjudication machinery comprising labour courts, industrial tribunals or national tribunal, the judgement of which is a binding on both the parties, that is, the employers and the workers. However, adjudication is not preferred as it is a time-consuming process and its judgements leave a bitter taste in the mouth of the losing party which continues, and at times even aggravates its efforts, to show down the winning party at an appropriate time—thus disturbing industrial harmony.
2. **Arbitration**: It has also been observed that when the workers and the employers fail to resolve their differences on wage issues, both may agree to refer the issue to an arbitration whose decision is binding on both the parties. When both the parties at their own agree for referring the wage issue to an arbitrator, it is known as voluntary arbitration. However, if the government at its own refer the issue for arbitration, even if both the parties or either of the two parties do/does not agree for it, then it is known as compulsory arbitration. In such a case also, the mandate of the arbitration is a binding on both the parties to comply with. Of course, compulsory arbitration is usually frowned upon.

Practices of Supplementary Base Pay

In addition to above practices of wage fixation operational in Indian organisations, base pay fixed through job evaluation and so on is also supplemented by many organisations through contingency pay comprising performance-related pay (PRP), competence-related pay, skill-based pay (SBP), shop-floor incentive and bonus schemes, salesforce incentive schemes, executive incentive and bonus schemes, employee and executive share schemes, team rewards, gainsharing, profit-sharing, then profit-related pay and beyond, other cash payments and so on (all of which have been given a fairly good treatment in Chapters 5 and 6).

All the aforesaid methods/systems of wage fixation have their own plus and negative points. There is always a scope for improvement, and therefore, the concerned parties should continue to overcome the flaws involved in the aforesaid methods.

Management Strategy

Wage fixation is a highly sensitive issue for both the management and the workers. It is because the wages are the only source of income in the case of workers who, by and large, are poor as well. For employers also, wage fixation is very crucial because wages alone constitute a big chunk in the total cost of production, and therefore, their profits go down if the wages are fixed at higher side. Hence, it will be highly desirable for the management to formulate an appropriate wage strategy.

In this regard, the management should conduct job evaluation and job pricing on scientific lines so as to lay down a sound basis for wage fixation and then through collective bargaining fix the wages. In case the job evaluation and job pricing have been carried out justifiably, the workers' union will also appreciate the logic of the management in fixing wages in a particular fashion. It will be desirable if the management takes workers' union into confidence, while conducting the process of job evaluation and job pricing. In case the organisation concerned comes under the purview of wage board, the management should prepare itself with as an exhaustive information and documentation as possible so that it may convince the other parties to see reason in its contention and stand taken by it during the proceedings of the wage board. In case, the organisation constitutes a part of the unorganised sector, then also the wage strategy of the management should be such as may protect the interest of both its own as well as of workers also because it is the workers whose role is the deciding factor in making an organisation a success or a failure.

Chapter Review

1. It is desirable to have an idea about the current practices regarding wage fixation in Indian organisations. In case wages are not fixed appropriately, workers are likely to suffer not only economically but also emotionally, socially and psychologically. Hence, wage fixation deserves a great attention. In our country, there are divergent systems and institutions for fixation of wages, such as unilateral wage fixation, bipartite wage fixation, tripartite wage fixation, statutory wage fixation and third-party wage fixation.
2. As far as the wage fixation in the organised sector is concerned, it is usually done unilaterally, usually by employers, through the process of job evaluation and job pricing. The methods of job evaluation are classified into two categories: non-analytical methods (job ranking method and job classification method) and analytical methods (point method and factor comparison method). All these methods have their own plus and negative aspects. After the relative worth of jobs are determined and their hierarchy is determined through job evaluation, a price tag is attached to every job by following the process of job pricing. However, for pricing managerial jobs, job evaluation and job pricing are not the right answers. Hence, their jobs are priced through comparing data collected from different sources, determining their incentives and distinctive fringes, and deciding their pay packages.
3. Wage fixation in the unorganised sector is done unilaterally by the employer, which is usually on the lower side as there are neither the trade unions in this sector nor the process of collective bargaining is effective.
4. Bipartite wage fixation is common in a good number of organisations/industries through the process of collective bargaining. Tripartite wage fixation is prevalent in industries for which wage boards are constituted. Though wage boards' recommendations are not mandatory, yet in most of the cases, they are

accepted by the parties concerned. A good number of wage boards have been constituted, and in some cases, more than two/three wage boards have been constituted for certain industries.
5. Statutory wage fixation is another method wherein the government fixes wages, through legislative steps and constituting Pay Commissions.
6. Third-party wage fixation involves the role of adjudication and arbitration machinery per the provisions of the Industrial Disputes Act, 1947.
7. The base pay fixed through job evaluation and so on is also supplemented by many organisations through contingency pay, that is, paying for performance, competence, skills and so on.
8. Keeping in view the sensitive nature of wage fixation, the management should formulate such a strategy in this regard as may protect not only its own interest but also of the workers and the community.

Key Terms

adjudication machinery
arbitration
attitudinal structuring
bipartite wage fixation
Boulwarism bargaining
compensable factors
continuous bargaining
distinctive fringes
distributive bargaining
factor comparison method
going rates of wage
haggling bargaining
integrative bargaining
intra-organisational bargaining
job analysis
job classification
job description
job evaluation
job pricing
job ranking method
job specification
labour grades
national floor-level minimum wage
paired-comparison technique
Pay Commissions
point method
red circle rates
span of control
statutory wage fixation
tripartite wage fixation
unilateral wage fixation
organised sector
unorganised sector
wage board

Discussion Questions

1. Discuss why wage fixation is very important to both the workers and the employers.
2. Discuss what methods of wage fixation are prevalent in Indian industries.
3. Discuss how wages are usually fixed in the organised sector.
4. Discuss the methods of job evaluation and job pricing and point out which methods are more popular in Indian industries.
5. Discuss how managerial compensation is fixed in our country and how it is that job evaluation does not have any significant role in this regard.

364 *Compensation and Reward Management*

6. Discuss how wages are fixed in the unorganised sector.
7. Discuss the bipartite wage fixation in Indian industries. Also, discuss how far collective bargaining has been able to play its role in this direction.
8. Discuss how far the wage boards have proved their worth in the fixation of wages in Indian industries. Will it be desirable to give statutory force to the recommendations of the wage boards?
9. Discuss how far statutory wage fixation has been effective in our country.
10. Discuss whether the adjudication machinery and arbitration should be used for fixation of wages or not. What are the advantages and disadvantages of these mechanism?

Individual and Group Activities

1. In a group of two members, visit some big organisations in the private sector and discuss with the HR officials there how they fix wages of their employees. Do they go for job evaluation and job pricing or not and why? Prepare a brief report after the discussion is over.
2. Individually talk to the senior HR officials of a big manufacturing organisation and find out how their company fixes managerial compensation.
3. In a group of two members, visit a medium-scale organisation where wage board has fixed wages of its employees. Find out the reaction of trade union officials there with regard to the appropriateness of the wage board recommendations.
4. Individually discuss with the HR officials of a company where collective bargaining has played an important role in the fixation of wages of its employees. Find out from them how it has all been possible and what has been the role of workers' representations in this regard.
5. In a group of three members, visit a few big organisations and discuss the issue of wage fixation with both the HR officials and trade union leaders of each organisation. Prepare a management's strategy which can be used, of course with some modifications, in most cases.

Application Case 10.1

Incentive System of Wage Payment

Harry has been working as an operative staff in a company where wages were paid per time rate system. Accordingly, he was being paid on monthly basis like other operative staff. The company where he was employed has not been progressing well, and two years back the company suffered a substantial amount of loss. Having analysed the factors responsible for poor performance and also making a comparative study with some other companies in the same trade, it was revealed that in Harry's company labour cost per unit of output was considerably higher as compared to other companies.

The manager of the company convened a meeting of the concerned departmental heads as also the head of the HR department to take a fresh look of the wage system and find out a better alternate so that labour cost per unit of output may be reduced. All sorts of suggestions were put forward and deliberated upon. After a marathon session of the meeting, the general consensus of opinion emerged that in order to motivate individuals to produce more individually, incentive system of wage payment may be introduced wherein each worker will receive a guaranteed minimum wage whether he is able to produce standard output within the standard time or not. Further, those who produce more than the standard output will be entitled to payment per piece of their output at a pre-decided rate.

After a week when necessary preparations for the introduction of new method of wage payment had been made, the new system of wage payment was introduced. To a great satisfaction of the top management, the output per member of operative staff went up and the labour cost per unit of output came down by 30%, and the workers, especially those who were more efficient, were found extremely happy as their total earnings went up considerably. Even marginal workers had nothing to complain about as everyone was assured of minimum guaranteed wage.

Questions

1. Identify the main cause of reduction in the labour cost per unit of output after the incentive system of wage payment was introduced.
2. What is the difference between time rate system of wage payment and the incentive system of wage payment?

Notes

1 Quoted in *The Times of India*, 2 November 2022.
2 *The Times of India*, 12 November 2022.
3 ILO, *Job Evaluation, Studies and Reports, New Series*, No. 56 (Geneva: ILO, 1960), 8.
4 United States Department of Labour, Bureau of Labour Statistics, *Glossary of Currently Used Wage Terms, Bulletin 983* (Wellington: U.S. Government Printing Offices, 1950).
5 Flippo, *Principles of Personal Management*, 291–92.
6 G. T. Milkowich, *Compensation*, 9th ed. (New Delhi: Tata McGraw-Hill Education Private Ltd., 2011), 106–7.
7 Ibid.
8 Ibid., 108–9.
9 E. B. Flippo, *Personnel Management*, 6th ed. (New Delhi: McGraw-Hill International Editions, 1984), 303.
10 See Flippo, *Principles of Personal Management*, 309; Yoder, *Personnel Management and Industrial Relations*, 644.
11 See Yoder, *Personnel Management and Industrial Relations*, 643.
12 See T. A. Mahoney, 'Compensation Preference for Managers', *Industrial Relations* 3, no. 3 (May 1964): 135–44.
13 Yoder, *Personnel Management and Industrial Relations*, 644.
14 *The Economic Times*, 27 December 2016.
15 *The Economic Times*, 17 June 2016.
16 Ibid.

17 *The Times of India*, 5 December 2022.
18 Ibid.
19 *The Economic Times*, 19 March 2018.
20 Ibid.
21 Ibid.
22 *The Economic Times*, 14 January 2019.
23 Ibid.
24 *The Economic Times*, 20 March 2018 and Infosys put together.
25 Ibid.
26 Ibid.
27 Ibid.
28 Ibid.
29 *The Economic Times*, 20 June 2016.
30 Ibid.
31 Yoder, *Personnel Management and Industrial Relations*, 645–48.
32 See E. E. Lawler, 'Secrecy about Management Compensation: Are There Hidden Costs', *Organizational Behavior and Human Performance* 2, no. 2 (May 1967): 182–89.
33 For details, see Sharma, *Industrial Relations and Labour Legislation*, 102–49.
34 *The Economic Times*, 30 March 2017.
35 Ibid.
36 Ibid.
37 Ibid.
38 See Ministry of Labour & Employment, *Report of the National Commission on Labour* (New Delhi: Ministry of Labour & Employment, Government of India, 1969).
39 For a detailed study, see Sharma, *Industrial Relations and Labour Legislation*, 631–48.
40 https://tradingeconomics.com.
41 Ibid.
42 *The Times of India*, 28 December 2022.
43 Ibid., 28 December 2022.
44 Quoted in *The Times of India*, 28 December 2022.
45 *The Times of India*, 5 January 2023.
46 Ibid., 9 November 2022. Productivity (see Exhibit 10.8).
47 *Hindustan Times*, 30 March 2017.
48 *The Economic Times*, 23 April 2018.
49 Ibid.
50 Ibid.
51 *Hindustan Times*, 25 May 2018.
52 Ibid.
53 Ibid.
54 *Hindustan Times*, 5 September 2018.
55 Ibid.
56 Ibid.
57 New Labour Code for New India, *Ministry of Information and Broadcasting* (New Delhi: Government of India, 2021), 0.
58 Ibid., 10–11.
59 *Hindustan Times*, 13 September 2016.
60 *Hindustan Times*, 6 July 2016.

11 Fringe Benefits and Services, and Internal Audit of Compensation and Benefits (I)

Learning Objectives

After studying this chapter, the reader should be able to do the following:

1. Explain the importance of benefits in total compensation.
2. Explain the concept, philosophy and definition of fringe benefits as also its objectives and significance.
3. Explain the various types of fringe benefits.
4. Explain the origin of the concept of social security and highlight its objectives and need.
5. Point out the forms of social security and describe its scope.
6. List and describe the various acts related to social security passed in our country.
7. Understand and explain the recent biggest labour reforms initiated by the Government of India through Labour Reforms Bill, 2022.
8. Explain the Social Security measures initiated through the Labour Reforms Bill, 2022.

Introduction

Even though employee benefits and services constitute a significant part of total compensation, there is yet no clear answer to the following questions:

1. Do employee benefits and services facilitate an organisation's performance?
2. Does a sound employee benefits programme impact favourably an organisation's ability to attract and retain its employees?
3. Do employee benefits and services motivate employees to give their best to their organisation?

Although no research study has yet been able to provide a conclusive proof of answering the above questions in affirmative, the fact remains that benefits and services extended to workers have always been in vogue, though in different forms and under variety of titles such as 'non-wage benefits', 'employee benefits', 'wage supplements', 'perquisites other than wages', 'fringe benefits', 'social charges' and 'supplements'. However, the basic concept in the use of all these terms is the same.

DOI: 10.4324/9781032628424-15

The findings of a research study[1] also revealed that non-wage benefits cost 22.24% of the total labour cost. Almost a similar trend was found in a survey of comparison of wage and benefit costs (private versus state and local governments) conducted in 2005 wherein fringe benefits constituted 22.2% of total compensation in the private sector and 32.1% in the state and local governments.[2] The significance of benefits and services is further corroborated by the findings of the survey wherein it was revealed that 89% of executives feel that employee benefits play a vital role in attracting as well as in retaining good employees.[3] As a matter of fact, extension of fringe benefits is a great source of contentment to the workers as these benefits supplement their income, make their lives comfortable and improve their status and standard of living. Since a contended worker is an asset to an organisation, he is instrumental in overall progress of an organisation. That is why today a substantial majority of organisations provide fringe benefits to their workers, though their type, quantum and timings differ a great deal. A large majority of employees today prefer new benefits, like health insurance or paid time off, over a pay raise (see Exhibit 11.1).

Exhibit 11.1   Perks

Perks and benefits are among the top thing's employees consider when deciding whether to accept a job. Almost 80% of employees say that they would prefer new benefits, like health insurance or paid time off, over a pay raise.

Source: The Economic Times, 20 June 2016.

Before going ahead, it will be in the fitness of things to understand the concept, philosophy, definition and other relevant issues of fringe benefits.

Fringe Benefits

Concept, Philosophy[4] and Definition of Fringe Benefits

The term 'fringe benefits' is of recent origin and did not come into use till 1950,[5] though such benefits to workers, in some form or the other, have been in vogue for quite a long time. Although the labour economists[6] have realised the potentialities of fringe benefits in the execution of production plans, they have not been unanimous in giving a uniform definition of fringe benefits. Of course, they all agree that the main purpose of fringe benefits is to supplement money wages of workers, and thus narrowing the gap left between the money wages and the cost of living.[7] Fringe benefits are usually the extra benefits provided to the workers in addition to compensation paid in the form of wages or salary.

We come across different definitions of the term 'fringe benefits'. For example, Cockmar says that fringe benefits are 'those benefits which are provided by an employer to or for the benefit of an employee and are not in the form of wages, salaries and time related payments'.[8] Belcher defines these benefits as 'any wage cost not directly connected with the employee's productive effort, performance, service or sacrifice'.[9] Thus, the benefits provided to the workforce apart from the negotiated wages are nowadays termed as either fringe benefits or supplementary benefits or non-wage benefits. However, the substance of all these terms is the same.

As a matter of fact, fringe benefit is primarily a means in the direction of ensuring, maintaining and increasing the income of the worker or employee. It is a benefit which supplements a worker's ordinary wages and which is of value to him and his family insofar as it materially increases his comfort.

According to ILO, wages are often augmented by special cash benefits, by the provision of medical and other services or by payments in kind, that form part of the wage for expenditure on the goods and services. In addition, workers commonly receive such benefits as holidays with pay, low-cost meals, low rent housing, etc. Such addition to wage proper is sometimes referred to fringe benefits. Benefits that have no relation to employment or wages should not be regarded as fringe benefits though they may constitute a significant part of the workers total income.[10]

It is also worth noting that fringe benefits usually act as maintenance factors than as motivators.[11] One of the major factors responsible for a variety of definitions of fringe benefit is that some employers and employees interpret the meaning of fringe benefits in their own way, that is, as it suits them. In view of the differences in opinions of different authorities, and in order to have a proper understanding of its connotation and implementation in the Indian industrial structure, it may be desirable to refer to Section 2(vi) of the Payment of Wages Act, 1936; Section 2(b) of the Minimum Wages Act, 1948; Section 2(22) of the ESI Act, 1948; and some provisions made under the Employees' Provident Funds and Miscellaneous Provisions Act, 1952, and the Payment of Bonus Act, 1965. However, some clarifications with regard to fringe benefits are also found in the Industrial Disputes Act, 1947, and in certain rulings and judgments of different High Courts and the Supreme Court of India.

Objectives of Fringe Benefits

Broadly speaking, fringe benefits are instrumental in accomplishing certain social, human relations, and macroeconomic goals. The main objectives of fringe benefits may be as follows:

1. To meet the needs of employees and safeguard them against certain hazards of life, particularly the ones which an individual, especially of small means, cannot himself provide for
2. To attract and retain employees
3. To earn gratitude and loyalty of the employees[12]
4. To remain competitive in the market regarding the provisions of fringe benefits
5. To boost the image of the organisation
6. To seek meaningful cooperation of employees in production process
7. To infuse confidence, motivate and boost morale of the employees
8. To reduce rate of absenteeism and labour turnover
9. To reduce the influence of trade unions
10. To reduce statutory interference
11. To improve human and industrial relations
12. To promote employee welfare and provide qualitative work environment
13. To provide a tax-efficient method of remuneration which reduces tax liabilities compared with those related to equivalent cash payment[13]
14. To improve quality of life of workers and promote their well-being

Significance of Fringe Benefits

Fringe benefits benefit all the stakeholders in an industry in the following manner:

1. **Benefits to workers**
    a. Reduce gap between nominal wages and real wages of the workers.
    b. Provide contentment to workers.
    c. Improve their standard of living.
    d. Maintain their self-respect.
    e. Make workers more responsible.
    f. Help in their growth and development.
    g. Improve their productivity

2. **Benefits to employers**
    a. Present attractive areas of negotiation when large wages and salary increases are not practical.
    b. Help in attracting and retaining employees.
    c. Reduce the influence of trade unions on workers.
    d. Help in reducing cost of production.
    e. Help in reducing wastage and depreciation.
    f. Help in increasing productivity.
    g. Help in increasing profits.
    h. Help in increasing output.
    i. Help in improving quality.
    j. Boost the image of the organisation.
    k. Help in reducing the rate of absenteeism.
    l. Help in reducing supervisory expenses.
    m. Improve human and industrial relations.

3. **Benefits to society**
    a. Keep goods and services available at reasonable prices.
    b. Increase in gross national production.
    c. Achieve educational upliftment.
    d. Promote peace and harmony.
    e. Improve standard of living.
    f. Eliminate social evils.
    g. Reduce social costs.

Intangible Benefits

The power of intangible benefits is no less than that of tangible benefits. Rather, at times, intangible benefits prove more powerful and effective. Even at the time of applying for a job, an applicant weighs up both the tangible and intangible benefits offered by different employers. Some of the intangible benefits that may attract the attention of an applicant during the process of deciding whether to apply/join or not a particular organisation may include praise/recognition for achievements, power/authority, opportunities for growth, working environment, work-life balance, flexi timings, structure of the organisation, opportunities for career progression, dignity of labour and the like.

Factors Responsible for the Need and Growth of Benefits

The beginning of the need for fringe benefits can be traced back to wage and price controls initiated by certain countries during the Second World War. Consequently, the employees felt the pinch of inadequate rise in their wages and therefore, their trade unions started putting forward their demands for introduction and enforcement of new benefits in their then existing benefits. Besides, the cost-effectiveness of benefits also encouraged the demand for benefits because most of these were not taxable and some of them, such as accident insurance, life insurance and health insurance, can be obtained at concessional rates, if asked for on group basis.

In addition to this, statutory requirements also made it obligatory on the part of the employers to extend certain benefits. For example, in our country, the Employees Compensation Act, 1923; the Employees' State Insurance Act, 1948; the Factories Act, 1948; the Payment of Bonus Act, 1965; the Employees Provident Fund and Miscellaneous Provisions Act, 1952; the Payment of Gratuity Act, 1972; and so on have made it mandatory on the part of the employers to make benefits and facilities available to the employees. Employers also started extending certain benefits voluntarily to attract competent employees as also to create a good image of themselves. Humanistic considerations that a worker is a human being first also prompted employees to extend certain benefits. Paternalistic considerations on the part of the employers to take care of their workers in case of illness, employment injury, unemployment, poverty and so on were also instrumental in the extension of employee benefits. Keen competition among employers to acquire and retain competent employees also encouraged the extension of employee benefits. The recent labour reforms being introduced are going to play an important role in the promotion of benefits.

Benefit Policies and Practices

In order to control benefits costs and to accomplish the desired objectives, an organisation should formulate its benefit policy which should clearly specify the range of benefits, for example, holidays, leaves and so on, that is, what benefits would be available to all the employees and what will be the additional benefits among which an employee can exercise his choice, for example, transport facilities, housing facilities and the like. Similarly, the policy should also mention the size of each benefit and be made available to the employees taking into consideration its perceived value to the employees as also its cost to the company. Again, the percentage of each benefit to total compensation should be specified, though it will depend a great deal on the range and size of benefits made available to the employees. Then comes the issue of option given to the employees to choose a package of benefits according to their requirements. Not every hat fits on the head of every person. Similarly, a number of packages of benefits should be worked out, from which an employee may choose any one according to his personal requirements. The exercise of choice will be guided by an individual's typical needs depending on the size of his family, age group and so on. While formulating policies, harmonisation should also be taken into consideration, that is, there should be no distinction at any level in the hierarchy between the benefits provided. However, they may differ depending on the length of service and so on. In the same way, government policies, especially those that have tax implications regarding benefits, should also be kept in view while formulating benefit policy. Competition packages of benefits being offered by the competitors of the company also affect a company's benefit policy in determining what is necessary to enable the company to sustain itself in the market. The status of the trade union operating in the company has also to be taken care of while formulating the organisation's benefit policy. It is always desirable to keep the trade union into confidence while formulating a benefit policy; otherwise, there may be problems later. Trade union may help in the selection of typical benefits and how they should be administered.

However, when it comes to the practice of providing benefits to employees, it differs from industry to industry and from organisation to organisation. For example, there is a great variation in this regard in private and public sector organisations, and so is the case in organisations where labour costs constitute a small part of total costs and where such costs constitute a substantial part of total costs. Similarly, the practices of providing benefits differ depending on the employer's view or intention with which the benefits are being extended and so on.

However, it is always desirable to adopt a balanced approach so that while following the best practices, the benefit costs do not rise beyond a desirable level.

A detailed discussion on factors affecting fringe benefits and the coverage and types of fringe benefits available in Indian organisations is given as follows.

Planning, Designing and Administration of Benefits

The planning and designing of benefits depend a great deal on the compensation objective. Only those benefits should be introduced which meet the compensation objective. For example, if the compensation objective is to put a check on high rate of turnover, then there can be several options to achieve this objective such as increasing wages and introducing incentives. Having tried these objectives if you find that the objective of reducing turnover rate is not being achieved, another option can be to introduce employee stock option, that is, if an employee continues his job for three years, he will be entitled to company shares to the tune of 10% of his salary, if he continues for five years, then he will be getting the shares to the extent of 15% and if he continues for 10 years, he will be getting the shares to the tune of 20% of his salary. Similarly, typical benefits can be planned and designed if female employees need be attracted. In such a case, women-oriented benefits such as transport and crèche facilities, flexi-working hours, work from home, etc., can be thought of.

In the same way, an external survey regarding benefits offered by your competitors can be conducted so that your benefits are at least equivalent to those of the competitors, or if not, then some justification can be put forth for the same. Cost-effectiveness and affordability of the organisation are other issues to be taken care of while administering the benefits programme. There should be full justification for increasing a particular amount of expenditure on a specific benefit. Case benefit analysis in this direction can play an important role. Another issue that needs to be taken care of during the administration of benefits programme is who should be covered under a benefits programme, that is, whether all employees—males and females—or only permanent employees or both permanent and temporary employees or even probationers can be included, or even retired employees can also be covered, for example, medical treatment even after retirement and so on. Such decisions have a wide implication for administration of benefits.

The next administrative issue can be choosing a suitable benefit package. It needs to be decided if only a standard benefit package, which is uniformly applicable to all employees, is to be introduced or it has to be or not to be supplemented by a cafeteria-style package. In the latter case, an employee can choose any of the benefit packages which meets his/her requirements the most. Cafeteria-style packages are in the interest of both the employees and the employer.

The third issue related to the administration of employee benefits is whether the cost of benefit is to be borne extensively by the employer (non-contributory) or both by the employer and the employee (contributory) and, if so, in what proportion. However, it is always advisable to make benefit options contributory so that the beneficiary does not misuse it or waste it.

In case there is any legal requirement from the side of the government, then that also needs to be complied with. In case any benefit is not tax exempted, legal requirements should be taken care of.

Current Approaches

There are three main current approaches in the arena of fringe benefits which are given as follows.[14]

1. **Innovative approach**: Under the innovative approach, new dimensions are being added to certain benefits. Also, new benefits are being added to minimise the impact of tax. Benefits are being tailor-made to meet the needs of individual employees. Aligning benefits of blue- and white-collar employees is also part of innovation in the design and administration of fringe benefits.[15]
2. **Flexibility**: 'Flexible benefits' is a blanket term for employees giving employees more control over their reward packages without employee increasing extra costs.[16] Today, organisations have become sensitive to tailor-make the benefits to suit the requirements of individual employees instead of offering common standard packages. In our country, this is more applicable in the case of managerial employees and the staff and workers are yet to taste it. The flexible approach responds to an employee's needs helps recruitment and retention, makes the employer look flexible and forward looking, highlights the aggregate value of the package, makes employees more loyal and so on. Some of the examples of existing flexible benefits include private medical insurance, insurance benefits, company cars, pensions, holidays and so on.

    The following are the four main plan architectures[17] of flexible benefits:

    a. Individual plans operating independently
    b. Umbrella plan
    c. Flex fund plan
    d. Voluntary ('affinity') benefits

    While designing and implementing a flexible benefit project, it is advisable to associate employees concerned and realistic deadlines must be fixed for its implementation and whenever required to liaise with interested third parties. Of course, in the implementation of a benefit project certain barriers like communication of a benefit project and administrative problems are likely to be confronted with.
3. **Harmonisation**: Harmonisation seeks to bring in a measure of equity and fair play and is supposed to contribute to improvements in employee attitudes and performance and signification of payroll procedures and fringe benefits administration.[18] Under harmonisation, an attempt is made to have a single statue for the entire workforce of an organisation. However, it is specially in the case of deduction for coming

late on duty, marking attendance, working hours, distinction of pay and so on that the harmonisation process is involved, though it can be extended to all conditions of services and work practices.

Factors Influencing Choice of Benefits Package

There are several factors that influence benefit choice. For example, from an employee's point of view, his age, sex, marital status, size of the family and so on will be the determining factors, while choosing a benefit package.

Reviewing and Modifying the Benefits Package

Reviewing the effectiveness of a benefits package from time to time, that is, whether the extension of a particular benefits package could serve the desired purpose, is also very important because only then it may be decided whether a particular benefit should be allowed to be continued or discontinued, or its quantum needs to be reduced or enlarged and so on. However, measuring the impact and effectiveness of a particular benefit(s) is not an easy task. Of course, there are certain indicators which may provide a clue in this direction. For example, the enthusiasm of employees towards overtaking a particular benefit package, expression of a sense of satisfaction of employees regarding a particular benefit package, demand from the employee for more choice in the benefit packages made available to them, change in the policy of taxation by the several towards certain benefits and so on.

Keeping in view the feedback received at the time of the review of benefits packages as also the latest happenings, one may ask for rendering the benefits packages. It is, therefore, desirable to redesign them. However, while redesigning a benefits package, in addition to taking into consideration the feedback received from reviewing of existing benefits package, it is also essential to give due weightage to the new trends and best practices with regard to benefits package, especially the ones being adopted by your competitors, as also to the new aspirations of the employees, the demands being put forward by trade unions, taxation policy of the government related to benefits package, current stations of employee value proportion and so on.

Informing the Employees About Benefits Package

Simply having good benefits packages designed and making them available is not enough. What is equally important is to make the employees aware about them as also about their value to the employees and that how much it will cost the organisation per employee. It should also be communicated to the employees as to with what intention the benefits package has been introduced. This can be taken care of by mutual discussion, various publications of the organisation, display of attractive charts and so on.

Factors Affecting Fringe Benefits and Services

The extension and availability of fringe benefits are affected by many factors such as organisation's financial health, trade union's bargaining power, employers' philosophy with regard to fringe benefits, employers' consciousness to their social responsibility, the cost of fringe benefits, employees' needs, taxation policy of the government with regard to fringe benefits, statutory requirements regarding fringe benefits and utility of a particular item of fringe benefits to workers.

Coverage, Classification and Types of Fringe Benefits

Based on the study of relevant acts, rulings and judgments of various courts, the following types of payments fall in the category of fringe benefits:

1. They should be computable in terms of money.
2. They should not be part of any contract, indicating when the sum is payable.
3. The amount of such payment is not predetermined.

While Cockmar classifies fringe benefits into two categories—(a) those which are offered on the basis of status, such as car, foreign travel, telephones, secretarial services and company scholarships, and (b) those which are key benefits, such as retirement benefits and house purchase schemes—the US Chamber of Commerce divides fringe benefits under five heads: (a) payments to be made under any specific legislation (i.e. statutory benefits); (b) pensions and other payments as agreed; (c) paid rest period, lunch breaks, wash-up time, to-get-ready time, travel time and so on; (d) payment for time not worked at all such as holiday pay and lay-off pay; and (e) other items such as bonus and profit-sharing.

Again, while Hodge[19] classifies the fringe benefits into two categories—(a) extra pay for time worked, such as incentive bonus, old-age insurance, unemployment compensation and shift subsidy, and (b) payment for time not worked, such as paid rest, lunch breaks, travel time and vacation pay—Dale Yoder and Paul D. Standohar classify fringe benefits into four categories: (a) for employment security, such as unemployment insurance, overtime pay, maternity leave with pay and lay-off pay; (b) for health protection such as health insurance, medical care and hospitalisation; (c) for old age and retirement such as pension and gratuity; and (d) for personnel identification, participation, and stimulation, such as attendance bonus, housing, canteen and stress counselling.

According to another classification, fringe benefits may be for (a) payment for time not worked, such as paid holidays and paid vacation; (b) employee security, such as lay-off compensation and retrenchment compensation; (c) safety and health, such as safety measures and health benefits; (d) welfare and recreational facilities, such as housing, canteen, counselling, holiday homes, educational facilities, picnics and transportation facilities; and (e) old age and retirement benefits, such as pension, provident fund, gratuity and post-retirement medical benefits.

Benefits have also been divided as (a) direct benefits (which help the employees directly, e.g. medical facilities) and (b) indirect benefits (which help the employees indirectly, e.g. providing free furniture to the canteen contractor). Benefits have also been categorised as (a) statutory benefits and (b) voluntary benefits.

Fringe Benefits and Current Practices (I)

The three main categories of fringe benefits are (a) social security benefits, (b) labour welfare facilities and (c) bonus. While a brief discussion about social security is made in the following paragraphs, the discussion on labour welfare activities and bonus are contained in Chapters 11 and 12.

Social Security

In the modern industrial set up, workers are exposed to various contingencies of life, including employment injury, occupational diseases, illness, old age, death and so on. With almost no or very less savings with the workers, it is difficult for them to sustain themselves during such contingencies. Hence, there should be some mechanism that may enable them to face such contingencies when their earning capacity is lost either temporarily or permanently. It is here that social security comes into picture because it takes care of employees from womb to tomb. The provision of social security measures in an organisation makes workers feel more confident, more loyal and dedicated to their jobs and give their best to their organisations.

The Concept and Definition of Social Security

Although the concept of providing social security to workers has always been there in one form or the other, but it has always been less than required. The modern concept of social security became popular when the Beveridge Plan, prepared by Sir William Beveridge, was presented to the Parliament of the United Kingdom in December 1942. The Plan provides for a unified system of income maintenance to cover needs arising from variety of causes. However, the origin of the concept of social security can be traced to the general feeling that a worker in distress should be helped by the capable members of the community, or the employer, or the state or by all of them together. But such a distress should have been caused by the contingencies of life, such as industrial accidents, occupational diseases, illness, unemployment, old age and death. Although the desired funds to provide social security to the workers should come from their employers or state or the community, either individually or jointly, but it will be appropriate if the workers are also made a part of this joint fund, though in a very modest way. It is perhaps for this reason that an ILO publication defines social security as the security that society furnishes, through appropriate organisation, against certain risks to which its members are exposed. These risks are essentially contingencies of life which the individual of small means cannot effectively provide for by his own ability alone or even in private combination with his fellows.[20]

Objectives of Social Security

The objectives of social security are usually categorised under three heads: (a) to compensate (i.e. income security during the period of calamity), (b) to restore the earning capacity (i.e. restoration of earning capacity through re-employment or rehabilitation as well as medical treatment of the diseased or invalid worker) and (c) to prevent the contingencies (taking steps to avoid the loss of productive capacity caused due to illness, unemployment or employment injury or occupational disease[s]).

Need and Significance of Social Security in Indian Industries

Workers in lower-middle-income countries like India are more exposed to the various contingencies of life. Besides, workers in such countries are poor and physically weak. Hence, the need of social security measures is greater in such countries than for the workers of industrially advanced countries. The reasons that call for the need of social security for industrial workers in our country may be summarised as follows:

1. Indian industrial workers are more exposed to various contingencies of life and fall victim to such contingencies more frequently for a variety of reasons.
2. Because of their low wages, their capacity to save is either nil or extremely low.
3. In a good number of cases, Indian workers are indebted. It is said that Indian workers are born in debt, live in debt and die in debt.
4. The old joint family system is giving way to nuclear family system—thus leaving no dependable source to rely on at the time of contingency.
5. Social security maintains self-respect and dignity of workers as they get social security benefits as a matter of right.
6. Social security restores the lost working capacity of the affected workers at the earliest possible.

Forms of Social Security

Social insurance and social assistance are the two main forms of social security:

1. Social insurance: It aims at the maintenance of minimum standard of living of the employee during the period of contingency of life. It is obligatory for all employees to become its member once it is introduced in any organisation, industry or state. Its funds are drawn from employers, the state and the employees, though the contributions made by the employees are nominal. It maintains self-respect of the employees as benefits under it are granted to members as a matter of right and without any means lest.
2. Social assistance: It is a purely government affair and, therefore, financed exclusively by the government and benefits are granted on fulfilling prescribed conditions, though benefits are claimed as a matter of right. The overall objective is to help the people when they fall victim to certain contingencies of life.

Scope of Social Security

While social insurance is the main form of social security and, therefore, falls under the scope of social security, social assistance, too, is within the scope of social security. However, whether commercial insurance is a constituent of scope of social security is a little but controversial issue because, first, it is voluntary in nature; second, its aim is not the maintenance of minimum standard of living; and finally, the help available depends on the amount of premium paid by the beneficiary.

Social Security in India

Social security used to be provided in the past also to people, in general, and to the workers, in particular, which is evident from our ancient scripts such as manuscripts, Kautilya's Arthashastra and Naradasmriti. However, it used to be the joint families, orphanages, trusts, panchayats, other local bodies, philanthropists, widow homes and so on that were the main institutions for providing social security to the people in distress. But due to industrial revolution and gradual social changes happening over a period, these institutions failed to provide social security either at all or inadequately. Hence, the state had to intervene but not much could be done till very recently. Anyway, the Report of the Royal Commission on Labour in India, the publication of the Beveridge Report in the United Kingdom, the adoption of the ILO convention No. 102, Social Security (Minimum Standards), 1952, and the Directive Principles of State Policy enshrined in the Constitution of India provided the much-desired fillip to strengthen the institution of social security and the role of the government to be played in this direction.

Present Status of Social Security in Indian Industries

If compared with the industrially advanced countries, it will not be an exaggeration to say that in India we have just made a beginning both quantity-wise and quality-wise as far as social security to industrial workers is concerned, though it is a good beginning and a promising one. While voluntary social security (through trade unions) is as good as missing, the employers have done only a little bit in this direction. It is the statutory social security that is ruling the roost, though even in this respect also there remains much to achieve. The Government of India has passed certain acts to make provisions for employment injury, occupational diseases, health insurance, maternity benefits, provident fund, pension schemes, retrenchment, and lay-off compensation and so on. A brief description of various acts passed in this regard is as follows:

The Employees'[21] Compensation Act, 1923[22]

The act aims at paying some amount of compensation at the time of invalidity or death caused by employment injury or occupational diseases as laid down in the act. In case of temporary disablement, the amount of compensation payable to the eligible employee is a half-month by payment of the sum equivalent to 25% of the monthly wages of the employee in accordance with the provisions of the act. However, such half-monthly payments can continue for a maximum period of five years. The half-monthly payment is payable to employee on the 16th day from the date of disablement continues for a period of 28 days or more and thereafter half-monthly during the disablement or during a period of 5 years, whichever period is shorter. In case such disablement lasts for a period of less than 28 days, the injured employee will be paid after the expiring of a waiting period of 3 days from the date of disablement. If the injury results in his death, the employer is required to deposit an additional sum of not less than 5,000 with the commissioner, which will be payable to the eldest surviving dependent of the employee as funeral expenses. In case of permanent partial disablement, the amount of compensation payable to the eligible employee is calculated according to the percentage loss of earning capacity caused by injury, as laid down in Schedule I of the act. If the employee is 'permanently totally disabled', the amount of compensation shall be 60% of the monthly wages of the disabled worker multiplied by the relevant factor indicated in Schedule IV of the act or an amount of INR 140,000,[23] whichever is more, subject to a maximum of INR 5.48 lakh. However, in case of death of an employee, the amount of compensation is equal to 50% of the monthly wages of the deceased employee multiplied by the relevant factor indicated in Schedule IV of the act (linked to age) or an amount of INR 120,000,[24] whichever is more, subject to a maximum of INR 4.56 lakh. The act ceases to be applicable in those establishments where the ESI Act, 1948, is applicable. The wage ceiling limitation for eligibility has been increased to INR 8,000 per month effective from 18

January 2010. The affected employee is entitled for re-imbursement of the actual medical expenditure incurred by him for treatment of injuries caused during employment. There is no ceiling on it. Thus, the act is quite meaningful, though many scrupulous employers, especially in the small sector, play with the provision of the act to avoid payment of disability compensation to the affected worker.

The Maternity Benefit Act, 1961[25]

This act has provisions for granting 12 weeks (now revised to 26 weeks) maternity leave with average daily wages plus medical bonus of 25% (now revised to 3,500 from 19 December 2011)[26] if prenatal confinement and postnatal care is not provided free of charge. This leave can be further extended under certain conditions as laid down in the act. The act also entitles the mothers to avail two nursing breaks, over and above the initial normal rest, of prescribed duration for nursing the child until the child becomes 15 months old. Thus, the act provides a great help to expecting female workers both financially and physically, though certain improvements are still required. Per the latest amendment of the act in 2017, effective from 10 April 2017, the period of maternity leave has been increased to 26 weeks and the female employee will be deemed to be in continuous service for this period.[27] Besides, earlier in the year 2018, the High Court of Uttarakhand struck down as unconstitutional a state rule that denied maternity leave to a woman upon her third pregnancy. The High Court held that the rule violated the provisions of the Maternity Benefit Act, which did not authorize discrimination of this kind. However, the High Court also observed that the rule contravened the spirit of Article 42 of the Constitution, which mandates the State to provide for 'securing just and human conditions of work and for maternity relief.

The has been made applicable to adopting or commissioning mothers also from the date the child is handed over to the adopting mother. A commissioning mother refers to a biological mother who uses her egg to create an embryo implanted in any other woman.

Employers are required to provide a mandatory creche facility (within the prescribed distance from the establishment), either separately or along with other common facilities. At present there is no wage limit for coverage under the act.

There have been several instances of retrenchment of female employees or clamping down on women employment by firms afraid of a bloating salary bill after the government extended the period of maternity leave to 26 weeks from the earlier 12 weeks.

According to ISF, the Employees' Provident Fund Organisation (EPFO) contribution criteria should be limited to three months and government should consider reimbursing paid leave for 14 weeks instead of 7 weeks for a period of one year. 'This will help companies ease into the change in policy, where eventually government can reduce the compensation percentage over a period of three years', ISF suggested. Under the Maternity Benefit (Amendment) Act, 2017, the government extended maternity leave from 12 weeks to 26 weeks with effect from 1 April 2017. Following this, there have been several instances brought to the notice of ministry wherein employers have either retrenched female employees on flimsy grounds or are not hiring too many female workers fearing it will inflate their wage bill,[28] and that these female employees may not join back after availing six months of paid leave.[29] Trade unions welcome the move saying it will ease the burden of employers and bring in some formalisation to the country's workforce, they share ISF views threshold is not legitimate.[30]

The ESI Act, 1948[31]

The ESI Act is an integrated act taking care of many contingencies and is considered a very bold attempt in providing social security to industrial workers. The act applies to factories using power and employing ten or more persons.[32] ESI Scheme will be applicable to establishment preparing sweets with the aid of LPG (Employees' State Insurance Corporation V. Premlal, 2009. LLR [Kar HC]). An advertising agency is a 'Sharp' (Kuriacone V. ESI Corp. [1988] 2 CLR 301 [Ker.]). Employees of factories drawing monthly wages up to INR 15,000 per month and INR 25,000 per month for persons with disabilities are covered under the scheme.[33] The limit of wages for coverage of an employee under the act is subject to change as and when the central government so decides, following the set procedure. The scheme is financed by contributions from the employees at the rate of 1.75% and from employers at the rate of 4.75% of the wages of the employees. The state governments' share of expenditure on the provision of medical care is to the extent of 12.5% (1/8th within the capita ceiling).[34] The ESI scheme is now operated in 815 centres scheduled in 31 states/union territories. As of 31 March 2014, 1.95 crore insured persons, about 7.58 crore beneficiaries and about 6.70 lakh factories and establishments were covered under the scheme. Under the sickness benefit, the affected employee is entitled to cash payment at the standard benefit rate, corresponding to his daily average wages for a maximum period of 91 days in two consecutive benefit periods, extendable to 120 days in certain cases. Maternity benefit is payable at double the standard benefit for 12 weeks (now revised to 26 weeks) per the conditions laid down for the purpose. The benefit is available in case of confinement, miscarriage or sickness arising out of pregnancy, premature birth of a child and so on. The disablement benefit is paid in cash and in instalments to the insured person for the temporary, permanent (both total or partial disablement) disablement arising out of employment per conditions laid down for the purpose. Dependent's benefit comprises cash payments to the dependents of an insured person who dies as a result of occupational diseases or employment injury, per schedule and conditions laid down for the purpose. Medical benefit includes treatment of the insured person and the members of his family, covering primary health care to super specialist facilities, outdoor and indoor treatment, domiciliary visit, provision for drugs and dressings, supply of artificial limbs, dentures, spectacles and hearing aids free of cost when these are necessitated by employment injury. The Employees' State Insurance Corporation runs 36 hospitals (as on 31 October 2014), including 50 district centre hospitals in various states.[35]

There are some other benefits also which are available to an insured person. 'Other benefits' include funeral expenses, rehabilitation benefit and so on.

The Employees' Provident Fund and Miscellaneous Provisions Act, 1952[36]

The act aims at providing social security and timely monetary assistance to industrial employees and their families when they are in distress and/or unable to meet family and social obligations, and to protect them in their old age, disablement, or early death of the breadwinner and in some other contingencies. The act is applicable to establishments employing 20 or more persons, as also to undertakings owned by the central or state governments or by a local authority. Only those employees come under the purview of the act whose wages do not exceed INR 6,500 (revised to INR 15,000 with effect from 1 September 2014) per month, likely to be increased further. The central government is empowered to revise the wage limit for coverage of the employees. There are 1,183,905 establishments covered under this act with 220,513,525 employees.

There are provisions for the following in this act.

1. **Employees' Provident Fund Scheme:** Under this scheme, both employees and employers need to contribute mandatorily at the rate of 12% of the monthly wages (in case of general establishments) and 10% of the wages (in case of notified establishments) of the subscriber. The employee at the time of retirement or leaving the organisation is entitled to withdraw the amount (with interest) lying in his account, subject to certain conditions.
2. **Employees' Family Pension Scheme, 1971:** It was introduced in 1971 but ceased to operate since 1995.
3. **Employees' Pension Scheme (EPS),[37] 1995:** Members on attaining the age of 58 and having rendered minimum ten years' contributory service (including the membership period with the ceased Employees' Family Pension Scheme, 1971) shall qualify for superannuation pension. The other members will get the withdrawal benefit or as the rules permit. The scheme of 1995 provides several benefits to the members and their families such as monthly member pension, disablement pension, widow/widower pension, children pension, orphan pension, disabled children/orphan pension, nominee pension, pension to dependent parents and withdrawal benefit. The scheme is financed by transferring 8.33% of the provident fund contributions from employers' share and by contributions at the rate of 1.16% of the basic wages of employees by the central government. The pensioners who were drawing benefits under the erstwhile family pension scheme of 1971 will continue to draw family pension under the EPS, 1995.[38]
4. **Employees' Deposit Linked Insurance Scheme, 1976:** This scheme is applicable to all factories/establishments with effect from August 1976. All members of the Employees' Provident Fund Scheme are required to become the members of this scheme. Under this scheme, employers are required to contribute towards the insurance fund at the rate of 0.5% of pay. The benefit under para 22 of this scheme on the death of an employee has been further increased by 20% in addition to the benefits already provided therein. During the year 2013–2014, 28,441 employees' deposit linked insurance claims were settled and at the end of the year (2013–2014), the EPFO had cumulative investments of 13,711 crore under this scheme.[39]

Recent Developments

The government is likely to enhance the provident fund interest rate to 8.65% despite the decline in interest rates, benefitting over 60 million subscribers of the EPFO. Per the report in the *Economic Times*, of 18 February 2019, the Central Board of Trustees (CBT) of the EPFO was to meet on 21 February 2019 to consider the return for the current year besides an increase in the minimum pension for subscribers. The doubling of the minimum pension under the EPS of the EPFO will benefit nearly five million subscribers. 'The sub-committee on pension has reviewed the proposals of high-empowered committee to double the minimum pension to INR 2,000 for INR 1,000 now, restrict its withdrawal before retirement and introduce some amount of contribution from the beneficiaries during their work life'. Employees are automatically enrolled in the EPS if they are EPFO members. Subscribers pay 12% of their salary every month into the EPF account. Out of the matching contribution of 12% by employers, 8.33% goes to the EPS, subject to a maximum of INR 1,250 a month, 0.5% to the Employee's Deposit Linked Insurance Scheme and the rest to the provident fund. The central government contributes 1.16% of basic salary plus daily allowance to the EPS account. The hike in minimum pension will benefit five million EPS subscribers and will cost the government around the annual outgo of INR 9,000 crore per annum on the pension scheme. The EPFO presently covers 190 industries (mentioned in Schedule 1 of the EPFA Act) with over 2 million accounts in over 1.13 million establishments.

Proposal to Increase the Pension Limit under the Atal Pension Yojana (APY)

The government looked into the proposal to double pension limit under APY It was under active examination as there was a need to increase the value of pension under APY. The proposal was sent to the finance ministry with an aim to increase the subscriber base of APY, which stood at 10.2 million. Currently, there are five slabs of pension from INR 1,000 to INR 5,000 per month. There has been a lot of feedback from the market asking for higher pension amounts because many people feel that INR 5,000 at the age of 60 years, 20–30 years from now will not be sufficient. Pension Fund Regulatory and Development Authority (PFRDA) has sent two more proposals to the ministry—auto enrolment for APY and increasing the maximum age bar to enter the scheme to 50 years. At present, the age limit for enrolling for APY is 18–40 years. Increasing it to 18–50 years will help in expanding the subscriber base. About five million new subscribers were added under the scheme in 2017–2018, and it was hoped to add another six–seven million in the next financial year.[40]

Payment of Gratuity Act, 1972[41]

The act is applicable to employees engaged in factories, mines, oil fields, plantations, ports, railway companies, shops and other establishments or for matters connected therewith or incidental thereto, employing ten or more persons.[42] All the employees (including managers and supervisors) engaged in the aforesaid establishments are legally entitled to gratuity at the rate of 15 days wages multiplied by number of completed years of service, subject to fulfilment of certain conditions laid down under the act. The ceiling of the amount of gratuity has been increased from INR 3.5 lakh to INR 10 lakh with effect from 24 May 2010.[43]

With the passage of Payment of Gratuity (Amendment) Bill, 2018, with voice vote by the Rajya Sabha in March 2018[44] and subsequent signing into law by the presidents, the tax-free gratuity for public and private sector employees got raised to INR 20 lakh from INR 10 lakh. The Seventh Pay Commission had already raised it to INR 20 lakh for the government employees. The amendment has now ensured harmony among employees in the private and public sectors as well as autonomous organisations who are not covered under the Central Civil Services (Pension) Rules. The act is applicable to employees who have completed at least five years of continuous service.[45]

Exhibit 11.2 Withdrawal Limit Raised to INR 20 Lakh

The gratuity withdrawal limit has been raised to INR 20 lakh from the current ceiling of INR 10 lakh. The tax exemption limit on gratuity is also set to increase to INR

20 lakh. Mint cited a labour ministry spokesperson as saying on 23 February 2016 that all stakeholders—states, the Centre, unions, and industry representatives—agreed to this.

Now the gratuity withdrawal limit has been raised to INR 20 lakh from the current ceiling of INR 10 lakh (for more details, see Exhibit 11.2).

Retrenchment Compensation

1. Lay-off and retrenchment are two of the most serious problems employees are confronted with as they face a lot of economic problem while they remain laid off. The ongoing disturbances in the global economy and the danger of economic recession, which is looming large, are compelling many employers to lay off or terminate or retrench their employees on a large scale (see Exhibits 11.3 to 11.8)

Exhibit 11.3 Job Cut by Computer Manufacturer

HP said it expects to cut up to 6,000 jobs by end of fiscal year 2025, or about 12% of its global workforce, at a time when sales of personal computers and laptops are sliding as shoppers are tightening the budgets.

Source: The Times of India, 24 November 2022.

Exhibit 11.4 Airlines Push for Lone Pilot Flights to Cut Costs Despite Safety Fears

Airlines and regulators are pushing to have just one pilot in the cockpit of passenger jets instead of two. It would lower costs and ease pressure from crew shortages, but placing such responsibility on a single person at the control is unsettling for some.

Source: The Economic Times, 24 November 2022.

Exhibit 11.5 Google's Parent co Alphabet May Lay Off Up to 10K

Alphabet Google's parent company is reportedly gearing up to lay off about 10,000 poor performing employees. These form around 6% of its workforce. The move comes amid the Big Tech Lay-off season kicked off by Meta, Amazon, Twitter, Salesforce and more due to rough global conditions.

Source: The Economic Times, 23 November 2022.

384 *Compensation and Reward Management*

Exhibit 11.6   Meta Cuts 11K Jobs in First Big Lay-off in Co's History

Meta (which runs Facebook, Instagram, and WhatsApp) CEO Mark Zuckerberg said the company will cut more than 11,000 jobs in the first major round of lay-offs in the social media giant's history. Meta is taking steps to pare costs following several quarters of disappointing earnings and a slide in revenue. The reduction equal to about 13% of the workforce. The company will also extend its hiring freeze through first quarter.

Source: The Times of India, 10 November 2022.

Exhibit 11.7   Just a Dozen Staff Left in Twitter India

Meta (which runs Facebook, Instagram and WhatsApp) CEO Mark Zuckerberg said the company will cut more than 11,000 jobs in the first major round of lay-offs in the social media giant's history. Meta is taking steps to pare costs following several quarters of disappointing earnings and a slide in revenue. The reduction equal to about 13% of the workforce. The company will also extend its hiring freeze through first quarter.

Source: The Times of India, 10 November 2022.

Exhibit 11.8   Amazon Plans to Cut 10K Jobs in Co's Biggest Lay-off

Following Facebook and Twitter, Amazon plans to plans to lay off about 10,000 people in corporate and technology jobs starting as soon as this week, people with knowledge of the matter said, in what would be the largest job cuts in the company's history.

The cuts will focus on Amazon's devices organisation, including the voice assistant Alexa, as well as at its retail division and in human resources, said the people, who spoke on condition of anonymity because they were not authorised to speak publicly.

The total number of lay-offs remains fluid. But if it stays around 10,000, that would represent roughly 3% of Amazon's corporate employees and less than 1% of its global work force of more than 1.5 million, which is primarily composed of hourly workers.

Source: The Times of India, 15 November 2022.

---

2. Due to hard times and/or to increase their income, many employees are going for moonlighting in IT sector. As a result of which, many employers have terminated the services of such employees (see Exhibit 11.9)

> **Exhibit 11.9** Wipro Sacks 300 Staffers for Moonlighting on Sly
>
> The IT services industry is waging a war against moonlighting. Wipro chairman Rishad Premji said the company has fired 300 employees in the past few months for working for direct competitors while being on the rolls of Wipro.
>
> Source: *The Times of India*, 22 September 2022.

Most Tech companies like TCS, IBM India, Infosys, California-based Salesforce, etc., are rallying against moonlighting by their staff, though Tech Mahindra and some new age companies like Swiggy and Cred have a more generous view of the phenomenon.[46]

3. These people will also face difficulty during the period of their unemployment. Hence, those people who have been either laid off or terminated or retrenched need some sort of social security like retaining allowance, unemployment allowance, lump sum compensation and so on.

There are some provisions of social security under the Industrial Disputes Act, 1947,[47] which provide for payment of compensation to workers in the event of lay-off or retrenchment. In the case of lay-off, a laid-off worker is entitled to payment at the rate of 50% of total of the basic wage and DA which should not be more than 45 days at a stretch during any period of 12 months. In the case of retrenchment, the worker needs to be given one month's notice or wages in lieu thereof, and also 15 days average pay for every completed year of continued service. However, certain conditions apply in case of both lay-off and retrenchment. By amalgamating three labour laws into the Industrial Labour Code, 2020, the central government has taken some steps to secure the interest of workers in case of job loss or retrenchment of workers.

Other Steps

The other steps undertaken regarding social security include the following:

1. The Seamen's Provident Fund Act, 1966
2. The Assam Tea Plantations Provident Fund Scheme Act, 1955
3. Unemployment Dole Scheme (introduced in Kerala in 1982)
4. Old Age Pension Scheme introduced by many state governments

It is very much in the fitness of things if we follow the example of socialist countries whose avowed goal is to provide complete protection to every citizen from cradle to grave. For translating all these laws and regulations in practice, the major hurdle is that of funds. In our country, at present, the major burden is on the shoulders of the employers. Here, it may be suggested that the governments, both the central and state, should come forward and share a substantial part of the cost of social security benefits. The employees too should contribute according to their capacity to pay. Besides, the present fragmented character of our social security system also needs to be done away with. Moreover, whatever social security acts are operational at present in our country, their implementation also needs improvement as many scrupulous employers, especially in small organisations, play mischief and do not allow the workers to take full advantage of these acts. Finally, the lack of uniformity in the definitions of basic terms used in various social security acts also needs to be overcome.

It is praiseworthy that the present government has initiated the process of classifying all the 44 labour laws into four labour codes of which one will be that of social security. This is being done to bring uniformity of terms and definitions and remove anomalies.

Recent Biggest Labour Reforms[48]

The total number of workers in India, including both in the organised and unorganised sectors, is more than 50 crores. However, the workers in the unorganised sector used to be a neglected lot. It is for the first time that any government has bothered for the workers in both the organised and unorganised sectors and their families, and got the Labour Reforms Bill passed on 23 September 2022 in the Parliament. Hitherto, the entire workforce of the country was entangled in the web of labour legislations. In order to provide the working-class freedom from the aforesaid web, the central government has taken a revolutionary and historical step of codifying 29 labour laws into four codes. It will help workers getting security along with respect, health and other welfare measures which was overdue since long. Through these four labour codes, all workers of the organised and the unorganised sector will get the minimum wages and other benefits, including a large section of workers in the unorganised sector getting social security. Though the Second National Commission of Labour had recommended in 2002 that the then existing multiple labour laws at the central level, should be codified in four or five labour codes, no serious step was taken in this direction from to 2004 to 2014 and the topic of labour reforms had remained untouched even during the economic reforms carried out in 1991. Following detailed discussions at the level of Ministry of Labour and Employment, Government of India, the ministry uploaded all the draft labour codes on its website for stakeholders and public consultation. During 2015 to 2019, the Ministry of Labour and Employment organised nine tripartite discussions, involving central trade unions, employers' associations and representatives of state governments, inviting the opinions and suggestions of the aforesaid stakeholders on labour reforms. In addition, Parliament Standing Committee also examined all the four bills and finally made its recommendations to the central government. Prior to this, in order to give workers the benefit of portability through the Universal Account Number (UAN) so as to make it easier for the employees to access their EPF account and also enable them to withdraw their provident fund securely from anywhere in the country, the UAN mandate was brought into being on 1 October 2014. Besides, the system of 'inspector raj' was also removed and made the inspectors to play the advisory role or act as facilitator for workers. In order to ensure workers' right to minimum wages, the central government amalgamated four labour laws in the wage code, nine laws in the Social Security Code, thirteen laws in the Occupational Safety, Health and Working Conditions Code, 2020, and three laws in the Industrial Relations Code.49 (New Labour Code for New India, Ministry of Information and Broadcasting. Verified from https://labour.gov.in/sites/default/files/labour_code_eng.pdf).

Major Labour Reforms Undertaken Since 2014

- For transparency and accountability, the usage of IT-enabled system for inspection has been made mandatory.

- The ceiling limit of gratuity has been increased from Rs 10 lakhs to Rs 20 lakhs on 29 March 2018.
- On 16 February 2017, Payment of Wages Act enabled payment of wages to employees by cheque or crediting it to their bank account.
- Maternity Benefit Amendment Act, 2017, which came into effect on 1 April 2017, increased the paid maternity leave from 12 weeks to 26 weeks.[49]
- Passing of Labour Reforms Bill in 2020, which will ensure the protection of interest of workers like right to minimum wages, social security, occupational safety, health and good working conditions, etc. Besides, provisions in the Industrial Relations Code in addition to providing several other benefits to workers, will also remove the following:
    - Faster justice to the workers through the tribunal.
    - Workers disputes to be resolved within a year in the tribunal.
    - Industrial tribunals to have two members to facilitate faster disposal of cases.
- In industrial establishments, a trade union having 51% votes shall be recognised as the sole negotiating union which can make agreements with employers.
- In industrial establishments in which no trade union gets 51% votes, a negotiating council of trade unions shall be constituted for making agreements with employer.[50]

Benefits of Codification

Codification will be useful for the workers in the following manner:

- Single registration; single license; single statement; minimum forms
- Common definitions
- Reduction of committees
- Web-based surprise inspection
- Use of technology—electronic registration and licensing
- Reduction of compliance cost and disputes[51]

To conclude, it will be desirable to quote PM Narandra Modi, when regarding labour codes he said,

> We need to come out of the mindset that industry and labour are always in conflict with each other. Why not have a mechanism where both benefit equally? Since labour is a concurrent subject, the law gives flexibility to state governments to modify the codes further as per their unique situation and requirements. The right to strike has not been curtailed at all. In fact, trade unions have been conferred with a new right, enabling them to get statutory recognition. We have made the employer-employee relation more systematic and symmetrical. The provision of notice period gives an opportunity for amicable settlement of any grievance between employees and employers.[52]

He further stated,

> Until there are family sentiments among workers and employers, the feeling of belongingness does not arise. If the employer thinks that he feeds someone and if the Labour thinks his sweat is running in employers' world, then I do not think that the business will work smoothly. However, if family sentiments exist, if the sorrow of a worker

ruins nights of the employer and a worker does not sleep in the night, or some loss for the factory, with the arising of such family sentiments, the journey of development cannot be stopped by anyone.[53]

These reforms initiated through labour codes are pro-worker as now the workers can avail themselves of all benefits and social security even if hired for fixed term. These reforms will not only create huge employment but also protect the interest of workers by ensuring not only minimum wage reforms but also provision for social security for workers in informal sector and minimising government interference. The reforms will ensure priority to occupational safety of the workers and create better working environment.

Recent Labour Reforms and Social Security

Even after 75 years of independence, around 90% of the total workers who work in the unorganised sector do not have access to all the social securities. However, through continuous reforms and by taking care of the interest of workers, the Modi government started the initiative of providing social security to old age workers of unorganised sector. For this, the Pradhan Mantri Shram Yogi Man Dhan Yojana was started, in which provision was made for pension benefit of Rs 3,000 per month after reaching the age of 60.[54]

In order to ensure social security to all 50 crore workers in the country, the central government has amalgamated nine labour laws into the Social Security Code, 2020—thus, securing the right of workers for insurance, pension, gratuity, maternity benefits, etc. A comprehensive legal framework for Social Security has to be created so as to enable the workers to receive social security completely. Hence, a system would be institutionalised for the contributions received from employers and workers, in a phased manner. The main highlights of Social Security Code, 2020, are as follows:

- Through a small contribution, the benefit of free treatment is available under hospitals and dispensaries of ESIC.
- The doors of ESIC will now be opened for the workers of all sectors along with the workers of the unorganised sector.
- Expansion of ESIC hospitals, dispensaries and branches up to district level. This facility to be increased from 566 districts to all the 740 districts of the country.
- Even if a single worker is engaged in hazardous work, he would be given ESIC benefit.
- Opportunity to join ESIC for platform and gig workers engaged in new technology.
- Plantation workers to get benefit of ESIC.
- Institutions working in hazardous area to be compulsorily registered with ESIC.[55]

Expansion of Social Security

With the passing of the labour Reforms Bill by the Parliament in 2020, the availability of social security benefits has now been expanded as follows:

- Benefit of pension scheme (EPFO) to all workers of organised, unorganised and self-employed sectors.
- Creation of social security fund for providing comprehensive social security to the unorganised sector.

- Requirement of minimum service has been removed for payment of gratuity in case of fixed term employees.
- Employees engaged on fixed term to get same social security benefit as permanent employees.
- Creating a national database of workers of the unorganised sector through registration on Portal.
- Employers employing more than 20 workers to mandatorily report vacancies online.
- A Universal Account Number (UAN) for ESIC, EPFO and unorganised sector workers.
- Aadhaar-based Universal Account Number (UAN) to ensure seamless portability.[56]

Thus, the Social Security Code, 2020, focuses on the universalisation of social security as now the Employees' State Insurance Corporation will extend to all the workers medical care, sickness benefits, injury benefits, unemployment benefits, disablement and survivors' benefits and funeral expenses. Hitherto, the above benefits were available only to organised workers in 566 districts and was mandatory if more than 10 workers were working in an organisation. As such only 3.5 crore employees and 13.5 crore members were covered under it. But per Social Security Code, 2020, the benefits of the social security will be extended to entire country—740 districts. The scheme will be applicable to unorganised workers also including gig workers. There will be voluntary coverage by agreement of employees and employers even if the number of employees in an organisation is less than 10 workers. There will be no minimum limit of number of workers for hazardous or life-threatening occupations. Besides, the scheme is optional in plantations.[57] Besides, the provision of Employees Provident Funds Scheme, Employees' Pension Scheme and Employees' Deposit Linked Insurance Scheme, which are monitored by the Employees Provident Fund Organisation and are hitherto applicable to government employees and organised workers in scheduled industries and are mandatory if more than 20 workers are employed in an organised and voluntary if less than 20 workers are employed, will now, after the implementation of Social Security Code, 2020, be applicable to all industries, and voluntary for an organisation if employing less than 20 workers, and will also be applicable for all self-employed workers and any other class of workers including unorganised workers.[58]

These reforms provided under the Social Security Code, 2020, will be applicable to all workers even if hired for fixed term. Besides, certain provisions in Labour Codes other then

Social Security Code, 2020, will also be supportive in providing some social security to workers directly or indirectly. For example, under the Industrial Relations (IR) Code, 2020, the following provisions will provide some help to the workers at the time of their unemployment:

- In case of job loss, a worker will get benefit under the Atal Biit Vyakti Kalyan Yojna.
- Under the Atal Bimit Vyakti Kalyan Yojna, a worker of organised sector who loses his job gets financial aid from the government. This is a type of unemployment allowance, the benefit of which is admissible to the workers covered under the ESI Scheme.
- At the time of retrenchment, a worker would be provided 15 days' wages for re-skilling. The wages would be credited directly into the bank account of the worker so as to enable him to learn new skills.[59]

Management Strategy

While formulating its strategy with regard to fringe benefits, especially social security, the management should keep in view that wages are just one part of the total compensation—which the workers are entitled to for their contribution in the process of production. In order to enable the workers to lead a reasonably good life, they should also be extended social security and other fringe benefits. As far as the mandatory social security is concerned, the employers are legally bound to provide the same to their workers, and therefore, the management strategy should ensure that the social security measure, as provided under various social security acts, must be provided in both letter and spirit. In addition to that, the management strategy should provide for voluntary social security, in consultation with worker's representatives. The strategy should also ensure that all labour reforms, as envisaged under four labour codes, should be implemented in the right spirit.

Chapter Review

1. Although employee benefits and services constitute a significant part of total compensation, but no research study has yet been able to provide a conclusive proof about their impact either on organisation's performance or their ability to attract and retain employees or their effectiveness to motivate employees. Still, people have a favourable opinion about employee benefits, and therefore, fringe benefits in one form or the other have been in vogue since long because fringe benefits are a great source of contentment to workers as these benefits supplement their income, make their lives comfortable and improve their status as also their standard of living. Since a contented worker is an asset to an organisation, he is instrumental in the overall progress of the organisation concerned. That is why today greater attention is being paid to fringe benefits by a good number of organisations.

2. The concept of fringe benefit is of recent origin. The benefits provided to the workforce of an organisation apart from the negotiated wages are nowadays termed as either fringe benefits or non-wage benefits. These benefits are of great significance to workers as they reduce the gap between their nominal wages and real wages. Only those benefits which are computable in terms of money, are not part of any contract indicating when the sum is payable, and of which the amount is not predetermined fall under the category of fringe benefits. The main objectives of fringe benefits are to bridge the gap between money wages and real wages, attract and retain employees, seek commitment of employees and so on. Besides, benefits are of great importance not only to employees but also to employers and society.

3. Intangible benefits are as important as tangible benefits and at times even more important than tangible benefits. The Second World War, approach of trade unions, statutory requirements, cost-effectiveness of benefits, paternalistic

considerations and securing an edge over competitors have been the main factors responsible to realise the need of and promote the worth of employee benefits.
4. While framing benefit policies, range of benefits, size of benefits, percentage of each benefit to the total compensation, options available, harmonisation and so on should be clearly spelled out. In practice, benefits made available to the employees differ from organisation to organisation and from industry to industry. Planning and designing of benefits depend a great deal on the objectives of benefits envisioned by the management and the benefits package offered by the competitors. Options for choosing benefits package in a cafeteria style, formulation of appropriate benefits programme, coverage of employees' financial considerations, compliance of statuary obligations and so on are some of the other issues to be taken care of under planning, designing and administration of benefits. There are three current approaches in the field of benefits—innovative approach, flexibility and harmonisation. Age, sex, marital status, size of the family and so on are some of the main factors influencing choice of benefits package.
5. It is desirable to review benefits package from time to time and modify the same as and when required. However, communicating appropriately the benefits programme to the employees concerned is an important issue and demands adequate attention.
6. Payments included under fringe benefits can be categorised into (a) social security, (b) labour welfare benefits and (c) bonus. Social security, which is one of the major constituents of fringe benefits, is the security that society furnishes to a worker (or his dependents in case of his death) to sustain himself and his family in case he falls victim to any contingency of life. There is a greater need of social security for Indian industrial workers as they are poor, physically weak and highly exposed to contingencies of life. Social insurance and social assistance are the main forms of social security in our country. In Indian industries, social security is being provided mainly because of legal obligations. Employees' Compensation Act, 1923; ESI Act, 1948; Maternity Benefit Act, 1961; Employees' Provident Funds and Miscellaneous Provisions Act, 1952; Payment of Gratuity Act, 1972; and so on have been playing an important role in this direction. In other words, it is only the statutory provisions with regard to social security that have been playing an important role in the direction of making social security available to Indian workers. Very little has been done voluntarily either by employers or other agencies.
7. The initiation of the four labour reforms, which after amalgamation 29 central labour laws have given rise to four labour codes, will be extremely useful to the workers in both the organised and unorganised sectors across the country as they will ensure them right to minimum wages, social security, occupational safety, health, good working conditions, etc.

Key Terms

benefits package
commercial insurance
cost-effectiveness
contribution period
dependent's benefit
Directive Principles of State Policy
disablement benefit
employee benefit
Employees' Compensation Act, 1923
Employees' Deposit Linked Insurance Scheme
Employees' Pension Scheme
Employees' Provident Funds and Miscellaneous Provisions Act, 1923
Employees' State Insurance Act, 1948
fringe benefits
gratuity
Industrial Disputes Act, 1947
lay-off
maternity benefit
Maternity Benefit Act, 1961
medical benefit
Payment of Gratuity Act, 1972
permanent partial disablement
permanent total disablement
rehabilitation
retrenchment
retrenchment compensation
sickness benefit
social assistance
social insurance
social security
temporary disablement
total compensation

Discussion Questions

1. Discuss the objectives of social security and how social security is beneficial to employees.
2. Discuss the difference between social insurance and social assistance. Also, discuss whether commercial insurance should be included under the scope of social security or not.
3. Discuss the main provisions of social security under social security legislation in our country and what should be done to make them more meaningful.
4. Discuss the biggest labour reforms contained in the Labour Reforms Bill, 2020
5. Discuss the details of Social Security Code, 2019

Individual and Group Activities

1. Individually or in a group of two members, visit a big organisation and find out from the women employees if the Maternity Benefit Act, 1961, is being implemented both in letter and spirit in their organisation and whether they are satisfied with the benefits available under the act. Prepare a detailed report.
2. In a group of three members, visit a large manufacturing organisation and find out from trade union leaders if the ESI Act, 1948, is being sincerely implemented in their organisation. Take a note of their reaction towards the act and prepare a brief report.
3. Individually visit a small organisation to which the Employees' Compensation Act, 1923, is applicable. Discuss with the workers there if compensation for employment injury is paid to the injured workers per provisions of the act. Also, find out their observations on the act.

4. In a group of two members, visit some big manufacturing organisation and find out the reaction of trade union officials regarding labour reforms initiated by central government.
5. Individually discuss with the HR officials of some big organisation whether they visualise any difficulty in the implementation of labour codes in their organisation.

Application Case 11.1

John has been working as a welder in ABC Enterprise Ltd manufacturing special nuts and bolts for a reputed company. Initially John was appointed as an apprentice but by virtue of his hard work and quality work during the five years, he used to get appreciations from all concerned and rose to his present position. One day during the lunch hour, he went to the canteen of his organisation and took lunch along with his three colleagues. After having lunch, all the four enjoyed themselves for some time under the shadow of a big tree just in front of the canteen. While three of his colleagues dispersed from there, John went to the rest shelter of his organisation. As he felt sleepy, he saw a ceiling fan and slept on the bench which was placed just below the ceiling fan. Hardly five minutes had passed that the ceiling fan fell on John resulting in the fracture of his right-hand shoulder.

He was taken to the dispensary of the organisation. The medical officer took the X-ray and found that the injury was very serious and therefore, John was referred to a super specialist orthopaedician. After examining the X-ray report, he conducted operation of the shoulder of John. However, after about a fortnight, John found out that his right hand had no sensation, and hence, he felt that he won't be able to work with the right hand anymore in future. John contacted his supervisor and approached the HR department of his organisation for claiming compensation, but the HR department refused to entertain his claim on the ground that John was not working at the time of accident. John approached the officials of the union of workers. One of the senior officials of the union took John along with him to HR department and pleaded that though John was not working at the time of accident, but it was his official lunch period and was relaxing in the official rest shelter. However, the HR department did not agree with the contention of the union official.

Questions

1. Is the HR department justified in refusing the compensation claim of John?
2. Is John justified in claiming the compensation? If yes, why?
3. What future course of action should be adopted by John?

Notes

1 R. C. Sharma, 'A Critical Study of Non-Wage Benefits in Sugar Factories of Haryana and Punjab' (unpublished PhD thesis, Kurukshetra University, 1973).
2 See Milkovich, Newman, and Venkata Ratnam, *Compensation*, 355.

3 The Mckinsey Quarterly Chart Focus Newsletter, June 2006, member edition.
4 For an exhaustive study, see R. C. Sharma, 'The Concept of Fringe Benefits in Indian Industry', *Indian Journal of Industrial Relations* 13, no. 2 (October 1977): 243–52; and R. C. Sharma, 'The Concept and Philosophy of Fringe Benefits', *Integrated Management* XIII, no. 3 (March 1978): 22–28.
5 The term 'fringe benefits' has been traced to a gifted regional chairman of the National War Labor Board in the United States. James C. Hill, 'Stabilization of Fringe Benefits', *Industrial and Labour Relations Review* 7, no. 2 (January 1954): 221–34.
6 D. J. Robertson, *The Economics of Wages* (London: Macmillan, 1961); W. J. Bowen, *The Wage Price Issue* (New Jersey, NJ: Princeton University Press, 1960); D. J. Robertson, *Fringe Benefits, Labour Costs and Social Security* (London: George Allen and Union, 1965).
7 See Sharma, *Industrial Relations and Labour Legislation*, 405.
8 R. Cockmar, 'Employee Benefits for Managers and Executives', in *Management of Salary and Wage*, ed. A. M. Pavery (Sussex: Grover Press, 1975), 73.
9 D. Belcher, 'Fringe Benefits: Do We Know Enough about Them?' in *Wage and Salary Administration*, ed. A. Langsner and H. G. Zollitsch (Cincinnati, OH: South-Western Publishing Company, 1961), 488.
10 Quoted in P. S. Rao, *Essentials of Human Resources Management and Industrial Relations* (Mumbai: Himalaya Publishing House, 2000), 423.
11 'Herzberg's Two Factor Theory', in *Human Resource Management*, J. M. Ivancevich (New Delhi: McGraw-Hill, 2008), 243–52.
12 See Paul Pigors and C. A. Myers, *Personnel Administration* (Tokyo: McGraw-Hill Kogakusha, 1977), 547.
13 Ibid., 416.
14 Milkovich, Newman, and Venkata Ratnam, *Compensation*, 368–69.
15 Ibid.
16 Armstrong and Murlis, *Reward Management*, 443.
17 For details, see Ibid., 445.
18 Milkovich, Newman, and Venkata Ratnam, *Compensation*, 369.
19 R. H. Hodge, 'Pinning Down in Problematic Fringe', *The Personnel Function, A Progressive Report*: 113–15.
20 See Sharma, *Industrial Relations and Labour Legislation*, 417.
21 Substituted for 'Workmen's' by the Workmen's Compensation (Amendment) Act, 2009, and made effective from 18 January 2010.
22 For more details, see Sharma, *Industrial Relations and Labour Legislation*, 825–36.
23 Ministry of Labour & Employment, Government of India, *Pocket Book of Labour Statistics* (Shimla/Chandigarh: Labour Bureau, 2013).
24 Ibid.
25 For more details, see Sharma, *Industrial Relations and Labour Legislation*, 836–57.
26 Labour Bureau, Ministry of Labour and Employment, Government of India, *Pocket Book of Labour Statistics* (2013).
27 *The Economic Times*, 23 March 2018.
28 *The Economic Times*, 16 November 2018.
29 Ibid.
30 Ibid.
31 For details, see Sharma, *Industrial Relations and Labour Legislation*, 836–57.
32 Ministry of Labour & Employment, *Pocket Book of Labour Statistics*.
33 Ibid.
34 Ibid.
35 Ibid.
36 For details, see Sharma, *Industrial Relations and Labour Legislation*, 857–67.
37 For more details, see the Employees' Pension Scheme, 1995 in The Employees' Provident Fund and Miscellaneous Provisions Act, 1952, Lexi Nexis, Gurgaon (2022–2023), 203–52.
38 Ibid.
39 Ibid., 185–202.
40 *The Economic Times*, 13 June 2018.
41 For details, see Sharma, *Industrial Relations and Labour Legislation*, 877–86.

42 Ministry of Labour & Employment, *Pocket Book of Labour Statistics*.
43 Ibid.
44 *The Economics Times*, 23 March 2018.
45 *Hindustan Times*, 2 January 2018.
46 For details, see *The Times of India*, 22 September 2022.
47 For details, see Sharma, *Industrial Relations and Labour Legislation*, 767–85.
48 For details, see New Labour Code for New India, *Ministry of Information and Broadcasting*, 1–36.
49 Ibid., 8.
50 Ibid., 6.
51 Ibid., 20.
52 Ibid., 22.
53 Ibid., 21.
54 Ibid., 5.
55 Ibid., 13.
56 Ibid., 14.
57 Ibid., 28.
58 Ibid.
59 Ibid., 19–20.

12 Fringe Benefits and Services, and Internal Audit of Compensation and Benefits (II)

Learning Objectives

> After studying this chapter, the reader should be able to do the following:
>
> 1. Examine critically the various definitions of labour welfare as also its objectives and significance.
> 2. List and describe the principles of labour welfare.
> 3. Classify labour welfare work under different heads.
> 4. List and describe the statutory labour welfare work undertaken in our country.
> 5. List and describe the labour welfare work undertaken by employers and trade unions in Indian industries.
> 6. Explain the recent trends/development in the field of fringe benefits and services.
> 7. Explain the meaning of internal audit of compensation and benefits and also of related issues.
> 8. Understand and explain welfare measures initiated through the 'Labour Reforms Bill -2020'.
> 9. Understand and explain the labour welfare provisions contained in the Labour Codes.
>
> Explain the details of Payment of Bonus Act, 1965.

Introduction

Labour welfare is the second important ingredient of fringe benefits, social security being the first and bonus the third. It's just not enough to take care of social security of the workers because social security takes care of only contingent situations whereas labour welfare is concerned with physical, mental and economic betterment of the workers on regular basis, according to the requirement of workers. It many, therefore, differ from one set of workers to that of the another set of workers. Since labour welfare activities lead not only to the betterment of workers but also of the employers (as it is assumed that labour activities add to the contentment of workers and enhance their productivity), more and more organisations have started paying their due attention in this regard.

DOI: 10.4324/9781032628424-16

Fringe Benefits and Current Practices (II)

As stated earlier, after social security which is the first important constituent of the fringe benefits, there comes the labour welfare activities which are the second main constituent of fringe benefits.

Labour Welfare

The maintenance function of HRM aims at preserving and improving physical, mental and economic conditions of the employees as it helps all the stakeholders of an organisation. It is here that labour welfare comes into vogue. It is again, perhaps, for this reason that ever-increasing attention is being paid towards labour welfare activities in almost all the organisations, though in different degrees.

Meaning and Definition

Since labour welfare has been defined in several ways, it has been understood in various ways in different countries. The Royal Commission on Labour has also remarked, 'The term "welfare" as applied to the industrial workers is one which must necessarily be elastic, bearing a somewhat different interpretations in one country from another, according to the different social customs, the degree of industrialization and the educational development of the workers'.[1] Anyway, the *Oxford Dictionary* defines labour welfare as 'efforts to make life worth living for workmen'. According to the Labour Investigation Committee, welfare is

1. anything done for intellectual, physical, moral and economic betterment of the workers whether by employers, by government or by agencies over and above which is laid down by law or what is normally expected on the past of contractual benefits for which the workers may have bargained.[2]

    According to R. R. Hopking, 'welfare is fundamentally an attitude of mind on the part of management influencing the method by which welfare activities are undertaken'. The ILO has defined labour welfare as follows:
2. workers' welfare should be understood as meaning such services, facilities and amenities which may be established in, or in the vicinity of, undertakings to enable the persons employed in them to perform their work in healthy, congenial surroundings and to provide them with amenities conducive to good health and high morale.[3]

As a matter of fact, the term 'labour welfare' connotes anything that makes the conditions in the factory conducive to happiness, health and prosperity of workers. The labour welfare operates to neutralize the harmful effects of large-scale industrialisation and urbanisation. Provision of welfare amenities enables the workers to live a richer and more satisfactory life and contributes to their efficiency and productivity.

Objectives of Labour Welfare Work

The main objectives of welfare activities include the following:

1. To provide for economic betterment of the workers
2. To improve their health

3. To promote their intellectual betterment
4. To infuse confidence and boost morale of workers
5. To promote goodwill of the organisation
6. To attract and retain good employees
7. To increase productivity
8. To maintain good human and industrial relations
9. To treat workers as human beings first and workers thereafter
10. To combat trade unionism
11. To restrict government intervention
12. To earn loyalty of workers
13. To reduce rate of absenteeism and labour turnover

Increased Focus on Employee Well-Being

Of late, organisations have started taking more interest in their employees' health and well-being (see Exhibits 12.1 and 12.2). All-around steps are being taken including family outreach, but an overarching health and wellness strategy is largely missing. A study found that in 2018, over 80% of the organisations have taken at least one action in the following areas health risks, or condition management; weight management, physical activity and nutrition; and mental health. While 61% have taken at least one action to improve the financial well-being of employees in 2018, it is a matter of concern that almost half of the surveyed organisations still do not have a formally articulated health and well-being strategy.[4]

Exhibit 12.1 Companies Are Increasing Focus on Employee Well-being Study

Companies in India are beginning to take a more holistic view of employee health and wellness, going beyond physical well-being to include emotional and financial, according to the India Health and Well Being Study 2018 released by Willis Towers Watson, a leading global advisory, broking and solutions company.

Source: The Economic Times, 27 November 2018.

Exhibit 12.2 Companies Are Increasing Focus on Employee

Well-Being

More companies need to acknowledge that the day-to-day well-being of employees and their overall workplace experience is a clear management of priority if they want to focus on the long-term productivity of individuals and the company at large. Our workspaces, which are in our control, are designed to develop these building blocks in a healthy way and for long term. The organisations need to pay attention to sleep patterns, physical exercise, stress levels and diet.

Source: The Times of India, 23 November 2022.

It is immensely encouraging to observe this increased focus on employee health and wellness. However, to translate this into all-round well-being enhanced productivity and ultimately improved financial performance, companies must develop a coherent and holistic health and wellness strategy encompassing all four aspects—physical, emotional, financial and family.

According to Gardner study, enterprises focused on work and office-centric processes damage productivity and well-being of employees. What is needed in the future of work is to have an employee-centric approach.

A toxic management, even in hybrid mode, can cause severe stress, which can reduce performance by as much as 33%, and employees are 54% likely to leave the current employment. The aim must be to reverse these undesired side effects and drive sustainable progress, a growth mindset and loyalty. For this, build a culture of employee-centricity that provides open communication and feedback mechanism, imbibes trust, assures psychological safety and inspires creativity and innovation.[5]

It is always good for the organisation to start with employee well-being by having considerations for physical, emotional, mental and financial well-being for the employees. Considering employees just as customers redesign jobs, processes and workplaces on employee needs and requirements. Also provide space and opportunities for growth of employee besides ensuring psychological safety revamping feedback systems. Equally important is revamping compensation and rewards programmes.[6]

While a majority, 66%, of employers have already taken or will take steps in the next three years to develop a mental health strategy, 59% are planning to offer programmes to support chronic behavioural health conditions; currently offered by only 8% of employers. Similarly, 63% already have or are developing a strategy to improve financial well-being and 13% are considering it in three years' time. Towards this, 50% of companies are planning to deliver customised or personalised messages to help improve financial planning as compared to only 6% today.[7]

The number of employers recognising the role of family in the overall well-being of an employee and in turn their productivity is noteworthy. It is heartening to see that almost one in four organisations is beginning to engage the employees' family in one way or another. Some of them are inviting family members to participate in various programmes and activities (27%) organised by the companies, focusing communication to reach/involve family members (24%) and redesigning employee assistance programmes to better address emotional and financial well-being for employees and their dependents (44%).[8]

Significance of Labour Welfare in Indian Industries

An industrial worker in India is, by and large, a poor person and needs help for his economic, physical and intellectual betterment. Similarly, industrial units in India need higher rate of productivity, quality workers, stability of manpower, industrial peace and so on. Labour welfare activities undertaken by an organisation voluntarily, or even statutorily, are instrumental in the accomplishment of above aims and objectives.

Principles of Labour Welfare

Some of the main principles of labour welfare that should be kept in mind in the implementation of a labour welfare programme are as follows:

1. **Principle of self-help:** Labour welfare must aim at helping employees to help themselves in future.

2. **Principle of efficiency:** A welfare programme should also aim at increasing the efficiency of workers.
3. **Principle of democratic values:** Workers should be associated in the formulation, organisation and implementation of a welfare programme.
4. **Principle of meeting the real needs of the worker:** A welfare programme should aim at fulfilling the real needs of workers.
5. **Principle of social responsibility:** Industry, being a sub-system of the society as it draws its manpower from the society, has an obligation towards its employees to look after their welfare.
6. **Principle of evaluation:** A welfare programme must be evaluated periodically.
7. **Principle of re-personalisation:** Welfare should aim at the overall development of the employees.
8. **Principle of confirming the benefit in which the group is more efficient than the individual:** A welfare programme should aim at benefiting the group instead of an individual.
9. **Principle of flexibility:** The benefit should be flexible enough to incorporate any desirable change at any stage.
10. **Principle of financial adequacy:** A welfare programme should be calculable and adequate financial provisions should be made for it.
11. **Principle of publicising:** A welfare programme should be well publicised and communicated to all concerned.
12. **Principle of maintaining ego:** The employer should not assume a benevolent posture to indicate that it is due to generosity of the employer that a benefit has been given to workers.
13. **Principle of cafeteria approach:** A variety of packages suiting to different age groups, genders, family size, marital status and so on should be worked out and a worker should have an option of choosing any of these packages according to his preference or requirements.

Classification of Labour Welfare Work

Although there is no watertight classification of labour welfare work, yet for the sake of convenience, we may classify it into the following categories:

1. **Statutory welfare:** It refers to the welfare activities undertaken because of legislative compulsion. For example, it is mandatory, under the provisions of the Factories Act, 1948, for an employer to provide specified health (Sections 21–40) and welfare (Sections 42–50) facilities in a factory. Violation or non-adherence to these provisions may attract severe penalties under the relevant act.
2. **Voluntary welfare:** According to many authors, the real welfare work is that which is undertaken by an employer at his own sweet will and not under any legal pressure. That is why many employers undertake welfare activities such as medical, recreation, transport, library, games and sports, education, housing, uniforms and picnics.
3. **Mutual welfare:** As stated earlier also, trade unions or workers should also share a part of responsibility of undertaking welfare activities. Hence, we come across some welfare facilities like newspapers/reading rooms, some games such as volleyball and kabaddi, part-time homeopath doctor and so on being extended by some trade unions to their members.

According to another classification suggested by Broughtan, labour welfare activities can be grouped under two heads: (a) intramuralactivities, which are undertaken within the premises of the factory, such as health, welfare and safety measures, healthy working conditions and canteen, and (b) extramural activities, which are undertaken outside the factory, such as housing and medical facilities.

Labour Welfare Activities in Indian Industries

At the initial stages of industrial revolution in our country, there were hardly any welfare activities undertaken by any agency except a little bit undertaken by outside agencies and that too were provided on humanitarian considerations. It was the First World War (1914–1918) and progress made by the industrial revolution that prompted both the government and the employers to come forward in this direction. The government had to take initiative because public (workers are also a part of public) welfare is one of the major responsibilities of the government. The employers started coming forward because they also started realising that welfare activities are not only in the interest of workers but also benefit the employers because welfare activities are instrumental in improving health of the workers and make them feel satisfied which, in turn, help in improving the efficiency and productivity of labour. Welfare activities also help in reducing rate of absenteeism and labour turnover, infusing confidence, and boosting morale of the workers, and improving human and industrial relations. All these things together help in improving the health of the organisation—sometimes directly and sometimes indirectly. Hence, welfare activities should be well planned and properly undertaken. The trade unions have also initiated welfare work, though at a very modest scale because their capacity to spend on welfare work is highly limited.

The welfare activities undertaken in our country can be studied under the following heads:

1. **Welfare activities undertaken by the central government:** The government owes a great responsibility for looking after labour welfare as the workers constitute a significant part of people in general.
    a. **Directive Principles of State Policy:** The chapter on Directive Principles of State Policy (Articles 38–47) in our Constitution spells out the need for labour welfare as follows:

Article 38: State to secure a social order for the promotion of welfare of the people:

i. The State shall strive to develop a social system which will secure social, economic and political justice to all spheres of life.
ii. The State shall strive to minimize the inequalities in income, and endeavour to eliminate inequalities in status, facilities and opportunities, not only amongst individuals but also amongst groups of people residing in different areas or engaged in different vocations.

Article 39: Certain principles of policy to be followed by the State:

i. That the citizens, men and women equally, have the right to an adequate means of livelihood;

ii. That the ownership and control of the material resources of the community are so distributed as best to subserve the common good;
iii. That the operation of the economic system does not result in the concentration of wealth and means of production to the common detriment
iv. That there is equal pay for equal work for both men and women;
v. That the health and strength of workers, men and women and the tender age of children are not abused and that citizens are not forced by economic necessity to enter avocations unsuited to their age or strength;
vi. That children are given opportunities and facilities to develop in a healthy manner and in conditions of freedom and dignity and that childhood and youth are protected against exploitation and against moral and material abandonment.

Article 39A: Equal justice and free legal aid—The State shall secure that the operation of the legal system promotes justice, on a basis of equal opportunity, and shall provide free legal aid, by suitable legislation or schemes or in any other way, to ensure that opportunities for securing justice are not denied to any citizen by reason of economic or other disabilities.

Article 40: Organisation of village panchayats—The State shall take steps to organize village panchayats and endow them with such powers and authority as may be necessary to enable them to function as units of self-government.

Article 41: Right to work, to education and to public assistance in certain cases—The State shall, within the limits of its economic capacity and development, make effective provision for securing the right to work, to education and to public assistance in cases of unemployment, old age, sickness and disablement, and in other cases of undeserved want.

Article 42: Provision for just and humane conditions of work and maternity relief—The State shall make provision for securing just and humane conditions of work and for maternity relief.

Article 43: Living wage, etc., for workers—The State shall endeavour to secure, by suitable legislation or economic organization or in any other way, all workers, agricultural, industrial or otherwise, work, a living wage, conditions of work, ensuring a decent standard of life and full enjoyment of leisure and social and cultural opportunities, and in particular, the State shall endeavour to promote cottage industries on an individual or co-operative basis in rural areas.

Article 43A: Participation of workers in management of industries—The State shall take steps, by suitable legislation or in any other way, to secure the participation of workers in the management of undertakings, establishments or other organisations engaged in any industry.

Article 44: Uniform civil code for the citizens—The State shall endeavour to secure for the citizens a uniform civil code throughout the territory of India.

Article 45: Provision for free compulsory education for children—The State shall endeavour to provide, within a period of ten years from the commencement of this constitution, for free and compulsory education for all children until they complete the age of fourteen years.

Article 46: Promotion of educational and economic interest of Scheduled Castes, Scheduled Tribes and other weaker sections—The State shall promote with special care the educational and economic interests of the weaker sections of the people, and, in particular, of the Scheduled Castes and the Scheduled Tribes, and shall protect them from social injustice and all forms of exploitation.

Article 47: Duty of the State to raise the level of nutrition and the standard of living and to improve public health—The State shall regard the raising of the level of nutrition and the standard of living of its people and the improvement of public health as among its primary duties, and in particular, the State shall endeavour to bring about prohibition of the consumption except for medical purposes of intoxicating drinks and of drugs which are injurious to health.

Article 48: Organisation of agriculture and animal husbandry—The State shall endeavour to organize agriculture and animal husbandry on modern and scientific lines and shall take steps for preserving and improving the breeds, and prohibiting the slaughter of cows and calves and other milch and draught cattle.

Article 48A: Protection and improvement of environment and safeguarding of forests and wildlife—The State shall endeavour to protect and improve the environment and to safeguard the forests and wildlife of the country.

Article 49: Protection of monuments and places and objects of national importance—It shall be the obligation of the State to protect every monument or place or object of artistic or historic interest, declared by or under law made by Parliament to be of national importance, from spoliation, disfigurement, destruction, removal, disposal or export, as the case may be.

Article 50: Separation of judiciary from executive—The State shall take steps to separate the judiciary from the executive in the public services of the State.

Thus, India being a welfare State, it is obligatory on the part of the Central government to promote welfare of industrial workers also. Hence, the Government of India has passed several Acts to ensure welfare of the workers. Some of the main Acts are as follows.

b. **Factories Act, 1948:** Workers' well-being/welfare is closely related to their health, safety, and welfare. Factories Act, 1948, has taken a good amount of care in this regard. The relevant provisions regarding these aspects mentioned in the Factories Act, 1948, are as follows:

   i. **Health provisions**: The provisions pertaining to health are as follows:

   - *Cleanliness—Section 11(1)*: Every factory shall be kept clean and free from any drain, privy or other nuisance.

     Disposal of wastes and effluent—Section 12(I): Effective arrangement shall be made in every factory for the treatment of wastes and effluents due to manufacturing process carried on there to render them innocuous and for their disposal.
   - **Ventilation and temperature—Sections 13(I), 13(I)(a), 13(I)(b)**: Effective and suitable provisions shall be made in every factory for securing and maintaining in every room adequate ventilation by the circulation of fresh air, and such a temperature as will secure to workers therein reasonable conditions of comfort and prevent injury to health, etc.
   - **Dust and fume—Section 14(I)**: In every factory in which, by reason of the manufacturing process carried on, there is given off any dust or fume or other impurity of such a nature and to such an extent as is likely to be injurious or offensive to the workers employed therein, or any dust in substantial quantities, effective measures shall be taken to prevent its inhalation and accumulation in any workroom, and if any exhaust appliance is necessary

for this purpose, it shall be applied as near as possible to the point of origin of the dust, fume or other impurity, and such point shall be enclosed so far as possible.

- **Artificial humidification—Section 15(I):** In respect of all factories in which the humidity of the air is artificially increased; the State Government may make rules: (a) prescribing standards of humidification and (b) regulating the methods used for artificially increasing the humidity of the air.
- **Overcrowding—Section 16(I), 16(2):** No room in any factory shall be overcrowded.

  to any extent injurious to the health of the workers employed therein. Without prejudice to the generality of sub-section(I), there shall be in every workroom of a factory in existence on the date of the commencement of this Act at least 9.9 m^3 and of a factory built after the commencement of this Act at least 14.2 m^3 of space for every worker employed therein.
- **Lighting—Section 17(I):** In every part of the factory where workers are working or passing there shall be provided and maintained sufficient and suitable lighting, natural or artificial, or both.
- **Drinking water—Section 18(I), 18(2):** In every factory, effective arrangements shall be made to provide and maintain, at suitable points conveniently situated for all workers employed therein, a sufficient supply of wholesome drinking water. All such points shall be legibly marked 'drinking water' in a language understood by most of the workers employed in the factory, and no such point shall be situated within 6 m of any washing place, urinal, latrine, spittoon, open drain carrying sullage or effluent or any other source of contamination unless a shorter distance is approved in writing by the Chief Inspector. In every factory wherein more than 250 workers are ordinarily employed provisions shall be made for cold drinking water during hot weather by effective means and for distribution thereof.
- **Latrine and urinals—Sections 19(Ia), 19(I), 19(2), 19(3):** In every factory, sufficient latrine and urinal accommodation of prescribed types shall always be provided conveniently situated and accessible to workers at all times, while they are at the factory. Separate enclosed accommodation shall be provided for male and female workers. In every factory wherein more than 250 workers are ordinarily employed, all latrine and urinal accommodations shall be of prescribed sanitary types. The State Government may prescribe the number of latrines and urinals to be provided in any factory in proportion to the numbers of male and female workers ordinarily employed therein.
- **Spittoons—Section 20(I), 20(2):** In every factory, there shall be provided a sufficient number of spittoons in convenient places and they shall be maintained in a clean and hygienic condition. The State Government may make rules prescribing the type and the number of spittoons to be provided and their location in any factory and provide for such further matters relating to their maintenance in a clean and hygienic condition.

ii. **Safety Provisions:** Safety at the workplace is very important for the welfare of the workers. It is good that the following provisions have been made in Chapter IV (Sections 21–41) for the safety of workers in the Factories Act, 1948.[9]

Internal Audit of Compensation and Benefits (II) 405

iii. **Welfare Provisions**: The relevant welfare provisions in the Factories Act, 1948, contained in Chapter V (Sections 42 to 50), are as follows.

- *Washing facilities—Section 42*: In every factory, adequate and suitable facilities
    for washing shall be provided and maintained for the use of the workers therein.
- *Facilities for storing and drying clothing—Section 43*: The State Government may, in
    respect of any factory or class or description of factories, make rules requiring the provision therein of suitable places for keeping clothing not worn during working hours and for the drying of wet clothing.
- *Facilities for sitting—Section 44(I):* In every factory, suitable arrangements for sitting
    shall be provided and maintained for all workers obliged to work in a standing position, in order that they may take advantage of any opportunities for rest which may occur in the course of their work.
- *First-aid appliances—Section 45*: There shall, in every factory, be provided and maintained so as to be readily accessible during all working hours, first-aid boxes or cupboards equipped with the prescribed contents, and the number of such boxes or cupboards to be provided and maintained shall not be less than one for eveyone hundred and fifty workers ordinarily employed at any one time in the factory.
- *Canteens—Section 46:* The State Government may make rules requiring that in any specified factory wherein more than 250 workers are ordinarily employed, a canteen or canteens shall be provided and maintained by the occupier for the use of the workers.
- *Shelters, rest rooms and punch rooms—Section 47*: In every factory, wherein more than 150 workers are ordinarily employed, adequate and suitable shelters or rest rooms and a suitable lunchroom, with provision for drinking water, where workers can eat meals brought by them, shall be provided, and maintained for the use of the workers.
- *Crèches—Section 48*: In every factory, wherein more than thirty women workers are ordinarily employed, there shall be provided and maintained a suitable room or rooms for the use of children under the age of six years of such women.
- *Welfare officer—Section 49(I):* In every factory, wherein more than five hundred
    workers are ordinarily employed; the occupier shall employ in the factory such number of welfare officers as may be prescribed. (Refer Annexure 7.1)
- *Power to make rules—Section 50*: The State Government may make rules to supplement this Chapter.

In addition, Section 67 of the Factories Act, 1948, deals with the employment of young persons and states that no child who has not completed his 14th year shall be required to work in any factory. Section 68 deals with the employment of children and adolescents and Sections 69 and 70 deal with the certificate of fitness granted to adolescents. There are some other sections also under the Factories Act, 1948, which are related to the safety of workers.

Besides the aforementioned, the following officials/agencies have also been contributing towards labour welfare in one way or the other:

- Chief Inspector of Factories
- Directorate General, Factory Advice Service and Labour Institute (DGFASLI)
- National Safety Council
- Director General of Mines Safety
- National Commission on Labour

Not only that, but the Government of India has sanctioned grants-in-aid for implementing water supply scheme to mine managements in Maharashtra and Goa. Although most of the activities are administered directly by the welfare organisations under the Ministry of Labour and Employment, yet loans and subsidies are also provided to the state government and local authorities and to the employers for implementation of approved prototype schemes.

iv. **Welfare work under statutory funds**:[10] In order to supplement the efforts of the employers and the state governments in providing welfare amenities to the workers, the Ministry of Labour and Employment administers the following welfare funds for beedi, cine and certain categories of non–coal mine workers, which are financed out of the proceeds of cess levied under the respective Cess/Fund Acts on manufactured beedis, feature films, export of mica, iron ore, manganese ore, chrome ore and so on.

- The Mica Mines Labour Welfare Fund Act, 1946
- The Limestone and Dolomite Mines Labour Welfare Fund Act, 1972
- The Iron Ore, Manganese Ore, and Chrome Ore Mines Labour Welfare Fund Act, 1976
- The Beedi Workers' Welfare Fund Act, 1976
- The Cine Workers' Welfare Fund Act, 1981

The Labour Welfare Organisation, which administers these funds, is headed by a director general (labour welfare)/joint secretary from the Ministry of Labour and Employment, assisted by the welfare commissioner (headquarters) of director's rank, who supervises nine regional welfare commissioners for the purpose of administration of these funds in the states.[11]

Separate 'welfare funds' have also been formed for specified services, such as posts and telegraphs, ports, dockyards and railways. The welfare measures financed out of these funds relate to provisions of medical, housing, drinking water, educational, recreational, and family welfare facilities.

2. **Welfare work undertaken by the state governments/union territories**:[12] The state governments have enacted several welfare-related acts and have also set up welfare funds for different welfare activities. Maharashtra and Uttar Pradesh's governments were pioneers in this field and still have more broad-based programmes of welfare as compared to other states. We come across model welfare centres in most of the states and the facilities provided in these centres usually consist of medical aid, educational and recreational facilities. In some states, vocational training is given to men and women. The Directorate General Labour Welfare looks after these activities on

behalf of the State Government in Maharashtra. A special Labour Welfare Fund Act was passed in August 1965 in Uttar Pradesh, which provides for the provision of housing, general welfare and development. A brief account of some of the welfare activities of state governments/union territories is as follows:

As far as **Andhra Pradesh** is concerned, the Andhra Pradesh Labour Welfare Board implemented some welfare schemes, like scholarships, PH scholarship, medical aid, emergent economics ameliorative relief (FEAR), funeral expenses, daughter's marriage gift scheme, maternity benefit scheme, loss of limbs and family planning scheme.

It is the **Gujarat Labour Welfare Board**[13] that has been providing various welfare facilities to industrial workers and their dependents in Gujarat. Gujarat Unorganised Labour (Except Agriculture Labour) Welfare Board continues to implement various schemes to provide social security and safety net to the workers of urban areas, engaged in unorganised sectors. In order to enable the workers to avail benefits of social security and welfare schemes, 27,839 workers were registered and given unique ID numbers and identity cards during 2009–2010.[14]

The **Government of Meghalaya** has also initiated non-statutory labour welfare work. It has established five labour welfare centres in Meghalaya, which are providing basic elementary training in sewing, knitting and embroidery. These centres are usually located outside the precincts of the organisation of workers. The **Government of Nagaland** has also established labour welfare training centres at Dimapur, Tuli (Mokokchung) and Wazeho (Phek) imparting training in tailoring, knitting and embroidery to the family members and dependents of industrial workers to enable them to supplement their income by way of self-employment. This has helped in raising their standards of living.

The Goa Labour Welfare Board provides facilities such as training in embroidery, sewing, cutting and tailoring for the benefit of industrial workers and their families through the 17 labour welfare centres set up at different places in **Goa.**

In **Karnataka,** the statutory welfare facilities, such as payment of wages, minimum wages, maternity benefit, employees' compensation, and payment of gratuity are being extended in the state under the respective labour laws. In addition, 13 types of monetary benefits have been extended to the building and other construction workers by Karnataka Building and Other Construction Workers Welfare Board. Besides, the unorganised workers—head load workers, auto, taxi, lorry and bus drivers and conductors, small hotel workers, garage workers, tailors, washermen and so on—are covered under the Swavalamban scheme.

In **Jammu division**, library facilities and other recreational facilities are being provided to industrial workers by the Labour Welfare Centre at Bari Brahmana. Besides, some accommodation in Labour Sarai is also provided to migratory labourers. In **Kashmir division**, study tours are conducted for the industrial workers from different industries to familiarize them with new working techniques and methods adopted by industrial workers of different states.

In **Andaman and Nicobar Islands,** six labour welfare centres are functioning in different parts of the Andaman and Nicobar Islands.

In **Maharashtra,** more than 280 welfare officers were appointed during the year 2009 in various factories in the state who are doing a good job.

In **Tripura,** Tripura Building and Other Construction Workers Welfare Board constituted in July 2007 is continuously providing social security and welfare measures to the workers engaged in building and other construction work. Six Balwadi centres are run by the Labour Department in the tea and rubber plantations to impart primary education and to provide nutrition to the children of tea and rubber plantation workers in the age group of three to six years. About 600 students have been benefitted during the year 2009.[15]

As far as **Orissa** is concerned, in addition to statutory welfare facilities as provided under different labour enactments, non-statutory welfare facilities such as accommodation, dress allowance, soap allowance, transport allowance, leave and travel concession and education allowance have also been provided to the workers of different industries by virtue of bipartite and tripartite settlements as provided under Industrial Disputes Act, 1947.[16]

3. **Welfare work undertaken by the employers:**[17] Normally, the broad-based policy of the employers for providing welfare facilities comprises recreational and educational facilities in large units. In the smaller units, employers usually conform to those facilities which are prescribed by law. In the case of some large-scale and well-organised industries such as jute and tea, welfare activities have been taken up on a joint basis. Individual mills have also set up several welfare centres as well as dispensaries for the benefit of their employees. Some details of welfare work undertaken by the employers are as follows:

    In **Coal India Limited,** various statutory welfare facilities such as canteen, rest shelters and pithead baths are being provided to the coal miners. Non-statutory welfare measures too have also been undertaken. Central cooperative and primary cooperative stores have been established to provide essential commodities and consumer goods at cheaper rate. Cooperative credit societies have also been functioning. Besides, Coal India Limited has started scholarship scheme to encourage the children of its employees. Besides, good medical facilities are also provided to the workers and their families. There are 86 hospitals with 5,875 beds, 429 dispensaries, 673 ambulances and 1,646 doctors (including specialists) to look after the employees.[18] There are 12 Ayurvedic dispensaries also that provide treatment to the workers through the indigenous system. Besides, Coal India Limited is also providing education facilities.

    The **Chennai Port Trust** has been providing several welfare facilities. The Chennai Port and Dock Educational Trust Higher Secondary School has been functioning quite well since 1989. Many facilities are also being provided by the Trust. During 2009–2010, the Trust spent INR 47,297,602[19] crore on the welfare of the employees.

New Mangalore Port Trust, Kolkata Dock Labour Board, United Planters Association of Southern India, Visakhapatnam Port Trust, Mormugao Port Trust, and Mumbai Port Trust have been doing a lot for the welfare of the workers.[20]

4. **Welfare work undertaken by trade unions:**[21] Trade unions can also undertake some labour welfare work, though the Indian unions, in general, have so far neither the will nor the ability to undertake the welfare work. The biggest limitation in the case of trade unions is the lack of funds. Hence, not much can be expected from such bodies. However, there are some good examples like the **Textile Labour Association, Ahemdabad, Tata Trust,** etc.
5. **Labour welfare work undertaken by voluntary social service agencies:**[22] It is worth mentioning that, of late, several voluntary social service agencies such as the Bombay Social League started by the Servants of India Society, the Seva Sadan Society, the Maternity and Infant Welfare Association and the Young Men's Christian

Association (YMCA) have been doing a good job in the direction of welfare work. The activities of these organisation comprise promotion of mass education through night schools, libraries and lectures, Boy Scout organisations, promotion of public health, recreation and sports for the working classes and so on. The Seva Sadan Societies in Pune and Bombay have undertaken social, educational and medical activities for women and children and have also trained social workers.

In advanced countries, voluntary agencies have played an important part in enforcement of social legislation through conferences, propaganda and fieldwork and in ensuring a high standard of compliance with law. Voluntary social services agencies can also follow suit in our country.

Recent Trends/Developments

Some of the happenings in the very recent past, especially during 2016, are as follows:

1. **Adoption leave:** A few companies like Accenture have started giving adoption leave to its employees (see Exhibit 12.3).

Exhibit 12.3 Adoption Leave

Changes were made on this front across many companies—most recently at Accenture—acknowledging an increasing trend of employees opting for adoption.

Source: The Economic Times, 27 December 2016.

---

2. **Joining bonuses:** Joining bonuses went down especially at start-ups (see Exhibit 12.4).

Exhibit 12.4 Joining Bonuses

These went down, especially at start-ups with funds drying up. Such bonuses were offered to about 10% of the staff, down from 30–40% a year ago.

Source: The Economic Times, 27 December 2016.

---

3. **Maternity leave:** Maternity leave has been extended from 12 weeks to 26 weeks (see Exhibit 12.5).

Exhibit 12.5 Maternity Leave

The Rajya Sabha passed amendments to the Maternity Benefit Act, 1961, increasing the period of maternity leave from 12 weeks to 26 weeks.

Source: The Economic Times, 27 December 2016.

410 *Compensation and Reward Management*

4. **Paternity leave:** Now many companies, e.g. TCS, Wipro, Zomato, etc., have started giving paternity leave (see Exhibit 12.6). The central government has already introduced it for their employees.

Exhibit 12.6   Paternity Leave

In a step towards making work cultures inclusive and progressive, more organisations are increasing their secondary caregiver parental leave. Some companies are now calling paternity leave 'partner-led' to ensure it is gender-neutral.

Source: The Times of India, 5 November 2022.

---

5. **Yoga:** Of late, a good number of companies have started opting for yoga sessions (see Exhibit 12.7).

Exhibit 12.7   Yoga Sessions

An Assocham paper released this year noted that over 53% of corporate companies were opting for *yoga sessions* at the workplace to boost employee productivity, reduce sick days and combat fatigue.

Source: The Economic Times, 27 December 2016.

---

6. **Xmas gifts:** Despite the adverse impact of demonetisations of 500 and 1,000 notes, some start-ups offered several gifts to their employees (see Exhibit 12.8).

Exhibit 12.8   Xmas Gifts

Despite the impact of demonetisation, some start-ups are pampering staff this holiday season with overseas getaways, road trips, bonuses, gifts and even happiness funds.

Source: The Economic Times, 27 December 2016.

---

7. **On-site acupuncture and improv classes:** Some companies, like Twitter, provide acupuncture and improv classes (see Exhibit 12.9).

Exhibit 12.9   On-site Acupuncture and Improv Classes

Twitter is well known for providing perks, such as three catered meals a day, but some lesser-known benefits include on-site acupuncture and improv classes.

Source: The Economic Times, 20 June 2016.

8. **Death benefits:** It is good that some companies, like Google, provide the surviving spouse or partner of a deceased employee 50% of their salary for a few years (see Exhibit 12.10).

Exhibit 12.10 Death Benefit

Google provides the surviving spouse or partner of a deceased employee 50% of their salary for the next ten years.

Source: The Economic Times, 20 June 2016.

---

9. **Paid time off for volunteering and money for donation:** A new beginning has been made by some organisations, like Salesforce, whose employees are given paid volunteer time off and money to donate to a charity of their choice (see Exhibit 12.11).

Exhibit 12.11 Paid Time Off or Volunteering and Money for Donation

Salesforce employees receive, six days or paid volunteer time off a year, as well as $1,000 a year to donate to a charity of their choice.

Source: The Economic Times, 20 June 2016.

---

10. **Partial reimbursement on student loan debt:** Some companies partially reimburse on student loan debt (see Exhibit 12.12).

Exhibit 12.12 Partial Reimbursement on Student Loan Debt

Employees are offered a $1,200-a-year reimbursement on student loan debt.

Source: The Economic Times, 20 June 2016.

---

11. **Baby cash:** Some companies provide cash to employee at the time of birth of baby (see Exhibit 12.13).

Exhibit 12.13 Baby Cash

Facebook provides $4,000 in 'Baby Cash' to employees with a new born

Source: The Economic Times, 20 June 2016.

---

12. **Egg freezing:** An initiative has been taken by Spotify to provide parental leave and so on for parents returning to the office, and reimbursing costs for egg freezing and fertility assistance (see Exhibit 12.14).

> **Exhibit 12.14 Egg Freezing**
>
> Spotify provides six months of paid parental leave plus one month of flexible work options for parents retuning to the office. The company also covers costs for *egg freezing* and *fertility assistance*.
>
> Source: *The Economic Times*, 20 June 2016.

13. **Gender reassignment:** Some companies, like Accenture, have started covering gender reassignment for its employees (see Exhibit 12.15).

> **Exhibit 12.15 Gender Reassignment**
>
> Accenture covers gender reassignment for its employees as part of its commitment to LGBTQ right and diversity.
>
> Source: *The Economic Times*, 20 June 2016.

14. **Travel stipend:** An initiative has also been taken for giving employees an annual stipend to travel and stay in any listing of their company in the world (see Exhibit 12.16).

> **Exhibit 12.16 Travel Stipend**
>
> Airbnb gives its employees an annual stipend of $ 2,000 to travel and stay in any Airbnb listing anywhere in the world.
>
> Source: *The Economic Times*, 20 June 2016.

15. **ESOPs:** Amidst concerns of a valuation bubble rising, ESOPs were slashed across the board at many of India's new-age companies.[23]
16. **Low-cost housing:** For providing low-cost housing, an organisation has taken a highly appreciable initiative (see Exhibit 12.17).

    For building low-cost houses, the government will collaborate with public sector banks, housing finance companies, and state-owned construction firms like NBCC, and there will be a tripartite agreement with member, bank/housing agency and EPFO.

    The panel has suggested this scheme for low-income formal workers, who are EPFO subscribers and could not buy a house during their entire service period. At present, there are over 70% EPFO subscribers whose basic wages are less than INR 15,000 per month.

Exhibit 12.17   EPFO Plans to Introduce Low-Cost Housing Scheme for its Members

The retirement fund body, Employees' Provident Fund Organisation (EPFO) is working on plans to provide *low-cost housing* to its five crore subscribers.

The Central Board of Trustees (CBT), EPFO's highest decision-making body, will consider the report of the expert committee on the same in a meeting scheduled for next month.

A committee set up by the EPFO last year had recommended a scheme to facilitate subscribers to buy houses where they will be allowed to give advance from their Provident Fund (PF) accumulation and also pledge their future PF contribution as EMI (equated monthly instalment) payments.

Source: Hindustan Times, 23 May 2016.

17. **Flexi timings:** These days flexi timings matter a lot (see Exhibit 8.18)

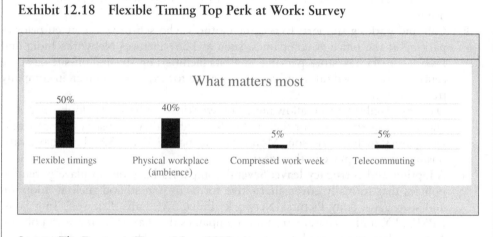

Exhibit 12.18   Flexible Timing Top Perk at Work: Survey

Source: The Economic Times, 5 June 2018.

The then labour minister Bandaru Dattatreya had said in the Lok Sabha about the plan to provide housing scheme for EPFO subscribers.[24]

18. **Other initiatives:** Some other initiatives undertaken by Indian Inc. are as follows:

   a. **Flexible timings:** Per TimesJobs survey of over 700 employers, flexible timings matter the most for the employee (see Exhibit 8.18).
   b. **Deloitte** is readying a programme called 'EmoFit+' geared specifically towards the evolving needs of young parents. In addition to other facilities, it will provide counselling services for new mothers and fathers.[25]
   c. At **Infosys**, employers get[26] access to online and in-person interactions with specialists, annual medical camps, parenting sessions and counselling sessions.

d. At **Mondelēz India Foods,** workshops[27] and sessions are conducted for new parents on topics like health of the child, health and financial wellness in perspective of becoming a new parent and changing priorities.
e. **Ericsson,** while offering crèche allowances and progressive maturity, paternity, and adoption leave, also sends gift hampers after the birth of a child.
f. At **PepsiCo,** an automated system called 'MatCare4U' keeps consistent information flowing t women on maternity issues via email and SMS.
g. **Enhanced maternity leave:** A host of companies, including PepsiCo, Godrej, PwC, GSK and KPMG, allow women to take maternity leave for six months or more. Tata Sons provides a seven-month maternity leave.
h. **Part-time or flexible work options:** Allow employees to vary working arrangements based on personal needs, such as work from home, reduced working hours and sabbaticals.
i. **Returning moms' programme** offers a sustainable solution to women on prolonged maternity leave. Companies, including EY and Genpact, have second career programmes that help to skill and retain women in the workforce.
j. **Secure performance rating** helps new mothers in maintaining their high performance. Companies like Tata Sons, PwC, Ericsson India, Godrej, and Citi have initiatives in place to let women retain their performance ratings. Also, this gives women a greater choice to plan their return to work while managing personal needs.
k. **Cab and parking support:** Expectant mothers who self-drive are given priority parking at the office at companies, such as Sony Pictures Networks India and PwC. Genpact has 'stork parking' at all its facilities, on-site and off-site day care centres at subsidised rates and reserved seating for expecting women in company transport vehicles.
l. **Day care facility/crèche allowance:** For working mothers who look for a safe and secure surrounding for their babies/kids when they themselves are at work. Companies such as Ericsson, Mondelēz, Genpact, EY and SAP Labs have various initiatives in place in this regard.
m. **Adoption and surrogacy leave:** Several companies have put in place parenting policies that formally cover alternative forms of parenthood such as adoption and surrogacy. Sony Pictures Networks India, SAP Labs, Ericsson, Tata Sons, KPMG, EY, and Accenture are some companies that have adopted such policies.
n. **Men as advocates of gender diversity:** As reported in *The Economic Times* of 12 August 2016, companies like Accenture have policies in place with the aim to ensure that the workforce comes together in an inclusive manner.
o. **Four-day work weeks:** A few organisations are floating a new possibility: a four-day workweek (see Exhibit 12.19).

Exhibit 12.19 Four-Day Workweeks

In recent months, various employers, such as Japanese electronics maker Panasonic, fintech start-up Bolt and the government of Belgium, have recommended giving employees the option to work four days but get paid for five, and Spain and Scotland are conducting their own trials of shorter weeks. They join a clutch of firms mainly in the tech sector that gravitated to a four-day format when the pandemic hit.

Source: *The Times of India*, 4 December 2022.

p. **Small bedrooms to stay overnight:** Now some organisations have started providing bedrooms for employees to enable them to stay overnight (see Exhibit 12.20).

Exhibit 12.20 Small Bedrooms to Stay Overnight

Elon Musk has converted rooms at Twitter headquarters in San Francisco into small bedrooms, featuring unmade mattresses, drab curtains and giant work monitors, media reported. The beds are prepared for remaining 'hardcore' staffers to be able to stay overnight at office, reports Forbes.

Source: *The Times of India*, 7 December 2022.

In one of its latest moves in the direction of providing social security, the Prime Minister's Office (PMO) gave approval to the labour ministry proposal on universal social security cover for 500 million workers, including those in the farm sector, seeking to start the process of putting in place a more secure welfare net a year before the General Election of 2019. The finance and labour ministries will work out the details of the scheme that will require nearly INR 2 lakh crore when fully rolled out for the lower 40% of the country's total workforce. The remaining 60% of the workforce was expected to make contributions out of their own pocket, either fully or partially.[28]

Recent Labour Reforms and Labour Welfare

In a tweet on the occasion of passing of the Labour Reforms Bill on 23 September 2020 in the Parliament, PM Narendra Modi said,

> Long due and much awaited Labour reforms have been passed by the Parliament. The reforms will ensure wellbeing of our industrious workers and give a boost to economic growth. These reforms will contribute to a better working environment, which will accelerate the pace of economic growth. These reforms also seek to harness the power of technology for the betterment of the workers and industry both.[29]

By getting the bills passed by the Parliament, 'the Central Government has made a headway towards changing the standard of living of workers in a fundamental manner. This will have a positive and far-reaching effect on workers. Employment creation and output of workers will also get enhanced'. Due to the passing of these four labour codes by the Parliament, the benefits of these for labour codes would be available to workers of both in organised and unorganised sectors. Hence, Employees' Provident Funds (EPF), Employees' Pension Scheme (EPS) and coverage of all types of medical benefits per Employees' Insurance Act will be available to the workers of both the organised and the unorganised sectors. With the amalgamation of twenty-nine labour laws in the four labour codes, the working class is going to be benefited directly or indirectly as these codes lead to economic, mental and physical betterment of the workers in both organised and unorganised sectors. For example, the amalgamation of the existing 13 labour laws into one code, the Occupational, Safety, Health and Working Conditions Code, 2020 (OSH Code 2020), will benefit the inter-state migrant workers in the following manner:

- Many provisions in the OSH Code will ease the lives of the inter-state migrant workers.
- Anomalies of the Inter-State Migrant Workers Act, 1979, have been exhaustively addressed in the OSH Code. For example, earlier, only workers appointed by a contractor were recognised as inter-state migrant workers but under the new provisions of the Code, workers can now be Aatmanirbhar as they can register themselves as inter-state migrant workers on the national portal. This provision will enable the workers to get a legal identity, which would allow them to get benefits of all social security schemes.
- A provision has been made for employers to provide travelling allowance annually to an inter-state migrant worker for undertaking a to-and-fro journey to his native place.
- If a worker is engaged in building and other construction work in one state and moves to another state, benefit from the Building and Other Construction Workers' Cess Fund will be provided.
- It has been made mandatory to issue appointment letters to the workers.
- Similarly, free annual health check-up of the workers will be mandatory and is to be provided by the employers.
- After the amalgamation of twenty-nine labour laws into four labour codes, an inter-state migrant worker would be entitled to get ration facility in the state he is working in, and the remaining members of his family would be able to avail of the ration facility in the state where they reside.
- There will be available mandatory helpline facility in every state for resolution of inter-state migrant workers' grievances.
- A national database will also be created for the inter-state migrant workers.
- Now if a worker has worked even for 180 days, he shall be entitled for one-day leave for every 20 days of work done, instead of the requirement of 240 days earlier.

Besides, the aforesaid four labour codes will also lead to women empowerment in the following manner

Women Empowerment Through the Labour Codes
- Women workers will have right to work in all types of establishments.
- Women will have the right to work at night with their consent, and further, the employer will have to make necessary arrangements to provide safety and facilities to women workers at night.
- Per the Maternity Benefit Act (amended), 2017, the paid maternity leave for women workers has been increased from 12 to 26 weeks, and a crèche facility has been made mandatory in all establishments having 50 or more workers.

The labour codes (per the Labour Codes Bill—2020) were to be implemented on July 1, 2022, in all the corporates and organisations under the registration of the Ministry of Corporate Affairs but due to multiple states not agreeing on the terms, the implementation of the above codes have been postponed as of now. The government has adopted a wait-and-watch policy because neither the trade unions nor the employers appear to be keen on the labour codes. With multiple states heading for assembly elections in 2023 and general elections in 2024 may be the other reasons, due to which the implementation of labour codes looks to be on the backburner. However, the central government has stepped up many schemes like Garib Kalyan, delivering of free food grains to the homes for the benefit of inter-state migrant workers and the poor in the country.

Bonus

As mentioned earlier, in addition to social security and labour welfare activities, which are the first and second constituents of fringe benefits, the third constituent of fringe benefit is bonus. There are three views about the concept of bonus. In the beginning, bonus was viewed as an *ex gratia* payment and, therefore, was considered derogatory from the point of view of employees. The second opinion about the concept of bonus is that once profits of an organisation exceed a certain base, workers have a *right to share it* because they play an important role in earning profit for an organisation. The opinion expressed by the Bonus Commission, 1964, Government of India, is also almost the same. The third view about bonus is that bonus is a *deferred wage*. According to this point of view, since it is difficult to instantly measure exactly the contribution of a worker in the process of production, a worker is paid a roughly estimated amount, and at the end of the stipulated period, his exact contribution is worked out, and the difference between his exact contribution and the amount already paid to the worker as his wages should be paid to him as wages.[30] It is, therefore, necessary that the worker should be paid his due. Keeping in view the diverse opinions on the issue and avoid any confusion, the Payment of Bonus Act was passed in 1965 making bonus a *statutory right of workers*, which can be claimed by them legitimately though under stated circumstances.

A few highlights of the act are as follows:

The Payment of Bonus Act, 1965, Repeated by the Code on Wages, 2019, with the Payment of Bonus Rules, 1975, as amended by (Amendment) Rules 2019[31]

The act extends to the whole of India and applies to every factory (as defined in Clause (m) of Section 2 of the Factories Act, 1948), every other establishment in which 20 or more persons are employed on any day during an accounting year (the appropriate government, by notification in the gazette, can reduce the limit of 20 persons). Every employee (other than apprentice) employed on salary or wage not exceeding INR 21,000 (earlier it was INR 10,000) per month, doing any skilled or unskilled, manual, supervisory, managerial, administrative, technical or clerical work for hire or reward, is entitled to a minimum bonus of 8.33% of the salary or wages earned by him or INR 100, whichever is higher, but not more than 20%, provided the employee has worked in the establishment for not less than 30 working days in that year.[32] An employee will be disqualified from receiving bonus in case he is dismissed from service for riotous or violent behaviour or fraud while on the premises of the establishment, and theft, misappropriation or sabotage of any property of the establishment. In case any financial loss is caused by the misconduct of the employee, the employer can deduct the loss from the bonus payable to the employee. The bonus should be paid in cash within a period of eight months from the close of the accounting year. The act also spells out under Section 15, the concept of 'set-on' and 'set-off' of allocable surplus.[33]

Internal Audit of Compensation and Benefits

Internal audit of compensation and benefits, including relational benefits, can bring not only transparency but also ensure that the process established in aligning and developing compensation packages is reliable, dependable, and credible and that it is made per law, internal regulations keeping in view the needs of employees. In order to make the compensation and benefit process efficient and effective in terms of risk management, control, delivery and proper governance, there should be internal audit of the system.

Planning and Definition of Internal Audit

Before moving further, it is essential to understand as to what internal audit is all about. As a matter of fact, internal audit is a method of independent and objective validation that results in enhanced value and improved operation and performance of an organisation. It also facilitates the effects of related processes to accomplish the goals and objectives of the organisation.

The Institution of Internal Auditors[34] defines internal auditing as an independent, objective assurance and consulting activity designed to add value and improve an organisation's operation. It helps the organisation accomplish its objectives by bringing a systematic and disciplined approach to evaluate and improve the effectiveness of risk management, control and governance process.

According to Kanello and Spathis,[35] internal auditing is a method of independent and objective validation, it not only increases the value and improves the operation and performance of the organisation but also facilitates the effects of related processes to accomplish the organisation's goals.

Internal audit is also defined as a multi-step process aimed to determine whether current processes and procedures comply with pre-decided rules and regulations or differ in any way from the standard.

While conducting internal audit in employee compensation and benefit, audit can focus on the philosophy and structure of compensation committee, compensation consultant's role and performance, pay and perks, and executive compensation. However, according to Wheeler,[36] wages can be audited from a number of dimensions such as record making, record keeping, minimum wage, overtime work, equal pay/non-discrimination issues, required deductions/withholding, other deductions, employee appraisals, vacations, holidays, personal leave, sick leave, other leaves, leaves of absence/disability, insurance benefits, pension benefits and deferred compensation. As a matter of fact, internal audit in HR compensation and benefits can be viewed as a process of determining if current processes and procedures of rewarding employees, including executives, synchronise with pre-laid down rules and regulations framed according to laws and statute of the organisation and adopted by committee, or deviate from it in anyway.

What Is Done in Internal Auditing?

Internal audit appraises the economy, efficiency and effectiveness of business operations and control, application of plans, procedures, and policies. It conducts special checks.

It also examines the functioning of accounting systems of the organisation as well as of related controls, credibility of financial and operational information. Burnaby and Hass have rightly observed for enterprises that the audit activity monitors the adequacy and effectiveness of management's control framework and contributes to the integrity of corporate governance, risk evaluation, and financial, operating and IT systems.

It is obvious from the foregoing discussion that corporate government, risk management and control are the three vital parts of internal audit process. For enabling internal audit functioning smoothly, International Standards for the Professional Practices of Internal Auditing (Standards) have been developed by the Institute of Internal Auditors for each part of the internal audit process. A few of the standards in this respect are as follows:

Standard 2110 (Related to governance)
Standard 2120 (Related to governance)
Standard 2130 (Related to governance)

Thus, the efficiency and effectiveness, that is, the performance of many functions, including HR function, can be improved through the process of internal audit. Over a period, there has been an overwhelming expansion in the scope.

Why Internal Audit of Compensation and Benefit Processes?

Of late, a greater need for financial reporting, according and auditing which are instrumental in providing relevant information on the financial position and performance of an organisation's business, is being felt across the corporate sector. According to Sabovic and Miletic,[37] this is due to emergence of the financial crisis and the crisis in corporate governance. Internal audit is specifically an interesting area of auditing. The main task of internal audit is to support the management of the organisation. The board, executive management, internal auditor, and external auditor are the main participants in corporate governance extent and types of information being audited. Today, auditing has spread its wings to almost all the financial areas of management and has become a critical tool to assess an activity, including compensation and benefits; for example, HR auditing provides the baseline data that is helpful to improve HR performance.

In his framework of HR audit, Bargerstock[38] emphasised the following four phases through which audit unfolds:

1. Ranking importance of the HRM Service Portfolio
2. HRM team self-evaluation
3. Measuring current service level
4. Developing action plan

There is no doubt that the compensation and benefits process is very complex. It is because reasons that compensation is operational cost for the organisation. It constitutes as much as up to 60% of total operational costs, though it may vary from organisation to organisation. All the same, it should not be forgotten that costs incurred on compensation and benefits are an investment in human capital that pays dividend all through it is made use of. Hence, such costs should be properly managed and duly audited to bring about improvement. Auditing of compensation and benefits is all the more important because it is a mechanism of corporate culture and also a vital source of employee motivation, and thereby affecting performance of the organisation through establishing link between effort and reward. Here, Vroom's expectancy theory can be referred to,[39],[40] which states that motivation is a product of the values one seeks and one's expectations of the probability that a certain action will lead to those values—that is, before expanding a given level of effort, an employee would be asking, 'If to make a strong effort on their job, will a superior level of performance be achieved? And if I do achieve such an outstanding level of performance, what kinds of rewards or negative outcomes will occur?' Besides, the employee also needs to know how valuable that outcome or performance level is to him/her. Vroom calls this value of valence. Besides, compensation and benefits are financial (tangible) and non-financial (intangible) rewards for employees and, therefore, they can be subject to many risks and frauds. They need to be thoroughly audited. It is also observed that in many cases there is little, and sometimes, even negative correlation with their contribution to the long-term performance of their organisations. Many executives have been generously paid even after their poor performances. Such lapses need to be identified through auditing and remedial steps must be taken. This sort of exercise will bring transparency to executive compensation and benefits. Not only this, but all possibilities of improving compensation and benefits processes by providing insight and recommendations depending on analysis and assessment of data available must be explained and action taken. It will also ensure that the processes established in aligning and developing compensation and benefit packages are available. All this is possible only through internal auditing. Hence, internal auditing is necessary. Internal auditing assumes added significance at the stage when the organisation is designing and recommending its own compensation and benefit packages. The structure and elements of aforesaid packages can be audited at this stage also and in case of any inconsistency, corrective action can be undertaken.

Researchers have revealed that a productive working relationship is the strongest when a risk managing internal audit is paired with a strategic HRM function. Besides, an internal audit planning process is more strategic in the presence of same pairing.[41]

Auditors, both internal and external, should not only be objective but also independent in the implementation of audits, and many cultural aspects or dimensions can make influences on auditor's assessment.[42]

There are many other reasons for doing internal audit in HR compensations and benefits. Also, there are some research studies carried out in the past that promote interest in and indicate the importance and benefits of internal audit in the contemporary production system. The request for cost efficiency, in terms of expenditures, and the effectiveness, in terms of corporate governance, high performances and above-average profits, are typical for modern companies. All those requirements are also related to the HRM process, and inside of it are compensations for employees. Besides the reasons and importance, it is significant to analyse tasks, areas and risks that are linked to compensation internal audit.[43]

Compensation and Benefit Structure, and Internal Audit Tasks Involved

There are two reasons that indicate the importance of HRM procedures and policies. The first is that they present the expected level of employees' behaviour and standards for functioning of HR activities in the organisation. In this regard, Savaneviciene and

Stankeviciute (2010)[44] laid emphasis on the work of Dietz and Boon where the authors in 2005 identifies 26 different practices that reflect the main objectives of most of the strategic HRM programmes used in more than 100 studies, of which top four are, in order of popularity: training and development, contingent pay and reward schemes, performance management (including appraisal) and careful recruitment and selection. The second reason is that these policies are standards which should be complied with and further that these policies are bases for conducting the internal control and internal audit. These policies are especially important in the areas of promotion and compensation, recruitment and selection, employee orientation, disciplinary action, evaluation and so on.

Since rewards impact employee satisfaction in the organisation, it is essential to audit the processes of compensation and benefits as also the main stages of it besides the structure of rewarding system. It will be quite relevant to mention here the basic stages of the compensation process, which comprise job analysis, job evaluation, determining the structure of compensation and benefits, performance measurement, implementation of payment systems, feedback and monitoring.

Methods of Conducting Audit

There are several methods of conducting audits, including surveys, interviews, observations, or a combination of the above and so on. However, the survey is the most popular approach.

Internal Audit of Compensation and Benefits: Risk Involved

Because of internal audit of compensation and benefit the organisations also carry several risks, such as compliance risk, employment market risk, reputation risk, operation risk and financial reports risk.

Another fact worth mentioning here is that only limited reviews of the justification of executive compensation and benefits are undertaken, and there are only a few organisations that get the compensation and benefits audited in the case of their executives.

Hence, to promote transparency and to raise the market's trust and confidence in an organisation, internal audit of executive compensation and benefits should be encouraged.

To sum up, internal audit is helpful in improving the efficiency and effectiveness of an organisation. It is usually done through insight and recommendations which are based on analysis relevant and data available from the organisation regard to compensations and benefits. Since compensation and reward systems constitute a very complex structure of activities and of many types of compensation, they need appropriate management and control. Compensations and benefits cost the organisation, on the one hand, and motivate and reward the employees, on the other hand. The process of compensation and benefits also causes a lot of complexities which can be sort out with the help of internal audit. For example, employment market risk, compliance risk, reputation risk, operation risk, financial reports risk and so on are the risks linked to HR compensation internal audit of compensation and benefit package.

Besides, internal audit is a support to HR management as well as to corporate grievance as a lot of information and data are collected in the process of audit which is very useful for the organisation in terms of improvement of business processes related to compensation and benefits. The main areas regarding compensation and benefit where internal audit should be conducted include overall plan, design, cash compensation, stock-based compensation, deferred compensation and various benefit-related areas, like pension and other retirement contributions. Besides, executive compensation and benefit programmes are the grey areas for conducting internal audit as the executives are accountable for managing organisation's business processes, functions and the organisation. The audit of executive compensation and benefit programmes assumes added importance because many a time it is observed that there is no correlation or even negative correlation between their contribution made to the organisation on the one hand and long-term performance of the organisation on the other hand. Hence, it needs a thorough analysis through internal audit so that corrective steps may be initiated. Above all, internal audit of compensation and benefits brings an element of transparency in the process.

Management's Strategy

The first and foremost vital thing for the management is to ensure that an employee benefit strategy should be an integral part of the total reward management strategy of the organisation, and more importantly, it should be supportive and instrumental in accomplishing the objectives of the organisation concerned besides being in line with the values and culture of the organisation. It should also add value to the base pay and performance-related pay policies of the organisation and create an impression among the employees that the organisation is genuinely concerned in the betterment of their working and living lives. It should also be instrumental not only in motivating the employees but also in infusing confidence among them as well as in boosting their morals, developing a sense of belongingness towards their organisation and create a feeling of commitment. The strategy should be formulated, as far as possible, in consultation with the employees so that the real needs of the employees could be identified and satisfied through the benefit strategy of the management.

The strategy should ensure that its implementation yields the desired results and that its implementation cost is more than that is compensated in terms of return by way of increase in output of the organisation through higher motivation, confidence, morale, commitment and sense of belongingness.

Besides, having adequate flexibility in operating the benefits package, tax implication regarding various fringe benefits should also get appropriate attention, while formulating an employee benefit strategy. The importance of intangible benefits should not be overloaded, and it should be ensured that the strategy should be innovative so as to secure an advantage over the employee benefit strategies of the competitors.

Chapter Review

1. Labour welfare which is another major constituent of fringe benefits. Broadly speaking, labour welfare is anything done for the intellectual, physical, moral and economic betterment of workers whether by employers, government or by other agencies over and above, what is laid down by law or what is normally expected based on contractual benefits for which the workers may have bargained for. Labour welfare has several objectives, such as promoting economic,

social, intellectual and physical betterment of workers, boosting their morale, infusing confidence and restricting union and government intervention. There are several principles of labour welfare, such as principle of social responsibility, principle of self-help, principle of flexibility and principle of democratic values, which help in making a labour welfare programme effective. Labour welfare may be classified in statutory welfare, voluntary welfare and mutual welfare. Labour welfare is also classified as intramural and extramural welfare activities. Although most labour welfare work in Indian industries has been undertaken by the central government, state governments, employers, trade unions and some other agencies, but it is primarily the central and state governments which have played an important role. However, there remains much to be done. Under the statutory welfare work, the Factories Act, 1948, which contains health provisions, safety provisions and welfare provisions, has made significant contribution. Besides, the Ministry of Labour and Employment administers several welfare acts, and a lot of welfare work has been undertaken under the auspices of these funds. The state governments have also been undertaking several welfare activities in their respective states. They have established welfare centres and welfare boards. A good number of employers, especially in jute, sugar and tea industries, have undertaken labour welfare activities. In coal mines, ports, plantations and so on also, a good number of welfare activities have been undertaken. Mutual welfare work undertaken by trade unions has not been able to make any contribution worth mentioning. Their poor finances are mainly responsible for this phenomenon. As a matter of fact, all concerned should make joint effort in a planned manner which will benefit all the stakeholders.
2. The passing of Labour Code Bill—2022 by the Parliament has enabled amalgamation of twenty-nine central labour laws into four labour codes. This will promote a lot of labour welfare of workers in both the organised and unorganised sectors, including inter-state migratory workers. It will also lead to women worker empowerment.
3. Bonus, the third ingredient of fringe benefits, is now being paid per the Payment of Bonus Act, 1965.
4. Internal audit of compensation and benefits is very important and should be conducted by all organisations.
5. While the management formulates its employees' benefits strategy, it should take the trade union into confidence and ensure that the benefits strategy is an integral part of the total management reward strategy. It should also create an impression that the management is genuinely concerned about the betterment of its employees and so on.

Keywords

bonus
labour welfare
labour welfare officer

mutual welfare
statutory welfare
voluntary welfare

Discussion Questions

1. Discuss the main definitions of labour welfare and main objectives of labour welfare work.
2. Discuss the classification of labour welfare work.
3. Discuss the steps taken by the central government to promote labour welfare, especially per the Factories Act, 1948.
4. Discuss the labour welfare work undertaken voluntarily by employers in Indian industries.
5. Discuss the impact of labour codes on labour welfare.
6. Discuss the main provisions of the Payment of Bonus Act, 1965
7. Discuss why benefits strategy should be an integral part of the total reward management strategy of an organisation?

Individual and Group Activities

1. Individually discuss with the HR officials of a big organisation and find out what voluntary welfare activities are undertaken by the employers in their organisation. Also, find out from them whether the employees are satisfied with these activities. If not, what are their expectations?
2. Visit a big organisation in a group of another two individuals and discuss with its trade union officials if the management of the organisation has been implementing the statutory labour welfare requirements satisfactorily or not. If not, what is the take of the management in this regard.
3. Visit a large manufacturing organisation, in a group of three members, and discuss with the union officials, what is the situation with regard to the implementation of labour codes.
4. Visit individually the union officials of a big organisation and find out the status of implementation of the Payment of Bonus Act, 1965.

   In a group of two students, visit a big factory and find out the status of internal audit of compensation and benefits.

Application Case 12.1

Fringe Benefits in Sugar Industry

Sugar industry enjoys a special status in Haryana and Punjab as the sugar industry draws its raw material, sugarcane, from the agriculture sector and the contribution of the agriculture sector constitutes a significant part of GDP of both the states. Hence, the significance of sugar industry in these two states. Since fringe benefits or non-wage benefits play a very important role in enhancing the employee contentment and its consequent positive impact on the quality and quantity of the product coming out from the concerned factories, a positive state of the availability of fringe benefits in sugar factories in these two states under study will be of great importance to the health of sugar industry.

The sugar factories in Haryana and Punjab provide fringe benefits under three heads: (a) social security benefits comprising compensation for employment injury, provident fund (including pension) and gratuity; (b) labour welfare benefits consisting of medical, educational and recreational benefits, canteen, uniform, housing and some other benefits in addition to retaining allowance; and (c) bonus.

However, not much has been done by sugar factories in this regard and leave much to be desired, especially in the case of fringe benefits extended by the employers at their own, that is, without any statutory obligation. The study reveals that social security benefits which are being provided by the sugar factories because of statutory obligations constitute 27.24% of the total expenditure on fringe benefits as a whole and another 40.81% of the total expenditure incurred on fringe benefits is spent as bonus which is also a statutory obligation. Thus, a total of 68.05% of the total expenditure on all the fringe benefits is being incurred because of statutory requirements. Only 31.95% of the total expenditure on all the fringe benefits taken together is incurred *voluntarily* on labour welfare, which is not a healthy trend and that is why the health of the sugar factories is not very sound. Thus, the expenditure on voluntary welfare activities needs to be increased substantially.

Source: The case study is based on the PhD thesis (unpublished) titled 'A Critical Study of Non-Wage Benefits to Workers In Sugar Factories of Haryana & Punjab', submitted by R. C. Sharma to the Kurukshetra University, Kurukshetra.

Questions

1. What types of fringe benefits are being extended to employees in the sugar factories of Haryana and Punjab?
2. Why does the expenditure on voluntary labour welfare needs substantial increase by the sugar factories in Haryana and Punjab?
3. Were you an authority to prepare a labour welfare plan for the sugar industry in Haryana and Punjab, what additions and attractions would you suggest?

Annexure 12.1

Duties, Status and Role of Labour Welfare Officer

The duties, status and role of labour welfare officer appointed under Section 49 of the Factories Act, 1948, are specified in detail in the Model Rules called Welfare Officers (Recruitment and Conditions of Service) Rules, 1951, as modified in 1957.

Duty Chart of Labour Welfare Officer

Supervision of Work

1. Safety, health and welfare programmes and housing, recreation, sanitation services as provided under law or otherwise
2. Working of joint committees
3. Grant of leave with wages as provided
4. Redressal of workers' grievances

Topics of Counselling for Workers

1. Personal and family problems
2. Adjusting to work environment
3. Understanding rights and privileges

Advisory Functions to Management

1. Formulating labour and welfare policies, apprenticeship training programmes
2. Meeting statutory obligation to workers
3. Developing fringe benefits and workers' education and use of communication

Liaison with Workers

1. To understand various limitations under which they work
2. To appreciate the need of harmonious industrial relations in the plant
3. To interpret company policy to workers
4. To persuade workers to come to a settlement in case of a dispute

Liaison with Management

1. To appreciate workers' viewpoints regarding various matters in the plant
2. To intervene on behalf of workers in matters under consideration of the management
3. To help different departmental heads to meet their obligations under the acts
4. To maintain harmonious industrial relations in the plant
5. To suggest measures for promoting general well-being of the workers

Work with Workers and Management

1. To maintain harmonious industrial relations in the plant
2. For prompt redressal of grievances and quick settlement of disputes
3. To improve productive efficiency of the enterprise

Work with Outside Agencies

1. Factory inspectors, medical officers, other inspectors for securing proper enforcement of various acts as applicable to the plant
2. Other agencies in the community with a view to help workers to make use of community services

It shall be observed from the duty chart that a labour welfare officer has direct responsibility for the administration of services pertaining to welfare and benefits, health and safety, joint committees, and leave with wages. He is also required to be concerned with the implementation of labour laws, proper working conditions, harmonious labour relations, industrial peace, plant productivity and workers' well-being. For this purpose, he must act as an advisor, counsellor, mediator and liaison man to both management and labour.

In order to ensure a proper discharge of the functions as stated above, the Model Rules lay down that a labour welfare officer should be a professionally trained person, be given the status equivalent to the head of a department, and be allowed to function as a 'neutral' person—a sort of buffer between management and workers.

Source: Welfare Officers (Recruitment Conditions of Service) Rules, 1951, Model Rules—Section 49, Factories Act, 1948.

Notes

1 Ministry of Labour & Employment, *Report of the Royal Commission on Labour in India* (London: H. M. Stationery Office, 1931), 261.
2 Labour Investigation Committee, *Report of the Labour Investigation Committee* (New Delhi: Government of India, 1946), 245.
3 International Labour Organization, *Second Asian Conference, Nuwara Eliya (Ceylone), January 1950, Report II, Provisions of Facilities for the Promotion of Workers Welfare* (Geneva: ILO, 1949).
4 *The Economic Times*, 27 November 2018.
5 Quoted in *The Times of India*, 2 November 2022.
6 For details, see Ibid.
7 *The Economic Times*, 27 November 2018.
8 Ibid.
9 For details of safety measures under Sections 21–41, see Sharma, *Industrial Relations and Labour Legislation*, 653–58.
10 Ministry of Labour & Employment, *Indian Labour Year Book 2009–10* (Shimla and Chandigarh: Labour Bureau, Ministry of Labour & Employment, Government of India, 2012).
11 Ibid.
12 Ibid.
13 Ibid.
14 Ibid.
15 Ibid.
16 Ibid
17 Ibid.
18 Ibid.
19 Ibid.
20 Ibid.
21 Ibid.
22 Ibid.
23 *The Economic Times*, 27 February 2016.
24 *Hindustan Times*, 23 May 2016.
25 *The Economic Times*, 12 August 2016.
26 Ibid.
27 Ibid.
28 *The Economic Times*, 12 August 2016.
29 New Labour Code for New India, *Ministry of Information and Broadcasting*.
30 Sharma, *Industrial Relations and Labour Legislation*, 714, PHI Learning, Delhi, 2016.
31 For details, see The Payment of Bonus Act, 1965 [Repealed by The Code on Wages, 2019 (29 of 2019)] with The Payment of Bonus Rules,1975 as amended by (Amendment) Rules, 2019, Bare Act, LexisNexis, Gurgaon, 2020, 1–45.
32 Season workers who have worked for not less than 30 working days are also entitled to bonus; J. K. Ginning and Pressing Factory V.P.O, Second Labour Court (1991) 62 FLR 207 (Bom).
33 The Payment of Bonus Act 1965 (Sec 15), 15 and [sec4(a)], 6.
34 The Institute of Internal Auditors, *International Standards for the Professional Practice of Internal Audit* (Florida, FL: Altamonte Springs, 2011) (Quoted by N. Berber, M. Pasula, M. Radosevic, D. Ikonov, and V. K. Vugdelija, 'Internal Audit of Compensation and Benefits: Tasks and Risks in Production Systems', *Inzinerine Ekonomika-Engineering Economics* 23, no. 4 (2012): 414–24).
35 A. Kanellou and C. Spathis, 'Auditing in Enterprise System Environment: A Synthesis', *Journal of Enterprise Information Management* 24, no. 6 (2011): 494–519.
36 S. Wheeler, 'Human Resource Audit', in *Human Resource Development for the Food Industries*, ed. W. A. Gould (Maryland, MD: CTI Publications, 1994).
37 S. Wheeler, 'Human Resource Audit', in *Human Resource Development for the Food Industries*, ed. W. A. Gould (Maryland, MD: CTI Publications, 1994).

38 S. Sabovic and S. Miletic, 'The Impact of the Crisis in Financial Reporting, Accounting and Auditing', *Technic Technologies Education Management* 5, no. 3 (2010): 613–20.
39 A. S. Bargerstock, 'The HRM Effective Audit: A tool for Managing Accountability in HRM', *Public Personnel Management* 29, no. 4 (2000): 517–27.
40 For details, see R. C. Sharma, *Human Resource Management: Theory and Practices* (New Delhi: SAGE Publications, 2018), 449.
41 Ibid.
42 M. A. Hyland and D. A. Verreault, 'Developing a Strategic Internal Audit–Human Resource Management Relationship: A Model and Survey', *Managerial Auditing Journal* 18, no. 617 (2003): 465–77.
43 M. Moradi, M. Salehi, and A. Fakharabadi, 'An Investigation Cultural Factors' Affection on Auditors' Assessment Estimation of Internal Control and Control Risk Determination', *Technics Technologies Education Management* 6, no. 3 (2011): 698–710.
44 Berber, Pasula, Radosevic, Ikonov, and Vugdelija, 'Internal Audit of Compensation and Benefits', 418.A. Savaneviciene and Z. Stankeviciute, 'The Models Exploring the "Black Box" between HRM and Organizational Performance', *Inzinerine Ekonomika-Engineering Economics* 21, no. 4 (2010): 426–34.

Part V

Integrating, Maintaining and Retaining Human Resources

13 Employee Motivation

Learning Objectives

After studying this chapter, you should be able to do the following:

1. Define the term 'motivation' and point out its objectives and importance.
2. Explain the process of motivation and types of motivation.
3. Describe the techniques/methods of motivation and also problems involved in motivation.
4. List and describe problems of motivation.
5. Explain the concept of executive motivation.
6. List and describe the theories of motivation.
7. Identify and explain the main elements of a sound motivational system.
8. Explain the meaning of incentives and classify them.
9. Explain the term 'group incentives' and point out its advantages.

Introduction

The primary task of a manager is that of maintaining an organisation that functions effectively. To do so, he/she must see that his/her subordinates work efficiently and produce results that are beneficial to the organisation. Organisational goals can never be achieved without subordinates' willingness to put their best efforts. Here arises the problem of motivation. 'The capacity to work' and 'willingness to work' are two different things. A person can be physically, mentally and technically fit to work, but he/she may not be willing to work, hence the need of motivation. Motivating a worker is to create a need and a desire on the part of him/her to better his/her present performance. Thus, performance is determined by two factors: level of ability to do certain work and level of motivation.

This can be expressed as follows:

Performance = Ability × Motivation

Hence, motivation is number one problem of management.

DOI: 10.4324/9781032628424-18

Meaning and Definition of Motivation

'Motivation' is a term derived from the word 'motive'. We can define 'motive' as which makes a person active in a particular way. It is an inner impulse causing man to action. A person works to satisfy his/her needs. So the human needs are the cause of action, and motivation is a process of causing a person realise these needs. In the context of HRM, motivation is a person's desire to do the best possible job or to exert the maximum efforts to perform the assigned tasks. Here are some important definitions of motivation:

According to Mitchell and Mickey,[1] 'Motivation is the set of attitudes and values that predispositions a person to act in a specific, goal-directed manner'.

According to Levine,[2]

> Motivation is an invisible inner state that energises human goal-directed behaviour, which can be divided into two components:
>
> 1. The direction of behaviour (working to reach a goal).
> 2. The strength of the behaviour (how hard or strongly the individual will work).

A few other definitions of motivation are as follows:

1. 'Motivation is the act of stimulating someone or oneself to get a desired course of action or push the right button to get desired results' (Michael J. Jucius).
2. 'Motivation can be defined as a willingness to expand energy to achieve a goal or rewards' (Dale Beach).
3. 'Motivation refers to the way in which urges, drives, desires, aspirations, strivings or needs direct, control or explain the behaviour of human beings' (McFarland).
4. 'Motivation means a process of stimulating people to action to accomplish desired goals' (W. G. Scot).

Thus, it is clear from these definitions that different experts have defined motivation in their own way. However, the basic contents are the same.

Characteristics of Motivation

1. **Motivation is an internal feeling:** Motivation is a psychological phenomenon which generates urge within an individual. Needs are feelings in the mind of a person that he/she lacks a certain thing. Such feelings affect the behaviour of the person.
2. **Person in totality, not in part, is motivated:** Every individual in the organisation is a self-contained and inseparable unit, and all of his/her needs are interrelated. These affect the behaviour in different ways. Hence, a person in totality, not in part, is motivated. Moreover, feeling of needs is a continuous process, as such, these create continuity in human behaviour.
3. **Motivation causes goal-directed behaviour:** Feeling of needs by the person causes him/her to behave in such a way that he/she tries to satisfy himself/herself so that he/she does not feel the lack of that specific thing. This can be expressed as in Figure 13.1.

Need, which is the feeling that something is required, creates tension in the mind and transforms itself into want depending on environment. This tension is released when this want is satisfied by certain behaviour again in the environment; that is, incentives exist to

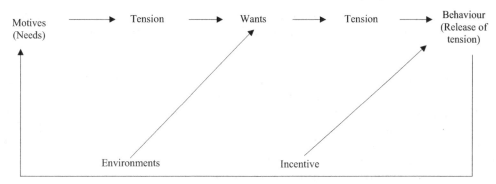

Figure 13.1 Need-caused Human Behaviour
Source: Based on discussion in K. Davis, Human Relations at Work (New York, NY: McGraw-Hill Book Company, Inc., 1962), 20–21.

satisfy the wants. Behaviour ends the moment tension is released. However, satisfaction of one need leads to feeling of another and the process goes on.

4. Motivation is the product of anticipated values from an action and the perceived probability that these values will be achieved by the action: The anticipated value is called 'value', and it is defined as the strength of a person's preference for one outcome in relation to others. The perceived probability is called 'expectancy', and it is defined as the strength of the belief that a particular act will be followed by a particular outcome. Thus, motivational relationship can be expressed in the formula.

   Motivation = Valence × Expectancy

Objectives of Motivation

Motivation aims at creating an environment which will make the personnel of an organisation:

1. Take initiative.
2. Show dynamism and curiosity.
3. Work willingly and cooperatively.
4. Work in a disciplined manner.
5. Take interest in their work.
6. Dynamic and enthusiastic.
7. Responsible and loyal.
8. Take pride in their job.
9. Have job satisfaction and high morale.
10. Have personal and group moral satisfaction.
11. Contribute their best to achieve their personal and organisational objectives.

Importance of Motivation

Motivation is an important function of management. Explaining the importance of motivation, S. L. McShane, M. A. V. Glinow and R. R. Sharma say that motivated employees are willing to exert a particular level of effort (intensity) for a certain amount of time (persistence), towards a particular goal (direction).[3]

As a matter of fact, motivation is one of the four vital drivers of individual behaviour and performance. Motivation is getting the members of the team to pull weight effectively, to give their loyalty to the group and organisation, to carry out properly the activities allocated and generally to play an efficient part in the purpose or task that the organisation has undertaken. Motivated employees are the real assets of any organisation. Technology, system and methods become effective only if these people have zeal and enthusiasm for work. All administrative action loses its point unless the members of the enterprise are willing to contribute their efforts for the fulfilment of their assigned tasks. The main function of management is to develop and increase a desire in every member of the organisation to work effectively in his/her position. This improves the morale of the employees. Good motivational measures result into increased productivity. These foster the cooperative spirit among the subordinates and their satisfaction level goes high. In a nutshell, to achieve organisational and individual goals in an economic and effective manner, motivation is an important tool in the hands of management to direct the behaviour of subordinates in the desired and appropriate direction and thus minimise the waste of human and other resources.

The importance of motivation in an organisation can be summed up as follows:

1. **High performance level**: Motivated employees put higher performance as compared to other employees. The high performance is a must for an organisation, and motivation is a vital requirement for high performance. Several research studies have proved the relationship between high performance and high motivation.
2. **Low employee turnover and absenteeism**: A motivated employee stays in the organisation for longer duration, and his/her rate of absenteeism is also quite low. High turnover and absenteeism create many problems in the organisation (see Exhibit 13.1). Although recruiting, training, and development of large number of new personnel not only take long time but are also expensive, in a competitive economy, this needs to be done because these keep workers motivated and motivation brings down the rate of turnover and absenteeism.
3. **Acceptance of organisational changes**: The changes in an organisation are a usual phenomenon due to various reasons, such as changes in technology and value system. The organisation must cope with these changes to cope with the requirement of time. When the changes are introduced in the organisation, there is a tendency to resist them by the employees. However, if they are properly motivated, they accept those changes with zeal and enthusiasm and support in their proper implementation too.

Exhibit 13.1 What Can Keep Employees Engaged and Motivated?

The belief that financial incentives work well for checking employee attrition is passes now. A good financial payout does help but cannot be called the main motivator in keeping the employees engaged and enthused enough to work for a particular organisation. This gives rise to a very essential question, as to what do some of the best employers across the globe do right, when it comes to keeping their employees engaged and motivated? With the change in the global work environment, it has been observed that an increasing number of professionals look for ethics where they can thrive well, both personally and professionally. The change in the perspective of the present-day employees has enabled a sea change in the way human resource looks at employee engagement. Today, HR is working towards reinventing strategies and initiatives to ensure that employees are enthused enough to be happy to stay back in the same organisation and help it involve to newer scales.

Source: The Economic Times, 15 March 2014.

Motives for Work

Why do people work? It is a fundamental question to be answered before preparing any plan for motivation. It is the intensity of human wants which motivates people to work. Employee motivation gets support and nourishment from the satisfaction of human wants. To increase individual work effectiveness, motivation aims at providing all sorts of stimulus and incentive to employees at work or at home. As incentives increase the intensity and duration of human efforts, motivation seeks to bring into operation the full play of such incentives. Incentives may be either economic or non-economic. Hawthorne experiments conducted by Elton Mayo, F. J. Roethlisberger and their associates have demonstrated that non-economic incentives are more impressive than financial incentives.

Motivation as the Central Task of Management

It is the central task of management to motivate the behaviour of organisational members towards working for common goals. This process also includes the task of conditioning and convincing the organisational members to integrate their own goals and needs into those of their organisation, preferably on a voluntary basis. It is getting the members of the team to pull weight effectively, to give their loyalty to the group and organisation, to carry out properly the activities allocated and generally to play an efficient role in contributing to the common purpose. Motivation is an internal instinct of initiating, energising, directing and sustaining certain patterns of human behaviour towards achievement of common goals. When it is discussed as an internal process, a person is supposed to motivate himself/herself without any external stimulus. On the other hand, as an external process, a person is motivated by an external agency to channel his/her behaviour towards certain ends set by himself/herself or that by external agency. In business enterprises, motivation is a double-edged sword. It is internal as well as external matter. The management has to motivate employees on a continuous basis so that they may be motivated to integrate their own goals and needs as well as efforts into those of their organisation. There are five variables or elements in this process:

1. Managers who motivate
2. Employees who are motivated
3. The work situation in which both operate
4. The actual work in which behavioural events and consequences are incorporated
5. Organisational goals and needs towards which behaviour is sought to be directed

The degree and level of motivation and its effects depend upon the managerial propensity (skill, desires and ability) to motivate. Only a self-motivated manager can motivate his/her employees because self-awareness on the part of managers as well as an interest in and understanding of the employees are very significant in this process. Motivation will also be effective to the extent the objects of motivation—namely, the employees who are to be motivated—are receptive for it. If they have requisite propensity for motivation, only then they can be motivated fully. The degree of propensity to be motivated differs from individual to individual. Even the technique varies widely in different circumstances. Because an individual has a multitude of motives, each influencing his/her behaviour in different degrees in different situations, the problem of motivation becomes really a complex problem. It is more a social and human problem rather than a technical problem. It requires a thorough understanding of human motives for work, their propensity for different people in different work situations and various techniques of motivation, that is, various incentives. Management can take certain steps to motivate employees (see Exhibit 13.2).

Exhibit 13.2   Keeping Employees Motivated

- Organisations can boost employee performance through transparency, meritocracy and clarity of role.
- Identifying the gaps in employee performance, addressing these by providing the right learning platforms and undertaking coaching and mentoring sessions to sustain their performance are critical.
- Employees should also be told how their performance impacts the organisation.

Source: Hindustan Times, 24 May 2016.

Precautions in Motivation

Although motivation is an important task of management, it is a part of the process of management. It should not be overlooked by the management. Management should have a balanced approach in this respect. Further, there cannot be a single source of motivation; a system of motivation requires a coordinated set of incentives, positive as well as negative, available for selective application to elicit the best efforts of individuals. Hence, a coordinated approach is required in this direction.

Self-motivation

Due to emotional reactions within, one may have a feeling of tiresomeness, which may prove a bottleneck to human action. Inner conflicts and anxiety also hamper a person's action. Hence, steps need to be taken to overcome these problems so that an individual can first motivate himself/herself because only thereafter will he/she be able to motivate others. An individual can better motivate himself/herself if he/she has definite targets and mission before himself/herself, adopts constructive thinking, gets determined and tough-minded and makes best use of his/her potentialities.

Processes of Motivation

In case the management really wants to proceed to motivate the personnel of the organisation, it has to carry out two types of activities: (a) what is to be done and (b) how and why what is done is done. While the former are steps in motivation, the latter are rules governing the steps in motivation. According to Jucius,[4] the main steps in motivation include the following:

1. **Sizing up**: The first stage of motivation involves ascertaining motivational needs of an individual or a group because due to individual differences, different individuals or groups need motivation in varying kinds of degrees.
2. **Preparing a set of motivating tools**: The second step involves selecting and applying specific tools of motivation. A manager can draw up a list of the devices that prove effective in motivating different kinds of people under different conditions.
3. **Selecting and applying motivational plans**: This step involves selection of the appropriate plan, the method of application and the timing and location of applications. This will also vary from situation to situation.
4. **Feedback**: Feedback is required to ascertain whether an individual or a group has been motivated or not. If not, then some other device may be used.

Rules of Motivation

While undertaking steps of motivation, it is desirable to be guided by certain rules. In this respect, Jucius[5] has suggested the following rules:

1. **Variability**: Since individual differences exist among people and further that even the same person is different from time to time, motivational programmes should change according to circumstances. Only then they can bring forth the desired results.
2. **Self-interest and motivation**: Motivation is based on selfishness. A man would feel motivated to help others only if he/she realises that his/her personal interest is best served by helping others.
3. **Attainability**: A person would feel motivated only when we establish such goals as are attainable by him/her, that is, within the reach of the motivated.
4. **Participation**: In case we want the employees to be motivated, we should make them participate in the plans of motivation. It will infuse confidence in them, and they will feel involved.
5. **Proportioning rewards**: Rewards in proportion to efforts made bring improvement and can serve to avoid under- or over-motivation.
6. **Individual–group relationships**: Motivation should be dependent upon group as well as individual stimuli.
7. **The human element**: In case an executive wants to motivate his/her subordinates, he/she should understand the feelings of them because their actions are caused by their feelings and thinking.
8. **Situational**: Motivation is affected by work situation.

Types of Motivation

An executive can motivate his/her employees in more than one way. The following are the important types of motivation:

1. **Positive or incentive motivation**: An employee can be motivated by offering him/her the possibility of rewards, promotion, prestige, praise, higher pay and so on.

2. **Negative or fear motivation**: While positive motivation is usually based on reward or incentives, negative motivation is based on force, fear, reprimands, punishment, loss of job and so on. Negative motivation compels an employee to act in a particular way because he/she knows that in the case of failure, he/she would have to face the consequences.
3. **External or extrinsic motivation**: Financial rewards, such as hike in pay, fringe benefits, social insurance schemes and holidays with pay, are also powerful motivators.
4. **Internal or intrinsic motivation**: Intrinsic motivation is concerned with the inner satisfaction that one gets after doing something concrete. The examples of intrinsic motivation may include appreciation (see Exhibit 13.3), recognition and compliments (see Exhibit 13.4), status, increased responsibility, more authority or power, more respect and so on. Mark Twain once said, 'I can live for two months on a good compliment'.[6] It sounds pretty good.

Exhibit 13.3   Craving for Appreciation

Psychologist and philosopher William James pens a letter to his class at Radcliffe College, with the quote 'The deepest principle of human nature is the craving to be appreciated'. He succinctly captures the essence of human motivation and its core connection to the power of recognition. He is probably clueless that an entire body of work will be built on this simple thought and it will continue to be relevant even centuries later, especially in the organisational context.

Source: P. Malhotra, 'To our Readers', *Human Capital* 17, no. 9 (February 2014): 8.

Exhibit 13.4   Employee Recognition

Employee recognition is no recent invention by any standards, but its implication for organisations is most definitely moving to higher grounds. After a comprehensive research study, Jean M. Twenge of San Diego State University and Stacy M. Campbell of Kennesaw State University concluded that Gen Y have personality traits like high self-esteem, unrealistically high expectations and a high need for praise. Their recommendations: organisations should upscale their recognition and praise programs to appeal to the psyche of this brave new workforce.

Source: P. Malhotra, 'To our Readers', *Human Capital* 17, no. 9 (February 2014): 8.

---

5. **Financial motivation**: It is concerned with money, which is supposed to be a very potential motivator. Financial motivators may include profit-sharing schemes, bonus, especially production bonus, higher salary and so on. A detailed account of financial (as also of non-financial) motivators is given elsewhere in this very chapter.
6. **Non-financial motivation**: Non-financial motivation is concerned with psychological rewards, that is, the inner-felt satisfaction. The following are some of the commonly used non-financial motivators:

- **Job enrichment**: Job enrichment is a new and popular non-monetary motivational technique. According to Flippo,[7] enrichment of jobs would include not only horizontal enlargement but also vertical enlargement to permit subordinate participation in managerial decisions concerning tasks assigned. Job enrichment involves vertical loading of job, adding more challenge to it. It is improvement of the job in such a way that it has more motivators than before and at the same time maintaining the degree of maintenance factors. Based on the assumption that in order to motivate personnel, the job itself must provide opportunities for achievement, recognition, responsibility, advancement and growth.

A good job enrichment should have the following approaches:

1. Due emphasis should be given on individual differences while taking a plan of job enrichment.
2. The employee should be given adequate benefit arising out of job enrichment.
3. People like to be consulted and to be given an opportunity to offer suggestions. So, it should be applied after their consultation.
4. The management should be sincere and honest in implementing the programme.

According to Robert Janson,[8] job enrichment may have the following:

1. Variety to allow use of multiple skills
2. Identity of task, thus permitting psychological closure
3. Task significance in the eyes of the incumbent and others
4. Feedback of task performance results
5. Autonomy in selecting methods of work, pace of work and determination of acceptable quality

- **Job enlargement**: In order to reduce monotony of repetitiveness and make the worker take more interest in his/her job, more responsibilities of a horizontal nature can be added to a job. 'The process of introducing variety by way of assigning additional responsibilities of a horizontal nature to a job is termed job enlargement'. Through job enlargement, a group of employees can be assigned a group of jobs and then allowed to decide for themselves how to organise the work. This will lead to more change of jobs and increased interaction among the group employees and thus motivate the employees due to increased interest in work.
- **Job rotation**: Job rotation involves shifting of an employee from one job to another job. The primary objective of job rotation is to increase the skills and knowledge of the employee about the related jobs. Job rotation is one of the important methods of executive development programme whereby managers and executives are rotated among positions in different functions or geographic locations to make them learn how to meet new situations and problems of different jobs. As job rotation reduces monotony and boredom, the employee feels motivated to work more enthusiastically on related jobs.
- **Job loading**: Many a time, in order to make a job more interesting so that the employee may feel motivated, job loading is also done. It can be a horizontal job loading, in which the employee may be assigned more work at the same level at which he/she is currently working, or it can be at a vertical job loading, which implies larger areas of responsibility. Jobs are restructured in a fashion that make them intrinsically more worthwhile, interesting and motivating.

Techniques or Methods of Motivation

Based on the previous discussion (under the head 'Types of Motivation'), it can be said that the following are the main techniques of motivating the personnel in an organisation:

1. **Monetary techniques**: These techniques are based on this popular belief that a person works for money. Hence, an attraction of getting more money will prove to be the most powerful motivator. Incentives such as more pay (through various premium plans), fringe benefits, security of tenure and condition of service are some examples of the monetary techniques of motivation.
2. **Job-based techniques**: These techniques are based on social, human and psychological beliefs. Job simplification, job rotation, job enlargement, job enrichment, freedom in planning for work, sense of recognition, responsibility and achievement are some examples of such technique.
3. **MBO technique**: Peter Drucker, a well-known author of management, has developed this technique which emphasises on self-control and self-motivation. It is a participatory technique of motivation whereby managers and their subordinates jointly participate in achieving the common goals. It requires an emphasis on the MBO policy in the concern.
4. **Leadership styles**: Leadership styles or supervisory techniques also have a great role in motivation of employees. Autocratic, democratic and free-rein techniques of leadership are important styles and have their own implications for employee motivation, morale and productivity. The management must try different supervisory styles in different circumstances for different employees.
5. **Group-based techniques**: Herbert Bonner, a well-known author, has advocated group-based techniques for motivating the employees. According to him, 'Motivation is not wholly, nor even primarily, an individual variable. Certainly, its force and direction are functions of the social situation in which it arises and is exercised'. Hence, management should foster group consciousness and cohesiveness among individual employees by laying down general norms and guidelines of work for the whole group.
6. **Sensitivity training**: This is a technique of training given to groups of managers (known as T-groups) themselves so that they behave with and motivate their subordinates better. The sensitivity training is imparted to make the managers understand themselves better, becoming more open-minded, developing insight into group process and cultivating a systematic approach towards the problem of motivation. A manager thus trained is supposed to be more consistently able and willing to communicate with his/her subordinates and inspire them to contribute their best to the common goals and objectives.

Techniques Based on Incentive Plans

Another classification of techniques or methods of motivation is based on incentive plans as shown in Figure 13.6, which gives a snapshot view of various types of incentives which motivate the subordinates.

It is clearly visible from Figure 13.6 that motivation is a function not merely of monetary incentives but is related to non-monetary factors also.

Employee Motivation 441

As a matter of fact, motivation is more a psychological problem than a financial or managerial one. It is impossible to understand and administer motivation without considering what people want and expect from their jobs. Hence, the study of needs, aspiration and individual motives behind the work is very important. Undoubtedly, financial incentives can provide the necessary encouragement for employees to work harder, but social and psychological factors also play a vital (and more important sometimes) role in the process of motivation. Both types of incentives, financial and non-financial, are essential for motivating employees.[9]

Problems in Motivation

1. **Problem of implementation**: The first problem in motivation is of implementation. It involves the decision as regards to deciding what should be done to motivate an individual. People differ in their expectations; hence, they require separate types of incentives to be motivated.
2. **Problem of elements**: The elements of motivation can be divided into four classes: motivator, motivated, motivation techniques and motivational circumstances. According to some experts, the success of motivational measures depends upon the social and psychological levels of individuals to be motivated. According to some other experts, the personality of the motivator is the main element. But all these concepts are incomplete. A coordinated approach of these four classes is essential.
3. **Problem of moderate motivation**: The motivators should keep this fundamental thing in mind that motivation can be achieved on a moderate scale. Although motivation is an important tool in the hand of management to direct the behaviour of subordinates in the desired direction, it has its own limitations also. Subordinates can be motivated to a limited extent only.
4. **Problems of uneven motivation**: The problem of uneven motivation is also important. An executive should know the individual characteristics which determine the effectiveness of motivational measures to a large extent. All individuals do not possess equal education, same attitudes and same level of aspirations. Educated and skilled employees can be motivated more in comparison to unskilled and uneducated workers. The basis of motivation is the needs of employees. They should be recognised, identified and then satisfied through various types of incentives.
5. **Limitations of employees**: The management should keep in mind the limitations of employees also. They are not only for business organisations. They owe certain responsibilities for their families, social circle, city and nation also. So the management should not expect their wholehearted loyalty and dedication for organisation only.
6. **Motivation is situation-oriented**: Implementing the concept of motivation is always situation-oriented. The management should try to understand the situation properly, and only then any measure should be taken to motivate the employees. To motivate others, the executive himself/herself must be well motivated. He/she will prove to be an example to be emulated. Subordinates get inspiration from him/her.
7. **Motivation is an internal instinct**: Last but not the least, the management should not forget it that motivation by nature is an internalised process. It comes from inside but some reinforcements are needed to utilise it for practical purposes. Managers can

give only start, but actual and effective motivation will depend upon the internal will of the subordinate himself/herself.

Executive Motivation

Motivational factors in the case of executives need to be necessarily the same as are in the case of subordinates or rank-and-file workers. Like workers, managers are also, no doubt, interested in money, but in the case of latter, competitive performance and pride in a job done well are equally and sometimes even more powerful motivators. Among the important factors which motivate executives, we can include the feeling that they (executives) are doing something important or useful, that they are doing something that they themselves have set for themselves and that they are doing something that they can see that they have done, as well as the feeling of increased responsibility and authority, feeling of an increase in status, bigger pay packets, more perks, job security, better working conditions, challenging work, freedom of initiative, faith in the value of work, recognition, opportunities for self-development and so on.

Needs

The central problem of motivation, as far as the management of an organisation is concerned, is how to induce a group of people to work. A manager, before planning for motivation, should invariably know why people do the work. The ability to make effective motivational decisions requires knowledge about the motives which bring about purposeful behaviour. Motivation has its roots in such motives within a person which induce him/her to behave in a particular manner. These motives are known as 'wants', 'needs', 'fears' and so on. These are the drives to work. They are the initiating and sustaining forces of behaviour. They have a direct influence on an individual since they determine, in part, his/her thoughts and actions. A person's needs, working in conjunction with his/her emotions and other psychological functions, act as the motives that dictate his/her actions and behaviour. What an individual perceives as the real world about him/her, how he/she feels, what old thought patterns come into play, his/her current activities, all these processes and many more are influenced by his/her needs and the means he/she uses to satisfy them.

Types of Needs

There are various ways to classify needs. A simple one is the classification of needs as (a) primary—basic, physiological or lower-order needs—and (b) secondary—social-psychological, higher-order or derived needs (see Figure 13.2).

Primary Needs

These are animal drives which are essential for survival. These needs are common to all human beings, though their intensities may differ. Some of the physiological needs are food, sex, sleep, air, satisfactory temperature and so on. These needs arise out of the basic physiology of life and are important to survival and preservation of species. These needs are also conditioned by social practices. According to the concept of economic man, these are the only wants of a human being and he/she attempts to satisfy them only. But

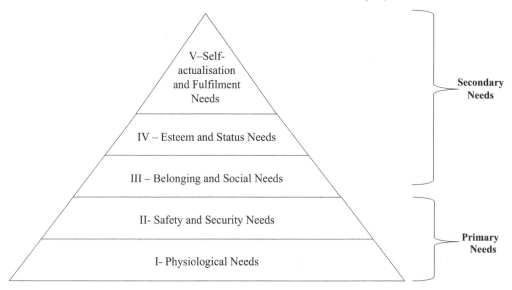

Figure 13.2 Maslow's Order of Priority of Needs

researches in human behaviour show that psychological needs are equally, rather more, important for human beings.

Secondary Needs

These needs are most nebulous because they represent needs of the mind and spirit rather than of physical body. They are also vague. These are learned through experience and environment and as such, they are also called learned or derived needs. Examples are rivalry, self-esteem, sense of duty and belongingness. A person's real secondary needs are often hidden so that even he/she cannot recognise them. They also change according to time and circumstances.

These may be further classified as follows:

1. **Social needs**: These are related to get high position and status in the society, to get praise from others and so on.
2. **Ego needs**: These are related to a person's ego. These may further be classified into two parts: (a) those needs that relate to one's self-esteem—needs of self-confidence, achievement, competence and knowledge—and (b) those needs that relate to one's reputation—needs for status, recognition, appreciation and so on.

Niles, in her book *Middle Management*, has classified the various needs as needs for security, achievement, recognition, sense of belongingness, monetary and opportunity for progress and worth. According to her, needs are the basic factors in motivation.

Maslow[10] has given certain priority to needs and has classified various needs as basic physiological needs, safety and security needs, belonging and social needs, esteem and status needs, and self-actualisation and fulfilment needs. He has given a need priority order of five levels, as shown in Figure 13.3.

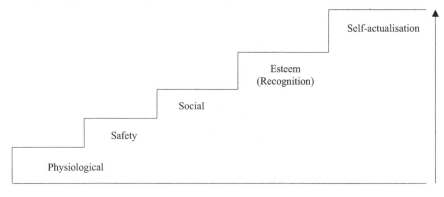

Figure 13.3 Maslow's Hierarchy of Needs

Source: Based on discussion in A. H. Maslow, 'A Theory of Human Motivation', Psychological Review 50, no. 4 (1943): 370–96, and A. H. Maslow, Motivation and Personality (New York, NY: Harper and Bros, 1954), 83.

Non-fulfilment of Needs

When a need is felt, a person tries to get it satisfied, resulting in a particular behaviour (desired one). However, because of some reasons, if the need is not satisfied, then he/she becomes
frustrated. He/she would try to modify his/her behaviour to eliminate factors responsible for the non-fulfilment of his/her need. However, the things blocking the person in achieving his/her goal are numerous, and many of them may be beyond his/her control. He/she fails to control these factors and frustration remains there. There will be great variations in the behaviour. However, this can be generalised as follows:

1. **Flight**: One way of handling a frustration is to leave the field or withdraw from the scene. Employees quit job that prove to be frustrating.
2. **Apathy**: Another method of withdrawal is showing indifference. If an employee does not leave frustrating jobs physically, he/she may remain absent psychologically, that is, reading on the job, daydreaming, thinking of almost anything except the work at hand and so on.
3. **Aggression**: A more common reaction to frustration is aggression, an act against someone or something. An employee being denied a promotion may become aggressive and verbally berate his/her superior.

Theories of Motivation

Some of the popular theories of motivation are as follows:

Maslow's Need Hierarchy Theory

Maslow was the pioneer in contributing to a systematic scheme of need hierarchy. He arrived at a conclusion, after proper research, that there are certain perceived needs of the employees and when they join organisation, they somehow believe that the needs can be better satisfied by doing so. Thus, they have a perceived expectation from the organisation they are working in. If their perceived needs are satisfied according to their expectation, they feel satisfied and motivated. On the other hand, if there is a gap between these, they become slow or they refuse to work.

The following are the important propositions advocated by A. H. Maslow about human behaviour:

1. **Man is a wanting being**: He is continuously wanting more and more. What he wants or will want depends upon what he already has. As soon as one of man's needs is satisfied, another appears at its place. This process is unending. It keeps man to work continuously.
2. **A satisfied need is not a motivator**: A man works to satisfy his needs. When a need is satisfied, it loses its capacity to induce a man to work. So only unsatisfied needs or fresh needs can motivate people to work.
3. **Man's needs have a hierarchy or importance**: Maslow thinks that a man's needs are arranged in a series of levels. As soon as needs on a lower level are by and large fulfilled, those on the next higher level will emerge and demand satisfaction. Thus, Maslow views an individual's motivation as a predetermined order of needs. Figure 13.3 shows this order or hierarchy of needs.

A brief description of these needs is as follows:

1. **Physiological needs**: At the lowest level of the hierarchy of needs are physiological needs. These are the needs which must be satisfied to maintain life. Food, air, water, rest, activity temperature and so on are included in it. Such needs have some common features: (a) they are relatively independent of each other, (b) they can be identified with a specific location, (c) they must be met repeatedly, and (d) in an affluent culture, these needs are usual rather than typical motivators.
2. **Safety needs**: These needs are often called as security needs also. These needs are concerned with physical and financial security. Physical security implies the freedom from bodily threat, and financial security is concerned with the security on the job and so on. When physiological needs of a person are reasonably fulfilled, needs at the next higher level, that is, safety needs, begin to dominate the person's behaviour.
3. **Social needs**: These needs refer to the needs of love and social security. Every individual aspires to be loved by others, to be associated with others and to get affection from his/her group members. Deprived of these things, he/she wants them as intensely as a hungry person wants food.
4. **Esteem needs**: Next in this hierarchy are esteem or egoistic needs. They include self-confidence, achievements, competence, knowledge of facts, self-respect and freedom. These all can be expressed in the three words—status, prestige and self-respect.
5. **Self-actualisation needs**: These needs are also known as self-accomplishment needs. These are the individual's needs for realising his/her own potentialities, opportunity for creativity and for continual development of his/her skill and powers.

Evaluation of Maslow's Classification of Needs

Maslow's classification of needs has been a landmark in the field of motivation. Its main utility is this that it has suggested the priority and nature of needs. This hierarchical concept of needs is important for understanding the managerial task in relation to human resources working in organisations. His approach is direct, simple and practical. He has himself pointed out that his hierarchy of needs is not rigid and fixed in order, and it is not the same for all individuals. Those individuals who are high in position in organisations are able to satisfy their high-order needs, but lower-level people are unable to do so. Once an individual has moved from a lower level of needs to a higher level of needs, lower-level needs assume a less important role.

Apart from the merits of this theory. Maslow's theory of human needs has certain weaknesses also. First, it is a general expression not specific. Second, the levels in the hierarchy are not rigidly fixed. The boundaries between them are hazy and overlapping. Third, it does not have any allowance for exceptions. Fourth, this approach overlooks the inner action of needs. An act is seldom motivated by a single need. Any act is more likely to be caused by several needs. These limitations should be kept in mind by the management when preparing any plan for motivation. Again people differ in their expectations significantly. The same need does not lead to the same response in all individuals. Hence, adversity in motivational efforts is also required.

Herzberg's Theory of Motivation

Needs priority, to a great extent, characterises the types of behaviour. It will be either directed towards achieving certain desirable positive goals or conversely towards avoiding other undesirable, negative consequences. Thus, a question may arise as to what variables are perceived to be desirable goals to achieve and, conversely, undesirable conditions to avoid. In this connection, a research study was conducted by Frederick Herzberg of Caste Western Reserve University and his associates. This study consisted of an intensive analysis of the experiences and feelings of some engineers and accountants in nine different companies in Pittsburgh area, USA. During the structured interview, they were asked to describe a few previous job experiences in which they felt 'exceptionally good' or 'exceptionally bad' about jobs. They were also asked to rate the degree at which their feelings were influenced—for better or worse—by each experience which they described.

In conducting the information from the interview, Herzberg concluded that there were two categories of needs essentially independent of each other affecting behaviour in different ways. His findings are that there are some job conditions which operate primarily to dissatisfy employees when the conditions are absent, but their presence does not motivate them in a strong way. Another set of job conditions operate primarily to build strong motivation and high job satisfaction, but their absence rarely proves strongly dissatisfying. The first set of job conditions has been referred to as maintenance of hygiene factors and second set of job conditions as motivational factors.

1. **Hygiene factors**: According to Herzberg, there are ten maintenance or hygiene factors. These are company policy and administration, technical supervision, interpersonal relationship with supervisors, interpersonal relationship with peers, interpersonal relationship with subordinates, salary, job security, personal life, working conditions and status. These are not an intrinsic part of a job, but they are related to conditions under which a job is performed. They produce no growth in a worker's output; they only prevent losses in his/her performance due to work restrictions. These maintenance factors are necessary to maintain a reasonable level of satisfaction in

employees. Any increase beyond this level will not provide any satisfaction to the employees; however, any cut below this level will dissatisfy them. As such, these are also called as dissatisfiers. Since any increase in these factors will not affect employees' level of satisfaction, these are of no use for motivating them.
2. **Motivational factors**: These factors are capable of having a positive effect on job satisfaction, often resulting in an increase in one's total output. Herzberg includes six factors that motivate employees. These are achievement, recognition, advancement, work itself, possibility of growth and responsibility. Most of these factors are related with job contents. An increase in these factors will satisfy the employees; however, any decrease will not affect their level of satisfaction. Since these increase level of satisfaction in the employees, these can be used in motivating them for higher output.

Herzberg maintains that the potency of various factors is not entirely a function of factors themselves. It is also influenced by the personality characteristics of the individuals. From this point of view, individuals may be classified into motivation seekers and maintenance seekers. The motivation seekers generally are individuals who are primarily motivated by the satisfiers, such as advancement, achievement and other factors associated with work itself. On the other hand, the maintenance seekers tend to be more concerned with factors surrounding their job, such as supervision, working conditions and pay.

Critical Analysis of the Theory

There are many related studies which support the view of Herzberg. The study of a group of supervisors[11] in utility industry substantially confirms the finding of Herzberg. Another study of scientists, engineers, manufacturing supervisors, hourly technicians and female assemblers[12] tends to confirm the results and theories from Herzberg's study. It should be added here that in this study, there are differences among the various groups of individuals (scientists, technicians and so on) about the relative importance of various satisfiers and dissatisfiers. Ishwar Dayal and Saiyadin have analysed the validity of Herzberg's theory. Their research findings of a study in the Indian context are highly supportive of Herzberg's motivation-hygiene theory.[13]

There are various studies, on the other hand, the results of which are against the model given by Herzberg. In a study,[14] it has been found that female employees perceive informal relationship with their fellow employees as motivational factor. Other studies show that motivation and maintenance factors are positively related with job satisfaction and many of the factors which are predominantly maintenance factors are considered motivational factors by lower-level employees.[15]

In India also, various such studies have been conducted. These, however, do not correspond with the research findings of Herzberg. In the study by Sawlapurkar et al.[16] of middle-level managers, it was found that for the managers, some of the maintenance factors such as job security, boss, company and working conditions were satisfiers and motivating factors. In the study by Lahiri and Srivastava[17] of middle-level managers, responsibility, domestic life, accomplishment, job and utilisation of abilities on the job were found to be motivational factors; the organisational policy and administration, promotion, salary, superior and growth were dissatisfiers. In India, more importance is attached to job security because of the fact that job opportunities are limited here considering the number of job aspirants.

Besides, in the research studies confronting the two factors—satisfiers and dissatisfiers—many writers and thinkers on the subject have argued against the theory as follows:

1. In fact, job satisfaction and dissatisfaction are two opposite points on a single continuum. Individuals on the job are affected by the change either in the job environment or in the job content.
2. Herzberg's model is 'method bound', and a number of other methods used for similar studies have shown different results not supporting his contentions. Thus, the theory has limitations in general acceptability.
3. This theory does not attach much importance to pay, status or interpersonal relationships, which are held generally as important contents of satisfaction.

In spite of these criticisms, Herzberg's model has been applied in the industry and has given several new insights. One of these insights is job enrichment, which applies to improvement of job in such a way that they have more motivators than before.

The idea behind job enrichment is to keep maintenance factors constant while increasing motivational factors. Job enrichment is different from job enlargement practised earlier to make job more attractive. In job enlargement, the basic idea is to change the job to become more complicated and varied so that monotony goes off, while job enrichment seeks to bring more motivators to the job—attaching more responsibility, more intrinsically satisfying work conditions and more power over the environment. Thus, Herzberg's model has solved the problems of managers who were wondering why their fancy HR policies failed to motivate their employees adequately.

Comparison of Herzberg and Maslow Models

When Herzberg and Maslow models are compared, it can be seen that both the models focus their attention on the relationship that is what motivates an individual. Maslow has given it in terms of need hierarchy and has suggested how people move to comparatively higher-level needs. Thus, any unsatisfied need becomes a motivating factor of the individual and governs his/her behaviour in that direction. In comparatively socially and economically advanced countries, most of the lower-order needs are fulfilled, and for people only higher-level needs remain motivating factors. This is what Herzberg has suggested. Most of his maintenance factors come under comparatively lower-order needs. Most of these needs remain satisfied and hence cease to be motivators.

However, there is a particular difference between the two models. Maslow emphasises that any unsatisfied need whether of lower order or higher order will motivate individuals. Thus, it has universality in its applicability. It can be applied to lower-level workers as well as higher-level managers. In underdeveloped countries, where, because of lack of socio-economic progress, even lower-order needs are not reasonably satisfied, such needs are motivating factors. According to Herzberg, these are hygiene factors and fail to motivate workers.

ERG Theory

Clayton Alderfer[18] propagated a new theory of motivation. He took Maslow's theory as a starting point and stated that Maslow's five levels of needs can be amalgamated into three: existence, relatedness and growth needs. Existence needs include Maslow's physiological and safety needs as well as money, relatedness needs include Maslow's social and esteem needs, and growth needs include needs like Maslow's self-actualisation needs. Alderfer's theory provides a more realistic explanation of everyday work behaviour than any other theory of motivation based on needs.

Goal-setting Theory

This theory, developed by Edwin Locke, suggests that the process of goal-setting in itself is motivating, provided the goal is perceived as realistic, just as a challenging task, provided it is achievable and is more motivating than an easy task.[19]

Vroom's Expectancy Theory

Victor Vroom[20] in 1964 presented a model about the process of employee motivation, known as expectancy theory (see Figure 13.4). Vroom argues that motivation is a product of the values one seeks and one's expectation of the probability that a certain action will lead to those values. According to Keith Davis,[21] an employee performs a kind of cost–benefit analysis. If the estimated benefit is enough to justify the cost of greater effort, then he/she is likely to put in greater efforts. In other words, we can say that before expending a given level of efforts, an employee would be asking, 'If I make a strong effort on this job, will a superior level of performance be achieved? And if I do achieve such an outstanding level of performance, what kinds of rewards or negative outcomes will occur?' Besides, the employee also needs to know how valuable that outcome or performance level is to him/her. Vroom calls this value a valence.

Thus, the motivation or force behind a specific level of work performance will be a function of two perceptions on the part of the employee:

1. The probability or perceived likelihood that certain outcomes will result from the person's effort.
2. The value (valence) or utility of such outcomes to the employee[22]

Theory of High Expectations

According to this theory, an executive's expectations are the key to subordinate's performance and development. The way an executive treats his/her subordinates is definitely

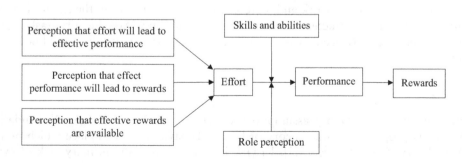

Figure 13.4 Expectancy Model

influenced by what he/she expects of them. In other words, we can say that a subordinate's performance is likely to fall or rise according to the executive's expectations.

Praise Theory

According to Professor Skinner's praise theory, personnel perform better in psychological satisfaction on the job when they are appreciated for their good work. Appreciation of positive achievements of a worker creates a pleasant environment in which the worker is likely to strive for more recognition by doing better work.

Attribution Theory

This theory involves finding out as to what people attribute their success or failure. Their attribution may then influence their future behaviour by changing their perception of the relation between effort, performance and reward.

Power Theory

A large number of managers are considerably motivated by power. Managers and administrators have a high need for power and a high need for achievement. The power attached with a particular office motivates the aspirants to put in their best so that they may be able to realise their objectives.

McGregor's Theory X and Theory Y

The management's action of motivating human beings in the organisation, according to McGregor, involves certain assumptions, generalisations and hypotheses relating to human behaviour and human nature. These assumptions may be neither consciously crystallised nor overtly stated; however, these serve the purpose of predicting human behaviour. The basic assumptions about human behaviour may differ considerably because of the complexity of factors influencing this behaviour. McGregor has characterised these assumptions in his Theory X and Theory Y (for details, see Theory X and Theory Y discussed in Chapter 1 of this book).

Job Characteristics Theory[23]

This theory, developed by Richard Hackman and Greg Old Hem, states that employees will be more motivated to work and more satisfied with their jobs to the extent that jobs contain certain core characteristics: skill variety, autonomy, task identity, task significance, feedback, experienced meaningfulness, experienced responsibility and knowledge results.

Theory Z

Criticising the contradictory assumptions under Theory X and Theory Y, Lyndall F. Urwick has proposed another theory of human behaviour at workplace which he has called Theory Z (see Figure 13.5). Urwick has viewed that the primary task of every

Employee Motivation

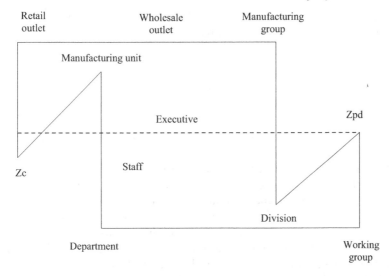

Figure 13.5 Model as Given by Urwick

manager is to make or distribute goods or services at prices which the consumers are able and willing to pay. And it is to this end that he/she must direct the efforts of those associated with him/her. In this context, he has given the following propositions:

1. Management is responsible for organising the elements of productive enterprise—money, materials, equipment, people—in the interest of economic ends.
2. In a free society, economic ends are determined by the choices of innumerable individuals in their capacity as consumers.
3. This involves a network of decisions and communications through which management postulates leadership.
4. Management groups these choices as (a) to facilitate economic production and distribution and (b) to enable these same people, in their capacity as producers or distributers, to satisfy their needs.
5. In a handicraft economy, the consumer communicates directly with the producer, while in modern machine economy, there are at least eight points at which consumer choice may be misinterpreted in terms of producer/distributor needs. A person has to move from point to point all round to Z instead of having direct contact.
6. A person as a consumer insists that the latest products of science and technology are at his/her disposal; he/she seeks change.
7. A person, as a producer or distributor, is not resistant to organisations' needs. But change threatens his/her human needs if it suggests the following:
   a. Loss of employment—physical and safety needs
   b. Change of working patterns—social needs
   c. Elimination of positions to which he/she may have aspired—egoistic and self-fulfilment needs

8. Management can overcome these difficulties of complex communications by devoting more attention to morale. This involves the following:

   a. Discipline—that is, the system of communication is precise and accepted by all concerned.
   b. Confidence—that is, each individual is assured that the institution is beneficent and will safeguard his/her needs.[24]

In order to clarify his propositions and human behaviour, Urwick has given a model which is in the shape of Z as shown in Figure 13.5.

According to him, the human behaviour in economic undertakings is best expressed not by the symbol X or Y but by the symbol Z. The whole economic process consists in relating the behaviour of the individual consumer at the top-left-hand corner of the Z (Zc) to the behaviour of the same individual as a producer or distributor at the bottom-right-hand corner of Z (Zpd). In between lie the two arms and the diagonal of the Z, representing a whole network of intermediate decisions involved in translating the behaviour Zc into behaviour of the same individual as Zp or Zd.

Urwick indicates that the individuals would be ready to direct their behaviour towards organisational goals under two conditions:

1. Each individual should know the organisational goals precisely and the contribution which his/her attempts are making towards the realisation of these.
2. Every individual should be confident that the realisation of organisational goals is going to affect his/her need satisfaction positively and that none of his/her needs are threatened or frustrated by membership of the organisation. Theory Z takes into account the organisational variables in shaping the behaviour of individuals. Thus, a particular individual may behave differently in different organisational conditions. From this point of view, the theory presents a more realistic picture of human behaviour in the organisation rather than making assumptions about human behaviour. Thus, the success of any organisation depends ultimately on the morale of all those engaged in it. The theory, however, could not get much popularity in management literature because such propositions have been given in one form or the other by different theories.

Important Elements of a Sound Motivational System

A critical analysis of the various motivational models reveals that there is wide scope of variability in the factors of motivation. As such, management will be in dilemma as to how to motivate their employees to get best results. Moreover, these models have been given by foreign contributors which are more applicable to their industrial system. In our country, because of different socio-economic conditions, these models are applicable with certain reservations. Thus, while adopting a motivational model, some important considerations should be kept in mind. These can be summarised as follows:

1. **Adequate motivation**: The motivation system should be adequate covering the entire human force in the organisation, and it should cover entire activities of the workforce. Sometimes, the presence of a motivational factor fails to produce any effective result, particularly when its amount is too small. In such a case, its energetic force should be increased so that it motivates strongly.

2. **Analysis of motives**: A good motivation system also attempts at analysing the factors which motivate the employees in the prevailing organisational environment. A study of the various needs of the employees, degree of intensity and the prospective consequences of satisfying them or continuing them dissatisfied on output should be conducted.
3. **Simplicity in motivational system**: The system should be simple in terms of both its understanding by the employees and its applicability in the organisation. Employees' efforts are directed to goal only when they perceive that a particular goal exists and this requires a particular type of efforts. The system should be simple to be adopted by the organisation at various levels.
4. **Uneven motivation**: In the organisation, all the employees are not of the same type. They differ in education, attitude, ambition and so on. Thus, more educated, ambitious people can be motivated up to very high level, while others cannot be. If such employees are motivated beyond a certain limit, this may create frustration in them as overloaded or unachievable goals create frustration.

Incentives

Management is the art of getting the work done through and with the people in formally organised groups. So the main task of the management is to motivate the employees to contribute their maximum towards the accomplishment of work. Generally, it is seen that workers produce only 60–70% of their capacity. However, if they are given some additional attraction or, in other words, incentives of any kind, they work more. This increase in their work is due to the incentive given by the management to the workers. As a matter of fact, work result and incentives have direct or positive correlation with each other.

Meaning and Definition of Incentives

The needs of individuals serve as driving forces in human behaviour. In the context of these needs, management tries to govern the behaviour of employees in satisfying their needs. The objects which are perceived to satisfy their needs are called incentives.

Dr Earnest Dichter has defined 'incentive' as follows: 'Incentive is a stimulus or a reason for producing action. Almost all of the human motivations can serve as incentives—anxiety, worries, fear, hope, prestige, money, security and so on. All are actual or potential incentives in our daily life'. Thus, incentive is a stimulus for more work. It incites action and motivates the people to do more and more work to increase their efficiency and to learn newer techniques of work.

Classification of Incentives

Incentives can be classified as follows:

1. Positive and negative incentives
2. Individual and group incentives
3. Financial and non-financial incentives

Positive and Negative Incentives

Positive incentives are those incentives which induce a worker to work more. They exercise good effect on the morale and efficiency of the workers. Appreciation, recognition and promotions are the frequent examples of such incentives.

On the other hand, negative incentives incite to production by creating feeling of fines, fear and punishment. They motivate an individual to abstain from doing something, such as avoiding breakages and absenteeism.

Individual and Group Incentives

When any incentive scheme is applied on personal basis or individual to individual, it is called individual incentive. This has the objective to give more profit to one who works more.

On the other hand, group incentives are given to the group as a whole, to the people of a department or to all employees working within the organisation. Profit-sharing, co-partnership and annual bonus schemes are the examples of group incentives.

Financial and Non-financial Incentives

Both financial and non-financial incentives are powerful motives at their own places. A detailed description of these incentives is given further.

Financial Incentives

In the context of existing economic system, money has become a means not only to satisfy the physical needs of daily life but also of obtaining social position and power. Human beings first take care of their primary needs of food, shelter, clothing and so on. Since money has the exchange value—we can fulfil these needs in exchange of money—it becomes a basic incentive for individuals. The organisations offer wages which become incentives for individuals to join the organisation. The wage structure should be such that it motivates the present and prospective employees of the organisation.

The traditional management thinkers have emphasised financial incentives to get best out of an individual. These financial incentives may be classified into two parts: individual and collective.

1. **Individual financial incentives**: This group of incentives includes all such plans which induce an individual to achieve higher output to earn higher financial rewards. Piece rate wages, Taylor's differential piece rate system and Halsey's efficiency plan are some of the examples of such incentives. The basic assumption behind these incentives is that an individual will be motivated for higher output to earn more money which satisfies his/her needs.
2. **Collective financial incentives**: This group of incentives tries to motivate individuals collectively. The basic idea of these incentives is the same as of individual financial incentives; however, the employees are given these collectively. Examples are bonus, profit-sharing and pension plan.

The financial incentives grouped into the aforesaid two points are shown in the chart depicted in Figure 13.6.

Non-financial Incentives

Financial incentives are used to motivate employees for higher work. However, individuals have various needs which they want to satisfy while working in the organisation.

Employee Motivation 455

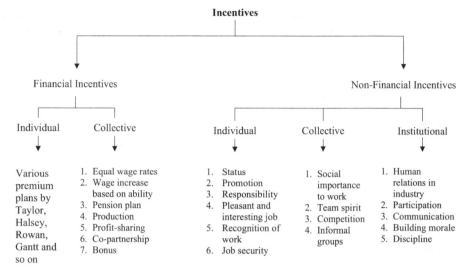

Figure 13.6 Financial and Non-financial Incentives

People at comparatively higher level of managerial hierarchy attach more importance to social-psychological needs, which cannot be satisfied by money alone. Thus, management, in addition to the financial incentives, provides non-financial incentives to motivate people in the organisation. The connotation of non-financial incentives does not mean that the organisation has nothing to spend on these. However, the emphasis of non-financial incentives is to provide psychological and emotional satisfaction rather than financial satisfaction. For example, if an individual gets promotion in the organisation, then it satisfies him/her psychologically more—that is, he/she gets better status, more challenging job, authority and so on than financially as he/she gets more pay also by way of promotion. The non-financial incentives can be grouped into three parts, as shown in the (Figure 13.6), and are explained further:

1. **Individual non-financial incentives**: These are incentives which motivate people on individual basis. Various forms of individual incentives are as follows:

    a. **Status**: Status, in general terms, is the ranking of people in the society. In the organisational context, it means the ranking of positions, rights and duties in the formal organisations' structure. Good status motivates the people to put more work and do hard work.

    b. **Promotion**: Promotion is defined as a movement to a position in which responsibilities and presumably prestige are increased. Promotion satisfies the needs of human beings in the organisation from various angles, such as money, prestige and status. The avenues of promotion, if they exist in the organisation, play an important role in motivating the employees.

    c. **Responsibility and challenge**: Many people prefer challenging and responsible jobs rather than monotonous and less responsible jobs. The management should provide such opportunities also by making the work challenging and more responsible.

d. **Making job pleasant and interesting**: The work should be made enjoyable and pleasant. If it is so designed, it will allow the employees to satisfy their natural instincts. This creates interest in the work and employees feel motivated.
   e. **Recognition of work**: Most people have a need for a high evaluation of themselves. They want that their work should be recognised by others. Recognition means acknowledgement with a sense of appreciation of work. When such appreciation is given to the work performed by employees, they feel motivated to perform work at similar or higher level.
   f. **Job security**: Job security and stability also play an important role in motivating the people. If job is secured, then worker will demonstrate more efficiency, will be highly motivated and will give more production.

2. **Collective non-financial incentives**: Employees work in groups. Their efficiency, aspirations, behaviour norms and standards are affected by the group. If the group in general is efficient, an employee tends to become more efficient. Hence, group incentives are also important. Some of the collective non-financial incentives are as follows:
   a. **Social importance of work**: People generally prefer a work which is socially acceptable. If the society gives importance and praise to the work, people like to perform. Sometimes people prefer a job of high social importance, even though the financial compensation would be less. The reason is simple. People have to live in society, and by performing a job of high social importance, they derive satisfaction of being important in the society.
   b. **Team spirit**: The management should encourage team spirit, that is, to work in cooperation and coordination. Teamwork is a coordinated action by a cooperative small group in regular contract, wherein members contribute responsibly and enthusiastically towards task achievement. If there is a team spirit among the employees, they will try to put in maximum efforts to achieve the objectives.
   c. **Competition**: Sometimes, for providing incentives to employees, competitions are organised between different individuals or different groups. There may be a case of self-competition where an individual tries to improve his/her earlier performance. When an individual performs very well because of any such competition, he/she should be given some advantages, not necessarily in terms of money, but it may be in terms of recognition, prestige, praise and so on. However, this method has a negative consequence also. Although all the employees try to put in maximum efforts, all of them cannot win. As such, they may feel frustration and their efficiency will go down. Hence, there is a need to have only healthy competitions.
   d. **Informal groups**: When people work together, they develop some sort of affiliation among themselves. These relationships are not officially prescribed but created on the basis of certain factors, both personality factors of the employees and other social factors. The creation of these informal groups provides social satisfaction to employees at workplace. People feel to achieve a sense of belongingness and security. Management should provide the way of creation of such informal groups so long as they are not detrimental to organisational efficiency and objectives because sometimes the informal groups may go against the interest of the organisation.

3. **Institutional non-financial incentives**: The incentives are related with the environmental factors in the organisation. Conducive and congenial atmosphere of the organisation motivates employees to produce better results. The following incentives fall in this category:

   a. **Human relations in industry**: Human relations in the industry are related with the policy to be adopted in the organisation to develop a sense of belongingness in the employees, improve their efficiency and treat them as human beings and not merely a factor of production. The emphasis is on providing greater satisfaction, both physiological and psychological, by creating such environment in the organisation where employees can work efficiently and pleasantly. In such an environment, employees are motivated to stay with the organisation and they also adopt productive behaviour.

   b. **Participation**: The superior–subordinate relationship emphasises that superiors take the decisions and subordinates implement them. However, in such a decision-taking process, subordinates do not feel very enthusiastic in implementing the decisions. As such, the subordinates should also be associated with the decision-making process. This not only motivates subordinates to take prompt and proper action on decision implementation but also makes them responsible for anything which goes wrong.

   c. **Communication**: Communication is the lifeblood of an organisation. The complex nature and big size of organisations require greater specialisation and division of work. Thus, for a particular goal, total activities are divided into parts and subparts to share the information about their functioning among themselves. This is done through communication, as communication is the process of passing ideas and understanding from one person or group to another person or group. A free and adequate flow of communication is necessary. This, besides providing base for successful organisational functioning, provides satisfaction to individuals in the organisation as they want to be informed properly about the matters concerning their interests. Thus, free flow of communication in the organisation motivates employees properly.

   d. **Building morale**: Although there are various definitions of morale, it can be defined as the attitudes of individuals and groups towards work environment and towards voluntary cooperation to the full extent of their ability in the best interest of the organisation. Generally, high level of morale results in high productivity. High morale of employees depends on the various facilities provided to them to satisfy their physiological and psychological needs, the latter being more important. However, management should attempt to measure employees' morale. If the morale level is low, then the factors should be analysed and proper action taken.

   e. **Discipline**: Discipline is, in essence, obedience, application, behaviour and outward respect shown by employees. It is employees' self-control to meet an organisation's standards and objectives. Management has the primary responsibility for developing and maintaining discipline. It maintains discipline by applying standards in a consistent, fair and flexible manner. This provides employees to behave in a particular direction as any employee whose behaviour is inconsistent with standards invites disciplinary action. Maintenance of proper discipline also motivates employees.

Financial vs Non-financial Incentives

This is an important, growing and alive controversy that whether financial incentives are more important or non-financial incentives are more significant. Some authors as well as practising managers give more importance to financial incentives. They claim that money in itself has no value for a person, but in the context of the existing economic organisation, money has become a means not only of satisfying the physical needs of daily life but also of obtaining social position and power. For this reason, financial incentives have assumed great importance. On getting money, a person first turns his/her attention towards the things he/she needs—food, clothes, house and so on. Then he/she satisfies the needs of health and education. Once these needs have been satisfied, he/she tries to obtain more and more luxuries. But some individuals continue to work even after having reached this stage because their social prestige and power increase with their bank balance. Individuals with this lust for money continue their search throughout their life, for this search never ends. People who do not feel any specific need for power do not like to earn money once their needs and comforts have been taken care of. In the same way, economic loss has diverse effects. Loss of money deprives the poor person of his/her bread, while the rich person loses his/her prestige, although he/she does not suffer from hunger. Despite this, the poor person suffers less on account of this psychological loss because only his/her body is directly affected. On the other hand, the rich person suffers a blow to his/her social prestige and self-respect, which is a mental injury.

Money has become the means of satisfying many needs because it is the medium of exchange. If social position and power are not based on money in any society, then money will cease to be a powerful incentive. Money is the most important incentive in a society where a person's success is measured by the money he/she earns. But where this does not happen, money is not a powerful incentive. This analysis shows the importance of financial incentives, which are offered in industries in two ways—either in the form of salary increase or in the form of occasional bonus. The financial incentives have the effect of increasing production and inducing the worker to work harder and better.

Exhibit 13.5   Motivating Staff in Tough Times

1. Recognise hard work
2. Balanced communication
3. Top management engagement
4. Circulate success stories
5. Lend an ear

Source: The Economic Times, 31 January 2017.

On the other hand, experts claim that 'man does not live by bread alone'. Hence, money cannot act as the only motivator. The workers, being human beings, need non-financial incentives more. Non-financial incentives satisfy their social, psychological and personal needs, and this satisfaction makes them happy and efficient. Nowadays, workers are more conscious as regards to their personality, behaviour of management, self-respect and self-satisfaction. These things cannot be provided by money only. Hence, non-financial incentives become a must. As a matter of fact, any one type of incentives cannot do in the absence of the other type of incentives. As both right and left feet are necessary for a person to walk smoothly, both types of incentives are necessary to establish industrial peace in the business.

Motivation Staff in Tough Times

It is very important that organisations keep their employees motivated in tough times. In this regard, the steps recommended in Exhibit 13.5 are suggested.

Group Incentives

Incentives can be of various types: positive and negative incentives, individual and group incentives, monetary and non-monetary incentives, and so on. When incentives are classified on the basis of number of the employees to whom the schemes are being applied, these can be personal/individual and group/collective incentives. Individual incentives are provided to the individuals in different ways, while group incentives are applied to a group of employees collectively. From monetary point of view, group incentives may be of both types: financial and non-financial; inviting suggestions from workers and workers' participation in management (hereafter WPM) are two peculiar examples of non-financial group incentives. Profit-sharing, distributing annual bonus and distributing prizes at department are some examples of group incentives.

Advantages of Group Incentives

Group incentives give the following benefits as compared to individual incentives:

1. They develop the group feeling and sense of cooperation.
2. Group has no quick demand of job changes, and everybody is engaged in the completion of the collective objective.
3. Group incentives put off the problems of absence and late coming.
4. Because of group incentives, other managerial problems like transfer decrease and labour problems come down.
5. The labour costs and production overheads are reduced.

Chapter Review

1. Motivation refers to the way in which urges, drives, aspirations, strivings or needs direct, control or explain the behaviour of human beings. Motivation is an inner impulse, causing a person to action. Motivated employees produce more, their rates of absenteeism and turnover remain low, and they are always willing to adapt. Motivation is, therefore, the central task of management.
2. The main steps in the process of motivation include sizing up, preparing a set of motivating tools, selecting and applying motivational plans, and feedback. Motivation may be positive or negative, extrinsic or intrinsic and financial or non-financial. Motivation is, however, a psychological and social problem.

3. Techniques or methods of motivation include monetary techniques, job-based techniques and sensitivity training. Techniques are also classified as financial and non-financial techniques or plans.
4. Motivational factors in the case of both the executives and subordinates are almost the same, but in the case of the former, competitive performance and pride in a job well done are equally and sometimes even more powerful motivators.
5. Motives are needs that drive a person to work. They are the initiating and sustaining forces of behaviour. Needs may be either primary or secondary needs.
6. Theories of motivation include Maslow's need hierarchy theory, Herzberg's two-factor theory, ERG theory, goal-setting theory, Vroom's expectancy theory, theory of high expectations, praise theory, attribution theory, power theory, McGregor's Theory X and Theory Y, job characteristic theory and Theory Z. All theories have their own positive and negative points.
7. Work results and incentives have direct or positive correlation with each other. Incentives can be positive or negative incentives, individual or group incentives and financial and non-financial incentives—all with their merits and demerits.

Key Terms

belonging and social needs
co-partnership
ego needs
employee turnover rate
esteem and status needs
existence needs
extrinsic/external motivation
financial incentives
financial motivation
fringe benefits
growth needs
Hawthorne experiments
human relations
hygiene factors
informal groups

intrinsic/internal motivation
job enlargement
job enrichment
job loading
job rotation
job satisfaction
maintenance factors
MBO
motivation
motivators
negative motivation
non-financial incentives
non-financial motivation
participative management
pension plan

physiological needs
positive incentives
positive motivation
primary needs
productivity
profit-sharing
relatedness needs
safety and security needs
secondary needs
self-actualisation needs
self-motivation
sensitivity training
valence

Discussion Questions

1. Examine critically the concept of motivation and also why motivation is said to be the central task of management of an organisation.
2. List and describe the main features of all the important theories of motivation and find out which theory/theories of motivation is/are more popular and why.

3. What are the types of incentives and also why non-financial incentives are equally important to motivate employees?
4. Identify and explain the main techniques and methods of motivation.
5. Write an exhaustive note on executive motivation.
6. List and describe the main elements of a sound motivational system.
7. Differentiate between individual incentives and group incentives.
8. Examine critically the concept of self-motivation.
9. Distinguish between primary needs and secondary needs, quoting suitable examples.
10. Discuss the rules of motivation as suggested by Michael J. Jucius.

Individual and Group Activities

1. As an individual, visit some big organisation and discuss with its HR officials whether its management practises positive motivation or negative motivation or both and why. Prepare a brief report on the whole discussion.
2. As a group of three members, discuss with the union officials of some big organisation to find out whether the members of their union prefer financial incentives or non-financial incentives and why.
3. In a group of three members, visit some big organisation and talk to some senior employees. Find out to what extent they appear to be self-motivated.
4. As a group of two members, visit a large manufacturing organisation. Discuss with both the HR officials and trade union officials and find out how the organisation promotes non-financial motivation.
5. As an individual, discuss with some HR official of some big organisation and find out the existing problem being confronted by the management in motivating the employees.

Application Case 13.1

Frequency of Promotion as a Source of Motivation

Mathew, a BTech from NIT, Kurukshetra, had joined ABC Company as an assistant engineer (mechanical) 13 years back. After three years, per the promotion policy of the company that if the performance of an assistant engineer is consistently satisfactory, he/she will be promoted to the next higher post after the completion of three years, he was promoted as an engineer (mechanical), and after the completion of another three years, he was promoted as senior engineer (mechanical). When he completed nine years of his service from the date of joining, he was promoted as assistant manager (production), and after the completion of another three years, he was promoted as deputy manager (production), and his salary was raised to 80,000 per month.

Thompson, a classmate of Mathew at the same NIT, had joined another company as assistant engineer (mechanical) where, per the promotion policy of the company, every assistant engineer is promoted as senior engineer after the completion of six years of satisfactory service and is further promoted as deputy manager after the completion of another six years of satisfactory service. As such, Thompson, after the completion of his 12 years of service, also became deputy manager (production) at a salary of 80,000 per month.

Thus, after the completion of 12 years of their service, both Mathew and Thompson were enjoying the same position and salary.

However, it was felt that Mathew was more motivated and also more satisfied in his personal life than Thompson throughout their service of 12 years in their respective companies.

Questions

1. What could have been the reason for the consistent more motivation in his company and also more satisfaction in his personal life in the case of Mathew as compared to that of Thompson in his company? Discuss.
2. Do you approve of the promotion policy of the company in which Mathew has been working or of the company where Thompson is employed? Give arguments for your stand.

Notes

1 T. R. Mitchell and A. E. Mickey, 'The Meaning of Money: An Individual Difference Perspectives', *Academy of Management Review* 24, no. 3 (July 1999): 568–78.
2 D. L. Levine, 'Piece Rate, Output Restrictions, and Conformism', *Journal of Economic Psychology* 13, no. 3 (1992): 473–89.
3 S. L. McShane, M. A. V. Glinow, and R. R. Sharma, *Organisational Behaviour* (New Delhi: Tata McGraw-Hill Education Pvt Ltd, 2008), 200.
4 Jucius, *Personnel Management*, 41–42.
5 Ibid., 42–44.
6 P. Malhotra, 'To Our Readers', *Human Capital* 17, no. 9 (February 2014): 8.
7 Flippo, *Principles of Personnel Management*, 74.
8 For details, see Robert Janson, 'Job Design Fir Quality', *The Personnel Administrator* 19, no. 7 (October 1974): 15.
9 'There cannot be a single source of motivation: a system of motivation is required—a coordinated set of inducement, positive and negative, available for selective application to elicit the best efforts of individual'. (Koontz and O'Donnell)
10 See A. H. Maslow, *Motivation and Personality* (New York, NY: Harper & Bros., 1954).
11 M. M. Schwartz, E. Jenusaitis, and H. Stark, 'Motivational Factors among Supervisors in the Utility Industry', *Personnel Psychology* 16, no. 1 (1963): 45–53.
12 M. S. Myers, 'Who Are You Motivated Workers?', *Harvard Business Review* 42 (January–February 1964): 73–88.
13 I. Dayal and M. S. Saiyadin, 'Cross-Cultural Validation of Motivation Hygiene Theory', *Indian Journal of Industrial Relations* 6, no. 2 (October 1970): 171–83.
14 Richard Centres and E. Bugental Daphne, 'Intrinsic and Extrinsic Job Motivation among Different Segments of the Working Population', *Journal of Applied Psychology* 50, no. 3 (June 1966): 193–97.
15 Keith Davis, *Human Relations at Work* (New York, NY: McGraw-Hill, 1967), 57.

16 M. P. Sawlapurkar, C. P. Dusad, and D. V. Khare, 'Job Motivation of Middle Managers', *Indian Journal of Applied Psychology* 5, no. 2 (1968), 243.
17 D. K. Lahiri and S. Srivastava, 'Determinants of Satisfaction in Middle Management', *Journal of Applied Psychology* 51, no. 3 (1967): 251–65.
18 For details, see C. P. Alderfer, *Existence, Relatedness and Growth: Human Needs. Organisational Settings* (New York: The Free Press, 1972).
19 For details, see David Guest, 'Motivation after Maslow', *Personnel Management* 8, no. 3 (March 1976): 29–32.
20 See Victor H. Vroom, *Work and Motivation* (New York, NY: John Wiley & Sons, 1964).
21 Davis, *Human Relations at Work*, 35.
22 Vroom, *Work and Motivation*.
23 For details, see Gomez-Mejia, Balkin, and Cardy, *Managing Human Resources*, 61–62.
24 Urwick, *The Elements of Administration*, 14–15.

14 Job Satisfaction, Employee Morale and Communication

Learning Objectives

After studying this chapter, you should be able to do the following:

1. Define the term 'job satisfaction' and explain factors related to job satisfaction.
2. Explain the ways and means to increase job satisfaction.
3. Explain how we can measure job satisfaction.
4. Define the term 'employee morale'.
5. List and describe the factors contributing to high morale.
6. List and describe the methods of measuring morale.
7. Define the term 'communication' and explain the elements of communication process.
8. List and describe the barriers to communication.
9. List and describe the types of communication.
10. Explain how the effectiveness of communication is evaluated.

Job Satisfaction

Meaning and Definition

Job satisfaction has been a subject of hot chase by researchers. There have been more than 3,000 published studies on job satisfaction during about last three decades. Job satisfaction is the attitude one has towards his/her job.[1] Stated another way, it is one's affective response to the job.[2] It is concerned with the 'feeling' one has towards his/her job. The importance of job satisfaction is fairly evident from the fact that it boosts the morale of a worker. If a worker is not satisfied with his/her work, then both the quantity and the quality of his/her output will suffer. If his/her job satisfaction increases, then there is an improvement in both the quality and the quantity of production. Factories in which the workers are satisfied with their work are also characterised by a high morale. However, job satisfaction is dependent on one's ability to execute the job well (see Exhibit 14.1).

> **Exhibit 14.1 Ability and Job Satisfaction**
>
> According to Kruger and Smit, in their book *Basic Psychology for HR Practitioners*, an individual's job satisfaction is a direct result of his or her ability to execute tasks.
>
> Source: A. Poddar, 'Empower, Execute and Excel', *Human Capital* 17, no. 9 (February 2014): 31.

Factors Relating to Job Satisfaction

Job satisfaction is derived from and is caused by many interrelated factors which cannot be completely isolated from one another for analysis. Besides, these factors may also change from one situation to another. Some such important factors are discussed further.

Personal Factors

1. **Sex:** Other things remaining the same, women are more satisfied with their work than men because, relatively, women are less ambitious.
2. **Age:** Usually young workers have higher level of job satisfaction, but by and by it shows a declining trend. However, certain studies on the subject have revealed positive results between advancing age and job satisfaction.
3. **Number of dependents:** The greater the number of dependents one has, the less job satisfaction he/she will have. Financial stress causes greater job dissatisfaction.
4. **Time on job:** Job satisfaction is relatively higher at the beginning of career, but by and by it starts dropping down by the time one reaches between fifth and eighth years on the job and surprisingly again starts going high with more time on the job.
5. **Level and range of intelligence:** Research findings reveal that the relation of intelligence to job satisfaction depends upon the level and range of intelligence and the challenge of the job.
6. **Level of education:** Research studies reveal different results on the relationship of education to job satisfaction. For example, some studies have revealed that less educated people have more job satisfaction, while the findings of some other studies have been contrary to it.
7. **Attitude:** People having positive attitude have more job satisfaction.
8. **Personality:** People having positive traits in their personality usually have job satisfaction.

> **Exhibit 14.2 Research Findings**
>
> Gallups' 142 country study on the State of the Global Workplace revealed that, per the State of American Workplace Report, 70% US workers don't like their job, creating an environment where many workers are emotionally disconnected from their workplace and less productive.
>
> Source: S. C. Saha, 'Enroute to Employee Engagement', *Human Capital* 17, no. 10 (March 2014): 44.

Factors Inherent in a Job

1. **Nature of the job:** If the type of work involved in a job is of varied nature, then it brings more job satisfaction than does a job having routine work; some jobs do not appeal to the job holders (see Exhibit 14.2).
2. **Skill required:** In case a job involves high skill requirement, it gives more job satisfaction than does a job in which skill demands are at a lower level.
3. **Occupational status:** Research studies have revealed that jobs having high social status and prestige give more job satisfaction.
4. **Size of the plant:** Usually, in small plants, people get more job satisfaction because of attention they receive from the management and also due to respect they get for their ability.
5. **Geography:** Workers in large towns are less satisfied with their jobs as compared to those working in small towns.

Factors Controllable by Management

1. **Security:** The higher the security of job, security of retirement benefits, security of life and security of finance provided by the management, the greater will be the job satisfaction to the employees.
2. **Fringe benefits:** Although the provision for fringe benefits affects the job satisfaction, these benefits occupy low position of importance.
3. **Co-workers:** The job satisfaction is likely to be more if the co-workers are good. Hence, management and workers all should try to create and maintain good human relations in the industry to create friendly environment.
4. **Flow of communication:** In case communication flows adequately and smoothly, workers are likely to have more job satisfaction.
5. **Working conditions:** Where working conditions are better, workers get more job satisfaction because good working conditions leave an impact on the mind of the worker.
6. **Responsibility:** Those jobs in which a lot of responsibility is involved give more job satisfaction, especially to the educated and highly educated people.
7. **Supervision:** Jobs supervised by good-tempered and human-relations-oriented supervisors are source of more job satisfaction, whereas ill-tempered supervisors become the source of dissatisfaction to the workers.
8. **Wages:** Jobs carrying attractive wages and pay scales give more job satisfaction. Wages are of more significance so long as physiological needs are not fulfilled.
9. **Opportunities for advancement:** Employees, especially the ambitious and potential ones, get more job satisfaction in jobs offering opportunities for advancement.

Increasing Job Satisfaction

In case the employers want to create job satisfaction for their employees, they should keep the following things into consideration:

1. **Grievance-handling procedure:** It is desirable that the complaints of the workers are heard patiently, and the problems solved as far as possible. Factories in which the workers' demands/grievances are not handled properly suffer because the workers lose confidence in the management and become frustrated.

2. **Satisfactory future**: Every worker is definitely concerned about his/her future prospects. If the factory rules clearly lay down the conditions for promotion and advancement, and if the worker gets the expected promotion and improvement in pay scales at the right time, then he/she feels more satisfied with his/her job and becomes confident of his/her future. If on the other hand, the worker feels that even good work will not be rewarded, then he/she becomes frustrated and slack in his/her work.
3. **Testing the worker's ability and progress**: Every worker, whether in a factory or in an office, desires that he/she should be paid according to his/her ability. If he/she has undergone some new training or has increased his/her ability to work in some way, then he/she should be compensated for his/her better ability through a rise in salary. Organisations in which the management keeps an eye on the ability and progress of its workers normally provide a high degree of job satisfaction to their workers. It is necessary that the management should give the workers some opportunity of progressing higher and higher. If, on the other hand, the organisation does not pay any attention to the abilities and increased efficiency of its staff, it suffers in the long run because the workers also lose interest in their jobs and do not often try to improve their level of efficiency. This happens because they feel that an increase in qualifications or efficiency is not related to progress or promotion.
4. **Respect for creative suggestions**: Generally speaking, a worker working under a particular set of conditions is best qualified to say how and where improvements can be made. If workers are encouraged to suggest ways and means of improving productivity and the conditions of work, they often come with very valuable ideas. This helps in increasing job satisfaction because when the worker is praised for giving a good practical idea, he/she tends to pay more attention to his/her work in to win more praise. If suggestions are neglected, then the worker feels dissatisfied and over a period, his/her creativity is killed.
5. **Cordial analysis or evaluation of work performance**: In every organisation, the manager or the supervisor has to offer critical comments of the work performed by the worker because he/she must point out the worker's mistakes and try to eliminate them. If this criticism is offered in a cordial and friendly way, more as a suggestion than criticism, then his/her job satisfaction is also thereby maintained. But if the worker is humiliated or bitterly criticised for his/her mistakes, then he/she loses his/her peace of mind.
6. **Increase in wages**: Rules governing increases in salary should be clear and explicit and should be acted upon impartially and regularly. If the worker gets the anticipated increase in salary at the right time, then he/she feels satisfied with his/her job. If this does not happen, then dissatisfaction is the result. Increase in salary is, in fact, the most important factor in job satisfaction.
7. **Praise for good performance**: If workers are not praised for exceptional performance in their work, then they lose interest in it and, as a result, the organisation suffers. Generally, the worker prefers to work well and remain occupied than merely to pass the time allotted to him/her. If he/she is also encouraged in his/her work by an occasional word of praise and respect, then he/she is further motivated to maintain a high level of efficiency and in fact to improve it. If he/she is not praised for his/her work, then his/her enthusiasm and zeal immediately fall.
8. **Promotion according to ability**: In every organisation, some people get retired after completion of their service period, leaving scope for promotion for the junior employees. If promotion is based upon the ability of the worker, then the worker's

mental satisfaction is maintained. If, on the other hand, promotion depends upon other factors such as casteism and personal favour, then the worker's interest in his/her work declines.

9. **Proper quantum of work**: If job satisfaction is to be maintained, it is essential that the expected quantity of work does not exceed the individual's ability to complete it. If he/she needs to work more than he/she comfortably can for a long time, then he/she is bound to become disgusted, depressed and tired.
10. **Equal wages for equal work**: Labour unions in almost every industry are demanding that there should be equal pay for equal work. In any factory or office, a worker must be paid as much as other workers are being paid in his/her or other organisations for similar work. The worker feels satisfied if this equality is maintained. If it is not, then the worker loses his/her satisfaction.
11. **Freedom to seek help in solving problems**: Very often the worker is faced by problems in his/her work that he/she cannot solve alone. In such a case, he/she should be free to seek help and guidance from other workers or his/her superiors. If it is so, then the worker gets more job satisfaction.
12. **Absence of unnecessary intervention and criticism**: No individual wants to sacrifice his/her self-respect. If the worker is unnecessarily shown disrespect or abused, then he/she quickly becomes dissatisfied. Hence, he/she should be protected from useless interruptions and criticism.
13. **Satisfactory hours of work**: The hours of work in any factory or office should be convenient and so arranged as to offer the least possible inconvenience to the largest number of employees. If this is not looked into, the workers become dissatisfied.
14. **Availability of leaves and rest:** In every industrial organisation, the workers should be given the proper amount of rest and holidays on festivals and other occasions of social celebrations. Nowadays, workers are allowed to avail themselves of around 10 casual leaves and 30 earned leaves every year in addition to the weekly holiday. Holidays given on festivals and on occasions of general celebration are in addition to this. Female workers are allowed fairly long leaves during pregnancy. It is generally seen that workers feel satisfied if the management in any organisation follows a liberal policy towards leaves to workers.

It is evident from this description of factors influencing job satisfaction that it necessitates the creation of certain conditions of work. Different factors may be important in different situations. An increase in wages is a common factor which is important everywhere. Promotion is another factor which plays an important role in maintaining or destroying job satisfaction. Apart from this, other factors may be more or less important, depending upon the situation. For example, an organisation in which the worker's educational degrees have great importance should also see to it that the worker is promoted when he/she adds to his/her qualifications. Finally, it can be said that job satisfaction depends on all those factors which influence morale.

The Measurement of Job Satisfaction

With a large number of studies on job satisfaction during the last three to four decades, there have evolved many different scales used to measure it. The scales can be divided into two general categories.[3] One is called tailor-made scales, which are constructed for a particular setting or project. The second set consists of standardised scales, which establish group norms on the scales and ensure the reliability and validity of the measuring instruments. Thus, we find that job satisfaction is an important and interesting concept and has duly received the attention it deserves. There are reasonably good instruments to measure it, and there are also well-formulated theoretical explanations of it. In case there exists a provision in an organisation to measure job satisfaction periodically, it may be possible to understand in a better manner the extent to which the organisation is meeting employees' needs and expectations.

Employee Morale

The satisfaction or dissatisfaction from the job gives rise to the psychological problem of morale, which is an individual's or a group's feeling of competence reinforced by job satisfaction and need fulfilment. It may precede or follow performance and productivity. It is a total attitude towards one's work and colleagues. In work situations, it is a product of need satisfaction and job satisfaction level.

Meaning and Definition of Morale

Different definitions of morale can be divided into three main categories:

1. **Classical approach**: The definition of Robert M. Guion can be put in this category. According to him, morale is defined as the extent to which individual needs are satisfied and the extent to which the individual perceives that satisfaction stemming from total job satisfaction.
2. **Psychological approach**: According to Edwin B. Flippo, E. F. L. Breach, Noah Webstor, Sara Niles and so on, morale is a psychological concept. According to them, morale is a state of mind and emotions, affecting willingness to work, which in turn affects individual and organisational objectives. Thus, it is a mental attitude of the individual which enables him/her to realise that the maximum satisfaction of his/her drives coincides with the fulfilment to the objectives of the company.
3. **Social approach**: Some modern writers describe morale as a social process. This concept is based upon Hawthorne experiments. The definitions given by Professors Elton Mayo, Keith Davis, F. J. Blankenship, W. A. Cohen and L. M. Moarse, and Dale Yoder can be put in this category. According to Keith Davis, morale can be defined as the attitudes of individuals and groups towards their work, environment and voluntary cooperation to the full extent of their ability in the best interest of the organisation. Similarly, to quote Leighton, 'Morale is the capacity of a group of people to pull together persistently and consistently in pursuit of a common purpose'.[4] According to Jucius, 'Morale is a state of mind and spirit, affecting willingness to work, which in turn affects organisational and individual objectives'.[5]

Thus, we see that on the one hand, morale is a personal matter, while on the other hand, it is a group problem. As a matter of fact, it is an inner impulse explaining the attitude of a member employee towards his/her work, working conditions, fellow workers, management, job satisfaction, total organisation and so on. It may be low or high. The high morale is reflected in zest, active cooperation, satisfaction, appreciation and so on, while the indicators of low morale are passive cooperation, feeling job unimportant and work a burden, hostility and apathy. According to T. Harell, high morale is a spirit of wholehearted cooperation in a common effort.

Importance of Morale

Morale, productivity of workers and their level of motivation are directly correlated. As we know, motivation is an intrinsic ability and desire for positive efforts towards performance. The word 'motivation' is derived from 'motive', which is defined as an inner state that activates a person to do some work or channelises his/her behaviour towards goals. So it is clear that if the level of morale is high, then the motivation degree will also be high. If both of these are high, then the quality of work done and level of performance will also be high. Conversely, positive efforts and sound performance of job will also lead to high morale and motivation. Thus, we can say that the level of morale of an efficient and capable worker will be high and, simultaneously, he/she will be highly motivated too. But research studies have been unable to establish a conclusive and consistent correlation between motivation and morale. Sometimes, it happens that the morale is high but productivity is low or vice versa. Similarly, in some cases, high morale and low motivation may also coexist. It is also possible to witness situations in which people suffering from low morale do nevertheless perform the assigned tasks rather well. But theoretically, we may say that motivation, productivity and morale move together.

The importance of morale can be illustrated with the statement of T. Harell who says that 'high morale' is a confident spirit of wholehearted cooperation in a common effort. Besides, today the importance of human relationships has come to be recognised in all industries. A high morale is the hallmark of good human relations in an organisation.[6]

W. W. Finlay, A. Q. Sartain and W. M. Tate have also pointed out that morale is essentially a feeling of belonging so dominating that the worker places the group's interest above his own.[7]

The importance of morale can be further illustrated with the statement of F. J. Roethlisberger who says that 'what physical health is to a physical organism, morale is to a cooperative system'.[8]

Keith Davis has compared morale to a lady when he writes, 'Never underestimate the power of a woman. Simultaneously, do not underestimate the power of morale'.[9]

As a matter of fact, the significance of high morale can be measured by recognising the disadvantages of low morale which are discussed further.

Disadvantages of Low Morale

Low morale may lead to the following:

1. Lowering down the production
2. Increase in work slackness and absenteeism
3. Increase in grievances and complaints
4. Increase in labour turnover rate
5. Lack of peaceful industrial relations (hereafter IR)
6. More accidents
7. More industrial disputes and so on

Real and high morale is the positive problem of a good organisation. That is why, every enterprise takes care of it nowadays.

Theory of Morale Development

Morale develops out of mutual satisfaction of interests. According to Jucius, 'employees who conclude that their interests are being served fairly when they contribute to the organisation's interests develop a favourable attitude of mind. Conversely, their attitude is poor when they perceive an unfair treatment of their interests'.[10] Thus, morale is in essence conditioned by a group's understanding of the relation between personal interests and organisation interests.

Factors Contributing to High Morale/The Process of High Morale Building

There are various factors which contribute to high morale among workers of an industrial organisation. The management of various enterprises use these factors in building the morale of their workers. Morale building is a continuous activity which means improving and maintaining the high level of morale of employees. It is a perpetual task and needs continuous efforts. C. E. Gregory has named it as the producer of climbing up a moving ladder. Just as a moving ladder has no end or steps, so also the process of morale building does not end. It implies that morale building is a continuous and complex process.

The steps of morale building can be divided into two groups—individual and group efforts. In this context, the group efforts are more practical, economical and effective. Hence, the managements generally try group efforts. Another way of classifying morale-building efforts is to divide them as physical and psychological factors. Their detailed description is as follows.

Physical Factors for High Morale

1. **Conditions of work**: The conditions of work have an important influence upon it. If the conditions of work favour the workers and create interest in the work, then morale is likely to be high. On the contrary, if the conditions of work are not favourable and serve to distract the interest of the worker, then morale is likely to fall. 'Conditions of work' being a comprehensive term include both physical and mental or psychological conditions. Various research studies have led to the belief that physical conditions of work have an important influence upon morale in the workers. Tindall and Cair have proved based on their experimentation that good conditions of work help to maintain a high morale. In this connection, Cair has pointed out the influence of music on the mental conditions of workers. Culier's experiments seem to indicate that in bad conditions of work, morale tends to fall because the worker evinces signs of worry, distaste, irritability, anxiety, sleeplessness, laziness, lethargy and so on.
2. **Position of promotion**: Studying the morale of various individuals in various positions of different companies, Arbrock concluded that the attitude of foremen is better than that of clerks, while that of clerks is more favourable than those of other classes of workers. This study reveals that the morale of individuals is also susceptible to such influences as the post that they are holding. The main psychological fact at the root of this phenomenon is that if the individual in questions does not get a position

that concurs with his/her psychological bent of mind, then his/her enthusiasm begins to wane, and he/she loses confidence in those who are in authority above him/her. Hence, if morale is to be kept high in any industry, then it is essential that posts be allotted in accordance with the ability and labour of the individuals, and that these posts be improved from time to time.

3. **Increase in salary**: It is a psychological fact that workers are primarily concerned with their salary or wages. Shepard has stressed the fact that if the workers' wages are reassessed from time to time and appropriate changes are made, then the morale tends to occupy a high level. On the contrary, if the wages remain stationary for a long time, and there is no increment, then the workers' enthusiasm is demeaned, and they tend to heap blame on their officers. Increase in pay should be made dependent upon hard work and other qualities. If increase in pay depends upon the personal idiosyncrasy of the individual in power, then most people become cynical as they do not like to cringe before such a person. Secondly, even the ingratiating types who win increases in pay and promotions through subservience rarely have a high morale. Hence, for pay increase to have a favourable influence upon morale, it is essential that the basis of increase be proper and the same for everyone.

4. **Method of distribution of salaries**: Morale is also influenced by the method of distributing salary no less than by increase in it. All studies to date on the subject have not led to any conclusive idea as to which method is the best. Some methods are, of course, better than certain others. Various methods will be examined briefly here:

   a. **Share of profits**: Under this method, the workers in companies and factories are given bonus and share of profit from time to time. The following facts need to be mentioned in connection with this method:

      i. This method engenders dissatisfaction in the better and more efficient workers because they find that others less efficient and less skilful than themselves are deriving the same benefits without deserving them.

      ii. In this method, the worker is never sure of his/her actual income in the future because neither the quantity of profit is definite, nor is the time of its distribution certain. Despite these difficulties and drawbacks, this method has been found to meet with the approval of approximately one-third of the workers. Besides, this method is also rather simplen because of which it is one of the most widely used methods today.

   b. **Remuneration according to work**: In this method, the worker is reimbursed according to the quantity of material he/she produces. The research made by Mathewson on this subject has made it abundantly clear that the method can succeed only if the worker is confident that the rate of payment will not fall, because he/she usually expects that if he/she works more, then he/she will earn more, but this might also create a reason for the company to reduce the rate of payment. Fear of this kind guides them to reduce their rate of working. It is evident that if the worker can be convinced of the stability of payment rates, then the piece wages method is superior to the bonus method, but it requires that the following facts be kept in mind:

      i. Attention should be concentrated not only on quantity but also on quality.

      ii. While paying the worker, it should be made abundantly clear to him/her that he/she is being paid according to a certain definite rate of a specific kind of work so that no doubt lingers in his/her mind and compels him/her to work slower.

 iii. In connection with remuneration, the rate should be constant, and there should be no fear of the rate of payment being reduced.

If these facts are kept in mind and the appropriate arrangements made, then the morale of the worker can be kept high through the piece wage method, because it is by this method that the worker is constantly inspired to work more and produce better results. It is also very good from the point of view of creating good incentives.

5. **Opportunity to share profit**: Among the physical requirements, another one is the possibility and opportunity of progress in any concern. If the workers in a company are being paid dividends out of its profits, then it should be equally distributed. In other words, all workers should be given equal opportunity of progress and to earn high wages, without any discrimination. If this is not done, then most of them tend to turn against the authorities in their company, while at the same time, a feeling of jealousy for those who have progressed is engendered in the unfortunate ones. This destroys not only collective organisation and administration efficiency.

Psychological Factors

1. **Praise/appreciation**: It is a matter of general psychological knowledge that praise of good work and effort helps to infuse further enthusiasm and energy in the worker. Studies conducted by such eminent psychologists as Thorndike and Harlock evinced that praise of a worker's effort helps to increase his/her motivation. In fact, the influence of the reward and punishment scheme of work is fairly evident and widely known. Any work that derives punishment for the perpetrator is shunned by him/her in future, while he/she desires to repeat any work that results in reward. Praise is a psychological reward. Praise by individuals for whom we have respect and in whose judgement we have faith matters a lot to us. If the authorities in the factory or office praise all good efforts, then morale becomes high among the workers. On the other hand, if good work and hard labour go unpraised or unnoticed, enthusiasm wanes in the worker, as he/she feels that he/she is not being valued according to his/her merits. This fact is one of the important reasons that work in an impersonal psychological organisation like a government office is rarely of a high order of efficiency. Direct praise or blame is rarely forthcoming, except from very conscientious individuals in authority.

2. **Knowledge of success**: Some other experiments have brought to light the fact that if the worker is aware of the degree of success, he/she is achieving in his/her work, then his/her interest and enthusiasm in it are maintained, and so is the high level of morale. In very big factories where the individual worker does no more than make only a very small cog in a very big wheel and is not aware of the effect of his/her own effort towards the completed wheel, boredom and disinterest are likely to set in very early. What is implied here is not the knowledge of the mere result. Result of work can be bad as well as good. Knowledge and failure can only serve to lower the morale, but if the worker is again encouraged to think in terms of success, then morale can be regained. As a rule, success ensures a high morale. It is the reward of effort. And reward is a favourable element in the creation and maintenance of morale.

3. **Fulfilment of collective needs**: A person works not only to meet the needs of his/her body such as food and clothing but also to satisfy certain other collective psychological requirements. He/she is also desirous of meeting others, expressing his/her emotions, thoughts, and beliefs, exhibiting himself/herself, knowing himself/herself and winning social prestige and recognition. Any kind of work that affords all these advantages to the worker is almost certain to create a very high morale in him/her, but if all these things are not made available to him/her, then morale is likely to fall, if it was ever high. Hence, in maintaining the morale of their workers, the organisers and authorities should keep in mind the fact that the workers' collective needs be also fulfilled and satisfied.

4. **Forbearance and good behaviour of authorities**: Workers attach much importance to the behaviour of inspectors, managers, and others in authority towards them. If conduct towards them is not all that can be desired, then general morale is likely to suffer. If the worker is constantly interrupted and scolded over his/her work, then he/she loses all respect for the officer. The only course of keeping workers contented, that is, open to the officer and authorities, is that of good and considerate behaviour towards them. In such circumstances, the workers are inclined to pay little attention to other conditions around them and are enthusiastic enough to do anything that is likely to benefit their factory or organisation.

5. **Autonomy and freedom**: If in any company or factory, a worker loses his/her identity to the extent of being reduced to the level of a small cog in the huge wheel, then he/she is likely to be dissatisfied with his/her work because it appears heavy and insipid to him/her. Hence, to maintain the worker's morale at a high level, it is essential that he/she be given the maximum degree of freedom that his/her function and position allow. He/she should also not be prevented from meeting other fellow workers, particularly those individuals who are in authority. It helps in creating a more intimate and knowledgeable atmosphere, in which he/she can tell his/her troubles to the proverbial daddy. But giving freedom does not imply that discipline should be done away with. Independence within the framework of laws is the most desirable state of affairs.

6. **Sense of unity, identity and equality**: It has been pointed out earlier that collective or group organisation is indicative of high morale. Hence, it is essential that a sense of organisation and unity should circulate freely among the workers. Psychologists such as May and Wright concluded from their examinations and study that in order to maintain a high morale among workers in industries, it is essential that the workers have in themselves a feeling of being organised, united or equal. The workers should be able to identify themselves with their factory or office or organisation and think of its interests as if they were their own. If this is achieved, then even the most difficult times can be successfully seen through by making a collective effort. An increase in the feeling of unity and identity can be facilitated by many things, such as a definite name of the company or organisation, a definite dress and a common badge. Besides these, certain group objectives can be set up, the achievement of which involves organised and collective effort on the part of the workers. Exerting oneself among many others striving for the same objective serves to lessen tension and increase mutual goodwill in the organisation. Workers should be made to realise that they are an important and responsible part of the industry. They should also be equipped with knowledge of the various aspects of the industry so that they come to look upon it as their own industry.

7. **Other factors**: Apart from the aforementioned physical and psychological determinants of morale, there are some other factors that influence it. For example, through his experiments and research, Super has established a relationship between age and morale. Similarly, the research of Arhork has shown that the level of morale is higher in the case of female workers than in the case of male workers. Maintaining a very high level of morale requires careful attention to be paid to all aspects of the worker's personality and to all aspects of his/her work handling grievances at proper stage and in time. Employee counselling, delegation of authority and introducing suggestion scheme are other factors which can be instrumental in improving the morale of employees.

Measurement of Morale

The measurement of morale is a very difficult task because it is basically a psychological issue and it is made up of several individual tendencies. Hence, in order to measure the level of morale in a worker, the management must observe characteristics of low morale in the behaviour of a particular employee. The following are some of the general features of low morale:

1. Antagonistic attitude towards those in authority
2. Lack of obedience or forced obedience
3. Feelings of hatred, jealousy, doubt and disrespect; lack of confidence towards those in authority
4. Disappointment; unenthusiastic insipidity
5. Lack of collective administration, unity and belief in one's efforts
6. Mental turmoil and unhappiness
7. Lack of system and productivity in work
8. Tendency of circulating all kinds of rumours
9. Poisoning mind of others towards authority behind its back
10. Lack of appreciation of work
11. Mutual conflicts and non-cooperation

Methods of Measuring Morale

The main methods of measuring morale are as follows:

1. **Common workers' opinion analysis**: One very popularly used method of measuring the morale is the common workers' opinion analysis method in which the opinions of the average workers are collected and analysed. For this, certain scientific questionnaires are prepared that reveal the workers' opinions regarding various aspects of the industry as well as towards the authorities. The workers do not have to reveal their names in answering these questionnaires. This has the initial advantage of assuring the workers of secrecy regarding their views. When the questionnaires are received back after having been filled and duly completed by the workers, it becomes possible to see the various scores and which the workers have complained. If some object or subject is a matter of complaint in a large majority of cases, then efforts can be made to rectify it. Success in this method depends upon the degree to which the questionnaire is scientific, and upon the degree of truth in the workers' responses.

2. **Exit interview method**: In this method, those individuals are directly interviewed who have departed from the unit in question for various reasons. One main advantage of this method is that it reveals the reasons that the workers feel compelled to seek jobs elsewhere so that future desertion on the part of present employees can be discouraged. Another feature of this method is that having left the employment of a particular concern or the unit, the ex-employee feels free to give expression to his/her frankest view on any and every aspect of the business. Another advantage of this method is that the views of departed employees cannot result in any harm to the administration or to those in authority. There can be no doubt that some workers may have grievances against the administration of their job that has no relation whatsoever with actual and real conditions. But if many workers leave their jobs on the same pretext, then evidently it is necessary to put an end to the source of complaint to maintain a high level of morale. In this manner, this method has proved extraordinarily useful in measuring the existing level of morale and suggesting methods of improvements. It also locates the cause of falling morale. If, however, most of the departed employees speak well and favourable of the work and the administration of the factory or business house, then there is very reason to believe that morale is at a high level.

3. **Attitude measurement**: As has been pointed out earlier, morale is an expression of attitude of the workers towards their work, the authorities and general administration or organisation. Hence, the workers' attitudes can be known in order to evaluate their morale. For example, if the answers to the following queries were supplied by workers, then their attitudes in these respects could be known:

    a. I work in the company under compulsion.
    b. The authorities in the company believe in the policy of paying as little wages as can practically be paid.
    c. If I can get the same salary in a different company, I am prepared to resign from my present position.
    d. I have no respect for or faith in those in authority above me.
    e. The conditions of work in which I work cannot be said to be good by any standards.
    f. I find no freedom, pleasure or satisfaction in my work.

The workers' attitudes can be discovered by requiring him/her to mark these queries right or wrong.

4. **Sociological method**: Nowadays, particularly in the case of group studies, the sociological method is very prevalent. Moreover, a method for measuring the morale can be used to discover characteristics of the workers' group organisation whereby the level of morale can be discovered. Accordingly, the worker is given a questionnaire containing certain questions intended to throw light on the characteristics of group organisation. For example, the workers are asked to name and enumerate the individuals with whom they would like to work, or under whom they would prefer to work, or in which sort of company they prefer to spend their time or have anything to do with. If the answers of many individuals to this question seem to speak favourably of any one individual, and the answers seem to show respect, love and confidence

for the individual, then it is fairly evident that he/she is capable of becoming a good administrator. If he/she is already in the administrative cadre, then it evidences a high level of morale in the workers, for respect and confidence in authority is a sign of high morale. But if he/she is not so situated, then the answers seem to show lack of confidence in the existing administration, a lack of confidence that can be rectified by promoting the desired individual into the administrative block, or otherwise by advising the existing administrative group to mend its ways and adopt other more calculated ways to win the confidence and respect of their subordinates.

In this manner, it is evident that no single method can help fully in realising the condition of morale in any unit and in discovering the means of improving existing morale.

5. **Company records and reports**: The records and reports of the company prepared for other reasons and purposes can be used to measure the morale of employees. These records can be analysed in the following manner: change of labour ratio, man-hours lost, absence and slackness, number of grievances reported by workers and resolved by the management, number and value of accidents occurred in the factory and so on. All these variables can be interpreted as an index of morale.

Warning Signs of Low Morale

In case low morale is not detected at the initial stages, it becomes a tough job for the management to get over it. Attentive managers, therefore, always keep a vigilant eye over the state of morale of their employees. In case it is observed that the employees are not taking pride in their work, or the rates of absenteeism and labour turnover are high, or the frequency of strikes or sabotaging activities is high, or the employees are not cooperating willingly, the management should deduce that the level of morale of employees is low.

Communication

In an era of accelerating economic and social change, the communication challenges facing managers are much more difficult than what was a decade ago (see Exhibit 14.3).

The process of communication, which must take place between one human mind and another, is fundamental to all aspects of life and is vital to the function of integration. Any business organisation is a human group constituted for certain specified objectives. The achievement of these objectives largely depends upon the fact that all human efforts are properly coordinated and integrated.

Individuals in the organisation performing different activities are functionally interrelated. The working and maintaining of this relationship is possible only through communication which provides for exchange of information. No business organisation can work without an effective communication network. It is an important human skill. The ability to communicate effectively is one of the major skills of a manager. According to the research conducted by Paul Pigors and C. Mayers, an executive, supervisor or manager spends nearly 70% of his/her time in communication. The face-to-face communication plays a vital role in managerial decision-making. As Benjamin Balinsky puts it, if there is any short-cut of executive effectiveness, it is the mastery of the art of face-to-face communication.

> **Exhibit 14.3 Power of Storytelling**
>
> According to Devdutt Pattanaik, mythologist and storyteller, 'The imperative of faster innovation, emergence of global network of partners, rapidly growing role of intangibles, increasing ownership of means of production by knowledge workers, escalating power of customers in the marketplace and burgeoning diversity, all these forces imply a capacity to communicate in the compelling manner'. Smart managers are often heard asking, how many people do we need in our organisation who can communicate compellingly, who can engage and inspire staff and clients to embrace change with enduring enthusiasm. The answer is 'everyone'. It is because the capacity to communicate difficult change message offers immediate impact on the bottom line.
>
> *Source:* M. Pathak, 'Power of Storytelling', *Human Capital* 17, no. 9 (February 2014): 52.

Meaning and Definition

The word 'communication' is derived from the Latin word 'communicare', literally meaning to make common, to share, to impart, to convey or to transmit.

Communication is the process through which two or more people come to exchange ideas and understanding among themselves. Newman and Summer[11] define communication as an exchange of facts, ideas, opinions or emotions by two or more people. Communication is also defined as an intercourse by words, letters, symbols or messages, and as a way that one organisation member shares meaning and understanding with another.[12]

Other definitions of communication are as follows:

According to Louis A. Allen, communication is the sum of all the things a person does when he/she wants to create understanding in the mind of another. It involves a systematic and continuous process of telling, listening and understanding.

According to M. W. Cuming, the word communication describes the process of conveying messages (facts, ideas, attitudes and opinions) from one person to another so that they are understood.

Thus, we see that communication in organisations has the following characteristics:

1. It involves more than one person.
2. It deals with the transmission of facts and feelings or both.
3. Media of communication may be numerous.
4. As a business organisation has continuity, the process of communication is also a continuous process.
5. The effectiveness of communication largely depends upon the proper understanding of what is being communicated and what is being received and then responded.

Thus, the different views on communication emphasise the understanding element in the communication. Sharing of understanding would be possible only when the person to whom the message is meant understands it in the same sense in which the sender of the message wants him/her to understand. Thus, communication involves something more than mere transmission of message and physical receipt thereof. The correct interpretation and understanding of the message is important from the point of view of organisational efficiency.

As such, the greater the degree of understanding present in the communication, the more the likelihood that human action will proceed in the direction of accomplishing organisational goals.

Communication Process

Communication is a process of changing rather than static existence. Events and relationships are seen as dynamic, continuous and flexible and are structured only in a relative sense. Communication process, as such, must be considered, as a whole, a continuous and dynamic interaction, both affecting and being affected by many variables.

The Elements of Communication Process

The communication process involves the following elements, as shown in Figure 14.1:

1. **Sender:** Anyone who intends to contact with the objective of passing information and ideas to other people is a sender.
2. **Ideas:** This refers to the subject matter of communication, which may include an opinion, attitude, feelings, views, order, suggestions or the like.
3. **Encoding:** As the subject matter of communication is abstract and intangible, its transmission requires the use of certain symbols, such as words, actions and pictures. Conversion of the subject matter into these symbols is the process of encoding.
4. **Channel:** These symbols are transmitted to the receiver through a certain channel or medium, such as telephone and radio.
5. **Receiver:** A receiver is the person to whom the message is meant for.
6. **Decoding:** The receiver converts the symbols received from the sender to give him/her the meaning of the message.
7. **Feedback:** Feedback is the process of ensuring that the receiver has received the message and understood in the same sense as the sender meant it.

Importance of Communication in Management

Communication is instrumental to a great extent in boosting productivity and performance (see Exhibit 14.4).

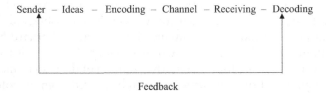

Figure 14.1 Elements of Communication Process

480 Integrating, Maintaining and Retaining Human Resources

The importance of communication was not very much highlighted by the traditionalists. They took organisation more as a technical and formal structure. Hence, the need of communication was undermined. But Hawthorne experiments conducted by Elton Mayo and his associates observed that organisations are social structures consisting of people working at different levels, having multiple differences. Proper interactions to them are necessary for achieving common goals. Therefore, the importance of communication was realised more after the 1930s, and the world of modern-day management is really a world of communication.

Nowadays, it is considered to be an important human skill. The ability to communicate effectively has become one of the major skills of a successful manager. According to research conducted by Paul Pigors and C. Mayers, an executive spends his/her near about 70% time in communication. In some cases, communication requires up to 90% of a manager's time. The lowest levels of managers, such as foremen, may spend less time in communication activities, but the higher one is in the organisational hierarchy, the more likely one is to spend greater time in communication.

Exhibit 14.4   Productivity and Performance

Productivity and performance suffer when employees are unable to communicate, collaborate and eventually innovate.

Source: Rachel McAlpine, *Global English: For Global Business* (New Zealand: Pearson Education Limited, 1997).

Exhibit 14.5   Various Forums Used by Canara, HSBC, Oriental Bank of Commerce and Life Insurance Company Ltd for Ensuring Open and Transparent Communication

Open and transparent communication is ensured through various forums like town hails, company intranet, coffee sessions with the CEO, open houses, newsletters, etc., in the company.

Source: *The Economics Times*, 15 March 2014.

Keeping in view the important role-played by communication, some companies such as Canava, HSBC, Oriental Bank of Commerce and Life Insurance Company Ltd ensure open and transparent communication through various forums (see Exhibit 14.5).

An ex-president of American Management Association once observed that the number one management problem today is communication. Chester I. Barnard has called it the foundation of all group activities. In the words of Gorge R. Terry, it (communication) serves as the lubricant fostering for the smooth operation of the management process. The importance of communication in management can be judged from the following points:

1. **Basis of coordination**: The importance of communication in the context of modern complex organisation is much greater. These big organisations being designed based

on specialisation and division of labour comprise several people. The larger the size of an organisation, the greater is generally the degree of specialisation and division of work. Hence, the more urgent is the need for coordination, which requires mutual understanding about the organisational goals, the mode of their achievement and the interrelationships between the work being performed by various individuals, and all this can be achieved through communication only. In the words of Mary Cushing Niles, good communications are essential to coordination. They are necessary upward, downward and sideways through all the levels of authority and advice for the transmission, interpretation and adoption of policies, for the sharing of knowledge and information and for the more subtle needs of good moral and mental understanding.[13]

Exhibit 14.6 Managers and Communication Skills

In 2007, Harvard Business Professors Linda A. Hill and Tarun Khanna wrote a case study that centred on a company that authorises employees to rate their managers publicly on a company intranet. Managers who cannot communicate effectively don't respect employees or fail to lead responsibly, risk receiving embarrassingly low ratings that can affect their employment.

Source: M. Pathak, 'Making Managers Responsible', *Human Capital* 17, no. 12 (May 2014): 50.

---

2. **Smooth working of an enterprise**: Communication makes possible the smooth and unrestricted running of an enterprise. All organisational interaction depends on communication. The job of a manager is to coordinate the human and physical elements of an organisation into an efficient and active working unit that achieves the common objective. It is only the process of communication which makes cooperative action possible. What objectives are desired, what activities are required, how will they be done, who will do what and when and how people will react all depend upon the internal and external communication processes of the organisation.

   Managers having poor communication skills do not prove effective (see Exhibit 14.6).
   In the words of Herbert G. Hicks also, communication is basic to an organisation's existence—from the birth of the organisation through its continuing life. When communication stops, the organised activity ceases to exist.

3. **Basis of decision-making**: Communication is a primary requirement for decision-making. In its absence, it may not be possible for the top management to take any meaningful decision. Relevant information must be received before any meaningful decision can be made. Again, to implement the decision effectively, it becomes essential to have a good communication system. That is why Chester I. Barnard says that the first executive function is to develop and maintain a system of communication.

4. **Increases managerial efficiency**: Communication is essential for quick and systematic performance of managerial functions. The management conveys through communication only the goals and targets, issues instructions, allocates jobs and responsibilities

and looks after the performance of subordinates. As a matter of fact, communication lubricates the entire organisation and keeps the organisation at work. In modern days, the skill of communication has become an essential quality of successful management.

5. **Promotion of cooperation and industrial peace**: More, better and cheaper production is the aim of all prudent management. It may be possible only when there is an industrial peace in the factory and cooperation between management and workers. The two-way communication promotes cooperation and mutual understanding between both the parties. The efficient downward communication helps the management to tell the subordinates what management expects from them. The upward communication helps the workers in putting their grievances, suggestions and reactions before the management.

6. **Establishment of effective leadership**: Communication is the basis of direction and leadership. By developing the skill of communication, a manager can be a real leader of his/her subordinates. A good system of communication brings them in close contact with each other and removes misunderstanding.

7. **Morale building and motivation**: An efficient system of communication enables management to change the attitudes, to motivate, to influence and to satisfy the subordinates. Most of the conflicts in business are not basic but are caused by misunderstood motives and ignorance of the facts. Proper and timely communication between the interested parties reduces the points of friction and minimises those that inevitably arise. Good communication assists the workers in their adjustment with the physical and social aspect of work. It improves good human relations in industry. Communication is the basis of participative and democratic pattern of management.

Thus, we see that communication is very vital for the existence and smooth running of an organisation. Emphasising the importance of communication, Chester I. Barnard has very aptly remarked: 'The first executive function is to develop and maintain a system of communication'.[14]

Factors Responsible for Growing Importance of Communication in Business Organisations

There are certain factors that can be held responsible for the growing importance of communication in business organisations. They are as follows:

1. **Growth in size of organisation**: Business organisations in modern times have grown, employing thousands of people, working at different places. Such large organisations have various levels in hierarchy in organisation structure. Direct contacts are not possible; hence, communication is of vital significance in directing these people.

2. **Growth of trade unionism**: After the Second World War, the trade unionism has flourished very rapidly. Today, management of a large business house is not possible without keeping trade unions into confidence. Their cooperation can be obtained through an efficient system of communication only.

3. **Technical developments**: The technology is developing very fast. The technical improvements affect the composition of groups, relationships between a subordinate and his/her superior and the methods of working also. The adjustment in social, organisational and physical aspects of work is possible only through communication.

4. **Emphasis on human relations in industry**: The growing importance of human relations in industry and the desire of management to maintain good human relations with their workers have also necessitated the communication. Now the nature of employer–employee relationship is changed from master–servant relationship to partnership. Communication helps in this process by changing the attitudes, perceptions, needs, feelings and so on.
5. **Other factors**: The idea of social responsibilities of business and the developments in the field of social sciences, such as sociology and psychology, have also increased the importance of communication.

Types of Communication

Figure 14.2 reflects upon the important types of communication in industry.

According to the Organisational Structure

1. **Formal communications**: Such communications are those which are associated with the formal organisational structure. They travel through the formal channels—officially recognised positions in the organisation chart. They are established mainly by the organisational structure. Formal communications are mostly in black and white. We generally hear the phrase 'through proper channel'. It explains the essence of formal channels. Such communications include orders, instructions, decisions of intentions and so on of the superiors. A detailed description of formal communication is given later on in this very chapter.
2. **Informal communications**: Informal communications are also known as 'grapevine' communications. They are free from all sorts of formalities, because they are based on the informal relationship between the parties such as friendship, membership of the same club or association or origin from the same place. Such communications

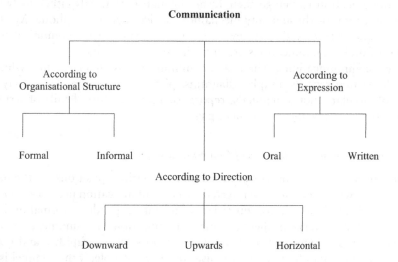

Figure 14.2 Main Types of Communication

include comments, suggestions or any other informal reaction also. They may be conveyed by a simple glance, gesture, node, smile or mere silence too. A detailed discussion of informal communication will follow in subsequent pages of this chapter.

According to Direction of Communication

1. **Downward communications**: Communications which flow from the superiors to subordinates are known as downward communications. They include orders, rules, instructions, policy directives and so on. Their nature is directive. It would be impossible to manage an enterprise without downward communications.
2. **Upward communications**: Upward communications are just reverse of the downward communications. They flow from the subordinates to their superiors. Such communications include reactions and suggestions from workers, their grievances and so on. Contents of the upward communications are reports, reactions, suggestions, statements and proposals prepared for the submission to the boss and so on. There was very little appreciation of this form of communication sometimes before as it did not fit into the traditional theory of organisations. But in modern times, upward communications are main source of motivation in employees.
3. **Horizontal communications**: When communication takes place between two or more people at the same hierarchical level of organisation, it is known as horizontal, lateral or cross-wise communication. The communications between functional managers or among superintendents of a department working under one boss and the meeting of general managers of various factories are examples of such communications. Horizontal communications may be oral as well as written.

According to Way of Expression

According to the way of expression, communication may be oral or written.

1. **Oral or verbal communications**: In oral communications, both parties to the process of communication exchange their ideas through oral words either in face-to-face communication or through any mechanical device such as telephone. Meetings and conferences, lectures and interviews are other media of such communications. More details of oral communications are given in subsequent pages.
2. **Written communications**: These are communications in black and white. These include written records, graphs, diagrams, pictures and so on. These may take the form of circulars, notes, manuals, reports or memos. More details of written communications are given in subsequent pages.

Communication Network or Channels of Communication

There are a number of channels or paths connecting various positions for the purpose of communication which together are referred to as 'communication network'. It comprises two types of channels which are interrelated and interdependent: formal and informal ones. Without the existence of these channels, organisational communication is not possible. Besides, these channels also determine the smoothness, rapidity and correctness with which the messages flow in an organisation. For example, if the channel is too narrow considering the volume of messages flowing through it, then the messages may be delayed or even blocked. On the other hand, if the channel is too long, then again the same thing may happen. Besides, the existence of a number of filter points in the channel may also affect the accuracy of the messages flowing through it. Something may either get added or may be deleted from the original message, thus defeating the very purpose of communication.

Communications Through Channel of Command (Formal Communication)

Formal channels of communication include established and organisational channels and officially recognised positions. So, the formal channel, as the very name implies, is the deliberately created, officially prescribed path for flow of communication between the various positions in the organisation. Thus, it is a deliberate attempt to regulate the flow of organisational communication so as to make it orderly and thereby to ensure that information flows smoothly, accurately and timely.

We often hear the phrase 'through proper channel'. It explains the essence of formal channels of communication. This officially prescribed communication network may be designed on the basis of single or multiple channels. A single-channel communication network prescribes only one path of communication for any particular position, and all communications to that position would have to necessarily flow through that path only. Ordinarily, this path is the line of authority linking a position to its line superior. It is also known as 'channel of command' and commonly referred to as 'through proper channel'. Its implication is that communication to and from a position should flow through the line superior or subordinate only.

Merits of Communication Through Channel of Command

The formal communication or communication through the channel of command has the following advantages:

1. **Maintenance of authority of the officers**: The formal communication helps in the maintenance of authority of the line officers. Subordinates respect their superiors. It helps in exercising control over subordinates and fixation of responsibility in respect of activities to be carried on by a person in the organisation.
2. **Sound and proper communication**: An immediate superior has a direct contact with his/her subordinates. He/she understands their attitudes, wants, level of intelligence and capacity well. He/she can determine it efficiently as to how, what and when the information is to be communicated and to whom. It is easy to be maintained properly.
3. **Other advantages**: Formal communication offers certain other advantages too. The formal organisation moulds the communication process along certain lines. It receives the support of line authorities, and closeness of the superior and the subordinate reduces the chances of misunderstanding.

Demerits of Formal Communication

The formal communication or communication through the channel of command has the following disadvantages:

1. **Overload of work**: In modern business organisations, there is a lot of information, messages and other things to be communicated. If all of that is transmitted through

formal lines of authority only, then it will increase the workload on line officers. They will not be able to perform their other functions well.
2. **Decay in accuracy**: It provides bottlenecks in the flow of information. It enhances the organisational distance also, and the chances of more transmission errors are likely to incur there. Screening of information at various positions reduces the accuracy of the message.
3. **Overlook by line officers**: Communication through chains of command is not suitable for upward communications at all. Line officers do not take any interest in the grievances of their subordinates. They do not like to forward the suggestions to the top management given by their subordinates. They naturally introduce their own views into information. The bias changes the nature and characteristics of information when it reaches at its destination.

Thus, we see that formal communication is useful in downward communications only. One way of overcoming these limitations is to provide a number of communication channels linking one position with various other positions. Thus, the system of multiple channels may improve the situation for some cases, but an unlimited use of this system may, however, cause confusion and also undermine the superior's authority. So, along with formal communication, the informal channels should also be developed for efficient and effective communication within an enterprise.

Informal Communication

The communication made through informal channels of communication is called informal communication. It is also known as grapevine communication. It is not the result of any official action but of the operation of personal, social and group relations of the people. Apart from their normal organisational relationship, people have social and personal relationships also. Such informal relations may be based upon personal friendship, membership of the same club or origin from the same place. Such channels of communication serve as a quick vehicle for messages. While formal communication exists to meet the utilitarian needs of the organisation, informal communication is the method by which people carry on their non-programmed activities within the formal boundaries of the system. Such communications are very fast, spontaneous and flexible. It is a very active channel of communication through which the information is carried immediately.

Merits of Informal Communication

Informal channels of communication perform a positive service to the organisation. It moves much faster. Besides, there might be certain subject matters of communication which do not require their transmission through the formal channel. The formal network of communication is often relatively static, while the organisation it seeks to activate is dynamic and must interact quickly to its changing environment. Consequently, the informal non-stable network of communication comes into frequent play in every organisation. The informal communication meets the needs of various people in the organisation, more particularly those people who freely mix up with others and rely upon informal relationships. A typical informal communication network involves people within the same hierarchy level of an organisation, for example, among various departmental managers. Such communication enhances the ability of the organisation to meet sudden problems.

Demerits of Informal Communication

Informal communication is also not without certain basic limitations. For example, many a time, messages communicated through the informal channel are so erratic that any action based on these may lead an organisation to a difficult situation. More often than not, it carries inaccurate information, half-truths, rumours and distorted information. In this case, the irresponsibility of the people communicating through the informal channel is the most important factor. Since origin and direction of the flow of information is not easy to pinpoint, it is difficult to assign responsibility for false information or morale-lowering rumours. Besides, each person conveying the message may add, or subtract or change the original message according to his/her motive, thus multiplying problems of informal communication. There is a possibility that by the time a communication completes its complex journey, it may be completely distorted or given a completely different colouring.

The informal communication is the integral part of the organisational process. The only thing management can do in this respect is to take suitable actions to minimise the adverse effects of such channels. A proper analysis of informal communication and a suitable classification in this respect would be helpful in making its use towards organisational efficiency.

Grapevine Communication

As mentioned earlier also, the informal channel of communication is also known as the grapevine. Therefore, it is not the result of any official action but of the operation of social forces at workplace. The term 'grapevine' arose during the days of the US Civil War when intelligence telephone lines were strung loosely from tree to tree in the manner of a grapevine, and the message thereon was often distorted. Hence, any rumour was said to be from the grapevine. But today, the term applies to all informal communications. As a matter of fact, informal communication is the method by which people carry on social, non-programmed activities within the formal boundaries of the system. Therefore, informal communication exists outside the official network, though continuously interacting with it. Informal channel is usually multiple in nature, that is, the same person having social relationships with a number of people working in the same establishment.

Types of Grapevine

There are four types of informal communication channels that have been identified so far. These include single-strand, gossip, probability and cluster as shown in Figure 14.3.

As far as the single-strand network is concerned, in it, the individual communicates with other individuals through intervening people. Regarding the gossip network, in it, the individual communicates non-selectively. In the probability network, the individual communicates randomly with other individuals according to the law of probability. In the cluster network, the individual communicates with only those individuals whom he/she trusts. Relatively, the cluster is most popular among all the types of grapevine.

488 *Integrating, Maintaining and Retaining Human Resources*

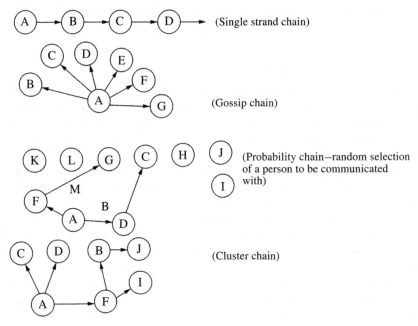

Figure 14.3 Informal Communication Network

Transmission of Communication

As messages, ideas, suggestions and so on, which are the subject matter of communications, are abstract and intangible, their transmission and receipt require use of certain symbols such as (a) words (either oral or written); (b) pictures, graphs, diagrams and so on; and (c) actions or gestures including facial expressions. These symbols become the media of communication. Each of these media may be either used exclusively, that is, to the complete exclusion of others, or two or more of these may be used to supplement each other. However, oral and written methods of communication are relatively more significant and popular also.

Oral Communication

In this form of communication, both the parties to the process, that is, sender and receiver, exchange their ideas through oral words either in face-to-face conversation or through any mechanical or electrical device. For example, today, telephones serve the purpose of oral communication.

Merits of Oral Communication

Oral communication proves very useful in face-to-face, two-way communication where people can exchange their feelings freely, and clarity regarding any doubt may by easily sought. It is very fast and is instrumental in complete interchange of information. Use of gestural communication along with oral one increases the effectiveness of this type of communication since actions speak louder than words. Most employees, including supervisors and managers, often prefer oral communication. They enjoy opportunity to ask questions and participate in the discussion. Face-to-face oral communication is sometimes supplemented by public address systems that permit managers to speak directly to workers at their workplace.

Demerits of Oral Communication

First of all, oral communication suffers from the disadvantages of absence of any permanent record of communication. Besides, at times, it becomes time-consuming, especially in meetings and conferences when after various deliberations, nothing concrete comes out. Again, many a time, oral communication is not taken seriously by the receiver and the basic objective of communication in such cases is not achieved. Besides, the spoken words may not be clearly heard or understood. Sometimes, due to previous strained relations of superior and subordinate, the word may be taken in the sense which was never intended.

Written Communication

The moment communication is reduced into writing, it is called the written communication. This may include written words, graphs, diagrams, pictures and so on. Written communications are frequently used in all organisations. In many cases, this form of communication becomes indispensable, for example, in the case of rules, orders, schedules or policy matters. The circulars, magazines, notes and manuals are some common forms of written communication.

Merits of Written Communication

One of the main merits of written communication is that it possesses the capacity of being stored as record for future references. Besides, the communication efforts may be minimised by simultaneous communication to various points, such as through circulars. It also enables the communications to take place between distantly placed parties without much cost. Written communication is more orderly and binding. It helps subordinates and superiors to take suitable actions in the organisation as desired in the written communication.

Demerits of Written Communication

Written communication is not without its faults. First, it is very time-consuming in terms of both preparation and understanding. There are also chances of communication being misunderstood. It is more costly in comparison to oral communications in most of the cases.

Oral and Written Communication: A Comparison

As a matter of fact, each of the different media of communication has its strength and weaknesses which determine its use and suitability for communication in any particular context. Therefore, in some cases, oral communication may be necessary, while in others, written communication may be more useful.

Hence, one cannot depend upon a particular medium of communication as both of these media are complementary to each other. Therefore, in practice, both these media are used. However, oral communication is more useful where the subject matter is complex and final decision needs more deliberations from the people concerned. While in day-to-day business and in routine type of activities, oral communication may be relied upon, in the case where the messages are to be kept for future reference, written communication is not the only alternative but it is better in all respects.

Principles of Effective Communication

The sole aim of communication is to keep people informed. Communication for the sake of communication only is fruitless and ineffective. It should serve the desired purpose. For this, the management should develop an effective network of communication. In evolving an effective system of communication, the management should keep the following relevant and useful principles of communication in its mind:

1. **Principle of information**: Commenting on the realism, Terry says that the first principle of effective communication is to 'inform yourself fully'. It implies that first of all, the sender must be clear in his/her mind what he/she wants to communicate. Better the understanding, effective the communication would be.
2. **Principle of clarity**: Communication should always be in a common and easily understandable language. The ideas should be clear and unambiguous. It should be kept in mind that 'words do not speak themselves but the speaker gives them meaning'.
3. **Principle of attention**: The principal aim of communication is to make the message understood by the recipient, not just the transmission of ideas from one person to another. It is possible only when the person being communicated evinces interest and pays proper attention to the communicator. The principle of 'actions speak louder than words' should be kept in mind by the executive in this respect.
4. **Principle of consistency**: This principle implies that messages should not be mutually conflicting, but rather they should be in line with the overall objectives, policies, programmes and procedures of the concern. It will not be out of place to remark that self-contradictory messages always create chaos and confusion in the organisation which is highly detrimental to the efficient running of the enterprise.
5. **Principle of adequacy**: This principle demands that the information being sent should be adequate and complete in all respects, as incomplete information turns out to be extremely dangerous from the viewpoint of the business. The adequacy of the information being transmitted depends upon the intellectual capacity of the recipient and also the individual circumstances of each particular case.
6. **Principle of timeliness**: Ideas must be conveyed at the proper time, and delay in this respect will make them mere historical documents as the information loses its importance on account of delay.
7. **Principle of integration**: The primary objective of every communication should be to strengthen the enterprise so that it may enable itself to accomplish its goals within the set framework. The executives should always attach due importance to the fact that communication is a means to an end, not an end in itself. It should be geared towards achieving a genuine spirit of cooperativeness among the organisational personnel so that they may put their potentialities in the attainment of enterprise goals.
8. **Principle of informality**: Formal channels of communication are important and useful in their own place, but experience and practice of many companies reveal that informal communication networks play a dominant role in spreading information, which is extremely useful for the purposes of the management. So management should identify the dignity of such channels besides using formal communication network for funnelling information in several directions.

9. **Principle of feedback**: The next most important principle of an effective communication system is the existence of feedback confirmation. Whether the message has been understood by the receiver in the same sense in which the sender takes it and also whether the recipient agrees or disagrees to the proposal of the communicator make it essential on the part of the sender to confirm it from the receiver. In the case of verbal communication, there exist a number of opportunities to secure feedback in comparison to written communication. But for written communication, the management should drive or evolve suitable means and ways in this regard for the sake of making communication more effective.
10. **Communication network**: Communication networks refer to the routes through which the exchange and transmission of ideas, information and opinions flow in the process of being transmitted to the destination person for whom it is intended. A number of such networks may exist in the organisation at a particular point of time. But management should figure out such networks only which will contribute a lot in boosting the morale of individual members working in the organisation.

Evaluation of Effectiveness of Communication

Communication is the lifeblood of an organisation. It is difficult for any organisation to exist without it. Therefore, management should ensure that adequate and smooth communication flows in all directions and it is effective as well. For this purpose, a periodical review of the existing pattern of communication effectiveness should be made. This review may serve two purposes. On the one hand, it may reveal the direction in which the existing situation falls short of organisational requirements, and on the other hand, it would reveal the underlying forces responsible for the prevailing state of affairs as also the actions required to improve the situation.

There are many methods available for evaluating the effectiveness of communication. These are as follows:

1. **Attitude and morale surveys**: Attitude and morale of the employees speak for the effectiveness of communication. Therefore, some evidence of the effectiveness of communication may be available from attitude and morale surveys of the employees. A questionnaire of attitude and morale surveys may include communication dimension, and thus, reactions and opinions about a particular practice of communication may be obtained.
2. **Employee relation index**: Generally, a good communication system produces good employee relations in the organisation. Such an index may be prepared to test the effectiveness and smooth flow of communication.
3. **Clarity**: An effective communication process must ensure clarity of communication, thereby facilitating exchange of ideas and avoiding unnecessary seeking of clarification. There are two methods which measure readability and understanding of written communication: one developed by Robert Gunning which is known as fog index and another one has been developed by Rudolph Flesch known as reading ease. Clarity involves expressing the communication in a language and transmitting in a way that is comprehended well by the receiver.
4. **Communication audit**: In the communication audit, a frequent approach measures the information known to various groups of managers and employees and compares that information with what has been made available to them. Normally speaking,

the process of communication must ensure that all those types of messages that are needed by the various individuals in the organisation in connection with the effective discharge of their official duties must flow up to them, and further that this flow in respect of different types of messages must be adequate.
5. **Assimilation of communication**: Communication audit may be directed to measure specific programmes, such as reading speed, comprehension, contents, forms, clarity, management and employee attitude towards transmission and receipt, and so on. This may be directed at readers, writers, spokespeople or receivers.
6. **Other methods**: Many a time, by studying the records and statements of safety, absenteeism, labour turnover, accidents and so on, we can have an idea about the effectiveness of communication.

Obstacles or Barriers to Communication

Communication is an important instrument in the hands of management. An all-effective communication system improves the relationship between workers and management. It helps a lot in establishing peaceful IR too. The morale of employees is improved, and their productivity also goes up. But sometimes communication does not give desired results. 'What is communicated?' and 'How is it communicated?' are not so important in comparison to 'How much is understood?' There are so many obstacles for barriers in the process of communication which contribute to its failure. It has been rightly said that the greatest enemy of communication is its illusion. The following are the main barriers of communication.

Semantic Barriers

These barriers arise from the linguistic capacity of the parties involved in the process of communication. The following are some of the important forms of semantic barriers:

1. **Badly expressed message**: A badly expressed message is one which lacks clarity and precision. Poorly chosen and empty words and phrases, lack of coherence, careless omissions, poor organisation of ideas, defective sentence structure, poor vocabulary, numbing repetition, failure to clarify implications, typical jargon and so on are other features of a badly expressed message.
2. **Defective translations**: Since a manager receives different types of communication from different personnel in the organisation, the information must be translated into a language suitable to each category of personnel. Hence, the message has to be put into words appropriate to the framework in which the receiver operates, or it must be accompanied by an interpretation which can be easily understood by the group of personnel it is meant for.
3. **Ambiguous or uncommunicated assumptions**: It has also been observed that there are certain uncommunicated assumptions which underlie practically all messages. Many a time, a message may appear to be specific, but its underlying assumptions may not be clear to the person it is meant for.
4. **Typical jargon**: It is also not uncommon that technical personnel or professionally trained managers or executives tend to develop a special or peculiar or technical language of their own using typical jargon. This increases their isolation from others and builds a communication barrier as well as gives rise to hostility from the receiver.

Psychological Barriers

Emotional factors, which are also known as psychological factors, are the main barriers in interpersonal communication. The meaning ascribed to a message depends to a great extent on the emotional or psychological status of both the sender and the receiver. The main emotional barriers are as follows:

1. **Premature evaluation**: It was in 1952 that Rogers and Roethlisberger for the first time pointed out this barrier.[15] Premature evaluation refers to the tendency of prematurely evaluating communications, rather than keeping an uncompromised position during the interchange. Obviously, such evaluation hinders the transfer of information and may even demoralise the sender.
2. **Lack of desired attention**: A preoccupied mind and not listening to the message attentively are also the major chronic psychological barriers. Quite often, people simply fail to react to notices, reports, bulletins and so on because they just do not pay the desired attention to all these things.
3. **Transmissional loss and poor retention**: Successive transmission of the same message through various levels in the organisation may affect the accuracy of the message. Research studies have established that about 30% of the information is lost in transit in the case of oral communications. Similarly, in the case of written communication, the loss of meaning might happen as far as the appended interpretation, if any, is concerned. Poor retention of information is another barrier. Certain studies have revealed that the employees retain only about 50% of information, whereas supervisors usually retain about 60% of it.
4. **Too much reliance on the written word**: Although written word is important at its own place, it is not a substitute for sound face-to-face relationships. It should be clearly borne into mind that employees cannot be persuaded to accept the organisation's viewpoints, policies and so on through 'slick', easy-to-read, well-illustrated publications, unless there is a fair degree of mutual trust and confidence between the employees and the management of the organisation.
5. **Lack of trust in communicator**: Ill-considered judgements or decisions lacking logic or frequent counter-mending of the original communication by the communicator create doubts in the mind of the receiver. If this kind of exercise is done repeatedly, then the receiver is likely to act unenthusiastically or may even lose interest in the message.
6. **Delay in or failure to communicate**: Many a time, executives fail to transmit the required message. It may be due to laziness or any other such thing on the part of the communicator or due to mere assumption on the part of the communicator that 'everybody knows' or sometimes due to wilful intention to embarrass someone in particular.

Organisational Barriers

These may include the following barriers:

1. **Policy of the organisation**: It is the general organisational policy regarding communication that provides overall guideline to everyone in the organisation as far as communication part is concerned. This policy might be in the form of explicit declaration in writing, or it has to be interpreted from the behaviour of the personnel

of the organisation, especially the top management people. In case this policy is not supportive to the flow of communication in different directions, communication cannot flow swiftly.
2. **Rules and regulations of the organisation**: Since organisational rules and relations prescribe the subject matter to be communicated as also the channels through which it is to be communicated, they affect the flow of communication in the organisation. The rules often restrict the flow of communication, especially that of formal communication. Communication 'through proper channel' often causes delay and proves a big bottleneck in the free and expeditious flow of communication.
3. **Status relationships**: The hierarchical placement of people in superior–subordinate capacity in the formal organisation structure also obstructs the flow of communication, especially in the upward direction. The big gaps between hierarchical positions in terms of their status may cause breakdown in the process of communication or obstruct the free flow of communication.
4. **Complex organisational structure**: A complex organisational structure having a number of managerial levels often delays the communication or gets the communication distorted. This is more applicable in the case of upward communication due to the universal fact that nobody likes to pass the adverse criticism either of himself/herself or of his/her superiors to the higher authorities.
5. **Inadequate organisational facilities**: Smooth, swift, adequate, clear and timely flow of communication is possible only if adequate organisational facilities are available. In the absence of such facilities, communication cannot flow in the desired fashion.

Personal Barriers

There are generally two types of personal barriers.

Barriers from Superiors

These may include the following barriers:

1. **Attitude of superiors**: The flow of message in different directions is greatly affected by the attitude of superiors towards communication in general or in any direction. If this attitude is not favourable, then chances are that messages may not flow adequately from or to superiors in the organisation.
2. **Resisting threat to authority**: In order to satisfy his/her ego, every person in the organisation tries to get a higher position and prestige. Hence, most executives try to withhold information coming down the line or going up because frequent passing of information is likely to expose their shortcomings.
3. **Too much emphasis on 'through proper channel'**: Supervisors would never like to be by-passed in communication. Hence, they always insist on sending communication 'through proper channel', which as has been stated earlier also is an obstacle in the free flow of communication.
4. **Inadequate or no confidence in subordinates**: It has been observed that generally, superiors undermine their subordinates and consider them less competent and capable of advising the superiors. Hence, they obstruct the downward flow of some information.
5. **Shortage of time**: There are superiors who always say that they are overburdened and have little time to talk to their subordinates.

6. **Inadequate awareness**: Many superiors may not be aware about the significance and utility of free flow of communication in different directions. Obviously, they do not make the desired efforts in smoothening the flow of communication.
7. **Deliberately ignoring communication**: Many a time, superiors deliberately ignore the communication from their subordinates so as to maintain their importance in the organisation. Hence, subordinates also react accordingly.

Barriers in Subordinates

There are two important factors in the case of subordinates which are responsible for obstructing upward flow of communication:

1. **Lack of willingness to communicate**: In case the subordinate feels that he/she may be adversely affected if a particular piece of information is passed on to superiors, then he/she may not be willing to pass on such information upward.
2. **Inadequate or no incentives**: In case there are no incentives to individuals for promoting free flow of communication, especially in the case of upward communication, the free flow of communication is likely to be adversely affected.

Thus, we find that the personnel of an organisation can perform their functions better if the contents of communication are effective and the concerned people believe in the efficiency of free flow of communication. In order to overcome barriers to communication, many leaders turn to storytelling.[16]

Chapter Review

1. Job satisfaction is concerned with the feeling one has towards one's job. Factors relating to job satisfaction include personal factors, factors inherent in the job and factors controllable by management. Factors which add to job satisfaction comprise grievance redressal procedure, praise for creativity and good performance, fair wages, promotion, availability of opportunities for growth and so on.
2. It is not easy to measure job satisfaction. Yet two scales have been developed to measure job satisfaction, which are tailor-made scales and standardised scales.
3. Employee morale is the total attitude towards one's work and colleagues. It is the product of need satisfaction and job satisfaction level. Classical approach, psychological approach and social approach have defined employee morale from their own point of view. Since morale, productivity and motivation are directly correlated, the importance of morale is obvious. Factors contributing to high morale or the process of high morale building include physical factors and psychological factors.
4. Measuring employee morale is a very difficult task as it is basically a psychological issue and is made of several individual tendencies. Hence, in order to measure the level of morale in a worker, the management must observe characteristics of low morale in the behaviour of a particular employee. However,

the main methods of measuring morale are common workers' opinion analysis, exit interview method, attitude measurement, sociological approach, and company records and reports.
5. Some of the main warning signals of low morale include not linking pride in their work, high frequency of labour turnover, repeated sabotages and so on.
6. Communication is the process through which two or more people come to exchange ideas and understanding among themselves. The process of communication or the elements of communication process comprise sender, ideas, encoding, channel, receiver, decoding and feedback.
7. The importance of communication can be gauged from the saying that 'communication is the lifeblood of an organisation'. Increasing size of organisations, growth of trade unionism, technical progress, importance of human relations and so on are the main factors for growing importance of communication in business organisations.
8. Communication can be classified on the basis of: organisational structure (formal and informal communications), direction of communication (downward, upward and horizontal communications) and way of communication (oral and written communications). Information, clarity, attention, consistency, adequacy, timeliness, integrity, informality, feedback and communication network are the main principles of effective communication.
9. The four main types of informal communication channels include single-strand, gossip, probability and cluster.
10. The barriers to communication include semantic barriers, psychological barriers, organisational barriers and personal barriers.

Key Terms

attitude
cluster network
communication
communication network
decision-making
decoding
downward communication
encoding
formal communication
fringe benefits
gossip network
grapevine communication
grievance
horizontal communication
human relations in industry
informal communication
job satisfaction
morale
motivation
oral communication
personality
probability network
productivity
semantic barriers
single-strand network
standardised scales
tailor-made scales
upward communication
written communication

Discussion Questions

1. Discuss 'Job satisfaction is concerned with the "feeling" one has towards his/her job'. Also list and describe the factors relating to job satisfaction.
2. How can job satisfaction be increased? Identify the factors and explain each of them.

3. Discuss how job satisfaction can be measured and also which of the two scales, tailor-made scales and standardised scales, is better to measure job satisfaction.
4. Why it is said that employee morale is the product of need satisfaction and job satisfaction level. Also discuss the factors that contribute to high morale.
5. Discuss how we can measure employee morale. Which of the methods of measurement of employee morale appears to be better and why?
6. Examine critically the elements of communication process.
7. Why communication is called the lifeblood of an organisation? Discuss in detail.
8. Discuss the classification of communication and also the principles of effective communication.
9. Discuss the barriers to communication with special reference to psychological barriers.
10. How effectiveness of a communication system is evaluated? Discuss in detail.

Individual and Group Activities

1. As an individual, discuss with the HR officials of an organisation what steps are usually taken by the management of their organisation to increase job satisfaction of its employees.
2. In a group of two members, discuss with the HR officials of any large organisation and find out how their organisation measures employee morale, and prepare a brief report.
3. In a group of two members, discuss with the officials of the union of some big organisation what is being done by the management to boost the employee morale in their organisation, find out how their organisation measures employee morale, and prepare a brief report.
4. As an individual, visit some big organisation and find out from the HR officials the main business that they come across in the free flow and effectiveness of communication.
5. As an individual, visit some manufacturing organisation employing around 2,000 employees. Discuss with its trade union officials whether there is a free flow of upward communication in their organisation or there are some bottlenecks in its free flow. Prepare a brief report based on the aforesaid discussion.

Application Case 14.1

Job Enrichment and Job Satisfaction

Nanavati, an MBA from XLRI, Jamshedpur, has been working as a senior HR manager (recruitment—middle-level managers) for the last three years. Prior to this, he had worked as HR manager in a big manufacturing organisation where he was appreciated a lot for his distinguished contribution in the HR activities. In his present position, he appears to be fed up doing the same routine activities—drafting advertisements and conducting the process of recruitment and selection in close association of some other senior officials of the company—though he is getting a handsome salary. He is even contemplating a change of his job to some other organisation. His way of verbal communication, body language, lack of enthusiasm and initiative, and some other activities convinced the director (HR) of his company that he (Nanavati) does not have job satisfaction; that is why he has been behaving in that fashion. The director (HR) also felt that if Nanavati's job is not made more demanding and interesting, then he may leave his present job and bid farewell to the organisation.

In view of this, the director (HR) convened a meeting of the whole of HR department, except Nanavati, and had a free and frank discussion on the issue of Nanavati so as to find out a solution to the problem because in view of high potential and rich, long experience Nanavati had, the company never wanted to lose him.

Having lengthy and meaningful deliberations on the issue, it was decided that Nanavati may also be assigned the task of recruiting senior-level managers also. Hence, the designation of Nanavati was revised to senior HR manager (recruitment—middle- and senior-level managers), with no change in his salary, and was made effective with immediate effect. The decision of the director (HR) showed a salutary effect on the working of Nanavati, who was found even sitting late after office hours to finish his work. His interpersonal behaviour also became more cordial, and he started feeling more involved in HR activities.

Questions

1. Why was Nanavati feeling bored in his job as HR manager (recruitment—middle-level managers)?
2. Do you think that the positive change in Nanavati was due to his job enrichment? If yes, then how and why?
3. Were you the director (HR) of the company, would you have thought of giving a little lift in his salary also? Yes or no? Why?

Notes

1. E. J. McCormick and D. Ilgen, *Industrial Psychology* (New Delhi: Prentice-Hall of India Pvt. Ltd, 1984), 303.
2. Ibid.
3. For details, see McCormick and Ilgen, *Industrial Psychology*, 309–11.
4. Alexander H. Leighton, 'Human Relations in a Changing World: Observation on the Use of Social Sciences', *American Journal of Sociology*, 55, no. 3 (November 1949): 305.
5. Jucius, *Personnel Management*, 430.
6. K. Davis, *Human Relations at Work* (New York, NY: McGraw-Hill Book Company, Inc., 1962), 77.
7. W. W. Finlay, A. Q. Sartain, and W. M. Tate, *Human Behaviour in Industry* (New York, NY: McGraw-Hill Book Company, Inc., 1955), 223–33.
8. F. J. Roethlisberger, *Management and Morale* (Cambridge: Harvard University Press, 1941), 192.
9. Davis, *Human Relations at Work*, 76.

10. Ibid., 431.
11. W. H. Newman and C.E. Summer Jr., *The Process of Management* (Englewood Cliffs, NJ: Prentice Hall Inc., 1961), 59.
12. R. M. Bellows, T. Q. Gilson, and G. S. Odiome, *Executive Skills* (Englewood Cliffs, NJ: Prentice Hall Inc., 1962), 59.
13. M. C. Niles, *The Essence of Management* (Bombay: Orient Longman, 1956), 390–92.
14. Chester I. Barnard, *The Functions of the Executive* (Cambridge, MA: Harvard University Press, 1968), 26.
15. C. R. Rogers and F. J. Roethlisberger, 'Barriers and Gateways to Communication', *Harvard Business Review* (July–August, 1952): 46–59.
16. M. Pathak, 'Power of Storytelling', *Human Capital* 17, no. 9 (February 2014): 52.

15 Supervision and Leadership

Learning Objectives

After studying this chapter, you should be able to do the following:

1. Explain the meaning and definition of supervision and also a supervisor's position, role and importance in an organisation.
2. List and describe supervisory techniques and contrast people-oriented and production-oriented supervision.
3. List and explain practices of effective supervision and also point out qualities and functions of a supervisor.
4. List and describe factors affecting supervision and also explain how a supervisor can be instrumental in improving human relations.
5. Explain the concept and definition of leadership and point out characteristics of leadership.
6. Distinguish 'leadership' from 'domination' and 'headship', and point out the relationship between leadership and motivation.
7. List and describe the qualities and functions of a leader.
8. List and describe the main theories of leadership.
9. List and describe the main leadership styles.
10. Point out the disadvantages of categorisation of leadership.
11. Point out the recent developments/emerging trends in the field of supervision and leadership.

Introduction

In the absence of appropriate supervision and effective leadership, no organisation can accomplish its objectives. Supervisors and leaders direct, monitor, control, guide and inspire the employees concerned.

It is they who infuse confidence, boost morale, lead, motivate and make them behave in the desired fashion. Hence, supervision and leadership are two vital concepts as discussed in the subsequent pages.

DOI: 10.4324/9781032628424-20

Supervision

Meaning of Supervision

'Supervision' comprises two words: 'super', that is, superior or extra, and 'vision', that is, sight or perspective. The literal meaning of the term 'supervision' is 'to oversee' or 'to inspect the work of other persons'. Thus, supervision refers to an act by which any person inspects or supervises the work of other people, that is, whether they are working properly or not. In business organisations, there are supervisors and subordinates. According to M. S. Vitoles, supervision refers to the direct, immediate guidance and control of subordinates in the performance of their jobs. Thus, the activity of supervision is concerned with the direction, guidance, control and superintendence of the subordinates. A supervisor performs these tasks. R. C. Allan has called it a 'responsibility job', which is above 'work job'.

According to the Toft Hartley Act, 1947 (USA), 'Supervisors are those having authority to exercise independent judgement in hiring, discharging, disciplining, rewarding and taking other actions of a similar nature with respect to employees'.

We can divide the definitions of supervision into three categories depending on the emphasis these have laid on a particular aspect:

1. **From the point of view of emphasis on maximising production**: The definition following under this category associates supervision with output—that is, because of their skills, expertise and experience, supervisors help their subordinates to improve their output in terms of both quantity and quality.

Thus, supervision implies guiding and looking after the work of the subordinates so as to ensure that the work is being done according to the norms laid down for the purpose. In this way, the primary objective of a supervisor is to help in getting the production maximised both quality- and quantity-wise.

2. **From the point of view of emphasis on workers' performance and human relations aspect**: In this category, we include those definitions that lay emphasis on workers' performance and human relations aspect, and which accept the worker as a part of the social system. Thus, according to this view, supervision is the process by which a supervisor helps the supervisee to adjust to his/her job, to develop team spirit and to assume even greater responsibility.
3. **From the point of view of emphasis on the development of the personality of the worker**: In this category are included those definitions that lay emphasis on the development of personality of the worker. According to the experts holding this view, supervision is the act of 'guiding the workers to develop their self in the best possible manner'.

In short, we can say that supervision involves motivating, guiding, inspecting, supervising, developing, coordinating and controlling the subordinates.

Levels of Supervision

As we have already seen, there are three levels of management: top management, middle-level management and supervisory (lower-level) management. Supervisors belong

502 Integrating, Maintaining and Retaining Human Resources

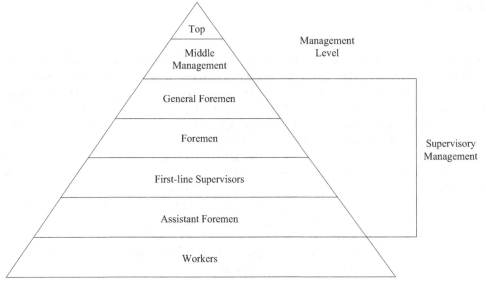

Figure 15.1 Position of First-line Supervisors in the Management Hierarchy Organisation

to the third level of management as shown in Figure 15.1 (a first-line supervisor is one who is just above the rank-and-file workers engaged in production).

It is obvious from Figure 15.1 that supervisors first receive instructions from the middle-level management and according to that take work from workers.

The main job of supervisors is to manage workers at the bottom level of an organisation. They have to head a non-management family. A supervisor has to interact in authority relationship with two groups: workers (his/her subordinates) and managers (his/her superiors). Supervisors are linchpins. Both upward and downward communications between the management and the workers flow through them.

Role and Position of a Supervisor in an Organisation

According to Keith Davis, there are five views regarding the position of a supervisor in an organisation or the supervisor's organisational role which are as follows:

1. **Supervisor as a key man in management**: A supervisor is the key figure in the organisation because he/she makes decisions, controls work and interprets policy of the management to the workers. He/she represents management to the workers. Therefore, management is judged as he/she is judged by the workers. He/she is also the main figure in getting the work done. However, in reality, he/she is less than a key figure.
2. **Supervisor as the person in the middle**: According to this view, a supervisor has to work between two forces: the management and the workers. On the one hand, management has a lot of technical and production-oriented expectations from him/her, and, on the other hand, the workers also have a lot of reward-oriented expectations from him/her. His/her position in the organisation is as shown in Figure 15.2.

Figure 15.2 Supervisor as a Person in the Middle

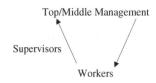

Figure 15.3 Supervisor as the Marginal Man

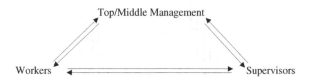

Figure 15.4 Supervisor as Another Worker

3. **Supervisor as the marginal man**: According to this sociological concept, supervisor is either left out of main activities and influences affecting his/her department or he/she is just on the margin of such activities as shown in Figure 15.3.
4. **Supervisor as another worker**: According to this view, a supervisor is just like a worker lacking authority and having a feeling that he/she is not part of management. Only his/her designation is changed. His/her position in the organisation is as shown in Figure 15.4.
5. **Supervisor as a human relations specialist**: Per this view, a supervisor is considered to be a human relations specialist looking after the human side of operations. His/her position in the organisation is as shown in Figure 15.6.

Importance of Supervisors in an Organisation

The status of supervisors, who are known by various names in different departments/organisations, such as gang boss, foreman, inspector or first-line supervisor, is very important in an organisation. A supervisor has the direct contact with the rank-and-file workers as well as with the management. He/she is the foundation or keystone in the organisational arch as shown in Figure 15.6.

Due to division of labour in industry, the work of a worker becomes monotonous due to its repetitive nature, but an effective supervisor can overcome such problems to a great extent by making the worker feel the significance of the contribution made by him/her in the total process of production. An effective supervisor can also be instrumental in

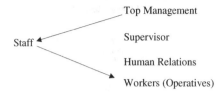

Figure 15.5 Supervisor as a Human Relations Specialist

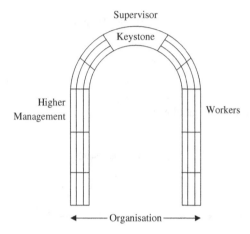

Figure 15.6 Supervisor as a Keystone in the Organisational Arch

promoting industrial peace by looking into and getting the workers' grievances redressed at the very initial stage. He/she can also give good advice, provide training, help in promotion and get the worker involved in the affairs of the organisation. As the status of a supervisor is multidimensional, he/she has to act as a friend, leader and guide of his/her subordinates. He/she is the very basis of sound human relations in an organisation.

He/she guides, trains and instructs the workers in the use of machines and equipment which may be sophisticated or otherwise, so that the same could be used optimally, safely and economically. High degree of specialisation makes the necessity of efficient supervisors all the more acute. A good supervisor tries to coordinate the highly specialised and separate units consisting of groups and individuals having individual differences in things such as temperament, qualifications, expertise, skills and ambitions.

Thus, we find that supervision is the most important activity in an industrial concern. The efficiency and prudence with which the task of supervision is performed determine the productivity of workers, quantum of production and, to a great extent, the cost of production also. The first-line supervisor is the most important person in the chain of management because he/she comes daily in direct contact or touch with the subordinates. As he/she understands the capacities, qualities and special characteristics of his/her workers individually, he/she can exercise effective control over them. As a matter of fact, he/she is the hub around which the whole organisation revolves. He/she assigns the work, trains and guides the workers to do that work, gives them necessary instructions, inspects their work while they are working, helps them in the times of difficulty and so on. He/she is instrumental in creating cordial human relations and an atmosphere for development.

He/she can make the changes easily acceptable. He/she can motivate them. He/she can improve their morale and win their loyalty for the organisation and respect for higher authorities. The following are some of the more important factors which explain the importance of supervision in effective industrial management:

1. **Importance as a middleman**: A supervisor is the first and most important link between the workers and the management. He/she is instrumental in getting the orders and instructions of high officials followed by the workers and in transmitting workers' grievances and problems to the higher management. Thus, he/she serves both the groups as a middleman.
2. **Motivating the workers**: A supervisor is always in direct contact with the workers, so he/she knows their efficiency, capabilities, differences in perception and level of motivation, and so on. So he/she can do a lot to suggest suitable motives for different groups of workers. He/she can prepare sound plans for their personal development and the like.
3. **Importance in good IR**: Peaceful IR depend to a large extent on the attitude and behaviour of the supervisor because he/she is the first-line manager. He/she has to deal with his/her fellow workers. He/she is the true representative of the HR philosophy of the industrial organisation.

Supervisory Techniques

By 'supervisory techniques' or 'supervisory styles', we mean the process of dealing with the fellow workers. It is a process of influencing the behaviour of subordinate workers. A supervisor guides people or their activities in an organised effort. He/she has the function of interpreting the objectives of a group, delineating the course of action most likely to lead to the achievement of the objectives and getting the support and cooperation of subordinates. These supervisory techniques (or styles) have a great role in the motivation of employees. There are mainly three types of supervisory techniques, which are as follows:

1. **Democratic or consultative technique**: This technique is based on the democratic principles of supervision and leadership. Under this technique, the advice of the workers should be taken on all important matters. The objective of the technique is to give chance to workers to suggest solutions to various problems related to company, and if these suggestions are appropriate and useful, then they should be taken into consideration. Thus, workers are instigated to give suggestions and advice. It makes workers feel their importance in their organisation. Their original thinking process is awakened and they work with more enthusiasm and interest and feel that the supervisor is helpful in their development and progress. This is an employee-centred supervisory style, giving importance to the needs and motives of the employees. It has a positive impact on their behaviour and efforts.
2. **Autocratic technique**: According to this technique, all rights are centred in the supervisor, and his/her orders are strongly obeyed. He/she fully controls his/her subordinates. While the workers tend to be unfaithful and undisciplined, this technique is used. In such circumstances, all acts of workers are controlled by the supervisor. Generally, nowadays, this technique is not used as it is based on time-worn Theory X of motivation.

3. **Free-rein technique**: This is just opposite of the autocratic technique. Herein, the supervisor gives complete freedom to workers to work and after seeing their abilities develops them. It can be said as a laissez-faire policy also.

This should be carefully understood that the supervisor should not depend on a single technique. As circumstances permit, techniques should be changed or adjusted. There cannot be one best technique of supervision for all.

In the words of R. Likert, 'There is no one best way to supervise. Supervisory practices that are effective in some situations yield to unsatisfactory results in others'.

People-oriented vs Production-oriented Supervision

The best supervisory style is the first style, that is, the democratic or consultative style as it is an employee-oriented style. The people-oriented supervisors give their primary attention to the human aspect of organisation. And in this way, they try to build an effective work group with high performance goals. As against this, the production or job-oriented approach is concerned with the performance of assigned tasks at prescribed rates, using standard methods, conditions and times. Likert[1] opines that a supervisor must always be interested in the development of people (his/her employees) so that their efficiency and productivity may increase. If employees are satisfied and have high morale and capabilities, then they will automatically produce more at economical costs and within reasonable time. The employee-oriented approach stresses the relationship aspects of employees and supervisors. It emphasises that every individual is important and takes interest in everyone, accepting their individuality and personal needs.

On the other hand, the production- or job-oriented approach emphasises upon production and technical aspects of jobs, and employees are taken as tools for accomplishing the jobs. This approach is akin to the authoritarian approach in the leadership behaviour. This approach mars the initiative and creativity of the employees, and they become indifferent to the organisational goals. The sense of belongingness is a must for purposeful action, and it is possible only through a people-oriented supervision.

Effective Supervision

On the basis of the research studies conducted by the University of Michigan, Harrell has mentioned the following four supervisory practices which are consistently related to the productivity of a group:

1. **Differentiation of supervisory role**: More productive supervisors perform functions more associated with leadership. Supervisors who spend most of their time in supervising have higher morale and higher productivity in their work groups.
2. **Closeness of supervision**: High-producing supervisors generally do not supervise as closely as low-producing supervisors. Close supervision may have negative response as far as morale and motivation of the employees are concerned.
3. **Employee orientation**: High-producing supervisors take more personal interest in their subordinates—their training, promotion, motivation and so on.
4. **Group cohesiveness**: High-producing supervisors believe in high group cohesiveness. High group cohesiveness coupled with employees' confidence in their supervisor leads to more production.

Qualities of a Supervisor

To be a successful supervisor, one must possess the following qualities:

1. **Technical competence**: A supervisor must have a thorough knowledge of the work, nature of work, processes of work and systems and so on. He/she should be able to demonstrate the work and to instruct about it.
2. **Team spirit**: A supervisor must believe in team spirit as he/she has to deal with subordinates working in groups. He/she should create such an atmosphere in which all workers would like to work with mutual cooperation. As such, team spirit makes hard work easier.
3. **Knowledge of various techniques of supervision**: A supervisor must know all the aforesaid three techniques of supervision and their merits and demerits also. He/she must apply them according to person, circumstances and work.
4. **Efficient administrator**: A supervisor is the manager of first line. He/she has to deal with people directly, so he/she must be an efficient administrator too. He/she has to control, direct and extract, so he/she must know the rules of the efficient administration and practise them also.
5. **Understanding of human relations**: An efficient supervisor must be capable of understanding the feelings, habits, perceptions, attitudes and the like of his/her subordinates. He/she must be able to understand and behave with them with an understanding as a human being.
6. **Other qualities**

    a. Impartiality
    b. Being people-oriented
    c. Balanced temperament
    d. Helping attitude
    e. Being realistic
    f. Not being dependent only on his/her formal authority
    g. Honesty and sincerity
    h. Ability to make quick decisions
    i. Encouraging suggestions
    j. Being a good listener to others' point of view
    k. Team spirit
    l. Being a good coordination
    m. Being inspiring and motivating
    n. Being a good disciplinarian
    o. Mental alertness
    p. Having good and attractive personality
    q. Recognition of responsibilities
    r. Regular improvement in work methods
    s. Maintenance of an improvement in work standards already achieved

Nature of Supervision

It has been divided into three categories:

1. **Substantive supervision**: It implies that the supervisor should be well versed about the nature of the work he/she is supposed to do.

2. Institutional supervision: It implies that care should be taken of the standard of the organisation, including that of punctuality and working.
3. Personal supervision: It implies close relationship with employees at personal level.

Functions of Supervisor

A supervisor has to do the following:

1. Help his/her workers to develop their innate qualities to improve their performance
2. Help his/her subordinates to adjust to their job requirements and to develop
3. Make the workers loyal towards their organisation
4. Provide expertise, skills, knowledge and experience to make workers learn without fear and hesitation
5. Encourage free communication
6. Develop employee potential to an extent where they need no supervision
7. Cooperate with other supervisors
8. Prove a good link between the management and workers
9. Solve personal problems of his/her subordinates to the extent possible
10. Maintain discipline
11. Correct the mistakes of his/her subordinates
12. Explore new fields of knowledge
13. Introduce new, useful and scientific methods of production and administration
14. Have a clear understanding about his/her plan of action
15. Know his/her job, duties, responsibilities, authority, accountability and so on
16. Divide responsibilities and duties to his/her subordinates rationally and scientifically
17. Listen and look into the grievance of his/her subordinates
18. Delegate authority and win their confidence

A Vigilant Supervisor

A vigilant supervisor is one who does the following:

1. Obtain approval of his/her boss before executing his/her plan
2. Work within budgetary constraints
3. Look impartial
4. Do not resort to self-praise
5. Have helping attitude
6. Point out drawbacks in the working of the organisation

Improving Supervisory Conditions

It is neither possible nor desirable to give absolute power and independence to supervisors. Therefore, in order to make a supervisor effective, the management should improve his/her conditions by taking the following steps:

1. According him/her higher status, keeping in view that the supervisor is the keystone in the organisation arch
2. Awarding him/her suitable pay and other benefits
3. Imparting him/her training on scientific lines

Supervision and Leadership

4. Restructuring his/her job, thus offering him/her greater job satisfaction and responsibility
5. Associating him/her in decision-making, policy formulation and so on
6. Encouraging him/her to become a member of different professional bodies
7. Encouraging him/her to attend conferences and seminars in related areas
8. Listening to and looking into his/her grievances and problems
9. Counselling him/her wherever necessary
10. Making him/her feel that he/she is a qualified and responsible leader of people

Rules for Successful Supervision

A well-known psychologist, Blum, has suggested the following rules for effective supervision:

1. Listening attentively and patiently whatever the worker says.
2. Taking no decision in hurry. It should be a well-thought-out decision after listening to his/her subordinates.
3. Avoiding argument with the workers.
4. Avoiding criticism of a worker in the presence of others.
5. Avoiding uncontrolled and autocratic leadership.

Factors Affecting Supervision

The following factors affect supervision and motivate the supervisor to improve his/her technique of supervision:

1. Nature of the organisational structure in which he/she is working
2. Nature and management techniques of top management
3. Nature of the work that he/she supervises
4. His/her own personality, level of education and training, experience and social background
5. Nature and temperament of his/her subordinates
6. Nature and extent of psychological and personality variations in his/her fellow beings

Supervisor and Human Relations

Supervisors can play a very effective role in cultivating good human relations in the organisation by taking the following steps:

1. **Participation**: A supervisor should encourage his/her subordinates to express their views freely. He/she should seek their options on all matters affecting them directly. His/her role is very important in promoting democratic supervision which helps in promoting good human relations.
2. **Communication**: A supervisor can be instrumental in the establishment of good human relations through free and systematic communication. He/she can interpret the policies and orders of the top management to the workers in the right perspective and can thus avoid many misunderstandings and confusions. This also helps in improving human relations.
3. **Democratic leadership**: Since a supervisor is the leader of a group of people, he/she should present the ideal of democratic leadership before them. He/she should take

full advantage of their abilities and experience by consulting them. This also leads to good human feelings among the workers.
4. **Work change**: By bringing about certain changes in the routine work or nature of work or conditions or methods of work, a supervisor can break the monotony of the worker and, therefore, can improve human relations.
5. **Personal contact with the workers**: A supervisor can improve human relations by maintaining informal contacts with his/her subordinates and taking interest in solving some of their personal problems. This will also lead to good human relations.
6. **Frequent feedback from workers**: A good and effective supervisor is one who interviews his/her subordinates from time to time in order to take feedback from them. Having done so, he/she can take remedial steps to solve their problems.
7. **Encouragement to the new concept of employer–employee relationship**: In place of traditional master–servant relationship, a supervisor should behave in and practise the new concept of employer–employee relationship which lays more emphasis on the recognition of the personality of workers and their active participation in the affairs of the organisation. This will promote good human relations.
8. **Employee orientation**: In order to improve human relations, a supervisor should be employee-oriented and keep their interest uppermost in his/her mind. He/she should always think in terms of development and progress of his/her subordinates.
9. **Coordination of interest**: For improving human relations, a supervisor should try to coordinate and integrate the interests of the management, of his/her own self and of the workers. This will give a sense of contentment to the workers.
10. **Organisational environment**: One of the most important requirements of maintaining good human relations is to prepare a suitable organisational environment conducive to the maintenance of good human relations. Since a supervisor is the keystone in the organisational arch, he/she has to play an important role in order to ensure the desired type of organisational environment.

Thus, we see that a supervisor can be effective in promoting good human relations in an organisation. However, we should not be over-expectant that a supervisor alone can be instrumental in promoting good human relations.

We should not forget that a supervisor also has limitations. He/she has to face many human problems. He/she has to tackle the workers individually as well as collectively. Individual problems of workers are different from the problems of workers as a group. Because of individual differences, a supervisor has to understand and appreciate the difficulties of each and every worker on an individual basis and thereafter solve them accordingly, which is not a simple task. Many a time, the management and the trade union take a decision ignoring the supervisor, which is not desirable. Whenever anything goes wrong, the supervisor is the first casualty.

If there is any positive development, then the management takes the entire credit. Because of these human problems, a supervisor has to face a lot of problems in maintaining good human relations. It is, therefore, very important that supervisors be trained in human relations and how to overcome or at least minimise the human problems.

Leadership

The function of direction involves the exercise of the function of leadership by management. Managers at all levels act as leaders because they have subordinates (followers) whose efforts have to be canalised in a definite direction. It is only the leadership of a management that guides, inspires and directs the members of an organisation for achieving common purpose. It is the quality of leadership that usually determines the failure or success of a business enterprise.

The Concept of Leadership

Leadership is an elusive concept because it often means different things to different people. McCormick and Ilgen[2] have considered three viewpoints in this regard which are as follows:

1. **Position:** To some, leadership resides in a position within the organisation. Most of the behaviour is seen as coming out from the power, authority and other aspects delegated to the position. Thus, according to this point of view, a position is a set of prescribed behaviours for the person assigned to it. In other words, a person assigned to a particular position is supposed to behave in a manner expected of him/her.
2. **Person:** The second viewpoint concentrates on a 'person'. It lays emphasis on the leader's personal characteristics. People having abilities, positive value interests and personality variables prove to be better leaders.
3. **Process:** The third view of leadership focuses on the 'process' by which leaders lead, that is, what the leaders do to lead. Leaders are supposed to influence others' behaviour and thus achieve group goals by seeking the willing cooperation and commitment of their subordinates. Influencing is not just exercising the routine power of the role or position. It is rather some degree of influence that can be attributed to the individual in the leadership position. In this way, the process of orientation towards leadership combines the position and the person by recognising that the major component of what is called leadership is the leader's ability to influence his/her subordinates. Similarly, the influence process is obviously affected by the situation which is primarily composed of properties of the leader's position.

Definition

It is difficult to define leadership in exact terms. Literally, the term 'leadership' has come from the word 'lead'. The verb 'to lead' has two meanings—'to excel or to be in advance' and 'to guide, govern and command others or to lead an organisation'. The first meaning hints at certain qualities of leaders, while it is the second meaning of leadership that is followed in business management. Now, let us examine how the term leadership has been defined and explained by management experts. According to Koontz and O'Donnell, leadership may be defined as the ability to exert interpersonal influence by means of communication towards the achievement of goals. Thus, leadership is a personal quality through which the leader motivates, directs and guides the activities of the personnel of his/her group. Almost similar views have been expressed by C. I. Barnard when he says that leadership refers to the quality of the behaviour of the individuals whereby they guide people on their activities in an organised effort. In the same way, Theo Haimann has also said, 'Leadership can be defined as the process by which an executive imaginatively directs, guides and influences the work of others in choosing and attaining specified goals by mediating between the individual and the organisation in such a manner that both will obtain maximum satisfaction'.[3] Ordway Tead has also remarked that

512   Integrating, Maintaining and Retaining Human Resources

leadership is the name of that combination of qualities that makes one capable of getting other people to do something; chiefly because of one's influence, others become willing to do so. In the same way, Terry has defined leadership as the ability to influence people to strive willingly for mutual objectives. Livingston regards it as the ability to awaken in others the desire to follow a common objective. Keith Davis has also pointed out that it is 'the ability to persuade others to seek defined objectives enthusiastically. It is the human factor which binds a group together and motivates it towards its goals'.[4] Bittel has also remarked, 'It is the knack of getting other people to follow you and to do willingly the things that you want them to do'.[5] According to Hodge, leadership is 'the ability to shape the attitude and behaviour of others, whether in formal or informal situations'.[6]

Thus, it is clear from these definitions that leadership is the process of influencing the behaviour, activities and efforts of an individual or a group for achieving common goals. A business manager is the leader of his/her subordinates.

Based on these definitions, certain characteristics of leadership may be specifically referred to as follows:

1. **Group of followers**: Without followers, leadership cannot be imagined. It does not exist in the vacuum. It is only on the followers or a group that a leader can assert his/her authority. A manager has a defined group of his/her subordinates as followers.
2. **Influencing behaviour**: Leadership envisages the idea of influence. As McFarland observes, the very essence of the leadership role in business is found in the context to which an executive can influence the behaviour of the fellow executives along the lines he/she himself/herself desires. The influence is exercised for the attainment of certain common goals.
3. **Reciprocal relationship**: Leadership is not domination. It is a mutual relationship based on reciprocity of the leaders and the led. A leader does not only influence his/her group but is also, at the same time, influenced by it.
4. **Common goals**: Leadership is the activity of influencing people to make efforts for the attainment of certain common goals. It is the leader who defines the common goals, makes them understood by all and reconciles the common objectives within the individual's ambitions and interest.

Nature of Leadership

Leadership plays a vital role in the management of people. It is the ability to secure desirable actions from a group of followers voluntarily, without use of coercion. It is a personal qualification which is used to direct the followers or subordinates. It may be formal and informal. Formal leadership is used through command and authority, while informal leadership is acquired through personal traits and courage. According to Robert Tannenbum. 'Leadership is the interpersonal influence, exercised in situations and directed through the communication process towards the attainment of goals'. Thus, leadership is a process of purposive behaviour. It is also an important instrument of motivation. Its acceptance by the group of followers is voluntary. It cannot be imposed.

Leadership may be positive and negative also. The positive approach towards leadership is based on rewards and incentives given to followers to get their energies channelised to the attainment of goals of their organisation. On the other hand, negative leadership is based on fear, force and punishments. In this type of leadership, the leader uses fear, force, reprimand, scolding and the like to direct his/her subordinates in a particular direction.

Distinction Between Leadership, Domination and Headship

It is essential to understand the distinction between leadership, domination and headship. Leadership is essentially informal in nature, while domination is the result of forcible assumptions of control and authority by one person over the will and affairs of another person. It is often the result of coercion or undue influence. Domination implies the imposition of authority and power over the group, while leadership is generated from within the group. Leadership is different from headship also. The former is essentially informal in nature and is related to the needs, aspirations and motives of the group. On the other hand, headship implies a formal power. In leadership, acceptance by the groups is voluntary, whereas in headship, it is formal and often imposed.

It is not necessary that a head has personal influence on the minds of the followers, while a leader gains influence over them by his/her qualities of head and heart. A true leader is always an ideal example for his/her followers, while a head may not be so.

Relationship Between Leadership and Motivation

Leadership and motivation are intimately related to each other. Good leadership following the dynamic leadership technique makes the members of the group faithful to the objectives of the enterprise and encourages them to work. The main object of leadership is to gain faith of the followers. On the basis of this faith, the leader becomes successful in taking work from them. In reality, management is the art of making people perform, and the development of this art depends on leadership.

An efficient leader encourages and instigates the subordinates to the desired job and gets them ready to do more work. In the execution of job, the efficient leader has to take their advice and look into their difficulties which are necessary to motivate the followers.

Hence, it can be said in the end that good leadership is a motivating power which forces others to work. It is really the positive source of motivation. An efficient leader will always be successful in getting his/her subordinates motivated. Thus, leadership and motivation are complementary to each other and a basis of sound organisational structure.

Qualities of Leaders

Following are the main attributes of an effective leader:

1. Willingness to assume responsibility
2. Ability to be perceptive
3. Ability to be objective
4. Ability to establish proper priorities
5. Ability to communicate
6. Ability to inspire
7. Maturity and stability
8. Integrity
9. Physical energy
10. Social skills
11. Conceptual skills
12. Being accommodating
13. Ability to make quick decisions

However, a large number of management thinkers and psychologists have pointed out the main attributes of a good leadership in their own ways.

Importance of Leadership

Leadership plays a vital role in management. Good leadership is an integral part of effective direction. It provides the vital spark to boost the morale, which has its roots in good human relations, which, in turn, can be fostered and toned up by leadership. The statement of Koontz and O'Donnell that 'managers should be leaders, leaders need not be managers' explains the importance of leadership in management. It is very true that the whole part of a manager's job, which involves getting things done through people, is undoubtedly made easier when the manager is a skilful leader.

Peter F. Drucker, an original thinker on management, considers leadership as a human characteristic which lifts a person's vision to the highest degree, raises his/her performance to higher standards and builds his/her personality beyond its normal situations. A manager, while performing the functions of a leader, does not only guide his/her subordinates but also provides a psychological shield to them. An average person wants to be led and guided by an efficient group leader. The presence of a manager makes the employee behaviour consistent, efforts cooperative, morale high and quality of worker improved. As a matter of fact, he/she guides every group, may it be small or big. It requires a strong leader to guide, inspire and direct the group members towards the attainment of a particular objective. George R. Terry has very aptly remarked that 'The will to do is triggered by leadership and lukewarm desires for achievements are transferred into a burning passion for successful accomplishment by the skilful use of leadership'.[7] Without leadership, a group disintegrates, destroys its team spirit and fritters away its energy.

Functions of a Leader Manager

The importance of leadership functions in a modern organisation can be understood by reviewing the various functions which are generally performed by managers as leaders. The main functions of a leader manager are as follows:

1. He/she formulates objectives for his/her group.
2. He/she leads the group/organisation.
3. He/she gives orders and instructions to do work.
4. He/she maintains discipline in the group/organisation.
5. He/she maintains communication in the group/organisation.
6. He/she listens to subordinates and responds to their needs.
7. He/she takes important decisions for the group.
8. He/she maintains unity and cohesiveness in the group/organisation.
9. He/she inspires and motivates the various members of his/her group.
10. He/she appraises performance and communicates the results of evaluation.
11. He/she represents the group to the outside world.

Thus, we see that a leader has to perform the function of leading the group of his/her subordinates. Managers at all levels should also act as leaders because they have subordinates whose efforts are to be channelised in a definite direction. As leaders, they have to not only show the way but also lead the groups towards it. In doing this, the manager leading the whole or a part of organisation has to set an example to his/her followers. Unsatisfactory performance in any organisation can be primarily attributed to poor leadership. Most of the failures of business establishments have been due to inefficient leadership. Good leadership performs the following functions:

1. It motivates and inspires the employees for high and better performance.
2. It creates confidence in the workers and subordinates.
3. It promotes morale which leads to high productivity and organisational stability.

What Indian Leaders Say About Leadership/Some Valuable Tips About Leadership

A lot can be learnt about leadership by understanding what eminent leaders think about it. A few observations of some of the leaders are discussed further.

Take Baby Steps: Pick Up Those Leadership Skills

The project manager of Work Better Training advises to take baby steps, quoted in *Hindustan Times* of 20 December 2016, as contained in Exhibit 15.1.

Exhibit 15.1 Take Baby Steps: Pick Up Those Leadership Skills

- Reflect the confidence your organisation has in you.
- Do an assessment—what specific qualities and actions does a good leader have?
- Understand the challenges faced by a leader and how he/she overcame them.
- Prepare your strategy and work out a plan as a leader.
- Have a 'we' mindset, not a 'you and I' mindset.
- Get to know what makes each member on your team tick, what motivates them.
- When working on a task, discuss the 'way ahead' together.
- You need to trust your team and the fact that they will do a good job.
- Be aware of what each one is doing, guide them if and when required.

Source: Hindustan Times, 20 December 2016.

Moving into a leadership role for the first time needs to be difficult—but it does mean changing your focus and adjusting your goalposts in a way that you can do justice to the new role. There are five ways[8] one should go about it which are as follows:

1. Be a mindful leader.
2. Understand team members.
3. Trust subordinates and delegate.
4. Focus on communication skills.
5. Be supportive, not a 'boss'.

A leader should set clear goals (see Exhibit 15.2).

516 *Integrating, Maintaining and Retaining Human Resources*

Exhibit 15.2   A Leader Should Set Clear Goals

According to Shaleen Sinha, chief operating officer of Zivame, a leader should have the ability to set clear goals, which can often be stretched, and then to give freedom to perform.

Source: The Economic Times, 17 January 2017.

Besides potential, a leader should have ambition and high energy (see Exhibit 15.3).

Exhibit 15.3   Besides Potential, Ambition and High Energy Matter

Shikha Sharma, CEO of Axis Bank, looks for people who do not just have potential but are very engaged and ambitious and have visible energy.

Source: The Economic Times, 9 August 2016.

Leaders should follow a process (see Exhibit 15.4).
Unhappy leaders in pursuit of greatness prove better in future (see Exhibit 15.6).
Om Manchanda, CEO of Lal Path Labs Ltd, says that it is important to be practical, and that to be a great leader, one should have the ability to be in the shoes of people who he/she manages.[9]

Exhibit 15.4   It Is Important to Break Big Problems into Small Problems

According to Amit Grover, co-founder of AHA Taxis, the best way (for a leader) to solve a big problem is to break it into many small problems and solve each of them one by one. As a leader, one has to be clear in one's communication about one's vision and let the expert team leaders handle things.

Source: The Economic Times, 3 June 2016.

Exhibit 15.5   Unhappy Leaders in Pursuit of Greatness

Vineet Nayar, founder of Sampark Foundation, looks for unhappy people. Unhappy with what they had done based on their conviction that they are capable of ten times more. Unhappy with just optimising resources and growing incrementally because they are capable of path-breaking ideas. Unhappy with themselves, thus hungry to learn and experiment more. He looks for unhappy leaders in pursuit of greatness and not happy managers who made small look big. According to him, such unhappy people become good leaders.

Source: The Economic Times, 9 August 2016.

Understanding of macro environment, disruption and its impact on the sector as well as leadership style is very important for a leader. Clarity of thinking is also very important (see Exhibit 15.6).

Exhibit 15.6 Qualities of a Future Leader

For Harsh Mariwala, chairman of Marico, the three crucial qualities of a future leader are clarity of thinking, purpose and communication.

Source: The Economic Times, 9 August 2017.

According to Pramit Jhaveri, CEO, Citi India, leadership is not just about being successful at work or in your career. It is also about how you grow as an individual and as a human being which contributes to how you become a leader.[10]

Acceptability by others as a leader is a very important quality of a leader (see Exhibit 15.7).

Exhibit 15.7 Acceptability of Leadership by Others

According to R. K. Mishra, director of Institute of Public Enterprise, a leader is one who is acceptable by others. A leader is one who has approval from others. He is a co-worker, goal-setter, motivator, constant inspirer and achiever. He transforms people and organisations and takes them to another level. He is a guru and guide. He renews the organisation's and people's energy.

Source: Hindustan Times, 9 August 2016.

According to Rajan Anandan, vice president of Southeast Asia and India at Google, energy and will to fight make a leader.[11]

Translation of the larger vision to simple workable goals is what is expected of a good leader (see Exhibit 15.8).

Exhibit 15.8 Translation of the Larger Vision to Simple Workable Goals

According to Harvinder Singh, country manager of India and director at United Airlines Business Services Pvt. Ltd, a leader is someone who can translate the larger vision to simple workable goals and create enough passion in the team to work towards those goals.

Source: Hindustan Times, 23 August 2016.

Top bosses should have an open-door policy. They should also be assertive, fair and willing to fly that extra mile. They are people who have no access barriers. They listen to their people (see Exhibit 15.9) and inspire them to aspire for more, achieve more and become much more. This is what the director of South Asia at Lufthansa Passenger Airlines feels.

Exhibit 15.9   How a Boss Can Become a Good Listener

A boss can become a good listener by adapting the following:

1. Undivided attention
2. Get to the root cause
3. Be perceptive
4. Never interrupt
5. It's not about you

Source: The Economic Times, 2 December 2016.

Theories of Leadership or Approaches to the Analysis of Leadership

Leadership is the process of influencing the behaviour and activities of an individual or a group for achieving common goals. Thus, the existence of a leader is very essential to guide, inspire and direct the activities of a group. Now, the question arises that how leaders are developed.

Basically, there are three approaches to leadership: the trait theory, the situational theory and the followers'/acceptance theory. However, some more theories have also come up into existence. A brief account of all main theories of leadership is given further.

The Trait Theory

It is a traditional approach to the theory of leadership. According to the trait theory, a leader has specific traits of mind and intelligence. These special qualities of head and heart generally include mental capacities and moral qualities. The trait theory holds the view that successful leaders possess these basic qualities and these are inherited rather than acquired. Out of this approach came the popular belief that 'leaders are born and not made'. For a long time, this theory has been widely accepted and it is still very common.

This theory suffers from the following weaknesses:

1. It is not clear as to which of the traits are most important ones and which are the least important ones. Various authorities have listed different qualities for successful leadership.

2. It does not consider the influence of situational factors in leadership.
3. It has not been possible so far to isolate and identity specific traits that are common to leaders.
4. It assumes that leadership can be examined in isolation. But it is not possible.
5. This approach does not suggest anything for developing future leaders since it is based on the assumption that leaders are born.

The Situational Theory

According to the situational approach to leadership, leadership is presumed to be specific and relative to the situation in which it occurs. These are the circumstances of a group which produces a leader. A leader may be good for a group at one level and under one set of circumstances, and he/she may not prove to be so in other circumstances. So the situational approach states that leadership phenomena are the product of situations in particular groups. Thus, the approach does not believe that leaders are born but asserts that leaders are made. Thus, it necessitates the executive training and development programmes for the development of future leaders.

This theory suffers from the following weaknesses:

1. It places much emphasis on the situational aspect and overlooks the qualities needed in a successful leader.
2. Leadership is a subjective consideration in which qualities of head and heart of a leader play well their part. But this theory overlooks it.

The Followers' Theory

This theory tells us that leadership is developed on the basis of acceptance from followers. Leadership cannot exist without a group. A study of the characteristics of a followers' group is also necessary to understand the nature of leadership. If a leader is successful in leading his/her group, satisfying them and motivating them, then he/she will be assumed to be a good leader.

There seems to be some justification for regarding the followers as the most crucial factor in a leadership event. It is, therefore, necessary that leadership function is analysed and understood in terms of the characteristics of the group of followers and their dynamic relationship (between leader and his/her group).

The major weakness of this approach is that it overlooks the quality aspect of leadership. A leader has certain qualities, whether earned or inherited, that is why he/she is able to lead the group.

The Contingent Theory

Taking the clue from the situational approach of leadership that any one of the single style of leadership cannot be considered suitable for all situations and for all kinds of subordinates, Fred E. Fiedler developed a contingency model of leadership, assuming that the effectiveness of the leadership is based on the leader's ability to act in terms of situational requirements. To approach his study, Fiedler postulated two major styles of leadership: lenient or human relations approach and task-directed style. The human relations approach is oriented primarily towards achieving good personal relations and a position of personal prominence. Task-oriented style is primarily concerned towards achieving tasks performed. Fiedler feels that 'the group performance will be contingent upon the appropriate matching of leadership style and the degree of favourableness of the group situation for the leader, that is, the degree to which the situation provides the leader with influence over his group members'.

Favourableness of situations has been defined as the degree to which a given situation enables the leader to exert influence over a group. Fiedler has identified three dimensions of favourableness of situation:

1. The leader–member relationship is the most significant variable in determining the situation's favourableness.
2. The degree of task structure is the second most important aspect in the favourableness of situation.
3. The leader's position power obtained through formal authority is the third most critical dimension of the situation.

Situations are favourable if all the three dimensions are high. The model presented by Fiedler has many significant implications to managers. It indicates that leadership effectiveness depends on various elements in the group environment. Thus, the effectiveness of the group performance can be affected by changing the leadership style for the situation in accordance with the described relationships. This also helps in designing the selection and training programmes for managers to be suitable for given situations.

The Interactionist Approach

According to this approach, leadership cannot be studied in isolation because it represents an interaction among members of a group. In this approach, the emphasis is on the quality of the leader–subordinate relationship which determines productivity morale and other goals. Experience has shown that leaders of highly productive units devote a greater part of their attention to human aspect of their subordinates' relationships and try to build effective work groups having high performance goals.

The Functional Theory

According to Dowling and Sayles, leadership acts are those which help a group to attain its goals and satisfy its needs. Therefore, an organisation first decides the leadership functions it needs and then these functions are distributed in an effective manner so as to achieve the desired objectives and also to maintain group cohesiveness.

The Path–Goal Theory

This approach, the credit for the origin and refinement of which goes to Robert J. House and Terence R. Mitchell, emphasises the leader's influence on his/her subordinates' perception of their work objectives, personal objectives and paths to achieve these objectives. According to House and Mitchell, a leader's behaviour can motivate and satisfy his/her subordinates to an extent which may promote the attainment of the subordinates' goals and make the path easier for attaining these goals. Per this approach, there are at least four basic styles of leadership: directive leadership, achievement-oriented leadership, supportive leadership and participative leadership.

The other theories of leadership such as Reddin's 3-D theory, Likert's System I through System IV and managerial grid are discussed further here.

Leadership Styles

Managers have to put the plans and the organisation into action. They do this by leading and controlling. Leading is a matter of dynamic man-to-man relationships between a manager and his/her subordinates. It is the process by which a manager directly and personally influences the behaviour of those people who work with him/her. Hence, leadership styles have a great role in affecting the interpersonal behaviour of managers as well as those of managed. The leadership styles are also known as leadership techniques. To define, leadership styles are the patterns of behaviour which a leader adopts in influencing the behaviour of his/her followers (subordinates) in the organisational context. Various styles adopted by leaders in relation to their followers are commonly classified on the location of decision-making into three distinct categories: autocratic style, free-rein style and participative style. Their brief description is as follows:

1. **The autocratic style**: Under this style of leadership, all decision-making power is centralised in the leader who allows a very nominal role, or does not allow at all, to his/her subordinates in the decision-making process. The leader adopting this style stresses his/her prerogative to decide and order and the subordinates' obligation to do what they are told to carry out. He/she does not give subordinates the freedom to influence his/her thinking, decisions or behaviour. He/she does not care to know the feelings of them. He/she does not respect their personality. He/she takes credit for accomplishment and blames his/her followers for failure. It is but natural that this type of leadership mars employee motivation, morale and productivity. Hence, such leaders are generally disliked by their subordinates, but some employees prefer such superiors as many of them feel comfortable under conditions of strong dependence on their boss.

2. **The free-rein style**: This leadership style is just like laissez-faire policy. Such leaders completely surrender all decision-making powers to a group of their subordinates. The leader completely abdicates his/her leadership position and leaves all responsibility and most of the work entrusted to him/her to the group which he/she is supposed to lead. Thus, it is a permissive style of leadership where there is the least intervention by the leader. The group operates entirely on its own under such leadership.

3. **The participative style**: Such leadership style is also known as democratic consultative or ideographic style of leadership. Such leadership allows the active participation of the subordinates in the process of decision-making. The leader adopting this style does not abdicate his/her authority and responsibility but actively participates and helps the group in coming to a decision. Such leaders believe in subordinate-centred leadership. They are friendly to their subordinates, they get approval from them, and they favour group decision-making.

    This participative leadership is preferred by not only subordinates but also the progressive managers. In general, employee-oriented leadership style, giving due importance to the needs, motives and feelings of the employees, has a positive and satisfying impact on their behaviour towards work. Such group is very adaptive and responsive. They welcome any change in work situations and conditions and the like.

4. **Bureaucratic or rules-centred leadership**: In this type of leadership, rules, regulations and procedures guide the behaviour of both the leader and his/her subordinates. Thus, administration becomes just a routine work, and due to this, the subordinates

do not take any initiative and become indifferent and usually do the minimum required work.
5. **Manipulative leadership**: In this sort of leadership style, the leader manipulates his/her subordinates in such a way as may lead to his/her achievement of desired goals. It usually exploits the ambitions and aspirations of the employees. Since it is based on manipulation, nobody prefers this style of leadership.
6. **Expert leadership**: In this style of leadership, the leader is looked upon by the members of his/her group as an expert who is, therefore, supposed to be talented, is a master of his/her job and possesses necessary skill in order to maintain his/her supremacy over others. The basis of this leadership style is leader's knowledge and ability.
7. **Likert's System I through System IV**: Another universalist framework of leadership style was developed by Renis Likert. He envisaged four basic styles:

   a. **System I—exploitative autocratic**: Management is seen as having no trust and confidence in its subordinates. Hence, goal-setting and decision-making are done by the top management. Control rests in the hands of top management. It works on the basis of power and positional authority and follows the philosophy of Theory X. It is the fear complex, punishment, coercion and occasional rewards that make the subordinates work. Due to this type of environment, there generally develops an informal organisation which tries to resist formal organisational goals.
   b. **System II—benevolent autocratic**: In this system, management seems to have confidence and trust in its subordinates. While majority of the decisions and goal-setting are done by the top management, many decisions are made at middle and lower levels also. Motivation is accomplished by rewards and punishments. There usually develops an informal organisation, but it does not always resist formal organisational goals.
   c. **System III—consultative leadership**: Although the management has substantial trust and confidence in its subordinates, still, broad policy and general decisions are made at the top management level. Subordinates are permitted to make specific decisions at lower level. This system moves from Theory X to Theory Y. Motivation is accomplished by rewards, occasional punishment and some involvement of the subordinates in the decision-making process.
   d. **System IV—participative group leadership**: In this leadership style, management has full faith and confidence in its subordinates. There is a free flow of communication in all directions. Decision-making is widely dispersed throughout the organisation, although well integrated and coordinated. Motivation is accomplished by participation and involvement in setting goals, developing economic rewards and methods for appraising progress towards goals, and widespread responsibility for the control process, with full involvement of lower units. This system has a strong Theory Y philosophy.

Thus, System I is a task-oriented and System IV is a relationship-oriented leadership style based on teamwork, mutual trust and confidence. Systems II and III are in between the two extremes.

8. **Managerial grid**: The management grid of Robert Blake and Jane Mouton is a well-known style scheme. They propose a managerial grid based on the

Supervision and Leadership 523

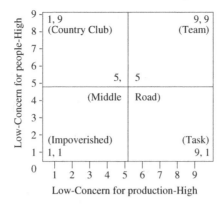

Figure 15.7 Managerial Grid Leadership Style
Source: Based on the discussion in R. Blake and J. Mouton, The New Management Grid (Houston: Gulf Publishing Co., 1978), 11–13.

styles of 'concern for people' (employee-oriented) and 'concern for production' (production-oriented or task-oriented).

In Figure 15.7, showing the managerial grid, five different types of leadership based on concern for production (task) and concern for people (relationship) are located in the four quadrants identified by the Ohio University Studies. 'Concern for people' is exhibited on the vertical axis. People become more important to the leader as his/her rating advances up the vertical axis. A leader with a rating of 9 on the vertical axis has maximum concern for people. As far as 'concern for production' is concerned, it is exhibited on the horizontal axis. Production becomes more important to the leader as his/her rating advances on horizontal scale. A leader with a rating of 9 on horizontal axis has a maximum concern for production.

The following five types of leadership styles have been shown on this grid (see Figure 15.7).

- **Impoverished (1, 1)**: This leadership style shows little concern for either people or output.
  Reddin calls it 'deserter' and is convinced about its ineffectiveness.
- **Task (9, 1)**: This style exhibits high concern for output and ignores concern for human element. Blake and Mouton call it 'autocrat'.
- **Country club (1, 9)**: Here, the manager shows little concern for production. Human factor is attached the maximum stress. Blake and Mouton refer to this as 'country club' management. Reddin calls it 'missionary'. According to both, it is not effective.
- **Middle road (5, 5)**: In it, the manager shows equal concern for people as well as task. Such a manager is called a 'compromiser'.
- **Team-based style (9, 9)**: In this style, the manager seeks high output through the medium of committed people. This commitment is due to mutual trust, respect and a feeling of interdependence. Reddin feels that this style is more effective than being

524 Integrating, Maintaining and Retaining Human Resources

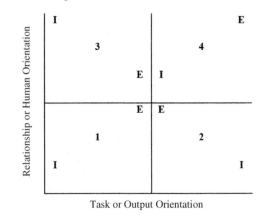

Figure 15.8 Reddin 3-D Styles

a compromiser, especially in situations calling for integration. He calls it 'executive'. Blake and Mouton also feels that only the (9, 9) style represents a successful integration of organisational and human values in all situations.

9. **Reddin's 3-D theory**: In this 3-D management style theory, Reddin was the first to add an effectiveness dimension to the task and relationship dimensions of earlier models. He places styles and situations into a grid format, utilising the dimensions of 'task orientation' and 'relationship orientation'. He uses 'I' for ineffective and 'E' for effective style. The total area has been divided into four cells as given in Figure 15.8.

In cell 1, the style is ineffective and, therefore, has been termed as 'deserter', implying that in such a situation, no one would like to be a leader.

In this situation, the more effective style is 1E, 'bureaucrat', stressing on enforcement of rules and procedures. In large organisations, we come across many such situations requiring bureaucratic leadership. In cell 2, the more effective is 2E, 'benevolent autocrat', and less effective is 2I, 'autocrat'. In cell 3, the less effective style is 3I, 'missionary', showing a disproportionate concern for people, while the more effective is 3E, 'developer', suggesting more concern for helping people develop skills that will be useful in task accomplishment. HR managers should like to use this type of style. In cell 4, the inner position is not effective and the less effective style has been termed 'compromiser' involving integration. The more effective style is labelled 'executive', stressing teamwork, coordination and confrontation to discover the law of situation.

Per Reddin's theory, there are four acceptable styles of leadership, the suitability of each of which will depend on situation, yet most higher-level managers use the executive style, though effectiveness of the style depends upon the leader, the followers and other situational variables.

Categorisation of Leadership Styles

These different styles of leadership are often treated as completely distinct from one another as if the distinction between them was clear-cut and water-tight. But such a situation does not exist in actual life; in actual practice, managers use a mixed leadership style. Such categorisation is neither practicable nor useful. Categorisation of leadership has the following disadvantages:

1. It encourages the tendency to classify people under particular personality groups, which is not practicable.
2. It builds up certain fixed expectations about the way a leader would be behaving and does not take into account either the need or the possibility of variations in the behavioural pattern at different times or under different circumstances.

Recent Development

Another leadership style, organisational behaviour modification (OBM) technique, popularised by Fred Luthans, is a refined form of the time-worn 'carrot and stick' style of supervision. This approach promotes desirable behaviour by rewarding the good employees and eliminates undesirable behaviour by punishing them for wrong activities or wrong behaviour.

HRM Strategy with Regard to Supervision and Leadership

Since supervision and leadership play a vital role in the success of an organisation, management should formulate an appropriate strategy in this regard. First, the management should appoint only those people as supervisors who possess all those qualities that a good and effective supervisor should have. They should be properly trained in interpersonal skills, and it should be ensured that they treat workers humanely, listen to their grievances and help them in getting them redressed. Besides, they should also help the workers in overcoming their operative problems. Similarly, leaders should not only be competent but also be inspiring and motivating. They should be able to take their subordinates and peers along with them. The management should ensure that all the leaders possess the required job knowledge, interpersonal skills, decision-making skills, behavioural skills and other special skills required to play their role well in the organisation. The management strategy should ensure that those leaders who come up to its expectations should be properly rewarded and encouraged. The leadership style should synchronise with the philosophy of management and should be instrumental in accomplishing the strategic goals of the organisation. The strategy should have a provision for getting adequate feedback about the way the supervisors and leaders are playing their role and necessary remedial steps be taken wherever necessary so that competitive advantage over the organisation's competitors could be secured.

Chapter Review

1. Supervision involves motivating, guiding, supervising, coordinating and controlling the subordinates. A supervisor may be viewed as a key man in the management, a person in the middle, the marginal man, another worker and a human relations expert. Hence, he/she has to play all the roles of all the aforementioned people.

2. A supervisor has a great importance in his/her organisation as he/she is the keystone in the organisation arch, handles the problems of workers, removes monotony of their routine jobs, motivates them, makes them feel proud of their contribution in the total process of production and helps in improving human relations. The main supervisory techniques comprise democratic/consultative techniques, autocratic techniques and free-rein techniques. A supervisor can be people-oriented as well as production-oriented, but relatively the former is preferable to the latter.
3. An effective supervisor performs functions more associated with leadership, avoids close supervision, follows the people-oriented approach and believes in group cohesiveness. A good supervisor should have technical competence, team spirit, knowledge of various techniques of supervision and understanding of human relations. He/she should be impartial and objective, honest, cooperative and helpful, quick in decision-making, and people-oriented. He/she performs several functions such as helping, training, developing, disciplining, grievance-handling and problem-solving.
4. A supervisor is supposed to not only maintain but also improve human relations through encouraging workers' participation and involvement, good communication skills, democratic leadership, personal contacts and win the hearts of his/her subordinates.
5. Leadership is a matter of 'position', 'person' and 'process'. It is the process of influencing the behaviour, activities and efforts of an individual or a group for achieving common goals. 'Leadership' is essentially 'informal' in nature, and the acceptance of it by the group is voluntary, whereas 'domination' implies coercion and undue influence and 'headship' implies a formal power and is often imposed. A good leadership is a motivating power which prompts others to work.
6. The main qualities of a leader comprise being able to inspire, to motivate, to communicate and to make quick and appropriate decisions; possessing good job knowledge and vision; being impartial and honest; being able to boost morale and infuse confidence, helping in raising production; providing guidance and psychological shield to employees; being inspiring; and improving quality of followers. A leader manager formulates objectives, imparts instructions, maintains discipline, looks into the needs of his/her followers, and inspires and motivates them.
7. There are several theories of leadership, such as the trait theory, the situational theory, the followers' theory, the contingent theory, the interactionist approach, the functional theory and the path–goal theory. Each theory/approach has its own positive and negative points. A leader should pursue the theory or a mix of theories whichever suits him the most.
8. Similarly, there are several styles of leadership, such as autocratic, democratic, free-rein, bureaucratic, manipulative, expert leaderships, Likert's System I through IV, managerial grid and Reddin's 3-D theory. Each style has its merits and shortcomings.
9. Another leadership style, OBM, promotes desirable behaviour by rewarding the good employees and eliminates undesirable behaviour by punishing them for wrong activities.
10. However, in practice, managers use a mixed leadership style.

Key Terms

benevolent autocratic
bureaucratic style
consultative leadership
contingent theory
country club
democratic/consultative technique
domination
expert leadership
exploitative autocratic
followers' theory
formal leadership
functional theory
headship
human relations aspect
impoverished
informal leadership
interactionist approach
keystone
leader manager
leadership
Likert's System I through System IV
management grid
manipulative leadership
marginal man
middle road
organisational behaviour modification (OBM)
participative style
path–goal theory
person in the middle
production-/task-oriented supervision
Reddin's 3-D theory
reciprocal relationship
situational theory
substantive supervisor supervision
team-based style
team spirit

Discussion Questions

1. Discuss what the supervision is all about and what is the position and role of a supervisor in an organisation.
2. Discuss why supervision is needed in an organisation and also the various techniques of supervision.
3. Discuss the implications of effective supervision. Also discuss the qualities and functions of good supervisors.
4. Discuss the factors affecting supervision.
5. Discuss how a supervisor can be instrumental in improving human relations in an organisation.
6. Discuss the concept of leadership and characteristics of leadership.
7. Discuss the differences between leadership, domination and headship. Also discuss the relationship between leadership and motivation.
8. Discuss the qualities, functions and importance of a leader.
9. Discuss the main features of all the main theories of leadership and point out which of these theories is the best and why.
10. Discuss the main leadership styles and point out which one is the best and why.

Individual and Group Activities

1. As an individual or in a group of three members, pay a visit to some big manufacturing organisation, talk to a few supervisors there and find out from them what role is being played by them in their organisation.

2. As an individual, visit some big organisation, meet a few workers and find out from them which technique of supervision is usually followed by their supervisors and whether they (workers) like it or not and why.
3. In a group of two members, visit some big manufacturing organisation, have a discussion with a few employees and find out whether their leaders are motivating and inspiring. Also ask them to give a few examples in this direction.
4. As an individual, discuss with a few leaders of a big organisation the functions they are performing in their organisation and what has been the reaction of their followers in this regard.
5. In a group of three members, discuss with union officials which leadership style is being followed in their organisation and whether they are satisfied with it or not and why.

Application Case 15.1

Change of Leadership Style

Keswani inherited a plastic goods manufacturing company, as a tradition, from his father, who was very much liked by his employees. Everyone was offering his willing cooperation in the process of production. The father was in touch with almost each group of workers and took personal interest in resolving their problems. But as ill luck would have it, he died in an accident, leaving the entire responsibility on Keswani, who was in his early 30s.

For some time, Keswani followed the footprints of his father, and because of the sudden rise in the demand for plastic goods manufactured by his company, the profits continued rising high year after year. The sudden, rapid favourable turn in the fortunes of Keswani made him indifferent towards the lot of his employees, and he ceased to take interest in their problems, which began multiplying over a period of time. At times, Keswani became hostile and started making decisions in an autocratic manner.

In the meantime, an advertisement by a newly set-up plastic goods manufacturing company inviting applications for almost all the positions came to the notice of the union leader of the company. He contacted the various groups of workers and suggested that they should en masse move to the newly established company. Receiving a favourable inkling from the work groups, he contacted the owner of the new factory, who agreed to appoint all the members of the union in his company. Consequently, most workers resigned and joined the new company as they had come to know about the employee-centred style of leadership of the owner of the new company.

Questions

1. What led to change in the leadership style of Keswani?
2. Was it ethical for the owner of the new company to take most of the employees of Keswani's company? Yes or no? Why? Give arguments.
3. Were you a union leader in Keswani's company, what would have been your initiative?

Notes

1. See Likert, *New Patterns of Management*, 279.
2. See McCormick and Ilgen, *Industrial Psychology*, 319–20.
3. Ibid.
4. T. Haimann, *Professional Management* (New Delhi: Eurasia Publishing House, 1966), 440.
5. Davis, *Human Relations at Work*, 96–97.
6. L. R. Bittel, *What Every Supervisor Should Know* (New York, NY: McGraw-Hill, 1974).
7. B. J. Hodge and H. G. Johnson, *Management and Organisational Behaviour* (New York, NY: John Wiley & Sons, 1970), 250.
8. For details, see *The Economic Times*, 23 December 2016.
9. See *The Economic Times*, 23 August 2016.
10. *The Economic Times*, 9 August 2016.
11. *The Economic Times*, 9 August 2017.

16 Managing Employee Discipline and Handling Grievances

Learning Objectives

After studying this chapter, you should be able to do the following:

1. Explain the meaning of discipline and its significance to different stakeholders in an organisation.
2. List and describe both the objectives and the principles of discipline.
3. Explain who is a 'difficult employee' and also explain the various approaches to discipline, and the factors responsible for indiscipline.
4. Explain disciplinary action and the procedure for taking disciplinary action.
5. Explain the meaning of the term 'grievance' and distinguish it from 'dissatisfaction' and 'complaint'.
6. List and describe the causes of grievances and also the principles of handling grievances.
7. List and explain the steps involved in the Model Grievance Procedure.

Introduction

When it comes to maintaining and retaining employees, the significance of discipline and grievance-handling procedure in an organisation hardly needs any elaboration. If handled properly, these help not only in boosting morale, infusing confidence, enhancing contentment of employees, increasing the quantum and improving the quality of output but also in motivating and retaining employees in the organisation.

Discipline and Disciplinary Action

No person ever grows until he/she is disciplined, and no organisation prospers unless it has disciplined workforce. Effective discipline is, therefore, a sign of any good organisation. The success of an organisation is possible when it has acceptable performance from its employees, which, in turn, is possible when its employees are willing to execute instructions and orders from their superiors; adhere to rules, regulations and procedures; follow norms; and behave in the desired fashion. Absence of discipline leads to chaos in the organisation. Despite numerous advantages of discipline, cases of indiscipline are

DOI: 10.4324/9781032628424-21

not wanting in organisations, which not only affect performance of the organisation adversely but also spoil human relations and IR as also the image of the organisation. An employee's attitude towards work is a crucial factor in productivity or performance, and discipline may play an important part in this attitude. Discipline is one of the most challenging areas in HRM function because, in dealing with difficult employees, HR managers have to diagnose both internal and external environmental factors in discipline situations, prescribe and implement appropriate remedial actions, and evaluate the effectiveness of their decisions.[1]

Meaning and Definition

Discipline is the orderly conduct by an employee in an expected manner. It is the force or fear of a force that deters an individual or a group from doing things that are detrimental to the accomplishment of group objectives. In other words, discipline is the orderly conduct by the members of an organisation who adhere to its rules and regulations because they desire to cooperate harmoniously in forwarding the end which the group has in view. Good discipline means that employees are willing to abide by company rules and executive orders and behave in the desired fashion. Discipline implies the absence of chaos, irregularity and confusion in the behaviour of a worker. According to Calhoon, 'Discipline is a force that prompts individuals or groups to observe rules, regulations and procedures which are deemed to be necessary for the effective functioning of an organisation'.[2]

Violation of rules, regulations, procedure and norms is considered as misconduct—that is, any act which is inconsistent with the fulfilment of the expressed and implied conditions of service—or is directly linked with the general relationship of the employer and the employee—has a direct effect on the contentment or comfort of men at work or has a material bearing on the smooth and efficient working of the organisation concerned. Every organisation wants its employees' behaviour to be in conformity with the required system which it has prescribed in order to achieve the organisational goals. Thus, in brief, discipline is orderly conduct by the employee in an expected manner. The purpose of discipline is to encourage employees to behave sensibly at work, that is, adhere to rules and regulations. Disciplinary action is called for when an employee violates one of the rules.[3]

Exhibit 16.1 Main Features of Discipline

- Discipline means orderly conduct by employees.
- Discipline is the training that corrects, moulds, strengthens and brings perfection.
- Discipline is the control gained by enforcing obedience.
- Discipline needs both constructive and remedial steps for its monitoring.

Features of Discipline

Based on the concept and various definitions of discipline, the main characteristics or features of discipline are shown in Exhibit 16.1.

532 Integrating, Maintaining and Retaining Human Resources

Significance of Discipline

Discipline in industry is beneficial to all the stakeholders. It not only motivates employees but also heightens their morale and infuses confidence in them. It makes them duty-conscious, develops positive thinking in them, makes them behave in a cooperative manner, improves human relations and IR and reduces their grievances. It helps a lot in the efficient and effective working of the organisation and thus is helpful in enhancing output, improving quality of product(s), reducing cost of production, requiring less supervision, promoting self-control and promoting safety and security of employees. Above all, it boosts the image of the organisation and ensures respect for seniors.

Objectives of Discipline

Discipline aims at promoting adaptability among employees so that they may adjust themselves according to the requirement and give their best to the organisation. It also aims at enabling the employees to behave in the desired fashion, to have respect for their seniors, to follow rules, regulations and procedures, to increase output at the least cost, to boost morale of the employees, to make them feel more confident, to improve human relations and IR, to discourage violation of rules and regulations by employees, and so on.

Principles of Discipline

The main principles which are instrumental in making a disciplinary system effective are enumerated in Exhibit 16.2.

Exhibit 16.2   Principles of Discipline

- Principle of natural justice
- Principle of consistency
- Principle of objectivity
- Principle of prompt action
- Principle of objectivity
- Principle of well-defined procedure
- Principle of fair action
- Principle of disciplinary action as a tool
- Principle of code of conduct
- Principle of preventive measure
- Principle of appeal

Exhibit 16.3   Guidelines for a Manager for Having a Consultation Discussion with an Ineffective Employee

- Identifying and analysing the root cause(s) for poor performance
- Preparing the disciplinary interview

- Conducting the interview in a professional manner
- Issuing the discipline (prescribing the disciplinary steps and making the undisciplined employee understand the discipline and what is expected of him/her)
- Not expecting to win popularities

Difficult Employees

There are always some employees in most organisations who are difficult to be handled. According to Ivancevich,[4] difficult employees may belong to any one or more than one of the following categories:

1. **Ineffective employees**: This category includes those employees whose performance is below acceptable standards. It may be due to several factors, such as lack of skills and abilities, shortcoming in the job itself and lack of appropriate motivation climate. In order to overcome the problem of ineffective employees, a manager may follow the guidelines as given in Exhibit 16.3.
2. **Alcoholic or substance-abusing employees**: Some employees have personal problems off the job (such as alcoholism, drug use and family problems), which affect their productivity on the job.
3. **Participants doing theft, fraud and other illegal acts**: There may be some employees who engage in various illegal acts, such as theft, misuse of company facilities or property, embezzlement, sabotage of products and parting with the trade secrets.
4. **Rule violators**: Difficult employees falling under this category consistently violate the organisational rules, such as by bringing weapons at work, sleeping on the job, coming late and being violent at the workplace. Such employees do not respond to supervisory reactions. At times, it is difficult to identify violence-prone people even by the best trained managers.

Organisations implement a variety of techniques and programmes to tackle difficult employees, but there remains much to be done.

Approaches/Aspects to Discipline

There are several approaches to discipline, though the positive discipline approach and the negative discipline approach have been in much limelight. The main approaches are as follows:

1. **The hot stove rule**: One view of discipline is referred to as the hot stove rule.[5] In case a person touches a hot stove, he/she is likely to sustain burn injuries. Hence, the hot stove rule involves the following:
    a. **Warning system**: It is expected of a good management to warn its subordinates the consequences of the undesirable behaviour.
    b. **Immediate burn**: In order to maintain discipline, action should happen immediately so that the accused should see the connection between the act and discipline.
    c. **Consistency**: As the hot stove burns everyone alike, any employee who performs the same undesirable act will be disciplined similarly.

d. **Impersonality**: Disciplinary action is not pointed towards a person; it is meant to eliminate undesirable behaviours.[6] Punishment should be impersonal in application.

2. **Negative discipline/progressive discipline approach**: Negative discipline is also known as punitive, enforced, autocratic or coercive discipline. In it, violators of rules and regulations suffer penalties. The purpose of negative discipline is to scare others, that is, to keep others in line and to ensure that they do not indulge in undesirable behaviour. It is deterrent in nature. It involves the use of techniques such as reprimands, fines, lay-offs, demotions, transfers and the like. In progressive discipline, a sequence of penalties is administered, that is, each subsequent one is slightly more severe than the previous one. For example, while the first violation may attract an oral warning within 24 hours of return to work and a written record of the act to be kept in the file of the employee concerned, the second violation may invite written warning which is to be kept in the employee's file. The third violation may result in two-week lay-off without pay, and the record of the same to be kept in the employee's file. The fourth violation may attract dismissal of the employee concerned. Proper documentation of everything is very important in this approach.

3. **Positive discipline approach**: In the foregoing two approaches, the focus is on the past behaviour. However, employees disciplined in a punitive way may not necessarily build commitment into their jobs. Hence, a better approach, known as positive approach, came into prominence, which is future-oriented and aims at solving the problems in consultation with employees in such a way that the problem does not arise again. It aims at reformation. In some organisations, instead of issuing a warning, if an act of indiscipline is committed, only a reminder about behaviour is issued. For repeated violation(s), instead of imposing fine or suspension, a decision-making leave is sanctioned. If the employee, even after the aforesaid leave, does not commit to the rules, his/her services are terminated. This approach recognises that people make mistakes. Although it de-emphasises punitive action, it uses the most punishing consequence of all, being discharged.[7]

    Positive discipline emphasises the concepts of self-discipline, team spirit, respect for rules, regulations and procedures, regard for supervisors, greater freedom for development, and willingness to cooperate and coordinate. It believes in talking to the employee and counselling him/her to behave. Positive approach is thus a soft approach and evokes better response when the management applies the principle of positive motivation.

4. **Human relations approach**: Human relations approach, which is also known as humanistic approach, is a soft approach and aims at healthy interpersonal relationship between the employees and their supervisors. In it, efforts are made to enable the accused employee to improve his/her behaviour. Hence, the problem is thoroughly analysed, its root cause is found out and remedial steps are taken.

5. **Judicial approach**: In this approach, the relevant acts such as the Industrial Disputes Act, 1947, and the Industrial Employment (Standing Orders) Act, 1946, play an important role in the maintenance of discipline. Employees know the consequences of violating the provisions of the acts and, therefore, take due precautions in respect of their work behaviour. There are many labour laws which also help directly or indirectly in maintaining discipline in an organisation.

Thus, we see that each of these approaches has its own advantages and disadvantages. Although it cannot be said that which of the discussed approaches is foolproof, positive

Managing Employee Discipline and Handling Grievances 535

discipline approach appears to be a relatively better option because it is not restrictive in nature and prompts employees to fall in line with the rules, regulations, procedures and guidelines issued by their respective organisations.

Factors Responsible for Indiscipline

There are several factors which may be responsible for lack of discipline in an organisation. For convenience's sake, these may be divided into the following categories:

1. **External factors**: There are several economic, social and political factors, which may cause indiscipline in an organisation. For example, the ideology of the ruling party, the character of political leaders, the general level of education among masses and the social and ethical values of the general public may also affect the climate of discipline in an organisation. Religious acrimony in the population of the country, caste feelings, regional feelings, high rate of inflation, economic turmoil in the country and so on may also affect discipline level in organisations.

Exhibit 16.4   Internal Causes Responsible for Indiscipline

- Ineffective leadership which cannot motivate, control and motivate employees
- Hasty and not-duly-analysed decisions by management affecting employees
- Improper placement of employees
- Defective supervision
- Favouritism by management
- Low wages
- Poor working conditions
- Lack of opportunities for personal growth of employees
- Absence of code of conduct
- Absence of or inappropriate grievance redressal procedure
- Biased attitude of managerial personnel
- Inappropriate trade union leadership
- Excessive workload
- Defective communication system
- Unfair labour practices
- Illiteracy among workers
- Outside leadership in trade union(s)
- Victimisation of workers
- Non-recognition of personality and sentiments of employees

Exhibit 16.5   Personal Factors Responsible for Causing Indiscipline

- Addiction to drugs, alcoholism and so on
- Poor upbringing
- Irritating temperament
- Aggressive attitude
- Negative attitude

536 Integrating, Maintaining and Retaining Human Resources

2. **Internal factors:** Internal factors are mainly responsible for causing indiscipline in an organisation (Exhibit 16.4).
3. **Personal factors:** Personal factors responsible for causing indiscipline, which are related to a few individuals, are shown in Exhibit 16.5.

Exhibit 16.6   Checklist of Possible Causes of Deficient Behaviour

- Problems of intelligence and job knowledge
- Encroachment problems
- Motivational problems
- Physical problems
- Family problems
- Problems caused by work group
- Problems originating in company problems
- Problems stemming from society and its values
- Problems from the work context and the work itself

Source: Based on discussion in John B. Miner, *The Challenges of Managing* (Philadelphia: W. B. Saunders Company, 1975), 958–66.

Miner[8] has provided a checklist of possible causes of deficient behaviour (causing indiscipline) as shown in Exhibit 16.6.

Types/Forms of Punishment

There can be various types of punishment depending on the severity of act of indiscipline. Punishments can be divided into two categories:

1. **Major punishments:** Major punishments are awarded when the act of indiscipline is of a very serious nature or when the minor punishments do not prove effective in the case of a particular employee(s). Major punishments may comprise stopping the annual increments temporarily or permanently, transfer to an odd place/position, demotion, punitive suspension, termination of services and so on.
2. **Minor punishments:** Minor punishments are mild in the beginning but can be a little bit harsh subsequently, such as oral warning, written warning, withdrawal of a certain facility/privilege, fines, suspension, forced leave without pay and so on.

Forms of Indiscipline

There can be a very long list of forms of indiscipline, but the major ones include violation of rules, regulations and procedures laid down by the organisation; insubordination; absenteeism; gambling; drinking; taking drugs; tardiness; idling; fighting; shouting; loafing; mishandling tools, equipment, machinery and other properties of the organisation; poor performance of duties; stealing; threatening; sleeping on duty; and so on.

Many union–management contracts spell out the types of discipline and the offences for which corrective action will be taken. Some of the infractions that are typically specified are shown in Exhibit 16.7.

Exhibit 16.7 Some of the Infractions Typically Specified in Many Union–Management Contracts

- Incompetence—failures to perform the assigned job
- Misconduct—insubordination, dishonesty or violating a rule, such as smoking in a restricted area
- Violation of the contract—initiating a strike though there is a no-strike clause, for example

Source: Ivancevich, *Human Resource Management*, 501.

Maintenance of Discipline: Whose Responsibility?

Maintenance of proper discipline in the organisation is a joint responsibility of all concerned. However, it is the line people who share greater responsibility. It will, therefore, be desirable if foremen and supervisory staff are well versed in the techniques of maintenance of discipline. The management of an organisation can play an important role in this direction by formulating appropriate policies which can be instrumental in maintaining good discipline in an organisation. In addition to taking preventive steps such as code of conduct, grievance redressal procedure, WPM, transparency in administration, publicising discipline-related rules and regulations and free flow of communication, it should also take immediate disciplinary action against violators of discipline, which should be progressive in nature.

Alternatives to Punishment

There are several options to punishment and improving behaviour of the employees in an organisation:

1. **Rewarding:** There must be some incentives and encouragement for behaviour which is physically incompatible with the undesired behaviour. For example, there may be special weightage for regularly disciplined workers at the time of promotion.
2. **Allowing reasonable period for adjustment:** In case of newly appointed employees or inexperienced people, a reasonable period of time should be given to them for learning and not repeating the acts of indiscipline.
3. **Environmental engineering:** By bringing about some changes in the features of environment, some acts of indiscipline can be avoided. For example, some employees may mark the attendance of their tardy colleagues. This can be avoided if biometric machines are provided for taking attendance.
4. **Extinction:** Efforts can be made to identify what it is that causes the unruly behaviour. For example, in order to avoid undesirable comments against female employees by some male employees at the time of exit after the duty hours are over, a few

marshals can be posted on the way of exit or a separate exit can be provided for female employees.

Disciplinary Action and Basic Elements of Disciplinary Action Process

Broadly speaking, disciplinary action refers to conditioning of future behaviour by the application of rewards, such as appreciation, participation and other incentives, or penalties such as fines, reprimands and lay-offs. However, disciplinary action is commonly confined to the application of penalties that deter employees from behaving in an undesired fashion. The basic elements of the disciplinary action process include assigning responsibility for the administration of disciplinary action; awareness and clarity among employees about what behaviour is expected of them; association of employees in the formulation of rules and regulations, which should be implementable, fair and just; uniform application of punishment; presence of constructive element in punishment policy; knowledge about the consequences of violating rules, regulations and procedures; prompt disciplinary actions; getting facts; implementation of the principle of natural justice; fairness in determining penalty; and normal behaviour of the supervisor towards the accused after the disciplinary action has been taken.

Procedure for Taking Disciplinary Action

Usually, the procedure is laid down in the Standing Orders (certified per the provisions of the Industrial Employment [Standing Orders] Act, 1946) and the same has to be followed. In case no procedure is laid down or the Standing Orders do not exist, the following procedure is adopted by most organisations:

1. Preliminary investigation in order to establish a prima facie case
2. Issuing a charge sheet
3. Suspension pending enquiry, if necessary
4. Notice of enquiry
5. Conducting enquiry and providing opportunity to the accused to defend himself/herself, that is, following the principle of natural justice
6. Recording of findings by the enquiry officer
7. Awarding punishment
8. Communication of punishment
9. Implementation of penalty
10. Proper follow-up

Jucius has suggested the following steps:

1. Accurate statement of the disciplinary problems
2. Collection of full information on the case
3. Selection of tentative penalties to be applied
4. Choosing among the alternative penalties
5. Application of the penalty
6. Follow-up of the case

Legal Framework

The main laws related to punishment are discussed further here.

Industrial Employment (Standing Orders) Act, 1946[9]

The Standing Orders of an organisation usually specify the acts of misconduct. The misconduct is punishable only if it is committed within the premises of the establishment or in the vicinity thereof, except in a few cases. Warning, fine, stoppage of promotion, demotion, stopping annual increment for a certain period, suspension, termination by giving a 15-day notice or paying wages in lieu thereof and dismissal, that is, immediate termination of service without notice, though in the latter case the accused has to be given an opportunity to defend himself/herself, are common disciplinary actions/punishments. The accused can challenge the punishment in a court under certain circumstances as stated under the act:

1. **Industrial Disputes Act, 1947:**[10] The relevant sections on punishment in the act are Section 11A and Section 33.
2. **Payment of Wages Act, 1936:**[11] The relevant section regarding punishment in this act is Section 8.

Alternative Dispute Resolution (ADR)[12]

Formalised and institutionalised in the USA in 1922, the ADR involves using methods other than formal court litigation to settle a dispute. In the USA, the method is being used extensively, and a good number of unionised contracts comprise some form of binding dispute resolutions. The commonly used ADR methods are shown in Exhibit 16.8.

Essentials of a Good Disciplinary System

A disciplinary system can be more effective if it has the following features:

1. Existence of Code of Discipline/Code of Conduct (see Annexure 16.1).
2. Awareness about the relevant rules, regulations and procedures among the employees and supervisors.
3. A well-publicised procedure to be followed to determine penalty.
4. Immediate action following the happening of the act of indiscipline.
5. Objectivity and constructivism/fairness in action.
6. Disciplinary action should be taken in private so that the accused does not feel humiliated. It should not be taken in the presence of one's subordinates.
7. Normal attitude towards the employee after disciplinary action has been taken.
8. Proper follow-up.

Exhibit 16.8 Common ADR Methods Used

Mediation
Arbitration
Summary jury trial
Ministerial

Source: 'Overview' section at www.adr.org (accessed on July 2005).
Note: The American Arbitration Association handles over 230,000 cases each year.

Role of HR Manager

An HR manager plays a crucial role in the maintenance of discipline in an organisation. He/she is involved in advising top management and assisting line management in the development of constructive disciplinary philosophy and then communicating it to all concerned. He/she is also instrumental in the implementation of this policy, and he/she ensures that disciplinary action is fair and based on sound principles and that the principle of natural justice is duly followed. He/she is also instrumental in training executives and supervisors in handling disciplinary problems. He/she is also expected to involve workers or their representatives in the formulation and implementation of disciplinary programmes. He/she is supposed to strive hard in inculcating positive discipline among the employees. He/she is also supposed to develop diagnostic skills so as to understand deep-rooted causes of symptomatic manifestation of disciplinary problems. He/she is, therefore, expected to probe deeper into deep-rooted deprivation of needs and perceived blockages to achievement of certain goals in such cases. He/she is supposed to be a role model for others to emulate. He/she has to play an important role in improving work culture and creating opportunities for self-growth for employees. All these prove that the HR manager has to play an important role in the maintenance of discipline in an organisation.

Managing Grievances

The true index of the level of contentment of employees in an organisation is the quantum and nature of grievances in existence. These grievances may be genuine or ingenuine, real or imaginary, and valid or invalid. When the expectations of an employee from the organisation he/she is working for are not fulfilled, he/she develops a feeling of discontent or dissatisfaction. When he/she feels that some injustice has been done to him/her or that the organisation is not fair towards his/her cause, he/she is said to have a grievance. There is hardly any organisation where there are no grievances, though there may be difference of degree or substance.

Meaning and Definition

A grievance may be expressed or even implicit, though it should have continuity along with dissatisfaction. Here, it may be pertinent to distinguish among dissatisfaction, complaint and grievance. While a dissatisfaction is any state or feeling of discontent, a complaint is a spoken or written dissatisfaction with regard to anything brought to the notice of the foreman or supervisor concerned. A complaint becomes a grievance when this dissatisfaction is concerned with work and is brought to the notice of the management or of a union steward. That is why Beach[13] has rightly remarked, 'Grievance is any dissatisfaction or feeling of injustice in connection with one's employment situation that is brought to the notice of management'. Calhoon has also defined a grievance in almost the same sense when he says that a grievance is 'anything that an employee thinks or feels is wrong, and is generally accompanied by an actively disturbing feeling'.[14] According to the ILO, a grievance is a complaint of one or more workers with respect to wages and allowances, conditions of work and interpretation of service conditions covering such areas as overtime (hereafter OT), leave, transfer, promotion, seniority, job assignment and termination of service. Here, it should be noted that while an individual grievance relates to one or a few individuals and, therefore, should be handled by the grievance procedure of the organisation concerned, group grievances are concerned with general issues with policy implications, which are usually dealt with through collective bargaining. Trade unions play an important role in handling group grievances and usually keep themselves away from individual grievances, which are redressed through the grievance procedure of the organisation concerned.

As indicated earlier, a grievance may be genuine or ridiculous, stated or unstated, valid or invalid, legitimate or illegitimate, and in writing or not. However, the discontent causing the grievance must be connected with the organisation concerned. Of course, grievances exist in the minds of individuals, are produced and dissipated by situations, are fostered or healed by group pressures, are adjusted or made worse by supervisors, and are nourished or dissolved by the climate in an organisation, which is affected by all the mentioned factors and by the management.[15]

A grievance is a complaint, whether valid or not, about an organisational policy, procedure or managerial practice that creates dissatisfaction or discomforts.[16]

Features or Characteristics of Discontent-causing Grievances

Based on the definitions of and opinions discussed earlier, the discontent-causing grievances should have the following features:

1. The discontent should be caused by something connected with the organisation concerned.
2. The discontent may be valid or invalid, genuine or ingenuine, real or imaginary, true or untrue, rational or ridiculous, and in writing or not.
3. The discontent may be expressed or implied.

Causes of Grievances

Grievances may be related to a number of factors, such as the organisation, work environment, work group, supervision, economic issues, violation of rules or worker's self. However, grievances are mostly related to supervision, working conditions, victimisation, promotion, transfer, retirement, increments, OT, wages, bonus, incentives, seniority, leave, fringe benefits, disciplinary action, fine, difference of opinion, doubts and fears, attitude of trade union, ego, impractical attitude to life, wrong placement and so on. Chandra's survey has also pointed out most of these causes.[17] However, at times, the apparent cause of a grievance may not be a real one. The shoe might be pinching elsewhere. Still, the management should make every effort to study every grievance very carefully, analyse its root cause(s) and take remedial steps including change in the relevant policy, if need be.

Principles of Handling Grievances

Handling of grievances can be more effective if certain principles are adhered to, though at times because of involvement of human element in grievances, even these principles may not prove foolproof. The main principles[18] in this regard are as follows:

1. Principle of interviewing (of the aggrieved employee)
2. Management's attitude towards employees (of winning employees' confidence and trust)

3. **Long-run principles** (In addition to keeping into consideration the immediate or individual effect of grievances, their long-term impact should also be kept into consideration. Human nature, effects of the past and danger of losing confidence also have to be kept into consideration.)

Forms of Grievances

A grievance may be as follows:

1. **Factual grievance:** That is, when a legitimate need of the employee remains unfulfilled.
2. **Disguised grievance:** That is, a grievance arising out of reasons not known to even the grievant employee.
3. **Imaginary grievance:** That is, a grievance arising out of any misinformation, rumour, doubt and the like, for example, arising due to a false rumour that some employees have to be retrenched.

Tracing the Grievances

The main methods of tracing/identifying/discovering grievances are as shown in Exhibit 16.9.

In order to uncover the mystery surrounding grievances, any one or more than one of the aforementioned methods should be used, depending on the circumstances existing at a particular period of time.

Effects of Grievances

If not redressed timely, grievances may prove fatal to the health of an organisation because non-redressal of grievances affect all concerned. For example, grievances cause and increase absenteeism and labour turnover; dampen their confidence and morale; reduce their loyalty, sincerity and dedication; cause safety problems; and so on. All of these, in turn, may affect adversely the quality and quantum of output and may increase the cost of production because the employees may become indifferent to the cause of the organisation as they may idle away their time, operate machinery carelessly causing damage to it, waste raw material and so on. Grievances may affect human relations and IR and cause indiscipline—sometimes resulting in strikes and lockouts. Presence of unredressed grievances may require additional supervision and may cause stress among managerial personnel. However, grievances need immediate redressal.

Exhibit 16.9   Methods of Tracing Grievances

- Exit interview
- Grapevine or gossiping
- Observation
- Grievance procedure
- Unusual behaviour of the employee(s)
- Open-door policy
- Suggestion box
- Opinion survey
- Change in attitude of employee(s)

Advantages/Need for a Grievance Procedure

The adverse effects of grievances on the contentment, efficiency of employees and also the cost of production and quality and quantum of output, as stated in the foregoing head, emphasise the need for a grievance procedure in an organisation. Employees have a right that their grievances must be looked into. They should not feel that they are totally at the mercy of their supervisors. They should have a judicial type of justice whenever they feel the necessity of it. They also have a right to know the status of their grievance, that is, where they stand so far during the course of hearing of their grievance from time to time and stage to stage. The provision of a grievance redressal procedure in an organisation overcomes the said issues and neutralises, to a very great extent, the adverse impact caused by the absence of a grievance redressal procedure.

Grievance Procedure

A grievance procedure is the method or procedure by which a grievance is filed and carried through different steps or stages, leading to an ultimate decision.[19] A grievance procedure provides an orderly system, whereby both employer and union determine whether some action violated the contract.[20]

A grievance procedure may be a stepladder procedure in which a grievant may first present his/her grievance to his/her supervisor. If the grievant is not satisfied, then he/she moves to the next level, that is, the head of the department, and then to the joint grievance committee (which may have representatives of both the employees and the management), and thereafter to the CEO, and then may appeal for arbitration if the grievant is not satisfied with the decision at the immediately preceding stage. At every stage, the decision is to be taken within a set time framework. As against stepladder procedure, there may be an open-door policy in which the grievant employee is allowed to directly approach the head of the organisation or the officer designated for the purpose and present his/her grievance. However, the open-door policy may not be feasible in a large organisation as due to large number of employees, it may not be possible for the head of the organisation or the officer designated for the purpose to spare time for going through the grievances of individual employees.

Prerequisites for the Effectiveness of a Grievance Procedure

Since unredressed grievances may prove dangerous to the success of an organisation, it is necessary for an organisation to have a systematic grievance redressal procedure. However, for a grievance redressal procedure to be effective, it should possess the following prerequisites:

1. *Acceptability* by all concerned
2. *Simplicity,* that is, easily understandable by all concerned
3. *Promptness*, that is, the grievance should be promptly handled
4. *Adequate training* to all concerned, especially to the supervisors and the union representatives
5. *Time framework*, that is, the decision to be taken within the time limit at every stage
6. *Follow-up*, that is, a periodical review of the procedure and remedial steps, if required

However, it should be kept in view that the grievance redressal procedure should be in conformity with the existing legislation and supportive to the existing machinery.

A Manager's Steps for Handling Grievances

Flippo[21] has suggested the following steps to be undertaken by a manager for handling grievances:

1. Receive and define the nature of dissatisfaction
2. Get the facts
3. Analyse and decide
4. Apply the answer
5. Follow up

Some critical dos which are useful guides in handling grievances[22] are shown in Exhibit 16.10.

Exhibit 16.10   Dos Which Are Useful Guides in Handling Grievances

1. Investigate and handle each case as though it may eventually result in arbitration.
2. Talk with the employee about his/her grievance; give the person a full hearing.
3. Require the union to identify specific contractual provisions allegedly violated.
4. Comply with the contractual time limits for handling the grievance.
5. Visit the work area of the grievance.
6. Determine whether there were any witnesses.
7. Examine the grievant's personal record.
8. Fully examine prior grievance records.
9. Treat the union representative as your equal.
10. Hold your grievance discussions privately.
11. Fully inform your own supervisor of grievance matters.

Source: Based on discussion in E. B. Flippo, *Principles of Personnel Management* (Tokyo: McGraw-Hill, Kogakusha Ltd, 1976), 435–43.

Steps in the Grievance Procedure

The steps involved in a grievance procedure may vary in number depending on the number of factors, but usually the following are the main steps that a grievance procedure should consist of:

1. **Define the dissatisfaction correctly**: Having received the grievance, the management should define the problem accurately and in correct perspective.
2. **Collect relevant information and data**: Having understood the grievance correctly, the management should gather facts, figures, opinions and all other relevant information regarding the grievance through all possible sources, such as interviews, discussions and records kept in the organisation.
3. **Analyse and resolve**: Once the relevant information is available, it should be properly analysed, all possible solutions should be worked out, a comparative study should be made and the best solution should be selected.

4. **Immediate redressal**: Having identified the best solution, it should be promptly implemented. A delayed implementation of the decision may lose its desired impact and may not prove a deterrent.
5. **Follow up**: It is very essential to find out whether the desired impact of the decision taken and implemented could be obtained or not. If not, then a fresh exercise in the whole issue should be undertaken and remedial steps be taken.

IIPM[23] has summarised a grievance procedure as shown in Exhibit 16.11.

Exhibit 16.11   Grievance Procedure as Summarised by IIPM

- First of all, the grievance should be resolved at the lowest level, that is, between the grievant and his/her immediate superior.
- The grievant should be apprised that he/she can appeal against the decision of his/her immediate superior and to whom.
- The grievance should be promptly dealt with.
- In case the grievance is against any instruction issued by the supervisor, the grievant must first carry out that instruction before the grievance-handling procedure can be set in motion.

Source: Indian Institute of Personnel Management, *Personnel Management* (Calcutta: Indian Institute of Personnel Management, 1973), 29–30.

Model Grievance Procedure

It was in the 16th Session of the Indian Labour Conference (hereafter ILC) held in 1958 that the Code of Discipline was adopted and the Model Grievance Procedure was formulated in pursuance to the said Code. It is voluntary in nature. The grievance procedures existing at present in most organisations are based on the aforesaid Model Grievance Procedure, with certain changes depending on the requirement of the organisation concerned. The Model Grievance Procedure has the following time-bound steps (see Figure 16.1):

1. In case the grievant employee is not satisfied with the discussion with his/her foreman, the first stage of the grievance procedure involves presenting the grievance by the aggrieved employee to his/her supervisor/officer designated by the management for the purpose, who is supposed to reply within 48 hours of the presentation of the grievance.
2. In case the aggrieved worker is not satisfied with the decision taken by the supervisor/officer or does not receive reply within the stipulated period, he/she can either in person or accompanied by the departmental representative present his/her case to the head of his/her department designated by the management for the purpose within the specified time during which on any working day the grievant employee could meet the departmental head for presentation of his/her grievance. The departmental head is supposed to reply within three days of the receipt of the presentation of grievance.

546 Integrating, Maintaining and Retaining Human Resources

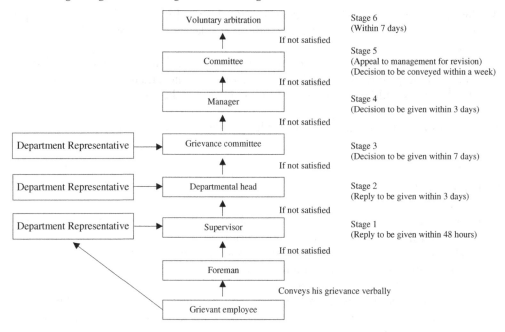

Figure 16.1 Model Grievance Procedure
Source: As adopted by the Indian Labour Conference (ILC) in May 1958.

3. In case the aggrieved employee is not satisfied with the reply of the departmental head, he/she may request that his/her grievance may be forwarded to the grievance committee, which has the representatives of both employees and management. The grievance committee is supposed to make its recommendations to the manager within seven days of the worker's request. The management is under obligation to accept the recommendations made by the grievance committee if the same are unanimous. In the case of difference of opinions among the members of the committee, their views along with the relevant papers shall be put up before the manager who shall communicate his/her decision within three days from the receipt of the grievance committee's recommendations.
4. If the decisions of the management are not communicated within the prescribed time or if the grievant is not satisfied with the decision, then he/she can appeal to the management for revision of the decision. The management is supposed to give its decision within seven days from the date of the grievant's revision petition.
5. If still the aggrieved employee is not satisfied, then the union and management may refer the grievance to voluntary arbitration within seven days of the receipt of the management's decision by the aggrieved employee.

However, the aforesaid procedure is not applicable if the grievance is caused due to dismissal of an employee. In such a case, the discharged or dismissed employee may appeal to the dismissing authority or to a senior authority specified by the management within a week from the date of dismissal or discharge.

Grievance Management in Indian Industries

On the legal front, it is usually the Industrial Employments (Standing Orders) Act, 1946; the Factories Act, 1948; and the Industrial Disputes Act, 1947, which deal with the grievances of industrial employees. However, these acts have not been able to tackle the problem and the progress made in this regard is far from satisfactory. In addition to these acts, the Model Grievance Procedure or the Grievance Procedures developed by different organisations on their own, which are usually based on the Model Grievance Procedure formulated based on the Code of Discipline, adopted by the 16th Session of the ILC, are commonly used to handle grievances. Per the findings of a study of 12 textile mills located in Coimbatore, which was jointly sponsored by the South India Textile Research Association and the National Productivity Council, no systematic and formal grievance procedure exists in any of the sample mills. There is a sort of informal procedure based on traditions and conventions that is operative in most organisations. However, some large-scale units do not have any procedure worth mentioning.

In most organisations in our industries, there is no systematic procedure of maintaining records of grievances. Union representatives play an important role in the settlement of grievances where there is only one majority union. In many organisations, it is the labour officers or the labour welfare officers who deal with some of the grievances in their respective organisations. In some cases, the works committees constituted under the provisions of the Industrial Disputes Act, 1947, also play some role in this direction, but it is not significant. Most of the grievances in Indian industries are related to wages and allied issues. The number of levels dealing with grievance differ from organisation to organisation and vary between two and six. It may be suggested that while in small organisations employing less than 500 employees, the grievance procedure may have three stages only, in medium-sized units employing 501 up to 2,000 employees, it may have five stages, and for even larger organisations, the grievance procedures may have six stages.

After all is said and done, there is no denying the fact that a formal grievance-handling procedure can play a highly significant role in redressing the grievances of employees, which, in turn, may give a boost to the morale of employees and be effective in increasing their productivity and subsequently the overall growth of an organisation.

Chapter Review

1. No organisation can sustain itself unless it has a disciplined workforce because discipline is the force that prompts individuals or groups to observe rules, regulations and procedures, which are necessary for the effective functioning of an organisation.
2. Maintenance of discipline in an organisation is in the interest of all the stakeholders because it infuses confidence and boosts morale of employees, improves working of the organisation, helps in improving both quantity and quality of its products, helps in reducing cost of production and so on. Adherence to the principles of discipline, therefore, makes the discipline system effective.
3. Almost all organisations have some 'difficult' employees who may be ineffective, may be violent, may be alcoholic and may indulge in theft, fraud and other illegal activities. The main approaches to discipline include the hot stove rule,

positive discipline, negative/progressive discipline, human relations approach and judicial approach. Factors responsible for indiscipline in an organisation may be external, internal or personal or a mixture of any two or all of these factors. Types of punishment may include major punishments as well as minor punishments.
4. Alternatives to punishment may comprise rewards, improvement in the working environment, allowing reasonable time for adjustment, extinction and so on. Disciplinary action refers to conditioning of future behaviour. The procedure for disciplinary action may include preliminary investigation, issue of charge sheet, suspension of the employee if necessary, notice of enquiring, conduct of enquiry following the principle of natural justice, recording of findings of enquiry, awarding punishment, communication of punishment, implementation of punishment and proper follow-up.
5. An HR manager is supposed to play an important role in the maintenance of discipline. He/she is, therefore, expected to have diagnostic skills to identify deep-rooted causes of symptomatic manifestations of disciplinary problems and be capable of taking necessary remedial steps.
6. Grievance is any dissatisfaction or feeling of injustice in connection with one's employment situation that is brought to the notice of management. Grievances may be caused by a number of factors, which may be organisation-related, worker-related or both. Grievances may be factual, disguised or even imaginary. Therefore, it is necessary to uncover the mystery surrounding grievances. The employers also have their grievances against their workers.
7. Employee grievances affect all the stakeholders adversely and spoil the working environment of the organisation. Hence, it is in the interest of all concerned to have a grievance redressal procedure in an organisation which is acceptable to all concerned, is simple to understand, encourages promptness in handling, has time framework, is handled by duly trained personnel and is properly followed up. Steps involved in a grievance procedure may consist of defining the dissatisfaction correctly, collecting relevant information/data, analysing and resolving, immediate redressal and proper follow-up.
8. A grievance procedure may be based on an open-door policy or a stepladder procedure.
9. The Model Grievance Procedure was formulated in pursuance of the Code of Discipline, which was adopted in the 16th Session of the ILC held in 1958. The Model Grievance Procedure suggests five time-bound stages whereby the grievant employee first approaches his/her supervisor, and if not satisfied, then to the head of the department, and then the grievance committee and then to the management. Thereafter, he/she can apply for review and if still not satisfied, then the grievance can be referred to voluntary arbitration.
10. In Indian industries, certain grievances are taken care of per the Industrial Employment (Standing Orders) Act, 1946; Factories Act, 1948; and Industrial Disputes Act, 1947. However, most organisations have evolved their own grievance procedure, which is usually based on the Model Grievance Procedure with minor modifications here or there per their requirement. Grievance procedure plays a significant role in redressing grievances wherever the same is in force.

Managing Employee Discipline and Handling Grievances

Key Terms

- absenteeism
- code of conduct
- code of discipline
- complaint
- difficult employee
- disciplinary action
- disciplinary procedure
- discipline
- disguised grievance
- dissatisfaction
- environmental engineering
- exit interview
- extinction
- grapevine
- grievance
- grievance procedure
- grievant employee
- hot stove rule
- human relations approach
- indiscipline
- judicial approach
- model
- natural justice
- negative discipline
- open-door policy
- outside leadership
- positive discipline
- prima facie case
- progressive discipline
- procedure
- stepladder procedure
- victimisation
- voluntary arbitration

Discussion Questions

1. Discuss how a disciplined workforce helps in improving the effectiveness of an organisation.
2. Discuss who a 'difficult' employee is and what the approaches to discipline are.
3. Discuss the factors responsible for indiscipline and also the alternatives to punishment.
4. Discuss what the term 'disciplinary action' means and the steps involved in the disciplinary process.
5. Discuss the role of an HR manager in the maintenance of discipline in an organisation.
6. Discuss what the term 'grievance' is all about and how it differs from 'dissatisfaction' and 'complaint'.
7. Discuss the causes and forms of grievances.
8. Discuss why it is important for an organisation to have a grievance procedure.
9. Discuss what is meant by grievance procedure and also the prerequisites necessary to make a grievance procedure effective.
10. Discuss in detail the genesis of the Model Grievance Procedure and various stages involved in it.

Individual and Group Activities

1. Either as an individual or in a group of two, visit some large organisation employing more than 1,000 employees and discuss with the HR officials so as to find out the status of 'difficult' employees in their organisation and how the management deals with them.

2. In a group of three members, discuss with the HR officials of a big manufacturing organisation the main causes of indiscipline in their organisation and what alternatives to punishment are used in their organisation.
3. As an individual or in a group of two members, visit some large organisation and discuss with the trade union officials whether the management follows all the main steps involved in a good disciplinary procedure while taking disciplinary action against its employee(s). Prepare a brief report in this regard.
4. In a group of three members, discuss with the trade union officials of a medium-scale organisation the main causes of grievances of workers and whether the management undertakes any steps to trace/identify the grievances in their organisation.
5. As an individual, discuss with the HR officials of a large organisation whether their organisation has a grievance procedure and whether it is based on the Model Grievance Procedure. If not, then what are the main deviations? Later on, prepare a brief report on it.

Application Case 16.1

2012 LLR 1074 MADRAS HIGH COURT

Hon'ble Mr K. Chandru, J.

W.P. No. 11726/2008, D/-28-6-2012

Management of Metropolitan Transport Corporation

(Now known as Metropolitan Transport Corporation, Chennai) Limited Vs

Presiding Officer, I Additional Labour Court, Chennai & Anr.

Important Points

- Assaulting a superior officer at the workplace is a serious misconduct and, if proved in the enquiry, awarding reinstatement even without back wages to the worker by the Labour Court is not justified and liable to be set aside.
- Discipline at the workplace is very important and should not be overlooked by showing sympathy towards the worker who had assaulted his/her superior at the workplace which has been proved.

Order

1. This writ petition is filed by the state-owned Transport Corporation having its headquarters at Chennai. In this writ petition, they have come forward to challenge the award dated 24 May 2006 passed in I.D. No. 623 of 1999 by the First Additional Labour Court, Chennai, the first respondent herein.
2. By the impugned award, the Labour Court directed the reinstatement of the second respondent workman without back-wages, but with continuity of service.
3. The writ petition was admitted on 9 June 2008. Pending the writ petition, an interim stay was granted. Subsequently, the second respondent workman filed two applications, one for vacating the interim order and another for grant of wages under section 17B of the Industrial Dispute Act, 1947. By an order dated 7 July 2009, this court disposed of the interim applications by making the interim stay absolute and

also issued direction to pay monthly wages in terms of section 17B of the Industrial Disputes Act. Subsequently, the matter was referred for resolution of dispute by Permanent and Continuous High Court Lok Adalat. But the Lok Adalat was unable to solve the dispute and returned the papers for deciding the matter on merits, vide order dated 25 October 2010.
4. Since the petitioner management does not file the documents filed before the Labour Court, this court directed the Registry to summon the records from the Labour Court, and accordingly, original records were summoned and perused by the court.
5. It is seen from the records that the second respondent workman was joined as a driver in the petitioner corporation and was suspended from duty on 16 January 1997, alleging four charges against him. The charges levelled against the petitioner was that on 14 January 1997, he entered the time keeper's room along with the duty conductor and shouted at the assistant engineer by name Jayakumar in a rough and rude manner that he made certain defects in his posting vehicle, and when the said Jayakumar replied that all the complaints were attended, the second respondent workman did not accept the word of the said assistant engineer and so he threatened the assistant engineer. At that time, the branch manager of Avadi depot was present in the time office, and he called the second respondent workman and enquired into the complaint. The second respondent made same complaint against the branch manager in a rude manner, who was present at that time in the time office. He tried to convince the second respondent and explained that the defects were rectified on 13 January 1997 itself, and if he is not satisfied, he can take another spare vehicle. Without listening to the word of the branch manager, the workman suddenly slapped on the left cheek of the branch manager and also made an attempt to assault the branch manager. The other staff, including the security guard, who were present in the spot, took away the workman from the place of incident and sent him outside the depot gate. On this incident, a detailed report was given to the petitioner corporation for taking necessary action and thereafter, the workman was placed under suspension, effective 16 January 1997. He was issued with a charge memo dated 17 January 1997, and his explanations were called for. The workman denied the allegations levelled against him. Subsequently, an enquiry was conducted. The enquiry officer, in his report, found him guilty of the charges. Along with the enquiry report, the second respondent workman was given a second show cause notice, and the workman gave his explanation to the petitioner corporation. Not satisfied with his explanation and taking into account his past conduct, the second respondent workman was dismissed from service on 23 July 1997.
6. As against the dismissal order dated 23 July 1997, the second respondent workman raised an industrial dispute under Section 2(A)(2) of the Industrial Disputes Act, 1947, before the government labour officer. The said conciliation officer, as he could not bring about mediation, gave his failure report dated 18 January 1999. On the strength of the failure report, the second respondent workman filed a claim statement dated nil.
7. The dispute was registered as I.D. No. 623/1999, and a notice was issued to the petitioner corporation. The petitioner corporation filed a counter-statement dated 7 March 2000. In the counter-statement, it was stated that not making any complaint to the police station will not minimise the gravity of misconduct of the workman.
8. Before the Labour Court, the workman examined himself as W.W.1 and marked ten documents as Exs. W1 to W10. The management examined one Janarthanan as

M.W.1, and on their side, eleven documents were marked as Exs. M1 to M11. Ex. M9 is the copy of the past service record of the workman. Ex. M11 series is the basic report given to the petitioner corporation regarding the incident.

9. The Labour Court, upon analysing the materials placed before it, both oral and documentary, came to the conclusion that there was no violation of principles of natural justice in the procedure adopted in the enquiry. The Labour Court also held that it did not find any justifiable reason to interfere with the findings of the enquiry officer. However, curiously, in para 7 of the award, the Labour Court recorded as follows:

> The evidence of the eye witness as well as the victim before the Enquiry Officer fortifies that wordy alterations between the workman and the Branch Manager resulted in slapping. The actual wordy alterations between the parties had not been elicited during domestic enquiry and, therefore, the utterances which actually provoked the petitioner to slap his own superior is not known. . . . Considering all the above facts, this Court feels in the interest of justice that lesser punishment in lieu of dismissal will be proper one. It is pertinent to note that the petitioner is now aged about 53 years and his service will also be for another 5 to 6 years only. Instead of dismissal, withholding of full backwages on the basis of 'no work no pay' will meet the ends of justice.

10. Ms. Rita Chandrasekar, learned counsel for the petitioner corporation, has stated that having found the enquiry valid and also having held that the charges are proved, there is no question of showing any sympathy to the workman, especially when he has assaulted his superior in the presence of witnesses, which, even according to the Labour Court, was clearly found proved. Once the enquiry is held to be fair and findings are recorded against the workman, then the question of invoking Section 11A of the Industrial Disputes Act, 1947, for a series of misconducts will not arise.

11. In the light of the findings recorded and the legal precedent referred to, it is not a fit case where any relief can be given to the second respondent workman, and the Labour Court clearly erred in directing reinstatement of the workman, though without back-wages, and it did not take into account the binding precedent of the Supreme Court made in this regard. Hence, the impugned award dated 24 May 2006 passed in I.D. No. 623/1999 by the first respondent Labour Court stands set aside and the writ petition stands allowed. However, there will be no order as to costs.

Questions

1. Do you approve of the judgement delivered by the Labour Court based mostly on the compassionate ground? Yes or no. Why? Give reasons.
2. Do you agree with the judgement given by the Madras High Court? Yes or no? Why? Give arguments.
3. Were you the final authority to decide the present case, what would have been your judgement and why?

Annexure 16.1

Code of Discipline in Industry

To maintain discipline in industry (in both public and private sectors), there has to be (a) a just recognition by employers and workers of the rights and responsibilities of either party, as defined by the laws and agreements (including bipartite and tripartite agreements arrived at all levels from time to time), and (b) a proper and willing discharge by either party of its obligations consequent on such recognition.

The central and state governments, on their part, will arrange to examine and set right any shortcomings in the machinery they constitute for the administration of labour laws.

To ensure better discipline in industry, management and union agree on not involving in some activities that are listed here.

Management and union(s) agree on the following:

1. No unilateral action should be taken in connection with any industrial matter and that disputes should be settled at appropriate level.
2. The existing machinery for settlement of disputes should be utilised with the utmost expedition.
3. There should be no strike or lockout without notice.
4. Affirming their faith in democratic principles, they bind themselves to settle all future differences, disputes and grievances by mutual negotiation, conciliation and voluntary arbitration.
5. Neither party will have recourse to (a) coercion, (b) intimidation, (c) victimisation or (d) go-slow.
6. They will avoid (a) litigation, (b) sit-down and stay-in strikes and (c) lockouts.
7. They will promote constructive cooperation between their representatives at all levels and between workers themselves and abide by the spirit of agreements mutually entered into.
8. They establish upon a mutually agreed basis a grievance procedure which will ensure a speedy and full investigation leading to settlement.
9. They will abide by various stages in the grievance procedure and take no arbitrary action which would bypass this procedure.
10. They will educate the management personnel and workers regarding their obligations to each other.

Management agrees on the following:

1. Not to increase workload unless agreed upon or settled otherwise.
2. Not to support or encourage any unfair labour practice, such as (a) interference with the right of employees to enrol or continue as union members; (b) discrimination, restraint or coercion against any employee because of recognised activity of trade unions; and (c) victimisation of any employee and abuse of authority in any form.
3. To take prompt action for (a) settlement of grievances and implementation of settlements and awards and (b) decisions and orders.
4. To display in conspicuous places in the undertaking the provisions of this code in local language(s).

5. To distinguish between actions justifying immediate discharge and those where discharge must be preceded by a warning, reprimand, suspension or some other form of disciplinary actions and to arrange that all such disciplinary actions should be subject to an appeal through normal grievance procedure.
6. To take appropriate disciplinary action against its officers and members in cases where enquiries reveal that they were responsible for precipitate action by workers, leading to indiscipline.
7. To recognise the union in accordance with the criteria (discussed later on in the chapter) evolved at the 16th Session of the ILC held in May 1958.

Unions agree on the following:

1. Not to engage in any form of physical duress.
2. Not to permit demonstrations which are not peaceful and not to permit rowdyism in demonstration.
3. That their members will not engage or cause other employees to engage in any union activity during working hours unless as provided for by law, agreement or practice.
4. To discourage unfair labour practices such as (a) negligence of duty, (b) careless operation, (c) damage to property, (d) interference with or disturbance to routine, normal work and (e) insubordination.
5. To take prompt action to implement awards, agreements, settlements and decisions.
6. To display the provisions of this code in the local language(s) in conspicuous places in the union offices.
7. To express disapproval and to take appropriate action against office-bearers and members for indulging in action against the spirit of this code.

Criteria for Recognition of Unions

1. Where there is more than one union, a union claiming recognition should have been functioning for at least one year after registration. Where there is only one union, this condition would not apply.
2. The membership of the union should cover at least 15% of the workers in the establishment concerned. Membership would be counted only of those who had paid their subscription for at least three months during the period of six months immediately preceding the reckoning.
3. A union may claim to be recognised as a representative union for an industry in a local area if it has a membership of at least 25% of the workers of that industry in that area.
4. When a union has been recognised, there should be no change in its position for a period of two years.
5. Where there are several unions in an industry or establishment, the one with the largest membership should be recognised.
6. A representative union for an industry in an area should have the right to represent the workers in all the establishments in the industry, but if a union of workers in a particular establishment has a membership of 50% or more of the workers of that establishment, it should have the right to deal with matters of purely local interest such as the handling of grievances pertaining to its own members. All other workers who are not members of that union might either operate through the representative union for the industry or seek redressal directly.

7. In the case of trade union federations which are not affiliated to any of the four central organisations of labour, the question of recognition would have to be dealt with separately.
8. Only unions which observe the Code of Discipline would be entitled to recognition.

Thus, we see that the striking feature of the code is that emphasis has been put on mutual agreement rather than on compulsory arbitration or adjudication. There is no legal sanction behind the code. Above all, the code is not superimposed from above, nor has it a statutory basis. However, it cannot be said that the code has no value. The code is helpful in maintaining industrial democracy. According to the code, representatives of management and unions should agree to encourage constructive cooperation between their representatives at all levels and between workers themselves.

For India, the Code of Discipline is essential to practise because its non-observance would cause harm not only to the individual worker but also to the whole nation. Keeping in view the same objective, the Code of Discipline provides that there should be no strikes and lockouts without notice, and neither party should have recourse to coercion, intimidation, victimisation or go-slow and also litigation and stay-in strikes.

Notes

1. Ivancevich, *Human Resource Management*, 520.
2. R. D. Calhoon, *Managing the Personnel* (New York, NY: Harper & Row, 1964), 206.
3. Bittel, *What Every Supervisor Should Know*, 308; P. Falcone, 'Fundamentals of Progressive Discipline', *HR Magazine* 19, no. 25 (February 1977): 90–92.
4. Ivancevich, *Human Resource Management*, 520–30.
5. See S. Ackroyd and P. Thompson, *Organisational Behaviour* (London: SAGE Publications, 2004).
6. Ivancevich, *Human Resource Management*, 532–33.
7. Ibid., 534.
8. J. Miner, *The Challenge of Managing* (Philadelphia, PA: Saunders, 1975).
9. For details of the act, see Sharma, *Industrial Relations and Labour Legislation*.
10. For more details, see Ibid., 767–83.
11. Ibid., 628–37.
12. See P. M. Armstrong, 'Georgia-Pacific's ADR Program A Critical Review after 10 Years', *Dispute Resolution Journal* 7, no. 1 (May–July 2005): 18–22.
13. Dale S. Beach, *Personnel: The Management of People at Work* (London: Macmillan, 1975), 583.
14. Calhoon, *Managing the Personnel*, 319.
15. Ibid., 321.
16. Ivancevich, *Human Resource Management*, 501.
17. S. Chandra, *Grievance Procedure: A Survey of Practices in Industries in India* (Hyderabad: Administrative Staff College, 1968).
18. For details see Jucius, *Personnel Management*, 465–67.
19. Sharma, *Industrial Relations and Labour Legislation*, 284–85.
20. A. A. Sloane and F. Witney, *Labour Relations*, 10th ed. (New Jersey, USA: Prentice Hall, 1985), 221–27.
21. For details, see Flippo, *Principles of Personnel Management*, 435–37.
22. For an excellent checklist, see M. G. Newport, *Supervisory Management: Tools and Techniques* (Eagan, Minnesota: West Publishing Company, 1976), 273. See also M. Lurie, 'The Eight Essential Steps in Grievance Processing', *Dispute Resolution Journal* 54, no. 4 (November 1999): 61–65.
23. Indian Institute of Personnel Management, *Personnel Management in India* (Calcutta: Indian Institute of Personnel. Management, 1973).

Part VI
Employee Relations and Personnel Records, Audit and Research

17 Human Relations and Industrial Relations

Learning Objectives

After studying this chapter, you should be able to do the following:

1. Explain the concept, meaning and all the main human relations approaches.
2. List and describe the aims of a human relations policy and also why good human relations are necessary in an organisation.
3. Explain the steps which can be instrumental in improving human relations in industry.
4. List and describe the Hawthorne experiments and the contributions made by them.
5. Explain the concept, meaning and characteristics of IR.
6. List and describe the theoretical perspectives and approaches to IR.
7. List and describe the main objectives of IR and also why good IR are necessary for the success of an organisation.
8. List and describe the factors affecting IR.
9. Explain the causes and effects of poor IR and how to improve IR.
10. Give highlights of IR in India since independence of the country, and also indicate what should be the strategy of management with regard to IR in an organisation.

Introduction

Satisfied and duly contented employees are a necessary prerequisite for effective collaboration in an organisation because subordinates cannot be forced into cooperation. Good human relations play an important role in making an employee feel contented. They are an indication that an employee is being treated as a human being and that his/her emotions, sentiments, feelings and personality are being duly recognised by his/her boss and other people that he/she interacts with. Similarly, good IR are an index that the organisation believes in and follows the principles of industrial democracy in its day-to-day operations and further that the management and the workers' union have mutual trust and faith in each other. Good IR also indicate that the process and institutions of collective bargaining, WPM, grievance handling, fixation of wages and allowances, fringe benefits and so on are in place and yielding the desired results. It is because of these reasons that every organisation aims at maintaining good human relations and IR.

Meaning and Definition of Human Relations in Industry

In the broadest sense, the term 'human relations' refers to the interaction of people in all walks of life—in schools, colleges, homes, business, government and so on. But when we talk of human relations in industry', then, in a wider sense, it signifies the relationship that should exist between the human beings engaged in industry. However, in actual practice, the term signifies the relationship that should be cultivated and practised by an employer or a supervisor with his/her subordinates.

As a matter of fact, the art of human relations involves getting along with people either as individuals or as a group. Good human relations are an effective instrument to motivate the personnel towards the achievement of individual as well as organisational goals. It is perhaps for this reason that W. E. G. Scott has remarked, 'Human relations are a process of an effective motivation of individual in a given situation in order to achieve a balance of objectives which will yield greater human satisfaction and help accomplish company goals'.

Keith Davis has also observed that from the viewpoint of a manager, human relations is the integration of people into a work situation that motivates them to work together productively, cooperatively and with economic, psychological and social satisfaction.[1] Effective human relations depend on fulfilment of economic, social and psychological wants (see Figure 17.1).

In literal terms, 'human relations in industry' is a term generally used for organisational behaviour. From the point of view of management, human relations is motivating people in organisations to develop teamwork spirit in order to fulfil their needs and to achieve organisational goals efficiently and economically. The approach of human relations deals with the psychological variables of organisational functioning in order to increase the efficiency of organisations. It is the process of integration of man-to-man and man-to-organisations.

Although land, labour, capital and enterprise are fundamental factors of production, without the willingness and cooperation of subordinates, it is not possible for management to produce anything. The management can obtain their cooperation through the human relations approach. To follow the human relations approach in an organisation is a major form of motivation. Modern managers realise this fact very well that a business organisation is a complex form of human relations and certain social variables. It studies those positive aspects which invoke positive response in work behaviour.

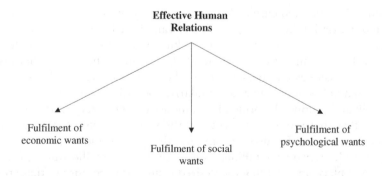

Figure 17.1 Effective Human Relations

Human Relations Approach

Keith Davis has defined human relations approach as follows: 'Human relations as an area of management practice is the integration of people into a work situation in a way that motivates them to work together productively, cooperatively and with economic, psychological and social satisfaction'.

Thus, Keith Davis views the human relations approach as humane treatment towards employees in the organisation. The problem of human relations is a moral and social problem, and its main object is to make man-to-man and man-to-group relations satisfactory. It is a process of integration between the organisational goals and individual motives. The following are the main features of this approach:

1. **Social factors in organisation**: An organisation is basically influenced by social factors. Elton Mayo has described an organisation as a social system of cliques, informal status system, rituals, and a mixture of loyal, non-logical and illogical behaviour. Thus, an organisation is more than a formal structure, and people are socio-psychological beings. These characteristics determine the output and efficiency in the organisation.
2. **Groups**: In the organisations, individuals tend to create groups. The group determines their norms of behaviour. Thus, management cannot deal with workers as individuals but as members of work groups, subject to the influence of these groups.
3. **Integrating process**: The process of human relations demands from the management a practice in leadership and communication in order to avoid conflicts among the group and individuals. Its main focus is on motivation. It involves the creation of a healthy and cooperative environment in the organisation. Democratic style of leadership is the best style, which ensures cooperation and active support of subordinates.
4. **Socio-psychological approach**: The human relations approach is a socio-psychological human behavioural approach. It concentrates on the study of human needs and the social and psychological aspects of the work. The approach emphasises upon the fact that a person is diversely motivated, and psychological factors play a more important role in his/her motivation.
5. **Other approaches**: The other approaches to human relations are as follows:

    a. **Rewards, soft or weak approach**: This approach is based on the assumption that the personnel in an undertaking are motivated to work to the extent to which they are rewarded. Reward and good working conditions play an effective role in making a worker work better and harder.
    b. **Fear and punishment or hard approach**: This approach is based on Theory X. It is the use of force, threat, fear and tight control that makes a worker work. But this approach is no more relevant in the modern context when trade unions have become a potential force.
    c. **Carrot and stick approach**: This approach is based on the assumption that people may be motivated to put in their best efforts either by rewarding or withholding rewards. The rewards are related to effective performance.
    d. **Path–goal approach**: This approach is based on the assumption that people work harder when they perceive that harder work is a path towards the goal they seek for.

Thus, the essential feature of the human relations approach is the interaction of management people and subordinates. It is an optimum relationship between productivity of organisation and human satisfaction. It is a problem of developing good relations in industry, to motivate subordinates and getting their willing cooperation for work. It is concerned with the problem of developing people and not techniques or skills.[2] It tells the management how to deal with people and to make them favourably responsive.

Fundamental Concepts of Human Relations in Industry

The concept of human relations is a noteworthy social approach towards the establishment of interpersonal relationship between superiors and subordinates. As management is a social science and like every social science, the approach of human relations requires certain fundamental concepts revolving around the nature of man and the nature of organisations which are imperative to be understood. In brief, they are as follows.

Concepts Relating to Nature of Man

As regards the nature of man, there are four basic assumptions which are as follows:

1. **Motivation**: In business organisations, the work is done by the workers. According to the need theory, both normal human behaviour and his/her course of future action are caused by a person's need structure. So management can influence the behaviour of individuals in the organisation by influencing their needs. The management can create suitable environment in the organisation conductive to the fulfilment of individual needs within the overall structure.
2. **Individual differences**: People have much in common, but they also differ in many respects—psychology tells us that each person has his/her own world. So management can get the subordinates motivated by treating them individually and differently. Only one measure of motivation cannot motivate all. Some are motivated by money, some others by status, and so on. Hence, an overall plan needs to deal with the subordinates individually. It is according to the saying that 'the whole philosophy of human relations begins with man and ends on man'.
3. **A whole person**: Some managers think that they have employed a person just for his/her labour, skill or brain. So they are concerned with his/her labour and work only. They have nothing to do with his/her personality, personal life, knowledge and other things. But this thinking is one-sided. Although a person's different traits may be separately studied, in final analysis, they all are an integral part of one system making up a whole person. His/her skill does not exist separately from his/her background knowledge. His/her work life depends upon his/her home life. His/her emotional conditions are based on his/her physical life and environment conditions. The functional idea should always be kept in mind by a manager that the whole person is to be dealt with, not a part of his/her personality.
4. **Human dignity**: Treating the subordinates as respectable human beings, appreciation of their skills and recognition of their personality are the basics of human relations. The commodity approach or a factor of production approach is not at all good for dealing with subordinates. As a matter of fact, it is a normal policy that confirms that subordinates are to be treated differently from other factors of production because they are human beings. They require and deserve human respect and dignity.

Concepts Relating to the Nature of Organisations

1. **Organisation as a social system**: Industrial organisations are social systems. Each organisation is a social group having a number of small groups. As people have needs, these organisations also have their needs, status and role. People working in organisations have relations of two types: formal and informal. An organisation should serve both the relationships.
2. **Mutual interests**: Organisation theory tells us about the mutuality of interest between individuals and organisation. Organisations are formed and maintained on the basis of some mutuality of interest among their participants. If this mutuality is lacking, no organisation can run for long. So the management should try to coordinate the common goals and individual motives in a nice manner because a member would like to continue within the organisation as long as he/she feels that his/her interests are being served by attaching to the organisation.

Differences Between Human Relations and Industrial Relations

Although it is difficult to draw a definite line of demarcation between the concepts of industrial relations (IR) and human relations, a broad distinction can be made.

IR refer to relations between the employers and employees (as two distinct groups) in an organisation or industry. Human relations, on the other hand, refer to the direct relationships existing between the employer and his/her employees considered as individuals, as distinct from IR, which denote collective relations. IR are viewed at the official level, whereas human relations are viewed at the personal level. Human relations in industry refer to a policy which should be followed to make the workers feel involved in the organisation, boost their morale and treat the workers as human beings and equal partners in the industry and not merely as a factor of production. Problems of human relations are personal in character and are related to the behaviour of workers where morale and social elements predominate.

IR are viewed at a particular period of time, say, in a particular month. For example, IR may be good in January but may be strained in February. Human relations, on the other hand, are built over a long period of time. They cannot be made good or bad in a month or so.

In case IR are bad, they may lead to strikes or lockouts. This may not be the case with poor human relations. On the other hand, if an organisation is successful in implementing its human relations policy effectively, it will also help in improving IR.

IR refer to the relations between the organisations of employers and the employees at a higher level of economy, whereas human relations are considered as the scientific investigation of the psychological and social interrelations produced in the collective performance of work.

The term 'industrial relations' is wider and comprehensive, and the term 'human relations' is a part of it. The human relations approach is a path leading to peaceful IR.

Aims of Human Relations Policy

Broadly speaking, a human relations policy aims at the following:

1. Making the workers feel involved in the organisation
2. Improving their efficiency

3. Treating the workers as human beings and equal partners in industry and not merely as a factor of production
4. Psychological integration of the workers within the undertaking

Need or Importance of Human Relations in Industry

The approach of human relations plays a significant role in today's organisations. The following are some of the important contributions of this approach:

1. **Economic and good production**: Maintenance of good human relations is the very basis of motivation. A highly motivated worker has an internal attitude to do more work. He/she tries to use his/her skill, ability and knowledge for more and more production. It lowers down the cost of production, improves its quality and increases the productivity of workers. Increased productivity brings economical and standard goods for the society.
2. **Maximum utilisation of manpower**: Human resources are the most valuable sources of production and basis for development. Although adequate finance, better quality of raw materials, improved machines and other infrastructure facilities are necessary to accelerate production, industries are not composed of only these things. They need human beings also who use these resources. This is only human factor which makes good and bad use of these resources. In the absence of trained and efficient personnel, the natural resources cannot do anything. It is only the human relation approach which motivates human beings to use these resources fully and efficiently.
3. **Psychological and moral grounds**: A sound justification for managerial interest in human relations is based on the psychological and moral grounds. Employees are also human beings just as are the members of management or ownership and are, therefore, entitled to human treatment. They should be treated with the same respect for their dignity that any other human being can claim. Psychological satisfaction is more valuable than physiological satisfaction.
4. **Development of trade unionism and government stress**: In modern times, the trade union movement is quite organised. Due to strong unionism and government's interference in the field of IR, an industrialist cannot afford to ignore the workers, their needs and their grievances. Although it is a negative approach to the significance of human relations approach, it is quite true.
5. **Development of industrial humanism**: The approach of human relations leads to the development of industrial humanism in industrial field. It focuses on job satisfaction rather than job remuneration. It makes the workers equally responsible for the growth of organisation. It prepares managers as true leaders. It is a study of group dynamics and interpersonal relationship which helps in understanding the behaviour of workers.

Suggestions to Improve Human Relations and/or Factors That Go to Make Up a Human Relations Policy

The resolution adopted at the Fourth Session of Metal Trades Committee of the ILO highlights certain factors that go to make up a human relations policy. Some other writers have also pointed out a few such factors which carry a lot of significance in a human relations policy and lead to improvement in human relations. Some of such important factors are as follows:

1. A sound organisational structure clearly specifying
    a. duties, functions and responsibilities;
    b. authority; and
    c. accountability

  of every one engaged in the organisation so that everybody in the organisation knows who is who, who is to do what and where, what the relationship is between two individuals and so on. For this, there should be an organisational chart.
  A specimen of an organisational chart is given in Figure 17.2.

2. Adequate conditions of employment such as
    a. fair wages and
    b. good working conditions.

3. Suitable policies for
    a. scientific and methodical recruitment and selection,
    b. placement and
    c. induction.

4. Education, training and development programmes for all.
5. Real and equal opportunities for advancement to all.
6. Promotion from within as far as possible.
7. Suitable policy for job termination.
8. Respect for the personality of workers—treating the subordinates as respectable human beings, appreciating their emotions and sentiments and recognising their personality. The commodity approach or a factor of production approach has become outdated. It is now a well-accepted fact that subordinates deserve human respect, and their dignity should be maintained by the management.
9. Personal knowledge about the subordinates.

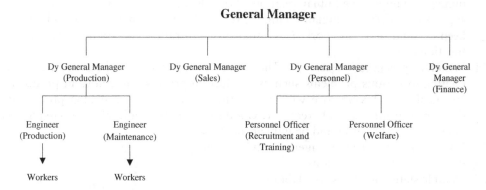

Figure 17.2 Organisational Chart of Central Safety Committee

10. Fairness, impartiality and frankness in the management's approach.
11. Frankness in dealing with people.
12. Direction without being commanding.
13. Keeping promises.
14. Understanding others' points of view.
15. Equal weightage for both workers and employers.
16. Employers must have a reputation for complete honesty, intelligence, flexibility and consistency of purpose.
17. Adequate provision for incentives and fringe benefits.
18. Positive approach towards collective bargaining, WPM, profit-sharing and labour co-partnership.
19. Development of personal and social forces: The Hawthorne experiments have proved that socio-psychological variables play a more prominent role in increasing efficiency and motivating the employees. The management should try to create a friendly atmosphere, exercise democratic style of supervision and emphasise the need of goal congruence.
20. Due recognition to groups and informal relations: In the organisations, individuals tend to create groups. Often workers tend to react as members of groups and not as individuals. The group determines their norms of behaviour. The management cannot deal with workers as individuals but as members of work groups, subject to the influence of these groups. Hence, the management must give due recognition to the group, norms and informal organisation structure existing within the organisation in order to maintain good human relations.
21. Communication: The Hawthorne experiments have proved that communication in the organisation is very important. Through communication, it can be explained to workers why a particular course of action is being taken. Participation of workers can be sought in the decision-making process concerning the matters of their importance and problems faced by them.
22. Personnel counselling: The management can establish a system of personnel counselling in the organisation. The workers should be provided timely guidance in their personal matters and difficulties. An expert can be appointed in the HR department for this purpose. This will also help in maintaining good human relations.
23. Supervision: The supervisory climate also has an important role to play in determining and improving human relations. Friendly, attentive and genuinely concerned supervisors affect the human relations favourably. The management should always keep in mind that teamwork is essential for cooperation and sound organisational functioning.
24. Introducing suggestion scheme: The suggestion from the workers can be invited relating to various problems such as production process, difficulties in production and facilities. This practice will involve them in the decision-making process and develop their interest and creativity. Good suggestions should also be remunerated financially, and they should be implemented too.
25. Mutual faith between management and workers.
26. Positive role by trade unions.
27. Suitable state policy towards labour.

Thus, we find that a large number of factors go to make up a human relations policy. The human relations approach is a complex and typical object. It is a philosophy which requires a complete change in the attitude of the management towards the workers. The managerial personnel cannot be trained in the human relations approach through any scientific training programme. What is required is the continuous practice of this philosophy. Although the human relations approach has been criticised by many experts on various grounds, even then it is a challenge for the modern management. Subordinates cannot be forced into cooperation. Strategy for some, psychology for others and understanding for a few have to be substituted for force in human relations.

Importance of Proper Diagnosis and Timely Action in Human Relations

Basically, organisation and management processes are human in nature since throughout human beings are involved. The human relations approach regards organisations as socio-economic systems and highlights the behavioural aspects of the individuals and groups that give character and content to organisations. Within the framework of such an approach, it is necessary to identify human problems in an organisation and solve them without loss of time so that areas of conflict and confrontation are reduced to manageable proportions.

It is agreed on all fronts that human beings are so many bundles of emotions, prejudices, preferences, motives, values, needs, fears and frustrations. Within an organisation, many of these characteristics find expression in words and deeds. Certain unpleasant feelings among the people often flow as undercurrents and erode organisational vitality unobtrusively. Several problems arise in the process which are to be tackled on a scientific basis, that is, through diagnosis, prescription and action.

The diagnostic process could be defined as an art of recognising the real problem, opportunity or threat from symptoms and signs. Many a time, actual problems get shrouded in a plethora of symptoms and are wrongly treated or even ignored. One knows that often there is personal pique behind a strike. Problem diagnosis is itself a specialised skill which calls for an open-minded, inquisitive, purposeful and objective approach. When problems are correctly diagnosed and defined, the tasks of searching for alternative solutions, final choice of an alternative and acting upon that alternative course of action become easier.

Prescription of a solution is the crucial intervening stage between a problem and an action. After diagnosing a human problem, it is necessary to search for an alternative way of tackling the problem. Several courses of action could be thought up and considered within the framework of the goals that are sought to be achieved by solving the problem. Ultimately, that alternative course which is believed to be most effective is to be chosen. Care should be taken to see that by solving one problem, others are not created as often happens, for example, when the wage demand of a group of workers is conceded in isolation of other groups. In the third stage, the chosen course of action is to be implemented which completes the cycle of problem-solving in human relations. Ideally, an action could be built into the decision itself so that little time is lost between decision and action. Timely action is of greatest importance for it stops the problem from growing and enables the real cause to be removed instead of being magnified.

Behind many a strike is a small but ignored grievance. Such an action will also put a stop to imaginary grievances and problems.

When human problems are approached in a scientific manner, tempered by pragmatism, humanism and dynamism, life in organisations becomes more tolerable. Organisational members find their places of work worthwhile centres to discover, develop and direct their capabilities to fulfil some of their cherished personal goals along with the organisational goals.

Hawthorne Experiments

Hawthorne experiments are an important landmark in the history of the human relations movement. The first intensive study of human behaviour in an industrial situation was made at the Hawthorne plant of the Western Electric Company, Chicago, by Elton Mayo and his associates. Professor Elton Mayo is generally recognised as the father of the human relations approach. He conducted these experiments from November 1924 with a group of psychologists and sociologists.

They conducted a series of experimental studies there between 1924 and 1932.

The perspective of Taylor and his lieutenants had its roots in the logic of engineering but in the Hawthorne experiments, there was applied a socio-psychological technique to managerial problems which gave impetus to development of a theory of human behaviour in organisations.

The series of experiments may be classified into three parts:

1. Illumination experiments (1924–1927)
2. Relay assembly test room experiments (1927–1932)
3. Bank wiring observation room experiment (1931–1932)

In most of the experiments, the researchers proceeded on the hypotheses of scientific management. A relationship of physical and social factors with the level of output was examined. The illumination studies were conducted with the usual controls of scientific experimentation. The original assumption was that there was a correlation between the intensity of illumination and worker output. Researchers found the difference in quantity and quality of production due to the change in physical conditions. Then they experimented with rest periods, shorter working days and wage incentives. They also tested the influence of fatigue and monotony on output. The findings were very confusing because in most of the cases, when original conditions were restored, still the output showed an increasing trend. Then they made a study of the psychological factors also that seemed to exert a greater influence on output than the changes in rest periods, wages, hours of work and the like.

The Hawthorne studies provided evidence that an organisation is not merely a formal arrangement of people and functions. More than that, it is a social system which can be operated successfully only with the application of the principles of psychology and other behavioural sciences. The researchers came to the conclusion that a factory is a social organisation. The non-financial incentives have much influence on their productivity and willingness to work in comparison to financial incentives. Subordinates cannot be compelled to cooperate. They can be better motivated through the human relations techniques.

The main contributions of Hawthorne experiments may be generalised as follows:

1. **Social factors**: These experiments proved that social factors play a more prominent part in determining the level of output. A business organisation is basically a social group. Elton Mayo has described an organisation as 'a social system, a system of rituals and a mixture of logical, non-logical and illogical behaviour'. People are

socio-psychological beings. These characteristics determine the output and efficiency in the organisation. Financial incentives have a limited role in motivating the people. Non-financial incentives affect significantly the behaviour of workers and their productivity.

2. **Groups**: In the organisations, individuals tend to create groups. Workers often tend to react as members of groups and not as individuals. The group determines their norms of behaviour. If a person resists a particular norm of group behaviour, he/she tries to change the group norm because any deviation from the group norm will make him/her unacceptable to the group. Thus, the management cannot deal with workers as individuals but as members of work groups, subject to the influence of these groups.
3. **Leadership**: Leadership is important for directing group behaviour. Leadership cannot come from superiors only as held by the scientific management approach. There may be informal leadership as is clear from bank wiring experiments. In some cases, an informal leader is more important than a formal one, as in the experiments; the supervisor could not exert pressure on the work group about the production norms because he/she was under considerable pressure to accept the group norm of which he/she was in charge. However, a supervisor is more acceptable as a leader if his/her style is in accordance with the human relations approach. In this context, the democratic style is the best which provides greater satisfaction to workers.
4. **Communication**: The Hawthorne experiments show that communication in the organisation is very important. Through communication, workers can be explained why a particular course of action is being taken; participation of workers can be sought in the decision-making process related to the matters of concern to workers.
5. **Conflicts**: The conflict is generated in the organisation because of the creation of groups with conflicting objectives. Thus, groups may be in conflict with organisation, though the creation of groups sometimes helps to achieve organisational objectives. Similarly, a conflict may arise because of maladjustment of individual and organisation. Thus, a conflict arises the problem of adjustment of individual to the organisation.

Exhibit 17.1 Human Relations Is Here to Stay

Human relations is here to stay because it concerns that great organisational variable and source of strength—people. 'By this time, even that hard bitten industrialist, the anti text book personnel agnostic, and the Teddy Roosevett type of material leader are ready to admit that human relations helps get the job done'.

Source: C. J. Berwitz, 'Beyond Motivation', *Harvard Business Review* (May–June 1960): 123, quoted in Davis, Human Relations at Work, 11.

---

6. **Supervision**: The supervisory climate also has an important role to play in determining the rate of output. The friendly to the worker, attentive and genuinely concerned supervision affects the productivity favourably. For example, in the bank wiring room, an entirely different supervisory climate existed—friendlier to the workers and less use of authority in issuing orders—which helped in productivity, while in

regular departments, supervisors were used to maintain order and control, and this type of supervisory arrangement produced inhibiting atmosphere.

The Hawthorne experiments opened a new frontier to the study of management which has been followed by many behavioural scientists later on. About the Hawthorne experiments, Henry Landsberger had observed that a most spectacular academic battle has raged since then, or perhaps it would be more accurate to say that a limited number of gunners has kept up a steady barrage, reusing the same ammunition. The beleaguered Mayo garrison, however, has continued its existence behind the solid protection of factory walls. Besides the Hawthorne experiments, other contributions to human relations have come from Bakke and Argyris (fusion process and integrating individuals and organisation); McGregor (human side of enterprise); March and Simon (problems of organisation); Likert (management system, theory of motivation); and so on.

However, a few people still cling to the idea that human relations is a fad and have interpreted this demise of the age of human relations as the death knell of the whole subject; that is, the 'happiness boys' are on the way out.[3] However, the fact remains that human relations is not almost finished; it has just started and its future is highly promising (see Exhibit 17.1).

Industrial Relations (IR)

Good IR in an organisation are an indication to a great extent of the contentment of employees engaged in that organisation. In case the employees are contented, they are likely to give their best to their organisation, resulting in higher productivity and consequent enhanced profits to employers and higher income/benefits to employees. It is perhaps for this reason that today every organisation pays due attention in the direction of maintaining good IR.

Concept, Meaning and Definition

The concept of IR has generally developed as a consequence of industrial revolution,[4] that is, the emergence of large-scale industries, which is responsible for creating two distinct groups in the industries: the workers on the one side and the employers on the other, with an estranged relationship between the two. The employers, being the owner of the means of production, started dominating the industrial scene and dictating the terms of employment.[5] This led to the exploitation of the working class as the trade unions were virtually missing in the early stages of the industrial revolution and so was the case with the role of the government, which adopted the laissez-faire policy.

Hence, the problem of IR was viewed as the problem of relationship between the employers and the workers. There was virtually a tug of war between these two groups, the workers being the losers most of the time. Consequently, the subsequent period witnessed a great deal of strikes and lockouts, resulting in substantial losses to the employers and affecting adversely the revenue of the government in terms of taxes and duties it used to get on the output/profits of the industries. Hence, in due course of time, the government started intervening in the affairs of IR and passed the Workmen's Compensation Act, 1923, and the Trade Union's Act, 1926, followed by many other acts, such as Industrial Employment (Standing Orders) Act, 1946, and Industrial Disputes Act, 1947, later on. Hence, people started viewing the problem of IR as the complex of interrelations

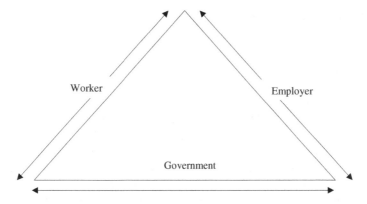

Figure 17.3 Industrial Relations as a Three-Dimensional Affair

among employers (or their associations), workers (or their trade unions) and the government, as shown in Figure 17.3.

Exhibit 17.2   Main Characteristics of IR

- IR are the outcome of the employment relationship in an industrial organisation; that is, it is the industry or organisation that provides the setting for IR.
- The employer and their organisations, employees and their trade unions, and the government are the main parties of IR.
- IR is an art of living together for the purpose of production.
- The IR system creates complex rules and regulations to maintain harmonious relations.
- The government plays an important role in shaping IR through labour legislation, rules, regulations, agreements, awards and so on.

Source: Hindustan Times, 6 June 2016.

It is John T. Dunlop to whom goes the credit of introducing the three-dimensional model of IR.[6] Thus, IR refer to the collective relationship between the management, employees and the government. According to the ILO also, IR deal with either the relationship between the state and the employers and the workers' organisation or the relation between the occupational organisations themselves. However, with the liberalisation and growing environmental concerns, consumers and community have also come to play a critical role in IR processes and outcomes.[7]

Thus, in order to have harmonious IR in an organisation, it is desirable to have an appropriate IR climate which is a subset of organisational climate that pertains to the norms and attitudes reflecting union–management relationship in an enterprise.

Characteristics of IR

The main characteristics of IR are as shown in Exhibit 17.2.

Theoretical Perspectives and Approaches to IR

There are several theoretical perspectives and approaches to IR, the main ones being as follows:

Unitary perspective: This approach does not hold water these days because it presumes that since management owns and controls an enterprise, decision-taking is the prerogative exclusively of the management and, therefore, management is the only source of authority in an enterprise. Hence, workers' unions have no role to play and conflict has no rationality to exist in an organisation.

Pluralist perspective: This approach is based on the writings of Clegg,[8] Flanders[9] and so on and assumes that since an organisation comprises varied groups, such as employers, employees, shareholders, consumers and the government, each group having its own objectives and interests, conflicts are inherent in an organisation. Hence, conflicts should be amicably resolved.

Human relations approach: This approach implies that the relationship between an employee and an employer should be as between two human beings because an employee is a human being first who needs freedom of expression, respect for his/her personality and sentiments, and so on.

Systems approach: The credit of evolving this approach goes to John T. Dunlop.[10] This approach views IR as a distinctive sub-system of society comprising managers, workers and the government as three principal actors who function in contexts (economic, technological, power relations and so on) aiming at the output (formulation and administration of rules) following certain ideology (shared value by all concerned), the equation being as follows:

$$r = f(a, t, e, s, i)$$

where
r = the rules of the IR system
f = function
a = actors
t = technical context of the workplace
e = economic context of budgetary constraints
s = power context and the status of the parties
i = ideology of the system

The approach is a little bit obscure and is, therefore, criticised on this account.

Industrial sociology approach: According to this approach, conflict is the basic concept that should form the basis of the study of IR. The crux of IR is the nature and development of conflict.[11] This approach is criticised because of its too much emphasis on conflict in IR.

Oxford approach:[12] This approach can be explained with the help of the following equations:

$$r = f(b)$$
or
$$r = f(c)$$

where
 r = the rules governing IR
 b = collective bargaining
 c = conflict resolved through collective bargaining

This approach is criticised because of its laying too much of emphasis on collective bargaining and ignoring economic, technological, sociological and ideological variables.

Fahlbeck's Views on Approaches to IR

Fahlbeck[13] has suggested the following approaches to IR:

1. **'My boat' attitude**: Get off, if you do not like it. That is, there is little or no concern for the other party, that is, the workers.
2. **'Shared boat' attitude**: We shall sail together. Do not rock the boat. That is, there is some concern for the employees.
3. **'Our boat' attitude**: It is our own enterprise, and let us confine our efforts to better it. That is, there is equal concern for the workers.
4. **'Your boat' attitude**: This prompts and motivating the employees to give their best to the organisation by giving them a feeling of ownership and pride.

An employer can follow any of these approaches, though 'your boat' attitude is likely to give better results, provided the workers are a matured and sensible lot.

Objectives of IR

The main objectives of IR are as follows:

1. To avoid misunderstanding, confusion and conflict between the management and workers and promote mutual trust and faith between the two
2. To improve productivity, output and profitability of the organisation
3. To avoid strikes and lockouts
4. To associate workers in the decision-making process and promote industrial democracy
5. To protect and promote the interest of all the stakeholders

Scope of IR

The constituents of scope of IR may be as shown in Exhibit 17.3.

Significance of IR

Neither the management nor the workers' unions can function in isolation. Hence, a fruitful cooperation between the two is inevitable; otherwise, the entire process of production will be paralysed and not only the organisations will suffer but also the community and the government will be adversely affected. Good IR promote industrial peace, mutual trust and faith between the management and the workers of an organisation;

boost morale of the workers; infuse confidence; give boost to output; help in improving productivity; and protect and promote interest of all concerned, hence the utility of harmonious IR.

Exhibit 17.3 Scope of IR

- Individual relations: concerning discipline and grievances of individuals.
- Collective relations: concerning trade unions, collective bargaining, functioning of joint committees (such as house allotment committee and library committee) and prevention and settlement of industrial disputes.
- Role of state: role played by the government in terms of labour legislation, labour reforms, rules, regulations and so on.
- International aspects: role played by the international organisations of employers and workers or the bodies like the ILO.

Principles of Promoting Harmonious IR

The main principles of promoting healthy IR comprise keenness of both employers' associations and workers' unions to deal with their mutual problems freely, independently and responsibly; firm determination of employers' associations and workers' union to resolve their problems through collective bargaining; and keenness of both workers' unions and employers' associations to associate with government agencies keeping in view the general, social and economic measures affecting labour management relations.

Major Actors and Their Roles in IR

There are three major actors in the arena of IR as follows:

1. **Workers and their unions**: Workers and their unions are one of the main actors of the IR system. The constructive approach of workers and their unions in protecting and promoting the interest of the workers play an important role in maintaining good IR.
2. **Employers and their associations**: Employers and their associations are another important actor in the arena of the IR system. The positive approach of management in dealing with workers also plays a significant role in maintaining good IR.
3. **Government**: The central government and the state governments are the third main actor in the field of the IR system as the aforesaid governments affect IR through labour legislation, labour policy, labour reforms, rules and regulations, and so on. The government is supposed to maintain balance between the employees and the employers.

Functions of IR Staff

The main functions of the IR staff comprise maintaining good rapport between the management and trade union(s), safeguarding the interest of all stakeholders, maintaining free flow of communication between the management and the trade unions, and all other steps necessary to maintain good IR.

Factors Affecting IR

It is both the external and internal factors that affect IR as follows:

1. **External factors**: External factors may include the following:
   a. **Economic factors**: These may comprise wages, DA, bonus and other allowances.
   b. **Psychological factors**: These factors may consist of management's approach, its philosophy and attitude towards its workforce; management's trust and confidence in the trade union(s) of the organisation concerned; workers' attitude towards management, their union, their fellow workers and the working environment; and so on.
   c. **Political factors**: These factors may include the labour policy of the government, ideology of the ruling party, labour legislation, labour administration, political stability in the country, role and attitude of opposition parties, and so on.
   d. **Global factors**: Globalisation also affects the state of IR. The approach of MNCs and transnational companies also affect IR of a country.
   e. **Social factors**: These factors may include level of enlightenment, level of education, culture, attitudes, beliefs, customs, rituals, traditions and so on of the people at large.

2. **Internal factors**: Internal factors are controllable. Hence, these factors should be paid due attention to maintain good IR. These consist of the IR policy of the organisation, WPM, profit-sharing, labour co-partnership, trade unions and their leadership and approach, work culture, working environment, wage policy, fringe benefits, mutual trust between labour and management, workforce diversity, grievance-handling procedure, discipline, opportunities for growth for employees, promotion policy, recruitment policy, transfer policy, quality of work life, training and development, machinery for prevention and settlement of industrial disputes, inter-group behaviour, human relations, bipartite and tripartite committees, transparency in the working of the organisation, collective bargaining, financial stability of the organisation, treatment towards workers and so on.

Prerequisites and Functional Requirements of Good IR

In order to have good IR, some of the main requirements are as shown in Exhibit 17.4.

Causes of Poor IR

There are a large number of causes responsible for poor IR, the main being as reflected in Exhibit 17.5.

Exhibit 17.4   Main Requirements of Good IR

- Positive/constructive approach of both management and trade union(s)
- Economic satisfaction of workers
- Transparency in the functioning of the organisation

- Free flow of communication
- Social and psychological satisfaction of workers
- Mutual trust between management and trade union
- Enlightened trade unions
- Faith in the institution of collective bargaining
- Appropriate labour policy and labour legislation
- Sound finances of the organisation
- Respect for the personality of workers
- Job satisfaction to employees

Exhibit 17.5   Causes Responsible for Poor IR

- Low wages
- Poor working conditions
- Inappropriate behaviour of supervisors towards workers
- Unfair labour practices
- Lack of job satisfaction to workers
- Defective human relations policies
- Lack of security of job
- Improper leadership of trade unions
- Ineffectiveness of collective bargaining
- Absence of appropriate grievance-handling procedure
- Poor discipline in the organisation
- Lack of mutual trust and faith between the management and the workers

---

Effects of Poor IR

Poor IR lead to strikes and lockouts which affect the economic, psychological, physical and social life of 'employees'. They lose their confidence, and their morale goes downwards. It affects their efficiency, effectiveness and productivity. Poor IR increase their stress and cause a number of problems to them. It is not only the employees, but the employers also suffer economically because due to poor IR, workers develop an indifferent and many a time negative attitude which may cause increased cost of production, reduction in output, increase in depreciation of machinery, reduction in productivity and consequent reduction in the profitability of the organisation. The government also gets less amount of revenue in terms of taxes, excise duty and so on. The community also has to pay a price for poor IR and consequent strikes and lockouts, causing shortage of goods and services, higher prices, irregular supply of goods and services, and so on.

Thus, poor IR are a bane for all the stakeholders.

How to Improve IR

Some of the suggestions to improve IR may be as shown in Exhibit 17.6.

It is good that employers have now started realising that they cannot function in isolation and that seeking cooperation of the trade unions is a must for the effective

Human Relations and Industrial Relations

functioning of an organisation. Hence, a good number of organisations have now started developing good relations with the workers' unions.

IR in India Since Independence

The Government of India has been playing an important role in improving the climate of IR in our country since Independence. The major steps taken by the Government of India in this regard are as follows:

1. Enactment/implementation of the Industrial Disputes Act, 1947
2. Sincere efforts by the ILC
3. Enactment/administration of
    a. The Factories Act, 1948
    b. The Minimum Wages Act, 1948

Exhibit 17.6   Suggestions to Improve IR

- Developing mutual faith and trust between the management and the workers and their associations
- Formulation of sound human relations/IR policies and proper implementation of the same
- Frequent and genuine discussion between the management and the union(s) to resolve their differences
- Increasing effectiveness of collective bargaining and WPM
- Proper wages, reward and incentives to workers
- Sharing increased productivity gains with the workers
- Increasing transparency in the working of the organisation
- Increasing HRD
- Avoiding litigation
- More focus on preventive steps

---

   c. The ESI Act, 1948
   d. The Employees' Provident Funds and Miscellaneous Provisions Act, 1952
   e. The Payment of Gratuity Act, 1972
4. Formulation of Code of Conduct (1958)
5. Industrial Trance Resolution (1962)
6. Establishment of the National Commission on Labour, 1969
7. Standing Labour Committee (SLC)
8. Constitution of National Apex Body (NAB; a bipartite body)
9. Encouragement to WPM and collective bargaining
10. Initiating labour reforms
11. Amendment of various labour laws

Indian industrial scenario has been a story of industrial peace and industrial conflicts, the latter being ruling the roost for most of the time. For example, during 2016, thousands of temporary workers were laid off due to cash crunch (see Exhibits 17.7–17.9).

578 *Employee Relations and Personnel Records, Audit and Research*

Exhibit 17.7 Temporary Laid-off Workers

A cash crunch following demonetisation has led to thousands of temporary workers being laid off, particularly in labour-intensive industries.

Source: The Economic Times, 27 December 2016.

Exhibit 17.8 Laid-off Workers

Many employees of Grofers, InMobi and Snapdeal were given the pink slip as start-ups across sectors—especially those in food tech—have been laying off people.

Source: The Economic Times, 27 December 2016.

Exhibit 17.9 Laying off Employees

In August, Ola shut down its Taxi For Sure business—acquired last year—and laid off nearly 700 employees.

Source: The Economic Times, 27 December 2016.

However, the aforesaid steps taken in our country have been able to promote good IR to a considerable extent. The employers and the workers' unions should also accelerate their efforts in improving IR by adopting a positive and constructive approach in this regard.

Prospects of IR in Indian Industries

The future of IR in Indian industries is likely to be relatively better than what it has been so far. Some of the reasons for this optimistic view include a noticeable change in the attitude of both the management and the trade unions that they cannot function in isolation, management becoming more tolerant with the existence and working of trade unions, the institution of collective bargaining beginning to play a greater role, WPM likely to be more and effective, positive amendments in labour laws, labour reforms initiated by the government, more roles being played by the ILO, the effect of IR policies of the MNCs operating in the country, increase in the extension of fringe benefits (including social security and labour welfare facilities) and so on.

Management Strategy

Since the employers also have to bear the brunt of poor IR, the management of an organisation should have a positive and reformative approach towards trade unions and, therefore, attach due importance to them. It should grant recognition to the major union and remain in close touch with it all through. It should win the confidence and trust of the union and consult it on all vital issues, especially those which affect workers. The strategy should aim at developing good human relations policies, focus on transparency, free flow of communication, good human relations, making collective bargaining and WPM effective, and so on. The strategy has to include a provision for educating workers that the integration of management's and workers' interests is the need of the hour.

Chapter Review

1. Maintenance of good human relations and IR in an organisation is a must if it has to accomplish its objectives.
2. Human relations in industry, in a wider sense, signify the relationship that should exist between the human beings engaged in an industry. The human relations approach refers to treating employees humanely so that they may be motivated to work together productively, cooperatively and with economic, psychological and social satisfaction. The main features of the human relations approach comprises social factor in organisation, tendency to form groups, integrating process and socio-psychological approach. Other than the human relations approach, the main approaches to human relations are rewards, soft or weak approach, fear and punishment or hard approach, carrot and stick approach, path–goal approach and so on.
3. The fundamental concepts of human relations in industry can be grouped under two heads: (a) concepts relating to the nature of a person (e.g. motivation, individual differences, a whole person and human dignity, etc.) and (b) concepts relating to the nature of an organisation (e.g. organisation as a social system and mutual interest). Human relations refer to the direct relationship existing between the employer and his/her employees, considered as individuals, as distinct from IR, which refer to collective relations. There are some other differences also between human relations and IR. Making the workers feel involved, improving their efficiency, treating workers as human beings and psychological integration of workers within the undertaking are the main aims of a human relations policy.
4. Good human relations are necessary in an organisation because they lead to higher output, maximum utilisation of manpower, psychological integration, reducing the impact of trade unionism, development of industrial humanism and so on. There are a number of factors that make up a good human relations policy, such as a sound organisational structure, fair employment conditions, suitable policies, and equality and social justice. It is always advisable to diagnose human relations problems and take appropriate action well in time. The main contributions of the Hawthorne experiments relate to the role of social factors, groups, leadership, communication, conflicts and supervision in group behaviour.
5. IR refer to the collective relationship between the management, employees and the government. Unitary, pluralist, human relations approach, systems approach, industrial sociology approach and Oxford approach are the main

theoretical perspectives and approaches to IR. However, Fahlbeck has suggested 'my boat', 'shared boat', 'our boat' and 'your boat' approaches to IR.
6. Good IR are in the interest of all concerned as they lead to industrial peace, higher output, greater productivity and more benefits to workers. Workers and their unions, employers and their associations, and the government are the three major actors in the realm of IR which are affected by external factors, which comprise economic, psychological, political, global and social factors, and internal factors, which include work culture, IR policy, status of WPM and collective bargaining, wage policy, human relations policies, grievance redressal procedure and so on.
7. All economic, political, social and legal factors which affect workers adversely are responsible for poor IR. Poor IR adversely affect all the stakeholders in an organisation.
8. Steps involved in improving IR include developing mutual trust, formulating appropriate human relations and IR policies, free flow of communication, proper wage, incentives and fringe benefit policies, and so on.
9. IR in our country have been a story of peace and conflict. Since the independence of the country, a lot of labour laws have been enacted, labour policies improved, ILC and SLC and WPM and collective bargaining encouraged, labour reforms initiated and many other steps taken to improve IR. Because of these steps, the future of IR in our country appears to be promising.
10. The management of an organisation should focus, in its strategy with regard to IR, on strengthening of collective bargaining, WPM, profit-sharing, increasing mutual trust, transparency, free flow of communication and so on.

Key Terms

carrot and stick approach
Code of Conduct
collective bargaining
communication
conflicts
fear and punishment or hard approach
globalisation
groups
human dignity
human relations
human relations approach
individual differences
industrial relations (IR)
integrating process
labour legislation
laissez-faire
leadership
lockouts
path–goal approach
personnel counselling
retrenchment
rewards, soft or weak approach
social factors
social system
socio-psychological approach
strikes
supervision
trade union movement
whole person
workers' participation in management (WPM)

Discussion Questions

1. Discuss what the term 'human relations in industry' is all about. Also discuss the human relations approach and all other main approaches to human relations.

2. Discuss the main factors that go to make up a good human relations policy and also discuss the contributions made by the Hawthorne experiments to promote the human relations approach.
3. Discuss what should be the strategy of the management to maintain and improve good human relations in an organisation.
4. Discuss the theoretical perspectives and approaches to IR.
5. Discuss the major actors in the arena of IR and what role they play in IR. Also discuss the significance of good IR to different main stakeholders in an organisation.
6. Discuss the factors influencing IR.
7. Discuss the prerequisites of a good IR programme.
8. Discuss the role of state in the field of IR.
9. Discuss the status of IR since Independence of the country.
10. Discuss what should be the strategy of management with regard to IR in an organisation.

Individual and Group Activities

1. As an individual, discuss with the HR officials of some big organisation and find out which approach to human relations their organisation practises and how far it has been effective.
2. As an individual, discuss with the union officials of a mid-sized manufacturing organisation the status of IR during the last five years in that organisation.
3. In a group of two members, visit some large organisation and find out from its HR officials the factors that affect IR in their organisation.
4. As an individual, visit a large organisation and discuss with the union officials whether the management of their organisation makes sincere efforts to maintain good IR. Yes or no? Prepare a brief report.
5. In a group of three members, discuss the strategy that the management of an organisation should formulate and implement to ensure that IR do not deteriorate.

Application Case 17.1

Poor IR Causing Violence

Anticipating the final verdict on 10 March 2017 in the case of Maruti plant violence on 28 July 2012, the district administration imposed prohibitory orders under Section 144 near the Maruti Suzuki plant, IMT, Manesar from 10–15 March 2017 in order to deal with the violence, if any, from the side of trade unions. And the final verdict was pronounced on the expected date holding 18 employees guilty of various offences committed during a riot at Maruti Suzuki factory at Manesar nearly five years ago, another 13 were found guilty of murdering Dev, and another 117 were acquitted of all charges. The sentences of the 31 convicted employees were to be pronounced later on.

The police had arrested 148 workers in connection with the case which was under trial at the district court. While 11 of them were still in jail, the rest were released on bail in different hearings. But all were facing trial as they were accused of various charges, including rioting with weapons, murder, attempt to murder, unlawful assembly, assault and trespassing.

Violence was triggered after a tussle between workers and the management over various demands. It was reported by some that an argument between a worker and a supervisor followed by the supervisor's casteist remarks instigated the incident. The worker allegedly physically hurt the supervisor and was punished with suspension. All this happened in the morning shift. The union failed to get the suspension reverted. Consequently, around 1,200 workers from the morning shift stayed on the factory premises to know the final outcome. Around 6 PM, they blocked the gates of the factory followed by large-scale violence. They attacked the managers, ransacked offices and set the company properties on fire. In the malady, Awanish Kumar Dev, GM (HR) was burnt alive beyond recognition and around 100 senior-level employees sustained injuries. Per an estimate, the total damages caused to the company worked out to be around $1 million. A day after, 91 employees were arrested and the magistrate ordered their 14-day detention in judicial custody. Later on, with the help of footage from the CCTV cameras of the neighbouring Suzuki Powertrain India plant, the attackers were identified, and 145 employees were charged and facing trial since then.

The prohibitory orders under Section 144 of the Criminal Procedure Code were imposed within 500 m of Maruti Suzuki plant in Manesar after members of several workers' unions held a meeting at Manesar on Tuesday and warned of protest if the court verdict was anti-workers. The unions decided to hold a meeting on the evening of 10 March 2017 and launch a protest if the decision was not in favour of the workers.

Several unions are in favour of the jailed and undertrial workers. They have unanimously decided to protest if the verdict is not in the workers' favour. Workers missed their food at the company's premises on 9 March 2017, said Kuldeep Janghu, general secretary, Maruti Udyog Kamgar Union. Local worker unions called the verdict anti-labour. One of the unions said that workers across industries in the Gurugram–Manesar–Bhiwadi–Bawal belt, an area near Delhi dotted with the factories of automobile and auto-parts manufactures, would go on a hunger strike on 16 March 2017—a day before the court was scheduled to pronounce the sentences. They were also considering approaching a higher court. Kuldeep Janghu said that close to 400 unions in and around Gurugram would participate in the hunger strike the next week. 'We will take the case up to a higher court if required', he said, adding that workers would meet to firm up further plan of action. However, the industries have welcomed the verdict. This case will never be forgotten in the history of poor IR.

Per the news report of *Hindustan Times* of 17 March 2017, a day before the announcement of punishment for 31 workers convicted in the July 2012 Maruti Suzuki Manesar violence case, workers across industries skipped their day's meal and protested silently. Workers later held a meeting at Maruti's Manesar plant and told the media that they had decided the future course of action but the execution would depend on the court announcement.

The canteens wore a deserted look on Thursday as the workers did not turn up for lunch. Several workers said that it marked their resentment against the system for not providing facts before the court during trial, resulting in the conviction of 31 colleagues.

The District Court of Gurugram convicted 13 employees of murder and 18 others of rioting and other charges on 10 March. As many as 117 workers were acquitted.

Awanish Kumar Dev, GM (HM) of Maruti Suzuki, was burnt to death and several other were injured in the violence.

The labour unrest and violence at Maruti's Manesar plant took place on 18 July 2012, in which 100 employees were injured and one senior executive of the company was killed.

Kuldeep Singh Janghu, general secretary, Maruti Udyog Kamgar Union, said, 'It is a sensitive moment for us, as on the one hand, we have respect for the court while on the other hand, we pray for our convicted friends who will be facing a tough time tomorrow. We are worried about their families and their financial conditions'.

(Based on news reports contained in *Hindustan Times*, 9 March 2017, *Hindustan Times*, 11 March 2017; *Hindustan Times*, 17 March 2017; *The Economic Times*, 11 March 2017.)

Questions

1. Do you approve the stand taken by the Maruti Udyog Kamgar Union in the present case? Yes or no? Why? Give reasons.
2. Present the highlights of the case in a small paragraph of about 10–15 lines.

Notes

1. Davis, *Human Relations at Work*, 4–5.
2. The definition of human relations contains a number of points. First, human relations focuses on people rather than on economics or mechanics. Second, people are in an organisational environment rather than in unorganised social contact. Third, a key activity in human relations is motivating people.
3. J. M. Black, 'Farewell to the Happiness Boys', *The Management Review* 7, no. 26 (May 1961): 38–47.
4. See Sharma, *Industrial Relations and Labour Legislation*.
5. Ibid.
6. J. T. Dunlop, *Industrial Relations Systems* (New York, NY: Henry Holt & Co., 1958), viii.
7. See Sharma, *Industrial Relations and Labour Legislation*, 6.
8. See H. A. Clegg, *A New Approach to Industrial Democracy* (Oxford: Blackwell, 1960).
9. See A. D. Flanders, *Management and Unions* (London: Faber, 1970).
10. Dunlop, *Industrial Relations Systems*.
11. C. Margerison, 'What Do We Mean by Industrial Relations? A Behavioural Science Approach', *British Journal of Industrial Relations* 7, no. 2 (July 1969): 273–86.
12. A. N. J. Blain and J. Gennard, 'Industrial Relations Theory: A Critical Review', *British Journal of Industries Relations* 8, no. 2 (July 1970): 91–113.
13. C. S. Venkata Ratnam, *Industrial Relations*, 17th ed. (New Delhi: Oxford University Press, 2014), 24.

18 Collective Bargaining and Workers' Participation in Management

Learning Objectives

After studying this chapter, you should be able to do the following:

1. Explain the meaning, definition and characteristic features of collective bargaining.
2. List and describe the forms of collective bargaining and also explain the prerequisites for the success of collective bargaining.
3. Explain levels and benefits of collective bargaining.
4. List and describe the steps involved in the process of collective bargaining.
5. Discuss the growth and status of collective bargaining in Indian industries and visualise the future prospects of collective bargaining in India.
6. Explain the concept, meaning and characteristics of WPM.
7. Describe the levels and forms/types of WPM.
8. List and describe the various schemes of WPM that have been introduced in Indian industries so far.
9. Explain the prerequisites for effective participation of workers in management and also if these are available in Indian industries.
10. Evaluate the effectiveness of WPM in Indian industries and also point out the main constraints in the way of WPM.

Introduction

Collective bargaining and WPM are the two vital elements of industrial democracy. The effectiveness of these two institutions in any organisation, industry or country is an indication that industrial democracy is at work in that organisation, industry or country. Since industrial democracy ensures the rights and privileges of workers, as a result of which they feel inclined to contribute their best towards the accomplishment of their organisation's objectives, the two institutions of collective bargaining and WPM assume added importance. In this chapter, these two elements have been dealt with.

Collective Bargaining

Collective bargaining is one of the three main approaches to labour–management negotiations, the other two being unilateral approach in which the employer alone decides the terms and conditions of employment and the tripartite approach in which in addition to the two parties (the workers and the employer), a third party, usually the government, also participates—a good example in this regard may be a wage board. As far as collective bargaining is concerned, it is a bipartite process in which the representatives of both the workers and the employer negotiate the relevant issue(s). Initially, individual employees negotiated directly with a potential employer on the wages they would receive for the services provided. However, with the advent of industrial revolution and consequent emergence of large-scale industries, a large number of people entered the labour market. Hence, it was not found convenient to negotiate individually due to paucity of time, variety of jobs, the resultant variation in rewards and a weak bargaining capacity of an individual vis-à-vis all-powerful employer. It adds to the bargaining power if it is done collectively, hence the emergence of the concept of the institution of collective bargaining which is today considered as an essential element of industrial democracy.

However, collective bargaining should not be confused with 'labour–management cooperation'. While the latter occurs only when 'the cards are face up on the table', in the former, each of both the parties, that is, the representatives of the workers and the employer, 'plays its cards close to its chest'. In the UK, the pay and conditions of employment of about 70% of the employees are fixed directly or indirectly through collective bargaining.[1]

Meaning and Definition

Collective bargaining is a process by which the representatives of the organisation meet and attempt to work out a contract with the employees' representatives—union. It is the process of cajoling, debating, discussing and threatening in order to bring about a favourable agreement for those representatives.[2] The term 'collective bargaining' was coined by Sydney and Beatrice Webb[3] who defined it as a method by which trade unions protect and improve the conditions of their members' working lives. According to the *Encyclopaedia of Social Sciences*, collective bargaining is a process of discussion and negotiation between two parties, one or both of whom are a group of people acting in concert. The resulting bargain is an understanding as to the terms and conditions under which a continuing service is to be performed. More specifically, collective bargaining is a procedure by which the employer and a group of employees agree upon the conditions of work.[4] Per the ILO Workers Manual, collective bargaining is 'the negotiations about working conditions and terms of employment between an employer, a group of employers or one or more employer's organisations on the one hand, and one or more representative workers organisations on the other hand, with a view to reaching an agreement'.

According to Perlman,

> [Collective bargaining] is a technique whereby an inferior social class or group exerts a never slackening pressure for a bigger share in social sovereignty as well as for more welfare and greater security and liberty for its members. It manifests itself equally in politics, legislation, court litigation, government administration, religion, education and propaganda.[5]

A very simple definition of collective bargaining given by Bhatia reads as 'The technique of collective bargaining is adopted by unions and management for resolving their conflicting interests'.[6]

Thus, we find that collective bargaining is a rational process in which appeal to facts and to logic reconciles conflicting interests in the light of common interests. Edwin B. Flippo has rightly remarked, 'collective bargaining is a process in which the representatives of labour organisation and the representatives of business organisation meet and attempt to negotiate a contract of agreement which specifies the nature of employee–employer union relationship'.[7] Michael J. Jucius has also stated that 'collective bargaining refers to a process by which, employers on the one hand, and representatives of employees on the other, attempt to arrive at agreement covering the conditions under which employees will contribute and be compensated for their services'. Collective bargaining is defined to cover the negotiation, administration, interpretation, application and enforcement of a written agreement between employers and unions representing their employees, setting forth joint understanding as to policies and procedures governing wages, rates of pay, hours of work and other conditions of employment. According to Dale Yoder, collective bargaining is essentially a process in which employees act as a group in seeking to shape conditions and relationships in their employment. As a matter of fact, collective bargaining represents voluntary conciliation and voluntary arbitration and never a compulsory adjustment.

Nature and Features/Characteristics of Collective Bargaining

Based on the aforementioned definitions, the following can be said:

1. Collective bargaining is industrial democracy at work.
2. It is a process as it consists of a number of steps.
3. It is a dynamic and an ongoing or continuous process.
4. It is a group action between two groups negotiating through its representatives at the bargaining table.
5. It is flexible in nature; that is, it believes in 'give and take'.
6. It is basically a political institution in which the rules are formed by the union(s) of workers and employers' associations to regulate the terms and conditions of employment.
7. It is a bipartite process.
8. It tends to improve IR and is an advanced form of human relations.
9. It is a formalised process.
10. It takes care of day-to-day developments, capacities, policies, interests and so on.
11. It is basically a political institution in which the rules are made by the trade unions of workers, employers and corporations/organisations.[8]

Need and Significance

Collective bargaining is needed by both workers and employers because it is beneficial to them in the following ways:

1. It is instrumental in increasing productivity.
2. It results in increased wages and better working and living conditions of workers.
3. It is likely to lead to better mutual understanding between the workers and the employer.
4. It creates a sort of industrial jurisprudence.

5. It leads to better implementation of decisions.
6. It promotes industrial peace.
7. It develops a sense of self-respect and responsibility among the employees.
8. It infuses confidence and boosts morale of workers.
9. It facilitates free flow of communication.
10. It helps in both prevention and settlement of industrial disputes.
11. It ensures fair treatment to workers at the hands of management.

It is obvious from these benefits that collective bargaining serves the interests of not only the employees but also the employers and the community.

Legal Framework

Employees in government industrial undertakings, such as Central Public Works Department (CPWD), Post and Telegraph (P&T) and Telecom, do not enjoy the right to collective bargaining as the Government of India does not permit it. Hence, their wages and salaries are based on Pay Commissions.[9] This is despite the fact that freedom of association as a fundamental right is provided under Article 19(c) of the Constitution of India, which has been duly recognised by the Trade Unions Act, 1926; Industrial Disputes Act, 1947; and Industrial Employment (Standing Orders) Act, 1946.

Bargaining Forms

Following are the main forms of bargaining (see Figure 18.1):

- **Distributive bargaining**: It is also called conjuncture bargaining. As the name suggests, it involves distribution of the pie. One party's gain is another's loss. In this regard, there are two possibilities: (a) each of the group (that is, employees and employers, may try to grab as much of the pie as it can [leaving a bitter experience for the loser]) or (b) both the groups together endeavour to increase the size of the pie so that each may get more (a better option as compared to the earlier one). It is usually the economic issues such as wages, allowances, bonus and benefits that are taken care of under this type of bargaining.
- **Attitudinal restructuring**: In this form of bargaining, an attempt is made to develop trust and cooperation between the two groups—the trade union and the

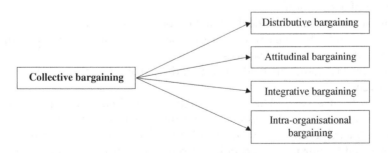

Figure 18.1 Forms of Collective Bargaining

management—so that the problems can be resolved amicably. For example, if the two groups are not pulling well in the past, there is a need of attitudinal restructuring from bitterness to cordiality and so on. In it, the focus shifts from the mere settlement of issues to evolving long-term bipartite relationships whereby the parties live and work together.
- **Integrative bargaining**: It involves mutual negotiations which result in benefiting both the parties such as increasing productivity, reducing cost of production and increasing profitability of the organisation, and if all this happens, both the employer and the union are likely to be benefited, the philosophy being to follow a win-win solution to the problem. Integrative bargaining is usually used for the issues such as designing interesting jobs and improving the quality of life.
- **Intra-organisational bargaining**: This form of bargaining aims at settling internal conflicts through developing consensus of opinion. Usually, both the employers' and unions' officials discuss the demands and arrive at a consensus of approach before they meet at the bargaining table.

Bargaining Agent

Deciding the bargaining agent (i.e. trade union that will represent the workers while negotiating an agreement) in an organisation has always been a contentious issue. There is no central law in our country according to which the bargaining agent can be chosen. However, in certain states, there are legal provisions for recognition of trade unions but where none (legal provision) exists, the usual practice is to follow the code of discipline which provides that the employer should recognise the union having the maximum membership.

Conditions/Prerequisites for the Success of Collective Bargaining

In order to make collective bargaining successful, certain prerequisites, as discussed further, are necessary:

1. Existence of a well-organised and fully recognised trade union with well-defined policies.
2. Mutual trust and faith between the employees and the management.
3. Favourable political climate, that is, the government and public opinion supporting the institution of collective bargaining.
4. Spirit of 'give and take' in both the management and the workers' union.
5. Freedom of association.
6. Strong, stable and democratically functioning trade unions.
7. Obligation on both the parties to bargain before resorting to any other measure.
8. Absence of unfair labour practices.
9. No uncertainty about the fields in which the parties are legally required to bargain collectively.
10. Topics to be discussed: The usual practice is to discuss all matters pertaining to wages, hours of work, holidays, leave, termination of services and other disciplinary matters. Issues pertaining to the establishment of grievance procedure, suggestion schemes and labour participation in various functions of the enterprise may also be discussed. The scope of collective bargaining itself is subject to bargaining, and no rigid framework can be provided initially.[10] An idea of the subject usually covered under collective bargaining can be had from Exhibit 18.1.

Exhibit 18.1 Contents of Collective Agreement

(a) The purpose of the agreement, its scope and the definition of important terms
(b) The rights and responsibilities of the management and of the trade union
(c) Wages, bonus, production norms, leave, retiring benefits, and other benefits and terms and conditions of service
(d) Grievance redressal procedure
(e) Methods and machinery for the settlement of possible future disputes
(f) A termination clause

Source: Indian Institute of Personnel Management, *Personnel Management in India.*

Exhibit 18.2 Indicators of Matured Collective Bargaining

While nothing is final, it is possible on the basis of the experience of the industrially advanced countries of the West, where collective bargaining is said to have made considerable advances, to identify some indicators of matured collective bargaining.

(a) A high degree of collective bargaining as mentioned in terms of the proportion of workers covered by collective agreements
(b) Qualitative conduct of the parties to collective bargaining both before a situation warranting negotiations develops and the methods followed at the time of arriving at agreements

Source: Abdul Aziz, 'Collective Bargaining in Karnataka: A Review', *Indian Journal of Labour Economics* 24, no. 4 (January 1982): C71.

In case the aforesaid prerequisites are available, an organisation can be hopeful of making a collective and successful move towards matured bargaining. Some of the main indicators of matured collective bargaining are shown in Exhibit 18.2.

Types of Collective Bargaining Agreements

Collective bargaining agreements can be classified into three categories: (a) bipartite agreements finalised voluntarily for their implementation; (b) bipartite settlements finalised primarily by the parties (the employer and the union), but registered before the conciliator to make it binding on themselves under the provisions of the Industrial Disputes Act, 1947; and (c) consent awards, that is, settlements arrived at while the disputes are pending before the tribunal. Such consent awards are recorded by the tribunal and thus the agreement negotiated gets legal sanctity.

Levels of Collective Bargaining

Bargaining may be at the plant level or industry level or the national level as follows:

- **Plant level:** Plant-level collective bargaining is quite common in Indian industries. To quote a few examples of some of the earlier popular plant-level collective bargaining agreements, we can make a mention of the agreements between Tata Iron and Steel Company (TISCO) and Tata Workers' Union at Jamshedpur (1956 and 1959)[11] (which contains provisions for union security, workers' cooperation in seeking for higher productivity, WPM, acceptance of the scheme for job evaluation and many provisions hitherto unknown in India, though well known in other industrially advanced countries),[12] the Bata Shoe Company agreement (1955, 1958 and 1962), Modi Spinning and Weaving Mills Company's Agreement (1956), the Metal Corporation of India Agreement (1960) and so on. The main feature of such agreements is that these are confined only to the plant concerned.

- **Industry level**: Industry-level collective bargaining agreement is finalised at the industry level and is applicable to the organisations belonging to that industry only. In industry-wide bargaining practice, employers may be represented by a bargaining committee, selected by individual firms and authorised to conclude an agreement for them. When bargaining is restricted to a single locality, employers may be represented by an employers' association. For the union, uniformity in local or regional agreements may be achieved by including representatives of the national organisation or by requiring that a national officer counter-sign each local agreement.[13]

One of the examples of industry-level collective bargaining agreements in India is the agreement concluded in the Iron and Steel Industry through bilateral negotiations at the industry level and signed on 27 October 1970.

Another example of such an agreement may be the agreement between the representatives of the Indian Tea Planters' Association and the Indian Tea Association and the representatives of the Hind Mazdoor Sabha (HMS), signed in 1956, regarding the bonus for plantation workers.[14] The bilateral agreement concluded between the Mysore government and Transport department and its employees is another example of industry-wide collective bargaining. Industry-level agreements are preferred because the representatives of the two sides are closely connected with the industry, know its complexities and realities and are always interested in the early solution of the problem. Besides, they can be more effective in the implementation of the agreement because they are continually involved in the industry.

- **National level**: Such agreements are not many in our country because of large number of workers' central federations and diverse conditions in different parts of the country, yet some national-level agreements have been concluded at the national level, such as the Delhi agreement related to nationalisation and allied matter, concluded at a conference of the representatives of labour and management on 7 February 1951. Agreements entered in the banking industry and also in the Life Insurance Corporation of India are some of the other examples of national-level collective bargaining. National-level agreements are generally bipartite and finalised at the conference of labour and management convened by the central government.

Benefits of Collective Bargaining

Collective bargaining is very useful because it develops better mutual understanding and empathy between the employer and his/her employees, and as they get an insight into the constraints of each other, they realise and appreciate the limitations of each other. Since both the parties are directly involved in the negotiations, they can take better care of their problems. Both the parties can meet frequently, as and when required, for negotiations to take care of working conditions in case there are any technological or other changes needing any adjustment. Collective bargaining enables the two parties to frame procedural rules that govern the behaviour of both the employer and the workers' union towards each other. Collective bargaining also enables the two parties, that is, the employer and the union, to frame substantive rules which regulate the relations between individuals instead of groups, such as economic relationship, political relationship and social relationship.

Negative Aspects of Collective Bargaining

Since collective bargaining is based on power and conflict, it does the most for the people who need it the least. We find that the strong trade unions in the labour market could protect their income because of their skills and unity, while the weakest workers have very limited ability to form unions and, therefore, are unable to get the benefits of collective bargaining. Besides, since it is difficult to have collective bargaining without the right to strike, there is always a problem of strike and its consequences. Another problem with collective bargaining is that there is always a possibility that the two parties—the employer and the workers' union—may have collusion and fix prices very high at the cost of customers.

Process of Collective Bargaining

The process of collective bargaining involves various steps which can be covered under two heads as discussed further.

Negotiation Stage

Following are the main steps which constitute the negotiation steps:

1. **Identification of the problem**: It is the starting point of the process. The success of the rest of the steps of the process of collective bargaining depends on the identification of the problem in its true perspective.
2. **Preparation for negotiations**: This step comprises the following steps:
    a. **Constitution of negotiating teams**: Both the management and the union constitute their teams who represent them at the negotiating table. Only such people should be selected who are well acquainted with the problem(s) on which negotiations are going to take place. However, additional and other useful information should also be provided to them by the side they will be representing at the negotiations. The representatives so selected should do their homework, should know themselves and their opponents, should know what they want and what is their reserve price, should also know the consequences if the deal does not materialise, should try to know as much as possible about the stand their opponents are likely to take and, above all, should gather as much relevant quantitative information to substantiate their own point of view as possible. Besides, the representatives should possess the desired attributes and negotiating skills, such as good communication skills; 'give and take' attitude; knowledge about haggling, Boulwarism and continuous bargaining; pat hand; trade-off and buyout; positive bargaining; complete knowledge about the working conditions, human

relations and IR policies of the company, its past history and agreements entered into earlier by counterpart organisations; knowing dirty tricks; ranking goals priority-wise; knowing where to assert and where to stop; anticipating their opponent's strategy; arguing power; and knowing how to allow the opponent to save face if he/she backs down.

b. **Bargaining power**: Before going to the bargaining table, each side should know its bargaining power; that is, it should know the maximum concession it can offer to the other side, keeping in view the estimated cost of strikes or lockouts if it is restored to.

c. **Data collection**: During negotiations, each party has to support its arguments with relevant facts and figures. Hence, both the parties collect data, which may enable them to stand in good stead. Data should be collected not only about their own organisation but also about the organisations located in their close vicinity and the organisations belonging to their industry.

3. **Negotiation of agreement**: Usually, it is the chief negotiator representing the management who initiates the problem, pointing out its nature and the views of both the parties. Then follows the discussion. Both the parties use their own strategies. Dale Yoder has suggested certain probabilities/tactics.[15] There may be table pounding which is regarded as a standard operating practice (SOP). Each party generally recognises both the usefulness and limitations of level noises. Each party pounds loudest when making assertions about which it is least certain.[16] Bluffing may be another strategy. Both parties recognise the opportunities to gain from bluffing. Either may make dire threats with no serious thought of carrying them out. Bluffing in the early stages may have real advantages because it helps in creating an impression that they have worked hard and accomplished a great deal.[17] Staff shoe is another stand. Per this approach, either or both parties may play it cool. They may evaluate the situation as one in which tempers need to be soothed rather than aroused. They may recognise that they have a good going thing; they strive not to spoil it. This approach is common in situations where the parties are committed to continuous bargaining.[18] In trade-off and buyout, either party may take the position that every concession has a price tag and anything can be agreed on for enough money. For example, the union may be persuaded to accept a smaller number of leaves or holidays for slightly higher wages. In the big deal, each party strives to put together—by bluffing, buyouts, trade-off and other tactics—the best possible (big) deal for constituents. Positive bargaining/strategy means introducing serious proposals for change. For example, employer demands for a less expensive escalator clause, union action to central wildcat strikes on reductions in complaints about production standards and so on. These can also be followed by the orthodox procedure of labour negotiations, that is, *haggling bargaining*, which may be of two kinds: (a) *piecemeal approach*, in which issues are settled one by one independently and ticked away, and (b) *total approach*, in which no issue is settled independently. Each issue is discussed and laid aside as others are brought forward, but every issue remains open until suddenly the whole complex is ready to crystallise into a total agreement because it is assumed that all issues are interrelated and independent.[19]

Another approach can be Boulwarism (known after its originator, Lemuel Boulware, former vice president of the General Electric Company) bargaining. In it, in addition to meeting with union representatives, the company conducts an extensive communication programme through which it tries to sell its offer directly to the union members and persuades them to make their opinions known to the union leaders. The company tries to give an impression that the company has offered it at its own and not under pressure from the union. Besides, the company wants to demonstrate that the offer is final with scope for any change because the offer is based on facts and sound logic.

Sometimes, this happens in continuous bargaining in which both the parties—the management and the union—try to explore the problem through joint meetings over a long period of time and try to narrow down their differences and finally reach a settlement.

Walton and Mckersie[20] point out that any settlement may have one or all the elements: (a) intra-organisational bargaining, (b) attitudinal structuring, (c) obstructive bargaining and (d) integrative bargaining (all discussed earlier).

Thompson and Weinstock have developed a model of employer and union strategies. Per this model, while employers follow the McGregor Theory Y, union representatives are Theory X-oriented.[21]

Formal negotiations create the collective bargaining agreement. (Informal negotiations can be regarded as the part of the total process of contract administration. It is a continuing process arising out of the day-to-day interpretations and applications of the formal agreement.)[22]

4. **Collective bargaining agreement**: The collective bargaining agreement is the outcome of negotiations between the employer and the union. Such an agreement is a written statement of terms and conditions mutually agreed between the two parties during collective bargaining. What should be included or excluded in a collective agreement is a matter of opinion. While some authors feel that an agreement may be divided into four parts—union security, worker security, economic factors and management protection—the IIPM[23] opines that the collective agreement should comprise the following:

   a. Purpose of the agreement, its scope and the definition of important terms
   b. Rights and responsibilities of the management and the trade unions
   c. Wages, bonus, production norms, leave, retiring benefits, and other benefits and terms and conditions of the service
   d. Grievance redressal procedure
   e. Methods and machinery for the settlement of future disputes
   f. A termination clause

5. **Follow-up action**: Once the collective agreement is finalised, it should be reduced in black and white and widely circulated among all concerned. Supervisors should be specifically briefed about the details of the agreement as it is they who play an important role in its implementation.

Contract Administration

Agreements, like public policy declarations in legislation, cannot implement themselves and carry out their provisions. Administration of an agreement, like administration of a law, is the real clue to effects and results.[24] The progress in collective bargaining is not determined by just signing of an agreement; it is rather measured by the effective administration of the collective agreement.[25] It is, therefore, desirable that both the parties should implement the agreement in both letter and spirit.

No agreement can reflect perfect foresight with respect to the problems to be encountered. Questions of meaning and intent will almost certainly arise. Contract administration must answer these questions and supply interpretations. That is why it is well said that contract administration involves the application, interpretation and enforcement of the terms which the parties have agreed.[26]

While the management may assign such responsibilities for administration of the agreement to foremen, supervisors, plant managers and HR department, the workers' union may assign this task to shop stewards, local presidents, business agents and so on. The major issues in this regard include communication, interpretation, amendment and revision, grievance settlement, arbitration and so on.

Growth and Status of Collective Bargaining in India

The pattern of collective bargaining in different countries is not the same nor is the collective bargaining at the same stage of development all over the world.[27] It is because the growth of collective bargaining is closely associated with the growth of trade unionism. Besides trade unionism which impacts the growth of collective bargaining, the other impacting factors in this regard include labour legislation, attitude and role of the government, changes taking place in technology, political environment, economic order, ownership of individual enterprises, structure of trade union organisations and so on.

In India too, the growth of collective bargaining is closely associated with the growth of trade unionism in India. The expansion in the number and types of subjects which collective bargaining covers has been mainly due to getting the trade unions stronger over a period of time, though the recent legislation and liberal attitude taken by the government have also played a role in this direction.

We can trace the origin of collective bargaining agreements in India back to around 1920 when, at the insistence of Mahatma Gandhi, the first collective bargaining agreement was finalised to regulate labour management relations between a group of employers and their workers in the textile industry in Ahmedabad.[28] However, there was no significant development in the status of collective bargaining until the country became independent in 1947. It was the First Five Year Plan that stated that collective bargaining is the fundamental basis of mutually satisfactory relationship.[29] Hence, efforts were made to popularise collective bargaining, though not much could be achieved. Of course, collective bargaining virtually touched most of the important segments of the national economy, as far as determination of wages and conditions of employment are concerned. Only about 32–49% of disputes could be settled through collective bargaining agreements during the period 1956–1960.

In our country, most of the collective bargaining agreements have been concluded at the plant level, though industry-level agreements in some industries like textile centres in Mumbai and Ahmedabad have been common. We come across such agreements in coal industry, ports and docks, banking industry, chemicals, automobile, oil refining and distribution and so on in the recent past. For example, the sixth bipartite settlements which came into being with effect from 1 November 1992 led to an improvement in wages by 10.5%. In addition to this, a 6% increase was achieved by unions in terms of pension from 1 November 1993.[30] The scope of agreements has been widening, and issues related to bonus, wages, OT, hours of work, promotion, retrenchment, lay-off, dismissal, labour productivity, rationalisation, pension, incentives, grievances procedure, disciplinary matters, WPM, settlement of industrial disputes, job evaluation, modernisation and so on have been the part of collective agreements, though with no uniformity. An idea regarding subjects covered by collective agreements can be had from the 1963 and 1969 surveys conducted by the Employers' Federation of India (EFI), as shown in Tables 18.1 and 18.2.

Table 18.1 Details of Areas Covered by Agreements Reported by EFI Survey 1963

Number of Agreements	First	Current
	136	275
Number of Units	117	162
	(%)	(%)
1. Wages, DA and bonus wages, salary scales	69	57
Revision of wages/workloads	1	8
DA	41	40
Bonus	49	37
Incentive wages/bonus	4	12
2. Other cash allowances OT	13	14
Acting officiating allowance	4	8
Shift allowance	4	11
Tiffin allowance	3	11
Travelling allowance	4	3
Duty allowance	3	4
Outstation allowance	1	3

Source: The Employers' Federation of India, *Collective Bargaining: A Survey Practices and Procedures*, Monograph No. 8 (Mumbai: The Employers' Federation of India, 1966), 75.

Table 18.2 Subjects Covered by the Collective Agreements of the EFI Survey 1969

Subject	Number of Agreements
Wages	96
DA	59
Tiffin allowance	20
Canteens	19
Retirement benefits	53
Bonus	50
Annual leave	40
Paid holidays	36
Casual leave	26
Job classification	26
OT	25
Incentives	23
Shift allowance	22
Acting allowance	22
Medical benefit	19
Grievance	14
Work study	13
Fresh supply of milk	13
Housing	12
Promotion	12
Rationalisation	11
Accident benefit	11
Permanency	10
Joint consultation	9
Sick leave	9

Source: The Employers' Federation of India, *Collective Agreements, Trends in the 60s*, Monograph no. 15 (Mumbai: The Employers' Federation of India, 1971), 53–54.**BLE t 18A7.2**

Long-time agreements of two to five years have also shown an increase. For example, only recently, Hero MotoCorp inked a wage agreement at its Gurgaon unit for three years (see Exhibit 18.3).

The Life Insurance Corporation of India had also entered into an agreement with the union in November 2015 affecting around 0.1 million employees (see Exhibit 18.4).

PSBs also usually enter into wage agreements for a period of five years (for details, see Exhibit 18.5).

Exhibit 18.3   Hero MotoCorp Inks Wage Agreement at Gurgaon Unit

Hero MotoCorp Ltd (HMCL) inked a wage settlement pact with its permanent workers at Gurgaon plant, entailing a hike of Rs. 12,500 spread over three years. The three-year agreement will be implemented with retrospective effect starting from 1 August 2015 till 31 July 2018. The earlier wage settlement was effetive from 1 August 2012 to 31 July 2015.

Source: The Economic Times, 5 July 2016.

Exhibit 18.4   LIC Management, Union Agree on 15% Wage Hike

The management of Life Insurance Corporation (LIC) and the Union representing around 1 lakh employees of the insurance behemoth have agreed on 15% wage hike, which will be effective from August 2012. The management also agreed to a five-day week for alternative Saturdays for LIC employees. The pact offers a 15% hike in salary which includes a 13.5% increase in the basic pay and a 1.5% raise in allowance like HRA, CCA and daily commuting allowance.

Source: The Economic Times, 26 November 2015.

Exhibit 18.5   Wage Agreement

Punjab National Bank plans to break ranks with other state-run banks and seek approval from its board to introduce performance-linked remuneration in a move aimed at retaining talent, managing director, Usha Ananthasubramaniam said. It is the Indian Banks' Association (IBA) that negotiates wage hike with officers' associations and employee unions. The wage hike is applicable for five years and the contract is due for renewal on 1 November 2017.

Source: Hindustan Times, 9 November 2016.

A new trend noticeable during the last few decades in some states is that after an agreement has been finalised between the management and the unions, it is got to be signed by the conciliation officer concerned so that it may be a settlement under conciliation and thus binding on both the parties. We also come across a great variation in the IR situations and collective bargaining practices due to a number of reasons.

The main factors affecting the growth of collective bargaining favourably and the present status of collective bargaining in Indian industries include tripartite conferences; industrial committees; Industrial Truce Resolution, 1962; amendments conducive to growth of collective bargaining in the Industrial Disputes Act, 1947; statutory provisions; Joint Consultative Boards; WPM, Workers' Education Scheme, Code of Discipline, Workers Committees, grievance-handling procedure, Joint Councils and so on. With a positive change in the attitude of both the employers and the workers' unions, it is expected that the institution of collective bargaining will grow more rapidly.

Assessment of Collective Bargaining in India

Since there is a lack of trust and faith between the employers and trade unions and further that except in a few states, there are no statutory provisions for the recognition of trade unions, collective bargaining in our country has not yet been able to make the desired headway. Not only this, but the spirit of 'give and take', which is the essence of collective bargaining, is also missing to a great extent between the aforesaid two parties. A good number of unions have got used to apply tactics, such as go-slow, sit-in strikes, union gate meetings and tool-down strikes, during the pre-negotiations period and shouting of slogans when the negotiation sessions are on as a means to getting their demands conceded. Some unions and employers use strikes and lockouts, respectively, as weapons to improve the prospects of a settlement in their favour. It is, therefore, no surprise to find in the process of collective bargaining conflict situations, third-party interventions, legal battles and so on, which are not consistent with a developed mature bargaining process.[31] Another author has also remarked,

> Since independence, collective bargaining has continued to grow at a steady pace, but there have been hurdles in its way. Notable among these hurdles are difficulty in recognition of unions, ineffective procedures, outside leadership, easy availability of adjudication machinery, restrictions on strikes and lock-outs, too many labour laws, inadequate unionization, etc.[32]

However, over a period of time, the changing attitude of both employers and the unions have helped in promoting the cause of collective bargaining. Through a sample study conducted by the EFI, it was revealed that during 1950–1960, the number of disputes settled by collective bargaining agreements ranged between 32% and 49%. Some of recent developments such as the active role being played by tripartite conferences, ILO's efforts, grievance-handling procedure, WPM, Workers' Education Scheme, greater awakening in managements' and unions' way of thinking, and government's efforts have encouraged the institution of collective bargaining.

Reasons for Slow Growth of Collective Bargaining in India

The main factors responsible for slow growth of collective bargaining in India can be summarised as follows:

1. Weak trade union movement
2. Inadequate support from the government and employers
3. Excessive dependence on adjudication machinery for resolving industrial disputes

4. Absence of any central law for compulsory recognition of trade union
5. Inter-union rivalry
6. Reduction in the area of collective bargaining due to emergence of several new institutions, such as wage boards, labour legislation and WPM
7. Politicalisation of trade unions
8. Lack of mutual trust between employer and his/her employees
9. Lack of proper understanding and appreciation of the concept of collective bargaining
10. Lack of spirit of 'give and take' in both the groups—the employer and the unions
11. Non-availability of factual information
12. The separatist tendencies of craft unions
13. Unfair labour practices
14. Unequal strength of both the parties—the employer and the unions
15. Indifferent attitude of some of the union leaders as also some of the employers towards collective bargaining

Future of Collective Bargaining

It is unfortunate that collective bargaining as a way of living in an industrial society is yet to be achieved. It is, therefore, necessary that in order to ensure a bright future of collective bargaining in Indian industries, both the management and trade unions follow certain principles,[33] such as granting of recognition by the employer to the union of workers, treating the union fairly, visualising workers' grievances and solving them timely, positive and cooperative approach of both the groups, avoiding unfair labour practices, extending due cooperation by the union in increasing the productivity of the organisation, respect for each other and making sincere efforts by both groups to establish all the prerequisites necessary for the success of collective bargaining. Although the principles are being followed to some extent, but they should be followed vigorously in both letter and spirit. Both the groups should give up their rigid attitude and follow the policy of 'give and take'. They should give up their approach of approaching adjudication machinery and if, at all, the two groups fail to reach an agreement, they should utilise mediation/arbitration machinery. We should go by the international consensus, which holds that collective bargaining should be recognised as a human right at par with the fundamental rights such as the right to vote and the right to free expression.[34]

Besides, neither the management nor the union should assume that it has won because at times, some victories may become hazardous. In case either of the two parties having got most of its proposals through gives an impression to the other party that it (the other party) has lost the battle, the other party will get revengeful and start preparing for showing down the so-called winning party at a later stage. Such an approach damages the very foundation of collective bargaining. Collective bargaining is just like a game in which parties keep on winning and losing the game, but the sportsman spirit remains intact. A declining trend has also been noticed in the proportion of unionised workplaces and also in the collective representation of employees on many issues, predominately due to reassertion of managerial power in the workplace and government support to management in the face of globalisation. The decline could also be attributed to the shift of jobs from the manufacturing to the service industries and unaggressive union leadership.[35] Today, we also come across the proactive approach being practised in some industries. For example, in software industry, either trade unions do not exist in most of the organisations or, if they do exist, they are as good as dead because of the proactive approach of the employers. They anticipate the problem and find out its solution, leaving no role for the trade union to play. As against this, we find that between 1980 and 2004, strong trade unions had been the backbone of collective bargaining. If the institution of collective bargaining is to be strengthened, trade unionism also needs to be strong.

Thus, it can be said that though the prospects of collective bargaining in Indian industries are not bleak, it can be shining and more shining if all concerned focus on ensuring the presence of prerequisites, as discussed earlier, necessary for its success.

International Scenario of Collective Bargaining

The international scenario of collective bargaining does not reflect a uniform trend. While the number of workers covered by collective agreements remained relatively stable, in some countries it fell, especially in countries having deregulated market and lacking support for collective bargaining. For an example, between 1980 and 2004, collective bargaining coverage in most of Western Europe had remained remarkably at approximately 80–90% of employees.[36] On the other extreme, in certain countries like China, there is no concept of collective bargaining. As far as the transition economies are concerned, they have just made a beginning with collective bargaining. It is good that at the international level, some collective agreements have taken place like the International Federation of Chemical, Energy, Mine and General Workers' Unions (ICEM) signed the first ever IR global agreement in the oil sector with Statoil (the Norwegian State oil company) in 1988.

While in certain countries, like those in South America, collective bargaining has remained underdeveloped, it has been stable in North America, and in countries like Brazil, in the banking sector, both the employers' organisations and unions have formed national industry-wide associations to coordinate strategies in the public and private sectors.

In 2008, there were about 149 million workers covered under collective agreements in China. There the government and social partners use tripartite mechanisms to promote collective bargaining. We also come across there a gradual spread of regional and sectoral bargaining. Some countries, such as Jamaica, Grenada and Bermuda in Caribbean have improved and developed new procedures to promote collective bargaining there. They have also introduced a duty to bargain in good faith. In Nepal also, collective bargaining at the sectoral level is being strengthened. Some countries such as Kenya and Nairobi in Africa have introduced and elaborated rules and procedures governing collective bargaining processes. Many other countries in Africa have created new IR institutions to encourage collective bargaining. Anyway, collective bargaining is still lagging behind in a number of countries in Africa. However, in South Africa, around one-third of all workers in W&S employment are covered under collective bargaining agreements.

As far as the APAC region is concerned, there is no uniformity, though enterprise-level bargaining is popular in the region. However, in Sri Lanka, we come across sectoral agreements in the plantation sector. In India also, we come across sectoral agreements in the plantation, cotton and textiles, and banking sectors, but enterprise-level collective agreements generally rule the roost. In Korea, though enterprise-level agreements are popular, we also come across sectoral bargaining in certain sectors such as health sector and banking sector.

It is the multiplicity of trade unions that has been restructuring the growth of collective bargaining in many countries such as Indonesia, Pakistan and Cambodia. In some countries, white-collar and knowledge workers in many organisations are not keen to join trade unions because their wages and other employment conditions are determined on their individual performance and innovativeness and not by collectivism as we find the scenario in the IT and ITES organisations in India. In Taiwan, collective bargaining is rapidly becoming a thing of the past.[37]

Collective bargaining takes place at the sectoral level in many of the EU15 countries and some of the new member states. In some countries, collective bargaining takes place at the sectoral level and in some other at the inter-sectoral level as well as centralised level.

In Finland and Denmark, sectoral-level bargaining is quite common. The EU15 countries—Australia, Belgium, Finland, Denmark, Germany, France, Greece, Ireland, Luxembourg, Italy, Portugal, Spain, Sweden, the Netherlands and the UK—have introduced procedural amendments to facilitate the adoption of collective bargaining structures, permitting greater articulation of issues at different levels.[38]

Workers' Participation in Management

In case workers are associated in the decision-making process, it gives them a great psychic satisfaction besides other advantages of WPM. Their ego is satisfied to a great extent, and they feel involved in the affairs of their organisation and start giving their best to the organisation. Besides, WPM is a big leap towards realisation of the concept of industrial democracy which is instrumental in establishing industrial peace and enabling an organisation to achieve its objectives.

The emerging changes in the working world point to the gradual transition from muscle to mind and brawn to brain in terms of human skills and their utilisation at the workplace. This emphasises the need for the management belief, initiative and commitment to management through joint consultation and cooperation.[39] It is here that workers' participation comes into vogue.

However, voluntary measures are more effective than those imposed through legislation and so on. In individual enterprises, depending upon management philosophy and the extent of interest and initiative that a management takes, there is no dearth of new initiatives for promoting and facilitating consultation and cooperation at the shop floor and enterprise levels. It is sure that any action plan to promote and facilitate consultation and communication within the enterprise can benefit immensely from the ideas, information and caveats contained in ILO Recommendation No. 129 on the subject.[40]

Concept and Meaning

The origin of the concept of WPM can be traced back to the writings of Fabian socialists headed by Sydney Webb, who highlighted the economic and social disorders of industrially developing countries and stressed the need for unity and cooperation among partners of production.[41] The origin and growth of political democracy in many parts of the world was another factor for giving a boost to the concept of WPM. Since political democracy and economic industrial democracies go along, it was argued that just as in political democracy people have the right to choose their government, the workers should also have the right to affect the managerial decisions (i.e. industrial democracy). It was Mahatma Gandhi who initiated the idea of WPM in our country through his concept of trusteeship. The concept received further impetus from the First World War and the Second World War when in the quest of industrial peace, some countries recommended to establish joint committees/bodies. The three recommendations of the ILO adopted in 1952, 1960 and 1976 further encouraged the process of consultation with the workers and recommended the establishment of tripartite machinery for consultation. With the passage of time, the idea of WPM got institutionalised in many countries, though the term of WPM varies from country to country depending on its economic, political and social circumstances. In India, the concept got further impetus through an amendment to the Constitution of India, providing for WPM and including it as a Directive Principle of State Policy (Article 43A). The enactment of the right to information in 2005 was another milestone in oiling the process of WPM.

However, 'participation', as it is understood today, has been fraught with multiple meanings and, therefore, it has acquired different meanings for different people defining it per their own convenience. For example, while workers regard WPM as a co-decision and right of co-determination, management interprets it as joint consultation prior to decision-making. To some, WPM is the method through which workers are able to collectively express their views on the functions of the enterprise. To others, WPM is sharing of power and authority between the workers and the management. However, the underlying point in all opinions being sharing the decision-making power with the workers in an organisation in an appropriate manner, that is, to eke out a say of the workers in the decision-making process. Thus, WPM is a movement from decision-taking to decision-making.

Characteristic Features of WPM

1. WPM increases the scope of employees' share of influence in decision-making.
2. It is presumed that workers will own responsibility.
3. Participation has to be at different levels so as to influence policy formulation and to help in its execution.
4. There will have to be forums and practices providing for association of workers' representatives.
5. It increases a worker's productivity through active cooperation between the worker and the management.
6. It boosts a worker's motivation.
7. It increases understanding between the two groups.
8. It recognises a worker's personality.
9. It puts industrial democracy into practice and makes the workers conscious of their democratic rights.
10. It makes a worker feel involved in the affairs of his/her organisation.

Some authors[42] have grouped these objectives under the heads such as economic objectives, social objectives and psychological objectives.

Decision-taking vs Decision-making

In normal course, people do not distinguish between 'decision-taking' and 'decision-making' and use the terms interchangeably. However, there is little difference between the two. While 'decision-taking' is an autonomous individual action, and at times, though rarely even unilateral, 'decision-making' is a group or consultative process wherein the concerned group is taken into confidence and the decision is made.

Direct Participation vs Indirect Participation

Indirect participation is usually through the elected representatives, whereas in direct participation, every individual worker is provided an opportunity to participate in the management, such as an employee suggestion scheme and as a member of a quality circle.

Participation vs Collective Bargaining

In order to accomplish organisation objectives, it is necessary that workers should be committed at the workplace, and commitment can be obtained through consensual processes involving cooperation, communication and consultation. It is here that WPM comes into picture. It is not easy to keep the labour, which has become highly conscious about its rights and privileges, contented unless it is actively involved and engaged in the affairs of the organisation. WPM takes care of all these issues.

Collective bargaining, on the other hand, is essentially a process in which employees act as a group in seeking to shape conditions and relationships in their employment; that is, its main focus is on collectively settling down conditions of employment.

Levels, Forms/Types, Structures and Network

Participation can take place at three levels in an enterprise—floor level, plant level and corporate level.[43] The forms of participation are the functions of the purpose:

- **Communication:** The purpose is to give and get information.
- **Consultation:** The purpose is to obtain other party's views.
- **Participation:** To let the people concerned take part in taking decisions.
- **Joint decision-making:** Management taking decisions together with workers/unions.[44]

It has, therefore, been rightly said that workers' participation can be as follows:

- Informative participation
- Consultative participation
- Administrative participation
- Decision-making participation

A brief description of these is as follows:

- **Informative participation:** This is the initial level of participation and refers to information-sharing concerning balance sheet, economic conditions of the plant, production and so on so that the workers can have an idea of what is going on in the organisation and may offer their suggestions on the matters of general economic significance.
- **Consultative participation:** This is at the next higher level. Here, the workers are consulted on matters such as welfare programmes, safety and methods of work.
- **Administrative participation:** Here, the workers have a greater share in participation, and they assume a greater responsibility for the discharge of management functions as workers enjoy a bit more autonomy in the exercise of administrative and supervisory powers in matters affecting workers, for example, to be a part of administration of 'canteen committee'.
- **Decisive and decision-making participation:** It being the highest level of participation, workers get an opportunity to participate in the final decision-making process.

Decisions are taken jointly on all matters—work-related issues or interest-related issues. Hence, it leads to oneness and total involvement.

However, according to P. Suba Rao,[45] forms of workers' participation are as follows:

- Workers' committees
- Joint management councils (JMCs)
- Joint councils
- Shop councils
- Unit councils

Other Forms of Workers' Involvement in Management

There are two other most talked forms of employees involvement: (a) autonomous work groups (e.g. autonomous work groups at Volvo's Kalmer Plant in Sweden and, to a lesser extent, at Calico Mills at Ahmedabad) and (b) quality circles.

Models in WPM

The main models in WPM are as follows:

- **Workers' councils model**: Workers' councils are exclusive bodies of the employees alone. Members of workers' councils are elected by the employees of sections concerned. They may discharge different functions in the management of an organisation. There is no fixed limit on the number of workers' councils in an organisation, which may vary from just one workers' council for the whole organisation or there may be a hierarchy of workers' councils from shop floor to the staff board. Workers' councils are also known as staff councils.
- **Collective bargaining model**: Theoretically speaking, collective bargaining is also a form of WPM. It is used as one of the important methods that affect managerial decisions relating to conditions of employment. Through collective agreements, it gives right to both the groups—the management and the workers—to frame rules for conditions of employment and termination of employment contract.
- **JMCs model**: JMCs comprise representatives of both the management and the employees and are the most common form of WPM in India. They are usually advisory and consultative bodies, the final decision mostly to be taken by the top management. JMCs are very common in the UK.
- **Workers' self-management model**: This model is practised in Yugoslavia. In this model, workers are part of main decision-making bodies. In this system, workers are either owners or they have the right to make use of the organisation's assets.

Thus, we find that there is no one model of WPM which is being used universally. Different countries follow the model of their own choice.

Benefits of WPM

WPM is beneficial to all concerned as follows:

1. WPM promotes industrial democracy and industrial harmony.
2. It releases the creative abilities of the individual.

3. Workers also have useful ideas. Hence, the same can be used in the interest of the organisation.
4. Workers may work more effectively if they participate in the decision-making.
5. Workers accept those decisions better in which they have been a party.
6. It facilitates upward communication.
7. It develops trust, faith, understanding and cooperation between the management and the workers (see Exhibit 18.6).
8. It may prove as a stimulus to management efficiency.
9. It also provides psychic satisfaction to workers.
10. It boosts the morale of workers and increases their commitment to the cause of the organisation.
11. It not only increases the productivity of the organisation but also enhances its profitability and smoothens its functioning.
12. It is a measure directed towards minimisation of class feelings at the workplace.
13. It is an important forum of self-expression for the workers.
14. It avoids the chances of external and political intervention in the affairs of the organisation.

Exhibit 18.6   Participative Decision-making Is a Way of Life

UTI, over a period of time, has built an environment of socialising decisions with all before implementations. This has instilled a lot of faith and trust amongst all. Standardisation of employee value proposition irrespective of levels, region, grades and nature of jobs is what gives them the extra edge over their competitors.

Source: The Economic Times, 15 March 2016.

Development of WPM in India

Before Independence of India

Surprisingly, in India, it was the government and not the trade unions which initiated WPM as until the end of the First World War, trade unions were too weak to counter the employers' decisions. It was Tata Steel that constituted Workers' Committee in 1919, which had the representatives of both the management and the union, though the committee could not last long. We can trace the beginning of joint consultations in the right sense of the word when in 1920, the Ahmedabad textile industry agreed to resolve their disputes through mutual discussion. Some printing presses followed suit in the same year. Following the recommendations of the committee constituted by the Government of Bengal in 1921, some workers' committees were set up. The Royal Commission on Labour in India (1931) appreciated the workers' committees, but the economic depression (1932–1934) hampered the progress of these committees.

Since Independence

The main developments regarding WPM in our country since independence are as follows:

In the context of our country, WPM is one of the Directives Principles of State Policy embodied in Article 43A, which was inserted in the Constitution of India by the 42nd Amendment. It reads as follows:

> The State shall take steps, by suitable legislation, or in any other way, to secure the participation of workers in the management of undertakings, establishments or other organisations engaged in any industry.

This speaks for the importance attached to WPM in our country. A brief description of the experiments made in the direction of giving effect to the aforesaid constitutional imperative and otherwise also is as follows.

Works Committees (1947)

Even before the Constitution of India came into being with effect from 26 January 1951, the Industrial Disputes Act, 1947, provided that every undertaking employing 100 or more employees is under an obligation to set up works committees as a scheme of WPM. It was provided that the total strength of a works committee should not exceed 20, and it should have equal number of representatives of both the employer and the employees. The tenure of the works committee is two years. Its task is only to smooth away friction that might arise between the management and the workers in the day-to-day work. The items which works committees can deal with are shown in Exhibit 17.7.

Certain items such as wages and allowances, bonus, profit-sharing, retrenchment and lay-off, provident fund (PF), gratuity, leaves and holidays, housing and transport facilities, and incentive schemes were excluded from the purview of works committees. However, these committees have not been able to serve the purpose they are constituted for.

The factors responsible for their ineffectiveness are shown in Exhibit 17.8.

In order to make works committees function successfully, some of the main suggestions made by the First National Commission on Labour (1969) include more supportive attitude of both the management and the unions, appropriate appreciation of the scope and functions of the works committees, proper coordination of functions of the multiple bipartite bodies functional at plant level and wholehearted implementation of the recommendations made by the works committees.

However, what is needed most to make the works committees successful is the positive intention of both the management and the employees. They should ensure that the recommendations made by the works committees are implemented in both letter and spirit.

Exhibit 18.7 Illustrative List of Items Which Works Committees Can Deal With

1. Conditions of work such as ventilation, lighting, temperature and sanitation including latrines and urinals
2. Amenities such as drinking water, canteens, dining rooms, and medical and health services
3. Safety and accident prevention, occupational diseases and protective equipment

4. Adjustment of festival and national holidays
5. Educational and recreational activities
6. Administration of welfare and fine funds
7. Promotion of thrift and savings
8. Implementation and review of decisions arrived at in the meetings of works committees

Source: Based on discussion in C. B. Mamoria, *Personnel Management* (Mumbai: Himalaya Publishing House, 1980), 805–6.

Joint Management Councils (1958)

The Study Group, set up in 1956 by the MoLE, examined the experiences of the UK, France, Sweden, Belgium, Yugoslavia and so on related to WPM. While the first part of the report of the Study Group comprised the evaluation and appraisal of WPM in the aforementioned countries, the second part of the report set forth the prerequisites for starting the joint consultation in Indian organisations. The report also provided a framework of the proposed scheme. The ILC approved the major recommendations, including the setting up of JMCs, in its 15th session, which was held at New Delhi in July 1957.

On the basis of recommendations of the ILC, a tripartite subcommittee was constituted to consider details regarding the scheme of WPM, which laid down the following criteria for selection of undertakings where JMCs could be introduced:

1. The unit should employ 500 or more employees.
2. The management and the workers should agree to establish JMCs.
3. The workers' union should be affiliated to one of central federations.
4. The employer in the case of private sector should be member of one of the leading employers' organisations.
5. The unit should have a fair record of IR.

Exhibit 18.8 Factors Responsible for Ineffectiveness of Works Committees

1. The recommendations of works committees are advisory in nature, and there is mostly delay in their implementation. There is no machinery to enforce the decisions of these committees. This also dampens the enthusiasm of the workers to make works committees successful.
2. Some employers consider these committees as substitutes for collective bargaining and, therefore, bypass the unions. Hence, the unions view these committees as a threat to their very existence and, in such apprehension, lose every interest in their constitution.
3. Some employers insist upon their prerogatives and consider it below dignity to sit on these committees with their employees.

4. Inter-union rivalries or the absence of provision to hold the election of representatives by secret ballot or to recall a member who forfeits the confidence of the workers in general are also reasons responsible for the ineffectiveness of these committees.
5. There is lack of interest among workers due to assignment of minor functions to the works committees and exclusion of issues such as wages and allowances, bonus, rationalisation, retrenchment and lay-off from the purview of these committees.
6. There is lack of competence shown by the workers' representatives on these committees.

JMCs were established with the objective of increasing the association of employers and employees so as to develop cordial IR, providing psychological satisfaction to employees, improving operational efficiency of employees, educating the workers and providing welfare facilities to the workers.

However, the experiment is a mixed story of success and failures. Some of the organisations where the experiment yielded good results include Tata Steel, Bharat Heavy Electricals Ltd (BHEL) and so on. The main reasons where JMCs did not prove effective are shown in Exhibit 18.9.

In some cases, workers' unions were exclusively responsible for the failure of JMCs. For example, the two unions operating in the Hindustan Cables Limited, Rupnarayanpur, could not agree on the mode of choosing workers' representatives to the JMC, though management of the company wanted to start a JMC.[46] In the public sector, the main reasons responsible for inefficient working of JMCs were the rivalry between unions and the bureaucratic machinery of the government. It was also alleged that JMCs and works committees appeared similar in scope and functions and that multiplicity of bipartite consultation bodies served no purpose.

Exhibit 18.9 Reasons for Unsatisfactory Working of JMCs

1. Management is often not prepared to give as much information to the workers as they need on proper decision-making.
2. There is also an apprehension that the workers, not having expertise in management, are likely to be at disadvantage vis-à-vis the management when complex matters are discussed.
3. Trade unions fear that the JMCs, by becoming alternative channels for articulating workers' interests, would weaken unions' hold over the workers.
4. Workers' representatives on these councils feel dissatisfied with their role, as decision-making is confined to welfare activities only. They want to be given authority to share decisions on more important subjects of collective bargaining, such as wages and bonuses, in which they say the workers are most keenly interested. To be asked to invest time and energy in discussing trivial matters, while important issues are forbidden, is infuriating.

5. Middle management and supervisors are generally hostile to workers' participation because they resent their actions being questioned on the shop floor. The fact that the management sometimes sides with the workers' representatives and reprimands the supervisors weakens their authority.
6. Employers, who already have the system of consultation with the workers in the form of works committees and the recognised unions, find the JMCs in their present form quite superfluous.
7. The absence of a representative union in a good number of organisations has made it difficult for the councils to work smoothly.
8. There is inherent contradiction between the role of union leaders at the bargaining table where they can put all kinds of pressure on management and their role as members of a Joint Council when they must subordinate their sectional interests to those of undertaking as a whole.

The First Labour Management Seminar (1958) and the Second Seminar on Labour–Management Cooperation (1960) organised by the MoLE discussed the issue of JMCs and made certain recommendations for making JMCs work effectively. The working of the JMCs was also examined by the National Commission on Labour (1966–1969) which also expressed its dissatisfaction about the progress made by JMCs.

Workers' Directors (1970)

Another experiment in WPM involved the launching of the scheme for the appointment of workers' representatives on the board of directors of nationalised banks. Subsequent to the nationalisation of banks under the Nationalised Banks (Management and Miscellaneous Provisions) Scheme, 1970, the government required all nationalised banks to appoint employee directors to their boards, one representing workers and the other representing its officers. The employee director was to be appointed by the government from out of a panel of three employees to be furnished by the representative union of that bank. The workers so suggested should have been in continuous service of one or more nationalised banks for a minimum period of five years and also that they should not reach superannuation age during the term of their office as director which was fixed as three years.

The scheme required verification of trade union membership and identification of representative union. This was perhaps the first exercise to place representatives of workers on the boards of sector corporations. The process of appointment of worker directors was carried through all right in 1971, but the second round of appointment took until 1981 in all the 14 banks. This scheme also did not prove a success because the worker directors were not well-versed in comprehending the intricacies of board-level matters. Besides, it was an additional burden on the worker directors. The unions were also not very cooperative as they felt that their powers were reduced. There was also a risk lest some of the bank secrets might be leaked to the unions. The management did not like to share their privilege of making decisions. Because of all these constraints, these directors were removed from the boards of nationalised banks.

New Scheme of Workers' Participation in Industry (1975)

Keeping in view the spirit of the amendment of the Constitution of India in 1975 and insertion of Article 43A in the Directive Principles of State Policy requiring suitable legislation or any other way to secure the participation of workers in the management of undertakings, the scheme of WPM, envisaging establishment of shop councils at the shop floor or departmental level and a joint council at the plant in enterprises level, was initiated in 1975 in manufacturing and mining industries, provided the concerned undertaking employed 500 or more workers irrespective of whether it was in public, private or cooperative sector. The scheme was also made applicable to departmentally run units. It was a part of 20-point Economic Programme. The scheme envisaged participation of workers in the decision-making process in the matters concerning production, productivity, safety measures, working conditions, absenteeism, overall efficiency of the shop or department, general discipline, management of waste reduction, maximising machine and manpower utilisation, and so on. The scheme is non-statutory, and the decisions of both shop council and joint council were expected on the basis of consensus and not by the process of voting. Their decisions were required to be implemented within one month. A brief description of shop councils and joint councils is as follows:

1. **Shop councils**: There should be a shop council for each department or shop or one shop council for more than one department or shop depending on the number of workers employed in different shops or departments. Each council shall have equal number of representatives of employers and workers. The term of the shop council shall be two years. The council should meet at least once a month. While the chairman of the shop council shall be nominated by the management, the worker members of the council shall elect a vice chairman from among themselves. The functions of shop councils are shown in Exhibit 18.10.
2. **Joint councils**: Following the other conditions as laid down in the scheme, there shall be only one joint council, and it shall function for a period of two years. The chief executive of the unit shall be the chairman of the joint council, and there shall also be a vice chairman who will be nominated by worker members of the council. One member of the joint council shall be appointed as its secretary. The joint council shall meet at least once a quarter. In some of the states, the minimum requirement of 500 or more workers was also reduced. The decision made by the council shall be on the basis of consensus and not by a process of voting, and the same shall be implemented within one month unless otherwise stated in the decision itself. The functions of a joint council are mentioned in Exhibit 18.11.

The scheme evoked some enthusiasm initially during the emergency but withered soon after lifting of the emergency and change of the government in 1977.

Second Scheme (Unit Councils) of 1977

In 1977, commercial and service organisations employing 100 or more employees were also brought within the purview of a participative scheme, broadly similar to the 1975 scheme. The scheme was extended to hospitals, Railways, P&T and State Electricity Boards. Due to problems such as the criterion for determining representation to the forums, inadequate sharing of information and lack of supportive culture, the scheme could not make any significant headway. In 1977, the new government led by Janata Dal constituted a special tripartite committee on WPM. The committee recommended on three-tier participation at board, plant and shop floor levels. However, the Janata Dal did not last for long to pursue the recommendations.

Exhibit 18.10 Functions of Shop Councils

1. Help management in achieving production targets
2. Help in improvement of production, productivity and efficiency
3. Assist in tackling the problems of absenteeism
4. Safety measures
5. Assist in maintaining discipline
6. Help in improving physical conditions of work
7. Welfare and health measures
8. Proper flow of communication

Source: Based on discussion in P. S. Rao, *Essentials of Human Resource Management and Industrial Relations* (Mumbai: Himalaya Publishing House, 2000), 640.

Exhibit 18.11 Functions of Joint Councils

1. Settlement of matters which remain unresolved by the unit-level councils and arranging joint meetings of two or more unit-level councils for resolving inter-council problems
2. Review of the working of the unit-level councils for improvement in the customer service and evolving methods for the best way of handling of goods traffic, accounts and so on
3. Dealing with unit-level matters which have a bearing on other branches or on the enterprise as a whole
4. Development of skills of workers and adequate facilities for training
5. Improvement in the general conditions of work
6. Preparation of schedule of working hours and holidays
7. Proper recognition and participation of useful suggestions received from the workers through a system of rewards
8. Discussion of any matter having a bearing on the improvement of performance of the organisation/service for ensuring better customer service

Source: Based on discussion in P. S. Rao, *Essentials of Human Resource Management and Industrial Relations* (Mumbai: Himalaya Publishing House, 2000), 641. New Scheme of Workers' Participation (1983)

Following the review of the working of WPM schemes introduced earlier, the government preponed and notified in December 1983 a new scheme of WPM and made it applicable to all central public sector enterprises exempting industries in defence sector, departmental undertakings of the central government and so on. State governments were also advised to introduce the scheme in their state undertakings and to encourage private sector to implement it. Per the scheme, WPM is to operate at the shop floor level and also at the plant level. There is a provision for board-level participation also. There will be an equal representation of both the parties at the shop floor and plant levels. It is to be ensured that there is a representation of different categories of workers such as unskilled and skilled, technical and non-technical, and supervisory and non-supervisory (managerial personnel are not to be included) at both shop floor and plant levels. The exact number of representatives will depend on the size of the people employed and will be determined by the management in consultation with the trade unions consensually. In case the organisation employs 10% or more women of the total workforce, representation will be given to female workers as well. The scheme has universal applicability irrespective of number of workers employed in the organisation concerned. While the forum at the shop floor level is to look into a wide range of functions, such as production facilities, storage facilities, wastage control, material economy, cleanliness, welfare measures, and hazards and safety problems, the forum at the plant level is to look into operational areas, economic and financial areas, personnel matters, welfare areas and environmental areas.

Convertible Debenture Scheme and Equity Participation Scheme/Worker Shareholders (1985)

In 1985, the central government decided to introduce two new schemes to encourage WPM. Per the first scheme, workers were to be given convertible debentures at 80% of the average market value. Such debentures were to be converted into shares after five years. However, workers were not allowed to sell those shares for a minimum period of three years. According to the other scheme, it was obligatory for all promoters of new issues to offer at least 5% of the total shares to the workers and staff of the organisation.

However, overall, the results of the aforesaid schemes of WPM have failed to yield the desired results. In order to make WPM effective, there is a dire necessity of bringing about attitudinal change in all the stakeholders, some other relevant acts (e.g. Trade Unions Act, 1926) need required amendments, the provision in the Companies Act requiring unanimous board decisions in certain matters compulsory should be suitably modified, penalties proposed in Participation of Workers in Management Bill (1990) should be made mild, sharing of all type of information should not be mandatory, and the functioning of the institution of collective bargaining should be strengthened. Of course, in a few cases such as Tata Steel and State Bank of India (SBI), the WPM has been effective to a great extent. Tata Steel has a three-tier set-up: Joint Department Councils (JDCs) for each department of the works, the Joint Workers Council (JWC) for the entire works and the Joint Consultative Council of Management (JCCM) at the apex. Due to the functioning of these bodies, the performance of the plant has been up to the mark, IR have been cordial, a cadre of well-informed and enlightened trade union leaders has emerged from the grass-roots level, and a high sense of commitment is visible among workers. Similarly, the example of effectiveness of WPM in the SBI, the leading PSB of the country, can also be cited.

The Participation of Workers in Management Bill, 1990

Being not satisfied with the implementation of earlier schemes which were, by and large, voluntary in nature, the government felt the necessity of some sort of legislative backup to. Make the workers' participation effective. Hence, it proposed the Participation of Workers in Management Bill and introduced it in the Rajya Sabha on 30 May 1990, but it could not be passed. The bill aimed at introducing workers' participation at all the three levels—board, plant, and shop floor—through legislation, the intention being to provide specific and meaningful participation of workers in management, to specify detailed criteria for determining the manner of representation of workers on different councils, following the principle of secret ballot, providing for rules to specify the power which an inspector may exercise, fixing the number of members of the monitoring committee and so on.

Prerequisites for Effective Working of WPM Scheme

If workers' participation is to succeed in Indian industries, it should be supported as follows:

1. Positive attitude of all concerned towards WPM
2. Easy access to all relevant information
3. Faith in industrial democracy
4. Absence of multi-unionism
5. Strong trade unions
6. WPM should be taken complimentary to collective bargaining
7. Free flow of communication
8. Attainable objectives
9. Suitable human relations policies
10. Limited number of levels for participation
11. Industrial peace
12. Proper and timely implementation of decisions taken by WPM forums
13. Clear-cut understanding of the WPM schemes
14. Dynamic leadership

What is actually needed is the sincerity of purpose on the part of all concerned.

General Evaluation of the Schemes of WPM

A cursory glance of the working of WPM in Indian industries reveals the following points:

1. Lack of bipartite initiative. Most of the WPM schemes introduced from time to time in our country have been at the instance of government. Hence, the desired results are, by and large, missing.
2. The worker directors usually lacked the skills and competence required for doing the job effectively.
3. Lack of access to the desired information is quite noticeable.
4. Apprehension of leakage of vital information scares the management not to be transparent.
5. Lack of interest in WPM on the part of unions many of whom consider WPM as a parallel institution which is likely to erode their power.
6. WPM initiated by employers at their own have proved more effective as in the case of Tata Steel and SBI.

7. Confusion and duplication created by the functioning of parallel joint bodies such as works committees and JMCs.
8. Multiplicity of trade unions has done irreparable damage to WPM.
9. Lack of trust between the two parties is quite visible.
10. Delay in the implementation (and sometime non-implementation at all) of decisions taken by joint bodies.

Chapter Review

1. The effective functioning of collective bargaining and WPM indicates the smooth functioning of industrial democracy in the organisation concerned. Since industrial democracy protects and promotes the interests of workers, they (workers) also put in their best for their organisation.
2. As far as collective bargaining is concerned, it is a bipartite process in which the representatives of both the employees and the employer negotiate and finalise the terms and conditions of employment, working conditions and the like. Collective bargaining is beneficial to both the workers and the employers as it secures better terms and conditions of employment for workers and the resultant increase in productivity which leads to higher profits to the employer. Distributive, attitudinal, integrative and intra-organisational are the four main forms of collective bargaining. Plant, industry and the national are the three levels of collective bargaining.
3. The process of collective bargaining comprises (a) negotiation stage, which includes identification of the problem, preparation for negotiation (constitution of negotiating team, bargaining power, data collection), negotiation of an agreement, collective bargaining agreement and follow-up, and (b) contract administration.
4. In India, the growth of collective bargaining is closely associated with the growth of trade unionism. The origin of collective bargaining in India can be traced back to 1920, when, at the insistence of Mahatma Gandhi, the first collective agreement to regulate labour management relations between a group of employers and their workers in the textile industry at Ahmedabad was finalised. In India, most of the collective agreements have been concluded at the plant level and a few at the industry level and still fewer at the national level. Collective bargaining has continued to grow at a steady pace and still continues to be confronted with a number of constraints, such as lack of a central law for recognition of union, inter-union and intra-union rivalries, lack of mutual trust and faith between employer and his/her employees and lack of spirit of 'give and take', which need to be overcome if we are interested to see a bright picture of collective bargaining in future.
5. The international scenario of collective bargaining does not reflect a uniform trend and differs from country to country. For example, while in Western Europe approximately 80–90% of employees are covered under collective bargaining, in China the concept of collective bargaining is almost missing.
6. WPM is another important element of industrial democracy. WPM is to eke out a say of the workers in the decision-making process of an organisation.

WPM can be at three levels—plant level, industry level and national level—which can be in the form of informative, consultative, administrative and decision-making participation. Participation can also be in the form of autonomous work groups, quality circles and so on.

7. WPM is beneficial to both the employers and the workers. It satisfies workers' social and esteem needs, promotes industrial democracy, motivates workers and boosts their morale and confidence, thereby prompting workers to contribute their best. Since WPM is instrumental in improving productivity and maintaining industrial peace, it enables employers to have more profit.

8. Although traces of WPM can be witnessed in our industries in the early part of the 20th century, it began with the setting up of works committees (1947), followed by initiation of JMCs (1958), workers' directors on the board (1970), New Scheme of Workers' Participation in Industry (1975) involving setting up of shop councils and joint councils, Second Scheme of WPM (1977) involving consultation of unit councils, New Scheme of Workers' Participation (1983) and the Convertible Debenture Scheme and the Equity Participation Scheme/Worker Shareholders (1985). The presentation of Participation of Workers in Management Bill (1990) in Rajya Sabha, though could not be passed, brought a lot of awakening among the relevant stakeholders about the intricacies of WPM.

9. The main reasons for limited success of WPM in India comprise lack of trust between the two groups (the employer and the unions), lack of proper understanding and appreciation of the concept of WPM on the part of both the groups, lack of support for the management (even some unions do not support WPM as they treat it as a parallel institution of trade unions), multiplicity of unions, lack of proper and competent union leadership, delay in the implementation of recommendations made by the bodies constituted to give effect to the concept of WPM and so on.

10. The future of WPM can be promising if the prerequisites required for the success of WPM are made available in Indian industries.

Key Terms

administrative participation
attitudinal bargaining
autonomous body
bluffing
Boulwarism bargaining
collective bargaining
collective bargaining agreement
consent awards
consultative participation
continuous bargaining
decision-making
decision-making participation
decision-taking
direct participation
distributive bargaining
'give and take' approach
grievance redressal procedure
haggling bargaining
indirect participation
industrial democracy
industry-level bargaining
informative participation
integrative bargaining
intra-organisational bargaining

joint councils
joint management councils
labour–management cooperation
morale
national-level bargaining
negotiating teams
negotiation stage
Pay Commission
piecemeal approach
plant-level bargaining
positive bargaining/strategy
productivity
quality circles
recognised trade union
staff shoe
shop councils
table pounding
total approach
trade-off and buyout
unfair labour practices
unit councils
workers' participation in management
works committees

Discussion Questions

1. Discuss the concept, meaning and various definitions of collective bargaining and justify its need in the context of Indian industries. Also discuss the various forms of collective bargaining.
2. Discuss the prerequisites required for the success of collective bargaining. Also discuss the levels of collective bargaining.
3. Discuss the various stage of the process of collective bargaining. Also discuss the negotiating skills required by the members of the negotiating team.
4. Discuss the growth and status of collective bargaining in Indian industries.
5. Discuss the factors responsible for limited success of collective bargaining in India and how you visualise the future of collective bargaining in Indian industries.
6. Discuss the concept and meaning of WPM and also the levels and forms of WPM.
7. Discuss the factors responsible for poor progress of WPM in Indian industries.
8. Trace the history and progress of WPM in Indian industries.
9. Discuss the salient features of Participation of Workers in Management Bill, 1990.
10. Discuss how do you visualise the future of WPM in Indian industries.

Individual and Group Activities

1. As an individual, discuss with the HR officials of some manufacturing organisation employing more than 1,000 employees the present status of collective bargaining in their organisation.
2. In a group of two members, visit some big organisation and find out from the trade union officials if the institution of collective bargaining is functioning well in their organisation or not. Prepare a brief report.

3. In two groups of two members each, visit some big organisation. While one group may discuss with the HR officials the other group may discuss with trade union leaders of that organisation as to what suggestions they have in order to strengthen collective bargaining in their organisation.
4. In a group of two members, discuss with the HR officials of some organisation the status of WPM in their organisation. Is there any mechanism of WPM functioning in their organisation at present?

As an individual, discuss with the HR officials of some medium-scale organisation the constraints they come across in making the WPM a true success.

Application Case 18.1

Workers' Participation in Management

(A case study of some selected units in Haryana)

Introduction

WPM, unfortunately, has not yet emerged as a powerful institution in Indian industries, though it appeals to all as an attractive idea. However, there have been some organisations like Tata Steel where it has yielded fruitful results and can inspire other organisations to go for WPM. In the present study, some of the sample units are making sincere efforts for implementing WPM.

Findings

The survey of six sample units, codified as A, B, C, D, E and F, conducted for the study under review revealed that as far as management's response to the desirability of WPM is concerned, while managements of units B, C, D and F opined that WPM was very desirable, the managements of units A and E opined that WPM was desirable. With regard to participative bodies operating in sample units, it was revealed that since establishment of constitution of works committees is a statutory obligation, the same have been constituted in all the sample units, though their functioning is questionable. Regarding shop councils, the same were functioning in units C, D and F only. While unit C had four shop councils, unit D had two shop councils and unit F had six shop councils. Joint councils were found operating in the same sample units where shop councils were functioning, that is, in units C, D and F. The survey revealed that though both shop councils and joint councils were non-statutory bodies, the same were viewed very favourably in units C, D and F. The joint councils of the concerned units were fairly active and, on an average, had one meeting every month. Joint councils were headed by the chief executive of the unit concerned. As far as 'quality circles' are concerned, units A and F had introduced them but crumbled very soon, though they still exist on paper. The suggestions made by these circles had no takers. Hence, they were doomed to disappear. Units B, D and F reported that in addition to the routine participative bodies, they had production committees, quality control committees and some other committees too.

With regard to managements' response to the level of WPM desired, information sharing was desired by all, but units C, D and F desired it at the consultative level also. Unit F still went ahead and desired to have participation at the decision-making level as well, though it was never implemented. The managements of other units were of the opinion that workers are not equipped with the skills necessary at the decision-making level. Coming to trade unions' response to the level of success of WPM in their respective units, most of the trade unions believed that WPM was a failure in their units. Only unit C and the unions of units D and F were willing to accede 'partial success' to the scheme of WPM. These findings are confirmed to a great extent by the opinion survey ('Do workers participate in management in their respective units?'), which revealed that only unit D had more than 50% of the respondents who partially agreed that there was WPM in their unit. In all other units, the majority of the respondents disagreed that there was participation of workers in management.

Conclusion

WPM is, by and large, on paper only, except in a few cases, where also it is in an elementary stage. This miserable condition of WPM is largely due to the fact that the government after recommending WPM through statutes or endorsing recommendations of certain committees constituted for the purpose never cares for their follow-up. The spirit of mutual trust, faith and cooperation between the management and the unions, which is a prerequisite for the success of WPM, is almost missing in most of the sample units. Besides, the managements are reluctant to recognise the ability of workers to take part in management.

There were only three sample units that had some kind of participative management. The shop councils and the joint councils were active to a very limited extent. While workers' representatives in unit F were satisfied and enthusiastic, it was not the case in units C and D who complained that most of the subjects taken up were inconsequential. With regard to desirability of WPM, managements of all the sample units were of the opinion that participation was desirable but the workers were ill-equipped for the role.

The study further revealed that the idea of WPM was confined only to the leaders and a few enlightened workers and that most workers were unaware of the concept of WPM. The failure of WPM is also due to the fact that it was an imposed scheme by the government and that adequate preparations are not made before launching any new scheme of WPM. While the managements, by and large, are not willing to share decision-making with the workers, the unions are also not willing to give up their hostile attitude towards managements and, consequently, mutual trust and faith between the two is missing, which is one of most vital prerequisites for the success of WPM.

Source: P. J. Philip, 'Workers' Participation in Management', *Industrial Relations in Haryana* (unpublished PhD thesis, Kurukshetra University, 1988).

Questions

1. Identify the factors responsible for ineffectiveness in WPM in sample units.
2. Which of the sample unit(s) is/are doing relatively better in respect of WPM and how?

Annexure 18.1

The Participation of Workers in Management Bill, 1990

Keeping in view the various weaknesses of different schemes introduced from time to time, the government realised that the time had come for some kind of legislative backup to make further progress. The government, therefore, prepared the Participation of Workers in Management Bill. The bill was introduced in the Rajya Sabha on 30 May 1990, but it could not be passed. Some of the highlights of this bill are as follows:

1. The term 'worker' in this bill includes all types of employees—managerial as well as non-managerial. Whereas workers doing managerial jobs are termed as 'other workers', those doing non-managerial jobs and getting wages of less than 1,600 per month are termed as 'workmen'.
2. The bill has the provisions for setting up of shop-floor councils at the shop-floor level and establishment councils at the establishment level in accordance with the provisions of the scheme to be framed and notified by the central government. The shop-floor council and the establishment council of an establishment will consist of equal number of persons to represent the employer and the workmen ('other workers' are excluded). The number of persons on both the sides shall be determined by the appropriate government on the basis of many considerations such as the number of levels of authority in that establishment, number of shop floors, number of workmen in each shop floor and so on.

The representatives of the employer shall be nominated by the employer in such a manner as may be specified in the scheme. The representatives of the workmen shall be elected by and from amongst the workmen of the establishment by secret ballot or nominated by the registered trade unions per the scheme. A person representing the workmen shall cease to be a member of the council when he/she ceases to be a workman in the establishment, and the vacancy so caused shall be filled in such a manner as may be specified in the scheme.

The chairperson of each shop-floor council and establishment council shall be chosen by and from amongst the members thereof. The term of office of the members of each council shall be three years from the date of the constitution of the council. Councils shall meet as and when necessary but not less than four times in every year.

While a shop-floor council shall exercise such powers and perform such functions as it may deem necessary in relation to the following matters: production and storage facilities, material economy, operational problems, wastage control, hazards and safety problems, quality improvement, cleanliness, monthly targets and production schedules, cost reduction programmes, formulation and implementation of work system, welfare measures related to the shop and design group working, the establishment council shall exercise such powers and perform such functions as it may deem necessary in relation to the following matters: evolution of productivity schemes, planning and implementation of monthly targets and schedules, encouragement of suggestions, machine utilisation, review of operating expenses, administration of social security and welfare schemes, pollution control, review of the working of shop-level bodies and resolution of matters not resolved at the shop level or concerning more than one shop.

There is also a provision in the bill that provides that in the board of management of every corporate body owning an industrial establishment, representation will be given both to the 'workmen' and 'other workers'. While the persons representing workmen shall be 13%, the persons representing other workers shall be 12% of the total strength of the board. In case the total strength of the board is not sufficient to give representation to workmen, the board shall include at least one such person. As stated earlier also, the representatives of workmen shall be either elected by secret ballot or nominated by the registered trade unions. Representatives of other workers shall be elected by secret ballot. The term of office of both classes of representatives shall be three years. Both classes of representatives shall exercise all powers and discharge all functions of members of the board and shall be entitled to vote. The board shall review the functioning of each shop-floor council and the concerned establishment council.

3. The bill also provides for punishment to the extent of imprisonment of two years or fine up to 25,000 or both for any person who contravenes any of the provisions of the act and the scheme.
4. The appropriate government (central/state) may appoint inspectors for purposes of this act, and each inspector shall be deemed to be a public servant within the meaning of Indian Penal Code.
5. The appropriate government (central/state) may constitute a monitoring committee to review and advise it upon matters arising out of the administration of this act and the scheme. The monitoring committee shall include an equal number of members representing the following:
   a. The appropriate government
   b. The workers
   c. The employers
6. The appropriate government may exempt any employer from all or any of the provisions of this act.
7. The bill omits Section 3 of the Industrial Disputes Act, 1947, relating to the setting up of works committees.

Notes

1 J. Goodman, *Employment Relations in Industrial Society* (New Delhi: Heritage Publishers, 1985), 145.

2. Ivancevich, *Human Resources Management*, 494.
3. S. Webb and B. Webb, *Industrial Democracy* (London: Longman Green & Co., 1920), 181.
4. *Encyclopaedia of Social Sciences*, vol. 3 (Northampton, MA: Edward Elgar Publishing, 1951), 628.
5. S. Perlman, 'The Principles of Collective Bargaining', *The Annals of the American Academy of Political Sciences* 16, no. 4 (March 1936): 154–59.
6. S. K. Bhatia, *Collective Bargaining: The Theory and Practice of Effective Industrial Relations* (New Delhi: Deep and Deep Publications, 1985), 22.
7. Flippo, *Principles of Personnel Management*, 486–87.
8. A. Flanders, ed., *Collective Bargaining* (Middlesex, England: Penguin Books, 1969).
9. So far seven Pay Commissions have submitted their reports.
10. Sharma, *Industrial Relations and Labour Legislation*, 117.
11. C. B. Memoria, *Personnel Management* (Bombay: Himalaya Publishing House, 1980), 846–47.
12. R. C. Saxena, *Labour Problems and Social Welfare*, 12th ed. (Meerut: K. Nath & Sons, 1968), 150.
13. Yoder, *Personnel Management and Industrial Relations*, 514.
14. U. S. Ruby, *Collective Bargaining: A Project Report* (Ahmedabad: IIM, 1983).
15. Yoder, *Personnel Management and Industrial Relations*, 517–18.
16. Ibid., 517.
17. Ibid.
18. Ibid.
19. Sharma, *Industrial Relations and Labour Legislation*, 113.
20. R. E. Walton and R. B. Mckersie, *A Behavioural Theory of Labour Negotiation* (New York, NY: McGraw-Hill, 1965).
21. See Arthur A. Thompson and I. Weinstock, 'Facing the Crisis in Collective Bargaining', *MSU Business Topics* 16, no. 3 (Summer 1968): 37–43.
22. Yoder, *Personnel Management and Industrial Relations*, 512.
23. Indian Institute of Personnel Management, *Personnel Management in India*, 194.
24. Yoder, *Personnel Management and Industrial Relations*, 511.
25. Sharma, *Industrial Relations and Labour Legislation*, 115.
26. Yoder, *Personnel Management and Industrial Relations*, 525.
27. V. V. D. Prasad, 'Collective Bargaining: Its Relationship to Stakeholders', *Indian Journal of Industrial Relations* 45, no. 2 (October 2009): 195.
28. H. M. Stationery Office, *Report of the Royal Commission on Labour in India* (London: H. M. Stationery Office, 1931), 336–37.
29. See Planning Commission, Government of India, *First Five Year Plan* (1951), 573.
30. B. Sakunthala and K. S. Nemali, 'Collective Bargaining in Banking Industry', *Indian Journal of Industrial Relations* 33, no. 4 (April 1998): 528–32.
31. Abdul Aziz, 'Collective Bargaining in Karnataka: A Review', *Indian Journal of Labour Economics* 24, no. 4 (January 1982): C72–C81.
32. Prasad, 'Collective Bargaining'.
33. For detailed study of principles of collective bargaining, see A. E. Campo, 'Outline of Collective Bargaining: A Union Man's Checklist' (paper no. 2, Division of Industrial Relations, Stanford University, 1999), 74.
34. R. J. Adams, 'Collective Bargaining: The Rodney Dangerfield of Human Rights', *Labour Law Journal* 28, no. 4 (1999): 204–09.
35. H. Rai, 'Managing Trade Unions at the Firm Level and the Dynamics of Collective Bargaining', *Indian Journal of Industrial Relations* 44, no. 1 (July 2008): 118–29.
36. J. Kelly and H. Kevslin, 'The Puzzle of Trade Union Strength in Western Europe', *Indian Journal of Industrial Relations* 45, no. 4 (April 2010): 647.
37. J. C. Lee, 'Globalisation Changing Industrial Relations in Taiwan's Banking Industry', *Indian Journal of Industrial Relations* 45, no. 4 (April 2010): 326–31.
38. For details, see Sharma, *Industrial Relations and Labour Legislation*, 137–40.
39. See Venkata Ratnam, *Industrial Relations*, 548.
40. Ibid.
41. P. C. Tripathi, *Personnel Management & Industrial Relations*, 18th ed. (New Delhi: Sultan Chand & Sons, 2005), 486.

42 For example, see Sharma, *Industrial Relations and Labour Legislation*, 222.
43 Tripathi, *Personnel Management & Industrial Relations*, 488.
44 Venkata Ratnam, *Industrial Relations*, 534.
45 P. S. Rao, *Essentials of Human Resource Management and Industrial Relations*, 2nd ed. (Mumbai: Himalaya Publishing House, 1999), 635.
46 See B. Singh, 'Participative Management in Public Undertakings: Some Experiences', *Indian Journal of Labour Economics* 34, no. 4 (1991): 403.

19 Trade Unions

Learning Objectives

After studying this chapter, you should be able to do the following:

1. Define what a trade union is all about, its main characteristics and objectives.
2. List and describe functions of trade unions.
3. Explain types and structures of trade unions.
4. Identify and explain the obstacles in the growth of trade unionism in India.
5. Explain the process of registration of trade unions.
6. Explain the issue of recognition of trade unions.
7. Describe, in brief, the growth of trade union movement in India and also the state of trade unionism in India today.
8. Discuss about the main national-level federations of workers' unions in India.
9. Describe the main employers' associations in India.
10. Make suggestions to strengthen trade union movement in India.

Introduction

It is the industrial revolution and consequent exploitation of workers at the hands of employers that prompted the emergence of trade unions. During the early stage of the industrial revolution, the workers realised that if they bargained as individuals, the employer would have a leverage, for an individual would not matter as much as a group in seeking better terms and conditions of their employment. Hence, workers could see the benefit of organising themselves through the platform of trade unions to improve the terms and conditions of their employment and thus protect and promote their interests. Once their interests are duly protected, the workers are likely to be a better lot and contribute significantly in the process of production.

Definition

There has been no uniformity among authors as far as the definition of a trade union is concerned. It is so because a trade union is a complex institution, and different groups have different perceptions about it. One of the earliest definitions given by Beatrice Webb and Sydney Webb defines a trade union as 'a continuous association of wage earners for the purpose of maintaining and improving the conditions of their lives'.[1]

DOI: 10.4324/9781032628424-25

According to Edwin B. Flippo, 'A labour union or trade union is an organisation of workers formed to promote, protect, and improve through collective action, the social, economic, and political interests of its members'.[2]

Cunnison has also aptly remarked that a trade union is a monopolistic combination of wage earners who stand to the employers in a relation of dependence for the sale of their labour and even for its production, and that the general purpose of the association is in view of that dependence to strengthen their power to bargain with the employers. V. V. Giri also says that a trade union is such an organisation which is created voluntarily on the basis of collective strength to secure the interest of workers. Thus, it can be observed that despite different wordings, all the aforesaid quoted definitions have much in similarity than dissimilarity. However, it is the [xxx][3] Trade Unions Act, 1926, that has widened the scope of trade unions. Per Section 2(h) of this Act,

> [A trade union] is any combination, whether temporary or permanent, formed primarily for the purpose of regulating the relations between workmen and employers, or between workmen and workmen, or between employers and employers, or for imposing restrictive conditions on the conduct of any trade or business, and includes any federation of two or more trade unions.

Trade unions are supposed to follow the principles such as unity is strength, security (of job and wages) and equal pay for equal work.

Characteristics of a Trade Union

An analysis of the aforesaid definitions of a trade union boils down to the characteristics of trade unions as reflected in Exhibit 18.1.

Objectives of Trade Unions

Exhibit 19.1 Characteristics of a Trade Union

A trade union may be an association either of the employees or employers or of independent workers.

- The origin and growth of trade unions has been impacted by a number of ideologies.
- A trade union is usually a permanent combination of workers.
- A trade union aims at safeguarding and promoting the interests of its members.
- The character of trade unions has been constantly changing.

There are twin objectives of trade unions, (a) economic and (b) non-economic, which are as follows:

1. **Economic objectives:** These may comprise the following:
    a. To secure for workers fair wages

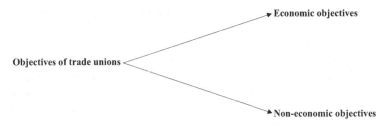

Figure 19.1 Objectives of Trade Unions

    b. To secure better and more fringe benefits
    c. To safeguard security of job of employees
    d. To secure better working conditions
    e. To improve productivity
    f. To secure opportunities for growth and development of employees
    g. To seek opportunities for promotion, training and so on

2. **Non-economic objectives**: Some of the main non-economic objectives of trade unions may include the following:
    a. To instil in its members a sense of social responsibility
    b. To influence the socio-economic policies of the community through civic participation in their formulation at various levels
    c. To contribute towards community development
    d. To strengthen political power of the workers
    e. To render social service
    f. To promote national integration and so on

Thus, trade unions aim at not only protecting and promoting economic, social and political interests of their members but also contributing towards betterment of the community.

Significance of Trade Unions

Trade unions are beneficial to all the stakeholders of an organisation, provided they (trade unions) have positive approach and mean business. Some of the main advantages of trade unions to some of the stakeholders are as follows:

1. **Benefits to workers**: Trade unions foster a sense of unity among their members, make collective bargaining instrumental in protecting and promoting the interests of their members, check their exploitation, promote their participation in management, get their working and living lives improved, help in their self-growth and development, and promote their economic, social, intellectual, physical and moral betterment.
2. **Benefits to employers**: Trade unions help in avoiding industrial conflicts through collective negotiations. They also help in reducing cost of production, reducing depreciation, increasing productivity, improving quality and output, and increasing the overall profitability of the organisation by getting their members' goals integrated with the goals of the organisation and also by fostering in them a sense of dedication towards their organisations.
3. **Benefits to the state and the community**: Trade unions make significant contribution in the formulation and implementation of labour policies and labour legislation by

the government. By preventing and resolving industrial disputes, trade unions are instrumental in ensuring regular supply of goods and services at reasonable prices to the community. The revenue of the government also gets a boost due to increased production of goods and services.

Functions of Trade Unions

Although there are great variations in the functions being discharged by trade unions in our country depending on the size of the union and other relevant factors, their functions are categorised under the following heads:

1. **Intra-mural/fighting/militant functions**: Such functions are usually performed within the premises of the factory and mainly aim at improving the economic and physical betterment of the workers. Thus, these functions may include ensuring fair wages, sharing gains of increased productivity, securing more fringe benefits, securing better working conditions, sharing profits, WPM and control over industry, if feasible. In order to carry out these functions, trade unions negotiate, enter into collective bargaining and, if not successful, may resort to strikes, boycotts, violence and similar means. That is why these functions are also called militant or fighting functions. These are the main functions carried out by Indian trade unions.
2. **Extra-mural/fraternal functions**: These functions aim at extending help to workers at the time of their needs like during the period of strike, and also improving the efficiency of the workers and making their life happier. These extra-mural functions may include helping the workers financially and otherwise during the period of strike, lockout or unemployment; extending legal facilities if required; providing welfare facilities; and so on. How far a trade union will perform these functions will depend on its financial position. Indian trade unions, by and large, have not been able to do anything significant in this regard.
3. **Political functions**: A number of unions contest elections and try to capture political power. Some of them have been successful in this regard as is the case in the UK where the Labour Party has been the ruling party several times. In India, the trade unions are not that well organised, but through their affiliated trade unions, every major political party tries to create and secure its vote bank.
4. **Auxiliary/supporting functions**: Besides the aforesaid functions, trade unions perform certain supporting functions also, like publishing its newsletters, bulletins, periodicals and magazines. Some unions collect relevant data and compile it for its use at appropriate time.

Types of Trade Unions/Structure of Trade Unions

Trade unions all over the world have a great variety and differ from each other in more than one way. They may be classified as follows.

Classification on the Basis of Composition of Membership or Structure

If classified on the basis of composition of membership, the unions may be:

1. **Craft unions**: The membership of such unions is drawn from among workers employed in a particular craft or trade or allied crafts or trades or occupations irrespective of the organisation or the industry they belong to. Such employees are craft

conscious and usually professionals or non-manual employees. The Ahmedabad Weavers' Union is an example that can be cited in this regard.
2. **Industrial unions**: In industrial unions, membership is open to all types of workers engaged in any one industry or a group of industries or service, that is, on industry-wise basis, for example, Rashtriya Mill Mazdoor Sangh, Mumbai.
3. **Labour unions**: In these unions, membership is open to all workers irrespective of their occupation, skill or industry, the philosophy being that all workers have common status and a common need for mutual help. Labour unions refer to both craft and industrial unions.
4. **General unions**: General unions believe in the solidarity of the working class. Hence, their membership is open to workers of different skills and trades engaged in different industries.
5. **Blue-collar workers' unions**: Blue-collar workers' unions constitute of employees usually performing operative jobs. They usually operate machines in the production and allied departments. Blue-collar workers constitute the bulk of membership of trade unions in the organised sector.
6. **White-collar workers' unions**: Such unions usually comprise office staff or who work off the shop floor and perform desk jobs or provide service over the counter or any such other job. White-collar category includes executives, managers, professionals, administrators, supervisors, clerks and the like. We come across such unions in banks, service sector, insurance companies, BPOs, software organisations, central and state government offices, and so on. Their members being educated and matured are aware of the capacity to pay of their organisations and, therefore, are more reasonable while they prepare their charter of demands.

Classification Based on Purpose

The unions can be further subdivided into two parts:

1. **Reformist unions**: These unions may be either business unions or revolutionary unions.
   a. **Business unions**: They are also known as 'bread and butter' unions and aim at securing economic interests of their members and follow the method of collective bargaining to accomplish their objectives.
   b. **Revolutionary unions**: Revolutionary unions are opposed to the capitalistic industry and replace it by the socialistic systems through radical means, such as strikes, boycott and gheraos. Revolutionary unions may be of any of the following forms:
      i. **Anarchist unions**: These unions endeavour to destroy the existing economic system and usually use violent means.
      ii. **Predatory unions**: Initiated by Professor Hoxie, such unions believe in plundering benefits and ruthless pursuit of the matter in hand by adopting any means irrespective of ethical, legal or moral considerations. Predatory unions may be of two types as follows:
2. **Guerrilla unions**: These unions can go to any extent, including resorting to terrorism and other violent means, to accomplish their objectives. It is the boss who rules the roost.

- **Hold-up unions**: The unscrupulous bosses of workers' organisations and unscrupulous employers conspire together to exploit the customers by selling their products at very high rates; the major chunk of the money so earned goes to the pockets of these unscrupulous elements, leaving very little, if at all, for the workers.

    iii. **Political unions**: Such unions aim at snatching the power of capitalists by political action so that workers may become more powerful.

3. **Friendly or uplift unions**: These unions mainly aim at improving the intellectual, moral and social life of their members. These unions are not craft conscious. They rather focus on the interest of workers. They are idealistic in nature. Since they are law-abiding, they believe in the institution of collective bargaining and also setting up of cooperative enterprises, mutual insurance, profit-sharing and the like.

Obstacles in the Growth of Trade Unionism in India

The growth of trade unionism in India has not yet been on sound footings. There is no doubt that the trade union movement has grown over a period of time but it needs to be stronger. It is unfortunate that it is primarily 'internal factors' pertaining to workers which are largely responsible for the slow development of trade unionism in our country. Such factors are as follows:

1. Lack of unity and awareness among workers
2. Small size of trade unions
3. Multiplicity of trade unions
4. Impact of outside leadership
5. Lack of appropriate leaders
6. Politicisation of trade unions
7. Lack of education among workers
8. Migratory character of labour
9. Intra-union and inter-union rivalry
10. Poor financial position
11. Lack of democratisation in the functioning of trade unions
12. Feeling of caste, religion, region, language and so on

Employers are also responsible for lack of sound development of trade unionism in India. Such factors are as follows:

1. 'Divide and rule' policy of some employers
2. Non-recognition of unions
3. Negative approach towards trade unionism
4. Creation of company unions

The government is also responsible to some extent. For example, the Trade Unions Act, 1926, allowed any seven employees of an organisation to form their trade union and, if they so liked, get it registered under the act. This led to multiplicity of trade unions defeating the very purpose of trade unionism. It is good that now this condition has been revised to 10% of the total number of workers or 100, whichever is less. Besides, the government has not put enough disincentives to discourage unions to go for adjudication. The government should encourage arbitration machinery for resolving industrial disputes instead of adjudication machinery. The political parties in the country have done a great disservice as each major political party has created its own central federation which grants affiliation to trade unions at organisation level. This has given rise to multiplicity of trade unions, thus striking at the very backbone of the trade union movement.

In case the workers themselves, the employers, the government and various political parties operating in the country take a genuine and united stand on creating a sound, positive and meaningful trade unionism in the country, it will be in the interest of all concerned.

Recommendations of National Commission on Labour for Strengthening Trade Unions

Some of the main recommendations made by the National Commission on Labour for strengthening trade unions have been regarding the following:

1. **Enlargement of functions**[4] of trade unions so that they may take care of basic needs of workers and involve the unions in the entire development process.
2. **Leadership:**[5] That is, focus on promoting internal leadership.
3. **Union rivalries**: Both inter-union and intra-union rivalries should be eliminated.
4. **Recognition of trade union**: There should be an independent authority for union recognition and recognition should be made compulsory under a central law with certain conditions.[6]
5. **Registration** of a trade union should be cancelled under certain conditions.
6. **Increase in the membership fee**[7] to improve the financial position of trade unions.
7. **Verification of membership** should be done by the Industrial Relations Commission to decide the representative character of a union.

Union Security

Per 'open shop', an employee is not required to be a union member before or after employment. But in order to keep the union members involved in union activities and seek their support, trade unions propose union security through the following measures:

1. **Closed shop**: Per this measure, the employment is routed only through the union; that is, employment is conditional subject to the membership of the trade union concerned.
2. **Preferential union shop**: Under this measure, an employee who is a union member is given first preference at the time of recruitment.
3. **Union shop**: In it, once employed, an employee is required to join the union if he/she is not yet a member of the union.
4. **Maintenance of membership**: Under this system, the union retains its members in good standing during the entire period of the contract as the main condition of employment.
5. **Agency shop**: Per this measure, the workers are required to pay the fees for the collective bargaining services, though they are not the members of the union.

It Is Difficult to Make Unions Happy

There have been a number of inherent weaknesses in the trade union movement in our country with the result that no government, even the government having a pro-workers communist union minister, could fulfil the demands of the trade unions. What is needed is both the genuine union leadership and the appropriate labour policy of the government.

Trade Unions and the Wages

The traditional view holds that trade unions cannot be instrumental in raising wages permanently because in the long run, rise in wages affects employment adversely. The classical economists hold the view that it is the marginal productivity of labour that determines wages; hence, trade unions have no role in this respect. Of course, per the modern economists, trade unions can play an indirect role in raising the wages by (a) improving the bargaining power of the workers (collective bargaining), (b) increasing the marginal productivity of labour (by infusing confidence, boosting morale, educating the workers, providing welfare facilities and getting the working and living conditions improved), (c) restricting the supply of labour to a particular trade and (d) formulating a suitable strategy.

Registration of Trade Unions

Although under the Trade Unions Act, 1926, it is not mandatory for a union to get itself registered. However, if interested to get itself registered, a union has to follow the procedure laid down in the Trade Unions Act, 1926. First of all, per an amendment of the act, the trade union intending to get itself registered should have at least 10% of the total workforce of the organisation or 100 of workers, whichever is less, employed in the establishment with which it is connected, as its members on the day application is made for registration. The application should contain all relevant information per the rules, and if the registrar is satisfied, he/she shall issue a certificate of registration in the prescribed form. After registration, a trade union so registered shall become a body incorporated by the name it is registered and shall have perpetual succession and a common seal. It shall have the power to acquire and hold property and to contract, and shall by the said name sue and be sued.

Although it is not mandatory to get a union registered, it is always advisable to get a union registered because a registered trade union has certain rights and privileges as also a few liabilities as discussed in the subsequent head.

Rights and Liabilities of a Registered Trade Union

Under the provisions of the Industrial Disputes Act, 1947, a registered trade union has certain rights. For example, no office-bearer or member of a registered trade union can be prosecuted under subsection (2) of Section 120B Indian Penal Code (45 of 1860), in respect of any agreement made between the members for the purpose of furthering any such object of the trade union as is specified in Section 15, unless the agreement aims at committing an offence

Again, no suit or legal proceeding shall be maintainable in any civil court against any registered trade union or any office-bearer; or furtherance of a trade dispute to which a member of the trade union is a party on the only ground that such act induces some other person to break a contract of employment; or that it is in interference with the trade, business or employment of some other person or with the right of some other person to dispose of his/her capital or his/her labour as he/she wills; and so on.[8]

There are also certain obligations/liabilities, such as submitting prescribed returns by a registered trade union. Again, a registered trade union is required to submit to the registrar, on or before such date as may be prescribed, a general statement in the prescribed form, audited in the prescribed manner, of all receipts and expenditure during the year ending 31 December next preceding such prescribed date, and its assets and liabilities existing on such 31 December. Besides, the account books of a registered trade union and the list of members of the trade union should remain open for members' inspection at such times as may be provided in the rules of the trade union.

Recognition of Trade Unions

As no provision pertaining to the recognition of trade unions is in operation at present, it is not mandatory under the Trade Unions Act, 1926, for an employer to recognise a trade union. However, as mutually agreed by the employers and trade unions under the Code of Discipline, the employer is required to recognise the union having the highest membership in the organisation. The trade union so recognised by the employer will become the sole bargaining agent and, therefore, shall represent the workers of the organisation concerned in the bargaining process.

Trade Unions' Reaction Towards Technical Changes, Privatisation, Liberalisation and Globalisation

Although there is no uniformity, in general, the attitude of trade unions towards technical changes, privatisation, liberalisation and globalisation has been negative if these result in retrenchment, downsizing of the organisation, overdemand for more skills, uncertainly in future, undue stress, reduction in the income of workers and so on. However, if the management takes necessary steps to neutralise the adverse impact of the aforementioned happenings preferably in consultation with the union, the trade unions have shown a cooperative attitude. For example, if the management has undertaken necessary steps for ensuring protection of income, security of job, adequate training and retraining, rehabilitation, outplacement and so on and is also willing to share with the workers the gains of increased productivity, the trade unions have extended necessary cooperation

Code of Conduct

In order to minimise inter-union rivalry,[9] the four central trade unions—All India Trade Union Congress (AITUC), Indian National Trade Union Congress (INTUC), United Trade Union Congress (UTUC) and HMS—accepted on 21 May 958 the following Code of Conduct:

1. Every employee or industry or unit shall have the freedom and right to join a union of his/her or its choice. No coercion shall be exercised in this matter.
2. There shall be no dual membership.
3. Democratic functioning of trade unions shall be respected.

4. There shall be regular and democratic elections of executive bodies.
5. Ignorance or backwardness of workers shall not be exploited.
6. Casteism, communalism and provincialism shall be eschewed by all unions.
7. There shall be no violence, coercion, intimidation or personal vilification in inter-union dealings.
8. Formation or continuance of 'company unions' shall be combated by all central unions.

Growth of Trade Union Movement in India

The roots of trade unionism in India can be traced back to the industrial revolution which was, by and large, capitalistic in nature. The growth of trade union movement in different periods in India has been impacted a great deal by the economic, political and social conditions existing during the then each period. Initially, it was the labour movement, which is 'for the workers', started from 1825. In the labour movement, it is the social reformers who endeavour to improve the lot of workers both inside and outside the factory premises. However, when the workers get united and form their associations to improve their lot, it becomes a movement 'by the workers' and is called trade union movement, which started in our country around 1918. Although there is no hard-and-fast rule to divide the trade union movement into stages, for convenience's sake, it can be divided into the following stages:

1. **Period from 1875 to 1918**: This period witnessed the labour movement in our industries which was totally unorganised. It was social in character and, therefore, is also known as social welfare period.
2. **Period from 1918 to 1924**: During this period, a good number of trade unions came into being, though their leadership was usually in the hands of advocates, politicians, doctors and so on. For example, in 1917, a trade union was established in the textile industry a Ahmedabad, and another union under the leadership of B. D. Wadia came into existence at Madras in 1918. AITUC, the first national-level union, came into existence in 1920.
3. **Period from 1924 to 1935**: This period, popularly known as the period of 'left wing trade unionism', was dominated by communists and was, therefore, militant in nature. Strikes were frequent and a number of communist leaders were sent behind the bars. In 1926, Indian Trade Unions Act was passed. All India Red Trade Union Congress was established in 1931. Many other unions came into existence. A few were bifurcated and some again reunited.
4. **Unity period from 1935 to 1939**: This period witnessed the efforts of Trade Union Committee of uniting some of the trade unions. There was a spurt in the number of strikes which increased from 101 in 1935 to 169 in 1939.
5. **Period of the Second World War to 1947**: Price rise due to the Second World War brought awakening among the workers and strengthened the trade unions, and collective bargaining and arbitration became popular. Trade unions got cooperation from both the employers and the government. Dissidents in AITUC formed the Indian Federation of Labour (IFL), and AITUC was captured by communists.
6. **Period from 1947 to 1970**: This period witnessed many changes in the trade union movement. Some new unions and federations were established such as INTUC in 1947, UTUC in 1949, Bharatiya Mazdoor Sangh (BMS) in 1955, Hind Mazdoor Panchayat in 1965, Centre of Indian Trade Unions (CITU) in 1970 and so on.

7. **Period since 1971**: In 1972, INTUC, AITUC and HMS agreed to form a National Council of Central Trade Unions (NCCTU) so as to bring coordination among the three unions and protect and promote the interest of the working class and also contribute towards the development of Indian economy. However, NCCTU did not prove effective and met its early death. All the trade unions protested against the promulgation of the Essential Services Maintenance Ordinance (ESMA). The Trade Unions Act, 1926, had many amendments during 2001. In 1999, there was a consensus of opinion among the main central federations such as INTUC, AITUC, CITU and BMS to protect domestic industry, strengthening the public sector units, amendment of labour laws, and including of rural and unorganised labour in the social safety net.[10]

Again, in order to oppose the government's efforts to rush through new legislations or amendments to the existing labour legislation and the so-called labour reforms without taking trade unions into confidence, around ten central trade unions—AITUC, INTUC, HMS, All India United Trade Unions Centre (AIUTUC), CITU, Trade Unions Coordination Centre (TUCC), UTUC, Self-employed Women Association of India and Labour Progressive Federation (LPF)—which altogether represent 0.47 billion of country's workforce, went on a general strike on 2 September 2015 and again on the same date in 2016. All central trade unions except BMS, to some extent, are dead against the labour reforms initiated by the government, though the government has been trying to persuade the trade unions to cooperate with the government's efforts.

Recent Happenings/Developments

Of late, in addition to their usual demands for increase in wages, DA and other related issues, trade unions have been raising some non-conventional demands also such as raising the income tax exemption limit, controlling price rise, reviving sick public sector units and social security for unorganised workers (see Exhibit 19.2).

Exhibit 19.2 Unions Seek Raising Income Tax Exemption Limit

Early in July 2016 the central trade unions demanded the raising of the income tax exemption limit to 5 lakh from the existing 2.5 lakh and minimum wages to 18,000 in a 15-point charter submitted to the government. Their charter also included measures to control price rise, revive sick public sector units and social security schemes for unorganised workers among others.

Source: Hindustan Times, 5 January 2016.

AITUC Secretary D. L. Sachdev also stated, 'We have also demanded 3,000 minimum monthly pension for all and asked for a special package for flood-ravaged Tamil Nadu to provide relief to workers as well as industry in the next budget'.[11]

On price rise, the charter said, 'Take effective measures to arrest the spiralling price rise, especially of food and essential items of daily use. Ban speculative forward trading in essential commodities, check hoarding and universalize and strengthen the Public Distribution System'.[12]

A check on 'relentless and increasing flow of import of industrial commodities including capital goods' to prevent dumping and also to protect and promote domestic industries and prevent loss of employment was also decided by the unions. Besides, 'FDI should not be allowed in crucial sectors like defence production, railways, financial sector, retail trade and other strategic sectors. In other areas, terms and conditions for FDI should be made public'.[13]

An interministerial committee on labour, headed by Finance Minister Arun Jaitley, was constituted which has so far held several rounds of tripartite consultations with trade unions and employers on labour reforms. On 28 December 2015, the committee had a meeting to finalise Wage Codes and Small Factory Bill.[14]

Exhibit 19.3 Demands Delinking of Labour Law Reforms from 'Ease of Doing Business'

In its pre-budget demands to the government, RSS affiliated trade union—Bharatiya Mazdoor Sangh—has demanded delinking of labour law reforms from 'ease of doing business' considerations of the government and called for regularising contract labour employed with government agencies.

Source: The Economic Times, 5 January 2016.

There has been a demand for delinking of labour laws from 'ease of doing business' (see Exhibit 19.3).[15] According to BMS, the government still feels labour cost reduction and relaxation of labour laws are priority indicators in ease of doing business.[16] Hence, BMS strongly demands that reference to labour cost or labour law relaxation should be removed forthwith in all documents related to ease of doing business in India.[17]

BMS further stated, 'Most jobs are gradually becoming temporary. Hence, regularize contract labour and provide contract workers wages and all benefits on par with regular worker in that industry'. It further asked for regularising contract labour employed with government agencies.[18]

A 14-point memorandum by more than half a dozen central unions was submitted to the government, including the demand that no labour law amendment should be undertaken without the consent of trade unions and workers.[19]

The labour ministry, led by Bandaru Dattatreya, vetted the Labour Code on Industrial Relations Bill, 2015. The Code proposes to combine the Industrial Disputes Act, 1947; the Trade Unions Act, 1926; and the Industrial Employment (Standing Orders) Act, 1946.[20]

Intense union heat forces labour ministry to think differently. Having run into stiff opposition from trade unions over a dozen proposed labour law reforms, the labour ministry is now taking the executive route to make key changes to existing legislation.

These include enabling women to in work night shifts, rationalisation of wages for contract workers, exempting low-wage workers from contributing to PF and introducing fixed-term employment to enable flexibility on hiring.

This government is adamant over creating a conducive environment for business in a way that it benefits both employers and the employees. Since trade unions are virtually blocking most of the proposed amendments, we now plan change some of the key provisions through executive orders.[21]

Protesting Snapdeal, the staff approached the labour department against the e-commerce major's decision of their illegal termination and lockout of the establishment with effect from 23 February 2016. The staff sought relief under Section 25(s), which clearly states that the employer has to give a one-month notice to employees if less than 100 are being asked to leave. If more than 100 employees are asked to go, then the employer should give a three-month notice.[22]

Trade unions oppose tax plan on PF. Rejecting the government's contention that proposed tax on EPF withdrawals was aimed at moving towards pensioned society, trade unions on Wednesday, 2 March 2016, said that retirement fund body EPFO, which has over 0.05 billion subscribers, already provides pension under its social security scheme. 'Seeing widest opposition to taxing the EPF withdrawals, Finance Minister Arun Jaitley is now trying to mince his words. EPFO runs a comprehensive scheme which has all components—PF, pension and insurance', AITUC Secretary D. L. Sachdev said.[23]

On 26 April 2016, trade unions, including INTUC, AITUC, CITU and AIUTUC, gave a call for day-long nationwide protest on Friday, 29 April 2016, against lowering the interest rate for PF subscribers lower than 8.8% decided by the EPFO (see Exhibit 19.4).

The Central Board of Trustees (CBT), which is headed by the labour minister, is the apex decision-making body of the EPFO. It is probably for the first time that the finance ministry has overruled the decision of CBT on the interest rate.

In September 2015, the movement led by hundreds of female workers in Munnar's tea garden (in Kerala) for helping increase in wages spread like wildfire but appeared on its last leg following a drubbing in the assembly polls, plummeting support and rampant factionalism (see Exhibit 19.5).

The female workers in Munnar's tea garden took on tea giants, trade unions and political parties and pulled off a miraculous victory in three local body seats in the Kerala panchayat polls last November.

Exhibit 19.4 Trade Unions to Protest on Friday against Lower EPF Rate

Union strongly denounces the 'unilateral reduction' in interest rate on Employees Provident Fund (EPF) from 8.8% to 8.7%, ignoring the unanimous decision of tripartite Central Board of Trustees (CBT) of EPFO, the statement added.

Source: The Economic Times, 27 April 2016.

Exhibit 19.5 Munnar Tea Workers Agitation Loses Steam in Political Arena

In September 2015, hundreds of women workers in Munnar's scenic tea gardens came together in protest, demanding a hefty hike in wages.

> The movement spread like wildfire through Kerala in a matter of weeks as women struck work, took out protest marches and grabbed the imagination of a state with a long history of workers' demonstration.
>
> Source: *Hindustan Times*, 6 June 2016.

Pembilai Orumai—a women's collective—was hailed as India's Jasmine Revolution, a reference to popular protests in 2011 that swept the president out of power in Tunisia. But barely six months later, the movement appeared to be on its last leg following a drubbing in the assembly polls, plummeting support and rampant factionalism.[24]

The decision of the Tamil Nadu government to allow IT workers to form unions is not likely to hurt the domestic industry in the short run, but it may have long-term impact. This is what the experts feels (see Exhibition 19.6).

The Tamil Nadu's principal secretary for labour and employment clarified that the IT sector is covered by the Industrial Disputes Act, 1947, which allows workers to form unions. There was high labour demand in the past, so employees could quit rather than raise their voice. But now, with automation, demand for labour will fall and that could spur creation of unions.[25]

According to Sagar Rastogi, analyst at Ambir Capital, when the industry is growing rapidly, there are above-average wage hikes of about 10% for junior employees and high mobility—attrition is 15–20%—there is no incentive for employees to form unions.[26]

> **Exhibit 19.6** 'Trade Unions Unlikely to Hurt IT in Short Terms'
>
> Tamil Nadu's decision to allow information technology workers to form unions is unlikely to hurt the domestic industry in the short term, but it may have a long-term impact as automation begins to hit demand for labour, experts said.
>
> Source: *The Economic Times*, 10 June 2016.

By now, several states, including Karnataka, have issued exemptions that prevent the forming of unions.[27]

The IT sector sees this as a retrograde gesture, while unions see it as an acknowledgement of employee rights.[28]

Railway unions had threatened and called for a nationwide indefinite strike by workers from 11 July 2016 to process their demands including review of new pension scheme and Seventh Pay Commission recommendations.

Banking employees' unions have criticised the Cabinet approval for the merger of SBI with its five associate banks, and have threatened action, including strikes, on fears that the move may result in job losses. According to the general secretary, Venkatachalam, All India Bank Employees Association (AIBEA), 'India does not need mergers or big banks. What happened to Lehman Brothers. Our country needs expansion, not consolidation. This is an unwarranted decision in the name of reforms'.[29]

The proposed two-day bank strike scheduled to begin on Tuesday, 12 July 2016, had been put on hold as Delhi High Court on Monday, 11 July 2016, restricted State Sector

Bank Employees Association (SSBEA) and AIBEA from going ahead with the strike. SBI associate banks had filed a writ petition in the Delhi High Court. 'In view of the Delhi High Court restraint order, our strike on 12th and 13th July, 2016 stands deferred', AIBEA General Secretary Venkatachalam said.[30]

The ILO has given the thumbs up to India' labour reforms but cautioned that the success of the country's growth story will lie in the government's ability to move towards formalisation of its workforce and provide universal social security to all.[31]

Stiff opposition from unions forced the government to go slow on plan to bring a raft of labour reforms during the last monsoon session (see Exhibit 19.7).

Another apprehension of trade unions is that if the Labour Code, which is one of the proposed laws, is enacted, then the companies will have the option of sacking nearly 300 employees without government approval.

The 'auto unions', which had formed a joint action committee, had threatened to launch a hunger strike if the government failed to initiate talks with them in two days (see Exhibit 19.8).

Exhibit 19.7   Labour Pains

- Centre proposed the labour reforms with an aim of making it easier for firms to operate and turn India into a manufacturing powerhouse.
- Trade unions, however, termed the proposals anti-labour. They said the new laws will allow industries to hire and fire at will.

Source: Hindustan Times, 18 July 2016.

Exhibit 19.8   Autos and Taxis on Indefinite Strike

As many as 85,000 autorickshaws and 18,000 black and yellow taxis will be off the roads on Tuesday (02 August 2016) as auto and taxi unions kick off an indefinite strike against the AAP government's alleged inaction against app-based cab services that are eating into their business.

Source: Hindustan Times, 26 July 2016.

Maruti workers' union seeks release of those workers who were convicted in March 2017 (see Exhibit 19.9).

The Lok Sabha on Wednesday, 17 August 2016, passed the Factories (Amendment) Bill, 2016, which includes a provision to increase the cap on OT in factories. The opposition alleged that the proposed amendments were pro-corporate and would not benefit the worker and walked out of the House before the bill was passed.

According to the Amendment Bill, the OT work hour, under Section 64, has been doubled from 50 to 100 in a quarter and to 125 under special circumstances through a special notification. The government pushed the bill through braving objections/

amendments from some opposition MPs—raised at the stage of introduction and later during passage.[32]

The ten trade unions that had collectively called a day-long nationwide general strike on 2 September 2016 to protest government's labour policies called it a historic success.

Industry body Associated Chamber of Commerce and Industry of India (ASSOCHAM) said that the strike, affecting trade, transport, key manufacturing facilities and banking services, may cause an estimated loss of 160–180 billion to the country's economy.

Unions claimed that 0.18 billion people joined the protest on Friday, 2 September 2016, a 20% increase over 0.15 billion people who went on strike on the same day last year.

Exhibit 19.9   Maruti Union Seeks Release of Those Convicted Recently

Around 500 workers affiliated to the Maruti workers' union held at protest at Kamla Nehru Park near the deputy commissioner's office on 4 April 2017.

They demanded the release of 13 workers who were sentenced to life imprisonment, and four others ordered to serve a five-year prison term in the case of violence in the company's Manesar plant in 2012 that left a manager dead. The union said that it will fight till justice is delivered. It is going to stage an all-India protest on 5 April 2017.

The union also demanded that workers found not guilty by the court be allowed to rejoin work at Maruti.

Source: Hindustan Times, 5 April 2017.

Tapan Sen, general secretary of the CITU, said,

The unprecedented response to the strike, despite the misinformation campaign unleashed by the BJP government aided by BMS (a central trade union affiliated to the RSS that did not participate in the strike), reflects the anger and resentment of the workers against the attacks on their working and living conditions by the neoliberal agenda of the BJP-led government.[33]

On 27 September 2016, Labour Minister Bandaru Dattatreya said that India is ready to ratify ILO conventions 138 and 182 related to child labour. 'India is now in a position to ratify the ILO conventions 138 and 182 concerning child labour and has started the process', the labour ministry said, quoting Dattatreya. The minister made the comments at the two-day BRICS labour and employment ministerial meeting, which began in the national capital on 27 September 2016. India has put a complete ban on employing children below 14 years of age and employment in hazardous occupations below 18 years, the ministry said. In another significant step, the government has presented amendment to the Maternity Benefit Act, raising the paid maternity benefit to 26 weeks from 12 weeks.[34]

The government has decided to double the PF investment in equities to 10% of the incremental corpus in 2016–2017 against 5% in the past financial year despite stiff opposition from labour unions.[35]

In a bid to bring more workers from unorganised sector under the health insurance scheme, the Employees' State Insurance Corporation has increased the monthly wage limit to 21,000, Labour Minister Bandaru Dattatreya said on Sunday, 3 December 2016. 'Coverage under ESIC scheme was enhanced to 15,000 in 2010. Now, government has taken a decision to hike the coverage to 21,000', he said.[36]

Tata Steel is edging closer to a deal with UK steel workers' unions to keep its troubled Port Talbot plant, the country's largest in South Wales, open until at least 2020, a media report said on Sunday, 3 December 2016.

Exhibit 19.10   Finance Minister Cracks the 'Code' on Archaic Labour Laws

In his Budget speech, FM Arun Jaitley said that legislative reforms will be undertaken to simplify, rationalise and amalgamate the existing labour laws into four codes—wages, industrial relations, social security and welfare, safety/working conditions.

Source: Times of India, 2 February 2017.

Union leaders will put a new rescue plan to its members this week (week ending on 9 December 2016), which could see investments into the UK's largest steel plant in return for concessions on staff terms and conditions, according to The Sunday Times.

Central to the plan is retention of Port Talbot's two blast furnaces, which turn iron ore and coke into molten iron.[37]

Shrugging off protests by central trade union, the Narendra Modi government signalled its commitment to press ahead with tough labour reforms (see Exhibit 19.10)

As a matter of fact, archaic labour laws have been cited by foreign investors as a major obstacle to investment.

Finance Minister Arun Jaitley's announcement in the budget that the government intends to simplify labour laws has not gone down well with the industry, which is apprehensive about action on the ground in the absence of any deadline given to rationalise the 44 labour laws.

Work on the four labour codes began immediately after the BJP-led NDA government came to power in May 2014, and at least two codes—the labour code on wages and the labour code on IR—are pending for Cabinet's approval for quite some time. Prime Minister Narendra Modi had in his Independence Day speech last year talked about labour codes, but the entire process was put on the backburner in view of the assembly elections in five states in early 2017.

'We are not sure whether any action will happen around this any time soon because there was no sense of urgency in the budget announcement related to labour codes', a labour expert in the staffing industry said, requesting not to be identified.

The expert further said, 'We understand that there is a political challenge to it but we have to work our way around considering manufacturing is the biggest need of the hour and that will not kick-start unless we ease our labour laws'.[38]

Can Union Workers Be Won Over, and How?

Can union workers be won over? It is a difficult question to answer. However, there are many examples, where union workers cooperate with the employers. Much depends on the philosophy of the employer towards his/her workers, his/her empathy, his//her humane approach, his/her positive attitude and also the approach of the union. Here, we can quote the example of Reserve Bank of India where the ex-Governor Raghuram Rajan could do this (see Exhibit 19.11).

Exhibit 19.11   Union Workers Were Won Over, and How

'We were against his lateral hiring policy but later we understood that he wanted to attract the best talent in RBI and get younger and sharper people in RBI', said Suryakant Mahadik, general secretary at All India Reserve Bank Workers Federation, a union of Class IV workers in the central bank. Mahadik was among the union leaders who met Rajan before the central bank's board meeting on 19 May.

Source: Hindustan Times, 20 June 2016.

Mr Rajan, governor at RBI, said, 'My unions come to me and say we fully trust you and we are going to fight hard for you. That makes me feel really good because these are the people I work with every day and who know me'. Both officers and workers' union unequivocally supported Rajan. So what changed between 2014 and 2016? According to workers associated with unions, they got to know Rajan better and understood that his ideas were all well-meaning and for the betterment of the central bank.[39]

According to Mahadik, general secretary at All India Reserve Bank Workers Federation, 'I have known 19 of the 23 RBI governors. All have been good but Rajan was the best because of his intelligence. As a citizen of India I believed he was the best man for the job'.[40]

National-level Federations of Workers' Trade Unions

Among the several federations of workers' trade unions, the following are the main ones:

1. AITUC
2. INTUC
3. BMS
4. HMS
5. CITU
6. UTUC
7. United Trade Union Congress-LS (UTUC-LS)
8. National Front of Indian Trade Unions (NFITU)

A few highlights of some of the major federations are discussed further here.

All India Trade Union Congress

It was established in 1920 and espouses a more radical approach in accomplishing its objectives. It is linked with the communist philosophy. It has affiliated unions (at unit/local level), provincial bodies (at state levels), general council and the delegates to the general or special sessions. The general session of the AITUC is convened once in two years, the general council meets once a year and the working committee at least twice a year. The general secretary and his/her administrative staff look after day-to-day operations and implementation side.

Indian National Trade Union Congress

Established in 1947 with the patronage of the Congress party, it believes in peaceful and non-violent solution of industrial conflicts. The basic pattern of organisation in the INTUC is the industry-level federation, whereby units are grouped together for the purpose of negotiating the terms and conditions of employment at the industry level which are finally implemented at the lower level. It is the regional branches and the councils which provide support services. The apex body takes an overall point of view regarding broader issues like government policies, and issues directions to the regional branches.

Hind Mazdoor Sabha

Coming into existence in 1948, HMS espouses the socialist philosophy. Its general council comprises the president, a maximum of five vice presidents, a general secretary, not more than two secretaries, a treasurer and other members representing different industrial sectors. It believes in and follows peaceful, legitimate and democratic methods to promote the economic, social and political interests of the workers and its other objectives.

Centre of Indian Trade Unions

Coming into being in 1971, it has its allegiance to CPI (M) and aims at promoting economic, political and social interests of workers. It comprises a central committee, a state committee and affiliated unions. It follows legitimate agitations, demonstrations and other such methods to accomplish its objectives.

Why Do Employees Join Unions?

It is basically to have security of job, to get their wages, allowances and fringe benefits increased, to get protection from exploitation and victimisation by employers, and to have a say in the affairs of the organisation that employees join trade unions.

Why Employees Do Not Join Unions?

Quite a good number of employees do not prefer to join unions. There may be several reasons responsible for it. Many such workers have no trust and faith in the effectiveness of leadership of the union of the organisation or if there is an environment of suspicion and doubt among the workers regarding union functioning and activities.[41] Another important reason is that many enlightened employers take proactive steps by anticipating the mood of employees and, therefore, the employees do not need the support of the union of their organisation. For an example, in most IT-related organisations, the employers take due care of their employees and do not let the employees feel the necessity of joining any union.

Suggested Steps to Make Trade Union Movement Successful

In order to make the trade union movement in our country more effective and successful, the following suggestions can be put forward:

1. Creating selfless, dedicated, effective and dependable union leadership
2. Eliminating political influence
3. Eliminating multiplicity of unions
4. Improving financial position of unions
5. Educating the workers
6. Positive approach of union
7. Integrating workers' and employers' objectives
8. Imparting training to union officials
9. Democratisation of functioning of trade unions
10. Transparency in the working of trade unions

State of Trade Unionism in India Today[42]

Some of the salient features of Indian trade unionism visible today are as follows:

1. While a good number of unions follow peaceful policies, Indian trade unionism is also witnessing militant attitude of some labour leaders. Many undesirable happenings have been taking place. Some of the examples of strikes involving violence are shown in Exhibit 19.12.

Exhibit 19.12 Showing Examples of Violence in Strikes

In October 2009, a RICO worker was killed in a clash with police when thousands of workers resorted to stone pelting outside the factory gates on Delhi–Jaipur road.

In September 2011, two Maruti union workers were arrested for inciting a worker to physically attack supervisors of the company. In July 2012, workers killed the general manager of Maruti Suzuki India Limited, Manesar plant, set the property on fire and injured about 100 managers and supervisors, including two Japanese engineers.

Source: Hindustan Times, 13 February 2015.

In July 2005, around 350 workers and over a dozen policemen were injured in an agitation started by workers of Honda Motorcycle and Scooter India plant.[43]

In March 2012, workers of Orient Craft Limited in Udyog Vihar turned violent when a contractor allegedly assaulted a worker. The irate mob pelted stones at the premises and set on fire 20 bikes, two trucks, one SUV and one police van. In March 2012, workers assaulted the vice-president of Suzuki Motorcycles after suspension of three union workers by the management.[44]

2. White-collar trade unionism is on the spread and getting active.[45] Even professionals have been moving in this direction.
3. Indian trade unionism is making a considerable headway, especially in the organised sector, in elevating the status of the working classes above that of mere slaves.
4. Inter-union and intra-union rivalry in a good number of cases is quite apparent.
5. Indian trade unionism is far away from organising the entire workforce of the country. More than 90% of the workers employed in the unorganised sector continue to be unorganised.
6. In a good number of cases, members of the trade unions behave irresponsibly, violently and aggressively.[46,47,48,49,50]
7. Indian trade unionism has grown up as an organisation operated mainly on business lines. It is no more an emotional struggle for a just labour cause as it used to be initially.[51]
8. As compared to the industrialised countries of the West, most strikes organised by Indian trade unions are short-lived and end in larger number of failures.
9. Because of having little bargaining power, a substantial number of trade unions depend on the support of political parties.
10. In certain sectors, such as ports and docks and air transport, there is a trend of forming craft unions, which is not in the overall interest of trade unionism.
11. Indian trade unions are becoming more and more litigation-oriented.
12. There is a dominance of quite a good number of unions by single individuals.
13. More and more trade unions are getting themselves registered under the Trade Unions Act, 1926.[52]
14. Most trade unions in our industrial organisations are small in size having very few members and, therefore, fail to protect and promote the interests of their members.
15. In many cases, trade unionism our country have realised the weak financial position of their organisations and have, therefore, offered their cooperation so as to help the managemnt.[53]
16. Indian trade unionism. has, by and large, not been successful in developing cooperation, patriotic feelings and sense of belongingness in its members towards their organisations.
17. Indian trade unionism has done little to make workers innovative and creative.
18. The income of registered workers' trade unions is very less and that too is fluctuating from year to year.
19. Indian trade unionism is doing little to educate the workers or to improve their living lives.
20. Not as much is being done to strengthen the institutions of collective bargaining and WPM as is desired. It needs to be followed up more vigorously.
21. Declining membership, dominance of outside leadership in many cases, multiple subscriptions of union membership and so on are some of the other features of Indian trade unionism noticeable these days.

Thus, Indian trade unionism today is suffering from many diseases which need to be overcome to strengthen the movement.

Employers' Associations/Unions/Federations/Organisations

Formation of the Bombay Mill Owners Association in 1875 and Indian Jute Mills Association in 1887 can be considered as pioneers of employers' organisations in our country. An employers' association can be formed and registered, as a non-profit organisation, under the provisions of the Trade Unions Act, 1926 (e.g. EFI), though they cannot invoke the dispute settlement machinery to intervene in their industrial disputes per the provisions of the Industrial Disputes Act, 1947. Employers' associations can also be registered under the Societies Registration Act, 1860 (e.g. Indian Tea Plantation Association [ITPA], All India Employer's Organisation [AIEO], Indian Postal Association [IPA] and Federation of All India Foodgrain Dealers Association [FAIFDA]), or the Companies Act, 1956 (e.g. All India Jute Mills Association [IJMA], Federation of Indian Chambers of Commerce and Industry [FICCI] and All India Rice Millers Association [AIRMA]). Such organisations can be constituted at the local level, regional level and central level (apex organisations/federations). While such organisations operating through the local chambers of commerce take care of the interests of the local entrepreneurs, the regional-level employers' associations, which are affiliated to the central employers' federation, offer consultancy service, organise seminars and conferences, take care of IR and undertake some welfare work also. Apex organisations or federations are central bodies and take care of the interests of the member entrepreneurs of the whole country. Some examples of apex bodies are All India Organisation of Employers (AIOE), EFI and All India Manufacturers' Organisation (AIMO). EFI and AIOE were recognised by the government as representatives of Indian employers. At present, the following are the main apex employers' organisations functioning in India:

1. **FICCI:** Established in 1927, several chambers of commerce and industrial associations are affiliated to it. It represents and coordinates the commercial interests of its affiliates. It also organises seminars, conferences, exhibitions and so on as well as conducts training programmes and publishes its magazines and literature useful to its member associations. FICCI consists of ordinary members (trade associations, chambers of commerce and industrial associates), associate members (manufacturing companies, insurance companies, banking companies, shipping companies and so on), Indian chambers of commerce functioning abroad and honorary members.
2. **EFI:** It was established in 1933 to safeguard the interests of its members, that is, employers engaged in trade, commercial and industrial activities. It consists of association members, ordinary members and honorary members. Its activities are undertaken by four regional committees and a central body, which comprises an executive committee and secretariat headed by a president and a general body. The EFI also keeps its members apprised about new proposals for legislation and other relevant issues. It also publishes *Industrial Bulletin*—a fortnightly publication—as well as an annual report.
3. **ASSOCHAM:** Initially, it was in December 1920 that the Associated Chamber of Commerce of India and Ceylon was registered under the Companies Act, 1913, but in 1932, its name was changed to Associated Chamber of Commerce of India, which was again changed to the Associated Chamber of Commerce and Industry in 1964. ASSOCHAM, besides giving an advisory service, undertakes representative and service functions. It is exclusively the local chambers of commerce that constitute the membership of ASSOCHAM.

4. **AIOE**: Established in 1953, AIOE aims at protecting and promoting the industrial development of India besides representing the country at the International Labour Conferences related to the interests of trade, commerce and industry. It also undertakes issues concerning the interests of its members. It comprises individuals and associations as its members. The general body, the executive committee and the secretariat are the three organs of AIOE. The general body meets once a year in which, in addition to other activities, office-bearers are also elected. It also advises and guides FICCI on labour related matters.

CII (1992), AIMO (1941), Standing Conference of Public Enterprises (SCOPE; 1973) and Council of Indian Employers (CIE), which comprises AIOE and the EFI, are some of the other employers' well-known organisations.

However, at present, it is the CIE along with SCOPE and AIMO that chooses delegates to represent Indian employers at tripartite forums as also at the International Organisation of Employers at Brussels.

Chapter Review

1. It is the industrial revolution and consequent exploitation of workers at the hands of employers that prompted the emergence of trade unions which prove instrumental in the protection and promotion of interests of their members. Per the Trade Unions Act, 1926, a trade union is any combination, whether temporary or permanent, formed primarily for the purpose of regulating relations between workers and employers, or between workers and workers, or between employers and employers, or for imposing restrictive conditions on the conduct of any trade or business, and includes any federation of two or more trade unions.
2. Trade unions have both economic and non-economic objectives. They promote the economic and non-economic interests of workers, increase profitability of the organisation for the employers, add to the revenue of the government and also benefit society. Trade unions perform intra-mural, extra-mural, political and auxiliary functions in order to achieve their objectives. Trade unions can be classified based on (a) composition of membership or structure (such as craft unions, industrial unions, labour unions, general unions, blue-collar workers' unions and white-collar workers' unions) and (b) purpose of trade unions (such as reformist unions and revolutionary unions).
3. There are several obstacles in the growth of trade unionism in India, such as illiteracy, ignorance, poverty, multiplicity of unions, politicisation of unions, inter-union and intra-union rivalries, lack of good leadership, lack of democratisation in the functioning of unions, company unions and outside leadership. In order to have union security, unions have several options such as closed shop, preferential union shop, union shop, maintenance of membership and agency shop. It is difficult to make unions happy irrespective of any ruling party. Trade unions can influence wages indirectly through collective bargaining, restructuring the supply of labour to a particular trade and so on.
4. Any 10% of the total workforce of an organisation or 100, whichever is less, can form their trade union per recent amendment of the Trade Unions Act, 1926, and get it registered if they so like (because registration is not mandatory)

after observing the formalities required under the act. The executive body and other members of a trade union are exempted from prosecution under certain sections of the IPC and civil suit.

5. There is no legal provision for recognition of a trade union. However, it is expected that an employer will recognise the majority union in his/her organisation as desired under the Code of Discipline.
6. In order to avoid dual membership of unions and minimising trade union rivalry, the four central unions—AITUC, INTUC, UTUC and HMS—adopted a Code of Conduct.
7. The growth of Indian trade union movement in India has been a story of unity and conflict among trade unions. Earlier it was a 'labour movement' starting from 1875 and by and by it took the shape of 'trade union movement'. The period of 1924–1935 was dominated by communists, and AITUC came into existence in 1926. The period of 1935–1939 is known as the period of unity of unions. During the period of the Second World War, trade unionism got strengthened, and collective bargaining and arbitration became popular. During 1947–1970, several unions and federations came into existence. Since 1970, a lot of developments have taken place. Of late, there is a confrontation between government and the central trade unions of workers over the unilateral steps being initiated by the government to bring the so-called labour reforms. Consequently, there have been two all-India general strikes by the central union—first on 2 September 2015 and the second on 2 September 2016. The government is trying to evolve a consensus of opinions with the unions on labour reforms, but the chances do not appear to be favourable.
8. There are around eight main national-level federations of workers' trade unions (central unions)—AITUC, INTUC, BMS, HMS, CITU, UTUC, UTUC-LS and NFITU. Even out of these, AITUC, INTUC, HMS and CITU are more popular.
9. Indian trade unionism today is suffering from many diseases such as inter-union and intra-union rivalry, poor finances, inapt leadership, ignorance among workers, dominance of quite a good number of unions by single individuals, almost absence of unions in the unorganised sector and militant attitude of good number of unions. All these shortcomings of Indian trade unions need to be overcome so that the movement may get acceleration.

Key Terms

agency shop
anarchist union
auxiliary functions
blue-collar workers' union
business union
closed shop
Code of Conduct
Code of Discipline
collective bargaining
company union
craft union

extra-mural functions
friendly union
general union
guerrilla union
hold-up union
industrial union
intra-mural functions
labour movement
labour union
migratory labour
national integration

open shop
political union
predatory union
preferential union shop
productivity
recognition of trade union
reformist union
registration of trade union

revolutionary union
trade union
trade union movement
union shop
uplift union
white-collar workers' union
workers' participation in management

Discussion Questions

1. Discuss how IR and subsequent emergence of large-scale production are responsible for bringing trade unions into existence.
2. Discuss the economic as well as non-economic objectives of trade unions.
3. Discuss the functions of trade unions and their importance to workers and the employers.
4. Discuss the main types of trade unions.
5. Discuss the obstacles in the way of growth of trade unionism in Indian industries.
6. Discuss the role of trade unions in the determination of wages.
7. Discuss the difference between the registration and the recognition of a trade union and the procedure for getting a trade union registered under the provisions of the Trade Unions Act, 1926.
8. Discuss the growth of Indian trade union movement in Indian industries and the obstacles it has been confronted with. Also discuss how to overcome these constraints.
9. Discuss the structure and functioning of any four of the main central federations of workers' unions.
10. Discuss the details of the main employers' associations functioning in our country.

Individual and Group Activities

1. As an individual, contact the union officials of a large manufacturing organisation and find out from them what functions are being performed by their unions.
2. In a group of two members, visit some big organisation and discuss with the HR officials the main difficulties they come across in dealing with the trade union officials of their organisation.
3. As an individual, discuss with the trade union officials of an organisation whether their union is recognised or not. Also find out whether the management discharges its obligations towards the recognised union.
4. In a group of two members, talk to the trade officials of a big organisation and find out how many trade unions are operational in their organisation. Are they

pulling on well among themselves? Also find out what are the main differences between them.
5. As an individual, discuss with some managerial personnel whether the concerned employers' association to which their association is affiliated is discharging its obligations properly. Do they have any suggestions to offer in this regard? If yes, then what? Prepare a brief report.

Application Case 19.1

Pitfalls of Outside Leadership

Raj Shoe Factory has been in existence for the last nine years, employing about 150 workers having little education, not to speak of legal expertise. Until five years back, there were two workers' unions when the two unions merged together. While the other members of the executive body of the current trade union are not educated, only one executive member of the union who is also the secretary of the union is a law graduate and happens to be from outside the organisation. He is a local advocate. He plays the leading role whenever any negotiation takes place with the management. The other members of the executive body of the trade union have full trust and faith in his leadership and, therefore, extend their full support as and when required. However, for the last two years, the union members have been observing that none of their demands have been met by the management and that the advocate member of the executive body of the union has always tried to highlight the helplessness of the management in meeting the demands of the union.

One Sunday late evening, the vice president of the workers' union was passing through the colony where the general manager of the shoe factory resides. The vice president of the workers' union saw that somebody was coming out from the residence of the general manager of the shoe factory and that while attempting to board his car, he fell down. When the vice president of the union and one more passer-by saw the person falling down, they ran towards him to help him out. When they reached near the car, the vice president was shocked to find that the person who had fallen down was none other than the advocate member of the executive body of the workers' union and that he was drunk. They helped the advocate member to board his car. Due to having taken a heavy dose of liquor, he could not recognise and remember that one of the two people who helped him enter the car was the vice-president of the union.

The next day, the vice president called an informal meeting of the executive body of the union without inviting the advocate member. He narrated the entire incident of the previous night to the members. All the members who attended this meeting got suspicious about the integrity of the advocate member and they decided that every Sunday late evening, the members, by rotation, will keep an eye over the activities of the advocate member, especially whether he goes to the residence of the general manager of the shoe factory. The advocate member was found paying visit to the residence of the general manager twice in the month. Now, all the members of the executive body of the union were convinced that with the connivance of the advocate member, the management was rejecting the demands of the union because it knew that the advocate member of the executive body of the workers' union will justify the stand taken by the management. In the next meeting of the executive body of the workers' union, a resolution was passed for expelling the advocate member from the executive body.

Questions

1. Do you think that outsiders be allowed to be the member(s) of the executive body of a workers' union, though it is permissible to do so under the provisions of the Trade Unions Act, 1926? Yes or no? Why? Give arguments.
2. Was it justified on the part of the executive body to expel the advocate member from it just because he was found visiting the residence of the general manager of the shoe factory once coming out from there in a drunken state?

Notes

1. Sydney Webb and Beatrice Webb, *History of Trade Unionism* (London: Longmans, Green and Company, 1920), 1.
2. Flippo, *Principles of Personnel Management*, 469.
3. The word 'Indian' omitted by the Indian Trade Unions (Amendment) Act, 1964, with effect from 1 April 1965. [xxx] refers to the deletion through amendment of the act.
4. See Government of India, *Report of the National Commission on Labour* (New Delhi: Ministry of Labour and Employment and Rehabilitation, 1969), 287.
5. Ibid.
6. Ibid.
7. Ibid.
8. See Sharma, *Industrial Relations and Labour Legislation*, 165–66.
9. M. G. I. Rao and P. S. Rao, *Human Resource Management in Indian Railways* (Delhi: Manas Publication, 1986), 115.
10. For details, see *The Economic Times*, 2 February 1999.
11. Press Trust of India, 'Raise I-T Exemption Limit to '5 lakh: Unions', Business Standard, 5 January 2016. Available at http://www.business-standard.com/article/pti-stories/raise-i-t-exemption-limit-to-rs-5-lakh-unions-116010400 795_1.html (Accessed on 5 December 2015).
12. 'Unions Seek Raise in I-T Exemption Limit', *Hindustan Times*, 5 January 216. Available at https://www.pressreader.com/india/hindustan-times-delhi/20160105/281779923106618 (Accessed on 6 December 2017).
13. Available at https://www.pressreader.com/india/hindustan-times-delhi/20160105/281779923106618 (Accessed on 6 December 2017).
14. For details, see *The Economic Times*, 28 December 2015.
15. *The Economic Times*, 5 January 2016.
16. See 'Better Not Cross Lakshman Rekha on Labour Laws: Bharatiya Mazdoor Sangh', *The Economic Times*, 5 January 2016. Available at https://economictimes.indiatimes.com/news/politics-and-nation/better-not-cross-lakshman-rekha-on-labour-laws-bharatiya-mazdoor-sangh/articleshow/50445648.cms (Accessed on 6 December 2017).
17. Ibid.
18. Ibid.
19. *The Economic Times*, 5 January 2016.

20 *The Economic Times*, 18 January 2016.
21 *The Economic Times*, 29 January 2016.
22 *The Economic Times*, 26 February 2016.
23 *The Economic Times*, 3 March 2016.
24 *Hindustan Times*, 6 June 2016.
25 *The Economic Times*, 10 June 2016.
26 Ibid.
27 *The Economic Times*, 9 June 2016.
28 *Times of India*, 9 June 2016.
29 *Hindustan Times*, 16 June 2016.
30 *Hindustan Times*, 12 July 2016.
31 *The Economic Times*, 7 July 2016.
32 *The Economic Times*, 18 August 2016.
33 *The Economic Times*, 3 September 2016.
34 *The Economic Times*, 28 September 2016.
35 *The Economic Times*, 30 September 2016.
36 *Hindustan Times*, 5 December 2016.
37 Ibid.
38 *The Economic Times*, 3 February 2017.
39 *Hindustan Times*, 20 June 2016.
40 Ibid.
41 A. M. John and G. D. Bino Paul, 'Workers Participation in Management: Insights from a Case Study', *Indian Journal of Industrial Relations* 49, no. 1 (July 2013): 64.
42 For a detailed study, see R. C. Sharma, 'Whither Goes Indian Trade Unionism?', *Haryana Labour Journal* 15, no. 4 (October–December 1984): 5–7; R. C. Sharma, 'Indian Trade Unionism: Recent Trends and Emerging Patterns', paper presented at the 25th Annual Conference of the Indian Society of Labour Economics, Lucknow University, Lucknow, 21–24 October 1983.
43 *Hindustan Times*, 13 February 2015.
44 Ibid.
45 See G. Cynax and R. Oakeshott, *The Bargainer: A Survey of Modern Unionism* (London: Faber and Faber, 1960), 147.
46 See *Hindustan Times*, 26 October 1986.
47 *Hindustan Times*, 21 October 1986.
48 R. S. Davar, *Personnel Management and Industrial Relations in India* (New Delhi: Vikas Publishing House, 1976), 304–7.
49 *Hindustan Times*, 13 February 2015.
50 Ibid.
51 Sharma, *Industrial Relations and Labour Legislation*, 194.
52 see For details, Labour Bureau, Ministry of Labour and Employment, Government of India, *Indian Labour Year Book 2009–10*, 95.
53 See Sunder Shyam, 'Emerging Trends in Employment Relations in India', *Indian Journal of Industrial Relations* 45, no. 4 (April 2010): 585–95.

20 International Human Resource Management

Learning Objectives

After studying this chapter, you should be able to do the following:

1. List and describe the various types of international organisations.
2. Explain the meaning of IHRM and differentiate between IHRM and domestic HRM.
3. Describe how to develop a more effective global HR system (GHRS) and how to make global HRM more acceptable besides how to implement GHRS.
4. List and describe the source of staffing international organisations and also the approaches to managing and staffing subsidiaries of MNCs.
5. Explain the cause of failure of expatriate managers and also the key traits of successful managers for global organisations.
6. List and describe the practices related to orienting, training and developing employees for international assignments.
7. Explain the practices related to compensating performance appraisal of international managers and repatriates.
8. List and describe the various dimensions of Hofstede's model and also its limitations and application.

Introduction

A good number of big companies do business abroad. Now even small companies are finding that success depends on marketing and managing overseas. The reasons that an organisation might expand its operations beyond its domestic markets are not far to seek. These may include searching for new and broader markets; taking advantage of large, inexpensive labour forces located in other countries; acquiring new and more efficient manufacturing technology; and so on. Consequently, the list of global companies that transcend national boundaries is growing steadily. It means that more employees are being sent overseas on temporary assignments. When abroad, such expatriates face typical challenges. They need to stay abreast of global economic, social and political trends and visualise the impact of these trends for their organisations. They come across diverse cultures and need to adopt a personalised approach with employees. They have to travel an extra mile to mix with the workers there, be social and avoid passing unpleasant remarks against them. For example, while hire and fire policies are quite common in the Western world, these may be vehemently opposed in countries such as India, Europe and Indonesia. Hence, there are several pressures of globalisation because global assignments are usually highly demanding. A survey of top international HR executives[1] has revealed certain challenges concerning international HR effectiveness such as finding suitable candidates, intercultural understanding, career management, employee retention, adjusting to environment, partner dissatisfaction and relocation reluctance. There are several complexities in global operations. International operations have more heterogeneous functions; there is more involvement in the personal lives of employees, more complex external influences, such as from societies and governments and more cultural differences with regard to languages, values, beliefs, ways of doing things and so on. Hence, there is a unique character of global HRM (GHRM) and, therefore, there is a need to understand the effects of national, cultural and global business differences on effective HR practices.

Type of International Organisations

Before we go forward, it will be best to know the types of international organisations, which are as follows:

- **International corporations**: International corporations are the companies that build on their existing capabilities to penetrate overseas markets. Such companies adopt their products to overseas markets without making changes in their normal operations. P&G and General Electric Co. are some of the examples which followed this approach to penetrate European markets.
- **MNCs**: An MNC has operations in many different countries, but each is viewed as a relatively separate enterprise supplying its products for the geographical region surrounding the country of operation of the unit. Thus, each separate enterprise within an MNC is responsible for adapting the company's products to the local culture, but most vital control remains either with the company's home offices or in the hands of an expatriate from the home country. The majority of the employees, including managers, are usually from the host country, especially in its earliest stages of internationalisation.[2] Xerox and Philips are examples in this regard.
- **Global corporations (GCs)**: A GC is structured so that the national boundaries disappear. It hires the best people for jobs irrespective of national origin. It sees the world as its labour source as well its marketplace. Hence, it locates an operation wherever it can achieve its objectives and goals in the most cost-effective manner. For example, McDonald's, Coca-Cola and Nestle believe in a world market for their products. A GC maintains control over its global operations through a centralised home office. It is the expertise of an employee in his/her particular area that matters most for a GC instead of his/her national affiliation. Its employees are often moved across national boundaries to meet the current needs of the organisation.[3]
- **Transnational corporations (TNCs)**: A TNC is an ideal type but hardly exists in reality. It provides autonomy to independent country operations and brings these separate operations into an integrated whole through a networked structure like Unilever. A TNC is a fine blend of local responsiveness of an MNC and the efficiency of a GC.

Anyway, irrespective of any of the forms discussed earlier, an organisation that conducts business overseas is usually known as an international organisation. It has to face a major challenge of locating and nurturing human resources required for implementing a global strategy.

What IHRM Is All About

IHRM is the result of an interplay among the three dimensions—HR activities, types of employees and countries of operation.[4] IHRM refers to the HRM issues and problems arising from the internationalisation of business, and the HRM strategies, policies and practices which firms pursue in response to the internationalisation process. IHRM, therefore, focuses on employees who are on international posting or on an international assignment.

Difference Between IHRM and Domestic HRM

IHRM requires a much broader perspective, encompasses a greater scope of activities and is subject to much greater challenges than is domestic HRM. IHRM is more complex than domestic HRM. The scope of domestic HRM is relatively narrow as compared to IHRM, which takes care of wide range of HRM activities and includes international taxation, foreign currencies, foreign locations, and the like. Again, while HR issues relate to employees belonging to single nationality, IHRM issues relate to employees belonging to more than one nationality, thus requiring setting up different HRM systems for different locations. Then, domestic HRM has to deal with limited external factors, while IHRM has to manage several external factors like government regulations of foreign country about staffing practices. A striking difference between the domestic HRM and IHRM is that while the former has limited involvement of the HR manager in the personal life of employees, IHRM requires greater involvement in the personal life of employees such as helping in the admission of children in schools and supporting the family in adjusting to a foreign culture through cross-cultural training. Besides, in domestic HRM, there is limited risk, whereas in international assignments, there is heightened exposure to risks such as health and safety of the employee and his/her family, terrorism, and human and financial consequences of mistakes committed in IHRM. Thus, a management style effective in the domestic environment may not be a success if applied in a foreign environment unless it is suitably modified.

Developing a More Effective Global HR System (GHRS)

For developing effective worldwide HR systems, an international company should engage itself in several best practices. It should form a global network in such a manner that its HR managers worldwide should not feel that they are merely local HR managers. They should rather have a feeling that they are the part of a greater whole—its GHRM network. It should form global teams to develop the new HR systems. It should also treat the local HR managers as equal partners and not just implementators. Besides, it should not forget that it is more important to standardise ends and competencies than specific methods. For example, in screening applications, it should be standardised as to what is to be assessed and be flexible how it is assessed.[5] Procter and Gamble can be cited as an example in this regard.

Making the GHRS More Acceptable

First, it should not be forgotten that global systems are more accepted in truly global organisations, that is, the organisations whose most functions and business units operate on a truly global basis. Such organisations along with their managers think of themselves as global in scope and perspective. Then, it is also advisable to investigate pressures to differentiate and determine their legitimacy instead of ramming through a change without ascertaining whether there may, in fact, be some reason for using a more locally appropriate system.[6] Again, in order to make the GHRS more acceptable, efforts should be made to work within the context of a strong corporate culture. For example, the corporate culture may encourage a relatively high degree of conformity among managers. Again, it may select, train and develop, and reward them in such a fashion that it may create a strong sense of shared values.

Implementation of the GHRS

Even if an international organisation has developed an effective GHRS, it is of no use if it is not implemented properly. For the effective implementation of a GHRS, the first important thing to be kept in mind is that there should remain a constant contact with the decision-makers in each country, as also with the people who are supposed to implement it as well as those who will use the system—that is, communicate, communicate, communicate, communicate!

Exhibit 20.1 Key Global Pressures Affecting HRM Practices

- Deployment: Easily getting the right skills to where we need them, regardless of geographic location
- Knowledge and innovation dissemination: Spreading state-of-the-art knowledge and practices throughout the organisation, regardless where they originate
- Identifying and developing talent on a global basis

Source: Based on discussion in J. M. Ivancevich, *Human Resource Management*, 10th ed. (New Delhi: Tata McGraw-Hill Publishing Company Ltd, 2008), 692.

Secondly, adequate resources should be made available to those who are supposed to implement the GHRS. Emphasis should be laid on what to measure but allow flexibility in how to measure. Then, work within the existing local system and treat local people as equal partners in system development. Local people should be trained to make good decisions about which tools to use and how to do so. Also assess common elements across geographies and create a global network for system development as global input is vital. But all the same, effort should be made to avoid doing everything the same way everywhere and also avoid forcing a global system on local people who should be used just for implementation. It is also desirable not to use the same tools globally unless it can be established that they really work everywhere and that they are culturally appropriate. There can be a long list of dos and don'ts in this regard.

The Global Challenges

The key global pressures[7] affecting HRM practices are shown in Exhibit 20.1

External Environment and IHRM

International business operations are affected a great deal by the external environment comprising economic, cultural and political factors. These factors differ from country to country. For example, if the business strategy and HR strategy of an international organisation are not consistent with the culture of the host country, the organisation is not likely to be a success story. It is, therefore, necessary to examine the 'fit' between organisational culture and the culture of the host country. Hence, there may be need of different HRM approaches and practices depending on the cultural environment of host countries.

Staffing the Global Organisation

Staffing a global organisation appropriately is critical to the success of an international organisation. Multinational organisations operating overseas may use any one or more than one of the following sources (see Figure 20.1) for staffing:

1. **Home country nationals or PCNs**: MNCs may employ the citizens of the country in which the MNC has its headquarters. They are not the citizens of the host country. For example, an American working for America-based General Motors' subsidiary in India is a home country national and also an expatriate. Hence, country nationals are usually appointed as managers, subsidiary heads, experts and heads of some key functions. For example, in India, Maruti has more than 15 Japanese heading key functional areas such as finance and production. PCNs are preferred because they know better about the functioning of the parent company; they can also better ensure proper linkage between foreign subsidiary and the headquarters. PCNs are also helpful in developing global capabilities in the organisation. But it should also be kept in view that PCNs are expensive and are not aware about the culture of the country where the subsidiary is located. But PCNs are usually preferred when the subsidiary is in its initial stage and when the host country does not have the required

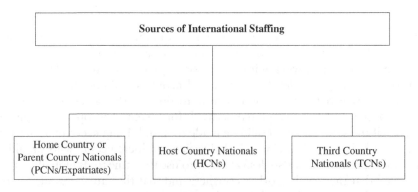

Figure 20.1 Sources of Staffing International Organisations

expertise. PCNs are also helpful in ensuring that the foreign subsidiary complies with the philosophy and policies of headquarters.

2. **HCNs:** Many people do not want to work in a foreign country. Besides, the cost of using expatriates is far greater than the cost of using HCNs, who are well versed with local language and dialect. They are also familiar with the local customs, norms, culture and so on. Hence, international companies prefer appointing HCNs, especially at middle and lower management levels. At times, even some governments also pressurise international companies for the nationalisation of local management. By appointing locals (HCNs), MNCs earn goodwill from local people. Sometimes, it is difficult to bring PCNs to the country where the subsidiary is located. For example, TCS has recruited many people, including some on senior positions as well, in Latin America. The main shortcoming of HCNs is that they have a local view rather than a global view about the operations of the subsidiary. At times, HCNs do not appreciate the needs of headquarters. However, HCNs are most suitable if the required technical expertise is available in them and when the subsidiary is well established. They may also be helpful in establishing a wide network for market as also for business expansion.

3. **TCNs:** TCNs are citizens of a country other than the parent or the host country. For example, a Chinese who works in an Indian subsidiary of an organisation having its headquarters in the USA is a TCN. It has been observed that usually TCNs are less costly than PCNs and have a considerable amount of international experience. However, it is not easy to get such competent and experienced people because of their short supply and they also pose greater challenges in terms of cross-cultural diversity management. All the same, TCNs usually prove their technical expertise.

It has usually been observed that when an organisation is in its early stage of global expansion, it depends mostly on PCNs/expatriates to give shape to operations and other vital activities—especially if the subsidiary is being set up in a developing country or relatively less developed economy and by and by it starts picking up people from the host country. TCNs are appointed when a typical talent or expertise is needed and the same is not conveniently available in the host countries and the like.

Approaches to Staffing Subsidiaries

It is the attitude of the top management at headquarters that affects the international staffing practices of an MNC with regard to employment of foreign executives at its subsidiaries as well as at the headquarters. The following are the main approaches in this regard (see Figure 20.2):

- **Ethnocentrism:** It is a cultural attitude marked by the tendency to regard one's own culture as superior to others.[8] Sending home country executives abroad—thinking that they will be able to deliver the goods—may be an appropriate strategy in the initial stages of expanding company operations worldwide as these officials know what to do immediately. For example, Korean firms in India, such as LG and Samsung, are normally headed by Koreans. Similarly, at Royal Dutch Shell, virtually all financial controllers around the world are Dutch nationals. Subsidiaries located overseas have little autonomy as all strategic decisions are made at headquarters. Most key positions at subsidiaries and headquarters are occupied by expatriates. The host country mid-level managers find it difficult to further careers in the global set-up as they rarely

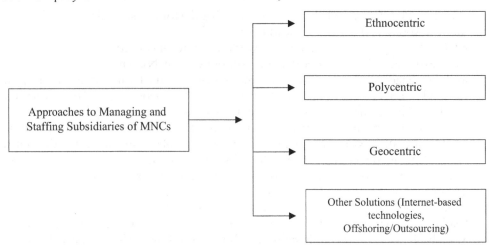

Figure 20.2 Approaches to Managing and Staffing Subsidiaries of MNCs

get exposure at strategy meets. Ethnocentrism reduces promotion opportunities for HCNs. Besides, PCNs take time to adopt to the culture of the host country and are, therefore, likely to commit mistakes in between. Not only this, but the foreign subsidiaries have to pay more to PCNs as they are costly as compared to HCNs. However, not all expatriates prove a success and many do not prove effective all the time because most expatriates are selected on the basis of their domestic track record, but they lack cross-cultural training and the like. All the same, ethnocentrism is justified in case there is a shortage of competent HCNs. It also helps in coordinating activities between the subsidiary and the headquarters.

- **Polycentrism**: It is the belief that only host country managers can actually understand the culture and behaviour of the host country market and, therefore, a foreign subsidiary should be managed by local people. HCNs do not have any language problem or cultural adjustment problems and do not need much training. Most Western MNCs have realised that the key to success of a foreign subsidiary is to appoint local people. Besides, HCNs are available at a low cost and there is no problem of cultural adjustment. It also overcomes the problem of turnover which is very high if PCNs are appointed in foreign subsidiaries. Under this approach, foreign subsidiaries are staffed with HCNs, while the staff at headquarters comprises exclusively of PCNs. HCNs are rarely, if at all, promoted to senior positions at headquarters. Polycentrism also causes gap between HCNs at subsidiaries and PCNs at headquarters.

- **Geocentricism**: Geocentricism involves searching candidates globally for managerial positions for both headquarters and foreign subsidiaries. They may be PCNs, HCNs or TCNs. Competence is the sole key to staffing. Such a staffing policy seeks the best people, irrespective of their nationality, for key positions throughout the organisation. Colgate-Palmolive can be cited here as an example. Since geocentricism focuses on competence, it leads to development of international executive team of competent people having cross-cultural skills. Geocentricism involves high training and relocation costs. It also needs centralisation of staffing process and a lot of monitoring.

- **Other solutions**: Outsourcing or offshoring is another vital international staffing issue. It involves having local employees abroad do jobs that the firm's domestic employees provisionally did in-house.[9] Besides, some organisations use Internet-based video technologies and group decision-making software[10] to enable global virtual teams to do business without either travel or relocation.

Organisations today need people with diversified global experience. Companies are keen to tap the global talent pool and seek professionals who have considerable global exposure.[11] Managers who have had multiple locations are better placed today to handle global operations.

Selecting Expatriate Managers

The importance of expatriates in foreign subsidiaries cannot be overlooked. In a good number of foreign subsidiaries, expatriates play an important role. Hence, their selection should be made cautiously, which first needs to identify the causes of failure of many expatriates so that the necessary care may be taken while selecting them.

Causes of Failure of Expatriate Managers

The causes responsible for failure of expatriates include the following:

1. Wrong selection—that is, the expatriate selected may not be right person for the assignment he/she has been selected for.
2. Failure of the expatriate to understand the work practices of the foreign subsidiary.
3. Poor performance—that is, below the minimum expected.
4. Inability of the family of the expatriate to adapt to the foreign subsidiary's environment.
5. Inadequate compensation.
6. Inappropriate relocation.
7. Cultural maladjustment (for details, see the discussion on the issue in subsequent pages), lack of imagination, sense of responsibility, attentiveness, industriousness, dedication to the assignment and initiative.
8. The spouse may not get the desired job or any job altogether.
9. Lack of ongoing support to the expatriate and his/her family.
10. Non-availability of formal 'global buddy'—that is, the local manager who can advise or guide the expatriate, especially the one who has been posted at the foreign subsidiary only recently, on issues related to norms of behaviour, office politics (if any) and medical help in case of emergency.
11. Difficulty in making close friends.
12. Children of expatriates getting pressure due to transfer of parents of their close friends.
13. Inappropriate education of school-going children.
14. A lot of other family and personal issues.

Currently, failure rates among expatriate managers are very high in many American corporations[12] (see Exhibit 20.2).

Exhibit 20.2 Major Reasons for High Failure Among Expatriate Managers in Many American Corporations

- Selection processes that focus too much on technical skills and too little on cultural factors
- Lack of systematic training for the overseas assignments
- Too little involvement of family members in the selection decision
- Lack of clean expectations about the role of the overseas assignment in the manager's career plans

Exhibit 20.3 Characteristics of a Successful Expatriate Manager

- Strong technical skills
- Good language skills
- Strong desire to work overseas
- Specific knowledge of overseas culture
- Well-adjusted family situation
- Complete support of spouse
- Behavioural flexibility
- Adaptability and open-mindedness
- Good relational ability
- Good stress management skills

Source: Ivancevich, *Human Resource Management*, 104.

Having identified the factors responsible for the failure of some of the expatriate managers, the next exercise to be carried out is to find out the traits of successful expatriate managers so that while making selection, it may be ensured that the candidate possesses those traits or most of those traits (see Exhibit 20.3).

Key Traits for Selection of Managers for Global Assignments

Following are the main traits that should be looked forward to in the process of selection of managers for foreign assignment:

1. **Personality**: Personality is one of the main factors responsible for the success or failure of an expatriate. It may include a number of things such as maturity, emotional stability, risk taking, coping with stress, flexibility, tolerance, agreeableness, extroversion, ambition for expatriate career, creativity, high motivation and perseverance.

Exhibit 20.4 Cross-Cultural Training

For companies that provide cross-cultural training, consulting and other services for global assignees, visit https://www.shrm.org/home.
Also visit http://www.cendantintercultural.com.

2. **Family factors:** Family pressures usually loom large in expatriate failures. Hence, while selecting an expatriate for foreign assignment, it is necessary to ensure that his/her family has a happy married life and to ensure willingness of the spouse to live abroad, the ability to adjust (that is, adaptability of spouse and family), positive attitude of the spouse, availability of the right type of education to the children of the expatriate in the host country, and taking due care of financial and other requirements.
3. **Organisational requirements:** Another thing to be taken care of at the time of selection of expatriates for foreign assignment is that he/she possesses the desired job knowledge and meets the organisational requirements. It may include organisational ability, administrative skills, managerial abilities, belief in the mission, belief in the job, accountability, and other related skills and knowledge.
4. **Communication skills:** Language capabilities—both verbal and written communication—in the host country's language, body language, knowledge about gestures, ability to resolve conflicting cultural issues and so on are some of the other traits of an effective expatriate. At the time of selecting them for foreign assignments, these should be kept in view.
5. **Cultural exposure:** One of the vital requirements of a good expatriate is the ability to adapt to new cultural situations. Interpersonal skills, diplomatic skills, global exposure, representing the parent country in the host country appropriately and so on play a vital role in the success of an expatriate (see Exhibit 20.4).

Thus, it is noticeable that in the selection of PCNs, the selectors must pay due attention to not only technical and administrative abilities but also their abilities to adapt to the new socio-cultural aspects prevailing in the host country. Adaptability screening should be carried out by a professional psychologist or psychiatrist so as to ensure family's probable success in handling the foreign assignment. The couple (the expatriate and his/her spouse) should be alerted about the issues related to their children's education and the like and reaction should be noted. It is perhaps for these reasons that several companies give future managers exposure to foreign cultures early in their careers. Some business schools arrange the internship of their students for short duration overseas. Japan and Germany have relatively better selection practices. Some other issues that should be addressed during the selection process relate to the willingness of the PCNs to join foreign subsidiary, their tolerance for ambiguity, their political sensitivity, their interest in foreign cultures, display of respect, frankness, empathy, kindness, integrity, resourcefulness and so on.

Orienting, Training and Developing Employees on International Assignment

Having screened the foreign assignees carefully, the next step is to orient and impart appropriate training to them.

Orientation

It is very important to arrange an extensive orientation for employees on international assignments so as to familiarise them with the culture, language and other typical aspects of the assignment. It may be desirable to arrange familiarisation trips for the prospective expatriates to the foreign country of their posting so as to give them a feel of the type of environment they are supposed to live in. Although there is no hard-and-fast rule, orientation programmes can be conducted in two phases: (a) The pre-arrival orientation may comprise cultural briefing so as to familiarise the prospective expatriates with the living conditions, customs and traditions of the host country, clothing and housing requirements and so on, and assignment briefing so as to give an idea about the nature and the duration of their assignment, the vacations/holidays they will be entitled to, their compensation package, incentives, taxes they are liable to pay, repatriation packing, residential accommodation in the host country and other such things. (b) The post-arrival orientation starts once the expatriates arrives in the host country and where they have to settle down. Hence, they should be guided and helped there with regard to such routine things as arrangement of residential accommodation, admission of their children in good schools, opening of bank accounts, obtaining driving license for self and drivers, awareness about the geography of the town, state and country, and so on. Cross-cultural training is another important aspect of expatriates' training. Since there is no culture uniform to the world, it is essential to impart training focusing on the impact of cultural differences and on raising trainees' awareness of such differences and their impact on business outcomes. In order to enable the expatriates to lead a normal life, they should be provided cross-cultural and language training; otherwise, they will experience culture shock, which, at times, forces the expatriates to return to their home country. They should, therefore, be apprised with the highlights of the culture of the host country including ethical and legal issues.

Career Development

Once an expatriate lands in the host country, he/she ceases to have direct and regular contact with his/her bosses and colleagues at headquarters. He/she starts feeling as if he/she is out of the system and that his/her future is blocked. To overcome this sort of realisation by the expatriate, it is advisable to have a monitoring system whereby the expatriate is mentored by a senior executive at the headquarters who remains in touch with the expatriate and pleads his/her case for promotion at headquarters at appropriate occasions. The mentor at the headquarters should also be instrumental in resolving problems of the expatriate related to headquarters. Another option in this regard can be that the expatriate and his/her family may be given opportunities to visit their home country at regular intervals, say every six months or annually, and thereby remain in touch with his/her bosses and other officials at headquarters. Yet another option can be organising development programmes at headquarters for expatriates on a regular basis, thus providing an opportunity to the expatriates to be in touch with the headquarters. Besides, an expatriate should be given such an assignment as may help him/her to have exposure in new things, enhance his/her knowledge and create a place for himself/herself in the organisation, enabling him/her to grow vertically within the foreign subsidiary and thus remain contented.

Some firms follow the steps as laid down in Exhibit 20.5 to meet the special training requirements of foreign subsidiaries.

Exhibit 20.5 Steps Being Followed by Some Firms to Meet Special Training Requirements of Foreign Subsidiaries

Step I: Focus on the impact of cultural differences; increasing trainees' awareness of such differences and their impact on business outcomes

   Step II: Getting trainees to understand how attitudes are formed and how they influence behaviour

Step III: Providing factual knowledge about the target country
Step IV: Skill building in areas like language and adjustment and adaptation skills

Source: Dessler and Varkkey, *Human Resource Management*, 707–8.

Recent Trends in Expatriate Training

Of late, different trends in expatriate training[13] have emerged as follows:

- Bringing the international managers together periodically for training seminars
- Providing continuing, in-country cross-cultural training during the early stages of an overseas assignment
- Using returning managers as resources to cultivate the 'global mindsets'
- Increased use of software and the Internet for cross-cultural training, guiding users to select the strategy to best handle the situation

Compensating Managers for International Assignments

The issue of compensation in the case of international employees is a tricky one. While it appears reasonable to maintain companywide pay scales and policies so as to reduce the risk of perceived inequities, if the cost of living is very high in the host country, maintaining companywide pay scales may not serve the purpose, as in that case no expatriate would like to go on foreign assignment. Besides, there may be certain legal requirements and tax policies in the host country which have to be complied with. It is, therefore, desirable to design a compensation plan in such a fashion that is strategically aligned yet flexible enough to accommodate specific needs of expatriates. Needs differ from individual to individual, from culture to culture and from location to location. Hence, actual cost of living should be worked out, and the expatriate may always be compensated for expenses accordingly. It should be ensured that expatriate compensation is fair, competitive and consistent with international compensation norms; otherwise, it may almost be impossible to get managers to take high-cost assignments. Maintaining an expatriate manager on an overseas assignment is a very costly proposition. It has been estimated that usually a middle-to-upper-level expatriate can cost an organisation from two to three times what it costs to maintain him/her on a domestic assignment.[14] A way out for this problem can be to pay a similar base salary companywide and then add on various allowances according to individual market conditions.

Some MNCs conduct their own local annual compensation surveys and use the information so collected to decide annual salary increases and proposed changes in benefits.

Many companies use the 'balance sheet approach' which tries to equalise purchasing power across countries. The companies using this approach estimate expenses for income taxes, housing accommodation, goods and services, and reserve and pay supplements to expatriates in such a way as to maintain the same standard of living he/she would have had at home. The balance sheet approach is one of the most popular international compensation approaches for US, European and Japanese firms. More than 85% of North American companies reportedly use this approach. In this approach, four groups of expenses—income taxes, housing, goods and services, and discretionary expenses, such as child support and car payments—are the focus of attention. The difference in these expenses incurred in the expatriate's home country and what these expenses will be in the host country is usually paid to the expatriate. However, in practice, some other expenses, if incurred by the expatriate in the host country, are also taken care of.

Another approach known as the 'global market approach' has also come into prominence, and many organisations have started following it for compensating global managers. It provides certain core components to all managers, no matter in which country they are posted. Many companies pay lump sum allowances directly to the relocating employees to take care of their relocation expenses. Although involving greater administrative exercise, this approach leads to a lot of uniformity in international compensation. Some US companies also pay foreign service premiums ranging from 10% to 30% of basic pay, hardship allowances and mobility premiums.

The common components of expatriate compensation include basic pay, cost of living adjustment, housing allowance, relocation allowance, home leave and travel allowance, hardship posting allowance, children's education allowance, currency differential payment, payments to protect from negative tax consequences and so on. For software companies, salary increases along with innovatively designed flexible benefit packages are considered part of global packages.

Incentives

These days performance-basis incentives are getting less popular in foreign subsidiaries. Incentives differ from country to country. For example, while US firms that offer long-term incentives to their overseas managers use overall corporate performance criteria (like worldwide profits) when awarding incentive pay, European firms focus on a guaranteed annual salary and companywide bonus.

Performance Appraisal of International Managers

Appraising the performance of international managers is not an easy task. The first concern in this direction is who should appraise the performance of the expatriates, that is, whether the home office managers or the host country bosses. Here, the cultural differences of the home and host countries may affect the appraisal. While the home country managers may not be fully aware about the situation the expatriate faces locally, and thus the appraisal may not be realistic, the host country bosses may also not be realistic in their appraisal because of various cultural differences and different work practices in the home and host countries. Anyway, while appraising the performance of the expatriates, factors such as compensation package, the task assigned to the expatriate, the support available to the expatriate from the headquarters, the environment in which he/she performs and cultural adjustments should be kept into consideration because if these factors are not conducive, the performance may be adversely affected for which the expatriate should not be held responsible. Hence, in the process of performance evaluation of expatriates, they should also be given opportunity to present their case.

Repatriation

Repatriation involves calling an expatriate back home after the completion of the international assignment. However, it has been observed that quite a good number of expatriates leave before the completion of their tenure abroad, and even out of those who return home after completion of their tenure abroad, a good percentage of them quit their job within three years of their returning home. This trend is to be checked as the parent company spends a lot on the transportation, living costs abroad, extending a number of benefits to their family, incurring cost on their training and development, paying premium for their insurance and so on. Formal repatriation programmes can be instrumental a great deal in addressing this problem as the formal repatriation programme ensures that the expatriate and his/her family do not feel that the company has left them adrift. For this, the company may arrange a psychologist trained in repatriation issues who meets the family before it goes overseas and discusses with it the challenges it is likely to be confronted with in the foreign assignment. He/she also assesses whether the family would be able to adapt to the new culture. The psychologist remains in touch with the family throughout its stay in the host country. The formal repatriation programme also ensures that the expatriate feels that he/she is still in the loop and keep him/her informed about the important happenings taking place at the headquarters. The expatriate is assigned a mentor for the purpose, and the expatriate is given opportunities to fly back to the home office periodically for meetings, interactions and socialisation with headquarter people. The formal repatriation programme may also involve providing formal repatriation services once the expatriate comes back to home office. The psychologist and a representative may be required to meet the expatriate and his/her family a few months before they are likely to return home and help them preparing for the return. They help the expatriate in planning his/her next career move, in updating his/her resume and in bringing him/her back in contact with the supervisors and do some other required things.

Sometimes it so happens that headquarters may not have planned properly to the expatriate's return home, and as a result of which, the expatriate may not be able to get a portfolio which is desirable. In order to avoid such an eventuality, the organisation should enter into an agreement with the expatriate before his/her departure to the foreign subsidiary, clearly specifying terms and conditions of the assignment and also mentioning the position and the salary the expatriate will be entitled to when he/she comes back to the home office. There may be many other apprehensions on the part of the expatriate in this regard. For example, he/she may be scared of the fact that in his/her absence, his/her peers at home office may be promoted or that due to his/her invisibility at parent company office, his/her career prospects may be adversely affected or that due to his/her failure at the foreign subsidiary, his/her career prospects may be adversely affected at the parent company or that on his/her return to the parent company, and his/her social status may come down as usually expatriates enjoy a higher social status in the foreign subsidiary. In order to alleviate all such apprehensions, the parent company may take certain steps such as appointing a senior manager at the parent company as the expatriate's mentor who can take care of the interests of the expatriate in his/her absence and also granting home leave periodically so that the expatriate may take all necessary steps to safeguard his/her interests.

The Cultural Nature of GHRM

Since some countries differ widely in their culture, that is, the basic values their citizens adhere to, and in the ways these values manifest themselves and ways of doing things,[15] it is essential to understand these differences and ensure that HRM and the cultural orientation of employees are congruent with one another. As a matter of fact, every aspect of

HRM can be influenced by cultural differences and, therefore, expatriates should adapt themselves according to the culture of the host country. It is here that the problem of cross-culture comes into prominence.

Although there are several models of how culture influences work behaviour, the most widely recognised is the Hofstede's theory of the cultural relativity of organisational practices.

Hofstede's Cultural Dimensions Theory[16]/Hofstede's Cultural Model

There are several models of how culture influences work behaviour. However, the most widely recognised is the Hofstede's 'theory of the cultural relativity of organisational practices'.[17] Hofstede argues that national cultural differences are not changing much at all, even though more superficial work-related norms and values might be. As a result, he feels that national culture will continue to have a strong influence on the effectiveness of various business practices.[18]

Hofstede developed his original model as a result of using factor analysis to examine the results of a worldwide survey of employee values by IBM between 1967 and 1973. Of course, it has been refined since then.

Hofstede established a personnel resource department of IBM which he managed until 1971. Between 1967 and 1973, he executed a large survey study concerning national values difference across the worldwide subsidiaries of this MNC. He first focused his research on the 40 largest countries and then extended it to 50 countries and 3 regions. He compared the answers of 117,000 IBM matched employee samples on the same attitude survey in different countries.

The original theory proposed four dimensions along which cultural values could be analysed: (a) individualism vs collectivism (IDV), (b) uncertainty avoidance, (c) power distance and (d) masculinity–femininity. These four dimensions regard four anthropological problem areas that different national societies handle differently, that is, the relationship of the individual with his/her primary group, ways of coping with uncertainty, ways of coping with inequality and the emotional implications of having been born as a boy or as a girl.

An independent research in Hong Kong[19] led Hofstede to add a fifth dimension to his model, long-term orientation, initially called as Confucian dynamism.

In 2010, Minkov's World Values Survey data analysis of 93 representative samples of national populations led Hofstede to identify a sixth last dimension: indulgence vs restraint. Now, let us discuss these six dimensions of the Hofstede's model in detail.

Individualism vs Collectivism

This dimension focuses on the relationship between the individual and the group. For example, in societies such as those in Asia, Africa and Latin America, the group's achievement and well-being are emphasised over the individual's. As against this, in individualistic societies, such as those in Australia, North America and Europe, more emphasis is placed on individual actions, accomplishments and goals. Individualistic societies have loose ties that often only relate an individual to his/her immediate family. They emphasise 'I' vs 'we'. People take care of themselves and make decisions based on individual needs.

Predictors of individualism are as follows:

Predictors	Individualism
Economic development	Developed/wealthy
Climate	Cold
Power–distance	Low

Consequently, in individualistic culture, people speak out, they question, they are confrontational and so on.

As against individualism, collectivism refers to a society in which tightly integrated relationships tie extended families and others into in-groups. These in-groups are local with undoubted loyalty and support each other when a conflict arises with another in-group. In collectivism, there is 'we' mentality.

Predictors of collectivism are as follows:

Predictors	Collectivism
Economic development	Underdeveloped/poor
Climate	Cold
Power–distance	High

Consequently, in collectivistic cultures, people blend in, avoid conflicts and use intermediaries.

Uncertainty Avoidance Index (UAI)

This dimension focuses on how cultures adapt to changes and cope with uncertainty. Emphasis is on the extent to which a culture feels threatened or is anxious about ambiguity. The uncertainty means not knowing what the future holds. Cultures such as Portugal, Japan and Latin American countries, with a high avoidance of uncertainty, endeavour to predict, control and influence future events. As against this, cultures such as China, Nordic countries and the Anglosphere, with low avoidance of uncertainty, are more willing to take things day by day. The basic traits of high uncertainty avoidance include having more formal rules, high expertise and belief in absolute truth, minimising risk, preferring details, having specific plans, being less tolerant of deviant ideas, consensus seeking and so on. As opposed to this, the basic traits of low uncertainty avoidance comprise having fewer rules, accepting relativity of belief, approval of risk taking, tolerating generalisation, tolerating deviation, seeking individual opinions and so on. Consequently, cultures with high anxiety avoidance are more resistant to change, often characterised by more elaborate rituals, whereas those with low anxiety avoidance tolerate dissent and deviance, accept conflict and so on.

Power Distance

This dimension focuses on the nature of human relationship in terms of hierarchy. Power distance refers to the extent to which the less powerful members of organisations and institutions, like the family, accept and expect that power is distributed unequally. Cultures vary in their view of power relationships. Human inequality is almost inevitable, but cultures with high 'power distance' emphasise these differences. For an instance, symbols of power and authority such as titles, big offices and luxury cars are witnessed in a culture with a high power distance. Such displays are given no or very less emphasis in a culture with a low power distance. In cultures with high power distance, such as Latin American, Asian, African and Arab countries, obedience to authority is expected, language is filled with power or hierarchy indicators, managers tend to be autocratic and subordinates accept direct supervision. In cultures with low power distance, like European countries, emphasis is on challenging decisions, expecting autonomy and independence.

Masculinity vs Femininity

Per this dimension, masculine societies give preference to achievement, heroism, assertiveness and material rewards for success. They are characterised with ambition, acquisition of wealth and differentiated gender role. On the other hand, feminine societies give preference to cooperation, modesty and quality of life. They are caring and have nurturing behaviours, sexuality, equality, environmental roles and so on. While cultures in warm climates tend to be masculine, in feminine cultures, cooler climates are witnessed. As a result, while masculine societies tend to see men as assertive and women as nurturing, and men tend to be competitive and visible, stress success and are non-vocation-oriented, feminine societies tend to have both men and women in nurturing roles and much less on assertiveness for either besides both men and women focusing on cooperation, awareness of those who are in need and importance to social accommodation. Masculinity is extremely low in Nordic countries, while it is very high in Japan and European countries such as Hungary and Switzerland, as well as Australia. In the Anglo world also, masculinity scores are relatively high.

Long-term Orientation vs Short-term Orientation

This dimension generally refers to the extent to which cultures think in terms of the future (the long term) or in terms of more immediate events (the short term).[20] This dimension associates the connection of the past with the current and future actions or challenges. A lower degree of this index (short term) indicates that traditions are honoured and kept while steadfastness is valued. On the other hand, cultures with a high degree in this index (long-term) view adaptation and circumstantial programmatic problem-solving as a necessity. For example, whereas long-term-oriented regions, such as Hong Kong and Japan in East Asia, continue to develop to a point, short-term-oriented poor regions, such as Africa and Latin America, including few Islamic nations, usually have less economic development.

Indulgence vs Restraint

This dimension is essentially a measure of happiness, that is, whether or not simple joys are fulfilled. 'Indulgence' refers to a society that allows relatively free gratification of basic and natural desires related to enjoying life and having fun. Such societies believe themselves to be in control of their own life and emotions. On the other hand, restraint refers to a society that controls gratification of needs and regulates it by means of strict social norms. Such societies believe that other factors dictate their life and emotions.

As a matter of fact, every aspect of HRM can be influenced by cultural differences along one or more of these dimensions. For an instance, there is evidence that national differences in uncertainty avoidance and power distance can affect the extensiveness of organisational selection practices.[21] Similarly, overall success of a training programme can be affected by differences in individualism and collectivism.

Correlations of Values with Other Country Differences

Research studies have revealed that low power distance is associated with consultative political practices and income equity, whereas high power distance is correlated with unequal income distribution and corruption in domestic politics. Again, the national culture measure of power distance is positively correlated with the ratio of companies with process innovation only over the companies with any of the three types of innovation considered in the country. Therefore, in countries with higher power distance, innovative manufacturing companies are somewhat more bound to resort to process innovations.

Application of Hofstede's Model

Importance of Cultural Difference Awareness

Culture is more often a source of conflict than of synergy. Despite the evidence that groups are different from each other, we tend to believe that deep inside all people are the same. However, cultural differences are still significant today and diversity tends to increase. Hence, in order to be able to have respectful cross-cultural differences, we have to be aware of these cultural differences. George Hofstede's model throws light on these differences. The tool can be used to give a general overview and approximate understanding of other cultures, what to expect from them and how to behave towards groups from other countries.

Practical Application of Theory

Hofstede is a well-known sociologist of culture and anthropologist in the context of applications for understanding international business because promoting cultural sensitivity helps people work more effectively when interacting with people from other countries and participate well to make sure that transactions are successful.

1. **International communication:** In international business, people have to interact daily with other people from different countries or with other companies abroad. The Hofstede's model gives insight into other cultures. For cross-cultural communication, awareness of cultural differences is essential because what is perfectly acceptable and natural in one country may be offensive in another.
2. **International isolation:** Proper understanding of cultural dimensions is likely to increase success in negotiations and reduce frustration and conflicts.
3. **International management:** While working in MNCs or other international companies, it is necessary for managers to provide training to their employees to make them sensitive to cultural differences and follow protocols across countries. The

dimensions of Hofstede's model offer guidelines for defining culturally acceptable approaches to corporate organisations.
4. **International marketing**: Hofstede's model is quite useful in international marketing also because it defines national values not in the business context but in general. For example, if you want to advertise cell phones in China, you may show a collective experience, whereas in the USA, you have to show how an individual uses it to save time and money.

Limitations of Hofstede's Model

The validity and the limitations of the Hofstede's model have been widely criticised. McSweeney is considered to be the most vocal critic of the Hofstede's model. Some of the limitations of the model are as follows:

1. **At the national level**: Hofstede's cultural dimensions enable users to distinguish countries but are not about differences between members of societies. They do not necessarily define individuals' personalities. Individual aggregate needs careful separation from national aggregate.
2. **At the organisational level**: Hofstede himself agreed that dimensions of national cultures are not relevant for comparing organisations within the same country because while national cultures are embedded in values, organisational cultures are embedded in practices. In order to manage international organisations, it is desirable to understand both national and organisational cultures.
3. **At the occupational level**: As far as occupational level is concerned, there is a certain degree of values and convictions that people hold with respect to the national and organisational cultures they are part of. For example, the culture of management as an occupation has components from national and organisational cultures which may not be the case at organisational level.
4. **At the gender level**: It is observed that while describing culture, gender differences are not taken into consideration, though there are certain factors that are useful to analyse in the discussion of cross-cultural communication. It is a matter of common knowledge that in each society, men's culture differs greatly from women's culture. For example, although men and women can often perform the same job from a technical standpoint, there are often symbols to which each gender has a different response. It is here that masculinity vs femininity dimension of the Hofstede's model comes into picture.

Despite all its limitations, the Hofstede's model is quite relevant as every aspect of HRM can be affected by cultural differences along one or more than or more of the dimensions of his model.

Management Strategy

In case an organisation already has or is in the process of having foreign subsidiaries, its recruitment and selection strategy should have adequate provisions for recruiting and selecting such people as are not only competent but also properly exposed to cross-cultural aspects. Not only this, it should also be ensured that their family, especially the spouse and children, would be able to pull on well in the new country of their posting.

The strategy should spell out which source(s) of human supply would be used to meet the requirements of manpower in the foreign subsidiary and how the expatriates and/or other incumbents would be provided cross-cultural exposure. Their compensation package as also their career development should be taken care of in the management strategy.

Chapter Review

1. Since the number of global companies that transcend national boundaries is growing steadily, more employees are being sent overseas. This phenomenon has given rise to the problem of IHRM. The main types of international organisations include international corporations, MNCs, GCs and TNCs.
2. IHRM refers to the HRM issues and problems arising from the internationalisation of business and the HRM strategies, policies and practices which firms pursue in response to the internationalisation process. IHRM requires a much broader perspective than the domestic HRM.
3. PCNs, HCNs and TCNs are main sources for staffing global organisation. The three approaches to staffing foreign subsidiaries include ethnocentrism, polycentrism and geocentricism. Outsourcing/offshoring is also followed by many international organisations to meet part of their staff required for foreign subsidiaries.
4. The main causes of failures of expatriate managers include wrong selection, their poor performance, inability to adapt to new culture, family problems and so on. The key traits that should be paid attention to at the time of selection of managers for global assignment include appropriate personality, proper family factors, organisational requirements, communication skills and cultural exposure.
5. Orientation and training and development programmes play an important role in making employees, appointed in foreign subsidiaries, effective. An orientation programme can be divided into two parts: pre-arrival orientation and post-arrival orientation. Cross-cultural training is very important for expatriate employees. Besides, career development of expatriate employees should be attached due importance.
6. When it comes to compensating managers in international assignments, it is a better proposition to pay them a similar base salary companywide and then add on various allowances according to individual market conditions. The balance sheet approach and global market approach are the two main approaches with regard to compensating managers in international assignments.
7. Performance appraisal of international managers involves many issues such as who should appraise their performance, that is, PCN or HCN bosses, environment in which they work, compensation they receive and cultural adjustments. Since repatriation involves a lot of problems for expatriates, it is better that an agreement specifying the details of their employment after their return to their headquarters be there, and there should be appointed a mentor for each at headquarters.
8. There are six cultural dimensions contained in the Hofstede's model and every aspect of HRM can be influenced by cultural differences along one or more of

these dimensions. There are correlations of values with other country differences. The Hofstede's model may have application in importance of cultural differences awareness and practical application of theory (international communication, international isolation, international management and international marketing).

9. The Hofstede's model also has certain limitations at the national level, organisational level, occupational level and gender level. But despite all limitations, it is quite relevant as every aspect of HRM can be influenced by cultural differences along one or more of the dimensions of his model.

Key Terms

balance sheet approach
career development
collectivism
cross-cultural training
ethnocentrism
expatriate
extroversion
geocentricism
global corporation
global market approach
Hofstede's cultural dimension
home country nationals
host country nationals (HCNs)
individualism theory

indulgence
international corporation
multinational corporation
offshoring
outsourcing
parent country nationals (PCNs)
polycentrism
power distance
repatriation
restraint
third country nationals (TCNs)
transnational corporation
uncertainty avoidance

Discussion Questions

1. Discuss the main characteristics of various types of international organisations and how they differ from one another.
2. Discuss what is meant by IHRM and how does it differ from domestic HRM.
3. Discuss (a) how to develop a more effective GHRS, (b) how to make the GHRS more acceptable and (c) how to implement the GHRS.
4. Discuss how the global organisations staff themselves, that is, what the main sources of their staffing are and what the main approaches to staffing subsidiaries overseas are.
5. Discuss why many expatriates fail abroad. Also discuss the main traits that should be kept into view while selecting expatriates for foreign assignments.
6. Discuss the contents of orientation and training and development programmes prepared for employees on international assignment.
7. Discuss the recent trends noticeable these days in expatriate training.
8. Discuss the issues involved in compensating, appraising performance and repatriation in the context of expatriate managers.
9. Discuss all the cultural dimensions of the Hofstede's model.
10. Discuss the limitations of the Hofstede's model.

Individual and Group Activities

1. In a group of two members, visit some subsidiary of an MNC and talk to the executives concerned and find out from them how their subsidiary has procured its staff members, especially at the middle and top levels, and prepare a brief report.
2. As an individual, talk to some of the officials of a subsidiary located in India and whose headquarters are located in London. Find out from them if they are satisfied with the approach their headquarters has followed with regard to staffing the subsidiary. In case they have any suggestion(s), it should be noted down and included in the report.
3. In a group of three members, pay a visit to an Indian subsidiary of an MNC having its headquarters at New York. Discuss with the expatriates working in the subsidiary and find out the problems being faced by them.
4. As an individual, find out from the officials of an Indian subsidiary of an MNC whose headquarters are in Germany, the way the orientation programmes are conducted for repatriates in the subsidiary.
5. In a group of two members of a group, find out from the officials of an Indian subsidiary how they expose the new joinees to the new culture.

Application Case 20.1

Problem of Cross-cultural Adaptation

Patrick, a management graduate with two-year experience at the headquarters of an MNC located in London, was promoted about a year back as senior marketing manager and posted at one of the subsidiaries of the MNC, located in New Delhi. His wife had earlier been working in a government office situated in London. After the posting of Patrick in New Delhi, his wife resigned from her government job and accompanied Patrick to New Delhi. Their 11-year-old son was studying in seventh standard in a reputed school in London itself.

Although Patrick was expecting his posting in any of the subsidiaries of the MNC he has been working for, he was hopeful that he would be posted in a European country and had never thought of being posted in New Delhi. In the initial months of his joining at New Delhi, he was not much disturbed as he was awfully busy with his official work. But with the passage of time, frustration started creeping in. He was missing his social life of London and experiencing a great difficulty in adapting to the culture of New Delhi. As his job involved travelling to some big cities of India, he found the varying culture of these cities very much unadaptable. The position of his wife was not much different from his own. She had now become a housewife and faced great difficulty in killing time gainfully. Their son also appeared to be frustrated. He had no friends and the environment at his new school in New Delhi was much different from what he used to have in London. With the passage of time, the whole family of Patrick felt miserable, and therefore, he wrote back to his headquarters that he would like to forego his promotion and will be happy to join back his old post at the headquarters.

Questions

1. What went wrong that made Patrick feel so uncomfortable at his new posting in New Delhi?
2. What should have been done by the headquarters before posting Patrick in New Delhi?
3. Were you the HR head at the headquarters of the MNC, how would have you handled the situation arising after the Patrick desired to forego his promotion and join back at headquarters?

Notes

1 See GMAC Global Relocation Services, National Foreign Trade Council, and SHRM Global Forum, *Global Relocation Trends 2003/2004 Survey Report* (Oak Brook, IL: GMAC Global Relocation Services, 2004), 118.
2 See Ivancevich, *Human Resource Management*, 101.
3 See D. J. Cherrington and L. Z. Middleton, 'An Introduction to Global Business Issues', *HR Magazine* 45, no. 6 (June 1995): 124–30.
4 P. J. Morgan, 'International HRM: Fact or Fiction', *Personnel Administrator* 45, no. 4 (1986): 31–37.
5 For details, see A. M. Ryan, D. Wiechmann, and M. Hemingway, 'Designing and Implementing Global Staffing Systems: Part 2—Best Practices', *Human Resource Management* 42, no. 1 (Spring 2003): 85–94.
6 Dessler and Varkkey, *Human Resource Management*, 698.
7 Ivancevich, *Human Resource Management*, 692.
8 Rao, *Human Resource Management*, 684.
9 Dessler and Varkkey, *Human Resource Management*, 701.
10 T. Dawyer, 'Localization's Hidden Costs', *HR Magazine* 49, no. 6 (June 2004): 135–44.
11 T. Agarwala, *Strategic Human Resource Management* (New Delhi: Oxford University Press, 2009), 773.
12 Ivancevich, *Human Resource Management*, 115.
13 Ibid.,708.
14 See J. S. Black, H. B. Gregersen, and M. E. Mendenhall, *Global Assignments: Successfully Expatriating and Repatriating International Managers* (San Francisco, CA: Jossey-Bass Publishing, 1992), 52–63.
15 Dessler and Varkkey, *Human Resource Management*, 63.
16 'Hofstede's Cultural Dimensions Theory', *Wikipedia*, last modified 18 October 2017. https://en.wikipedia.org/wiki/ Hofstede%27s_cultural_dimensions_theory
17 G. Hofstede, *Cultures Consequences: International Differences in Work-Related Values* (Newbury Park, CA: SAGE Publications, 1984).
18 Ivancevich, *Human Resource Management*, 100.
19 In 1991, Michael Harris Bond and colleagues conducted a study among students in 23 countries, using a survey instrument development with Chinese employees and managers.
20 Ivancevich, *Human Resource Management*, 100.
21 A. M. Ryan, R. A. Baron, and L. A. McFarland, 'An International Look at Selection Practices: Nation and Culture as Explanations for Variability in Practice', *Personnel Psychology* 52, no. 2 (Summer 1999): 359–91.

Bibliography

A. C. Hamblin, *Evaluation and Control of Training* (Maidenhead: McGraw–Hill, 1974).

Alan Price, *Principles of Human Resource Management: An Active Learning Approach* (Oxford: Blackwell Publishers, 2000).

Andrew Solomonson and Charles Lance, "Examination of the Relationship Between True Halo and Halo Effects in Performance Rating," *Journal of Applied Psychology*, 82, no. 5 (1997): 665–74.

Anne M. Bogardus, *Human Resources Jumpstart* (Alameda, CA: Sybex Inc, 2004).

Arthur James Todd, *Industry and Society: A Sociological Appraisal of Modern Industrialism* (New York: Holt, Rinehart and Winston, 1933).

Arthur R. Pell, *The Complete Idiot's Guide to Managing People* (Indianapolis: Alpha Books, 2003).

Arun Monappa and Mirza S. Saiyadain, *Personnel Management*, 2nd ed. (New Delhi: Tata McGraw-Hill, 1996).

Casey Ichniowski et al. (eds.), *The American Workplace: Skills, Compensation, and Employee Involvement* (New York: Cambridge University Press, 2000).

Charles Ehin, *Unleashing Intellectual Capital* (Woburn, MA: Butterworth-Heinemann, 2000).

Charles Halliman, *Business Intelligence Using Smart Techniques: Environmental Scanning Using Text Mining and Competitor Analysis Using Scenarios and Manual Simulation* (Oregon: Quality Books, 2006).

Charles M. Cadwell and Michael G. Crisp (eds.), *New Employee Orientation: A Practical Guide for Supervisors* (Menlo Park, CA: Crisp Publications, 1988).

Cherrie Jiuhua Zhu, *Human Resource Management in China: Past, Current and Future HR Practices in the Industrial Sector* (Abingdon, Oxon: Routledge Curzon, 2005).

Christine Ellis and Sarah Gale, "A Seat at the Table," *Training*, (March 2001): 90–96.

Clint Parry, "Make Position Description Work for You," *Inside Tucson Business*, 15 (22 August 2005): 17.

Clinton Wingrove, "Developing an Effective Blend of Process and Technology in the New Era of Performance Management," *Compensation and Benefits Review*, 81, no. 1 (January–February 2003): 27.

Clyde E. Witt, "The Right Stuff: Be a Better Talent Scout," *Material Handling Management*, 61 (March 2006): 44–49.

D. A. Ramasubramanian and P. Sridevi, "Recruitment Advertising," *Indian Management*, 23, no. 8 (1984): 33–38.

D. E. Guest, "Human Resource Management and Industrial Relations," *Journal of Management Studies*, 24 (1987): 503–22.

D. N. Bulla and P. M. Scott, "Manpower Requirements Forecasting: A Case Example," in D. Ward, T. P. Bachet and R. Tripp (eds.), *Human Resource Forecasting and Modeling* (New York: The Human Resource Planning Society, 1994).

Dale S. Beach, *Personnel: The Management of People at Work* (New York: Macmillan, 1975).

Dale Yoder, *Personnel Management and Industrial Relations* (Englewood Cliffs, NJ: Prentice-Hall, 1970).

Dale Yoder et al., *Personnel Management and Industrial Relations* (New Delhi: Prentice Hall of India, 1975).

David A. Decenzo, *Personnel/Human Resource Management* (New Delhi: Prentice Hall of India, 1996).
David A. Decenzo and Stephen P. Robbins, *Personnel Human Resource Management*, 3rd ed. (New Delhi: Prentice Hall of India Learning, 1973).
David Allen Baldwin, *The Library Compensation Handbook: A Guide for Administrators, Librarians, and Staff* (Westport, CT: Libraries Unlimited, 2003).
David E. Guest and Robert Horwood, "Characteristics of Successful Personnel Managers," *Personnel Management* (May 1981): 18–23.
David Guest and Derek Fatchett, *Worker Participation: Individual Control and Performance* (London: Institute of Personnel Management, 1974).
David Hon, "The Videodisc Microcomputer and the Satellite," *Training and Development Journal*, (December 1980): 28–34.
Deakin University, Faculty of Commerce, Open Campus Program, Institute of Distance Education, *Industrial Relations* (Delhi: Tata McGraw-Hill, 1992).
Donald L. Caruth and Gail D. Handlogten, *Managing Compensation (and Understanding It Too): A Handbook for the Perplexed* (London: Greenwood Publishing Group, 2001).
Donald Schwab, Herbert Heneaman III and Thomas Decotiis, "Behaviorally Anchored Scales: A Review of the Literature," *Personnel Psychology*, 28 (1975): 549–62.
Doris M. Sims, *Creative New Employee Orientation Programs: Best Practices, Creative Ideas, and Activities for Energizing Your Orientation Program* (New York: McGraw-Hill Professional, 2001).
Doug Bartholomew, "Taking the E-Train," *Industry Week*, 254 (June 2005): 34–37.
E. E. Lawler, "Job Design and Employee Motivation," *Personnel Psychology*, 22 (1969): 426–35.
E. E. Lawler, *Pay and Organizational Effectiveness: A Psychological View* (New York: McGraw-Hill, 1971).
E. H. Schein and W. G. Bennis, *Personal and Organizational Changes Through Group Methods: The Laboratory Approach* (New York: Wiley, 1965).
E. L. Levine, *Everything You Always Wanted to Know About Job Analysis* (Tampa, FL: Mariner Typographers, 1983).
Eddy Madiono Sutanto, "Forecasting: The Key to Successful Human Resource Management," *Journal Manajemen dan Kewirausahaan*, 2, no. 1 (March 2000): 1–8.
Edwin B. Flippo, *Personnel Management* (New York: McGraw-Hill, 1984).
Ernest J. McCormick and Joseph Tiffin, *Industrial Psychology* (Upper Saddle River, NJ: Prentice Hall, 1974).
"For Success with Corporate Coaching, Begin with Assessment," *HR Focus*, 83, no. 7 (July 2006): 8.
G. G. Alpander, *Human Resources Management Planning* (New York: AMACOM, 1982).
G. M. Stephenson and C. J. Brotherton (eds.), *Industrial Relations: A Social Psychological Approach* (New York: Wiley, 1979).
G. Roberts, *Recruitment and Selection: A Competency Approach* (London: Institute of Personnel and Development, 1997).
Gary Dessler, *Human Resource Management* (Delhi: Pearson Education, 2005).
Gary Gregures et al., "A Field Study of the Effects of Rating Purpose on the Quality of Multi-Source Rating," *Personnel Psychology*, 56 (2003): 1–21.
Gary P. Latham and Lise M. Saari, "The Application of Social Learning Theory to Training Supervisors Through Behavioral Modeling," *Journal of Applied Psychology*, 64, no. 3 (1979): 239–46.
George T. Milkovich and Jerry M. Newman, with the assistance of Carolyn Milkovich, *Compensation*, 7th ed. (Boston: McGraw-Hill, 2002).
George T. Milkovich and John W. Boudreau, *Human Resource Management* (Homewood, IL: Irwin, 1998).
George Thornton III, "Psychometric Properties of Self-Appraisal of Job Performance," *Personnel Psychology*, 33, no. 5 (Summer 1980): 263–72.
Georgia T. Chao, "The Socialization Process: Building Newcomer Commitment," in Manuel London and Edward M. Mone (eds.), *Career Growth and Human Resource Strategies: The Role of the Human Resource Professional in Employee Development* (New York: Quorum Books, 1988), 37.

Marshall Goldsmith. "Getting There with Executive Coach Marshall Goldsmith," in *Indian School of Business* (Hyderabad: ISB, August 2007).
Gill Palmer, *British Industrial Relations* (London: George Allen and Unwin, 1989).
Gordon Bitter Davis (ed.), *The Blackwell Encyclopedic Dictionary of Management Information Systems* (Cambridge, MA: Blackwell Publishers, 1999).
H. Koontz and C. O'Donnell, *Principles of Management* (New York: McGraw-Hill, 1972).
H. L. Tosi and S. J. Carroll, "Management by Objectives," *Personnel Administration*, 33 (1970): 44–48.
Howard P. Smith and Paul J. Browner, *Performance Appraisal and Human Development: A Practical Guide to Effective Managing* (Reading, MA: Addison-Wesley, 1977).
Howard Wilbert Miller, *Reengineering Legacy Software Systems* (Newton, MA: Digital Press, an imprint of Butterworth-Heinemann, 1998).
Human Resource Planning, *The Human Resource Planning Society* (Orient Blackswan, 1999).
Ian Beardwell, Tim Claydon and Julie Beardwell (eds.), *Human Resource Management: A Contemporary Approach*, 5th ed. (Harlow, Essex: Prentice-Hall, 2007).
Inga Pioro and Nina Baum, "How to Design Better Job Application Forms," *People Management*, 11 (16 July 2005): 42–43.
Institute of Personnel Management, *Personnel Management in India* (Bombay: Asia Publishing House, 1973), 29–30.
International Labour Organization Report, *Job Evaluation* (Geneva: ILO, 1960).
J. A. Conger and R. N. Kanungo, "The Empowerment Process: Integrating Theory and Practice," *Academy of Management Review*, 13, no. 3 (1988): 471.
J. P. Guilford, *Psychometric Methods* (New York: McGraw-Hill, 1954).
Jacqueline Durett, "Mentors in Short Supply," *Training*, 43, no. 7 (July 2006): 14.
James W. Walker, *Human Resource Planning* (New York: McGraw-Hill, 1980).
Janet R. Andrews, "Where Doubts About the Personnel Role Begin," *Personnel Journal* (June 1987): 84.
Jeffery J. Hallet, "Why Does Recruitment Cost So Much?" *Personnel Administration*, (December 1986): 22.
Jerald Greenberg (ed.), *Organizational Behavior: The State of the Science* (Mahwah, NJ: Lawrence Erlbaum Associates, 1994).
Jeremy Bugler, "The Invaders of Islington," *New Society*, (15 August 1968): 226.
Jerome Joseph, *Industrial Relations: Towards a Theory of Negotiated Connectedness* (London: Response, 2004).
Jim Kirkpatrick, "Transferring Learning to Behavior," *Fundamentals T+D*, 59 (April 2005): 19–20.
John E. Kelly, *Industrial Relations: Critical Perspectives on Business and Management* (London: Routledge, 2002).
John G. Belcher, Jr, *How to Design and Implement a Results-oriented Variable Pay System* (New York: AMACOM, a division of American Management Association, 1996).
John M. Moore, "The Role Relocation Plays in Management Development," *Personnel Administration* (December 1982): 31–34.
John P. Wanous, *Organizational Entry: Recruitment, Selection, and Socialization of Newcomers* (Reading, MA: Addison-Wesley, 1980).
John van Maanen, "People Processing: Strategies of Organizational Socialization," *Organizational Dynamics*, 7 (1978): 23–36.
John W. Jones, Brian D. Steffy and Douglas-Weston Bray, *Applying Psychology in Business: The Handbook for Managers and Human Resource Professionals* (Lexington, MA: Lexington Books, 1991).
Jonathan T. Scott, *The Concise Handbook of Management: A Practitioner's Approach* (New York: Haworth Press, 2005).
Joseph J. Martocchio, *Strategic Compensation*, 2nd ed. (Upper Saddle River, NJ: Prentice-Hall, 2001).
Joseph Matthews, Dorothy Matthews Berman and J. L. Matthews, *Social Security, Medicare & Government Pensions: Get the Most Out of Your Retirement and Medical Benefits* (Berkeley, CA: Nolo, 2008).
Joseph Prokopenko (ed.), *Management Development: A Guide for the Profession* (Geneva: International Labour Office, 1998).

Julia R. Galosy, "Curriculum Design for Managerial Training," *Training and Development Journal* (January 1983): 48–51.

Julia Vowler, "Away Days Promote Team Working," *Computer Weekly* (5 May 2005): 28.

K. Albrecht, *Successful Management by Objectives: An Action Manual* (Englewood Cliffs, NJ: Prentice Hall, 1978).

K. Eresi, "Personnel Practices in SSI in Bangalore City: A Survey," *SEDME*, 28, no. 2 (2001): 1–15.

K. Murphy, "Explaining Executive Compensation: Managerial Power Versus the Perceived Cost of Stock Options," *University of Chicago Law Review*, 69 (2002).

Karen Lawson, *New Employee Orientation Training* (Oxford: Elsevier, 2006).

Kathryn Tyler, "Performance Art," *HR Magazine*, 50 (August 2005): 58–63.

Kenneth M. York, David S. Strubler and Elaine M. Smith, "A Comparison of Two Methods for Scoring an In-Basket Exercise," *Public Personnel Management*, 34, no. 3 (Fall 2005): 271–80.

Kenneth N. Wexley and Gary P. Latham, *Developing and Training Human Resources in Organizations* (Glenview, IL: Scott Foresman, 1981).

Kenneth N. Wexley and Gary P. Latham, *Developing and Training Human Resources in Organizations* (Upper Saddle River, NJ: Prentice Hall, 2002).

Kevin Carlson, Mary Connerley and Ross Mecham, "Recruitment Evaluation: The Case for Assessing the Quality of Applicants Attracted," *Personnel Psychology*, 55 (2002): 466.

Kevin R. Murphy and Joseph Constans, "Behavioral Anchors as a Source of Bias in Rating," *Journal of Applied Psychology*, 72, no. 4 (November 1987): 573–77.

L. E. Davis, "The Designs of Jobs," *Industrial Relations*, 6 (1966): 21–45.

L. G. Reynolds, S. H. Masters and C. H. Moser, *Labour Economics and Labour Relations*, 9th ed. (Englewood Cliff, NJ: Prentice Hall, 1986).

L. Hough (eds.), *Handbook of Industrial and Organizational Psychology*, 2nd ed. (Palo Alto, CA: Consulting Psychologists Press, 1991).

Lee J. Cronbach, *Essentials of Psychological Testing* (New York: Harper and Row, 1960).

Leon C. Megginson, *Personnel and Human Resources Administration* (Homewood, IL: Irwin, 1982).

M. A. Campion, "Interdisciplinary Approaches to Job Design: A Constructive Replication with Extensions," *Journal of Applied Psychology*, 73, no. 3 (1988): 467–81.

M. Armstrong and A. Baron, *Performance Management: The New Realities* (London: Institute of Personnel and Development, 1998).

M. J. Duane, *Customized Human Resource Planning* (Westport: Quorum Books, 1996).

M. K. Gandhi, *From Yervada Mandir: Ashram Observances*, Translator: V. G. Desai (Ahmedabad: Navajivan Publishing House, 1957).

M. Srimannarayana, "Human Resource Management in Small Business," *Indian Journal of Industrial Relations*, 41, no. 3 (January 2006): 318–22.

M. T. Brannick and E. L. Levine, *Job Analysis: Methods, Research, and Applications for Human Resource Management in the New Millennium* (Thousand Oaks, CA: Sage Publications, 2002).

Manuel London and Arthur Wohlers, "Agreement Between Employees and Self-Rating in Upward Feedback," *Personnel Psychology*, 44, no. 2 (Summer 1991): 376.

Martha Peak, "Go Corporate U!" *Management Review*, 86, no. 2 (February 1997): 33–37.

Michael A. McDaniel, D. L. Whetzel, F. L. Schmidt and S. D. Maurer, "The Validity of Employment Interviews: A Comprehensive Review and Meta Analysis," *Journal of Applied Psychology*, 79, no. 4 (1994): 599.

Michael A. Tucker, "E-Learning Evolves," *HR Magazine*, 50 (October 2005): 74–78.

Michael Armstrong, *A Handbook of Human Resource Management Practice*, 8th ed. (London: Kogan Page Limited, 2001).

Michael Armstrong, *A Handbook of Personnel Management Practices*, 3rd ed. (London: Kogan Page, 1988).

Michael Hammer and James Champy, *Reengineering the Corporation: A Manifesto for Business Revolution* (New York: Harper Collins Publishers, 1993).

Michael J. Jucius, *Personnel Management* (Homewood, IL: Irwin Professional Publishing, 1980).

Michael Marquardt, "Harnessing the Power of Action Learning," *Training and Development*, (June 2004): 26–32.

Michael Poole, *Industrial Relations: Origins and Patterns of National Diversity* (London: Routledge, 2003).

Milton M. Blum, *Industrial Psychology and Its Social Foundations* (New York: Harper and Row, 1956).
Mohammad Abdul Mannan, *Workers' Participation in Managerial Decision-Making: A Study in a Developing Country* (New Delhi: Daya Books, 1987).
N. Perry, "Saving the Schools: How Business Can Help," *Fortune*, (7 November 1988): 42–52.
N. R. Chatterjee, *A Study of Some Problems in Indian Industry, Department of Business Management and Industrial Administration* (Delhi: University of Delhi, 1965).
Norma Chalmers, *Industrial Relations in Japan: The Peripheral Workforce* (London and New York: Routledge, 1989).
Ordway Tead and Henry Clayton Metcalf, *Personnel Administration: Its Principles and Practice* (New York: McGraw-Hill, 1920).
Orville G. Brim and Stanton Wheeler (eds.), *Socialization After Childhood* (New York, NY: Wiley, 1966).
P. C. Pant, "Interviewing: A Tool for Selection and Placement," *Indian Management*, 29, no. 7 (1990): 16–18.
P. Ward, "A 360-Degree Turn for the Better," *People Management*, (February 1995): 20–22.
Paul Michelman, "Methodology: Do You Need an Executive Coach?" *Harvard Management Update*, 9, no. 12 (December 2004).
Paul Pigors and Charles A. Myers, *Personnel Administration* (New York: McGraw-Hill, 1973).
"Performance Management: Getting It Right from the Start," *HR Magazine*, 49 (March 2004): Special Section 2–10.
Peter W. F. Davies (ed.), *Current Issues in Business Ethics* (London: Routledge, 1997).
"Plan for the Most Effective Internship Programs," *HR Focus*, 82 (September 2005): 7–11.
R. E. Walton and G. I. Susman, "People Polices for the New Machines," *Harvard Business Review*, 86 (1987): 71–83.
R. Wayne Mondy, *Human Resource Management* (Upper Saddle River, NJ: Pearson Prentice Hall, 2007).
R. Wayne Mondy, *Human Resource Management* (Upper Saddle River, NJ: Pearson Prentice Hall, 2008).
Randall S. Schuler and Ian C. Macmillan, "Gaining Competitive Advantage Through Human Resource Practices," *Human Resource Management*, 23, no. 3 (Fall 1984): 247–48.
Raymond F. Veilleux and Louis W. Petro, *Tool and Manufacturing Engineers Handbook, Vol. 5: Manufacturing Management*, 4th ed. (Dearborn, MI: Society of Manufacturing Engineers (SME), 1988).
Rensis Likert, *New Patterns of Management* (New York: McGraw-Hill, 1961).
"Report of the Labour Investigation Committee," *Main Report*, (Rege, D.V., 1946). Government of India.
"Report on the Provision of Facilities for the Promotion of Workers' Welfare," *ILO* (Nuwara Eliya: Asian Regional Conference, 1950).
David Sirota, Louis A. Mischkind and Michael Pfau, ""Report to Respondents: Survey of Views Toward Corporate Education and Training Practices"(New York: Sirota, Alper and Pfau, 1989).
"Research on Performance Appraisals Wins Award," *HR News*, 16 (July 1997): 13.
Richard B. Freeman and James L. Medoff, *What Do Unions Do?* (New York: Basic Books, 1984).
Richard C. Grinold and Kneale T. Marshall, *Manpower Planning Models* (New York: Elsevier North-Holland, 1977).
Richard D. Arvey and Robert H. Faley, *Fairness in Selecting Employees*, 2nd ed. (Reading, MA: Addison-Wesley, 1988).
Richard D. Rosenberg and Eliezer Rosenstein, "Participation and Productivity: An Empirical Study," *Industrial and Labor Relations Review*, (April 1980): 355–67.
Richard Hayman, *Industrial Relations: A Marxist Introduction* (London: Macmillan, 1975).
Richard Henderson, *Compensation Management*, 10th ed. (Upper Saddle River, NJ: Prentice Hall, 2005).
Rick Stoops, "Recruiting as a Sales Function," *Personnel Journal* (December 1982): 890.
Robert L. Mathis and John H. Jackson, *Human Resource Management*, 10th ed. (Mason: Thomson South-Western, 2004).
Robert L. Mathis and John H. Jackson, *Personnel: Contemporary Perspectives and Applications* (New York: West Publishing, 1982).
Robert T. Golembiewski, *Handbook of Organizational Consultation* (London: CRC Press, 2000).

S. E. Jackson and R. S. Schuler, "Human Resource Planning: Challenges for Industrial and Organizational Psychologist," *American Psychologist*, 45 (1990): 163.

Shaun Tyson and Alfred York, *Essentials of HRM* (Oxford and Woburn, MA: Butterworth-Heinemann, 2000).

Som Naidu, *E-Learning: A Guidebook of Principles, Procedures and Practices*, 2nd rev. ed. (New Delhi: Commonwealth Educational Media Center for Asia (CEMCA), 2006).

Stephen J. Carroll and Henry L. Tosi, *Management by Objectives* (New York: Macmillan, 1973).

Stephen L. Magnum, "Recruitment and Job Search: The Recruitment Tactics of Employees," *Personnel Administration* (June 1982): 96–102.

Sunit Arora, "How to Hire for a Fit," *Business Today*, 7–21 (January 1996): 68–70.

T. D. Wall and J. A. Lischeron, *Worker Participation: A Critique of the Literature and Some Fresh Evidence* (New York: McGraw-Hill, 1977).

Terence F. Shea, "'Sink-or-Swim' Is Not an Option," *HR Magazine*, 50 (March 2005): 14.

Terry L. Leap and Michael D. Crino, *Personnel and Human Resource Management* (New York: Maxwell Macmillan International Editions, 1990).

The Indian Institute of Personnel Management, *Personnel Management in India* (Kolkata: Asia Publishing House, 1973), 221.

Thomas A. Porterfield, *The Business of Employee Empowerment: Democracy and Ideology in the Workplace* (Westport, CT: Greenwood Publishing Group, 1999).

Thomas H. Stone, *Understanding Personnel Management* (New York: CBS College Publishing, 1989).

Toyohiro Kono and Stewart Clegg, *Transformations of Corporate Culture: Experiences of Japanese Enterprises* (New York: Walter de Gruyter, 1998).

V. V. Giri, *Labour Problems in Indian Industries* (Bombay: Asia Publishing House, 1958).

Vinayak Chaturvedi (ed.), *Mapping Subaltern Studies and the Postcolonial* (London: Verso, 2000).

Wayne F. Cascio, *Managing Human Resources: Productivity, Quality of Work Life, Profits*, 6th ed. (New Delhi: Tata McGraw-Hill, 2003).

Wayne F. Cascio and Elios M. Awad, *Human Resource Management* (Virginia: Reston Publishing House, 1981).

William B. Werther and Keith Davis, *Human Resources and Personnel Management*, 4th ed. (New York: McGraw-Hill, 1993).

Glossary

360-degree feedback In it, ratings are collected 'all around' an employee, from supervisors, subordinates, peers, and internal and external customers.

a whole person Although a person's different traits may be separately studied, they all are an integral part of one system making up a whole person, and all these traits together affect his/her behaviour.

achievement tests Achievement tests measure what the applicant can do and what task he/she can perform now.

action learning In it, an executive trainee is allowed to work full time, analysing and solving problems in other departments.

adjudication It refers to legal machinery as provided in the Industrial Disputes Act, 1947, to resolve industrial disputes.

affiliation needs These are social needs such as the need to belong and the need to be accepted by others.

agency shop In it, the workers are required to pay the fees for the collective bargaining services, though they are not the members of the union.

alternative staffing It involves meeting requirement of additional workforce through the use of non-traditional recruitment sources.

anarchist unions Such unions attempt to destroy the existing economic system and usually use violent means.

another worker A supervisor is just like a worker lacking authority and having a feeling that he/she is not part of management.

application blank It is a device commonly used by employers to gather relevant information from the applicants.

apprenticeship Apprenticeship is a process by which people become skilled workers, usually through a combination of formal learning and long-term OJT

aptitude tests Such tests measure the latent ability of a candidate to learn a given job if he/she is given required training.

arbitration It refers to the scenario when the parties involved in an industrial dispute, mutually agree to refer the disputes to an arbitrator for its settlement.

attitudinal bargaining In it, the focus shifts from the mere settlement of issues to evolving long-term bipartite relationships whereby the parties live and work together.

attribution theory It involves finding out as to what people attribute their success or failure. Their attribution may then influence their future behaviour by changing their perception of the relation between effort, performance and reward.

autocratic style Under this style of leadership, all decision-making power is centralised in the leader who gives a very nominal role, or does not allow at all, to his/her subordinates in the decision-making process.

autocratic technique In it, all rights are centred in the supervisor and his/her orders are strongly obeyed.

auxiliary functions These are supporting functions and include publication of newsletters, periodicals, magazines and so on.

averaging It involves simple averaging of forecasts made by individual experts.

balance and debt system of wages In it, a worker is paid minimum wages even if he/she produces less than the standardised output in the given time, in the expectation that he/she will make up the deficiency of work in future by doing more work.

680 Glossary

balance sheet approach This approach tries to equalise purchasing power across countries.

bargaining theory This theory states that there are always upper and lower limits and wages will be somewhere between these two limits depending on the bargaining strength of the two parties.

basic compensation It is the basic compensation that an employee receives for the work performed by him/her. It tends to reflect the value of the work and ignores differences in individual contribution. It is also known as basic pay.

basic wage Basic wage is a stable wage paid over a period of time which could be on a monthly, weekly or daily basis. This wage is the normal rate for a given level of output.

behavioural modification It is individual learning through reinforcement.

blue-collar workers' unions These unions constitute of employees usually performing operative jobs. They usually operate machines in the production and allied departments.

bluffing In it, either party or both may make dire threats with no serious thought of carrying them out.

bonus Bonus is a statutory right of workers which can be claimed by them legitimately under stated circumstances.

Boulwarism bargaining In it, the company in addition to meeting with union representatives conducts an extensive communication programme through which it tries to sell its offer directly to the union members and persuades them to make their opinions known to the union leaders.

brainstorming Brainstorming is a creative training/development technique in which participants are given the opportunity to generate ideas openly, without fear of judgement.

budgeted expense bonus Under this plan, bonus is based on the savings in actual total expenditure compared with the total budgeted expenditure. The percentage of bonus is the predetermined share of saving in budgeted expenditure.

bureaucratic or rules-centred leadership In this type of leadership, rules, regulations and procedures guide the behaviour of both the leader and his/her subordinates.

business or management games In this technique, teams of managers compete with one another by making computerised decisions regarding realistic but simulated organisations.

business unions These unions aim at securing economic interests of their members and follow the method of collective bargaining to accomplish their objectives.

career development It refer to those personal improvements that one undertakes to achieve a personal career plan.

career planning It is a deliberate process through which an employee gets aware about his/her personnel skills, interests, knowledge, motivation and other characteristics, and establishes action plans to attain specific goals.

carrot and stick approach This approach is based on the assumption that people may be motivated to put in their best efforts by either rewarding or withholding rewards or awarding punishment.

case studies Case method uses a written description of a real decision-making situation in the organisation or a situation that occurred in another organisation. Managers are asked to study the case to identify the problems for

casual applicants Casual applicants are unsolicited applicants who apply for jobs at their own.

central tendency It refers to the phenomenon when the rater marks all or almost all his/her personnel as average.

'centralised' recruitment In centralised recruiting, all the recruiting is conducted companywide from a central office.

classical approach Morale is the extent to which individual needs are satisfied and the extent to which the individual perceives that satisfaction stemming from total job satisfaction.

close supervision It refers to strict supervision with almost no freedom to employees.

closed shops In it, the employment is routed only through the union, that is, employment is conditional, subject to the membership of the trade union concerned.

cluster network In it, the individual communicates with only those individuals whom he/she trusts.

coaching Coaching involves direct personal instructions and guidance, usually with extensive demonstration and continuous critical evaluation and correction.

coaching Coaching involves teaching by example. It is a face-to-face counselling wherein the coach explains the relevance of information provided and how to generate alternatives to the problems.

Code of Conduct In order to minimise inter-union rivalry, the four central trade unions—AITUC, INTUC, UTUC and HMS—accepted on 21 May 1958 a Code of Conduct, stipulating certain conditions.

Code of Discipline (1958) The Code of Discipline lays down the criteria for trade union recognition. Normally, the union with largest membership will be recognised by the employers.

collective bargaining model In this model, the representatives of management and employees decide the terms and conditions of employment and the like.

collective bargaining It is a bipartite process in which the representatives of both the workers and the management negotiate the terms and conditions of employment.

collective bargaining It is a bipartite process in which the representatives of workers and employers negotiate employment terms and conditions and other related issues.

collective bargaining It is the method by which trade unions protect and improve the terms and conditions of their employment as well as their working lives.

collectivism In this, in-groups are local and supportive of each other. Therefore, in collectivistic cultures, people blend in, avoid conflicts and use intermediaries.

committee assignment In it, trainees are assigned to temporary committees that function as a task force to diagnose a specific problem, generate alternative solutions and recommend the best solution.

communication network Various channels or paths which connect various positions for the purpose of communication are together referred to as communication network.

communication Communication is the process through which two or more people come to exchange ideas and understanding among themselves.

compensable factors It refers to those job factors for which compensation should be paid to the job holders.

compensation of personnel Compensation function involves the payment of adequate and equitable remuneration to the employees for their contribution towards the accomplishment of the objectives of the enterprise.

competitive advantage It is defined as having a superior market position relative to competitors.

computerised forecast It involves determination of future HR needs by projecting sales, volume of production and human resources required to maintain this volume of output, using software package.

conciliation machinery, adjudication machinery, and arbitration These are the main provisions under the Industrial Disputes Act, 1947, to resolve industrial disputes.

contingent theory It states that the effectiveness of the leadership is based on the leader's ability to act in terms of situational requirements. It postulates that there are two major styles of leadership lenient or human relations approach and task-directed style.

continuous bargaining In it, both the parties—the management and the union—try to explore the problems through joint meetings over a long period of time, and try to narrow down their differences and finally reach a settlement.

controlling It involves comparing the achievements with the targets and, in the case of any drawback, taking remedial steps. It is, thus, a measuring and corrective device.

conventional philosophy of personnel management It takes a pessimistic view of human nature and believes in the pattern of close control and strict or task-oriented supervision of personnel.

cost premium plan In it, if the actual cost of production comes less than its standard cost of production, a part of the saving is distributed among the workers as their bonus.

craft unions Membership of such unions is drawn from among workers employed in a particular craft or trade or allied crafts or trades or occupations irrespective of the organisation or the industry they belong to. Such employees are craft conscious and usually professionals or non-manual employees.

cross-cultural training It refers to exposing the trainees to cultural aspects of different countries.

dearness allowance (DA) DA protects the wage earners' real income by neutralising the increased cost of living due to increase in prices.

decision-making participation It being the highest level of participation, workers get an opportunity to participate in the final decision-making process.

decision-making When a decision is made in consultation with others.

decoding It refers to converting the symbols received from the sender to give the receiver the meaning of the message.

decreasing piece rate Under this method, the rate of wages per unit goes down as the production increases.

dejobbing Dejobbing refers to broadening the responsibilities of a company's jobs and encouraging employers not to limit themselves just to what is on their job description.

Delphi techniques In order to overcome the limitations of individuals, per Delphi technique, estimates are sought from several individuals in an interactive manner, which are then revised by each individual based on the knowledge of other individuals' estimates, and in this way, a final estimate is worked.

democratic leadership It refers to involving the employees in decision-making.

democratic technique Under this technique, the advice of the workers should be taken on all important matters.

development of personnel Development programme involves workers' and supervisors' training programmes, executive development programmes, promotions and transfers, and the like, aiming at developing competencies of employees enabling them to perform their present and future jobs well.

development Development aims at longer-term development, focusing on developing the capabilities required for improving current or future performance.

directing Directing involves leading, guiding, motivating, supervising, communicating and inspiring personnel towards improved performance.

disablement benefit It is paid in cash and in instalments to the insured person on fulfilling certain conditions.

discipline Discipline is the orderly conduct by the employee in an expected manner.

disguised grievance It is when the cause of grievance is not known even to the grievant employee.

distributive bargaining It involves distribution of the pie. One party's gain is another's loss.

domination It is the result of forcible assumptions of control and authority by one person over the will and affairs of another person. It is often the result of coercion or undue influence.

double burden syndrome It refers to women struggling to balance work and family in a culture where both men and women feel that the family and household duties are primarily the women's responsibility.

downward communication It flows from top to bottom such as conveying orders, instructions and policy directives.

economic factors These primarily consist of wages and allowances, fringe benefits, bonus and so on.

economic man Economic man is one who is governed by materialistic considerations.

education Education is usually concerned with increasing general knowledge and understanding of our total environment.

electronic performance support system (EPSS) EPSS are sets of computerised tools and displays that automate training, documentation and phone support.

employee advocacy It refers to the HR responsibility for spelling out how managers should treat employees, represent employees' interests and so on.

employee compensation It is the reward that employees get for their contribution in the process of production.

employee orientation Giving primary attention to the human aspect in the organisation.

employee turnover rate It is the rate at which old employees are being replaced by new employees.

Employees' Deposit Linked Insurance Scheme, 1976 This scheme is applicable to all eligible factories/establishments with effect from August 1976. All members of the employees' provident fund scheme are required to become the members of this scheme.

Employees' Pension Scheme, 1995 The scheme provides a number of benefits to the members and their families, such as monthly member pension, disablement pension, widow/widower pension, children pension, orphan pension, disabled children/orphan pension, nominee pension, pension to dependent parents and withdrawal benefit.

Employees' Provident Fund Scheme Under this scheme, the member's and the employer's contributions along with interest are payable to the member of the scheme at the time of his retirement or leaving the service, per rules.

employment interviewing Interviewing aims at obtaining significant information about the interviewee in a face-to-face interaction.

encoding It refers to the use of certain symbols, such as words, actions or pictures, in transmitting the message.

Glossary 683

environmental engineering It refers to introducing some changes in the features of environment such as incorporating new devices and mechanisms.

equity theory This theory stated that both internal and external equities should be maintained while determining wage rates; otherwise, it will be difficult to attract and retain good employees.

equity It is concerned with felt justice according to natural law or right.

ERG theory ERG theory amalgamates Maslow's five needs into three: existence, relatedness and growth needs.

esteem needs These are esteem or egoistic needs such as status, prestige and self-respect.

esteem needs These needs refer to the want to be held in esteem both by a person and by others.

ethnocentrism It evolves sending home country executives to manage foreign subsidiaries.

executive development Executive development is a systematic process of training and growth by which individuals gain and apply knowledge, skills, insights and attitudes to manage organisation effectively.

exit interview It is conducted at the time when an employee leaves the organisation forever.

expatriates These are the citizens of the parent country (where headquarters are located) employed in foreign subsidiaries.

expert leadership In this, the leader is looked upon by the members of his/her group as an expert who is, therefore, supposed to be talented, master of his/her job and who possesses necessary skill in order to maintain his/her supremacy over other.

external equity It refers to market rates of jobs (outside the organisation) which should be reflected in the salary structure of an organisation. A compensation survey can provide the basis for external equity.

external factors These include the ideology of the ruling party, political leadership in the country, level of education of masses, and social and ethical values. Such factors are usually beyond the control of management.

extra-mural functions These are related to helping the workers financially and otherwise during the period of strike, lockout or unemployment; extending legal facilities, if required; providing welfare facilities; and so on.

extramural welfare activities Welfare activities which are undertaken outside the factory such as housing and medical are known as extramural activities.

extramural welfare activities Welfare activities which are undertaken outside the factory such as housing and medical are known as extramural activities.

factual grievance It arises when a legitimate need of the employee remains unfulfilled.

fair wage A fair wage is above the minimum wage but somewhat below the living wage, depending on the capacity to pay of the organisation.

fear/punishment/hard approach Per this approach, it is the use of force, threat, fear and tight control that makes a worker work.

financial incentives These incentives are monetary incentives given to the employees.

First Five Year Plan The duration of the First Five Year Plan was from 1 April 1951 to 31 March 1956.

followers' theory It states that leadership is developed on the basis of acceptance from followers. Leadership cannot exist without a group.

formal communication It travels through the formal channels—officially recognised positions in the organisational chart. It is usually in black and white.

formal HR policies Formal HR policies are deliberately and consciously formulated, usually by the top management, though not always.

formal leadership Formal leadership is used through command and authority.

free-rein style It is a permissive style of leadership where there is the least intervention by the leader. The group operates entirely on its own under such leadership.

free-rein technique In it, the supervisor gives complete freedom to workers to work and after seeing their abilities develops them.

friendly or uplift unions These unions mainly aim at improving the intellectual, moral and social life of their members. They believe in the institution of collective bargaining.

fringe benefits The benefits provided to the workforce apart from the negotiated wages are nowadays termed as either fringe benefits or supplementary benefits or non-wage benefits. These benefits reduce the gap between the nominal wages and the real wages of the workers.

fringe benefits The benefits provided to the workforce apart from the negotiated wages are nowadays termed as either fringe benefits or supplementary benefits or non-wage benefits. These benefits reduce the gap between the nominal wages and the real wages of the workers.

functional job analysis (FJA) After getting the description from DOT, the job analyst uses the FJA to elaborate and describe exhaustively the contents of a job in a common language.

functional theory It says that leadership acts are those which help a group to attain its goals and satisfy its needs.

functional/staff authority It empowers the HR manager to advise other managers or employees in the organisation.

gaming Gaming involves two or more teams. Each team is given a firm to operate for a number of periods. Each team makes decisions on various matters, and the result of one team affects all other teams as the same are competitive of each other. Decisions of all the firms are fed into a computer, and the team scoring the largest profit is declared the winner.

Gantt task and bonus plan In this plan, if a worker's output in a task time is equal to or more than the stipulated task, then he/she is paid a bonus at a certain percentage of guaranteed basic wage. The guaranteed basic wage is always a time rate wage.

gap sheet It indicates the areas where the employee lacks and needs training to enable him/her to do a new job well in future.

geocentricism Geocentricism involves searching candidates globally for managerial positions for both headquarters and foreign subsidiaries.

global corporations A GC maintains control over its global operations through a centralised home office. It is the expertise of an employee in his/her particular area that matters most for a GC instead of his/her national affiliation. Its employees are often moved across national boundaries to meet the current needs of the organisation.

global factors These may include the IR policy of MNCs and transnational companies in a country.

global market approach It provides certain core components to all managers, no matter in which country they are posted. Many companies pay lump sum allowances directly to the relocating employees to take care of their relocation expenses.

globalisation In it, the whole world becomes like a village market with no restrictions on the production and marketing of goods and services.

goal-setting theory Since motivation is goal-directed behaviour, goals that are clear and challenging will result in higher levels of employee motivation than goals that are ambiguous and easy.

gossip network In it, the individual communicates non-selectively.

grapevine It is a sort of rumour which is usually not dependable.

grievance committee It is a bipartite body comprising representatives of both workers and management in equal number.

grievance A feeling by an individual that some injustice has been done to him/her.

grievance Grievance is a state where an employee feels that some injustice has been done to him/her.

grievance It is a complaint lodged when the employee feels that some injustice has been done to him/her or management is not fair to him/her. It is with regard to employment conditions.

grievance It is any dissatisfaction or feeling of injustice in connection with one's employment situation that is brought to the notice of the management or union steward.

group/collective bonus plans Such plans which are useful when individual workers' output cannot be easily measured aim at ensuring higher productivity and more production and creating a sense of mutual cooperation.

group-based techniques In it, the management fosters group consciousness and cohesiveness among individual employees by laying down general norms and guidelines of work for the group as a whole.

groups In the organisations, individuals tend to create groups which determine their norms and behaviour.

guerrilla unions Guerrilla unions can go to any extent, including resorting to terrorism and other violent means, to accomplish their objectives. It is the boss who rules the roost.

haggling bargaining It may be either piecemeal approach or total approach.

halo effect Halo effect exists where the rater is influenced by the ratee's one or two outstanding good (or bad) performance, and he/she evaluates the entire performance accordingly.

Halsey-Weir plan Per this plan, a worker gets 30% of the time saved, that is, standard hours minus actual hours. Besides, a minimum wage is guaranteed under this plan.

Glossary 685

Hawthorne experiments Hawthorne experiments were conducted by Elton Mayo, Roethlisberger and their associates at the Hawthorne Plant of the Western Electric Company between 1927 and 1932.

Hawthorne experiments These experiments were conducted at Hawthorne Plant of the Western Electric Company between 1917 and 1932.

headship It implies a formal power. It is not necessary that a head has personal influence on the minds of the followers, while a leader gains influence over them by his/her qualities of head and heart. A true leader is always an ideal example for his/her followers, while a head may not be so.

Herzberg's two-factor theory According to this theory, awards have two aspects: (a) hygiene factors, whose absence creates dissatisfaction, and (b) motivation factors, which induce the employees to put in their best efforts. Hence, while determining wages, the role of the aforesaid factors should also be kept into view.

Herzberg's two-factor theory It states that if appropriate hygiene factors (such as working conditions, security, salary and company policies) are provided, then employees will not be dissatisfied with their jobs, but neither will they be motivated to perform at their full potential. Hence, the employees should be provided with some motivators (such as work itself, recognition, achievement, opportunity for advancement and responsibility).

hold-up unions In such unions, the unscrupulous bosses of workers' organisations and unscrupulous employers conspire together to exploit the customers by selling their products at very high rates; the major chunk of the money so earned goes to the pockets of these unscrupulous elements, leaving very little, if at all, for the workers.

home country/parent country nationals (PCNs) When the citizens of the country in which the MNC has its headquarters are employed in a foreign subsidiary, they are known as PCNs.

horizontal communication It takes place between two or more people at hierarchical level of organisation.

horizontal fit An SHRP should be in alignment with other functional areas' plans (horizontally).

host country nationals (HCNs) HCNs are the people who are the citizens of the country where the overseas subsidiary is located.

hot stove rule It implies warning system, immediate burn, consistency and impersonality.

HR policy An HR policy indicates the line of action or the attitude the management is likely to adopt in future towards its personnel and their problems.

HR strategies HR strategies refer to the specific HR courses of action the company plans to pursue to achieve its aims.

human capital Human capital is the sum total of an employee's skills, knowledge and competencies which an organisation uses to further its goals.

human relations approach It aims at maintaining good human relations between the worker and the supervisor, enabling the worker to improve himself/herself, probing the problem and solving it appropriately.

human relations approach It implies that the relationship between the employee and the employer should be as between two human beings because an employee is a human being first who needs freedom of expression, respect for his/her personality and sentiments, and so on.

human relations specialist A supervisor is considered to be a human relations specialist looking after the human side of operations.

human relations These are at personal level between two or more individuals in an organisation.

human relations These signify the relationship that should exist between the human beings engaged in industry.

human resource development (HRD) HRD aims at developing competencies which help in meeting out the requirements of not only a person's current job but also of the job(s) that he/she is likely to undertake in not-so-distant future.

human resource management (HRM) HRM is the planning, organising, directing and controlling of the procurement, development, compensation, integration, maintenance and separation of human resources to the end that individual, organisational and social objectives are accomplished.

human resource management (HRM) HRM is the planning, organising, directing and controlling of procurement, development, compensation, integration and maintenance of human resources for an organisation.

human resource planning (HRP) HRP is the process to ensure that the organisation has the right amount and the right kind of people to deliver a particular level of output or services in future.

human resource planning (HRP) It involves making the future plans for manpower, visualising the number and kind of personnel required at different times, determining the possible source of supply of the required manpower, preparing training and development plans, and working out programmes for effective use of the human resources.

hygiene/maintenance factors These are external to job and located in work environment. If these factors are provided to employees, then they will not be dissatisfied with their jobs, but neither they will be motivated.

illusive concept It refers to a false concept.

in-basket In it, a trainee is given material (e.g. a file) containing information on the company and its related issues to make a series of decisions within a fixed time. The trainee is given feedback on the quality of decision taken, the manner in which items were prioritised and how well the time was utilised.

incentive An incentive is a stimulus for doing more work.

incentive/bonus (premium) scheme It is a system of wage payment which induces a worker to produce more and known as incentive system. However, the worker is assured of a guaranteed-minimum wages.

incident method In the incident method of giving all the details of case, only bare outlines of a problem are put forth initially and the participants are given a role in which to view the incident. In case any additional relevant information is sought, it is provided. Initially, each participant solves the case, followed by formation of groups based on similarity of solutions. Each group so formed is expected to formulate a strong statement of position. Then groups debate their solutions, followed by comparison of their solutions with the results.

increasing piece rate Per this method, as the production increases, the per-unit rate also increases.

indiscipline It involves violation of rules, regulations, procedures and so on.

individualism This dimension focuses on the relationship between the individual and the group. It emphasises 'I'.

induction/orientation Induction/orientation is a short-term programme to equip the new hire with the information he/she needs to settle down quickly and happily and start his/her work confidently.

indulgence vs restraint This dimension is essentially a measure of happiness, that is, whether or not simple joys are fulfilled.

industrial relations (IR) IR denote the collective relationship between the management, employees and government. These are the complex of interrelations among employers (or their associations), workers (or their associations) and government.

industrial relations These are collective relations, that is, between two groups—workers on the one side and management on the other side.

industrial sociology approach It assumes that a conflict is the basic concept that should form the basis of the study of IR. The crux of IR is the nature and development of conflict.

industrial unions Membership in such unions is open to all types of workers engaged in any one industry or a group of industries or service, that is, on an industry-wise basis.

industrialisation Industrialisation refers to emergence, intensification and expansion of large-scale industries.

industry-based wage variation It refers to wage rates varying from industry to industry.

industry-level agreement An industry-level collective bargaining agreement is finalised at the industry level and is applicable to the organisations belonging to that industry only.

informal communication It is free from all sorts of formalities because it is based on the informal relationship between the parties.

informal HR policies Such policies are just grown. Hence, their framing or establishment cannot be analysed.

informal leadership Leadership is acquired through personal traits and courage.

integration It involves integration of individual and organisation goals.

integrative bargaining It involves mutual negotiations which result in benefiting both the parties such as increasing productivity, reducing cost of production and increasing profitability of the organisation. Consequently, employers are in a better position to compensate workers adequately.

integrity It refers to honesty.

intelligence tests Such tests are conducted to measure the general level of intelligence of the applicant through the measurement of his/her IQ.

interactionist approach This theory lays emphasis on the quality of the leader–subordinate relationship which determines productivity, morale and other goals.

interest tests Such tests identify a certain field of interest and also the kind of work that will satisfy the employee.

internal equity It refers to salary relativities between jobs within the organisation depending on the values attached to different jobs. Job evaluation can be used as a tool for ensuring internal equity.

internal factors These factors are manageable and include ineffective leadership, unfair practices, favouritism, biasness, defective supervision and so on.

internal factors These may consist of the IR policy of the organisation, WPM, profit-sharing, labour co-partnership, trade unions and their leadership and approach, work culture, working environment, wage policy, fringe benefits, mutual trust between labour and management, workforce diversity, grievance-handling procedure, discipline and opportunities for growth for employees.

internal or intrinsic motivation It is caused through appreciation, recognition, better status, more authority and the like.

international corporations These companies build on their existing capabilities to penetrate overseas markets and adopt their products to overseas markets without making changes in their normal operations.

international human resource management (IHRM) IHRM refers to the HRM issues and problems arising from the internationalisation of business and the HRM strategies, policies and practices which firms pursue in response to the internationalisation process.

intra-mural functions These functions are usually undertaken within the four walls of the factory and are related to increase in wages, allowances, fringe benefits, improvement in working conditions and so on.

intramural welfare activities Welfare activities which are undertaken within the premises of the factory, such as health, welfare and safety measures, healthy working conditions and canteen, are known as intramural activities.

intramural welfare activities Welfare activities which are undertaken within the premises of the factory, such as health, welfare and safety measures, healthy working conditions and canteen, are known as intramural activities.

intra-organisational bargaining Both the employers' and unions' officials discuss the demands and arrive at a consensus of approach before they meet at the bargaining table.

JMCs Model In this model, JMCs have representatives of both the groups and are usually advisory and consultative bodies.

job analysis It is a process of deterring the duties and skill requirements of a job and the kind of person who should be hired for it.

job analysis It is a process of obtaining information and facts about the job.

job analysis Job analysis is a systematic process of collecting information about the job—its duties, responsibilities, relationship with other jobs and so on.

job characteristics theory It states that employees will be more motivated to work and more satisfied with their jobs to the extent that jobs contain certain core characteristics—skill variety, autonomy, task identity, task significance, feedback, experienced meaningfulness, experienced responsibility and knowledge results.

job description A job description is a written statement of what the worker actually does, how he does it, what the working conditions are and so on. It represents a written summary of the job as an identifiable organisational unit.

job description It is mainly a statement of duties, responsibilities and other relevant details of the job.

job design Job design is the process of organising work into tasks required to perform a specific job.

job enlargement It is adding to a job more responsibilities of a horizontal nature, requiring almost the same skills and expertise as are held by the incumbent of the present job. It is just the process of expanding a job's duties.

job enlargement It refers to assigning employees additional same-level activities, thus increasing the number of activities they perform.

job enrichment It involves vertical loading of a job like making it more challenging.

688 Glossary

job evaluation Job evaluation establishes the relative value of jobs based on their contents, independent of link to the market.

job families Job families cover the idea of groupings of small jobs.

job instruction training (JIT) In this method, the trainers first train the supervisors who, in turn, train the employees.

job loading It can be horizontal job loading or vertical job loading.

job posting Publicising an open job (including its attributes such as its pay rate, working conditions and eligibility conditions) to the employees of the organisation concerned.

job pricing Job pricing is attaching a price tag to each job and creating a wage structure that equitably relates jobs to their calculated values.

job rotation In this system, the trainee is rotated periodically from one job to another.

job rotation It is shifting the employee from one job to another so as to broaden his/her organisational awareness.

job specification A written explanation of the knowledge, skills, abilities, traits and other characteristics (KSAOs) necessary for effective performance on a given job.

job specification It is a statement of human qualities needed for the job.

job specifications A job specification spells out what human traits and experiences are required to do a particular job well.

job A job is a collection or aggregation of tasks, duties and responsibilities that as a whole is regarded as the reasonable assignment to an individual employee.

joint council Per the New Scheme of Workers' Participation in Industry, there shall be only one joint council in an organisation, and it shall function for a period of two years. The decision made by the council shall be on the basis of consensus and not by a process of voting, and the same shall be implemented within one month unless otherwise stated in the decision itself.

key man A supervisor is a key man in the management as he/she makes decisions, controls work and interprets the policy of the management to the workers.

labour grades Labour grades are established, each grade representing a range of point values, with one wage rate or range for the entire grade.

labour turnover It refers to the movement into and out of an organisation by the workforce.

labour unions Membership is open to all workers, irrespective of their occupation, skill or industry.

labour welfare Any activity of management that leads to economic, physical, social or educational betterment of employees.

labour welfare Labour welfare is anything done for intellectual, physical, moral and economic betterment of the workers, whether by employers, government or agencies over and above which is laid down by law or what is normally expected on the past of contractual benefits for which the workers may have bargained.

labour welfare Labour welfare is anything done for intellectual, physical, moral and economic betterment of the workers whether by employers, government or agencies over and above which is laid down by law or what is normally expected on the past of contractual benefits for which the workers may have bargained.

laissez-faire policy It refers to non-interference and maintaining an indifferent attitude.

laissez-faire It involves giving complete freedom to all with no interference from the superiors.

lay-off It is a state wherein employment is not offered to a worker temporarily due to certain reasons which are beyond the control of the employer. However, the worker is entitled to a certain quantum of wages per rules.

lay-off Lay-off refers to a situation where an employer, for a reason beyond his/her control, is unable to offer employment temporarily.

lay-off/retrenchment compensation Under the Industrial Disputes Act, 1947, a worker who is laid off or retrenched is entitled to payment, per rules.

leadership It is the knack of getting people to follow you and to do willingly the things that you want them to do. It is essentially informal in nature and is generated from within the group. Acceptance of leadership by the group is voluntary.

learning zone In this zone, an individual takes his/her own time to familiarise himself/herself with skills, knowledge, attitude and so on needed to become fully conversant and competent for the job.

liberalisation It involves freedom from inspector raj.

Likert's System I through System IV Likert envisaged four basic styles—System I, exploitative autocratic; System II, benevolent autocratic; System III, consultative leadership; and System IV, participative group leadership.

line authority The authority which an HR manager exerts in his/her own department and also in service areas (e.g. organisation's library).

line functions Line functions are those which have direct responsibility for accomplishing the objectives of the enterprise.

living wage It represents the highest level of wages including all amenities which a citizen living in the modern civilised society is entitled to and expects when the economy of the country is sufficiently advanced, and the employer is able to meet the expanding aspirations of his/her workers.

lockouts It refers to not allowing the workers to work by the employer usually due to workers' unreasonable demands.

long-term orientation vs short-term orientation This dimension generally refers to the extent to which cultures think in terms of the future (the long run) or in terms of more immediate events (the short term).

maintenance of personnel Maintenance refers to sustaining and improving the conditions that have already been established.

management by objectives (MBO) In an MBO programme, there is a special provision for mutual goal setting and appraisal of progress by both the appraiser and the appraise(s).

management position description questionnaire (MPDQ) MPDQ, which is a checklist of 2008 items related to the concerns and responsibilities of managers, is designed to be a comprehensive description of managerial work.

managerial functions These include planning, organising, staffing, directing and controlling.

managerial grid Managerial grid is based on the styles of 'concern for people' (employee-oriented) and 'concern for production' (production-oriented or task-oriented).

manipulative leadership In this style, the leader manipulates his/her subordinates in such a way as may lead to his/her achievement of desired goals. It usually exploits the ambitions and aspirations of the employees.

Manning table It clearly indicates the number of employees in each category and each employee's personal inventory, having full details about each employee.

marginal man According to this sociological concept, a supervisor is either left out of main activities and influences affecting his/her department or he/she is just on the margin of such activities.

marginal productivity theory Per this theory, any industry would go on employing additional labour until the marginal productivity becomes equal to marginal cost.

masculinity vs femininity Per this dimension, masculine societies give preference to achievement, heroism, assertiveness and material rewards for success.

Maslow's hierarchy of needs Maslow classified needs into five categories and arranged them into a hierarchical order and said that first a person would try to satisfy his/her lower-order needs (physiological needs) and then his/her safety and security, social, esteem and self-actualisation needs.

MBO techniques It is a participatory technique whereby managers and subordinates jointly decide targets and evaluate the achievements so as to accomplish common goals.

mentor A mentor is a senior person who facilitates a junior person's career enhancement by a range of activities such as coaching, exposure, visibility and protection.

mentoring In it, a senior person acts as a guide, teacher, counsellor, developer of skills and so on and helps the mentee in realising his/her vision and getting him/her integrated with the organisation.

Merrick multiple piece rate plan In this plan, there are three-piece rates and the lowest piece rate is equal to the ordinary piece rate, which becomes the base piece rate.

middleman In the context of supervisor, a middleman means a link between the management and the employees.

migratory labour Those workers who do not stick to the industrial towns where they work and keep on moving from their place of work to their native villages/towns.

minimum wage It refers to that minimum amount which the labour department thinks necessary not only for the bare sustenance of life but also for the preservation of the efficiency of the worker.

Glossary

misconduct It involves violation of rules, norms, regulations, terms and conditions of employment contract, or any act which has a material bearing on the smooth and efficient working of the organisation concerned.

modern philosophy of personnel management It propagates that the constructive forces in people can be better realised through a participative or democratic attitude underlying management's personnel programmes.

modern theories of wages Modern theories assume that, on the one hand, wages are governed by the laws of demand and supply and, on the other hand, various external factors and constraints such as the institutions of trade unions and collective bargaining also affect the determination of wages.

morale Morale is the attitude of individuals and groups towards work environment and towards voluntary cooperation to the full extent of their ability in the best interest of the organisation.

morale Morale is the level of confidence of an individual or a group.

morale Morale is the level of confidence reflected by an employee.

motivation Motivation is that which energises, directs and sustains human behaviour.

motivational approach This approach focuses on satisfying employees' needs, and it is best illustrated by Herzberg's two-factor theory of work motivation. Employees feel motivated by jobs that increase their feelings of job worth. Hence, job design should result in increasing the worth of the job.

motivators/motivational factors These are internal job factors that lead to job satisfaction and higher motivation and consequently to higher output.

MP3/instant messaging In it, an Internet audiobook provider creates an audio learning site within the organisation's firewall. The employees use it to download training materials to their iPods.

multinational corporations (MNCs) Each separate enterprise overseas (of an MNC) is responsible for adapting the company's products to the local culture, but most vital control remains either with the company's home offices or in the hands of an expatriate from the home country.

multiple management Multiple management refers to the use of committees.

multiple management The trainee is assigned to an ad hoc committee functioning as a task force to diagnose a specific problem, generate alternative solution and recommend the best solution.

'my boat' attitude It has little or no concern for the workers.

national-level agreement National-level agreements are generally bipartite and finalised at the conference of labour and management covered by the central government.

negative motivation It is due to fear, use of force, reprimands, punishment, loss of job and so on.

negative/progressive discipline approach Through awarding punishment to discipline violators, it works as a deterrent to other employees.

nominal (money) wages Nominal or money wage refers to the monetary form of wage payment.

nominal group technique (NGT) In it, individual generation of estimates is followed by a group brainstorming session in the hope of generating one group decision that is preferred over any of the group decisions.

nominal wages The nominal wages are the wages which are paid in the form of money and are, therefore, also called money wages.

non-financial incentives These incentives provide psychological and emotional satisfaction and prompt employees to do more work.

non-financial motivation It is usually concerned with psychic rewards.

obsolescence Obsolescence may be due to age, temperament, lack of motivation, inability to adapt to changed technology and so on.

occupation An occupation is a group of jobs that are similar as to the kind of work and are found throughout an industry or the entire country.

on-demand recruiting services (ODRS) It refers to agencies providing short-term specialised recruiting to support specific requirement/projects without the expense of retaining traditional search firms.

on-the-job experience In it, interactions with fellow professionals and observations on the job help a trainee to learn the tricks of the job.

open shop In it, an employee is not required to be a union member before or after employment.

open-door policy In it, a grievant employee is allowed to directly approach the head of the organisation or the designated officer for the purpose, and present his/her grievance for solution.

operative functions Operative functions are the specialised functions related to a particular functional area.

oral communication In it, both parties to the process of communication exchange their ideas through oral words either in face-to-face communication or through any mechanical devices, such as the telephone.

organisation chart (OC) OC presents the relationship among several departments and units of the organisation and spells out line and staff functions.

organising It involves the establishment of an organisation structure through determination and grouping activities, the assignment of activities to the specified individuals and departments, defining their role, establishing relationships, the delegation of authority to carry out the responsibilities and provision of coordination of men and work.

'our boat' attitude It shows equal concern for the workers.

outsourcing/offshoring It involves having local employees abroad do jobs that the firm's domestic employees provisionally did in-house.

Oxford approach This approach states that rules governing IR are the functions of collective bargaining.

paired comparison technique In this technique, each job is compared with every other job, one at a time, and thus ranked in order of their merit, and wage rates are fixed accordingly.

participative style In this type of leadership style, leadership allows the active participation of the subordinates in the process of decision-making.

participative/democratic management In it, employees are associated in the decision-making process.

path–goal approach This approach assumes that people work harder when they perceive that hard work is a path towards the goal they seek for.

path–goal theory It states that a leader's behaviour can motivate and satisfy his/her subordinates to an extent which may promote the attainment of the subordinates' goals and make the path easier for attaining these goals.

Pay Commission It is constituted by the central government to recommend the pay rates and allowances of central government employees. Many other agencies follow these rates in full and a few partially only.

Payment of Gratuity Act, 1972 Per the act, all the employees (including managers and supervisors) engaged in the eligible establishments are legally entitled to gratuity at the rate of 15 days wages multiplied by number of completed years of service, subject to fulfilment of certain conditions laid down under the act.

peer appraisal It means the appraisal of an employee by his/her peers.

people-oriented supervision In it, the primary attention is given to the human aspect, and effort is made to build an effective work group with high performance goals.

perceptual motor approach and biological approach These two approaches stress on the integration of human–machine systems and suggest that equipment design should be as suits the operators.

performance appraisal Performance appraisal is a systematic, a periodic and, as far as humanly possible, an impartial rating of an employee's excellence in

person in the middle A supervisor is a person in the middle as he/she works between two forces the management and the workers.

personal factors These refer to typical features of an individual worker, such as aggressiveness, negativity and irritating temperament.

personality tests Personality tests measure the basic make-up or characteristics of an individual.

Philips hi-low matrix In it, a two-by-two matrix is used to elevate performance and potential in a single process.

Philips NV Holland model This model includes a five-point scale, ranging from excellent to inefficient, and provides for evaluation of employees on a few qualities—conceptual effectiveness, operational effectiveness, personal effectiveness, interpersonal effectiveness and achievement motivation.

physiological needs These are basic needs which must be satisfied to survive.

physiological needs These are the basic needs necessary for sustaining human life.

piece rate method Under this system, wages are paid based on the of quantum of output of a worker. The worker is paid at fixed rate per unit of output.

placement Placement is the determination of the job to which the accepted candidate is to be assigned as also the supervisor under whom he/she will work as well as location where he/she is to work.

planning It is a deliberate and conscious effort, well in advance, to utilise the resources to achieve given ends following a set procedure.

plant-level agreement These agreements are concerned with and implemented at the plant level only.

pluralist perspective This perspective assumes that since an organisation comprises varied groups such as employers, employees, shareholders, consumers and government, each group having its own objectives and interests, conflicts are inherent in an organisation.

policy A policy is a rule or a predetermined course of action established to guide an organisation towards its objectives.

political factors These may include ideology of the ruling party, labour policy of the government, labour legislation, political stability and so on.

political functions These functions include contesting elections, capturing political power and so on.

polycentrism Appointing people from host country (i.e. where the foreign subsidiary is located) is known as polycentrism.

position analysis questionnaire (PAQ) A PAQ contains 195 items, placed in six major sections, to be filled by a trained job analyst and to be followed by getting PAQ rating scores (with the help of computerised programmes), which enable the development of profiles and the comparison of jobs.

position rotation Position or job rotation involves moving a trainee from department to department to broaden his/her experience and identify strong and weak points.

position A position consists of responsibilities and duties performed by an individual.

positive bargaining/strategy It means introducing serious proposals for change.

positive discipline approach It encourages self-discipline, team spirit, reformation, involving and engaging workers, consulting workers and the like so as to prompt workers to behave in the desired fashion.

positive incentives These are incentives which induce a worker to work more.

positive motivation Motivation by offering the possibility of rewards, promotions, higher pay, praise and so on.

power distance This dimension focuses on the nature of human relationship in terms of hierarchy.

power theory It states that the power attached with a particular office motivates the aspirants to put in their best so that they may be able to realise their objectives.

praise theory Employees perform better if they are appreciated for their good work.

preferential union shop Per this system, an employee who is a union member is given first preference at the time of recruitment.

premature evaluation It refers to the tendency of prematurely evaluating communications rather than keeping an uncompromised position during the interchange.

premium or bonus plan Such a plan is a unification of time rate and piece rate systems and aims at providing suitable monetary incentives to both employers and employees of the time saved by the worker in completing his/her task.

premium zone In this zone, those who do not get opportunities for promotion despite the competence and good performance are encouraged by rewarding them approximately.

Priestman's production bonus plan In this plan, the bonus will be payable to that department which gives results higher than the standard output set jointly by a committee representing the management and the workers' union, well in advance every week or every month.

principle of adequacy It states that information being sent should be adequate and complete in all respects.

principle of integration Communication should be geared towards achieving a genuine spirit of cooperativeness among the organisational personnel so that they may put their potentialities in the attainment of enterprise goals.

principle of natural justice It involves providing an opportunity to the accused to defend his/her case.

privatisation In it, the means of production are owned and controlled by individuals.

probability network In it, the individual communicates randomly with other individuals according to the law of probability.

problem children The employees who have low grading in both performance and potential.

process chart A process chart spells out how a specific set of jobs is related to another.

procurement of personnel It is concerned with obtaining proper kind and right number of personnel at the right time and at the most economical rates so that the organisational goals could be easily accomplished.

production or job-oriented super-vision This is concerned with the performance of assigned tasks at prescribed rates, using standard methods, conditions and times.

productivity It is the ratio of output to input.

productivity It is the ratio of output to input.

productivity It is the ratio of output to input.

productivity Productivity is the ratio of output to input.

productivity Productivity is the ratio of output to input.

productivity Ratio of output to input.

profit-sharing plan Such a plan provides for sharing of the profits of the enterprise with the workers in a predetermined ratio.

promotion Promotion means the change to a higher job accompanied by higher responsibilities, higher status and increased pay.

promotion Promotion refers to advancement to positions of increased responsibilities, higher pay and better status.

proportioning rewards Rewards in proportion to efforts made.

psychological approach Morale is a state of mind and emotions affecting willingness to work which in turn affects individual and organisational objectives.

psychological factors These are emotional factors which may also prove barrier to communication.

psychological factors These may comprise management's attitude towards workers and their unions, and workers and their unions' attitude towards management, their fellow workers, working environment and so on.

psychometric tests Such tests try to capture the abilities of the employee on several fronts such as aptitude, logic, deduction and inference.

purchasing power theory According to this theory, if the rates of wages are high, it will increase the purchasing of workers, which will increase aggregate demand for goods and services, which, in turn, will increase the level of output, and thus, the demand of labour will also go up, and so will be the case with the wage rates, which will further go up.

qualified zone In this zone, an individual having passed through the learning zone makes efforts to increase his/her capacity so as to improve his/her performance and efficiency.

ratio analysis It determines future manpower requirement by using ratios between some causal factors and number of employees required.

real wages Real wage represents the actual exchange value of money wage.

realistic job previews (RJP) RJP refers to providing the prospective employee with realistic full picture of the job including its positive and negative features.

reciprocal relationship It is a mutual relationship based on the reciprocity of the leaders and the led.

recognised trade union Such a union becomes the representative union and becomes the sole bargaining agent.

recognition Recognition refers to acknowledging and appreciating the contribution of an employee.

recorded want ads In recorded want ads, job seekers are enabled to pick up a telephone and hear a short-recorded recruitment message containing job description, job specification and details of how to contact the organisation.

recruitment Recruitment is the process of searching for prospective employees and stimulating them to apply for jobs in the organisation.

red circle rates When some current rates generally show up as distinctly out of line, such 'over' rates are red-circled and are temporarily regarded as personal rates, to be protected as long as present employees remain in these jobs and are eliminated as soon as the employees concerned leave their jobs.

Reddin's 3-D theory This theory places styles and situations into a grid format. According to this theory, there are four acceptable styles of leadership, the suitability of each of which will depend on situation, yet most higher-level managers use the 'executive' style, though effectiveness of the style depends upon the leader, the followers and other situational variables.

reformist unions These unions may be either business unions or revolutionary unions.

regional wage variation It means when wage rates differ from region to region.

regression analysis It is a mathematical procedure that predicts the dependable variable based on the factors known as independent variables.

repatriation It involves calling an expatriate back home after the completion of the international assignment.

retrenchment It refers to termination of service for any reason whatsoever but does not include voluntary retirement on reaching the age of superannuation, dismissal inflicted by way of disciplinary action or termination of service as a result of non-renewal of contract of employment or on ground of ill-health.

review appraisal Conducted by the immediate supervisors/departmental heads. Such tests provide insight into the potential of the employee.

revolutionary unions These unions are opposed to the capitalistic industry and replace it by the socialistic systems through radical means such as strikes, boycott and gheraos.

rewards, soft, or weak approach This approach is based on the assumption that the personnel in an undertaking are motivated to work to the extent to which they are rewarded.

role-play Role-playing is spontaneous acting of a realistic situation involving two or more people under classroom situations.

role-playing In this technique, trainees act out the part of people in a realistic management situation.

Rowan plan It is a variable bonus sharing plan, and the proportion of the bonus a worker earns varies if the time saved by the worker varies.

safety needs These needs concern with the physical and financial security.

salary progression curves These curves are usually meant for professional, scientific or other highly qualified personnel linking increases in their salary over a considerable long time to their increased maturity, expertise and experience.

salary progression systems These refer to increases in salary in relation to merit or performance. In it, salary ranges are divided into defined zones through which an employee passes through while he/she progresses.

scatter plot It is a graphical method which is used to identify the relationships between two variables.

scientific and mechanistic approach This approach suggests a job structure according to which the job should be broken down into simple repetitive tasks to improve the efficiency of the workers.

Second World War It was fought from 1939 to 1942.

security needs These needs refer to the security of job, property, food, shelter, physical protection and so on.

selection Selection is the process of dividing the candidates into two groups—those who are selected and those rejected.

selective reading It facilitates the executives to avail selected literature through either the libraries of the organisation or free time to read assigned books or allowances for purchase of relevant books, periodicals and so on.

self-actualisation needs These needs are related to the desire to become what one is capable of becoming.

self-assessment In it the manager assesses his/her performance and work behaviour himself/herself. It should be taken as complimentary to the appraisal done by the superiors.

self-rating It means appraisal by the employee himself/herself.

self-realisation needs These are the individual's needs for realising his/her own potentialities and opportunities for creativity and for continual development of his/her skills and powers.

sensitivity training It is a technique used for increasing trainees' insights by candid discussions in groups led by special trainers.

sensitivity training Sensitivity training is imparted to make the managers understand themselves better, becoming more open-minded, developing insight into group process and cultivating a systematic approach towards the problem of motivation.

'shared boat' attitude It reflects some concern for the workers.

shop council Per the New Scheme of Workers' Participation in Industry, there should be a shop council for each department or shop or one shop council for more than one department or shop depending on the number of workers employed in different shops or departments.

Glossary 695

simulation models Such models are probabilities of future events to estimate future employment level based on certain assumptions.

simulation In the simulation method, instead of taking participants into the field, the field is simulated in the training session itself. It is, therefore, the presentation of a real situation of the organisation in the training session.

single-strand network In it, the individual communicates with other individuals through intervening people.

sit-in strike In it, workers report for duty but usually do not work and keep sitting on their duty place.

situation tests Situation tests measure the applicant's reaction when he/she is placed in a peculiar situation.

situational theory It states that there are circumstances/situation(s) of a group which produce a leader.

skill inventory It usually contains full information about each employee such as personal details, educational and training achievements, experience, and skills.

social approach Morale is a social process. According to this approach, morale is the capacity of a group of people to pull together persistently and consistently in pursuit of a common purpose.

social assistance It is a purely government affair and, therefore, financed exclusively by the government and benefits are granted on fulfilling prescribed conditions, though benefits are claimed as a matter of right.

social factors An organisation is a social system and people are socio-psychological beings. Their characteristics determine the output and efficiency of an organisation. These factors may include level of enlightenment, level of education, culture, attitudes, beliefs, customs, rituals, traditions and so on of the people at large.

social insurance It aims at the maintenance of minimum standard of living of the employee during the period of contingency of life.

social needs These needs refer to the needs of the love and social security.

social security It is the security that the society (all the agencies concerned) provides to a worker to enable him to sustain himself and his family in case he falls victim to any contingency of life.

socialisation Socialisation is a long-term process as compared to induction, which enables the new hires to acclimatise themselves to the new organisation, under its culture, and know what is expected of them by the organisation.

socio-psychological approach This approach emphasises the facts that a person is diversely motivated and socio-psychological factors lay a more important role in his/her motivation.

staff functions Staff functions are those that help the line people in accomplishing the organisational objectives, and are advisory in nature.

staff shoe Per this approach, either or both parties may play it cool. They may evaluate the situation as one in which tempers need to be soothed rather than aroused.

staffing Staffing is a process of manning the organisation and keeping it manned

standardised scales These establish group norms on the scales and ensure the reliability and validity of the measuring instruments.

stars Those employees who are very good in both performance and potential.

status relationships It refers to the hierarchical placement of people in superior–subordinate capacity in the formal organisational structure which also obstructs the flow of communication, especially in the upward direction.

statutory obligations Obligations which have to be discharged because of legal requirements.

statutory welfare Welfare activities undertaken because of legal compulsions are known as statutory welfare work.

stepladder procedure In it, a grievance is presented to the first-line supervisor and then to other authorised officers/bodies step by step, if the grievance is not resolved at the previous step.

stock options Stock options are offered to employees in the form of company stock with the objective of attracting, motivating and retaining them.

straight piece rate system with minimum wages In this system, a worker is paid minimum wages even if he/she produces less than the standardised output in a given time; otherwise, he/she is paid on the basis of straight piece rate.

straight piece rate In it, the worker gets per his/her output; his/her per-unit output is multiplied with the pre-fixed per-unit rate.

strategic human resource management (SHRM) SHRM means formulation and execution of HR policies and practices that create and develop human capital the organisation requires to accomplish its strategic objectives.

strategy A strategy is a determination of the long-term goals and objectives of an organisation, allocation of resources and an action plan to achieve the stated goals and objectives and secure an edge over its competitors.

strikes It refers to abstaining from work by the workers and affecting the working/production of the organisation adversely due to refusal of the employer to accept their demands.

structured insight This technique helps in understanding one actual behaviour in comparison with preferred behaviour. This method provides self-insight into leadership practices of top-level executives.

subsistence theory Per this theory, wages tend to settle at the level just sufficient to maintain the worker and his/her family at the minimum subsistence.

succession planning It is an ongoing process of systematically identifying, assessing and developing organisational leadership to increase performance and fill internal key positions whenever they fall vacant.

supervision Supervision is concerned with the direction, guidance, control and superintendence of the subordinates.

supplementary compensation These are benefits for the time not-worked such as vacation and holiday pay and sick pay.

surplus value theory According to this theory, in the capital wage systems, the supply of labour always tends to be kept in surplus, that is, in excess of the demand for it—thus, the workers do not get full compensation for the time and labour they spend on their duty.

system approach This approach views IR as a distinctive sub-system of society comprising managers, workers and the government as three principal actors who function in certain contexts.

System I—exploitative autocratic In it, control rests in the hands of top management. It works on the basis of power and positional authority and follows the philosophy of Theory X.

System II—benevolent autocratic In this system, management seems to have condescending confidence and trust in its subordinates. While majority of the decisions and goal-setting are done by the top management, many decisions are made at middle and lower levels also.

System III—consultative leadership In it, though the management has substantial trust and confidence in its subordinates, still, broad policy and general decisions are made at the top management level. Subordinates are permitted to make specific decisions at the lower level. This system moves from Theory X to Theory Y.

System IV—participative group leadership In this leadership style, management has full faith and confidence in its subordinates. There is a free flow of communication in all directions. Decision-making is widely dispersed throughout the organisation, although well integrated and coordinated.

table pounding In it, each party pounds loudest when making assertions about which it is least certain.

tailor-made scales These are constructed for a particular setting or project.

take-home salary It is the amount of salary left to the employee after making authorised deductions, such as income tax, provident fund and life insurance premium.

tasks Tasks are coordinated and aggregated series of work elements used to produce an output like a unit of production.

Taylor differential piece rate plan Per this plan, there are only two piece rates, high rate and low rate, for each job or task. In other words, if a worker performs the work within or less than the standard time, he/she is paid a higher piece rate, and if he/she does not complete work within the standard time, he/she is given a lower piece rate for low production, that is, he/she would be able to earn just an ordinary day's pay.

tele-training In it, groups of trainees located at different places are taught by a trainer in a central location via telephone hook-ups.

theory of high expectations The theory states that a subordinate's performance is likely to fall or rise according to the executive's expectations from his/her subordinate.

theory Z Theory Z was propounded by Lyndall F. Urwick.

third country nationals (TCNs) These are the employees of a foreign subsidiary who belong neither to the country where the headquarters of the MNC are nor to the country where the foreign subsidiary is located.

time method or time rate method Per this method, an employee is paid based on time-worked, that is, hourly, daily, weekly or monthly, irrespective of the quantity of work done.

time-based wage variation It refers to wage variation from one period to another.

Towne gain sharing plan This plan provides for calculation of bonus on the reduction in costs (usually the labour cost) as compared with predetermined standard. An individual is entitled to half of the savings pro rata with wages earned. The supervisory staff also gets a part of this bonus.

trade union A trade union is an organisation of workers formed to protect and promote the social, economic and political interests of its members through collective action.

trade-off and buyout Either party may take the position that every concession has a price tag and anything can be agreed on for enough money.

training Training is a process by which the skills, abilities and attitudes of employees to perform specific jobs are improved.

training Training typically focuses on providing employees with specific skills or helping the employees correct deficiencies in their performance.

trait theory This theory is based on the belief that 'leaders are born'—that is, leaders have certain inherited traits of mind and intelligence which make them leaders.

transfer Transfer is the process of an employee's adjustment with the work, time and place with no material change in his/her responsibilities, status or scenario.

transfers Transfers refer to reassignments to similar positions in other parts of the organisation or to a different place at which the plant/office of the organisation is located. There is no change in salary or status and so on.

transnational corporations (TNCs) These provides autonomy to independent country operations and bring these separate operations into an integrated whole through a networked structure.

trend analysis It is the study of an organisation's past employment needs over a period of years to predict future needs.

tribunals Tribunals are constituted to decide industrial disputes under the provisions of the Industrial Disputes Act, 1947.

uncertainty avoidance This dimension focuses on how cultures adopt to changes and cope with uncertainty.

understanding element It means that the recipient of communication should be able to understand the message as the sender wanted him/her to understand.

understudy In the understudy, the trainee acts as an assistant to the current job holder. The trainee learns by observation, experience, imitation, interaction and discussion of decisions with his/her supervisor of whom he/she is the understudy.

understudy In understudy approach, the trainee works directly with the person he/she is likely to replace. The latter is in turn responsible for the former's development.

unilateral wage fixation In it only one party, that is, the employer fixes wages.

union shop Under this measure, an employee is required to join the union if he/she is not yet a member of the union.

unitary perspective This perspective presumes that since management owns and controls an enterprise, decision-taking is the prerogative exclusively of the management and, therefore, management is the only source of authority in an enterprise.

upward communication It moves from bottom to top such as suggestions from employees to their superiors or grievances of workers placed before superiors.

variable compensation It ties pay to productivity or profitability, usually as one-time lump sum. It keeps fluctuating depending on productivity or performance of an employee.

vertical fit An SHRP should be in alignment with the corporate strategy (vertically).

vestibule schools In vestibule schools, shop conditions are duplicated, but instructions, not output, are major objectives, which are provided by trained instructors.

videoconferencing In it, the trainer sitting at one location communicates with the trainees at other places with the help of audiovisual equipment.

voluntary welfare Welfare activities undertaken by an employer at his own sweet will and not under any legal pressure are known as voluntary welfare.

Vroom's expectancy theory Motivation depends on (a) the expectation that a given level of effort will result in a desired outcome and (b) the value (or utility) of that outcome to the person concerned.

Vroom's expectancy theory Per this theory, motivation of employees depends on an individual's expectations about his/her ability to perform tasks and receive the desired awards.

wage board It is a tripartite body constituted by the government for an industry for fixing wage structure of employees.

wage board It is a tripartite body constituted to fix wages and the like for the employees of a particular industry.

wage fund theory This theory states that a fixed amount of wage fund is available for distribution at any one time, and the level of wages depends on the number of labourers seeking employment.

wages Wages mean the amount paid to the labour for his/her services to the employer.

walk-ins It means the submission of direct applications/direct interviews in the office of the organisation.

waste reduction plan Such plans provide incentives to workers to reduce wastage. The plan takes the form of a percentage

white-collar workers' unions These unions usually comprise office staff or who work off the shop floor and perform desk jobs or provide service over the counter or any such other job. White-collar category includes executives, managers, professionals, administrators, supervisors, clerks and the like.

workers' councils model These are exclusive bodies of the employees alone. Members of workers' councils are elected by the employees of the sections concerned. They may discharge different functions in the management of an organisation. There may be one or more such councils in an organisation.

workers' participation in management It refers to the association of workers in the decision-making process.

workers' self-management model In this model, workers are part of main decision-making bodies. In this system, workers are either owners or they have the right to make use of the organisation's assets.

written communication It is written in black and white.

Index

360 degree feedback 273–76, 280, 285, 291

abstract reasoning tests 164
accelerated competency system method 210
Accenture 18–19, 169, 189, 279–81, 409, 412, 414
achievement motivation 294
achievement tests 163–64, 179, 209
adaptability tests 164
adjudication 350, 361, 555, 597–98, 628
Administrative Reforms Commission 228
adoption leave 409, 414
advancement or promotion: benefits of 250; definition of 249; elements of 249; merit basis 252; policy of 250; seniority basis, advantages and disadvantages 251–52
advertising 138–39, 148, 380
Aerial Delivery Research and Development Establishment (ADRDE) 326
agreeableness 164, 658
All India Institute of Management 241
All India Management Association 198, 217, 236, 241
All India Manufacturers' Organisation (AIMO) 643
All India Organisation of Employers (AIOE) 643
All India Technical Education Society 240
All India Trade Union Congress (AITUC) 630
allowances 307, 414, 540, 559, 575, 587, 605, 607, 640, 661–62; designing and operation of 303
Amazon 146, 383–84
analyst 170, 198, 239, 360
appraisal interview: definition of 267; employee role in 268; types of 268
Apprentices Act 1961 197, 214–15
apprenticeship 194, 196–97, 204
aptitude tests 164, 169, 209
arbitration 301, 351, 361, 539, 543, 546, 553, 555, 586, 594, 598, 628, 631
ARDM model for HRM 25
Argyris, Chris 3, 4, 7, 29
assessment centres 168–69, 247, 276–77

Associated Chamber of Commerce: and Industry of India (ASSOCHAM) 637, 643
astrology 153
attitudinal restructuring 587–88
attribution theory 450
audiovisual-based training 194, 200
autocratic leadership 509
averaging method 75–76

Babbage, Charles 5
baby cash 411
Bajaj, Jamuna Lal 241
Banerjee, Padmakali 170, 239, 277
bargaining agent 588, 630
basic compensation 305
basic wage 306
behavioural description interview (BDI) 165
behaviourally anchored rating scales (BARS) 268, 276
Bhoothalingam Study Group (1978) 310
bidding approach 136
bi-partite wage fixation 336, 350
Bombay Disputes Conciliation Act 1934 26
Bombay Mill Owner's Association 26
Bombay Textile Inquiry Committee 9
Bombay University 240
bonus 307; plans 316, 318–21; scheme 314, 320; sharing plans 316–18
brainstorming 198–99
budgeted expense bonus plan 329
bureaucratic or rules-centred leadership 521
business plan 74

California Test of Mental Maturity (Adult Level) 165
career: definition 242; goals 243; management 243; path 243; in present day world 243
career development: actions 246; challenges in 247; methods to overcome challenges 247; policies for effective 247; practices adopted by organisation in 248; steps and policies in establishment of 247; steps in 246; strategic thinking about 247

Index

career planning: definition of 244–45; individual component in 245; organisational component in 245; steps in 246
case studies 198
caste 153
casual applicants 143
casual appraisal 268
centralised recruitment 134
central tendency 288
Centre of Indian Trade Unions (CITU) 640
Chakrabarty Committee (1974) 310
Chamber of Commerce 26
character references 160
checklist appraisal method 271
checkpoint model 280
collaborator 170
collective bargaining: agreements, types of 589; assessment of 597; benefits of 590; contract administration 593; definition of 584; forms of 587; future of 598; in India, growth and status of 597; international scenario of 599; legal framework 587; levels of 589–90; need and significance of 586; negative aspects of 591; negotiation stage 591–94; and participation, difference between 602; slow growth, reasons for 597
commercial insurance 377
commission 325
common metric questionnaire (CMQ) 113
communication: in business organisations 482; through channel of command, merits of 485; channels of 484; characteristics of 478; definition of 478; elements of 479; evaluation of effectiveness 491–92; formal, demerits of 485; informal, merits and demerits of 487; in management, importance of 479; obstacles or barriers to, oral 492–95; principles of effective 490; process of 479; transmission of 488; types of 483; written 489
company in-house programmes 202
company or local school programmes 202
compensation 48, 304
competency: based interview 168; based job analysis 118; based training, identification of methods 209; models 209
competency alignment process (CAP) 126
competency mapping: definition of 208; methods of 209; steps in 208
Comprehensive Test of Verbal: Intelligence 165
computerised information systems 82
computerised systems 78
conceptual effectiveness 294
Confederation of Indian Industry (CII) 12
conferences 194
conscientiousness 164
consistency 490, 532–33

constant errors 289
Constitution of India (1951) 310
consumer price index (CPI) 307
contentment 5
contextual model of HRM 24
contingent employment 150
contingent theory 519
controlling 47
conventional philosophy of management 4
co-partnership 5
Council of Indian Employers (CIE) 644
counselling 69
crash programmes 240
creativity training 202
creed 153
crisis training 202
cross-functional training 202
customer service training 202
customised generic method 209

Dattatreya, Bandaru 413, 633, 637–38
Dave Ulrich HR Model 24
dearness allowance (DA) 306
decentralisation 17
decentralised recruitment 134
decision-making 232, 481, 601
decision-taking 601
de-jobbing 126
Deloitte 170, 280, 413
Delphi technique 75
demotion 83
descriptive evaluation appraisal method 272
Dessler, Gary 11, 13, 37–38, 66, 80
development, definition of 227
differential piece rate plans 315
difficult employees 533
digital tools, use of 167
directing 47
Directive Principles of State Policy (Article 43) 310
direct participation 602
disciplinary action: definition of 538; elements of 538; procedure for taking 538–39
disciplinary system, essentials of good 539
discipline: approaches or aspects to 533; definition of 531; HR manager role in maintenance of 540; maintenance of 537; objectives of 532; principles of 532; significance of 532
disguised grievance 542
distance based training 201
distributive bargaining 587
diversity training 202
downsizing 17
Drucker, Peter 4, 440, 514

Index 701

economic depression 7
efficiency rating 264
egg freezing 411
ego needs 443
e-learning method 201
electronic performance support systems (EPSS) 194
emotional stability 164
employee advocacy 38
employee compensation: components of 306–307; definition of 304; and equity 307; factors affecting 305–306; importance of 304; objectives of appropriate 305; planning, steps in 307–308
employee development programmes 5
employee leasing 150
employee relations 40
Employees Compensation Act 1923 371
Employees Deposit Linked Insurance Scheme 381
Employees' Pension Scheme 1971 381
Employees' Pension Scheme 1995 381
Employees Provident Funds and Miscellaneous Provisions Act 1952 369
Employees Provident Fund Scheme 381
Employees' State Insurance Act 1948 371
employee value proposition (EVP): definition of 146; importance of 146; steps 147–48
Employers' Federation of India (EFI) 643
Employment (Standing Orders) Act 1946 27
employment agencies: private 140; public 139
employment interviews 171
employment planning 66
employment test 162
energetic 170
entrepreneur 170
environmental scanning 72
Equal Remuneration Act 1976 310, 355
e-recruiting 144
ERG theory of motivation 448–49
ESOPs 304, 321–22, 347–48, 412
Estimates Committee of Lok Sabha 240
ethnocentrism 655
executive development: components of programme 239–40; decision-making skills 232–33; general knowledge 236; in global organisation 242; interpersonal skills 234; job knowledge 235; needs of 232; organisation knowledge 235–36; principles of 232; procedure of programme 238–39; programmes, need for 230; specific individual needs 237; success, criteria for 242
expatriate managers: failure causes 657; selection of 658
expatriate training 661
expert leadership 522

external or extrinsic motivation 438
extraversion 164
extrinsic rewards 324

factor comparison method 340
Factories Act 1948 27, 371, 400, 403–405, 417, 425, 547, 577
factual grievance 542
fair wage 305, 310, 352, 565, 623, 625
Fazalbhai, Y. A. 240
Federation of Indian Chamber of Commerce and Industry (FICCI) 643
field review method 272
financial motivation 438
First National Commission on Labour 1969 310, 605
flat rate system 307
flexible job competency model method 210
Flipkart 146
Flippo, E. B. 8, 50, 100, 110, 119, 123, 134, 161, 163, 188, 190, 232, 249, 263
followers' theory 519
forced choice description appraisal method 271
free-rein leadership style 521
fringe benefits: categories of 375; definition of 368–69; factors affecting 371; labour welfare 397–408; need and significance in Indian industries 376; objectives of 369; origin of 368; significance of 370; social security 376–90
full time management courses 241
functional job analysis (FJA) 112
functional theory 520

gaming 194, 199, 205
Gandhi, Jehangir 240
Gantt, Henry L. 6, 316
Gantt task and bonus plan 316
GEC 280
gender reassignment 412
geocentricism 656
Gilbreth, Frank 6
Gilbreth, Lillian 6–7, 29
global corporation (GC) 651
global HR system: challenges faced by 654; cultural nature of 663–64; development of effective 652; implementation of 653; making more acceptable 653
goal setting theory 449
go-getter 170
graded salary structure 301–302
grapevine communication: definition of 487; types of 487
graphic rating scales appraisal method 270
graphology 153

grievance(s): advantages or need for procedure 543; causes of 541; characteristics of discontent causing 541; definition of 540–41; effects of 542; forms of 542; identification or tracing 542; management in Indian industries 547; manager handling of 544; model procedure 545; prerequisites for effectiveness of 543; principles of handling 541; procedure 543
group incentives: advantages of 459; definition of 459
group or collective bonus plans: advantages of 319; disadvantages of 319; types of 318–19

halo effect 288
Halsey plan 316–18
haphazard appraisal 267–68
Harvard HRM model 22, 103
Hasley-Weir plan 317
Hawthorne experiment 568–70
Herzberg's theory of motivation 446–48
highly systematic appraisal 268
high morale of employees: physical factors 471–73; psychological factors of 473–75
Hind Mazdoor Sabha (HMS) 640
hiring game 170
Hofstede's cultural model: application of 667; dimensions of 664; establishment of 664; limitations of 668
home country or parent country nationals (PCNs) 654
honesty tests 165
horizontal fit 68, 84
host country nationals (HCNs) 654
Hot Stove rule 533
HR audit 81, 419
HR demand: qualitative methods of forecasting 75; quantitative methods of forecasting 76
HR forecasting factors 78
HRIS learning portals 201
HR manager: functions of 39; roles of 21, 540
HR strategies model: best practices 102; integrating strategic change 102–103; with regard to HRP 103
HR supply, forecasting: of external candidates 82–83; of inside candidates 81–82
HR supply internal sources 136–37
human capital 240, 419
human capital management 8; definition of 11; significance of 11
human factor 6, 9, 14, 25, 35–37
human relations approach 519, 534, 561; aims of 563–64; definition of 560; features of 561–62; and industrial relations, difference, between 563; proper diagnosis, importance of 567–68; steps to improve 564–66

human relations in industry 457, 483; definition of 560; nature of man 562; nature of organisations 563; need or importance of 564
human relations (HR) strategy: challenges to 14; selection of 14
human resource accounting 277
human resource activities 13, 37, 73, 420, 652
human resource development (HRD): aims of 12; importance of 13
Human Resource Information System (HRIS) 81
human resource management (HRM) 10; changing environment of 14; a closed-loop system 37; environmental challenges 15–16; importance of 35; individual challenges 20; job analysis and design, strategy for 134; managerial functions of 46–47; models of 22; nature of 40; operative functions of 46–47; origin of 3; phases of 10; primary and secondary objectives of 42; principles of 45–46; recruitment and selection, strategy for 174; scope of 40
human resource planning (HRP) 84; definition of 66; HR department responsibility 68; long-term planning 70; macro perspective 86; micro perspective 89; process of 72; short-term planning 68–70; significance of 67; techniques of forecasting demand for employees 75
human resource (HR) policy: characteristics of ideal 54–55; contents of 53; control of 56–57; controversy over declaration of 55–56; framing of 52–53; implementation of 56; meaning of 50; nature of 50; need and justification of 50–52; sound basis for decisions 51

IBM 189, 280, 283–84, 292, 385, 664
iCount platform 279
imaginary grievance 542, 567
immediate burn 533
impersonality 534
incentive plans 54, 308, 314; advantages of 319
incentives 453, 662; classification of 453; definition of 453; difference between financial and non-financial system 458; financial 454
incentive system of wage payment, principles of 320
incentive wage plans, pre-requisites: for successful 320
incident method 198, 272
independent observer 111
Indian Engineering Association 26
Indian Institute of Management (IIM): Ahmedabad 241; Bangalore 241; Lucknow 241

Indian Institute of Personnel Management (IIPM) 41
Indian Institute of Social Welfare and Business Management, Calcutta 240
Indian Institute of Technology (IIT), Kharagpur 240–41
Indian Jute Mills Association 26, 643
Indian Labour Conference 1957 306, 310–11, 545
Indian Tea Association 26, 590
Indian Trade Union Congress (INTUC) 630–32, 634, 639–40
indirect participation 602
individual plan and group bonus plan, comparison between 320
induction or orientation 174; definition of 175; information to new employee, methods to provide 177; objectives of 175; process of 176–77; significance of 175–76
industrial development 214, 228, 240
Industrial Disputes Act 1947 369, 385, 408, 534, 539, 547, 551–52, 570, 577
Industrial Employments (Standing Orders) Act 1946 547
Industrial Policy Resolution (1948) 309–310
industrial relations 40, 563, 570; actors and their role in 574; characteristics of 571–72; definition of 563, 571; effects of poor 576; factors affecting 575; Fahlbeck views 573; functions of 574–75; in India since independence 577–78; management strategy 578–79; methods for improvement of 576–77; objectives of, poor, causes of 573; pre-requisites of good 575–76; principles for promotion of 574; prospects in Indian industries 578; scope of 573; significance of 573–74; theoretical perspectives 572
Industrial Truce Resolution (1947) 309–310, 597
industry-based wage variations 323
informal learning 201
Infosys 171, 273, 278–80, 345, 385, 413
innovator 38, 170, 239
instant messaging 194, 200
Institute of Chartered Accountants 241
Institute of Cost and Work Accountants 241
Institute of Personnel Management 241
Institute of Production Engineers 241
integration 48
Integration Devolvement Model of HRM 25
integrative bargaining 351, 588, 593
intelligence tests 163, 165
interactionist approach 520
interest tests 164
internal or intrinsic motivation 438
international assignments: compensation to managers in 661–62; orientation and training of employees for 659–60

international corporations 651
international human resource management (IHRM): definition of 652; vs. domestic HRM 652; and external environment 654
international managers, performance: appraisal of 662
internet: based training 201; recruitment through
interpersonal effectiveness 294
interviewing 165–66, 168, 172
interviews 112; in schools and colleges 141–42
intra-organisational bargaining 588, 593
intrinsic rewards 324
Ivancevich, J. M. 67, 237, 265–66, 533

job: classification or grading 338; descriptions 115; enlargement 69, 439–40, 448; enrichment 439–40, 448; holders questionnaires 111; identification 111; incumbent diary or log 112; information, sources of 111; loading 439; posting 136, 144, 148; previews, realistic 150; ranking method 337; rating 337; re-engineering 118; relationships 111; rotation 196, 235, 247, 439; rotation training 196, 235–36; specification 48, 80, 83, 337
job analysis 41, 47–48, 72, 76, 337, 421; competency-based 118–19; conduct of 113; data collection 114; definition of 109–310; filling of job descriptions 121; in jobless world 125–26; quantitative techniques to obtain information 112–13; research areas 111; and strategic human resource management 118; uses of 116
job characteristics theory 450
job competence assessment method 209–10
job description 48, 80, 337–38; advantages of a 122–23; characteristics of 122; contents of 119–20; definition of 119; general purpose form for 120–21; internet use for writing 122
job design: approaches 126–27; definition of 127; work-family balance and 127
job evaluation 117; analytical or quantitative methods 338–339; definition of 336; non-analytical or non- quantitative methods 337–38; process of 337; single vs. multiple plans 336–37
job families definition of 109–10
job instruction training (JIT) system 196
job pricing: conversion of point values into monetary value 342; definition of 342; labour grades, establishment of, red circle rates 343–44
job satisfaction: controllable by management 466; inherent in job 466; measurement of 468–69; methods to increase 466–68; personal factors 465

704 Index

job specification 83, 115–16; contents of 125; definition of 123
John Storey Model of HRM 24
joining bonuses 409
Jucius, Michael J. 4, 8, 50, 52, 57, 110, 125, 156, 432, 437, 469, 471, 538, 586
judicial approach 534

Kaufman Adolescent and Adult Intelligent Test 165
knowledge of results (KR) 170
KPMG 99, 279, 283–84, 414
Kuder Preference Record 164

laboratory training 199–200
labour grades 343
Labour Investigation Committee 27, 397
labour management 36, 40, 49, 229, 284, 287, 574, 584–85, 594, 608
Labour Market Information System (LMIS) 215
labour organisations, role in employment 143
labour relations 27, 41, 118, 426
labour turnover: definition of 100; high rate, causes of 100–101; measurement of 101; significance of 101–102
labour welfare: activities in Indian industries 401; classification of 400; definition of 397; objectives of 397–98; principles of 399–400; significance in Indian industries 399
lay-offs 74, 80, 83, 137, 172, 534, 538
leadership/leaders 170; categories of style 528–29; characteristics of 512; definition of 511–12; and domination, difference between 513; and headship, difference between 513; HRM strategy to 529; importance of 514; Indian leaders perception about 515; managers, functions of 515; and motivation, relationship between 513; nature of 512; qualities of 514; styles of 524–25; theories of 518–21
learning organisation: definition of 207–208; dimensions of 208
learning theory 189
leasing on demand recruiting services (ODRS) 143
lectures 177, 197, 201, 217, 234, 236, 409, 484
letters of recommendation, categories of 160–61
Likert, Rensis 4
Likert system I through system IV 520
line organisation 38, 250
literacy training 202
living wage 305, 308, 310, 402
long-term HR planning 70
low cost housing benefit 412

MakeMyTrip 98, 146
management by objectives 44
management by objectives (MBO) method 7, 276
management development: definition of 227; programme, contents of 230
management position description questionnaire (MPDQ) 113
management strategy: for foreign subsidiaries 669; for wage fixation 361–62
management training and development in: India establishment of industrial management institutes 240–41; training facilities 241–42
managerial appraisals 238–39
managerial development, objectives of 229
managerial grid leadership style 523
managerial judgement 75
managerial or executive compensation 348–49
managerial training: in India 228; need and importance of 228; objectives of 229
managers for global assignments, selection procedure 658–59
manipulative leadership 522
manpower management 40
manpower planning 66, 73, 277
man-to-man comparison appraisal method 269–70
manual systems 82
Markov analysis 76
Maslow, Abraham 10
Maslow's need hierarchy theory 444–45
Massachusetts Institute of Technology 198, 241
Maternity Benefit Act 1961 379, 409, 416
maternity leave 409
McGregor Theory X 450
McGregor Theory Y 4–5, 450
McKinsey 146
membership-based rewards 325
mental models 208
mentoring 201, 245, 247, 292
merit pay plans 325
merit rating: definition of 264; objective of 264
Merrick multiple piece rate plan 315–16
methods to convey 289–90
Micro, Small and Medium Enterprises (MSME) 215
Microsoft 279–80, 292
Miller analogies tests 164
Mill, J. S. 5
minimum wages 305
Minimum Wages Act 1948 305, 309–10, 353–55, 369, 577
minimum wages revision, by Delhi government 357
Ministry of Labour and Employment (MoLE) 386, 406

Minnesota Paper Form Board Test (MPFB) 165
minority groups employees 140, 143–44
modern philosophy of management: emergence of, factors for 4–5; of personnel management 4
modified job competence assessment method 210
monetary rewards 323–24, 344
morale development, theory of 471
morale, employee: categories of 469–70; definition of 469; disadvantages of 470; importance of, low 470; low, warning signs of 477; measurement of 475; methods of measurement 475–77
motivation: characteristics of 432; definition of 432; elements of sound system 452; executive 442; importance of 433–34; objectives of 433; precautions in 436; problems in 441; process involved in 437; rules of 437; techniques or methods of 440; theories of 444–45; types of 437–39; for work 435
motor ability tests 165
MP3 194, 200
multinational corporations (MNCs) 575, 578; staffing approaches 655–57
multiple management 194, 197, 205, 236–37
Munsterberg, Hugo 6–7

national wage policy in India 310–11
needs: definition of 442; primary 442–43; secondary 443
negative discipline approach 533
negative feedback fear of, methodology to overcome 290–92
negative or fear motivation 438
networker 170
networking sites, recruitment through 144–45
neurotic 165
Nominal Group Technique (NGT) 75
nominal/money wage 305
non-financial incentives 325
non-financial motivation 438
non-monetary rewards 325
numerical ability test 162

objective tests 165
occupation 110
occupational counselling 117
occupational informational net-work 113
offshoring jobs 146
on specific job 194–95
on-the-job (OJT) method 195–97
openness to experience 164
operational effectiveness 294
optimism: definition of 170; index 170; measurement of 170; origin of 170
optimism index 170, 277

oral communication: definition of 488; demerits of 489; merits of 488–89
organisational restructuring 17
organisation chart 113
organisation charts 80
organisation planning 238
organising 46
outplacement 17, 206, 630
outsourcing training 219–20
outsourcing white-collar jobs 145
overtime 83, 102, 120–21, 150, 176, 375, 418, 540
Owen, Robert 5
ownership plan 321

paired comparison technique 269, 337
partial reimbursement on student loan debt 411
participation: administrative 602; *vs.* collective bargaining 602; consultative 602; direct 602; indirect 602; informative 602; levels of 602
participative leadership 5, 520–21
participative leadership style 521
participative management 4
path-goal theory 520
pay commissions 359–61, 587, 635
Payment of Bonus Act 1965 307, 310, 355, 369, 371, 417
Payment of Gratuity Act 1972 371, 382, 577
Payment of Wages Act 1936 309, 359
peer appraisals 267
people-oriented supervision 506
performance appraisal: advantages or utility of 287; appraising performance of employees, options for 266; casual approach of 267–68; definition of 264; effective programme, introduction of 284–85; evaluation criteria for 267; faulty assumptions 287–88; importance of 265–66; in Indian organisations, practices followed 278–80; innovations in 280; and merit rating, difference between 264–65; modern methods of 273–75; need to appraise 265; need to do away with 292–93; objectives of 266; obstacles, methods to overcome 289; process of 266; psychological blocks 288; sound plan, characteristics of 286; technical pitfalls 288; traditional and highly systematic appraisal 268–72
performance-based rewards 324, 351
performance bonus 275, 324, 347
performance management advantage of 287; definition of 265
performance next 279
performance tests 164
personal interviews 114

personality tests 164–65
personal mastery 208
personal observation 114
personnel administration 8–10
personnel / HR management: characteristics of 8; development of 25–28; fifth phase of 8; first phase of 5–6; fourth phase of 6–7; second phase of 6; third phase of 6
personnel management 40–41
personnel procurement 47–48, 109, 143; maintenance of 49; development of 48
personnel records 39, 41
personnel replacement charts 82
Philips Hi-Lo Matrix model 294
Philips NV Holland model 294
phrenology 153
physical ability tests 165
physical examination 166
physiognomy 153
piece rate system 311, 313–16, 454
piecework 324
pigmentation 153
placement 41, 47, 65
planning 66–67
plans for action, development of 83
point method or manual system 338
point system 272
polycentrism 656
polygraphy tests 165
poor performer, shedding tag of 285–86
position analysis questionnaire 113
position replacement card 82
positive discipline approach 534
positive or incentive motivation 437
potential appraisal: best practices of 295; definition of 293; importance of 293; methods of 293–95; need of 293
power theory 450
praise theory 450
premium plan 316–18
pricing managerial jobs: factors affecting, methods of 349–50
Priestman's production bonus plan 318
Prime Minister's Shram Award 326
production linked incentive 326
production-oriented supervision 506
professionally managed enterprises 229
professional management 5
proficiency rating 264
proficiency tests 164
profit-sharing 321
programmed learning 200
programme targeting 238
progressive discipline approach 534
projective tests 165
promotion 69
psychological tests: additional tool of employment office 162; areas of usage 162–63; definition of 162; principles of 163; types of 163–65
psychometric tests 294
public relations 41
punishment: legal framework 538–39; major 536; minor 536; options to improve employees behaviour 537–38
Purdue test for machinists and machine operators 164

questionnaires 114

rater's liking and disliking 289
rating committees 267
ratio analysis 77
Ratnam, C. S. V. 583, 620
realistic job preview (RJP) 150
real wage 305
recruiter, attributes of effective 151
recruitment: alternatives to 150; blind audition to remove gender bias 171–72; centralised 134–35; decentralised 134–35; definition of 133; direct methods of 148; of diverse workforce 150; effectiveness of 149–50; employment section and department 134; evaluation of 149–50; independent function of 135; in Indian industries, practices followed 149; indirect methods of 148; objective of 133; recent developments and trends 151–52; third party methods of 148
red circle rates 343–44
Reddin's -D theory 524
references: check 161; definition of 160; limitations of 161; types of 160
refresher courses 189, 203, 216
Regional Directorate of Apprenticeship Training (RDAT) 215
regional wage variations 323
regression analysis 76
rehabilitation 17, 139, 376, 380, 630
re-hire of employees 137, 161
repatriation 662–63
research orientation 229
retirement 118
re-training 202–204, 206, 220
retrenchment 6, 17, 83–84, 100, 375
retrenchment compensation 383
return on investment (ROI) on training 202
review appraisal 295
reward system: aspects of 323; characteristics of 323–24; determinants of 324; extrinsic 324; in Indian industries 326; intrinsic 324; pros and cons of 326
role-playing method 199
Rorschach Blot Test 165
Rowan plan 317

salaries, definition of 304
salary administration: collective objectives 303; functions of 303–304; individual objectives 303; organisational objectives 303
salary progression curves 302
salary progression system 302
salary reviews, administration and control of 302
salary structure: graded salary structure 301–302; salary progression curves 302
scatter plot 77
school references 160–61
Scott, Walter Dill 7
selecting benchmark jobs 337
selection: accuracy in, steps to improve 154; cost benefit analysis of decision on 170; criteria, reliability and validity of 154–55; definition of 152; factors influencing 154; preliminary requirement before 153; procedure 155; pseudo-scientific methods of 153; scientific methods for, need of 153
selection of critical incident appraisal method 272
selective reading 196
self-actualisation 5, 443–45, 449
self-assessment 277–78
self-control 5, 118, 165, 277
self-direction 4–5, 277
self-discipline 5, 534
self-evaluation 277, 291
self-motivation 436–37
self-rating 267
sensitivity training 440
service appraisal 264
Sharma, R. C. 224, 333, 393, 394, 425, 428, 649
short-term courses 241
short-term HR planning 68–70
simple long-run trend projection/analysis 76
simulation 199
simulation models 76
situational interview (SI) 166
situational theory 519
situation tests 165
skill assessment 213
skill inventory 80–82
skills training 202
slides 200
Slosson Intelligence Test 165
Snapdeal 146, 578, 634
social assistance 377
socialisation: categories of 178; definition of 178
social needs 443, 445, 451
social ownership 213
social security: definition of 376; forms of 377; in India 377–78; objectives of 376; present scenario of Indian industries 378–81; scope of 377

special course 197–98
special events recruiting 144
special letters 161
special projects 196
specific aptitude tests 164
staffing 47
staffing international organisations 655
Standing Conference of Public Enterprises (SCOPE) 644
Stanford-Binet Scale Test 164
start-ups 172, 409–10
statutory minimum wage 305
stochastic method 78
stock option 321–22
straight piece work plan 315
straight ranking method 269
strategic human resource management (SHRM) 13; advantage of 13; objectives of 13; pattern of planned human resource deployments 13
strategic human resource planning (SHRP): changing environment and 85–86; model of 85
Strong Vocational Interest Blank 164
structural interview 165
subordinates 501–502
succession planning 137
suggestion schemes 326, 588
summer internship 145
supervision: categories of 501; definition of 501; effective 506; factors affecting 509; HRM strategy to 525; levels of 501–502; nature of 507–508; people-oriented *vs.* production oriented 506; rules for successful 509
supervisor: conditions to improve supervisory 508–509; functions of 508; and human relations, relationship between 509–10; in organisation, importance of 503–504; qualities of 507; techniques of supervisory 505; vigilant 508
supplementary compensation 305, 322
supportive management 4, 289
surprise appraisals 283–84
synergist 170, 239
systems method 210
system thinking 208

tailor-made tests 164
take home salary 305
Tata Consultancy Services (TCS) 91, 278–79, 347–48, 385, 410, 655
Taylor differential piece rate plan 315
team learning 208
team training 202
tele-training 194, 200–201
temporary assignment 69, 650
temporary employment 150

termination 83, 304
Textile Research Associations 241
Thematic Apperception Test 165
theory of high expectations 449
Theory X 4–5
Theory Y 4–5
Theory Z 450–452
third-country nationals (TCNs) 654
third party wage fixation 336, 361
time-based wage variations 323
time rate system 312
total quality management (TQM) 238
trade tests 164
trade unions: classification of 626–27; code of conduct 630–31; definition of 622–23; employees joining 640; functions of 625; movement in India, growth of 631–32; movement, steps for successful 641; national level federations 643; Nation Commission on Labour recommendations 628; objectives of 623–24; obstacles in growth of 627; present day developments 632; reaction towards changes 630; recognition of 630; registered, rights and liabilities of 629; registration of 629; significance of 624–25; and wages, relationship between 629
traditional appraisal 276
training: avoiding pitfalls 202; challenges in 201–202; definition of 187–88; *vs.* development 227; difficulties during evaluation of programmes 214; and education, relationship between 188; evaluation of programmes in organisation 213–14; facilities, evaluation of 217–18; good, features of programme 210; HRM strategy for 220; increase in investment on 219; in India, practices followed 214; within industries (TWI) 242; in large organisation, process 205–207; learning theory applicability to 189; link with business strategy 219; models for evaluation of programmes 213; and motivation, relationship between 189; need and importance of 189; objective of 188; off-the-job training methods 197–201; on-the-job training method 195–97; outsourcing 219; principles of 193; programmes and employee level 202–204; programmes at different levels 204; return on investment on 211–12; strategic goals 214; subject matter expert in assessment, use of 220; types of 202
training and development programme, evaluation of 242–43
training within industry (TWI) 195
trait theory 518
transfers: definition of 252–53; objectives of 253–54; policy 254; production 253;

remedial 253; replacement 253; shift 253; versatility 253
transnational corporations (TNCs) 651
travel stipend 412
tripartite wage fixation 351–52

unilateral wage fixation: analytical or quantitative methods of 338; in organised sector 336–38
unit-demand forecasting 75
University of Allahabad 241
University of Bombay 241
unorganised sector, wage fixation in 350
unstructured interview 165
unsystematic appraisal 267–68

variable compensation 305
vertical fit 14, 68, 84
vestibule schools 197
video-based simulation test 165
videoconferencing 200
videotapes 200
virtual workforce 145
visual confirmation 213–14

wage boards 351–52
wages: behavioural theory of 309; definition of 308; differentials or variations 323; economic theory of 308–309; essentials for satisfactory 322; functions of 303; payment, methods of 311; policies at organisational level 310–11; potent motivator 48; problems in India 311
walk-ins 145
warning system 533
Wechsler Adult Intelligence Scale 165
weighted application blank 160
welfare work: by employers 408; by state governments and union territories 406; under statutory funds 406; trade unions 408; voluntary social service agencies 408–409
Wide Range Intelligence Test 165
Wipro 273, 278–79, 346, 348–49, 410
Wonderlic Personnel Test 165
workers participation in management (WPM) benefits of 616–17; characteristics of 601; definition of 600; evaluation of schemes 612–13; forms of 603; in India, development 604; Management Bill 1990 611–12, 618; models in 603; prerequisites for effective scheme 612
workload analysis 76, 78, 80
work references 160–61
written communication 484, 489–91
written narratives 114

yoga 410